HISTORICAL DICTIONARIES OF RELIGIONS,
PHILOSOPHIES, AND MOVEMENTS
Edited by Jon Woronoff

1. *Buddhism,* by Charles S. Prebish, 1993
2. *Mormonism,* by Davis Bitton, 1994. *Out of print. See No. 32.*
3. *Ecumenical Christianity,* by Ans Joachim van der Bent, 1994
4. *Terrorism,* by Sean Anderson and Stephen Sloan, 1995. *Out of Print. See No. 41.*
5. *Sikhism,* by W. H. McLeod, 1995
6. *Feminism,* by Janet K. Boles and Diane Long Hoeveler, 1995
7. *Olympic Movement,* by Ian Buchanan and Bill Mallon, 1995. *Out of print. See No. 39.*
8. *Methodism,* by Charles Yrigoyen Jr. and Susan E. Warrick, 1996
9. *Orthodox Church,* by Michael Prokurat, Alexander Golitzin, and Michael D. Peterson, 1996
10. *Organized Labor,* by James C. Docherty, 1996
11. *Civil Rights Movement,* by Ralph E. Luker, 1997
12. *Catholicism,* by William J. Collinge, 1997
13. *Hinduism,* by Bruce M. Sullivan, 1997
14. *North American Environmentalism,* by Edward R. Wells and Alan M. Schwartz, 1997
15. *Welfare State,* by Bent Greve, 1998
16. *Socialism,* by James C. Docherty, 1997
17. *Bahá'í Faith,* by Hugh C. Adamson and Philip Hainsworth, 1998
18. *Taoism,* by Julian F. Pas in cooperation with Man Kam Leung, 1998
19. *Judaism,* by Norman Solomon, 1998
20. *Green Movement,* by Elim Papadakis, 1998
21. *Nietzscheanism,* by Carol Diethe, 1999
22. *Gay Liberation Movement,* by Ronald J. Hunt, 1999
23. *Islamic Fundamentalist Movements in the Arab World, Iran, and Turkey,* by Ahmad S. Moussalli, 1999
24. *Reformed Churches,* by Robert Benedetto, Darrell L. Guder, and Donald K. McKim, 1999
25. *Baptists,* by William H. Brackney, 1999
26. *Cooperative Movement,* by Jack Shaffer, 1999
27. *Reformation and Counter-Reformation,* by Hans J. Hillerbrand, 2000
28. *Shakers,* by Holley Gene Duffield, 2000

Historical Dictionary of Prophets in Islam and Judaism

Scott B. Noegel
Brannon M. Wheeler

Historical Dictionaries of Religions,
Philosophies, and Movements, No. 43

The Scarecrow Press, Inc.
Lanham, Maryland, and London
2002

SCARECROW PRESS, INC.

Published in the United States of America
by Scarecrow Press, Inc.
A Member of the Rowman & Littlefield Publishing Group
4720 Boston Way
Lanham, Maryland 20706
www.scarecrowpress.com

12 Hid's Copse Road
Cumnor Hill, Oxford OX2 9JJ, England

British Library Cataloguing in Publication Information Available

Library of Congress Cataloging-in-Publication Data

Noegel, Scott B.
    Historical dictionary of prophets in Islam and Judaism / Scott B. Noegel,
    Brannon M. Wheeler.
       p.cm. — (Historical dictionaries of religions, philosophies, and movements;
    no. 43)
    ISBN 0-8108-4305-6 (alk. paper)
      1. Prophecy—Judaism—Dictionaries. 2. Prophecy—Islam—Dictonaries.
    3. Prophecy—Dictionaries. 4. Prophets—Biography—Dictionaries. I.
    Wheeler, Brannon M., 1965– II. Title. III. Series.

BM6455.P67 N64 2002
296'.092'2—DC21
    [b]   2002022372

To our students

Contents

Editor's Foreword

At a time when differences between religions are too often highlighted, it is worthwhile to recall points of agreement, some of which are amazingly central and significant. Prophets and prophecy are extremely important to Judaism and Islam, both in their early and formative periods and today, as we interpret the doctrines of two religions that are most often seen as being at odds with one another. But so far there have been no reference works that deal specifically with prophets and prophecy in an accessible manner. This *Historical Dictionary of Prophets in Islam and Judaism* fills a notable gap in the literature, and also in Scarecrow's Historical Dictionaries of Religions, Philosophies, and Movements series.

The core of this volume is the dictionary section, which focuses on four main areas: prophets; texts; scholars and scholarship; and issues, concepts, and themes. The entries deal with a broad array of prophets and related figures, from Adam and Eve to Isaac to Moses to Jesus and his disciples to Muhammad. What we know about these figures is derived from essential texts, especially the Bible and Quran but many more as well, some barely known beyond specialist circles. The specialists and scholars are thus included, since it was they who interpreted and transmitted the texts. The loop is closed with entries on issues, concepts, and themes, among them prophecy, shamans, and oracles, but also ritual and law, ethics and mysticism, angelology and demonology. A selective bibliography can guide readers to further works of interest.

The authors have somewhat different backgrounds that come together in this balanced, comparative work. Scott B. Noegel specializes in the ancient Near East, biblical studies, and Judaism. Brannon M. Wheeler is a scholar of Islamic studies and comparative religion. Between them they have expertise in a variety of original languages, including Akkadian, Egyptian, Hebrew, Aramaic, Arabic, Greek, and Latin. This unique cooperation was facilitated by the fact that both are professors in the Department of Near Eastern Languages and Civilization at the University of Washington. It was further strengthened when they team-taught a course on prophets in Islam and Judaism at the university. This latest historical dictionary should consequently be accessible not only to academics but to students and lay readers as well.

Jon Woronoff
Series Editor

Preface

We began working on this book shortly after co-teaching a course at the University of Washington on the subject of prophets and prophecy in Islam and Judaism. The course allowed us to explore a number of comparative and methodological issues often neglected in the research of our separate fields, and confirmed for us the importance of bringing our disciplines into greater dialogue. The course also demonstrated to us the need for comparative research tools for students. The goals, methods, and perspectives that we employed and encouraged in this course have been integrated into this work, which thus represents a collaborative enterprise between disciplines as well as individuals.

The study of biblical prophecy has long benefited from comparative materials from elsewhere in the ancient Near East. The discovery of prophetic and divinatory texts from Assyria and Mari, and oracular texts from Egypt, have allowed scholars to place biblical prophecy on a long continuum of mantic experiences. In the last few decades scholars have increasingly taken a more interdisciplinary approach to the subject of prophecy, and so our understanding of the phenomenon in ancient Israel has profited from a number of models derived from the fields of anthropology, sociology, gender studies, folklore, sociolinguistics, literary criticism, and the comparative study of religions. Nevertheless, despite these advances, biblical scholars rarely have looked to the Quran and later Islamic exegetical views of prophecy for comparative data.

The situation in Islamic studies has fared even worse. Quranic and Islamic views of prophecy have been studied largely in isolation, and though some efforts have been made in recent years to examine the Quran's mention of Israelite prophets in conjunction with biblical traditions, these studies seldom have taken into consideration the ancient Near Eastern comparative materials or the interdisciplinary advances in biblical studies. Moreover, of those works that have considered the biblical materials, many have attempted to demonstrate the dependence of Islam on earlier notions of prophecy. Consequently, some scholars have explained the appearance of Israelite prophets in the Quran as the result of literary borrowing, if not the tendentious manipulation of biblical source materials, rather than as evidence of shared and variant traditions. Such approaches, in our opinion, have created methodological obstacles to the comparative study of prophecy in Islam and Judaism. At the very least, they have relegated scholarly discussion to a debate over historical precedence and privilege of tradition, rather than the purpose and meaning of prophetic traditions in the respective cultural matrices.

In this work, we have attempted to encourage a greater interdisciplinarity by treating each entry as a compilation of relevant data culled from biblical, Quranic, and later Jewish and Islamic traditions. At the same time, we have taken care to cite specific sources so as to retain the distinctiveness of each of the traditions included. While our primary focus has been the prophetic traditions of Islam and Judaism, at times it was necessary to include information found in early Hellenistic, Christian, gnostic, Mandaic, Manichaean, and Zoroastrian sources, in addition to those from the ancient Near East (Mesopotamia, Egypt, Syria, and Anatolia). Our goal is not to be exhaustive or to trace historical influences, but rather to provide heuristic models and avenues for the more detailed philological and historical research required of innovative comparative work.

An effort to promote interdisciplinary dialogue also has motivated our selection of entries, which intends to take the reader beyond the expected parameters of research (i.e., peoples, places, and texts), by facilitating a greater understanding of a few of the literary and methodological issues surrounding the study of prophecy generally. Thus, to name just a few examples, one will find entries on acrostic, asceticism, astronomy and astrology, Atbash, canon lists, cosmology, divination, drugs, ecstatic, form criticism, gematria, glossolalia, magic, medicine, mysticism, parallelism, poetry, possession, prophetic nudity, shaman, speech act theory, therianthropism, witchcraft, and word play. We also have found it necessary to include a number of entries on subjects that, while not always central to the study of prophecy, nevertheless, figure prominently in prophetic texts and narratives about prophets. One will find, for example, entries for angel, Ark of the Covenant, demon, mountain, music, sacrifice, tablets, temple, teraphim, and Tree of Life. Such entries have been treated with an interdisciplinary breadth that is designed to promote fresh inquiry.

The subject of this dictionary necessarily moves us beyond the Hebrew Bible and Quran and into a wealth of textual materials of later date that preserve traditions about prophets and prophecy. Some of these traditions echo earlier accounts found in the respective sacred canons. Others appear only in later exegetical and historical texts. We take seriously, however, the caveat that later written works often preserve earlier oral traditions, and are aware that the historical "original" of any text is unrecoverable. We do attempt to provide dates for texts, figures, and concepts, but these should not be interpreted as absolutes or as indicating dependence. We see our efforts as consistent with the recovery and assembly of mythical paradigms, figures, and motifs that are dispersed and ensconced in a variety of textual contexts.

Nevertheless, we have limited the scope of this work to what might broadly be called a "biblical" or "Near Eastern" tradition, which finds expression in the narratives of the Bible and Quran and in the exegesis of those texts. The sheer quantity of extracanonical textual remains has made exhaustiveness an impossibility, but we have defined exegesis in broad terms, including texts that overlap and share in the narratives of the Bible and Quran. Our consideration of Jewish prophetic traditions has focused primarily on the Hebrew Bible (Old Testament), Mishnah, Talmud, and a variety of midrashic works. This has led us into the New Testament and Christian exegesis of the Bible, though a fuller examination of prophets and prophecy in Christianity is beyond our purview. Where relevant, we also have included later traditions found in Jewish mystical works, such as the Alphabet of Rabbi Aqiba and the Zohar, and have drawn upon late pseudepigraphical works such as the *Chronicles of Jerahmeel* and the *Book of Jasher*.

Islamic sources consulted have focused primarily on the Quran, hadith collections and their commentaries, and the works of a number of later Muslim exegetes ranging from classical to modern and including Sunni, Shi'i, Mu'tazili, and Sufi works. In addition, the entries include information from histories, geographical and biographical dictionaries, stories of the prophets [Ar. qisas al-anbiya'], Quranic studies [Ar. 'ulum al-Quran], and prophetological texts [Ar. dala'il al-nubuwah]. An effort has been made to represent a wide diversity of interpretations and approaches, but the selections focus on the classical Arabic tradition. The integration of these extracanonical texts brings into relief the enormous productivity of the various prophetic traditions in the Jewish and Muslim communities of late antiquity, and often demonstrates an active interdisciplinary dialogue between ancient Jewish and Muslim exegetes lacking in current scholarship.

Throughout the writing process we have envisioned the work as an initial resource for students of biblical and Islamic studies, and for interested lay readers. Thus, the citations that accompany each of the entries, and the bibliography that concludes the volume, are intended to facilitate advanced interdisciplinary research. In a few cases, the texts we have referenced unfortunately appear only in their Hebrew, Aramaic, or Arabic originals. Nevertheless, we have felt it important to include them and have provided separate entries for all texts cited, regardless of whether they are available in English. This should provide the interested reader with a general sense of the citations' historical and literary contexts.

The entries themselves are arranged alphabetically. The majority are English terms, though in some cases we have retained a transliteration of the original Hebrew, Aramaic, or Arabic terms and titles. Cross-references have been kept to a minimum since we have endeavored to provide separate entries for all of the terms, figures, and texts that appear in the course of an entry. We have included a list of reference works in the bibliography for terms not found as entries. Where there is an overlap of entries we have indicated a *see* or *see also* cross-reference rather than repeating the information. We also have placed a general index at the end of the book to facilitate further research. We would like to thank Gary Martin for his invaluable help in creating this index.

Throughout we have attempted to make the entries accessible for a wide audience. All dates are indicated as BCE or CE, though subsequent dates in a single entry may not repeat this information unless it is ambiguous. In the entries we have tried to indicate uncertainty about dates with the use of "c." or by offering broader dating categories such as centuries, though we have not reproduced the multiple dates given in primary and secondary sources. Readers should be aware of the tentative nature of all exact dates when dealing with ancient textual sources and archaeology, compounded by the fact that the dating system we employ was not used by the peoples who wrote the texts we read. To facilitate reference, exact dates in the chronology are not differentiated from approximate dates.

With a few exceptions, diacritical marks have been omitted from the transliteration of foreign words. Most citations of foreign words are placed in brackets, not italicized, with an indication of the original language being transliterated. We have included this information only in select cases when it bears on the definition of the term involved, and especially when it suggests comparison. More exhaustive linguistic information can be found in one of the etymological dictionaries listed in our bibliography.

All references to the Bible are taken from the JTS Tanakh, which corresponds to the Hebrew Masoretic Text, and can at times be different in English Bibles based on the Septuagint or Vulgate. Books of the Bible are cited with the full title when the reference is to the whole book or whole chapters, and abbreviations are used for references to specific verses. All references to the Quran are to surah and verse divisions following the Egyptian standard edition, as are the identification of surahs by number according to their order in the Egyptian standard edition. Readers should be aware that there are several different schemes used, not always consistently, for numbering verses in other published translations of the Quran. Midrashic and talmudic citations follow the standardized references, as do all citations of Hellenistic literature such as Philo, Josephus, and Eusebius. Quran commentary references are according to the surah and verse being interpreted. All abbreviations used in the entries appear in the list of abbreviations included at the beginning of the book. We have eschewed italicizing titles of pseudepigraphical and apocryphal works as well as midrashic texts, but have italicized some works such as those of Josephus and Eusebius.

Hebrew and Arabic names are translated consistently, and are consistent with the standard equivalents familiar from most English translations of the Bible. Thus the Hebrew "Iyyub" and Arabic "Ayyub" are rendered as "Job" and the Hebrew "Yehezqel" and Arabic "Hizqil" are rendered "Ezekiel" in English. The name "Yahweh" is used for God when the biblical text is specific about the term, and "Elohim" is rendered as "God." The Arabic "Allah" is taken to be the Arabic word for "the God" and is translated throughout as "God" with a capital "G." We also have been consistent in avoiding the privileging of certain terms and traditions with capitalization (thus "prophet" as a title is always lowercase, as is "temple" even when it refers to the one in Jerusalem), but have retained capitals for the proper names of specific items (e.g., "Ark of the Covenant" and "Ka'bah").

The bibliography is not intended to be exhaustive, only representative, and we have cited only those works that bear on the subject of prophets and prophecy. We have separated the bibliographic data into categories that we feel will best assist advanced research. Thus, we provide categories for individual prophets and figures associated with prophecy regardless of whether the figure is considered a prophet in both Islam and Judaism: the reader will find bibliographic categories for Adam and Eve, Noah, and Daniel, though these figures are considered prophets only in Islam. We have divided the bibliographic entries for the Israelite prophets into pre-exilic and post-exilic categories and subdivided each of these groups by individual prophet. Preceding these entries is bibliographic data for the study of prophecy generally, which we have grouped into the following categories: Ancient Near East and Israel, Judaism, and Islam. Historically speaking, the formative stages of Judaism, as a religious system distinct from Israelite religion, overlap with the end of prophecy as an Israelite cultural institution. Thus, in the bibliographic category on Prophecy in Hellenism, Judaism, and Late Antiquity we include works that discuss prophecy from later Jewish perspectives or are relevant to the topic of Jewish mantic (and mystical) practices generally. Throughout, we have included relevant works dealing with exegesis as they relate to the stories of the prophets and prophecy. A table for the bibliography precedes the entries.

Abbreviations

Akk.	Akkadian
Antiquities	*Jewish Antiquities* of Josephus
Ar.	Arabic
Aram.	Aramaic
Av.	Avestan
b.	"son of" [Ar. *ibn*]
Bab.	Babylonian
Bar	Baruch (1, 2, 3, 4)
BCE	Before Common Era (or B.C.)
c.	circa
CE	Common Era (or A.D.)
ch.	chapter
Chr	Chronicles (1 and 2)
Cor	Corinthians (1 and 2)
Dan	Daniel
Deut	Deuteronomy
Ebl.	Eblaic
Eccl	Ecclesiastes (Qohelet)
e.g.	exempli gratia (for example)
Eg.	Egyptian
En	Enoch (1, 2, 3)
Eng.	English
Eph	Ephesians
Esdr	Esdras (1 and 2)
esp.	especially
Esth	Esther
Eth.	Ethiopic
Exod	Exodus
Ezek	Ezekiel

f.	floruit (flourished)
Gal	Galatians
Gen	Genesis
Ger.	German
Gk.	Greek
Hab	Habakkuk
Hag	Haggai
Heb	Hebrews, Epistle to the
Heb.	Hebrew
History	*Church History* of Eusebius
Hit.	Hittite
Hos	Hosea
Isa	Isaiah
Jas	James
Jdt	Judith
Jer	Jeremiah
Jub	Jubilees
Judg	Judges
Kgs	Kings (1 and 2)
Lam	Lamentations
Lev	Leviticus
lit.	literally
LXX	Septuagint
Macc	Maccabees (1, 2, 3, 4)
Mal	Malachi
Mand.	Mandaic
Matt	Matthew
Mic	Micah
Neh	Nehemiah
NHC	Nag Hammadi Codex
Num	Numbers
Obad	Obadiah
Pahl.	Pahlavi
passim	throughout
Pers.	Persian
Pet	Peter (1 and 2)
Phoen.	Phoenician
pl.	plural

Preparation	*Preparation for the Gospel* of Eusebius
Prov	Proverbs
Ps	Psalms
Q	Quran
Qoh	Qohelet (Ecclesiastes)
r.	reigned
Rev	Revelation (Apocalypse of John)
Rom	Romans
SAE.	South Arabian Epigraphic
Sam	Samuel (1 and 2)
sing.	singular
Sir	Wisdom of Jesus Ben Sira (Ecclesiasticus)
Sum.	Sumerian
Syr.	Syriac
TB	Talmud Bavli (Babylonian Talmud)
Thess	Thessalonians
Tob.	Tobit
TY	Talmud Yerushalmi (Jerusalem Talmud)
Ug.	Ugaritic
Zech	Zechariah
Zeph	Zephanaiah

Chronology

BCE

2400–2250	Cuneiform texts from Ebla
2100	Oldest versions of Epic of Gilgamesh
2040–1750	Middle Kingdom in Egypt
1750–1697	Mari Tablets
1400–1300	Lives of the Patriarchs: Abraham, Isaac, Jacob, Joseph
1400–1200	Prophethood of Zoroaster
1150–1020	Period of Judges of Israel
1020–1000	Reign of Saul
1000	Founding of Jerusalem
1000–961	Reign of David
961–922	Reign of Solomon
922–901	Prophethood of Ahijah
869–850	Prophethood of Micaiah
869–849	Prophethood of Elijah
850–800	Prophethood of Elisha
775–750	Prophethood of Amos
750–698	Prophethood of Micah
746–736	Prophethood of Hosea
738–689	Prophethood of Isaiah
721	Fall of Samaria and deportation of Israel by the Assyrians
640–587	Prophethood of Jeremiah
631–609	Prophethood of Huldah
605–598	Prophethood of Habakkuk
587	Lachish Letters
586	Jerusalem destruction by Nebuchadnezzar

570–500	Pythagoras
559–530	Reign of Cyrus II
559	Prophethood of Deutero-Isaiah
555–539	Reign of Nabonidus
520	Prophethood of Haggai
520–515	Second temple built in Jerusalem
490–425	Herodotus
431–404	Peloponnesian War
404–358	Activities of Ezra and Nehemiah
400	Redaction of book of Chronicles
388	Plato founds Academy in Athens
334–323	Conquests of Alexander the Great
331	Founding of Alexandria
300 BCE–100 CE	Dead Sea Scrolls Written
175–164	Reign of Antiochus IV
167–164	Maccabean Revolt
166	Redaction of Book of Daniel
64 BCE–25 CE	Strabo
40 BCE–4 BCE	Reign of Herod the Great
25 BCE–50 CE	Philo of Alexandria
4 BCE–30 CE	Jesus Christ

CE

37–100	Josephus
45–58	Missions of Apostle Paul
50	Death of King Abgar V of Edessa
66–70	First Jewish Revolt against Rome
70	Destruction of second temple in Jerusalem
70–160	Philo of Byblos
100	Elchasai in Syria
106	Nabataean lands made into Roman province of Arabia
130–165	Justin Martyr
130–200	Irenaeus
132–135	Second Jewish Revolt against Rome (Bar Kokhba)
150–215	Clement of Alexandria
180–216	Bardaisan in Edessa
185–251	Origen

205–270	Plotinus
216–277	Mani
226–632	Sasanian Empire in Iran
232–305	Porphyry
245–330	Iamblichus
260–339	Eusebius of Caesarea
267–272	Queen Zenobia rules Eastern Empire from Palmyra
297–373	Athanasius of Alexandria
306–373	Ephrem the Syrian
325	Council of Nicaea
331–395	Gregory of Nyssa
339–397	Ambrose of Milan
342–420	Jerome
345	Death of Aphrahat
347–407	John Chrysostom
350	Nag Hammadi Codices copied
350–428	Theodore of Mopsuestia
354–430	Augustine of Hippo
399–466	Theodoret of Cyrrhus
399–503	Narsai
440–523	Philoxenus of Mabbug
451	Council of Chalcedon
570–632	Prophet Muhammad
575–650	John Climacus
619–687	Ibn Abbas
622	Hijrah
633–708	Jacob of Edessa
634–644	Caliphate of Umar b. al-Khattab
642–738	Hasan al-Basri
652	Death of Ka'b al-Ahbar
650	Major redaction of Mandaean texts
650–749	John of Damascus
654–728	Ibn Sirin
655–732	Wahb b. Munabbih
661	Death of Ali b. Abi Talib
676–759	John of Damascus
700–765	Ja'far al-Sadiq
705–767	Ibn Ishaq
744–828	Isho' bar Nun
762–840	Manicheism state religion of Uighurs

780–855	Ahmad b. Hanbal
800	Pesiqta d'Rab Kahana
801–862	Kindi
810–870	Bukhari
839–924	Tabari
909–1171	Fatimids in Egypt
980–1037	Ibn Sina
995	Death of Ibn al-Nadim
995–1067	Tusi
1009	Death of Dinawari
1036	Death of Tha'labi
1040–1105	Samuel ben Yitzhaq (Rashi)
1075–1144	Zamakhshari
1092–1167	Abraham Ibn Ezra
1126–1198	Ibn Rushd
1135–1204	Moshe ben Maimon (Maimonides, Rambam)
1150–1210	Fakhr al-Din al-Razi
1153	Death of Tabarsi
1153–1191	Suhrawardi
1160–1233	Ibn al-Athir
1160–1235	Rabbi David Qimhi (Radaq)
1165–1240	Ibn al-Arabi
1171	Death of Dionysius bar Salibi
1174	Death of Samuel ben Meir (Rashbam)
1194–1270	Moses ben Nahman (Nahmanides, Ramban)
1203–1283	Qazwini
1225–1286	Bar Hebraeus
1225–1295	Shem Tov Ibn Falaquera
1240–1305	Moses de Leon
1272	Death of Qurtubi
1300–1373	Ibn Kathir
1372–1449	Ibn Hajar
1437–1508	Don Isaac Abravanel
1445–1505	Suyuti
1453	Constantinople captured by Ottoman Turks
1475–1550	Obadiah ben Jacob Sforno
1545–1563	Council of Trent
1571–1640	Mulla Sadra
1580	Death of Kashani
1903–1982	Tabataba'i

Introduction

A Brief History of Prophecy in the Near East

Some of the earliest evidence for prophecy as a cultural institution in the Near East comes from the Syrian site of Ebla, modern Tel Mardikh (c. 2400–2250 BCE). The prophets mentioned in Eblaic tablets appear to be rather peripatetic, plying their trade in various cities in and around Ebla. Some are mentioned as coming to Ebla from cities in the region. In fact, some of them are designated by the cities from which they hail. Since the references to such figures is rather parenthetic, and the texts in which they appear often fragmentary, it is scarcely possible at this time to reconstruct any coherent picture of the prophet in Eblaic society, much less a clear conception of the social role of prophecy there. About all one can say is that the term used for *prophet* [nabiutum] at Ebla is cognate to the word used to designate prophets in the Hebrew Bible more than 1,200 years later. It is not necessary, however, to conclude that the prophets at Ebla and those found in the Bible represent the same social or cultural institutions, for the Semitic word for *prophecy* [nabû], can designate a wide variety of mantic practices and behaviors. Even within the biblical corpus alone, the word *prophet* is used of people who represent a diverse array of social classes, religious leanings, and community functions. The Eblaic texts do not make explicit, for example, whether these prophets received their prophecies "directly," by means of perceived intuition, or "indirectly," by way of deductive "divinatory" devices and techniques. Nevertheless, the appearance of the "nabiutum" at Ebla does indicate that prophecy, broadly conceived, was an active social phenomenon in the region of Syro-Canaan at a very early date. Since the study of these texts is still in its infancy, it is probable that they will shed a great deal more light on the early history of Syrian prophecy.

Roughly 500 years later, the related word *prophet* [nabû], appears to the east of Ebla at a site on the mid-Euphrates known as Tel Hariri, or ancient Mari (c. 1750–1697 BCE). Though more than 600 years earlier than the formation of ancient Israel, the Mari texts provide our closest parallels to the biblical prophets, and thus form an important link between the institution of prophecy in Israel and that mentioned in the texts from Ebla. In fact, according to the records at Ebla, Mari is one of the cities designated as the point of origin for some of the prophets, and both Ebla and Mari represent the civilization of the Amorites, a people to whom the famous Hammurapi of Babylon (c. 1792–1749 BCE) also was related. Unlike the later biblical texts that place prophets and prophecies within literary contexts, the cuneiform tablets from Mari mostly appear in epistolary contexts, most of which date to the final decade of King Zimri-Lim (c. 1730–1697 BCE). The tablets of Mari show that both intuitive and deductive forms of prophecy existed side by side as legitimate techniques of divine communication. Numerous types of prophets appear in the Mari letters, and often they possess overlapping mantic expertise. For example, five kinds of prophets are attested: a priest-prophet [shangûm], male cultic prostitute and transvestite [assinum], proclaimer [qabbatum], ecstatic [muhhu], and answerer [apilum]. This last type apparently also prophesied in groups. Some of these figures serve as dream interpreters, while others seek the divine word in the entrails of animals (extispicy) or through other means of divination. Still others appear to receive divine missives directly. In some cases, the same figure appears familiar with multiple methods of accessing the divine, thus demonstrating that no divinatory means was deemed illegitimate, much less illegal, as is found later in Israel.

Scholars have distinguished the intuitive prophecies of Mari from the biblical prophecies by pointing to the former's tendency to be concerned with the material welfare, personal safety, and legitimation of the royal house, rather than with its excesses and the social and moral inequities that it creates for the average citizen. Yet it is important to point out that the number of prophetic texts discovered at Mari is still relatively small, and the prophets' lack of focus on the average person may be more apparent than real. In fact, one prophecy from Mari does command the king in the name of Adad, the god of Aleppo, to judge the cases of his wronged subjects, a prophecy not unlike that found in the biblical book of Jeremiah (Jer 21:12, 22:3) and elsewhere.

Roughly contemporaneous with the materials from Mari are a series of cuneiform tablets that were unearthed at the site of Emar (modern Tel Meskene), a city that lies between Ebla and Mari on the mid-Euphrates

River. Though Emar was a regional player from the 24th century BCE until its destruction in 1187 BCE, most of its tablets date to the period 1550–1200 BCE. The core of the archive at Emar was found in a temple, and its tablets indicate that a number of divinatory and performative techniques were practiced there, including the use of lots, extispicy, and necromancy. The tablets found in this archive identify them as belonging to the "diviner of the gods of Emar." Since this title is closely associated with the word *prophet* [nabî], known also at Ebla and Mari, the archive of Emar allows the conclusion that prophecy was a widespread phenomenon in the region of Syro-Canaan long before the prophets of biblical fame.

In Mesopotamia proper, deductive divinatory techniques are attested quite early. Already in Sumerian times (c. 3100–2350 BCE), there are references to dream interpretation, oracles, the casting of lots, and other such techniques. In the centuries following, but especially after 1500 BCE, even more evidence is found for an even wider range of divinatory techniques, including the reading of animal livers, malformed human and animal births, lecanomancy, and astrology, to name but a few. Such omens could be provoked or unsolicited, and the literate priests of Mesopotamia took great pains to record the many omens that they observed.

Despite the pervasiveness of the divinatory sciences in Mesopotamia, more intuitive or "direct" forms of prophecy do not appear to have been major cultural phenomena until the reign of the Assyrian king Esarhaddon (c. 680–669 BCE). Since Esarhaddon is known to have summoned foreign diviners to his court, even from as far away as Egypt, some scholars have concluded that intuitive prophecy was imported to Assyria from Syro-Canaan. The evidence for this, however, is not definitive, and indeed, cultural exchange is seldom unilateral. In fact, a number of clay liver models discovered at Hazor in Israel and at Ugarit (modern Ras Shamra) in Syria demonstrate the huge impact of Mesopotamian divinatory culture in that region. In fact, Ugarit's priestly archives contain spells for curing snakebites, as well as dream, birth and astronomical omina, and necromantic materials. Nevertheless, Ugaritic texts have produced no reliable evidence of prophets or prophecy.

The Assyrian prophets who appear to employ intuitive methods for accessing the divine are mostly associated with Ishtar, a goddess of love and fertility, and their prophecies, like those at Mari, primarily serve the royal house. Sometimes these prophets are women; at other times, they appear to be transvestites. In each case the prophets appear to serve also as priests of the goddess. Male gods too appear in dreams and visions, though it is only Ishtar who apparently speaks directly through her prophets. Tools by which the prophets invoke intuitive prophecies in Assyria include excessive weeping, sighing, and praying. Devotees of the goddess Ishtar are often called "criers of lamentations." The appellative is informative, for the term *nabû*, which is used in Assyria in reference to prophecy, also appears to mean "weep" and "lament" (in addition to its usage "speak, prophecy"). Such a usage perhaps sheds light on the cognate term for prophecy found at Ebla, Mari, Emar, and in ancient Israel. It is noteworthy that among later Jewish mystics, Christian ascetics, and Islamic Sufis, ritual weeping similarly served as a tool for ushering in the divine revelation and obtaining God's mysteries.

The land of Egypt also possessed prophets, and as in Assyria, they are intimately connected with the priesthood. The Egyptian term used to designate a prophet, in fact, was ḥm-nṯr, literally "servant of the god," a title that also designated priests. Predicting the future does not appear to have been a significant function of the Egyptian priestly-prophet. Instead, his primary duties included offering the temple sacrifices, overseeing the procession of the sacred boats, ministering the food and drink offerings at the altar and at funerals, caring for sacred utensils, and the anointing of the king. Nevertheless, some Egyptian prophets are said to have foretold agricultural yields and failures, atmospheric and celestial phenomena, the appearance of diseases on humans and livestock, and the coming of floods and earthquakes.

Some of the earliest evidence for prophets in Egypt comes from a number of steles from Saqqara, which date to end of the Fifth Dynasty (c. 2465–2325 BCE). These refer to the "prophets of Heka," the Egyptian personification of magic, and interestingly, identify them also as physicians. Later Egyptian works similarly assert a close connection between those who practice "hekah" and those who prophesy about the future.

Though magic has a long history in Egypt, divination does not appear to have been a widespread practice there, or at least not as widespread as it was in Mesopotamia. The Middle Kingdom period (c. 2040–1750 BCE), for example, knows of a few hemerologies, as well as the practice of reading omens from vessels of water, but beyond this, there is scarcely any evidence for divination at this time. A manual, dating to the

New Kingdom Period (1551–712 BCE), was used for dream interpretation (oneiromancy), but it is difficult to discern if it was simply an arcane item in the library of its owner or whether it represents a growing interest in oneiromancy during this period. It is clear, however, from a later dream manual written in Demotic (c. 700 BCE–400 CE), that an interest in oneiromancy did grow, and by the Graeco-Roman period, the practice of seeking divine oracles through dreams (i.e., incubation) was fairly well known, especially in areas where a Greek presence was strongest.

Egyptian literary papyri also make reference to prophets. Perhaps the most famous among them is the prophecy of Neferti (also known as Neferohu), a text that dates to the Middle Kingdom, but claims to have taken place in the time of Fourth Dynasty pharaoh Snefru (c. 2613 BCE). It is thus a classic example of an *ex eventu* prophecy. The story relates how King Snefru summoned the magicians of his court for entertainment. One expert, named Neferti, then prophesied to Snefru that a series of catastrophes would devastate Egypt, and that a pharaoh would arise afterward, by the name Ameni (i.e., Amenemhet I), who would restore order. The name of the pharaoh subtly references the ruling king Pharaoh Amenemhet I (c. 1991–1962 BCE), the first king of the Twelfth Dynasty, who usurped the throne of Mentuhotep IV (c. 1992 BCE). Though this tale is clearly a pious fiction, the "prophecy" would not have been useful to the king had there not been present a widespread belief in the reliability of prophecy as a cultural phenomenon.

Another Egyptian literary text that reports a prophetic experience is the Tale of Wen-Amon. The text dates to the 11th century BCE and describes the journey of a high-ranking Egyptian official named Wen-Amon to Byblos in Phoenicia. In the story, Wen-Amon witnesses a young man, perhaps working in the court of the Phoenician king, who is seized one night in a state of frenzied prophetic ecstasy. While the story tells nothing about prophecy in Egypt, it does attest to the presence of prophetic activity in the Phoenician court in a period roughly contemporaneous with the Israelite kings David and Solomon.

Given the colossal cultural impact that the great centers of learning in Mesopotamia and Egypt had on the Levant, it is no surprise that prophecy can be found in the Hebrew Bible (Old Testament), the product of ancient Levantine culture. For the average reader, however, it is the Hebrew Bible that is the most famous source of information on prophets and prophecy, though the ancient Near Eastern context of the Israelite prophecy and the biblical prophets is less known.

As at Mari and in Mesopotamia proper, Israelite prophets display a wide variety of prophetic behaviors and experiences, and hail from a number of different social contexts. Some are central to the royal house, or have close access to it, while others appear as peripatetic and marginalized figures, even at odds with the ruling family. Still others, like Deborah, serve military functions and localized authority. A few have priestly status, whereas others have more humble beginnings. The prophet Amos, for example, appears to have been a sheep breeder by profession. Some prophets appear to cross more than one social context. Biblical texts often also reference non-Israelite prophets, and call into question (with heavy polemic) the cultic status and religious authority of a number of Israelite prophets. As in the records from Ebla, Mari, Mesopotamia proper, and Egypt, the biblical texts reference both male and female prophets, though male prophets are more widely attested.

Though the Hebrew Bible portrays a few prophets as employing somewhat mechanical means for inducing prophecy, overall the image the Bible projects is one that characterizes the act of prophesying primarily as an intuitive process. Terms employed in the Hebrew Bible in reference to both sanctioned and unsanctioned forms of prophecy are identical and include [massa'] "a burden, a lifting up," [hazah] "envision," [ra'ah] "see," and [na'am] "utter." Even the dream [halom] can serve a prophetic function. The most frequently used term for prophecy, however, is naba', meaning "speak." Cognates for this term occur in the archives found at Ebla, Mari, and Emar. Also used are the expressions "man of God" and "servant of Yahweh," titles that recall the Egyptian ḥm-nṯr, "servant of the god." Though visual modes of divine communication appear with some frequency, the great majority of biblical references to prophecy underscore the central role that speaking plays in the prophetic experience, either as a medium of divine communication or in delivery of the prophecy. Hence, the English term *prophesy*, a word that derives from a Greek word meaning "speak before."

Prophecy as a cultural phenomenon clearly played a role in the early history of Israel, but as a cultural institution it appears to have taken root and burgeoned especially from the eighth to the fifth centuries BCE. This period often is called the time of the "Classical Prophets," a phrase used in reference to those prophets to whom are attributed literary works. This label, however, masks a great deal of continuity that exists between earlier forms of prophecy as characterized by prophets like Abraham and Moses, and the later classical forms. While the former figures appear only in narratives and not in prophetic works, per se, the form and style of their prophecies, and the prophetic behavior these figures exhibit, is hardly distinguishable from the so-called classical types. In both periods one can find prophetic dramas, pronouncements of weal and woe, performative mantic practices, and the delivery of prophecies in literary, indeed poetic, forms. Both periods give witness to prophetic discipleship societies in which divine and ritual knowledge is safeguarded and transmitted from a master to his disciples (often called "sons" in the Hebrew text). These traits are visible even with regard to the prophets mentioned in the Bible whom the ancient writers chose to vilify.

While Israelite prophets are best known for their predictions of future events and for their miraculous acts, biblical texts portray them also, if not primarily, as social activists and political analysts. They often decry the abuses of wealth and privilege, even of the royal house, and cry for justice and action in the face of inequity, crisis, and complacency. Such a social role is a far cry from that portrayed in the Mesopotamian and Egyptian materials relating to prophets. Given such a social context, it is easy to understand why many of the Israelite prophets had enemies.

At the same time, it must not be forgotten that the Bible's books represent centuries of careful editing by redactors who have played a formative role in shaping the books' religious and political ideologies. Thus, Moses is portrayed as a paradigmatic prophet, and the narratives about his life experiences provide theological and literary frames for some of the later prophets. Moses' successor Joshua, for example, is portrayed as another Moses, as is the later prophet Elijah. Foreign prophets and modes of prophecy, and the kings who support them, are cast as enemies of Yahweh. This vilification often represents tensions between competing prophetic and priestly groups, each vying for influence in an effort to position itself as an authoritative mediator of God's word.

Such tensions also reflect a number of historical changes in Israel's political and economic landscape. The formation of a monarchy under Israel's first king, Saul (c. 1020 BCE), engendered a great deal of debate. The prophet Samuel, for example, warned the people that such a drastic shift in social and economic structure would not come without cost. Monarchies require changes in land tenure, corvée labor, and of course, taxation. They also diminish the authority of prophets, who often served the ritual (sacrificial) needs of many different population groups. Samuel, for example, is known to have performed his ritual services on several different mountains and in a number of different villages before and during the reign of Saul. Indeed, after the Jerusalem temple was constructed under King Solomon (c. 960 BCE), the cost of the monarchy that Samuel forecast was everywhere present, and the cult and its hierarchy were centralized. The mountain sanctuaries that formerly served prophets and worshippers alike were now illegal. Prophetic schools either worked within the new political structure or were forced to live a more marginalized existence.

The cessation of Israel's northern tribes from the united monarchy in 922 BCE only seemed to entrench the problems against which the anti-monarchic contingents had railed against. Coercion by the state, a continued legitimization of various cultic regimes, and a broad basis of serfdom were reaching into every aspect of social life. The monarchy's practice of distributing land grants in exchange for services began to threaten the traditional tribal system of land tenure. This resulted in the emergence of a new urban wealthy elite responsible for perpetuating a form of rent capitalism in which a failed harvest could cause forfeiture and indentured servitude. These changes to the traditional economic structure and the inequity they caused brought upon prophetic rebuke, especially against the idle rich. It is in this context that the prophet Isaiah harangues against "those who join house to house, who add field to field" (Isa 5:8), and in which the prophet Micah pronounces doom upon "those who oppress a man and his house, a man and his inheritance" (Mic 2:2).

At the same time, the divided monarchy exacerbated developing tensions between the various prophetic "schools." The indictments against other prophetic "schools" that are present at this time often served as polemical tools of self-identity: tools that also must be understood in the light of the growing Assyrian political, military, and presumably cultural dominance of the period. It is during this period that aspirations for political independence are reflected in the nature of Israelite prophecy, specifically in the form of legislation that defines sanctioned (Israelite and direct) forms of access to the divine from unsanctioned (foreign and indirect) forms. See, for example, the following Israelite law.

Let no one be found among you who consigns his son or daughter to fire, or who is an augur, a soothsayer, a diviner, a sorcerer, one who casts spells, or one who consults ghosts or familiar spirits, or who consults the dead. . . . Yahweh your God will raise up for you a prophet from among your own people, like myself; him shall you heed (Deut 18:10–11, 18:15).

The impact of Assyria during this period also informs a number of changes that are found in the form that Israelite prophecies take and the audience to which they are delivered. The Assyrians, for example, had a complex system of vassalage with a highly developed ambassador network. Rebellion against Assyrian power was frequently quelled by killing the rebellious king and installing a puppet regime. Unlike in previous eras of Mesopotamian rule, from the reign of the Assyrian king Tiglath-Pileser III (c. 744–727 BCE) and onward, torture, mass deportation, and military atrocities marked Assyria's formal response to rebellion. Such is the case, of course, with the Northern Kingdom of Israel, which the Assyrian king Sargon II eventually destroyed and deported in 721 BCE. Interestingly, it is roughly at this time that biblical prophets, like Micah and Hosea, threaten exile for disobedience to Yahweh.

It is also with the Assyrians that heraldry first becomes a widely used tool of persuasion and agitation. Hence, the biblical story of the Assyrian herald Rabshaqeh standing outside of Jerusalem's walls questioning the political savvy of its king, Hezekiah, and threatening the populace with exile if they do not conform to Assyrian policy (2 Kings 18). Such a practice may have provided the model for those prophets whom Yahweh commands to "Go and proclaim in the hearing of Jerusalem" (Jer 2:1), and who direct their prophecies not at the reigning king, but at the "people of the land." After the eighth century BCE, in fact, the prophets' primary object is no longer the ruling houses of the twin kingdoms Judah and Israel, but rather the people of Israel as a whole. Mesopotamian conceptions of heraldry also may lie behind an innovative usage of the Hebrew term *messenger* [malakh] at this time. Formerly it had been applied only to royal messengers and angels, but after the sixth century BCE, it begins to be used in reference to prophets (Hag 1:13; Mal 3:1). Some scholars have suggested that contact with Assyrian and later Babylonian cultures, which privilege written over oral forms of prophetic delivery, also lie behind the appearance of literary prophecies during this period.

The exilic and post-exilic periods (after 586 BCE) again begin to see changes in the manner and style of the prophetic experience and its literary forms. It is during this period that prophecy becomes more apocalyptic, baroque, and eschatological in content. Visual modes of prophecy (e.g., dreams, visions) that once held less privilege over auditory and direct modes resurface at this time with renewed authoritative vigor. Hence, the apocalyptic views found in the Book of Daniel and the prophetic authority of dreams and visions as expressed in the Book of Joel. Some of these changes may reflect Babylonian, or later Hellenistic, influence, but it is likely that the impetus and momentum for such changes were already well underway in the pre-exilic period.

It should not be concluded, however, based on these proposed points of influence, that Israelite prophecy was a derivative, much less monolithic, enterprise. On the contrary, Israelite prophecy was very much a native and dynamic development. Moreover, the Israelite prophets themselves demonstrate a diverse array of ideological and religious positions that can be understood only within their individual historical contexts. Indeed, there is sharp disagreement among the biblical prophets on a number of important topics including responsibility for ritual authority; the role of Israel's historic (and mythic) past; the utility of political isolationism; the role and meaning of sacrifice; the vulnerability of the temple; and corporate versus individual responsibility for sin.

In 586 BCE, the Babylonian king Nebuchadnezzar destroyed Yahweh's temple in Jerusalem, a monument that had stood at the center of Israel's religious life for almost four hundred years. The priestly families were deported to Babylon along with the other important figures of Israelite society. The threat of destruction that had loomed heavy since the Assyrian destruction of Israel to the north, and the sense of profound loss felt by the exiles now living in Babylon, similarly inform the changes in prophetic discourse that occur during this period. In particular, there are increasing references to a "New Jerusalem" ruled by a future messiah (i.e., anointed king) who will descend from the line of Judah. The political stability and independence that Jerusalem once enjoyed in times past now became the very model upon which to construct messianic hopes. For this reason, the political institutions of Jerusalem (e.g, king, city) ironically became central elements in prophetic idealism in ways that the religious institutions (e.g., temple, sacrifice, priests) never did—though the promulgation of Yahweh's law had always been central to the prophetic mission. Indeed, the prophets Hosea, Amos, and Ezekiel, who might never have visited Jerusalem, appeal to Zion traditions and beliefs about a future Davidic king. In fact, the only prophetic books that do not mention the city (i.e., Daniel, Jonah, Habakkuk), belong to a time when the centrality of Jerusalem and its temple were not in doubt.

The last few centuries before the Common Era mark the gradual decline of Israelite prophecy as a cultural institution. Though prophecy continued to be a productive social phenomenon in the region generally, its place within ancient Israelite religion was greatly diminished. The reduced role of prophecy in Israelite society was due to a series of historical events that shaped the religious culture of Judaism, which at this time can be said to be a religious system distinct from that of Israel before the exile. The return of the Judahites from Babylon in the mid-fifth century BCE required them to establish a new administrative infrastructure. The Jerusalem temple was rebuilt and a new priestly hierarchy put in place; this hierarchy eventually took over the roles of administration and justice that in former times had belonged to a council of elders. The high priest now served as the primary mediator between Yahweh and the people, and his authority, at least on a cultic and state level, gradually replaced that of the prophet. Indeed, even some of the last of the Israelite prophets (i.e., Haggai, Zechariah, and Malachi) fall back on the authority of the "former prophets" as a means of establishing authoritative precedent for their own prophecies and credentials.

When the Romans destroyed the second temple in 70 CE, Israelite prophecy, as a viable cultural institution within the folds of Pharisaic Judaism, came to an end. Nevertheless, Pharisaic tradition, as embodied in the Talmud, testifies to the survival and prophetic import of divine echoes (bat qol) and dreams, though only as greatly reduced forms of prophecy. It also reveals how the biblical prophets continued to serve an important theological role as integral links in the transmission of the Torah, standing between Moses and Joshua, on the one hand, and the men of the synagogue, on the other. Some later Jewish mystical traditions also recognize intuitive prophecy as an active phenomenon. They describe a process by which "God's glory" speaks through the mouth of the practitioner during mystical union.

Despite the demise of prophecy as an institution in Pharisaic Judaism, the phenomenon of prophecy did not come to an end elsewhere in the Hellenistic and late antique world. Even early non-Pharisaic Jewish groups such as the Essenes and early Christians continued to believe in the efficacy and authority of prophecy. Prophets can be found throughout the Hellenistic world, and in Egypt among so-called gnostic groups, as well as in Mesopotamia and Iran among Zoroastrians and Manichaeans. Prophets also are known to have served vital roles among the peoples of pre-Islamic Arabia. The Quran records the stories of a number of pre-Islamic Arab prophets including Hud, Salih, and Shuayb. Other figures familiar from the Bible, such as Seth, Abraham, and Ishmael, are considered by Muslim exegetes to be "Arab" prophets. Of course, the primary role of Muhammad in his establishment of Islam was as a prophetic figure, sent to the Arabs, but as the culmination of all earlier prophets and with a message for all peoples.

Although the biblical books comprising the Hebrew Bible were canonized in the early centuries of the Common Era, and the traditions they contain fixed in the religious discourse of ancient Judaism, stories about the prophets not found in the Bible continued to develop and circulate. Such stories were passed down through the generations and preserved by a number of Jewish and Muslim exegetes. These "stories of the prophets" can be found in authoritative rabbinical works such as the Mishnah and Talmud, and were the focus of much commentary in later midrashic texts. Muslim scholars produced a number of significant works dedicated exclusively to the stories of the prophets [Ar. qisas al-anbiya']. These accounts were drawn primarily from the Quran and its exegesis, but also from Jewish and Christian sources, folklore, pre-Islamic Arab sources, and other oral accounts. Many of the stories preserved in Islamic sources are not otherwise extant in written form, and scholars have recognized the rich symbiotic relationship between Jewish and Islamic discourses on prophets and prophecy.

In both Jewish and Muslim contexts are found greatly expanded legends about biblical and extrabiblical prophets. In Jewish tradition, for example, the prophet Elijah becomes a figure whose role and activities are largely *sui generis* of the biblical stories. He becomes a shapeshifter and member of the cabinet of the coming messiah who visits later rabbis and instructs them on the secrets of the universe. Muslim exegetes report that the prophet Muhammad and a band of his followers once met Elijah on a journey outside of Mecca. Sufis associate Elijah with the immortal prophet Khidr, and accounts of both Khidr and Elijah circulated throughout medieval Europe. The many and various recensions of the Alexander Romance, which include stories of Khidr, can be found in Ethiopia, Iran, Central Asia, France, Russia, and Iceland. That such stories circulated well beyond the confines of Judaism and Islam can be seen by the importance of such prophetic figures in a number of Christian works including the New Testament, apocryphal and pseudepigraphical texts, and a wide variety of popular stories. Whether such traditions represent expansions of the biblical stories or whether they preserve otherwise unattested ancient accounts is often difficult to discern. Nevertheless, the presence and prominence of such stories both in Jewish and Muslim sources calls out for close comparative study.

At the same time, it is important to note that although prophecy was not always seen as a continuing active social phenomenon in Judaism and Islam, it continued to be the object of careful examination and inquiry. Medieval Jewish and Muslim scholars focused on the definition of prophecy, prophecy's process in relation to history and soteriology, and how prophecy as a more general phenomenon could be understood through the extant stories of specific prophets in particular times and places. In large part, the emphasis of Jewish and Muslim scholars was upon the Bible and Quran as primary receptacles for the written remains of prophecy. But as well, Jews and Muslims enjoyed the close interaction of their written work and personal contacts in places of learning such as Spain, Egypt and North Africa, Iraq, and the Arabian Peninsula. Although Jewish and Muslim scholars may have insisted on the relative values assigned to certain sources and methods of interpretation, they shared a common language, a common archive of stories, and common interests in the focus upon the application of revealed discourse and its relationship to the means by which the discourse was revealed.

Jewish and Muslim scholars, for example, began to ask whether prophecies found in the Bible and Quran constituted poetry, indeed, whether the text of the Bible and Quran might be considered "literary" in any way. Though certainly these questions were informed in part by the trends in Humanistic learning prevalent during that time, they were far from being only contemporary concerns. Already in antiquity the biblical prophet Ezekiel had registered his unease with the tension between poetry and prophecy by asserting that the titles "proverb maker" and "singer of songs" were synonymous with "false prophet" (Ezek 21:5, 33:32). The early Greeks too had perceived such a tension, but had long ago proposed that the muse inspired the poet and prophet alike. Faced with the new conceptual paradigms of Humanism, however, these ancient tensions began to resonate with new significance. Thus, Shem Tov Ibn Falaquera (c. 1225–1295 CE) suggested that the Bible's poems fall into three levels. Some are conveyed through prophecy; some are composed through the holy spirit (but not as prophecy), like the Psalms, Proverbs, and the Song of Songs; and others were composed by skilled poets. Muslim scholars likewise made distinctions between revealed texts and redacted texts, and sought to understand the nature of language as an instrument of both human and divine communication.

Jews and Muslims also questioned the literary nature of prophecy by examining subtle differences in the ways that biblical texts refer to prophecies. In his work *The Nature of Prophecy: Moses and Other Prophets*, the Jewish scholar Profiat Duran (c. 15th century CE) argued that the words "Thus said the Lord" signified "the substance of the Lord's message, couched in the prophet's own language." Don Isaac Abravanel (c. 1437–1508 CE) similarly wrote on the method(s) by which prophecies were written down. Muslim scholars such as Suyuti (1445–1505 CE) made careful inventories of the type of language employed in the Quran, and worked toward a theory of language that was derived from the divine origins of the speech used in revelation. In his work *The Bezels of Wisdom*, the Sufi Ibn al-Arabi (1165–1240 CE) details the close connection between prophecy and the human characteristics of individual prophets. In general, Jewish exegetes recognized a human hand in shaping prophecy: all the Bible's prophetic writings were invested with divine authority, and inspired by the Holy Spirit, yet they also were conditioned by the personality and capacity of the prophet. Such a view explained the diversity of prophetic styles and types found in the Bible. Muslims equated prophetic speech with revealed speech, explaining that the whole text of the Quran was the word of God. Yet Muslim scholars were also sensitive to the multivalent use of language, and a distinction between language as God's speech and language as the vehicle for human communication. Some Jewish scholars too argued that the text of the Torah was ultimately dictated by God, even if the personal touch of Moses was evident. At roughly the same time, other Jewish groups, such as the Karaites, were asserting the prophetic significance of biblical texts such as the Psalms, and the intimate relationship between the human language of the text and divine revelation.

Clearly the institution of prophecy in the ancient Near East has a long and rich history, one that illustrates the organic nature of religious traditions. The meaning and significance of ancient Near Eastern prophecy, and its reflection in later Jewish and Islamic tradition, cannot be appreciated fully without recourse to the specific historical and social contexts that bore them. At the same time, one may learn a great deal about the ancient prophets and their stories by approaching the subject comparatively. This is especially important with regard to prophecy in Islam and Judaism, for both draw significantly upon the vast prophetic "heritage" of the ancient Near East. It is this heritage that we hope this book makes evident. If, in certain cases, the entries themselves do not provide incontrovertible evidence of the intercultural transfer and exchange of ideas, we hope that the broad range of similarities and correspondences that are provided will be enough to budge both biblical studies and Islamic studies from their disciplinary isolation.

The Dictionary

– A –

AARON. Brother of Moses and Miriam, Aaron is the eponymous ancestor of the priestly Aaronites in biblical tradition. The etymology of the name Aaron [Heb. Aharon, Ar. Harun] is uncertain, but the pseudepigraphical Testament of Aaron and later Jewish exegesis fancifully derive the name from a Hebrew expression "Woe to this pregnancy" [Heb. ah ha-ron]. Biblical scholars, however, point to Egyptian cognates for the name.

Since the Aaronites are the central clan within the priestly tribe of Levi (*see also* LEVITE), Aaron's descendants are considered high priests (Exod 28–29; Lev 8–9). Exodus and Leviticus mention specific duties under the supervision of the Aaronite priests, and Aaron receives a special revelation from God restricting him and his sons from drinking wine when approaching the Tabernacle, distinguishing between the sacred and profane and the pure and impure, and teaching God's statutes to the Israelites. Some scholars see a parallel between the revelation of these three things to Aaron and Muslim traditions that report the revelation of three Quran verses to Umar b. al-Khattab, the prophet Muhammad's closest companion. In the Bible, Aaron was given charge of the Urim and Thummim (Exod 28:30; Lev 8:5–9; *see also* URIM AND THUMMIM).

Throughout biblical and Quranic narratives, Aaron frequently accompanies Moses. Both accounts describe how God offered Moses his brother Aaron as his spokesperson (Exod 4:10–17; Q 28:33–35). Q 19:53 considers Aaron a prophet, and Exod 7:1 states that God made Aaron to be the prophet of Moses. Nevertheless, Aaron plays less of an active role in these texts than his brother Moses. Before the pharaoh, Aaron does, however, play a significant role. Jewish exegesis notes that

Aaron was responsible for the three plagues that involved the earth and water, and it is Aaron's rod, said to have been created along with nine other items before the earth, that sprouts buds in Numbers 17. Aaron has no dialogue in the Quran, nor does he play a role in the plagues according to the Quran (Q 7:127–136). Q 10:75 refers both to Moses and Aaron being sent by God, but other verses indicate that Moses was sent alone (Q 11:96, Q 40:23, Q 43:46). In Q 20:49 the pharaoh asks Moses, "Who is the Lord of you (both)," presumably referring to Moses and his brother, but Aaron does not appear in the exchange that follows.

In both the Bible and the Quran, Aaron is linked to the making of the golden calf by the Israelites in the wilderness of wandering. Exod 32:4 states that Aaron made the golden calf, and Q 7:150–51 indicates that Moses held Aaron responsible for it. In Q 20:80–98, Aaron is present, but it is "al-Samiri" who creates the golden calf. Muslim exegesis explains that al-Samiri threw some dust from the hoof of Gabriel's horse into the jewelry being melted by the Israelites, causing it to emerge making noises as though it were alive (Q 20:88). In Exod 32:24 Aaron also claims that the calf emerged by itself after he threw the jewelry into the fire, but no noises are mentioned.

Numbers 12 gives an account of another incident when Aaron confronts Moses. The narrative describes how Aaron and Miriam reproached Moses for marrying a Cushite woman, at which point God appeared and afflicted Miriam with leprosy. In verses 11–12, Aaron intercedes on her behalf and she is healed after being shut out of the Israelite camp for seven days. The Aboth d'Rabbi Nathan explains that Aaron and Miriam confronted Moses because they claimed that prophets did not need to abstain from sex in order to receive revelations, and that Moses' abstinence was intended only to underscore his holiness.

The Bible states that the death of Aaron occurred before that of Moses (Deut 32:50) and that after he died, his priestly office passed to his son Eliezer (Num 20:22–29). Muslim exegesis of Q 5:26 reports that Aaron died before entering the Holy Land. Later Muslim exegesis and Jewish midrashic texts preserve extended accounts of Aaron's death. According to these stories, Moses and Aaron found a cave, and when Aaron entered he died. Upon his return, Moses is said to have been accused by the Israelites of killing Aaron, and was threatened until angels intervened and demonstrated that Aaron was not killed.

Some Muslim exegetes report that the "Seventy" in Q 7:155 were punished because they accused Moses of killing his brother.

ABD AL-MUTTALIB. Paternal grandfather of the prophet Muhammad, son of Hashim b. Abd al-Manaf. There are no sources external to Muslim tradition with information about Abd al-Muttalib, and the accounts of his life may be influenced by his later relationship to Muhammad. In the biography of Muhammad, Abd al-Muttalib is best known for his role in the rediscovery of the well of Zamzam and the buried temple implements in the pit of Zamzam. *See also* HIDDEN TEMPLE VESSELS; WELL.

ABGAR LEGEND. Account of an exchange of letters between Abgar V the king of Edessa (d. 50 CE) and Jesus. The letters are mentioned first by Eusebius, who claims to have seen them in the archives of Edessa. The *Doctrine of Addai*, a fourth- or fifth-century CE Syriac work, includes the text of the letters and the account of Addai's conversion of the city. Ephrem the Syrian mentions Addai the apostle in connection with the conversion of Edessa, but not the letters. When the pilgrim Egeria visited Edessa at the end of the fourth century CE she was told about the letters, but apparently not about Addai. At the end of the fifth century CE the letters were included in the apocrypha listed in the Gelasian Decree. The account of the letters was popularized by the Latin translation of Eusebius in the West, and the *Doctrine of Addai* was translated into Armenian, Arabic, Persian, Old Church Slavonic, and Coptic.

In the first letter Abgar invites Jesus to visit him in Edessa, heal him from his affliction, and stay in the city safe from the Jews. In his reply, Jesus blesses Abgar for believing without seeing and explains that he must remain in Jerusalem to complete his mission, but will send an apostle to Edessa after his heavenly ascension.

ABIGAIL. Wife of Nabal, the Carmelite (1 Sam 25:14, 27:3, 30:5; 2 Sam 2:9, 30:5). When Nabal, who is described as a churlish man from the "House of Caleb" (1 Sam 25:3), denied David and his famished troops provisions from among his flocks, David sought to retaliate by killing him. Abigail's smooth words, however, prevented David from taking action. After hearing that his wife had succeeded in assuaging

David's wrath, Nabal became terrified and died 10 days later (1 Sam 25:37–38). When David heard about Nabal's death, he married Abigail. The mention of Abigail as David's sister elsewhere in the Bible (2 Sam 17:25; 2 Chr 2:16) has prompted some scholars to reconstruct Abigail's marriage to David as a kinship marriage. Though Abigail is not called a prophet in the Bible, talmudic tradition lists her, along with Sarah, Miriam, Deborah, Hannah, Huldah, and Esther, as one of seven female Israelite prophets (TB Megillah 14a).

ABOTH D'RABBI NATHAN. Forty-chapter extracanonical tractate known in two primary recensions that was joined to the Babylonian Talmud, and thus constitutes a supplement (*see also* TOSEFTA) to the Talmudic tractate named Aboth. It is a rather composite and unique Jewish literary work that contains a variety of material including parables, narratives, formulaic numerical sayings, midrashic materials, and interpretations of biblical verses. The work is named after Rabbi Nathan (c. 130–160 CE), which some scholars see as anachronistic, though much of the material contained in Aboth d'Rabbi Nathan must precede c. 200 CE. Nevertheless, the work underwent some editing and revision in the centuries following, and some of its passages date no earlier than the sixth to seventh centuries CE.

ABRAHAH AND THE ELEPHANTS. Muslim exegetes interpret Q 105 as a reference to the attack of the South Arabian king Abrahah against Mecca and the Ka'bah in the year of the prophet Muhammad's birth (570 CE). According to Greek historical sources, Abrahah, originally an Ethiopian slave of a Roman merchant, took control of South Arabia around the middle of the sixth century CE. South Arabian inscriptions also attest to the reign of Abrahah, but not to his attack on Mecca. According to early Muslim sources, Abrahah sought to attack Mecca and destroy the Ka'bah during the lifetime of Muhammad's grandfather Abd al-Muttalib because a church Abrahah built in San'a, designed to lure pilgrims from other parts of Arabia, had been desecrated. Abrahah is said to have come to the outskirts of Mecca, guided by Abu Righal, with an army that included elephants. Abd al-Muttalib met with Abrahah, but Abrahah refused to turn from his mission, so Abd al-Muttalib and a group from the Quraysh stood at the door of the Ka'bah and prayed for God to save them from

Abrahah. In the morning, the elephants refused to enter the sanctuary at Mecca, and birds flocked down upon them, dropping stones of hardened clay [Ar. sijjil]. Abrahah and his men fled home, struck with a disease, and most of them died along the way except for Abrahah, who died once he arrived back in San'a.

Modern scholars have questioned the historicity of Abrahah's attack, but it is evident from Muslim sources that the account of the attack and its association with Q 105 was understood as heralding the dawning of a new prophetic age. In some aspects the account also parallels Jewish accounts of attacks against the temple in Jerusalem, and the punishment of being rained upon with stones of hardened clay is also found in the Quranic version of the destruction of Sodom.

ABRAHAM. Formerly called Abram (Gen 17:5), Abraham is recognized as the "founding father" and patriarch of ancient Israel and its religion. The Quran (Q 2:130–140, 3:65–68, 4:125, 16:120–124) depicts Abraham as the founder of the true religion, which was revived by the prophet Muhammad, and thus, Islam is called the "Religion of Abraham." According to the Bible, Abraham was the son of Terah (Gen 11:27). Q 6:74 seems to indicate that Abraham's father was named Azar, but Tabari claims Abraham's father was named Terah and gives the same genealogy as that found in Genesis 11, though he inserts Canaan as the son of Arpachshad, where the Bible gives Shelah as his son (Gen 11:12).

The dating of Abraham's life is debated, but biblical texts appear to place him c. 1400 BCE (not the often heard 2000 BCE). Abraham's homeland is said to be Ur of the Chaldeans (Gen 11:31), a city probably to be identified with the modern town of Urfa in northern Iraq. According to the Talmud, Ur was in Babylonia (TB Baba Batra 91a). Muslim exegetes preserve a variety of opinions regarding the place of Abraham's birth. Tabari reports that some say his birthplace was Sus, understood by Muslim geographers to be somewhere in Khuzistan. But perhaps Sus is to be related to the ancient Iranian city of Susa. Other Muslim exegetes assert that he was born in Babylon or that he was born near Kaskar, or in Haran, but later moved with his father to Babylon. The Bible also states that Abraham spent some time in Haran with his father (Gen 12:1–5), an interpretation evident in the New Testament as well (Acts 7:2–4; Jdt 5:8–9).

The biblical cycle of Abrahamic stories appears in Gen 10:26–25:18 and begins with Abraham as an adult, but the Quran provides numerous details about his birth and youth. Both Jewish and Muslim exegesis contain accounts of Abraham's nativity that closely parallel those of Moses and Jesus. According to these accounts, Abraham's birth was heralded by a star that, the local astrologers told Nimrod, signified the birth of a man who would destroy his kingdom. Nimrod ordered the slaughter of all male children, but Abraham was born in a cave, at which time he matured and miraculously began to speak. The Quran narrates Abraham's attempts to convince his father and his people of the error in worshipping idols (Q 19:41–50, 21:51–70, 37:83–99). Q 21:68–69 refers to the fiery furnace into which Abraham was cast by Nimrod for opposing the idols, a reference that is found also in Jewish exegesis on Gen 15:7 (Pirqe d'Rabbi Eliezer 25). The Apocalypse of Abraham, Genesis Rabbah, and Muslim exegetes add that Abraham's father was himself an idol maker (perhaps in reference to Josh 24:2). Q 9:114 refers to Abraham's renunciation of his father on account of his enmity toward God, and Jubilees 11:16 states that Abraham separated himself from his father because of his idolatry.

The Bible portrays Abraham as a man rich in theophoric experiences, some of which occur near trees with oracular associations. In the dream of a foreign king (Abimelech of Gerar), God refers to Abraham as a prophet (Gen 20:7), and later prophetic and historical tradition understands him as a "friend of God" (Isa 41:8; 2 Chr 20:7). Q 4:125 similarly states that God took Abraham as a friend, and seems to connect this with the appellation "Hanif" given to Abraham 10 times in the Quran. According to the Bible and the Quran, Abraham received visits from angels (Genesis 18; Q 11:69–74, 15:51–56, 51:24–30). Q 6:74–87 describes how Abraham arrived at monotheism after observing astral phenomena, an event that Muslim exegetes place just after his birth. Josephus also asserts that Abraham was the first monotheist (Antiquities 1.8.2). Hellenistic and late antique sources refer to Abraham as the original "Chaldean," having knowledge of the heavenly bodies and their interpretations. Elsewhere, the same verse is interpreted to indicate that Abraham ascended to the heavens, where he observed astral phenomena, a notion perhaps also reflected in Q 6:75. 2 Baruch and the Apocalypse of Abraham also refer to Abraham's visions of heaven, hell, and the future of Israel, including the temple in Jerusalem. Jewish writings, however, read Gen 15:5 as referring to God's command to Abraham to renounce astrology (Genesis Rabbah 44:8–12; TB Shabbath, 150a; Nedarim 32a).

Muslim tradition most closely associates Abraham's prophetic activities with establishing the sanctuary at Mecca and the pilgrimage there. Gen 12:6–7 and 13:18 describe Abraham's building of altars at the site of special trees. Jewish exegesis and some of the Targums on Gen 21:33 understand Abraham's planting of a "tamarisk" tree at Beersheba as the establishment of a sanctuary like the Garden of Eden. Josephus (Antiquities 1.10) and the Zohar (Zohar I, 102b) treat the tamarisk of Gen 21:33 as having come to Abraham from paradise where it had been kept since its creation at the time when the world was founded. The Genesis Apocryphon describes Abraham's vision of two trees concerning Sarah's interaction with the Egyptians. Muslim exegesis narrates how Abraham and Ishmael built the Ka'bah and instituted the pilgrimage to Mecca (Q 2:125–29, 3:96–97, 22:26–27). Q 14:35–41 also alludes to the discovery of Zamzam, which Muslim exegetes relate to the account of Beersheba in Genesis 21.

Jewish exegesis recounts the life of Abraham as a series of 10 trials. The Pirqe d'Rabbi Eliezer lists these as: Abraham's hiding at his birth, imprisonment and fiery furnace, migration from his homeland (Gen 12:1–9), famine that takes him to Egypt (Gen 12:10), Sarah being taken by the Egyptians (Gen 12:11–20), battle with the eastern kings (Gen 14), vision between the pieces (Gen 15), covenant of circumcision (Gen 17), casting away of Ishmael and Hagar (Gen 21), and the binding of Isaac (Gen 22). Q 37:106 calls God's command that Abraham sacrifice his son "a clear trial." Q 2:124 refers to the "words" that Abraham fulfilled, making him an example [Ar. Imam] for all people to follow. Muslim exegetes interpret this as being "ten words" referring to Abraham's institution of Muslim purity rites.

Other episodes from the life of Abraham are expanded in Jewish and Muslim exegesis. Talmudic and midrashic writings recall that in his battle against eastern kings, Abraham threw dust, which turned to swords, and chaff, which turned to arrows. Q 2:260 refers to the resurrection of four birds that Abraham had been instructed to dismember, perhaps related to Abraham's sacrifice of the birds in Genesis 15:9–10 (Gen 15:9 states that he sacrificed five animals). The

Genesis Apocryphon extends Abraham's migration to include a journey around the boundaries of the land promised to him, and his meeting with the Canaanite king of Shalem. The figure of Melchizedek (Gen 14:17–20) is elaborated, in some of the texts from the Dead Sea Scrolls and in the texts of the Nag Hammadi codices.

Abraham's attempted sacrifice of his son plays an important role in Jewish, Christian, and Muslim exegesis. Jewish exegesis views the willingness of Isaac as atoning for the sins of Israel, and Christian texts see Isaac as foreshowing Christ's suffering for Christians. Muslim exegetes are divided over whether the intended victim was Isaac or Ishmael. Many of the earliest and most respected exegetes claim that it was Isaac, but the view that it was Ishmael is predominant in later exegesis, especially when the account of the sacrifice is attached to Abraham and Ishmael's building of the Ka'bah at Mecca. A significant note of difference separating the Jewish and Muslim accounts is the description of the sacrifice itself. According to Gen 22:9, the sacrificial victim was to be burnt on the altar, whereas Q 37:103 indicates that Abraham was to slaughter his son but does not mention a sacrificial pyre. In Muslim exegesis Abraham also attempts to cut his son's throat at least one time before God stops him and provides a special ram, which appears as the "great sacrifice" in Q 37:107.

The Quran mentions the "Scriptures of Abraham" (Q 53:36–37 and 87:18–19), and Muslim sources give brief quotations from these books, which were supposed to have been revealed to Abraham. These traditions might refer to certain apocryphal texts attributed to Abraham such as the Testament of Abraham and the Apocalypse of Abraham. The Talmud also credits him with having written Psalm 89, by reading the incipit's reference to Ethan the Ezrahite as a pen name for Abraham (TB Baba Batra 15a).

ISAAC ABRAVANEL (1437–1508 CE). Jewish Bible exegete. Abravanel was born and studied in Spain, where he wrote on the natural sciences and on prophecy. He served as the treasurer for King Alfonso V of Portugal and wrote a commentary on the whole of the Hebrew Bible. His commentary focused on the practical aspects of the Torah and the Prophets, and included an introduction to each of the separate books.

ABU RIGHAL. Muslim scholars report that Abu Righal was one of the people of Thamud who was buried with the Golden Bough, which is thought to be a sign of the destruction of the people of Thamud, and their rejection of the prophet Salih. According to an early report, the prophet Muhammad pointed out Abu Righal's grave to his followers on the road between Mecca and Ta'if. Abu Righal is said to have been visiting Mecca at the time the people of Thamud were destroyed, but once he left the sanctuary of Mecca he too was struck down like his people. Other reports associate Abu Righal with hamstringing the she-camel of the prophet Salih. Still others identify Abu Righal as the one who guided Abrahah to Mecca in his attempt to destroy the Ka'bah in the year of the prophet Muhammad's birth.

ACROSTIC. A compositional device periodically employed by Hebrew poets in which each successive poetic line begins with a successive letter of the alphabet. Thus, to demonstrate using English, the first line would begin with the letter "A," the second with "B," the third with "C," and so on. Several biblical texts contain acrostics, including Neh 1:2–8; Psalm 37, 111, 112, 145; Prov 31:10–31; and Lamentations. Acrostics also appear in the extracanonical psalms among the Dead Sea Scrolls. The acrostics in Psalms 25 and 34 spell out the word *aleph* ("teach, alphabetize"), which has led some scholars to suggest that acrostics served a mnemonic function, assisting the memorization of the text, but since acrostics were employed also in Mesopotamia and Egypt, often in mantic contexts, others have suggested that they served a performative purpose, perhaps as a means of establishing cosmic order through language.

ACTS OF PAUL. Account of the missionary activities of the apostle Paul including his martyrdom. The text is dated to the second century CE, and parts of it are attested in a third-century CE Greek papyrus and a long Coptic papyrus of the fourth or fifth century CE. No complete text exists. The core of the text appears to have been organized around the stories of Paul's missions to major cities on his way to Rome, where he is martyred by Nero. Paul's main theme is the celibate or virginal life, which was seen as a threat to Roman society. The part of the text that deals with his conversion of Thekla was transmitted and preserved separately as the Acts of Paul and Thekla. At odds with the account of Paul's missions in the canonical Acts of the Apostles in the New Testament is the absence, in the Acts of Paul, of references to the hostility of the Jews.

ACTS OF PETER. Apocryphal text recounting some of the deeds of the apostle Peter including a contest with the magician Simon Magus and his martyrdom (*see also* MAGIC). The best attested copy of the text is a Latin manuscript dated to the sixth or seventh century CE, but the composition of the text is dated to the end of the second century CE on the basis of references in other Christian writers. Greek, Coptic, Syriac, Ethiopic, Arabic, Armenian, and Old Church Slavonic recensions demonstrate that the concluding chapters of the text were transmitted as a separate treatise entitled the Martyrdom of Peter. Among the fantastic deeds of Peter are his endowing of a dog and an infant with prophetic powers to speak, repairing a statue of the emperor, and raising three people from the dead. The text ends with Peter's martyrdom, being crucified upside down, apparently signifying his alien status in the world.

ACTS OF PETER AND THE TWELVE APOSTLES. Coptic text from Nag Hammadi (VI,1) describing the missions of Peter and the other disciples of Jesus. The first part of the text is an allegorical tale of a merchant who offers pearls to the poor who journey to his city. This is taken as a reference to Jesus and his mission on earth. In the second part of the text, Peter and the other disciples journey to the city of the pearl merchant, where Christ commissions them to return to the earth and heal the poor.

ACTS OF THE APOSTLES. Title given to a number of texts that report the activities of the early Christian apostles and focus primarily on their missionary activities and fantastic deeds. The canonical Acts of the Apostles, found in the New Testament, is considered to be a single unit with the Gospel of Luke and describes the ascension of Jesus; the Christian community in Jerusalem; and the earliest missions of Stephen, Philip, Peter, and Paul. There is also a group of five apocryphal acts that were treated as a unit in a Manichaean collection thought to date to the fourth century CE. The five apocryphal acts include the Acts of Peter, Acts of John, Acts of Andrew, Acts of

Thomas, and the Acts of Paul. Each of these texts exists only in part, and all appear in multiple Christian recensions. Each is cited by a variety of later Christian writers. The Acts of Peter and the Twelve Apostles appears in Coptic and was discovered also at Nag Hammadi (VI,1). Numerous later texts contain similar accounts of the acts of various apostles including Bartholomew, Mark, Barnabas, Philip, Luke, James son of Zebedee, James the brother of Jesus, Simon the Canaanite, and Judas Thaddeus.

ACTS OF THOMAS. Stories of the apostle Thomas consisting of 13 parts. The text is thought to have been composed in Syriac sometime in the third century CE and translated into Greek around the same time, though the extant Syriac recension is not considered to be the original. This text, along with four other apocryphal acts texts, were included in the Manichaean canon.

The apostle Thomas is known from other writings such as the Coptic Gospel of Thomas and the Book of Thomas. He also is called Judas Thomas, the twin of Jesus, in the Old Syriac version of John 14:22 and the Abgar Legend. In Eusebius and Origen, Thomas is said to be the apostle sent to Parthia, but in the Acts of Thomas he appears as the apostle sent to India. The transfer of Thomas's relics to Edessa (*see also* RELICS) also is mentioned by Ephrem the Syrian and the pilgrim Egeria who visited Edessa in the fourth century CE.

The Acts of Thomas includes a number of loosely connected episodes narrating the miracles and fantastic deeds of the apostle. Many of these are modeled upon the biblical narratives of the patriarchs and prophets. In many respects, the figure of Thomas is portrayed as a symbol for the ideal soul, a notion reinforced in the "Hymn of the Pearl," which appears in the text's ninth section. This interpretation of the acts is particularly prevalent in the Manichaean notion of the apostle. Throughout, the contrast between the beauty of the soul and the sinful condition of the body is represented in terms made familiar by stories of other prophets that contrast worldly existence with obedience to God (*see also* ASCETICISM).

The text ends with an account of the martyrdom of Thomas. Accused of being a magician, Thomas is said to have been slain by four soldiers but then buried in the tomb of earlier kings. The day after his death Thomas appeared to his followers, and sometime later the local king opened the tomb to take the bones of Thomas only to find that they already had been removed. The dust from where the bones had lain, however, was still able to rid the king's son of his possession by a demon (*see also* DEMON; POSSESSION).

AD. The People of Ad appear in the Quran in relation to the prophet Hud. Muslim exegetes provide the genealogy of Hud as descending from Shelah b. Arpachshad b. Shem b. Noah but also Eber b. Shelah b. Arpachshad b. Shem b. Noah. The Ad are said to be descendants of Uz b. Aram b. Shem b. Noah, and are said to be among the "Original Arabs," a grouping of peoples including the Ad, Thamud, Jurhum, Tasam, Amim, Midian, Amalek, Abil, Jasim, Qahtan, and the Banu Yaqtan. It is possible that the Ad are to be identified with the "Iyad" known from Aramaic inscriptions or the "Oaditai" mentioned by the Greek geographer Ptolemy (second century CE). Other scholars have argued that the proper name comes from an Arabic word [Ar. 'adi] meaning "ancient." There is also a reference to "Admah" as one of the cities of the plain mentioned in Gen 10:19.

In Muslim exegesis, the Ad are known for their great size and for their buildings. The exegesis of Q 7:69 includes reports that the Ad were over 100 cubits in height (i.e., 125 feet) and had great strength. The "artifices" mentioned in Q 26:129 are interpreted as castles, great buildings, and artificial water basins created by the Ad. Q 89:6–14 also refers to Ad and "Iram of the lofty supports," which Muslim exegetes understood as the great city of the Ad, which moved around the earth and was made out of gold and silver. In later Muslim sources, this city is given the name Ubar, and some scholars identify it with sites along the trade route from Oman.

ADAM AND EVE. The primordial couple credited with parenting the human race. In the Bible, the story of Adam and Eve appears in two creation accounts. The first (Gen 1:1–2, 1:4) employs the name Adam as a metonym for all humankind; man and woman are created simultaneously (Gen 1:27). The second treats Adam as an individual from whom God takes a rib and fashions the first woman after putting him into a deep sleep (Gen 2:7–25). Eve is the name given to the first woman by Adam (Gen 3:3), because it means "living" [Heb. havah] and she is "the mother of all living." Later Jewish and Muslim sources relate that God took soil from different parts of the earth to create Adam.

On the basis of Q 7:172, Muslim exegetes relate that all humanity was taken from the loins of Adam before their birth and made to testify that God is their Lord. Muslim sources also narrate how the angels failed to retrieve from earth the clay with which to fashion Adam until the Angel of Death was able to take it from different spots, mixing together red, white, and black soil. In the Quran, the story of Adam and Eve is intertwined, and closely paralleled with the story of Iblis and the origins of Satan (*see also* SATAN). Q 2:30–33 begins with the angels protesting God's plan to place Adam on the earth. Muslim exegetes explain that before the creation of Adam the Jinn had lived on earth for a thousand years, but had become so corrupt that God sent his angels to banish them to the islands of the seas and the edges of the mountains (*see also* JINN). The Quran (Q 7:11–18, 15:26–44, 17:61–65, 18:50–51, 38:67–88) states that after he created Adam, God commanded the angels to prostrate themselves to Adam, but Iblis refused and so was cast out of paradise. The notion that Satan was cast out of the Garden of Eden, because he was jealous of God or other angels, also appears in 2 Enoch and 3 Baruch. That Satan was jealous of Adam is found in the Life of Adam and Eve and the *Book of the Cave of Treasures*. The Babylonian Talmud relates that Eve copulated with the serpent (TB Yebamoth 103b), who wanted to kill Adam and marry her (TB Sotah 9b). Genesis Rabbah (15.6) sees the creation of Satan as coinciding with the creation of Eve, and thus, takes the reference to her as the "mother of all living" to include also the demons (*see also* DEMON).

According to Genesis 1, Adam was created at the end of creation, and the Talmud asserts that Adam was created on the eve of the Sabbath, a view it states is meant to distance itself from the Sadducean (Zadoqite) belief that Adam was a partner in God's creation (TB Sanhedrin 38a). Gen 2:7 states that Adam was created from the earth. In several passages the Quran (Q 15:26, 28, 33) describes Adam as being created from "dried clay" and "stinking slime," and Q 55:14 refers to Adam's body as being from a substance "like potter's clay" [Ar. salsal]. Tabari explains that Adam's body was left lying around for some time before God brought it to life, and during that time Iblis would come by and kick it with his foot, and the body would make hollow sounds. In Q 7:12 and 38:76 Iblis refuses to prostrate himself to Adam, because Adam is made of clay whereas Iblis is made of fire. Muslim exegetes also report that because the angels and God were solid, but Adam was hollow, Iblis was able to enter Adam's mouth and exit his anus. Genesis Rabbah emphasizes that Adam was created as a fully developed adult (Genesis Rabbah 14:7), and the Talmud records traditions in which Adam was created with two faces and Eve was formed from his "tail" (TB Erubin 18a).

The naming of the animals is interpreted as a lesson for the angels and a trial to prove Satan wrong according to Jewish and Muslim exegesis. Q 2:30 reports that God told the angels that he knew something they did not know, and Q 2:31 states that God taught Adam the names of all the things of the earth and challenged the angels to tell the names. In Q 2:32 the angels abdicate, and Adam reveals the names, which God says is the knowledge of what is hidden in the heavens and the earth. The notion that Adam had secret knowledge that he passed down to his sons and future prophets is found also in the Apocalypse of Adam and Testament of Adam. The Talmud relates that Adam is said to have had intercourse with every animal until Eve was created, and to have begotten ghosts and male demons before begetting "a son in his own likeness, after his own image" (Gen 5:3, TB Erubin 18b). The latter view is reflected in the Alphabet of Ben Sirah, which sees the she-demon Lilith as Adam's first wife (*see also* LILITH).

The test of Adam and Eve is recorded in Genesis 3, Q 2:34–39, and Q 20:115–26. According to the Bible, God prohibited Adam from the Tree of the Knowledge of Good and Evil (Gen 2:16–17). The rationale for the prohibition is interpreted to be that after acquiring knowledge of good and evil (divine knowledge), Adam and Eve must be barred from immortality (Gen 2:17, 3:3). Q 20:120 identifies the prohibited tree as the Tree of Immortality, indicating that eating from it was an act of sheer disobedience since Adam and Eve already were immortal in the Garden of Eden. Some Muslim exegetes explain that the tree was such that whoever ate from it would defecate and as such the tree was forbidden because feces were not allowed in the Garden of Eden (*see also* TREE OF LIFE).

The punishment for Adam and Eve's transgression is their expulsion from the Garden of Eden, which results in the spread of human civilization. Later prophets refer to Adam and Eve as the first example of sin in the world. The prophet Hosea refers to the sin of Adam and Eve as paralleling the sins of the tribe of Ephraim (Hos 6:7), and Job questions why he has been punished by comparing himself to Adam (Job 31:33). The Christian notion of "original sin" (Rom 5:12) also refers to the transgression of Adam and Eve. The Quran makes it clear that the sin of Adam and Eve resulted in their "Fall" from the Garden of Eden (Q 2:38, 20:123). Muslim exegetes describe Adam as having fallen to Sri Lanka and Eve to Jeddah. Adam and Eve are not said to have met until after Adam was sent to Mecca, where he established the sanctuary as a temporary earthly substitute for the Garden of Eden. Because of their sins, Adam and Eve were forced to live on their own; Adam had to cultivate the ground for food and Eve was made to bleed and give birth to compensate for the loss of immortality. Muslim exegetes interpret Q 2:37 to mean that God promised Adam and his descendants that if they repented and followed him they would return to the Garden of Eden in the future. Such a notion is embodied in the Muslim concept of Eden as the "Promised Land" of eschatological times.

Though Adam is never called a prophet in the Hebrew Bible, he does communicate directly with God. Muslim exegetes refer to Adam as a prophet. A report from the prophet Muhammad states that Adam was one of four "Syrian" prophets (including Seth, Noah, and Enoch). Muslim exegetes also report that "Scriptures" [Ar. suhuf] were revealed to Adam and that he passed on the legacy of his prophethood to his son Seth.

ADAM, SECOND. Term applied to prophet and savior figures in Islam and Christianity. The prophet Muhammad is related to the second Adam in a number of ways. According to Islam, Adam was the first prophet and Muhammad is the last. Adam was a prophet to all humanity, as is Muhammad. Similar associations between Adam and Jesus are developed in the New Testament. Luke 3:23–38 provides a genealogy of Jesus that goes back to Adam. Adam first established the sanctuary at Mecca, and Muhammad reestablishes Mecca as a sanctuary to God. The bodies of Adam and Jesus are also contrasted in the New Testament, such as in 1 Cor 15:35–53 where the spiritual body, like the risen Christ, is compared to the physical body of the earthly Adam. The apostle Paul contrasts Adam, through whom sin entered the world, with Christ, through whom resurrection and immortality come in Romans 5 and 1 Corinthians 15. Rev 22:12–14 also describes Jesus as "the first and the last." Adam's resurrection and its significance for the resurrection of all people also are tied with the fall from the Garden of Eden and the atonement of Adam in the Greek Apocalypse of Moses. The Quran compares the likeness of Jesus to the likeness of Adam, created from the earth (Q 3:59). Muslim exegetes read Q 2:37 as a reference to God's promise to let Adam and his descendants reenter the Garden of Eden at a future date. The prophet Muhammad is said to be waiting at the entrance to paradise, ready to usher in his followers on the Day of Resurrection.

AHIJAH. An Israelite prophet of Yahweh and a Levite (1 Chr 26:20) mentioned several times in the Bible who appears to have centered his work at Shiloh (e.g., 1 Kgs 11:29, 12:15, 14:2, 15:29; 2 Chr 9:29). He is responsible for pulling aside King Jeroboam I (922–901 BCE) while leaving Jerusalem, tearing his garment into 12 pieces and giving him 10 (though the Septuagint credits this act to the prophet Shemaiah [*see also* SHEMAIAH]). According to Ahijah, this prophetic drama was to represent Yahweh's rending of the northern 10 tribes from Solomon's kingdom (*see also* PROPHETIC DRAMA). He also predicted the death of Jeroboam's son when his wife came to him at Shiloh in disguise (1 Kgs 14:12). According to 2 Chr 9:29, Ahijah authored a prophetic book that contained information about Solomon's reign, though this text has not survived. Rabbinic tradition sees Ahijah as having lived an extraordinarily long life span, one that forms a link with seven other figures (Adam, Methuselah, Noah, Shem, Jacob, Amran, and Elijah) connecting creation to the end of the world (TB Baba Batra 121b). It also credits him with having taught King Jeroboam I and the prophet Elijah the mysteries of merkabah mysticism (TB Sanhedrin 102a; TB Erubin 5; 22a, Seder Olam 1; TB Baba Batra 121b. *See also* MERKABAH [CHARIOT] MYSTICISM).

AHMAD B. HANBAL. Ahmad b. Muhammad b. Hanbal (780–855 CE); also called the "Imam of Baghdad" or "Imam Ahmad." The *Musnad* of Ibn Hanbal is a collection of roughly 30,000 hadith reports, organized according to the Companions of the prophet Muhammad who first circulated the report (*see also* HADITH). Ibn Hanbal is well known as the eponymous founder of the Hanbali school of Islamic law and for his role against the Abbasid Caliphate in the inquisition of the ninth century CE over the status of the Quran as a created or uncreated text.

ALCHEMY. Science of transforming base metals into precious ones corresponding to the transformation of the base soul into the spiritual soul. Though the tenets and aims of alchemy differ depending upon the culture and place in which it is practiced, one of the general notions is the divine unity of the cosmos and the interpretation of natural phenomena as emanations and manifestations of God.

There are a number of different traditions regarding the origins of alchemy, but the earliest alchemical texts appear to be those preserved in Arabic. The word *alchemy* may derive from the Egyptian name for "Egypt" [Egypt. kemet, lit. "black land"] understood simply as "Egypt" through Arabic sources [i.e., al-khemet, lit. "the Egypt"]. Arabic texts purport to be translations of earlier Greek texts, which, in turn, are claimed to have been derived from more ancient sources. The earliest extant Greek alchemical manuscripts date to the 11th century CE, but there is a large body of Arabic texts attributed to Jabir b. Hayyan and Muhammad b. Zakariya al-Razi, the earliest of which seem to date to the ninth and 10th centuries CE. There also are a few Latin texts that claim to be translations of Arabic originals composed by Khalid, the grandson of the first Umayyad Caliph, but the Arabic texts are not extant, and the Arabic texts attributed to earlier figures may be pseudepigraphical.

Muslim sources attribute the origins of alchemy to Greek philosophers, but primarily to Hermes Trismegistos through the intermediary of his disciple Apollonius of Tyana. To Hermes is attributed the discovery of the Emerald Tablet at an ancient temple in the city of Akhmim in Upper Egypt. A commentary on the Emerald Tablet, entitled *The Secrets of Creation*, is attributed to Apollonius, as is a book, *On the Seven Metals*. Other figures from the stories of the prophets such as Mary, the Wise Men, Mani, Adam, Moses, and Korah are credited with the origins of alchemy, as are figures from early Islamic history such as Ali b. Abi Talib, the Imam Ja'far al-Sadiq,

Hasan al-Basri, and Dhu al-Nun al-Misri. The Arabic *Book of the Meeting*, translated into Latin as *Turba Philosophorum*, depicts a meeting of alchemists with Pythagoras at their head. Many of the works attributed to Jabir b. Hayyan and Muhammad b. Zakariya al-Razi were translated into Latin beginning in the 12th century CE. Best known among the Latin scholars of alchemy were Roger Bacon and Arnald of Villanova in the 13th century and Paracelsus in the 16th century. Later Arabic texts were also prepared, such as the work of Muhammad b. Umayl in the 10th century, Muhammad b. Abd al-Malik in the 11th century, and Husayn Ali al-Tughra'i and Ibn Arafa Ra's in the 12th century. Compendia of alchemical knowledge were prepared by Abu al-Qasim al-Simawi in the 13th century and Aydamir b. Ali al-Jildaki in the 14th century.

Arabic alchemy is based on the principle that all metals are of a single essence but are differentiated only by accidents that can be reversed by artificial means. Metals are believed to mature from base to precious deep inside the earth, but the alchemist can accelerate this maturation process through the mixing of various elements according to specific formulae. Many of the alchemical writings are composed using various technical terminology and code words, which resulted in the production of alchemical lexicons.

ALEXANDER ROMANCE. Term applied to a diverse group of stories related to the legendary exploits of Alexander the Great (356–323 BCE). The earliest of the Alexander Romances is represented by a Greek manuscript that is thought to have originated in the fourth century CE. It is attributed to Callisthenes, Alexander's official historian. Multiple recensions of this text, known as "Pseudo-Callisthenes," exist, the best known of which are in Greek, Syriac, Ethiopic, Latin, Persian, Hebrew, French, and German. The accounts deal primarily with Alexander's quest for immortality. They include his search for the water of life, attempts to fly to the heavens, journeys to the ends of the earth, and adventures to the bottom of the sea in a diving bell. Some of these accounts resemble stories found in the Epic of Gilgamesh (*see also* EPIC OF GILGAMESH) and other stories otherwise unknown after the Hellenistic period.

Alexander's quest for immortality is found in Jewish and Muslim exegetical sources. Muslim exegetes identify Alexander with Dhu al-

Qarnayn, mentioned in Q 18:83–101, and link the story of Alexander's search for the water of life to Moses' search for the "meeting place of the two waters" in Q 18:60–65. According to the Talmud, Alexander traveled to the Garden of Eden, following the water of life, where he was given a heavy eyeball that symbolized his insatiable pride (TB Tamid 32b). A similar account is found in the Latin text known as the *Iter ad Paradisum*, thought to be of Jewish provenance. Many of the versions of the Alexander Romance that appeared in the Islamic period refer to Alexander as "Dhu al-Qarnayn" and introduce the prophet Khidr as his companion or general of his forces.

ALEXANDRIA. City on the northern coast of Egypt founded by Alexander the Great in 331 BCE. The Lives of the Prophets states that the remains of the prophet Jeremiah were transferred by Alexander and placed in a circle around the city. The city was known as the first to bear the name of its founder rather than that of a god or hero. During the Ptolemaic period (304–330 BCE) the cult of Alexander the Great was established in the city, and Alexander's remains were interred in the Necropolis.

An important Jewish community had been established in Alexandria under Alexander's reign (Josephus, Jewish Wars 2.487), but it was decimated by the emperor Trajan after he crushed a Jewish revolt in 115 CE, and nearly annihilated completely by the persecutions of Archbishop Cyril in 415 CE. Among the most famous Jews living there during this period was the philosopher and biblical exegete Philo (c. 20 BCE–40 CE), a man active also in public affairs. According to later Christian writers, Christianity came to Alexandria around 60 CE with the apostle Mark after his persecution in Rome. It was in Egypt that Mark is said to have written the "secret" parts of his gospel. Mark is considered the founder of Christianity in Egypt. During the second century CE, Alexandria became a significant center for Christianity and was the home of a number of well-known Christian exegetes including Clement (c. 150–215), Origen (d. 185), and Athanasius (296–373). Muslims conquered Alexandria in 641 CE, at which time the political and cultural focus of Egypt shifted to the new capital of Fustat (Old Cairo). Among the many Muslim sites in Alexandria is a mosque dedicated to the prophet Daniel, which may go back to the site of an earlier shrine.

ALI B. ABI TALIB (d. 661). Abu al-Hasan Ali b. Abi Talib b. Abd al-Muttalib b. Hashim b. Abd al-Manaf b. Qusayy was the prophet Muhammad's paternal cousin, his son-in-law, and the fourth caliph (r. 656–661). Ali is regarded by many Shi'i Muslims as the first in a line of imams who succeeded the prophet Muhammad. Because of the importance of this position, many of Ali's sayings appear in Shi'i commentaries on the Quran, some of the more esoteric of which are said to have been compiled in a book entitled the *Jafr*, which was passed down to the sixth Imam Ja'far al-Sadiq, but subsequently lost. In alchemical and Nusayri Shi'i texts, Ali is considered one of the three divine hypostases (Ali, Salman, Muhammad), from whom the esoteric knowledge of the imam emanates, having originated with Muhammad and passed through Salman to Ali.

ALLAH. Common Arabic word for "God" found more times than any other noun in the Quran. The Arabic word appears to be constructed by combining the Arabic definite article "al" with "ilah," a common Semitic word for deity, thus making "al-ilah" or "allah," meaning "The God." Though some Muslim scholars claim Allah is one of the names of God, it is not always included in the various lists of the so-called "Ninety-Nine Names of God" found in later Muslim sources. Many of the names listed are derived from epithets found in the Quran referring to God's attributes such as mercy, knowledge, glory, and power. The Quran states that by whatever name God is called, to him belong the Most Beautiful Names [Ar. al-asma al-husna] (Q 17:110). Other words also appear in the Quran as nouns meaning "God," such as "Allahumma" (Q 3:26, 5:114, 8:32, 10:10, 39:46), which often is interpreted as a vocative form of "Allah," but perhaps is related also to the common Hebrew plural "Elohim," used for God in the Hebrew Bible.

ALPHABET OF BEN SIRAH. A midrashic text found in two main recensions attributed to the apocryphal sage Jesus ben Sirah (*see also* WISDOM OF JESUS BEN SIRAH) that consists of two lists of proverbs, one in Hebrew and the other in Aramaic, arranged alphabetically. Accompanying the proverbs are imaginative midrashic commentaries that depict the author as a divinely inspired sage, even as a baby. The text dates to sometime in the 11th century CE.

AMALEKITES. A tribe mentioned in the Bible and in Muslim exegesis, especially in conjunction with their interactions with the immediate descendants of Abraham and the Israelites. In extrabiblical sources they do not appear by name. According to the Bible, Amalek was one of the "chiefs of Elphaz in the land of Edom" (Gen 36:15–16), and the Amalekites are mentioned as dwelling in central Canaan (Judg 12:15) and in the Negev (1 Sam 30:1–2; Num 13:29). Muslim sources state that the Amalekites migrated from Iraq to the Arabian Peninsula, and they are reported to have lived in the Hijaz, southern Arabia, and in Syria. Muslim exegesis on Q 2:250–51 reports that Goliath was an Amalekite (the Bible says he is a Philistine in 1 Sam 17:4), and the Amalekites are also closely related to the Jurhum who settle with Ishmael and Hagar in Mecca. In some Muslim sources, it is said that Ishmael's first wife was an Amalekite, and that his second was from the Jurhum. The territory of the Amalekites mentioned in 1 Sam 15:7 is the same as that attributed to Ishmael in Gen 25:18, an association strengthened by the links between Ishmael, the Jurhum, and the Amalekites in Muslim exegesis.

AMBROSE (c. 339–397 CE). One of the "Four Doctors of the Western Church" along with Augustine, Jerome, and Gregory the Great. Ambrose received training in Roman law and became the consularis of Aemilia and Liguria (near Milan) in 370 before converting to Christianity and being ordained bishop of Milan (374–397). His sermons rely heavily on passages from the Hebrew Bible, and his exegetical style draws upon the approaches of Philo and Origen (*see also* PHILO OF ALEXANDRIA; ORIGEN). Ambrose applied a threefold interpretation to exegesis, interpreting the literal, moral, and allegorical meaning of select passages.

AMOS. The oldest prophetic book in the Bible and the name of a prophet who prophesied during the reign of Jeroboam II (775–750 BCE). The prophet was a shepherd from the southern town of Tekoa, but prophesied mostly in northern Israel. He appears to have denied that he was a prophet (Amos 3:10–15), though his assertion simply could represent an attempt to distance himself from cultic prophets or those working for the royal house. Amos prophesied during a time of relative peace and prosperity, marked by northern and southern expansion. This expansion led to frictions with various regions (e.g., Edom, Tyre, Moab), which Amos incorporated into his judgments against the nations (Amos 1:3–6, 2), but also against Israel and Judah (Amos 1:4–16). The relative prosperity also led to the people's abuses, idleness, and oppression, which he also denounced (Amos 6:1–7). Amos's message challenged the popular belief that Israel's election would protect them from harm, and reminded Israel that its election brings with it greater responsibility (Amos 3:1–7). Ignoring this, Amos proclaimed, would lead inevitably to an Assyrian invasion (Amos 3:10–12, 4:1–3). In the Talmud, Amos is listed, along with Jesse, Saul, Samuel, Zephaniah, Zedekiah, the Messiah, and Elijah as one of the eight "princes among men" who will appear in the end of time when Assyria treads the holy land (Mic 5:4). These princes are to appear with the "seven shepherds": David, Adam, Seth, Methuselah, Abraham, Jacob, and Moses (TB Sukkah 55b).

ANGEL. A divine figure that is able to cross the liminal zone between the sacred and profane. The generic Hebrew [mal'akh] and Greek [angelos] terms for this figure mean "messenger," referring to their role as deliverers of divine messages to mortals. The Vulgate distinguishes between divine messengers [Lat. angelus] and human messengers [Lat. nuntius].

In earlier biblical traditions, angels appear indistinguishable from humans. In fact, the Bible refers to them variously as "messengers," "men," and "God" (Gen 18:1, 18:2, 19:1). Their divine nature is apparent in that they have access to the divine and perform miraculous acts. Angels are designated as the "sons of God" (Gen 6:2; Job 1:6, 2:1, 38:7) and "sons of gods" (Ps 29:1, 89:7), phrases reminiscent of earlier Israelite and Canaanite (i.e., Ugaritic) beliefs that the gods had children (*see also* UGARIT). Such a belief is echoed also in Deut 32:8 (in the Septuagint and Qumran versions) and in the reference to the "holy ones" of Ps 89:6–8. The Quran similarly refers to some angels who are "close to God" (Q 4:172), but associates this epithet with Jesus (Q 3:45).

In post-exilic biblical texts generally, such as Job (also Dan 7:10, 9:21), angels appear to represent a hierarchically organized group of semidivine beings, some of whom have specific names. This hierarchy is modeled on the monarchy and perhaps receives its definitive stamp in the Persian period under the influence of Zoroastrianism. Jewish texts organize angels into higher and lower realms. Among the named angels are Michael (Dan 10:13, 21; Jude 9; Rev 12:7–9), Gabriel (Dan 8:16–27, 9:21–27; Luke 1:11–38), and Raphael (Tob 3:17, 1 En 20:13). The Quran describes angels as messengers with wings (Q 35:1), and Muslim scholarship describes many of the angels in fantastic terms. Muslim angelology holds that there are four archangels: Gabriel, Michael, Israfil, and Azrael, the Angel of Death. Each of these has a specific function, Gabriel being the most significant as the angel who brings revelations to the prophets, though Israfil also is attributed with that task in some traditions. Israfil also is said to be the angel in charge of blowing the trumpet on the Day of Resurrection from one of the gates in Jerusalem. Muslim exegesis of Q 2:97–98 preserves a debate between the prophet Muhammad and the Jews of Medina over the angels Michael and Gabriel, making Michael to be the angel of the Jews and Gabriel the angel of the Muslims.

In the Bible, some angels are assigned to watch over human affairs; for example, there are "watchers" (Dan 4:10–20; Jub 4:15–22, 1 En 1:5) and "ministers" (Ps 103:21). The Quran similarly characterizes the "Keepers" and "Watchers" as angelic beings (Q 82:10). Daniel (7:10) and 1 Enoch (89:61–77, 90:14–20) refer to an angel who guards the records that are to be opened on the Day of Judgment. The Quran mentions two guardian angels who sit and record the deeds of people (Q 50:17), and some Muslim exegetes regard the word Qa'id (meaning "sitting") to be the name of an angel who records evil deeds. A number of Muslim exegetes identify the "Scroll" [Ar. sijill] of Q 21:104 as an angel who is in charge of guarding scriptures. Muslim tradition also refers to Munkar and Nakir as angelic beings who torture human souls in death before the Day of Resurrection (Q 14:31, 40:46–48, 71:25). In the Bible and apocryphal works, other angels have a military function. Thus, angels are designated as "armies" (Ps 89:9, 103:21), "authorities" (1 En 61:10), and one angel as a "commander" (Josh 5:14). Like the Bible, the Quran also sees the "heavenly host" as a reference to the host of angels who worship God in the heavens (Q 37:8, 38:69). Some Muslim exegetes maintain that Dhu al-Qarnayn was an angel, or that the guardian of Dhu al-Qarnayn was the angel Raphael (see Q 18:83–101).

Harut and Marut are the "angels of Babylon" mentioned in Q 2:102 and are understood to be fallen angels who brought magic to human beings (*see also* MAGIC; SATAN). Other names are given to the leader of the fallen angels, such as Melchiresha, Belial, Beliar, and Mastema in the Dead Sea Scrolls and in Jubilees. The Quran refers to "Thunder" in a way that forces some Muslim exegetes to understand it as the name of an angel in charge of thunder (Q 13:13). Muslim exegetes also designate "Barq" [lit. "Lightning"] as the angel of lightning. 3 En 17–27 gives numerous names to the various angels of the heavenly hierarchy, many of them related to terms of natural phenomena such as thunder and lightning. Galatians 3–4 refers to the "elements of the world," which some interpret as celestial bodies or angelic powers that control earthly phenomena. Rev 1:20 also refers to the "angels of the seven churches," which some scholars see as corresponding to the Iranian notion that individuals and peoples have heavenly counterparts [Pers. fravashi], or the mystical notion of the 70 peoples of the earth represented by 70 angels, itself related to Deut 32:8, which credits 70 nations with having 70 angels (The Qumran text reads "sons of god" here, the Septuagint "angels," and the Masoretic text "Israel").

Q 40:49 refers to the "Treasurer of hell," which many Muslim exegetes equate with the name of an angel [Ar. malik] mentioned in Q 43:77. Elsewhere, the Quran refers to the "angels of punishment" and the "guardians of the fire," which also appear to relate to the angelic Treasurer of hell (Q 74:31, 96:18). Other heavenly beings include the "Holy Spirit" who is associated most closely with Jesus (Q 2:87, 2:253, 5:110) and with Gabriel (Q 16:102). Another "Spirit" mentioned several times in the Quran is said to be an angel created greater than the others (Q 16:2, 17:85, 70:4, 78:38, 97:4). Q 9:40 also refers to the "Presence of God" [Ar. sakinah] as an angelic being, a concept and term closely related to a Hebrew term understood as "God's glory" [Heb. shekhinah].

ANOINT. The process of consecrating individuals by pouring oil over their head and/or hands. In the Bible, anointing is performed by religious figures, either priests, prophets, or angels. Typically anointed are priests (Exod 28:41, 40:12–15), kings (Judg 9:8), and prophets (1 Kgs 19:16), though objects also can be anointed, such as the sacred vessels of the Tabernacle (Exod 29:36, 30:26; Lev 8:10) and weapons (2 Sam 1:21; Isa 21:5). The Hebrew word for "anointed" [Heb. meshiah] has come into English as "Messiah" or "Christ" from the Greek translation of the term [Gk. Christos].

Anointing was more than a symbolic gesture. It was a performative act of power that resulted in conferring the spirit of Yahweh upon the anointed. Thus, after his anointing King Saul was taken up by Yahweh's spirit and began to prophesy (1 Sam 10:10). David similarly was gripped by the spirit when the prophet Samuel anointed him (1 Sam 16:13). The rite was intended to sanctify the king to enable him to perform religious duties, and serve as a representative of the divine—though he himself was not considered divine. The ritual act of anointing was in place in Canaan long before the monarchy, as is seen by Jotham's parable concerning Abimelech (Judg 9:8, 9:15), and appears to have been widespread, since Hazael, the Aramaean king (842–806 BCE), is similarly said to have been anointed (though by the Israelite prophet Elisha) in 2 Kgs 8:9–15. The rite is probably Egyptian in origin, since many high officials in Egypt are anointed when they take office (though the pharaoh was not anointed, most likely because his office already was considered divine). The Amarna letters also mention the anointing of Canaanite kings as vassals for the pharaoh. Mesopotamians do not appear to have employed the rite of anointing. Regardless of its ultimate origin, the rite appears wholly Israelite by the time of the Judges.

ANTICHRIST. Eschatological figure described in apocalyptic texts as coming at the end of time to persecute believers and destroy the worship of God. The Antichrist appears as a character in a number of the stories of the prophets and is the subject of many prophecies. The Antichrist is not mentioned in the Quran, but in later Muslim sources he is called the "Dajjal," a term meaning the "False One" in Arabic, apparently derived from Syriac (*see also* DAJJAL).

The Antichrist is commonly associated or identified with Satan, and Rev 12:9 relates the names "great dragon" and "primeval serpent" to Satan. Perhaps referring to Daniel's dream of the four beasts in Dan 7, Rev 13:1 refers to the Antichrist as a beast that emerges from the sea. The imagery of the combat myth between God and Chaos represented by the sea, nature, or a beast is common from ancient Near Eastern myths that describe combats with primordial watery entities, often depicted as serpents. Such stories include the Babylonian struggle between Markduk and Tiamat, the Ugaritic fight between Baal and Yam, and the Egyptian nightly bout between Ra and Apophis. Many apocalyptic texts provide descriptions of the Antichrist. The Apocalypse of Ezra relates that he will appear as a man restrained with iron bars, an image repeated in Muslim texts in which the Antichrist is chained to a mountain. Jewish mystical traditions similarly assert that God chained fallen angels to mountains and punished them by suspending them between earth and heaven (Zohar I, 96, 126a, III, 208a and 221a). The Antichrist also is described in giant and cosmic terms in the Apocalypse of Ezra, the Coptic and Hebrew Apocalypses of Elijah, and in numerous traditions going back to the prophet Muhammad.

Later interpretations of Ezekiel 38 describe the prophet's reference to "Gog, the king of Magog," as a horde of barbarians associated with the Antichrist (*see also* GOG; MAGOG). The Quran relates Dhu al-Qarnayn's building of the gate against Gog and Magog who are to surge out upon the world at the end of time (Q 18:94–99). Such a conception of the Antichrist is found also in apocalyptic literature influenced by the experience of homeland invasions by foreigners. Muslim tradition preserves reports from the prophet Muhammad that the Antichrist is to lead the armies of Gog and Magog against the cities of Mecca and Medina.

The New Testament reflects an image of the Antichrist as one falsely claiming to be God (2 Thess 2:3–12). This idea is related to the "abomination of desolation" mentioned in Daniel (9:27, 11:31, 12:11) and to 1 Macc 1:54 as a reference to the desecration of the temple in Jerusalem by the Seleucid ruler Antiochus Epiphanes in the second century BCE. The "abomination of desolation" also is mentioned by Jesus (Matt 24:15; Mark 13:14), in reference to a future incident, and is taken by Christian exegetes as an allusion to the Antichrist. In the Quran, it is Nimrod of the Abraham story and the pharaoh of the Moses story who epitomize the Antichrist. Muslim tradition also describes the Antichrist in perverted messianic terms as riding on an ass, being followed by Jews, and miraculously providing sustenance for all people. The Apocalypse of Daniel portrays the Antichrist as a descendant of Dan, who as king and Messiah of the Jews, is to persecute Christians and attempt miracles.

In some accounts, the appearance of the Antichrist who heralds the eschaton is tied to the disappearance of revealed scripture, destruction of the temple, and rapture of the righteous (*see also* ESCHATOLOGY). Some Muslim traditions report that when the Antichrist appears the Quran will have been recalled from the earth and from people's memory, the people of faith will be taken away by God, and the Antichrist will destroy the Ka'bah. Muslim exegesis on Q 17:4 describes the destruction of the temple in Jerusalem by Nebuchadnezzar and the Romans in similar terms. 1 Thess 1:10 is cited by Christian exegetes as proof of the rapture of the saints before the coming of the Antichrist.

In most accounts, a messianic or prophetic figure is described as destroying the Antichrist. In Jewish, Christian, and Muslim texts the Antichrist is to be confronted by Elijah and Enoch, the two figures who have escaped death. Other messianic figures including Jesus and the Messiah ben David are described as leading the armies of God and his angels against the Antichrist in a final apocalypse at Armageddon. Some Muslim traditions foretell the return of Jesus and the Mahdi, a future savior figure sometimes associated with the Twelfth Imam who went into occultation in the second half of the ninth century CE.

ANTIOCH. Name given to various cities founded by Seleucid rulers, but most commonly associated with the Antioch of the Orontes River, located in modern southeast Turkey just north of the Syrian border. This city was important in early Christianity, and as a seat of regional power in late antiquity until at least the fifth century CE when coastal cities gave way to the inland cities of the caravan routes. According to Acts 11:26, it was at Antioch that the term *Christians* was first used, a fact noted also by some Muslim scholars in their exegesis of Q 36:13–29. The city or district [Ar. qaryah] mentioned in Q 36:13, to which were sent three messengers, is reported to be Antioch in Muslim exegesis. Some of the exegetes report that the three messengers were disciples of Jesus, an opinion supported by a report given on the authority of the prophet Muhammad that Jesus came before the messengers sent to the city. Other exegetes maintain that the messengers were sent to ancient Antioch when it was ruled by an idol-worshipping king named Antiochus.

APHRAHAT (d. c. 345 CE) Known as the "Persian Sage," Aphrahat was a Christian scholar, apparently of Iranian origin, who is known from 23 treatises he composed in the early fourth century CE. Little is known about him outside of his writings, but he was a monk and may also have been a bishop. The treatises of Aphrahat were written between 337 and 345 CE and address a variety of topics, making copious reference to the Bible and competing interpretations of select passages. His treatises are particularly rich in references to Jewish exegesis and have led some scholars to claim a close connection between him and the Jews of his time.

APOCALYPSE OF ABRAHAM. This text, preserved in Old Church Slavonic and Russian, contains an account of Abraham's youth and a series of visions seen while Abraham ascended through the heavens. The earliest Slavonic manuscript dates to the 14th century CE and several date to the 16th century CE, though the text is believed to be derived from an earlier Greek or Hebrew original. References in early Christian writers to a Sethian "Apocalypse of Abraham" seem to refer to a work with different content than what is preserved in Slavonic. The motif of Abraham ascending to heaven and having visions of the world also is found in the Testament of Abraham and in Q 6:75.

Chapters 1–8 describe several episodes from Abraham's youth, which parallel those found in Jewish sources, the Quran, and Muslim exegesis. In chapters 1–6 Abraham is said to have discovered that the idols sold by his father are false gods. Chapter 7 narrates how Abraham deduced the existence of God through the observation of natural phenomena. Chapters 9–32 recount Abraham's visions. After performing a sacrifice and fasting (9), he is said to have been greeted by an angel who is described in fantastic terms (10–11). The sacrifice of the birds, a theme that runs throughout the text, also may relate to Abraham's sacrifice of the birds in Gen 15:9–10 and Q 2:260. Abraham is described as first visiting Horeb (12) and then meeting the angel Azazel (13–14). He then has a vision of different angels (15–16); fire and the throne (17–18); the eight firmaments and the stars (19–20); the world, including a vision of Adam and Eve in the Garden of Eden (21–23); the sins of the world (24–26); the destruction of the temple in Jerusalem (27–28); and the final judgment (29–32).

APOCALYPSE OF ADAM. An account of the secret knowledge transmitted from Adam at the time of his death to his son Seth. The text is preserved in a unique Sahidic Coptic manuscript, found among the Nag Hammadi texts, and dated to the second half of the fourth century CE. Chapter 1 introduces the apocalypse and recounts the fall of Adam and Eve as a result of the false god who created them and was jealous that Eve had obtained and given to Adam secret knowledge of the true God. The vision of Adam (chapters 3–5) begins with an account of the great deluge and a fire, catastrophes through which the false god is to attempt a destruction of the descendants of Seth. Chapters 6–8 describe the coming of the "Illuminator of Knowledge" who will demonstrate the superiority of the descendants of Seth and their secret knowledge, which is equated with a baptism of living water.

APOCALYPSE OF DANIEL. Text describing a vision of the prophet Daniel regarding the appearance and activities of the Antichrist at the end of time. The text dates no earlier than the ninth century CE and is extant in three Greek manuscripts dating to the 15th and 16th centuries CE. It is divided into 14 chapters, with chapters 1–7 depicting historical events that took place in the eighth century CE, and chapters 8–14 foretelling the coming of the Antichrist. The Antichrist is identified as a descendant of the Israelite tribe of Dan who will gather together the Jews in Jerusalem and persecute the Christians. The Antichrist is to be born by entering the body of a fish and impregnating a virgin who touches the head of the fish. The text describes his size as gigantic, and he is said to bear an inscription on his forehead. The text predicts that he will cause an abundance of food and will be made king by the Jews in Jerusalem, where he will be confronted by three prophetic figures (perhaps Enoch, Elijah, and the apostle John). The text ends abruptly with the three prophetic figures being killed and the Antichrist persecuting Christians who attempt to hide in mountains and caves (*see also* CAVE).

APOCALYPSE OF JOHN. There are four apocalypses known by this title. The first is the canonical book, also known as the book of Revelation, which is described as a revelation given by Jesus Christ through the intermediary of an angel to John. This book is not included in all Christian canons, such as the Peshitta, and its status as canonical has been questioned by many Christian exegetes. The book assumes the form of a letter, written in the first person, to the seven churches of Asia. It reports a single vision related in two parts. The first is a vision of the risen Christ who tells John to write down his vision. This takes place on earth. The second part of the vision appears to make reference to John's ascent to heaven. There John is described as seeing the throne of God (4–5); the breaking of seven seals (6:1–8:1); the sounding of seven trumpets (8:2–11); the interaction of a woman, dragon, beast, false prophet, and the seven plagues (12–16). Much of the vision is given in symbolic terms, which are explained as references to earthly events and people. Chapters 17–18 describe the punishment of Babylon, and chapters 19–22 describe an eschatological battle, the reign of 1,000 years, the Day of Judgment, and the eschatological Jerusalem.

A second Apocalypse of John describes details of the eschaton in terms of a question and answer format. The text is extant in Greek, Old Church Slavonic, and Arabic, with the earliest manuscripts dated to the ninth century CE, though the composition of the text is placed as early as the fifth century CE. Among the topics discussed are a description of the Antichrist, the resurrection of the dead, and the punishments and rewards of hell and heaven. A third Apocalypse of John is extant in a Coptic manuscript dating to the 11th century CE, and a fourth Apocalypse of John appears in a Greek text dated to the seventh century CE.

APOCALYPSE OF MARY. There are two independent texts with this title, both of which refer to visions revealed to Mary, the mother of Jesus. One of these dates to the ninth century CE and is preserved in Greek, Armenian, Ethiopic, Cretan, and Old Church Slavonic. It recounts Mary's vision of hell and the punishments of the damned for whom she intercedes. The other text is extant only in Ethiopic and is thought to date to the seventh century CE, though the manuscripts are later.

APOCALYPSE OF MOSES. An account of the death of Adam and his instructions to his son Seth. The title comes from the opening lines of the preface, considered to be a later addition to the text, in which the account is said to have been revealed to Moses when he received the tablets of the Law. This text relates closely to the Life of Adam and Eve, a text preserved in Latin. The Apocalypse of Moses is preserved in Greek manuscripts, the earliest of which dates to the 11th century, though these manuscripts are considered copies or translations of an earlier version. Various recensions, apparently derived from the Greek text, are found in Armenian and Old Church Slavonic. The Syriac *Book of the Cave of Treasures* and the Ethiopic *Conflict of Adam and Eve* also adopt the format of placing future events into the context of Adam's prophesies at the time of his death. After a preface summarizing the penance of Adam and Eve in the Jordan and Tigris Rivers, the text opens (chapters 1–4) with an account of Cain's killing of Abel and the birth of Seth. In chapters 5–9, Adam is said to recount to his children the fall from paradise. Chapters 10–15 tell the story of Seth and Eve's quest for the oil that flows from the Tree of Life in paradise and the prophecy that only at the end of time will the oil become available. Chapters 15–30 contain Eve's account of the fall, and the repentance of Adam and Eve. Chapters 31–43 provide a description of the death of Adam and the angels' preparation of his body for burial, including its being washed three times in Lake Acheron.

APOCALYPSE OF PAUL. This title refers to two different texts that describe the apostle Paul's ascent through the heavens. The motif of Paul's heavenly ascent was widespread in late antiquity and in the medieval period, and was based on an exegetical expansion of his mention that he was taken to the third heaven (2 Cor 12:2–4). Many of the various recensions of the Apocalypse of Paul may reflect traditions not directly dependent upon other texts.

The first is a lengthy text, extant in Greek, Latin, Syriac, Coptic, Old Church Slavonic, Welsh, and Ethiopic, attesting to its popularity among early Christians. In the *Catalogue of the Sixty Books*, the Apocalypse of Paul is listed as a nonsanctioned apocryphal book, and it is mentioned also by Augustine as not authoritative. The text contains many parallels to other accounts of heavenly ascensions and visions of paradise, including Paul's vision of the fate of righteous and sinful souls, the ocean surrounding the earth, the lake of paradise in which the archangel Michael washes sinners so that they may enter paradise, and the four rivers of paradise (honey, milk, wine, oil). Paul also is described as meeting earlier prophets and biblical figures including Noah, Abraham, Isaac, Jacob, Lot, Job, and David. Enoch and Elijah are said to greet Paul at the entrance to paradise, and at the end of the text Paul is said to meet Mary, the mother of Jesus. The text also describes Paul's tour of hell and of paradise where he sees the tree from under which the four rivers of paradise flow.

The second text entitled the Apocalypse of Paul is attested in the Nag Hammadi collection (V,2) in Coptic. In this brief text, Paul is first greeted by a child, probably echoing his encounter with the risen Christ in the New Testament (Gal 1:11–17, 2:1–2). He then is made to ascend through 10 heavens, having a vision in each one. The visions include the 12 disciples, the punishment of sinful souls, various angels, an old man seated on a throne, and the Ogdoad. At the end of the text, Paul greets the 12 disciples who ascend with him to the 10th heaven.

APOCALYPSE OF PETER. Title of a number of texts associated with the heavenly visions of the apostle Peter. The best known of these texts is that extant in Ethiopic, describing the ascent of the apostle Peter into the heavens and his visions of the fates of sinful and righteous souls. This seems to be the Apocalypse mentioned by several early Christian writers. The Ethiopic manuscripts date to the seventh or eighth century CE, but this text is attested also in a partial Coptic (Akhmimic) recension and a couple of Greek fragments, one of which dates to the fifth century CE. Another Ethiopic recension is sometimes identified as independent of the first. In addition to these Ethiopic recensions there is also another Apocalypse of Peter known in two Arabic recensions, both of which closely parallel the Ethiopic recensions, but which also contain independent material.

The Coptic Apocalypse of Peter is among the texts found at Nag Hammadi (VII,3). This text contains visions given to the apostle Peter shortly before and at the time of the crucifixion of Jesus. The visions reveal a dualism that contrasts material existence with spiritual truth, and the physical body of Christ with his immortal existence. The text appears polemical in character, often challenging other Christian positions on Christology and the crucifixion.

APOCALYPSE OF SEDRACH. Account of Sedrach's ascension into the heavens and his dialogue there with God. The text is extant in a single Greek manuscript dating to the 15th century CE, but some scholars think it represents a Christian redaction of an earlier Jewish apocalypse. The identity of Sedrach is uncertain. The name may refer to Shadrach the companion of Daniel mentioned in chapter 3 of the book of Daniel. Others claim that it is a corruption of "Esdras," and maintain that the Apocalypse of Sedrach relates closely to other apocalyptic works attributed to Ezra.

APOCALYPSE OF ZEPHANIAH. Text describing the prophet Zephaniah's visions of the fates of righteous and sinful souls. The text is extant only in fragmentary form, and primarily in two Coptic texts from the White Monastery of Shenuda, both of which also contain the Apocalypse of Elijah. The Sahidic Coptic manuscript is only two pages in length, whereas the Akhmimic Coptic manuscript is 18 pages. Clement of Alexandria also quotes a Greek version of the text. The *Stichometry of Nicephorus* mentions a "Book of the Prophet Zephaniah," and an "Apocalypse of Zephaniah" is listed among the apocryphal works in the *Catalogue of the Sixty Books*.

The excerpt from Clement of Alexandria describes Zephaniah's vision in the fifth heaven with angels set upon thrones and praising God. The Sahidic text describes a soul punished by 5,000 angels, and another enigmatic vision of myriads of people with loose hair and unusual teeth. The Akhmimic Coptic text is divided into 12 chapters. It is missing the beginning, two pages between chapters 7 and 8, and four pages at its end. Among the visions recorded therein are the angels who record the deeds of people; the angels who carry away the souls of sinners; a city surrounded by bronze gates and iron bars; the angel Eremiel who presides over hell; two scrolls describing the righteous and sinful deeds of Zephaniah; saved souls; souls in torment; and the intercession of Abraham, Isaac, and Jacob.

APOCRYPHA. Term applied to texts not considered part of the canon of the Bible. Properly, the Greek term [Gk. apokrypha] means "hidden," and there are many traditions that attest to the importance of secret books. One of the earliest references to hidden books occurs in 4 Ezra 14:44–48, where Ezra is said to have authored 24 public books and 70 secret books. Numerous texts describe how Enoch was raised to heaven and ordered to compose 76 books that he delivered to his descendants. Muslim and Jewish traditions attribute secret books to Solomon, which some identify with extant Aramaic and Hebrew magic texts (*see also* MAGIC). The Quran refers to God's teaching Jesus the "Wisdom" (Q 3:48), a knowledge revealed to Lot (Q 21:74), Joseph (Q 12:22), Moses (Q 28:12), Abraham (Q 26:83), and John the Baptist (Q 19:14), apparently denoting secret knowledge.

As a technical term, the Apocrypha refers to a small number of writings that were left out of Jerome's Latin translation of the Bible (*see also* VULGATE) because he translated from a Hebrew version that excluded certain texts found in the Greek Septuagint. These books include the Epistle of Jeremiah (1 Bar 6), Tobit, Judith, 3 Ezra, additions to Esther, additions to Daniel, 1 Baruch, Ben Sira (Ecclesiasticus), Wisdom of Solomon, and 1 and 2 Maccabees. The Apocrypha were added later to the Vulgate and proclaimed to be a second canon by the Council of Trent in 1546 CE. The same books were rejected by Martin Luther, and thus they do not appear in Protestant Bibles.

In a more general sense, the adjective *apocryphal* refers to texts that are related to, but considered separate from, canonical biblical texts. This is the case with the so-called New Testament Apocrypha, which includes a large number of Christian texts both extant and nonextant, such as gospels, apocalypses, treatises, acts, letters, and liturgical texts. The corpus of Christian apocrypha is not fixed, nor is there scholarly agreement on the criteria for inclusion in such a list, though earlier Christian catalogs of canonical texts often included lists of nonauthoritative or apocryphal works (*see also* CANON AND CANON LISTS).

APOCRYPHON OF EZEKIEL. The name of a text distinguished from the canonical book of Ezekiel, which is attributed to the prophet Ezekiel and which is attested only in short fragments quoted in other sources. Josephus mentions it and the *Stichometry of Nicephorus* also lists a second book of Ezekiel among the apocrypha.

The longest fragment is found in Christian heresiography, and a similar, but not identical, text is cited periodically in later Jewish writings (TB Sanhedrin 91a–91b). It tells the parable of a lame man and a blind man in a garden, presumably referring to the resurrection of the dead and God's judgment of people on their own merits. A second fragment is quoted in 1 Clement 8:3 and also in the Nag Hammadi text entitled Exegesis of the Soul (II,6). A third fragment appears in a number of works by early Christian writers and in the apocryphal Acts of Peter. A fourth fragment is cited in more than 30 sources, the earliest of which is Justin Martyr's *Dialogue with Trypho* (c. 130–165 CE). A fifth fragment occurs in Clement of Alexandria, Origen, and the Manichaean Psalmbook.

APOSTLE. Term deriving from the Greek, meaning "one who is sent." Depending on the context, the term can designate a messenger or prophet who is sent or inspired by a deity to bring messages, usually of a divine origin, to humans. Though perhaps most famously used in reference to the apostles of Jesus in the New Testament, the term also appears in pre-Christian Greek literature to refer to an envoy or messenger, albeit rarely. In later non-Christian contexts an apostle is a legally authorized agent and representative of the sender. Thus, the Septuagint employs the word [Gk. apostolos] in its translation of 1 Kings 14:6 in reference to the prophet Ahijah who was commissioned with a message to the queen. This latter meaning is similar to the significance of an Aramaic term [Aram. sheliah] that designates an authorized agent in the Bible (Ezra 7:14, Dan 5:24). In postbiblical times, the Aramaic term was used to designate an authorized agent sent by the Great Sanhedrin (after 70 CE).

In the New Testament and in early Christian contexts, the term *apostle* appears in different, but related ways. The earliest Christian use of the word *apostle* occurs in the writings of Paul, found as a self-description at the head of many of the epistles. Paul's usage seems to have expanded the earlier conception of an apostle beyond the 12 disciples of Jesus who witnessed his resurrection (2 Cor 5:16). It is used also of those envoys sent as missionaries of early Christianity (Acts 1:21–26, 13:1–3). Hebrews 3:1 designates Jesus as an apostle, consistent with the description of Jesus in the Gospel of John, as one "sent" into this world. Later Christian writers use the term in reference to Moses, Isaiah, Jeremiah, and John the Baptist.

The Greek term, and its equivalent in Aramaic and Iranian languages, is also employed in other late antique religions. The Mandaean savior figure is called the "apostle," and the Mandaean *Ginza* mentions as apostles Abel, Seth, and Enosh. Manichaean writings refer to Mani as the "Apostle" standing in a chain of apostles that includes Jesus, Enoch, and Seth. The Sabians of Haran referred to Adam as a prophet and the Apostle of the Moon. Ephrem the Syrian describes Jesus as an apostle who is the last in a chain of the "Sons of Light" including Abel, Enoch, Noah, Abraham, Moses, Joshua, Samuel, and Joseph.

The Arabic term normally translated as "apostle" [Ar. rasul] is found more than 200 times in the Quran. The Quran uses another term, however, in reference to the Christian apostles, one related to the word used for apostles in the Ethiopic New Testament [Ar. hawari, Eth. hawarya]. In the Quran, the word *apostle* [Ar. rasul] is used also for angels (Q 11:77), and interchangeably throughout the text with other terms, such as "the one who brings news" [Ar. nabi] and "the one who warns" [Ar. nadhir], terms usually used for prophets (*see also* NABI). Muhammad, in particular, is called the "apostle of God" and "seal of the prophets" in Q 33:40 and elsewhere. Throughout the Quran one finds references to the notion that to each people was sent a different apostle. This concept parallels the early Christian idea of apostles dividing up the world among themselves in order to spread the Gospel.

Later Muslim scholars distinguish the term *apostle* [Ar. rasul] from the term *prophet* [Ar. nabi], though the usage of these terms as distinct types is not consistent in the Quran. According to this later distinction, an apostle is a special category of prophet who is sent with a book or a particular message for his people. This understanding is consistent with the notion of the apostle as authorized agent bringing a legal document from God to humanity. Likewise, the account of the prophet Muhammad's Ascension through the heavens parallels descriptions of other prophetic and apostolic figures ascending to heaven and receiving their commission.

ARAM. Northwestern region of Mesopotamia lying between the Euphrates and Tigris Rivers and the place where a number of Aramaean tribes dwelled, a people who spoke a tongue related to ancient Hebrew. The biblical tradition sees Aram as the region where Abraham stayed when stopping in Haran (Gen 11:28–32). Abraham's descendant Jacob also spent several years in Aram (Gen 21:1–35:26; Deut 26:5). The Israelites' historical connection to this region is recollected by the genealogical tradition that lists Aram as a son of Shem, the son of Noah (Gen 10:22). The Aramaeans became a major force in the time of David (2 Sam 8:3), and according to 1 Kings 20, in the time of King Ahab (869–850 BCE). The Aramaean stronghold continued until 722 BCE, when the Assyrian king Shalmanezer V (r. 726–722 BCE) defeated the forces of the Aramaean king Rezin (r. 740–732 BCE; 2 Kgs 16:9).

ARK OF THE COVENANT. Early Israelite portable shrine and relic containing a wooden box with a lid, overlaid with gold, on top of which were mounted two griffin-like figures [Heb. cherubim] placed face-to-face with wings touching (Exodus 25). The Ark and its lid were envisioned as a type of throne and footstool for Yahweh (Ps 132:7–8; 1 Chr 28:2), which the priests carried on golden poles like a palanquin. The Bible's description of the Ark as a throne matches iconographic representations of Canaanite and Phoenician royal thrones flanked by griffins.

According to the Bible, the Ark not only contained the tablets of the ten commandments (Deut 10:4), but also Aaron's rod (Num 17:10) and a jar of manna (Exod 16:33–34). Commenting on the Quranic conception of the Ark (Q 2:248), various Muslim exegetes report that it also contained some or all of the following: rods of Moses and Aaron, clothes of Moses and Aaron, shoes of Moses and Aaron, the broken tablets of the Torah, and some manna.

In the Bible, the Ark is first built by the Israelites in the wilderness of wandering, and the Song of the Ark (Num 10:35–36) reports a similar context. The Ark is brought by Joshua to a sanctuary at Gilgal (Josh 4:19) and is later transferred to Bochim or Bethel (Judg 2:1). It is later located at Shiloh (Judg 21:19; 1 Sam 1:3) and at Kiriath-Jearim (1 Sam 6:2) in the time of Samuel, but was taken into battle by Eli's sons and captured by the Philistines (1 Sam 4–6). In Philistine territory the Ark caused a plague of hemorrhoids and mice, and so it promptly was returned to the Israelites, to Beth-Shemesh, along with golden mice and golden hemorrhoids that served as offerings to the Israelite God (1 Sam 6:11–17).

The supernatural power of the Ark also is apparent in several biblical stories in which the Ark is consulted as a source of oracles (1 Sam 5:19) or in which Yahweh inflicts his wrath upon people who look into the box (1 Sam 6:19), or who touch it improperly. Thus, the Bible narrates how the oxen responsible for transporting the Ark back from Philistine territory stumbled, causing a man named Uzzah to grasp the Ark. For profaning the Ark by touch (Uzzah apparently was not a priest [Levite]), Yahweh struck him dead (2 Sam 6:7; 1 Chr 13:10). Direct contact with the Ark was avoided by way of the poles and rings by which it was carried (Exod 25:12–13).

From Beth-Shemesh, the Ark made its way to "the threshing floor of Nachon" (2 Sam 6:6), and then back to Kiriath-Jearim (also called the territory of Jaar in Ps 132:6). David then transferred the Ark amidst great pomp and glory to Jerusalem, where it was placed at a threshing floor (*see also* THRESHING FLOOR), eventually the same spot on which Solomon would build Yahweh's temple (1 Kgs 8:1–12; *see also* TEMPLE).

The lack of biblical reference to the whereabouts of the Ark after the Babylonian destruction of the temple in 586 BCE has given rise to a number of speculations concerning its current location or demise. In fact, the last biblical reference to the Ark appears in conjunction with King Solomon (1 Kgs 8:6–9). No text concerning a later period mentions it. The Ark is not listed as one of the temple vessels taken by Nebuchadnezzar to Babylon when he captured Jerusalem (2 Kgs 25:13–17; Jer 52:17–23), and Nebuchadnezzar's own account of the destruction does not mention it, though it does list many other temple items (*see also* HIDDEN TEMPLE VESSELS). Some suggest that it was destroyed or taken by the Egyptian pharaoh Shishak (c. 935–914 BCE; 1 Kgs 14:25–28) or by the Judaean king Jehoash (2 Kgs 14:8–14), and placed perhaps at Elephantine. Others say it was removed or destroyed during Manasseh's renovation of the temple (2 Kgs 21:4–6). According to 2 Macc 2:4–8, the prophet Jeremiah hid the Ark and other temple implements in a cave on the mountain outside of Jerusalem (*see also* CAVE). The Talmud records that Josiah hid the Ark under a rock in Jerusalem (BT Krithoth 5b; cf., Yoma 53b; Sanhedrin 26b). 2 Baruch 6:7 claims that an angel removed the vessels from the temple during the destruction of Jerusalem, but does not say where the angel put them. Several sources mention that the Ark will reappear at the end of time, in the custody of Elijah or the Messiah. In Ibn Ishaq's biography of the prophet Muhammad, it is reported that when Abd al-Muttalib (Muhammad's grandfather) recovered the well of Zamzam he also uncovered golden implements from an earlier temple including items from a mountain in Syria.

Biblical and ancient Near Eastern scholars have long been interested in the cultic power and significance of the Ark, and its relationship to the Egyptian divine boats with which the priests transported gods and deceased pharaohs (also gods). Both the Ark of the Covenant and the divine boats of Egypt were carried on poles and served oracular functions (Judg 20:27). It also is striking that both the Hebrew and Arabic words used for the Ark [Heb. 'aron, Ar. tabut] also mean "coffin" (*see also* LEVITE; THRESHING FLOOR). In fact, the same word appears in Gen 50:26 in reference to the sarcophagus containing the mummy of Joseph, which the Israelites brought back from Egypt. Like the Ark that contained the tablets of the Law, a metonymic embodiment of the nation's sacred texts and the power of Yahweh, the mummies of the pharaoh often were wrapped in sacred texts and performative amulets, and together with the pharaoh himself, constituted a metonymic embodiment of all that Egypt held powerful and sacred.

ARMENIAN BIBLE EXPANSIONS. Expression that refers to the stories about the biblical prophets, from Noah through Moses, written in Armenian, and closely related to Armenian translations of the Bible. The manuscripts for these texts date as early as the 15th century CE, and are preserved in multiple copies. The "History of Adam, His Sons and Grandsons" begins with Adam and continues through Enosh. The "History of Noah" includes an account of the great flood, the generations of Noah, Tower of Babel, Abraham, Sodom and Gomorrah, Abraham's descendants, the binding of Isaac, Isaac's marriage and death, Isaac's blessing of Jacob, Jacob and Laban, and Jacob's return to Canaan. The "History of Joseph" covers the biblical story of Joseph, the birth and childhood of Moses, and Moses' trip to Midian. The "History of Moses" includes the account of Moses in Egypt, the Israelites in the wilderness, and the death of Moses.

Throughout, these expansions contain long quotations and paraphrases from the Bible, adding details found in other exegetical treatments of these stories. Christian allegory is common, such as the association of the rock that Moses strikes and the manna in the wilderness as symbols of Christ. Other exegetical details appear related to Muslim exegesis, such as Satan assuming the form of crows and instructing Cain how to kill and bury his brother. In an unusual passage, perhaps related to the Three Steles of Seth, one of the expansions mentions that Enosh set up two pillars against the sons of Cain and wrote on them a prophecy concerning the future destruction of the earth by fire and water.

ARMENIAN PROPHET LISTS. Expression that refers to a series of lists of the names of prophets, some including significant events from the prophets' lives. The lists are written in Armenian and date to the 17th and 18th centuries CE. Some of the information contained on these lists parallels accounts in other Jewish and Muslim stories, such as Isaiah being martyred by being sawn in half, and how all the idols fell down at the virgin birth of Jeremiah. In another list, Jeremiah's scribe, Baruch, is said to have written a book that the Jews do not read. Often, the interpretation is explicitly Christian, such as the claim that the Israelite prophet Hosea prophesied about Christ rising on the third day and that the prophet Joel prophesied concerning Christ and the Holy Spirit, though the Jews interpreted the prophecy as relating to contemporary events. According to the Lists, Jerome remarked that Habakkuk was the prophet who brought food to Daniel when he was in the lion's den, information also found in the Greek Lives of the Prophets and the Apocryphal Bel and the Dragon (Bel and the Dragon 14). Listed among the prophets are David, Solomon, John the Baptist, Miriam, Deborah, Huldah, Elizabeth, Hannah, "Three Children," Zakok, Akia, Salamut, and Telemos the Cyclops son of Poseidon who prophesied to Polyphemus concerning Odysseus in Homer's *Odyssey* (9.509).

ASAPH. Referred to in 1 Chr 25:1 as a father of prophetic musicians established by David, along with Jeduthun and Heman. Asaph's sons, Zakkur, Joseph, Nethaniah, and Asarelah, served as musical prophets for Yahweh's temple (1 Chr 25:2). Since they "prophesied according to the order of the king" (1 Chr 25:5), they must be seen as prophets serving the royal house. Later, Ahab's Queen Jezebel (c. 860 BCE) would similarly employ the prophets of Baal (1 Kgs 18:19). The biblical Psalms that credit Asaph with authorship (Psalm 50, 73–83) are attributed to David in the Talmud (TB Baba Batra 14b).

ASCETICISM. In the past asceticism has been defined as a fellowship or communion with the transcendent order involving severe self-discipline and denial in an effort to achieve spiritual perfection. Recently, however, historians of religion have begun to recognize a diversity of behaviors inherent in asceticism and thus have expanded the concept to denote a form of religious behavior or expression marked by self-induced suffering, severe abstinence, or rigorous self-discipline, which in its more extreme forms can involve pica, self-induced pain, and self-mutilation. Ascetic behavior can be temporarily imposed or be maintained as a permanent lifestyle. Its goals include, but are not limited to, piety, penance, the denial of human pleasures, closeness with the divine, the invocation of the prophetic spirit, and ritual participation with the divine. Temporary forms of ascetic behavior include fasting, self-induced crying, prophetic nudity, and self-inflicted injuries. Permanent forms can include celibacy, self-induced poverty, sleep or food deprivation, and scarring.

Asceticism in its various forms can be found throughout the ancient Near East, but is attested in mantic contexts with greater frequency after the seventh century BCE, and then mostly in the Levant. In Assyrian records fasting and self-induced weeping are found as means of inducing prophetic dreams and visions (*see also* PROPHECY), but other forms of asceticism are noticeably absent. Asceticism does not appear to have been a common practice in ancient Egypt until the Christian era.

The Hebrew Bible records the ascetic behavior of a number of prophets who engage in fasting (Daniel 10), prophetic nudity (1 Sam 19:20–24; Isa 20:2–3), pica (Ezek 3:2, 4:12), and self-inflicted discomfort (Ezek 4:4; Jer 27:2; 1 Kgs 22:11). The practices of the Nazir (Num 6) also demonstrate ascetic aspects, and there is ample evidence to suggest that Nazirite customs were practiced late in the postexilic period (*see* NAZIR). Foreign prophets too practiced some forms of asceticism. Thus, the prophets of the god Baal gashed themselves with flints and spears while prophesying (1 Kgs 18:28–29).

Some of the texts found among the Dead Sea Scrolls, which date from the third to first centuries BCE, testify to the ascetic practices of an entire community, and according to the New Testament, John the Baptist and the early Christians also engaged in some forms of asceticism, including fasting (Matt 3:4, 6:16–17; Mark 2:20; Luke 7:33; Acts 10:10), and possibly also self-induced weeping (Luke 22:45–46), as well as sleep deprivation (Mark 13:37–41). Some late antique figures performed self-castration in an effort to avoid the temptations of carnal desire, and this activity continued in the Byzantine world at least until the 11th century CE, despite legal prohibitions against it. Tensions over the question of how ascetic one should be are also apparent in the Talmud. Some Jewish mystics of the Middle Ages participated in the suffering of "God's glory" [Heb. shekhinah] by way of fasting, weeping, and beating one's own face and pulling hairs from one's own head and beard.

Some Muslim mystics also practiced asceticism (*see also* SUFISM). Some of these practices are modeled upon the life of the prophet Muhammad, but the origins of many of them are specifically attributed to Jesus. Muslim exegetes stress that Jesus was poor, never had food for more than one meal, and shunned the activities and accoutrements of this world. Muslim asceticism is not commonly dualistic, but is explained as a suppression of the body for the purpose of purifying both it and the soul.

ASHERAH. Representation and name of a goddess who often appears in conjunction with a standing stone [Heb. massebah] and sometimes is considered a consort of the god Baal (Judg 3:7; 2 Kgs 23:4), though Ugaritic texts refer to her as the wife of El, the chief deity of the Canaanite pantheon. The object that represented the goddess was fashioned of wood (Judg 6:26) and trimmed and maintained by its worshipers (Exod 34:13; Judg 6:25). Some texts treat it as a living tree planted, or perhaps transplanted, for cultic reasons (Deut 16:21). In general terms, the Asherah may be seen as a form of sacred tree, and a form of worship widely attested in the ancient Near East (*see also* RHABDOMANCY). According to 1 Kgs 18:9, Asherah's cult involved the employ of prophets and the use of sacred utensils (2 Kgs 23:4). Asherah was popularized in the north of Israel during the reign of Ahab (by Jezebel, 1 Kgs 18:19, 869–850 BCE), and King Manasseh (687-642 BCE) in Judah (2 Kgs 21:7). Asherah's association with Canaanite worship naturally led to its prohibition (Exod 34:13) and prophetic attack (Isa 17:8; Jer 17:20; Mic 5:14). Archaeological finds at Kuntillet 'Ajrud and Khirbet el-Qom in the northern Sinai have unearthed several inscriptions from the eighth to seventh centuries BCE that refer to blessings in the names of Yahweh and his Asherah. The inscriptions provide evidence for a competing conception of Yahweh in ancient Israel, one that saw him as having a divine consort (2 Kgs 11:5). Though the Asherah was not sanctioned as an object of worship by Israelite state religion, some scholars believe that its physical representation may have persisted into later times, albeit in demythologized form, as the menorah (i.e., plant-like candelabra with seven candles). Numerous references in the Talmud demonstrate that the Asherah was still in existence as a living tree and perhaps cultic object long after the biblical period (e.g., TB Erubin 78b; Abodah Zarah 42a).

ASTRONOMY AND ASTROLOGY. Astronomy is the study of the position, motion, and distribution of celestial bodies and phenomena. Astrology is the study and application of astronomical principles for ascertaining their influence on human affairs. The peoples of the ancient Near East did not draw a sharp distinction between these two disciplines. The study of astral phenomena is often associated with prophecy and occurs as a literary motif in several stories of the prophets.

A serious technical interest in the night sky and its patterns appears in Mesopotamian records as early as the third millennium BCE in the form of bilingual lists of stars and constellations. In the two millennia that followed, this interest burgeoned into a full-blown science that recorded the observations of the moon's phases, solar and lunar eclipses, heliacal risings of planets, and the movements of the planets through the constellations. Since the planets were associated with particular gods, the science of tracking heavenly bodies was closely tied to astral worship. In fact, the earliest cuneiform sign used to write the word *deity* appears in the shape of a star. The sun, moon, and planets (five were known at the time) were considered gods, and therefore capable of influencing the natural world. They were worshipped like other gods and, in some cases, played significant roles in performative rituals of power and divination.

Mesopotamian diviners regularly sought the good will of the divine judge and sungod Shamash before performing extispicies (*see also* EXTISPICY). Astral omens, like all other types of omens, were understood as divine messages and interpreted according to the diviner's understanding of the assigned roles of the gods in the heavens; but it is not until the fifth and third centuries BCE that Babylonian and Seleucid horoscopes are found predicting one's future based of the date of one's birth. At roughly the same time, Near Eastern peoples began to come into greater contact with Greek-speaking peoples and the cultural exchange resulted in an adoption and adaption of some forms of Near Eastern astral worship by the Greeks. Along with these cults came Near Eastern knowledge of astronomical and astrological sciences, including the practice of determining individual (but not daily) horoscopes. The influence of Mesopotamia in this regard was felt elsewhere as well, and in fact, astrology is the divinatory art for which Mesopotamia was most famed in late antiquity.

References to Babylonian astrology appear already in the Hebrew Bible, but always in pejorative contexts that denigrate idolatrous forms of divine communication and worship. In Deutero-Isaiah there is the ridicule of Babylonian astrologers and the star gazers for their inability to save Babylon from the destruction that Yahweh will bring upon it (Isa 47:13–14). The book of Daniel also uses the word *Chaldean* (i.e., Babylonians) in conjunction with magicians and diviners (Dan 2:10; *see also* DIVINATION; MAGIC) who cannot achieve what Daniel can without recourse to these arts. Despite the Israelite attitude toward Mesopotamian astral worship, its impact is evident. It already had pervaded Israelite worship before the time of King Josiah (640–609 BCE) for it is recorded that one of his religious reforms involved deposing the priests who burned incense "to the sun, and to the moon, and to the constellations, and to all the host of heaven" (2 Kgs 23:5). Nevertheless, the struggle of state-sanctioned forms of Yahwism against Mesopotamian influence in this regard would only be victorious in part, for while Israelites in the post-exilic period would come to reject all forms of astral worship and astrology, they could do so not by denying the importance of astral bodies as divine signs and portents (*see also* SIGNS), but by relegating them to the control of Yahweh who created the constellations and zodiacal signs (Job 38:31–33).

Postbiblical references to the prophets often associate astrological knowledge with prophets and prophecy. According to 2 Enoch, and in fragments found among the Dead Sea Scrolls, the art of astrology was brought to humankind by a fallen angel named Kawkabel [Heb.

kokab, lit. "star" and Heb. 'el, lit. "God"] (2 Enoch 6–8). Muslim sources report that the fallen angels Harut and Marut brought astrological knowledge to earth. Jewish sources assert that the extraordinary life spans of the antediluvian sages enabled them to study the movements of the stars and to pass on their astrological knowledge to future generations (Genesis Rabbah 26:5; Antiquities I.2.3). The Testament of Adam records that calendrical and astronomical information passed from Adam at the time of his death to his son Seth. The Treatise of Shem is an astrological text based on the signs of the Zodiac. Abraham is frequently referred to as a "Chaldean," meaning one with astronomical and astrological training, and in some texts he is the one credited with bringing these disciplines from Babylon (Antiquities 1.8.2; Preparation 9.17.3–4). Many of the accounts of Solomon, including the Testament of Solomon and Muslim sources, report that Solomon had astrological knowledge along with the other arts he acquired in his mastery over the demons and Jinn (*see also* DEMON; JINN).

The Bible's rather uniform negative outlook toward Mesopotamian astral worship and astrology may represent more of a projected ideal than a reality, for as the Dead Sea Scrolls discovered at Qumran reveal, some forms of ancient Judaism were extremely receptive to astrological omens and horoscopes. Later Jewish writings record a number of astronomical traditions, especially with regard to the fixing of calendrical festivals, but register a certain amount of ambivalence with regard to the place of astrology within Jewish tradition. The Talmud, for example, contains a great deal of information on the planets and constellations, demonstrating a continued rabbinic interest in astronomical observations (TB Berakhoth 59b; Pesahim 94a–94b). Some rabbis are even said to have included astronomy as part of their regular course of study (TB Baba Batra 134a). The Talmud, perhaps in reaction to traditions to the contrary, attempts to distance Abraham from astrology (TB Shabbath150a; Nedarim 32a; Yoma 88b), and later traditions paint Israel's enemies as astrologers (Zohar I, 140b, III, 113b).

ATBASH. A performative linguistic cipher in which the first letter of the alphabet stands for the last, the second for the penultimate, the third for the antepenultimate, and so on. By way of Atbash, the prophet Jeremiah transforms "Babylon" into "Sheshak," a meaningless "rubble heap" of letters (Jer 51:4). Jeremiah also employs the device in Jer 51:1 in the words "heart of my enemies" [Heb. leb-qamay], which constitute an Atbash cipher for the "Chaldeans." The device has its origins in divinatory word play and derives from a belief in the power of words (*see also* WORD PLAY). Atbash continued in use in the talmudic period as an exegetical device (TB Shabbath 104a; Ketuboth 19a; Sanhedrin 22a, Horayoth 12b).

ATHANASIUS (c. 297–373 CE**).** Christian scholar born in Alexandria and later appointed as bishop. He lost the see of Alexandria in 335 and spent many years in the Egyptian desert. His writings include a treatise that preserves a number of biblical exegetical comments.

AVESTA. A Persian term referring to the whole of Zoroastrian scripture and the language in which the earliest scriptures were composed. The term *Avesta* probably derives from the Avestan *upasta*, denoting "the scriptures" as distinguished from the "Zand," which are later exegetical works often paraphrasing the contents of the Avesta. Much of the Avesta is presumed lost based on a comparison of the extant texts with what is claimed and summarized in the later Zand texts. The Avesta was divided into 21 books called Nasks, which themselves were divided into three groups of seven books each, but what is extant is normally divided into two groups for ritual purposes. The first group consists of the Yasna and Gathas, Vendidad, and Visparad. The Yasna is a liturgical text recited during the Yasna ritual and describes the preparation and offering of the special preparation of the juice of the Haoma plant. Five extant Gathas (psalms) contain the teachings and revelations of the prophet Zoroaster. Added to the Yasna is the Visparad, a collection of some 24 chapters. There are 22 chapters in the Vendidad, which include an account of creation, the legend of Yima, and extensive laws pertaining to purification rites. The second group of Avesta texts consists of the minor prayers and the Yashts. Among the minor prayers are the Nyaishes, which are five short prayers of praise to the Sun, Moon, Water, Fire, and four angels associated with the elements. Also included among the minor prayers are those used for special seasonal festivals and for funerals. The Yashts is a book of 21 hymns praising the angels and heroes of

Zoroastrian history. There are also a number of fragments of otherwise nonextant Avesta texts.

AZARIAH. Prophet mentioned only briefly in the Bible as the son of the prophet Oded (2 Chr 15:1). Azariah is credited with having prophesied to King Asa of Judah (913–873 BCE), along with his father, that Yahweh would be with Asa if he followed God's ways. The two prophets were influential enough to inspire the king to cease the worship of foreign deities and reinstitute the worship of Yahweh (2 Chr 15:8).

AZRAEL. Also pronounced "Izrael," this name is given to the Angel of Death in Muslim sources. Along with Gabriel, Michael, and Israfil, he is one of the four archangels. The Quran states that the Angel of Death will take every person and return them to God (Q 32:11), and Q 31:34 reports that only God knows where each person will be taken by death. Several of the stories of the prophets describe encounters between prophets and the Angel of Death.

– B –

BAAL. God of storms and fertility widely worshipped in the ancient Near East, especially in Syro-Canaan. At Ugarit, "Prince Baal" appears to be the son of the chief god El (or perhaps an outsider who usurps his sovereignty). Ugaritic texts also preserve his own liturgy (an entire epic) that reports how Baal took the throne from the god Yam (lit. "Sea"), went to battle against the god Mot (lit. "Death"), and commissioned the building of a great palace for himself. The texts also describe his stormy relationship with his sister and consort Anat, and report his bestiality with a heifer, a performative ritual that does not appear to have been viewed as taboo in Canaan.

The worship of Baal also was known in Egypt after a period of Levantine influence (c. 1400–1075 BCE), and was brought to Babylonia in the form "Bel" by the Amorites. Eventually Baal was adopted by the Greeks, who identified him with Zeus. Baal's epithet as "(Chariot) Rider on the Clouds" describes his role as rain-bringer, and is adopted for Yahweh in Ps 68:5. The Phoenicians later referred to him as "Baal of the Heavens." In the Bible, Baal appears in his various manifestations often as the object of prophetic harangue. Thus, in 1 Kgs 18:20–40, the prophet Elijah competes against the prophets of Baal and mocks their cultic drama by ridiculing their own mythology. His appearance in Israelite personal names indicates that his status was much greater prior to the rise of Classical Prophecy. The judge Gideon is also called Jerubbaal (Judg 6:32), and the component "Baal" also appears in the names of prince Ishbaal, the son of Saul (1 Chr 8:33), and Meribaal, the son of Jonathan (1 Chr 8:34), each of whom later editors refer to by replacing the component "Baal" with the word "boshet," meaning "shame." Attestations include Jerbosheth (2 Sam 11:21), Ishboshet (2 Sam 2:8), and Mephiboshet (2 Sam 4:4).

BAALBEK. City located west of Damascus and northeast of Beirut at the northern end of the Baqa Valley. According to Muslim exegetes, the prophet Elijah was sent to the people of Baalbek, as recounted in the Quran (Q 37:123–132). The association of the city with Elijah may be due to the mention of Baal in the Elijah story, though most modern scholars do not identify Baalbek with any sites mentioned in the Bible. Before the third century BCE the city was the site of a cult centered on the god Baal, and after this time the shrine served as a locus of worship for Zeus, Aphrodite, and Hermes. The extensive remains, dating to the early Roman period, may have been in better condition in the early Islamic period, and could have represented God's victory over Baal as told in the Elijah story (1 Kings 18).

BALAAM. Transjordanian prophet from the region of Moab who is hired by the Moabite king Balak to curse Israel, but who offers blessings instead (Num 23–24). Though not an Israelite, Balaam speaks with Yahweh, who tells him not to curse the Israelites but to go with the men sent by Balak (Num 22:2–21). While on the road, God speaks to Balaam through the mouth of his donkey (Num 22:22–35) and Balaam has a vision of the Angel of God. Balaam delivers four oracles blessing, instead of cursing, the Israelites (Num 23:7–10, 19–24, 24:3–9, 15–24). The last oracle includes a passage (Num 24:17) that was taken as a messianic prediction by early Christians, at Qumran, and in other Jewish contexts. Based on this oracle, some

Christian sources also identify Balaam as the founder of the order of the Magi who visited Jesus. Other biblical references credit Balaam's blessings to Yahweh (Deut 23:4–6; Neh 13:2; Josh 24:9–10).

Some scholars identify Balaam's homeland as Pitru on the upper Euphrates, based on the reference in Num 22:5, but others argue for a location farther south. In 1967, a series of seventh-century BCE inscriptions on plaster fragments were discovered at Deir Alla in the Transjordan. They were written in Aramaic, or in a dialect of ancient Hebrew closely akin to Aramaic, and report to be the account of Balaam, "seer of the gods." Unfortunately, the texts are extremely fragmentary, a fact that has given rise to a number of widely divergent interpretations. Nevertheless, texts do attest to the presence of prophetic traditions concerning Balaam in the Transjordan.

In later Jewish exegesis, Balaam is said to be the last of the gentile prophets who included Shem; Job; and Job's companions Eliphaz, Zophar, Bildad, and Elihu (TB Baba Batra 15b). Balaam also is portrayed as a magician, and the Targum Yerushalmi identifies the companions Balaam takes with him on the road (Num 22:22) as Jannes and Jambres, the two magicians mentioned in later tradition as competing with Moses before the pharaoh in Exodus 7 (though the Hebrew Bible offers no names). Jewish tradition also attributes Balaam's parables in Numbers 23–24 to Moses (TB Baba Batra 14b), and regards him as "the wicked Balaam" who has no portion in the world to come (TB Sanhedrin 90a, 105a, 105b). Philo treats Balaam as a gentile who claimed to be a prophet, but who was only just a soothsayer (De Migratione Abrahami 20.113–115). Josephus (Antiquities 4) defines Balaam as a diviner. By way of exegetical word plays on his name, the Talmud associates him with corrupting the people, and with bestiality (TB Sanhedrin 105a).

BAR HEBRAEUS (1225–1286 CE**).** Abu al-Faraj Gregory Bar Hebraeus is the author of Syriac and Arabic works, well known for his Syriac translations of selected Arabic works by al-Ghazali and Ibn Sina, his Syriac grammar, and his universal history in Syriac, which he also abridged into Arabic. Bar Hebraeus was a monk and the West Syrian or Jacobite bishop of Gubbash and Lakabbin, the metropolitan of Aleppo, and the head of the Jacobite Church in Persia. His universal history is of particular importance for the stories of the prophets, treating history from the creation to his own time and incorporating biblical materials, Jewish and Christian exegetical traditions, and Islamic materials.

BARLAAM AND JOSEPHAT. A legend of Indian origin that combines elements from the life of the Buddha, Christian parables, and other narratives of unidentified origin. The story probably originates from a Sanskrit original that relates to works known in Central Asian Buddhist Soghdian texts and to Manichaean fragments found at Turfan. In these texts the Buddhist designation "Bodhisattva" is shortened to "Pwtysf" or "Bodisaf," a name that also appears in a Muslim list of false prophets where it is said to be conflated by the Sabians with Enoch and Hermes Trismegistos. The story then seems to have been transmitted into Arabic where the term *Bodisaf* was read as "Yudasaf" (replacing the one dot of the "b" with the two dots of the "y" in the Arabic script). The Arabic recensions of the story of Bilawhar and Yudasaf are said to have been transmitted into Arabic from Pahlavi in the eighth or ninth century CE, but are only preserved in later recensions. The story is mentioned in the *Letters of the Ikhwan al-Safa* [Ar. Rasa'il Ikhwan al-Safa]. Later recensions include Arabic texts that incorporate the story into a longer work, Persian translations of the Arabic, a Georgian translation found in Jerusalem, and a Hebrew paraphrase of the 13th century CE. The Georgian recension, which was translated into Greek around the 11th century CE, gives the names as Balahvar and Iodasap. This Greek recension was later attributed to John of Damascus (676–759 CE), and became widespread in medieval Europe. It was translated into Latin, Old Church Slavonic, Armenian, and French. Barlaam and Josephat were recognized by the Roman Catholic Church as saints, and a number of churches were dedicated to them.

The story begins with an introduction that tells of a prince named Josephat whom an astrologer predicts will be not of this world. A king tries to keep the prince confined to a special city in which he does not encounter suffering, but one day the prince leaves and meets the holy man Barlaam from Sri Lanka. Much of the remainder of the text cites a series of parables through which Barlaam instructs Josephat, and a debate in which the king is converted to the religion of Barlaam. Some of the versions, especially those popular in medieval Europe, include explicit references to Jesus Christ, but the Arabic versions do not appear to contain any specific Islamic allusions.

BARUCH. The son of Neriah, the scribe and apparent disciple of Jeremiah the prophet. He is said to have taken dictation for the prophet Jeremiah (Jer 36:4, 36:17–18), and while Jeremiah is in prison, Baruch reads the prophet's scroll in Yahweh's temple, an act that suggests he has privileged access (Jer 36:8). Jeremiah, after all, was a priest of Anathoth (Jer 1:1). The discovery in Jerusalem of a sixth century BCE bulla (seal impression) bearing the name of Berekhyahu son of Neriyahu seems to confirm his existence. Baruch's role as a prophet is nowhere mentioned in the Bible, but is assumed based on what later Jewish sources perceive to be his discipleship under Jeremiah.

Rabbinic traditions differ on whether Baruch is a prophet. The Talmud records one tradition in which Baruch is considered a prophet descended from the harlot Rahab (TB Megillah 14b), and assigns similar prophetic roles for Jeremiah's other apparent disciples Hanamel and Serayah (see Jeremiah 32, Rashi on Jeremiah 32, and TB Megillah 15a). On the other hand, at least one tradition states that he is not a prophet (Mekilta Bo, Petihta). He also is identified with Ebed-Melech the Ethiopian (Aboth d'Rabbi Nathan 43, 122; Pirqe d'Rabbi Eliezer 26, 130b). Some traditions see Baruch as having been "sent away" by God prior to the destruction of the temple, and thus having "not tasted death" (Sifre Numbers 99; TB Mo'ed Qatan 16b; Pirqe d'Rabbi Eliezer 53), having entered paradise while he was still alive (TB Derek Erez Zuta, 1). Nevertheless, Jewish tradition records several accounts of miraculous events at Baruch's tomb. One such event, told in a highly polemical style, involves a visit to Baruch's tomb by a Muslim prince. Having entered Baruch's tomb the prince found that Baruch's body had not decomposed (TB Shabbath 152b, Baba Mezi'a 84b). The prince was so impressed that he founded a Jewish academy on the spot, and went to Mecca, where he became convinced of the errancy of Islam and promptly converted to Judaism.

2 BARUCH. A text preserved in Syriac and Arabic describing the destruction of the first temple in Jerusalem (586 BCE), but probably written sometime after the destruction of the second temple (70 CE).

Based on historical references and the relation with 4 Ezra, scholars date 2 Baruch to the second century CE. The most reliable Syriac manuscript is dated to the sixth or seventh century CE, though there are Syriac fragments dated as early as the fourth century. There is a single Arabic manuscript dated to the 10th or 11th century CE, which appears to be written from a perspective familiar with Muslim eschatology. The theme of the destruction of Jerusalem and the temple is dominant in biblical prophetic sources, early Judaism and Christianity, and Muslim exegesis.

The text is divided into 87 chapters. Chapters 1–8 describe the destruction of Jerusalem, including an account of an angel removing the temple vessels and hiding them in the earth until the end of time (6:5–9). The rest of the text consists of visions received by Baruch and his exhortations to the righteous. Among these are a number of eschatological motifs such as the coming of the Messiah, the Resurrection, and the Day of Judgment. Many of the visions are preceded by Baruch's fasting for seven days, and several of the visions involve symbols that must be interpreted for Baruch (35–43, 53–74).

3 BARUCH. Preserved in Greek and Old Church Slavonic, this text depicts the destruction of Jerusalem and Baruch's ascension through five heavens. Many scholars date the origins of this text to the early third century, though the earliest clear reference to the work is the use of chapter two in the History of the Rechabites (sixth century CE). The Greek manuscripts date to the 15th century CE, and the Slavonic manuscripts (assumed to be translations of a lost Greek original) date from the 13th to 18th centuries CE.

The text is divided into 17 chapters and includes much material on angelology, astronomical features, natural wonders, and various references to biblical motifs and stories. Though related to other apocalyptic texts, 3 Baruch does not focus on eschatological themes. Each of the heavens visited by Baruch contains different items, many of which are found in other cosmological journeys. The first heaven is a plain on which men with cattle bodies graze. These beasts are identified as the people who built the Tower of Babel. In the second heaven is a prison with dog-faced creatures identified as those people who planned and forced others to build the Tower of Babel. The third heaven contains a giant serpent, numerous rivers, the Garden of

Eden, the chariot of the sun, and the Phoenix. In the fourth heaven, Baruch sees a lake with unusual birds, and in the fifth he sees the angels who bring gifts to people on earth. Michael carries a large bowl in which are the virtues and good works of the righteous. At the end of the Slavonic text Baruch is given permission to intercede on behalf of the sinners, and in both the Greek and Slavonic texts he is returned to earth with a commission to tell others about what he has witnessed.

4 BARUCH. Extant in a number of versions and languages, this text gives an account of Jeremiah, Abimelech, and Baruch's activities surrounding the destruction of the temple in Jerusalem. There are numerous Greek manuscripts of different versions of this text, the earliest of which dates to the 11th century CE, and also recensions in Ethiopic, Armenian, Old Church Slavonic, and Romanian. The title of the text in Greek is "Things Omitted from the Prophet Jeremiah," and the Ethiopic version gives the title as "The Rest of the Words of Baruch."

The text includes several narratives in nine chapters. Chapters 1–4 describe the vision given to Jeremiah that Jerusalem would be destroyed. Jeremiah then warns Baruch and Abimelech about the destruction, and is himself instructed to entrust the keys of the temple to the sun and the temple vessels to the earth, which swallows them. Chapters 5–7 relate how Abimelech fell asleep outside of the city and slept there for 66 years. When he awakes he finds his figs still fresh, and he is disoriented because of the passing time. An old man then gets Baruch, who sees Abimelech's return as a resurrection from the dead. In Chapters 8–9 Jeremiah returns from Babylon with the exiles, but is stoned to death for proclaiming Jesus Christ as the coming Messiah. These narratives have much in common with the stories attributed to Ezra and Jeremiah in the Muslim exegesis of Q 2:259.

BAT QOL. Hebrew term meaning literally a "daughter of a sound." The Bat Qol is considered a minor form of prophecy in early Jewish literature. Scholars often associate it with the divinatory practice of kledonomancy, and it probably is to be connected with the Babylonian prophetic omen known in Mesopotamia as an egirrû (*see also* EGIRRÛ). The Bat Qol could include many types of sounds, but at times appears to be interpreted as a human voice. In one instance, a child's recitation of a biblical verse overheard by the rabbis constitutes a Bat Qol. The Talmud states that the Bat Qol came into vogue after the deaths of the prophets Haggai, Zechariah, and Malachi, which also marked the departure of the Holy Spirit from Israel (TB Sanhedrin 11a; Yoma 9b). According to the Talmud Yerushalmi, this period also marked the cancellation of the Urim and Thummim, the destruction of the sanctuary, and the end of the "Shamir-worm" (TY Sotah 9:12–13). The latter is defined in the Tosefta version of Sotah 9:13 as a creature associated with the six days of creation, which was capable of splitting open stones, wood, or iron when placed on them. Some scholars relate the "Shamir-worm" to the worm that eats the staff of Solomon in Q 34:14.

BEERI. Prophet whose extant prophecies, according to Jewish tradition, appear in only two verses, which are included in the book of Isaiah (Isa 8:19–20). He is regarded as the father of the prophet Hosea and is identified with Beerah (1 Chr 5:6), who was taken into exile by the Assyrians (TB Pesahim 87b; Baba Batra 14b; Pirqe d'Rabbi Eliezer 33).

BEERSHEBA. Southernmost city in ancient Israel for much of Israelite history, often used along with the northernmost city Dan in a merism (i.e., "from Dan to Beersheba"), meaning "all of Israel" (Judg 20:1; 1 Sam 3:20; 1 Kgs 5:5; Amos 8:14). The name Beersheba probably means "Well of the Seven," and some scholars understand it as meaning "Well of the Seven (Stars of the Pleiades)." The Bible reinterprets it as meaning "Well of the Oath," based on the tradition of Jacob and Esau's oath (Gen 26:31–33). The prophet Samuel later attempted to establish his sons Joel and Abijah as hereditary judges in Beersheba (1 Sam 8:2). Beersheba is the site where Abraham made a covenant with Abimelech, the Philistine king, and planted a sacred tamarisk for calling on El 'Olam (Gen 21:32–33). According to Tabari, it was Dhu al-Qarnayn (Q 18:83–101) who presided over the dispute between Abraham and the Philistines at Beersheba. Beersheba is also the place where Abraham sent Hagar when his first wife Sarah drove her out (Gen 21:14). Gen 22:19 relates that Abraham lived there after nearly sacrificing his son. Muslim exegetes identify the well of Beersheba with the well of Zamzam, a well that appears after Hagar runs between Safa and Marwah seven times. The sanctuary established at Beersheba by Abraham (Targum Onqelos on Gen 21:31) is identified with the sanctuary at Mecca by Muslim exegetes, and the biblical Paran mentioned in Gen 21:21 is said to be the Hebrew name for Mecca.

BEN SIRA. *See* WISDOM OF JESUS BEN SIRAH.

BENJAMIN. The son of Jacob and Rachel (Gen 35:18) and eponymous ancestor of the Israelite tribe of the same name. It is from the tribe of Benjamin that King Saul descends; King David descended from the tribe of Judah. The tribe of Benjamin's land rested between that of the tribes of Judah and Ephraim. According to Judges 20, a bloody friction with the rest of Israel forced the tribe to become dependent on the tribe of Judah. When the monarchy divided upon Solomon's death, Benjamin was annexed into Judah (Neh 11:7). The tainted relationship between the tribes of Benjamin and Judah remained in Israelite consciousness long after the united monarchy (1 Sam 22:7; Rom 11:1; Phil 3:5). The prophet Jeremiah also belonged to the tribe of Benjamin (Jer 1:1).

BIBLIOMANCY. The divinatory practice of deriving import from the random reading of biblical verses, which came into vogue following the canonization of the biblical text and the destruction of the temple. The Talmud refers to several instances of bibliomancy (TB Berakoth 55b) and appears to treat the practice as a form of Bat Qol (*see also* BAT QOL). Early Jewish texts attest to the bibliomantic application of roughly 180 biblical verses.

BOOK OF ARDA VIRAF. Zoroastrian text dating from the fifth or sixth centuries CE describing Arda Viraf's vision of heaven and hell. The work opens with an account of the destruction of Zoroastrian scriptures and the religion in the time of Alexander the Great (356–323 BCE). Arda Viraf is chosen to journey through heaven and hell to ascertain reliable information about the rituals and beliefs of the Zoroastrian religion. Arda Viraf is escorted by various angels on a tour of the fate of different souls, both pious and sinful, in heaven and in hell, and visits God on his throne. Many of the righteous deeds and sins correspond directly to obligations and prohibitions in Zoroastrianism. While the descriptions of the sins are specific to Zoroastrianism, the general structure of the text closely parallels other visions of heaven and hell in Jewish, Christian, and Islamic apocalyptic texts such as the Greek Apocalypse of Ezra, 3 Baruch, and the Ascension of Isaiah.

BOOK OF JASHER. A Hebrew exegetical compilation [Heb. Sefer ha-Yashar] dated as early as the 13th century CE, incorporating many elements from Jewish and Islamic exegesis and concerning biblical and Israelite history from the creation to the time of Joshua, Moses' successor. The text is divided into 91 chapters, each with an average of 30 verses. The work is composed in an archaic Hebrew style reminiscent of the Bible, which led some early scholars to connect it with the "Book of Jasher" mentioned in Josh 10:13 and 2 Sam 1:18–19.

BOOK OF JOSIPPON. A medieval Hebrew version of the writings of Josephus beginning with Genesis 10 and ending with the fall of Masada. The text seems to have been composed in Italy, in the middle of the 10th century CE, drawing on a fourth-century CE Latin paraphrase of Josephus and the Apocrypha. Ibn Hazm translated the text into Arabic in Spain during the 11th century CE, and Jewish exegetes (including Rashi) used the Book of Josippon, apparently believing that it was written by Josephus.

BOOK OF THE CAVE OF TREASURES. A Syriac text recounting history from the creation to Jesus Christ. The book is commonly attributed to Ephrem the Syrian (306–373 CE), and some scholars argue that its contents date back to the second century CE, though many consider the book to combine a number of earlier traditions and to have been redacted much later. There are multiple versions of the text in Syriac (esp. the "Western" and "Eastern" versions) as well as Arabic, Ethiopic, Coptic, and Georgian recensions. The "cave" is supposed to be the one in which the secret books of Adam were hidden, along with the frankincense and myrrh that the Wise Men took as presents to the infant Jesus (*see also* CAVE). Closely related to this text is the *Book of the Bee*, attributed to a Solomon, bishop of Basra, in the 13th century CE. The *Book of the Bee* contains much of the same information as found in the *Book of the Cave of Treasures*, but continues the story through the early history of Christianity in outline form.

BOOK OF THE GIANTS. This text is extant only in Aramaic fragments from the Dead Sea Scrolls (and is classified with the Enoch materials) and from passages in a Manichaean version of the work. A reference in the Gelasian Decree indicates that this work was known also in late antiquity. The text contains different narratives of the sons of the watchers and their women, and closely relates to the accounts found in the Ethiopic Book of Enoch, also known as 1 Enoch.

BUKHARI (810–870 CE). Abu Abdallah Muhammad b. Ismail b. Ibrahim b. al-Mughira b. Barbizbah al-Ju'fi al-Bukhari is the compiler of the most widely authoritative collection of prophetic hadith reports (*see also* HADITH). This work, said to have taken 16 years to complete, is a standard reference for many later scholars. It includes 2,762 hadith reports, many of them repeated numerous times, and Bukhari is said to have winnowed these authoritative reports from a total of around 600,000 that he collected. The authoritative reports are arranged in 97 books and 3,450 chapters. Numerous commentaries have been written on Bukhari's authoritative collection, the best known being those of Ibn Hajar and Qastillani. Bukhari also wrote a biographical dictionary devoted to the names of the people mentioned as transmitting the hadith reports in his authoritative collection.

BUKHTNASAR. Arabic name given to a character largely associated with the Babylonian king Nebuchadnezzar II (605–562 BCE), but also with other foreign rulers linked to the destruction of the temple in Jerusalem. According to some Muslim sources, Bukhtnasar is named as one of the four people who in their times ruled over all the earth, a list that elsewhere includes Nimrod, Dahhak, Solomon, and Dhu al-Qarnayn. Muslim exegetes also report that it was Bukhtnasar who destroyed the temple in Jerusalem and carried off the Israelites in exile to Babylon. He was the king who saw the vision interpreted by Daniel, threw Daniel into the lion's den, and was turned into a wild beast by an angel for seven years. Among the other prophets of the period of the Babylonian exile with whom Bukhtnasar is associated are Hananiah, Azariah, Mishael, Ezra, and Jeremiah. In the Islamic exegesis of Q 17:4–8, it is reported that Bukhtnasar destroyed Jerusalem in the time of John the Baptist, and was compelled to kill the Israelites on account of their killing of John the Baptist. Muslim sources also record the tradition, associated with the Roman emperor Titus in the Babylonian Talmud (TB Megillah 11a), that God caused a mosquito to enter and live inside of Bukhtnasar's head. The expedition of the Babylonian king Nabonidus (555–539 BCE) against the pre-Islamic Arab site of Tema is associated with Bukhtnasar in some Muslim historical sources (*see also* NABONIDUS).

BUNDAHISHN. A Zoroastrian text preserved in Pahlavi containing an account of the creation of the world and definition of the various elements related to its creation. The *Bundahishn* is a commentary [Av. zand] on lost Avestan works that originally may have been put into writing in the fifth century CE, and may be traced back to earlier traditions in oral transmission. The extant redaction of the *Bundahishn* is dated to the ninth century CE along with a number of other Zoroastrian texts. Among the topics discussed in the text are the origins of Ohrmazd and Ahriman, formation of the cosmos, the primeval ox, seven archons of the planets, conflicts of the evil spirit with the elements of creation, the mountains, seas, five classes of animals, humans, procreation, fire, plants, various mythological beasts, rivers, 17 types of liquid, lakes, the ape and the bear, human hierarchy, calendar, distances, geography, future resurrection of the dead including the appearance of the Soshyant savior-figure, and the genealogies of the major Iranian families.

– C –

CAIN AND ABEL. Two sons of Adam and Eve. According to the Bible and Quran, Cain killed his brother while working in the field (Genesis 4; Q 5:27–32). Cain harbored jealous thoughts because Yahweh had accepted Abel's offering, but not his. For killing his brother, Yahweh cursed Cain, making him a fugitive and a wanderer (Gen

4:11–12). In order to protect him from being killed by others, he put a "sign" on him of unknown type and on an unknown location (Gen 4:15), though later Jewish tradition places it on his forehead (Rashi on Gen 4:15). In the Armenian biblical expansion on the story, the sign on Cain is said to be a horn that called out that Cain killed his brother. Jewish exegesis of Gen 4:18–24 claims that Cain was killed by his descendant Lamech when his horn caused him to be mistaken for a wild animal (Genesis Rabbah 22:12–13).

The question of why God accepted only the sacrifice of Abel is not clear in Genesis. Muslim exegetes interpret Abel's statement in Q 5:27 to indicate that Cain's sacrifice was not accepted because he was not of upright character. Other exegetes explain that Abel offered the best of his flocks while Cain offered only the undesirable parts of his produce. Since "Abel was a keeper of sheep, but Cain was a tiller of the ground" (Gen 4:2), some scholars see this story of the first fratricide as reflecting early tensions between nomadic and settled societies. The mythological context of the pericope is underscored by Cain's name. Though related in the text to the verb for "acquire" (Gen 4:1), Semitic cognates suggest that the name derives from the process of metallurgy, an association supported by Cain's descendant Tubal-Cain, a "forger of every sharp instrument in bronze and iron" (Gen 4:22). The name Cain also is identical to a Hebrew word used for spear (2 Sam 21:16).

The reason for the sacrifice and the murder also relates to the twin sisters of Cain and Abel according to Jewish and Muslim exegesis. According to a tradition preserved in the Talmud, both Cain and Abel were born with twin sisters (TB Yebamoth 62a). Genesis Rabbah (22:7) describes the fight between Cain and Abel as having been over who had the right to marry Abel's twin sister, and the *Book of the Cave of Treasures* indicates that Adam wanted Cain to marry Abel's twin and Abel to marry Cain's twin, but Cain insisted on marrying his own twin. Ibn Kathir and other Muslim exegetes repeat this same account though sometimes switching the names of the twin sisters, and adding that Adam set up the sacrifice to decide which brother would marry Cain's twin sister. Tabari reports that Eve gave birth 120 times, and Ibn Ishaq says there were 20 pregnancies, which produced 20 sets of boy and girl twins.

According to the Targum Yerushalmi (Gen 4:16), the moment Abel was murdered, the vegetation began to wither, and the fruit trees that were accustomed to bearing a variety of fruits only bore one type, a state of affairs that will continue until the messianic age. The Quran refers to Cain as one of the "lost ones" (Q 5:30), and Ibn Kathir reports that Cain carried Abel's corpse on his back for a year until he learned from two crows how to bury him (Q 5:31). Other sources claim that Cain was the offspring of Eve and Satan (1 John 3:10–12; Targum Yerushalmi on Gen 4:1; Pirqe d'Rabbi Eliezer 21). The Tanhuma (Bereshith 25) has Cain excuse the murder of his brother by asserting that God put the evil impulse in him.

CAIRO GENIZA. A collection of documents preserved in a storeroom of a medieval synagogue in old Cairo, also know as Fustat. The Hebrew word [geniza] means "hidden" or "treasure" and refers to the place where documents were cached. They were placed there and not destroyed because Hebrew was regarded as a sacred tongue and script, and because many of the texts contained the sacred name of God. The Cairo Geniza was discovered when the synagogue to which it was attached was refurbished at the end of the 19th century CE. Most of the 10,000 documents discovered, the bulk of them fragmentary, date to the 10th through 13th centuries CE, and are written in Arabic with Hebrew characters (Judeo-Arabic). The documents include court records, letters, and contracts providing detailed information about the social and economic life of the Mediterranean during this period. Letters also represent communities in India, North Africa, and Spain. Much of the documentation is connected with the Jewish communities of these areas, but also reflect the larger milieu of Islamic civilization. Among the documents were also found examples of biblical, apocryphal, exegetical, and other religious texts that relate to Jewish and Islamic practices and beliefs, as well as a community manual found elsewhere only among the Dead Sea Scrolls.

CANON AND CANON LISTS. Both Jewish and Christian scholarship produced lists of the books considered to be authoritative and thus worthy of inclusion in the Bible. Often the lists included other noncanonical but important works related to canonical books. Such lists demonstrate a widespread familiarity with, and concern for, certain authoritative texts and traditions related to them. Even in those cases where listed works are otherwise unknown or not extant, the titles indicate circulation and knowledge of certain textual traditions, references to which are found in other texts.

The Jewish Bible is designated as "TaNaK," referring to its three constituent parts: Pentateuch [Heb. Torah], Prophets [Heb. Nebi'im], and Writings [Heb. Ketubim]. The Torah appears to have been an authoritative unit of material already in the fifth to fourth centuries BCE, since it is mentioned in Neh 8:1. The Torah and the Prophets also appear as established categories for Christians in the first century CE, as cited in the New Testament. According to the Mishnah, the Jewish canon of 24 books was completed after 70 CE (Mishnah Yadaim 3:5), and several talmudic texts discuss "hidden books," a term employed for those books not accepted into the canon (TB Shabbath 13b). 4 Ezra 14:44–48 reports that the canon consisted of 24 public books and 70 hidden books, the latter of which may or may not imply their rejection from the canon. Josephus, Origen, and Jerome attest to only 22 books, and some Jewish exegesis preserves a number of 35 apparently counting the minor prophets as separate books.

The Christian Bible includes both the Hebrew Bible (Old Testament) and New Testament. The arrangement of the former differs from the Jewish canon and, depending on whether it is a Catholic or Protestant Bible, contains additional books (*see also* APOCRYPHA). The canon of the New Testament seems to have remained fluid among different groups, but the basic outlines of the canon appear to have been settled by the fifth century CE as a series of canon lists attests. One of the earliest lists is found in the fourth century CE work of Eusebius, who divides the known texts into acknowledged books, disputed books, and heretical works. Other early lists from the fourth century CE include the Canon Muratori, the Claromontanus Canon, the Cheltenham Canon, and the list provided by Athanasius bishop of Alexandria. Later canon lists include the Gelasian Decree (sixth century CE), *Catalogue of the Sixty Books* (seventh century CE), and the *Stichometry of Nicephorus* (who was patriarch of Constantinople, ninth century CE). These later lists are of particular importance for their catalog of apocryphal works, some of which are no longer extant nor otherwise known.

The notion of certain texts as canonical or revealed is extremely important in Muslim exegesis of the Quran, especially related to the stories of the prophets. Q 87:18, 26:196, and 20:133 mention the "first scriptures" or "scriptures of the first ones," which some exegetes say refers to the books revealed to Adam, Seth, and Enoch. Q 87:19 and Q 53:36–37 refer to the "scriptures of Abraham and Moses," and Muslim exegetes identify numerous references to the revelation of the Torah to Moses, the Psalms to David, and the Gospel to Jesus. Many of the texts mentioned by Muslim exegetes as having been revealed to certain prophets can be identified with apocryphal apocalyptic texts listed in Jewish and Christian canon lists.

CANON MURATORI. Catalog of New Testament texts discovered in an eighth-century CE manuscript by L. A. Muratori (1672–1750), but thought to date as early as the third century CE. Additional fragments of the catalog have been discovered since, but the fullest Latin text is still incomplete. Included among the canonical texts are the Apocalypse of John and the Wisdom of Solomon. The Shepherd of Hermes also is permitted for private reading.

CATALOGUE OF THE SIXTY BOOKS. Catalog of 60 canonical books followed by a list of nine noncanonical and 25 apocryphal texts. The catalog is thought to originate in the seventh century CE and was widely circulated throughout the Greek Church. Among the writings outside of the 60, but not considered apocryphal, are the Wisdom of Solomon, Wisdom of Sirach, four Books of Maccabees, Esther, Judith, and Tobit. The apocryphal texts include Adam, Enoch, Lamech, Patriarchs, Prayer of Joseph, Eldad and Modad, Testament of Moses, Assumption of Moses, Psalms of Solomon, Apocalypse of Elijah, Vision of Isaiah, Apocalypse of Zephaniah, Apocalypse of Zechariah, Apocalypse of Ezra, History of James, Apocalypse of Peter, Acts and Teachings of the Apostles, Epistle of Barnabas, Acts of Paul, Apocalypse of Paul, Teaching of Clement, Teaching of Ignatius, Teaching of Polycarp, Gospel of Barnabas, and Gospel of Matthias.

CAVE. Natural or man-made caves used for cultic and mantic purposes are well attested in the ancient, late antique, and medieval Near East, both in the archaeological and textual records, and may be phenomenologically related to more ancient cave paintings attested in a variety of locations.

Caves have been found to hold different sorts of objects. One such cave is located in Khirbet Beit Lei (c. 8th to 7th centuries BCE), near Lachish. It was found to contain a number of drawings (ships, a lyre player, and other figures) and inscriptional prayers and prophecies in the name of Yahweh. Archaeologists also discovered a cultic cave in Jerusalem dating to this same period that contained more than a thousand cultic objects (vessels, animal and human figurines), though this cave contained no inscriptions. Some scholars feel that the burial of cultic vessels in caves may inform the widespread Near Eastern literary motif of the temple vessels being hidden in the earth until the end of time (*see also* HIDDEN TEMPLE VESSELS). Placing objects in caves may have also had a cultic function, perhaps associated with rituals of initiation, apart from the objects being stored and hidden from exposure to noninitiates. Herodotus, for example, writes of a number of pre-Classical cults that used caves and deep underground holes for their cultic practices.

Other caves are reported to have been the setting for prophecy and other mantic practices. The Hebrew Bible tells the story of how the prophet Elijah received the word of Yahweh in a cave (1 Kgs 19:12–14), and how caves were used as hiding places for prophets in times of persecution (1 Kgs 18:3–5). It is possible that the incipit of Psalm 142:1 reports a similar mantic experience of King David. Hebrews 11:32–40 also indicates that prophets and prophetic figures hid in caves in the wilderness. Christian monks often lived ascetic lives in caves, and many monasteries in Egypt and Palestine are built into the sides of mountains. Arabic Hermetic sources commonly place the site of revelation and secret knowledge to be in a cave or other opening in the earth. The prophet Muhammad is reported to have received his first revelations in a cave on Mount Hirah, and other Arabic sources state that retreat in such caves was common in the late sixth and early seventh centuries CE. The cave as the site for the reception of divine or secret knowledge is also widespread in shamanistic and other astral practices in the Middle East and Central Asia.

CHRONICLES. The Hebrew book that comprises the end of the Jewish canon, typically divided into two major sections (1 and 2 Chronicles). Its English title derives from the Vulgate translation, which understands the book's Hebrew title [Heb. Dibrei ha-Yamim, lit. "words of the days"] to denote a "chronicle" of events in Israel's sacred history. The product of a later hand, sometime around 400 BCE, Chronicles is largely a revisionist repeat of the material found in the books of Samuel and Kings. Where the book does deviate, often considerably, one can see the theological and political preoccupations of the post-exilic period.

The first nine chapters of Chronicles detail a genealogy starting with Adam and ending with Saul. This allows the chronicler to focus on the kingdoms of David and Solomon, both of whom receive a far more positive treatment than they do in the books of Samuel and Kings (e.g., an account of David's affair with Bathsheba is absent). Also unlike these other books, Chronicles pays no attention to the divergent religious practices of the northern tribes following the split of the kingdom, but instead focuses only on the tribe of Judah, its cult in Jerusalem, and the later reformations of Judaean kings like Josiah (640–609 BCE). After describing the Babylonian destruction of Jerusalem (2 Chr 36:15–21), the chronicler concludes by mentioning the edict of Cyrus the Persian (559–530 BCE) permitting the exiles to return and rebuild Yahweh's temple (2 Chr 36:22–23). Most scholars see the chronicler as responsible also for the books of Ezra and Nehemiah, which take up the history of Judah where the book of Chronicles ends.

CHRONICLES OF JERAHMEEL. Hebrew text dated to the 11th or 12th century CE, attributed to a certain Jerahmeel b. Shelomoh, detailing biblical and Israelite history from the creation to the Maccabees. The text is preserved in a longer 14th-century CE collection attributed to the copyist Eliezer b. Asher. Much of the material in the *Chronicles of Jerahmeel* appears also in earlier Jewish and Islamic exegetical works, but some of the accounts are otherwise unattested or are developed more fully in this text.

CHRONICLES OF MOSES. Hebrew text [Heb. Dibrei ha-Yamim shel Moshe Rabbinu] describing the life of Moses. The manuscripts date to the 16th, 17th, and 18th centuries CE, but they may be related to an earlier Arabic recension of the story. Many of the elements in the chronicle parallel other accounts in Jewish and Muslim exegesis including Josephus, the *Book of Jasher*, and the Testament of Moses. Among the details of the life of Moses, the Chronicles of Moses includes an account of the nativity of Moses, the activities of Aaron before Moses is called, the reign of Moses over the Cushites for 40 years, the sojourn in Midian, Moses' vision of God, the contest with the Egyptian magicians, and the passing of leadership of the Israelites to Joshua.

CLASSICAL PROPHECY. The expression applied to the form of prophetic behavior and prophetic literature that appears in ancient Israel in the eighth century BCE and continues until the fifth century BCE (*see also* POETRY). This period saw an increase in prophetic activity, at least as portrayed in the biblical record. Beginning with the prophet Amos and ending with the prophet Malachi, the prophets of this period are credited with producing most of the prophetic literary texts contained in the Bible.

CLEMENT OF ALEXANDRIA (c. 150–215 CE). Titus Flavius Clement was one of the earliest Christian scholars in Alexandria. He traveled extensively and eventually studied with Pantaenus at a Christian school in Alexandria, which he later came to direct. During the final years of his life, Clement left Alexandria for Asia Minor under the persecutions of Septimius Severus (r. 193–211 CE). His writings include a treatise on gnostic teachings and exegetical notes (*see also* GNOSIS AND GNOSTICISM). Clement's exegetical approach, focusing on an interpretation that would allow for a synthesis of Christianity and Hellenistic culture, was influential on the work of Origen.

1 CLEMENT. Letter sent from the early Christian authority Clement in Rome to the Christians of Corinth in the late first century CE. Many early Christians include this letter in the canon of the New Testament, and manuscripts of the text often include other portions of the New Testament in Coptic and Syriac. Eusebius (History 3.16, 4.23) reports that the letter was read in Christian worship, and the text is cited as authoritative by other early Christian writers. The text outlines the authority of the Church based on the biblical example of prophethood, especially that of Moses.

2 CLEMENT. Short letter included in some of the manuscripts along with 1 Clement, though believed to be of different origins. The letter focuses on Christian conduct, using as examples the life of Jesus Christ. It quotes extensively from biblical texts and makes reference to a "prophetic word," which may refer to an unknown or unidentified early Christian text.

COLOPHON. An inscription placed at the end of a tablet that records the name of the author or compiler of the information contained on the tablet. In the biblical books, the colophon appears at the head of the text. The names of the prophetic books derive from their colophons.

CORPUS HERMETICUM. Collection of texts preserved in various languages related to revelations received by Hermes Trismegistos from the Egyptian god Thoth. The overall collection of Hermetic texts can be divided into several categories. The first includes astrological, alchemical, and talismanic texts usually dated to the second through seventh centuries CE. Another influential work is the philosophical Hermetical text entitled *Asclepius*, which appears to be a Latin adaptation of an earlier Greek text, but is also extant in Syriac, Armenian, Coptic, and Arabic. There are also a number of texts from the Nag Hammadi codices (VI.6–8) that relate to *Asclepius*. The *Stobaei Hermetica* consists of fragments and treatises quoted by Joannes Stobais (c. 500 CE). There is also an Armenian text on the *Definitions of Hermes Trismegistos for Asclepius* translated from Greek around the sixth century CE. A large and varied collection of texts dating sometime between 500 and 1000 CE was compiled in the 16th century CE under the title of *Corpus Hermeticum*. Arabic Hermetical texts account for a large portion of the corpus, preserving many extant and nonextant, or apparently original, Hermetical treatises. The Arabic texts are particularly rich in alchemical information as evidenced by the tradition of the "Emerald Tablet" said to have been discovered by Hermes Trismegistos in Egypt where it was stored by the first Hermes, who received it as a revelation from Thoth sometime before the flood of Noah's time.

COSMOLOGY AND COSMOGONY. Terms referring to the worldview or "map" of the world as an encompassing system capable of being comprehended, and to theories concerning the origins and creation of that world. The Bible and the Quran share some cosmological and cosmogonic views rooted in ancient Near Eastern conceptions of the world, such as the notion of a male creator God and his battle against the watery forces of Chaos, the division of the world into lower and upper realms in which the upper realm holds sway over the lower, and a teleological view of time with a definite beginning and end with which historical existence is contrasted.

In terms of the structure of the world, Jewish and Muslim texts basically hold to the concept of a three-storied universe. The bottom level is often described as hell or the chthonic realm that is beneath the earth. In the biblical tradition, the earth is conceived of as floating on a vast body of water. Exod 20:4, for example, delineates the heavens above, the earth below, and the water underneath the earth. The Quran depicts hell as consisting of liquid or boiling water with the earth spread out on top of it (Q 22:19–22, 55:43–44, 56:42–44). Hell also is described as a pit in which are the fires beneath the earth (Q 2:9–11). The great deluge is described as gushing forth from the earth (Q 54:12) and underground fountains (Gen 6:11), perhaps reflecting an older cosmic battle myth in which water is personified as the monster of chaos that a god or hero conquers in creating and ordering the world.

Much like the classical Greek conception, the earth or the middle realm of the cosmos is envisioned as a flat disc surrounded by the world ocean on all sides. The Quran describes the earth as flat and spread out (Q 71:19), wide and expansive (Q 29:56). There are points on the earth that serve as conduits or points of contact with the lower realms (pits, caves, water sources) and the upper realms (mountains, trees, high buildings). Muslim exegetes describe Mt. Qaf (Q 50:1) as a "world mountain," which surrounds the earth and holds up the sky, thus connecting the heavens and the earth. Mt. Zion also is described as a point connecting the earth and the heavens in the Bible and in Jewish exegesis. This parallels geographical conceptions in other traditions such as Mt. Sumeru in Indian tradition and Mt. Burz in Iranian tradition (*see also* MOUNTAIN).

The heavens are generally conceived of as being seven in number, and are described as the "courses" of the planets and the stars. Q 2:29 and 23:17 Quran states that there are seven "courses" in the heavens, and Q 67:3 describes the seven heavens as being stacked one on top of the other. Throughout late antiquity, astral mysticism depicted the heavens as being seven or nine, and sometimes 10 in number based on the calculation of the number of planets and other astral phenomena.

COVENANT. A binding agreement or treaty [Heb. berit, Ar. mithaq] between two parties, often accompanied by a symbolic action. The Bible refers to a number of covenants between individuals such as that between Abraham and King Abimelech of Gerar (Gen 21:32), between Jacob and Laban (Gen 31:44), and between Nahash the Ammonite and the people of Jabesh-Gilead (1 Sam 11:1), but much of biblical tradition is taken up with a series of covenantal agreements between God and Israel. Thus, God established a covenant with Noah (Gen 9:8), which is symbolized by a rainbow, and a covenant with Abraham (Gen 17:8–23), which is symbolized with circumcision. The first and most important covenant in the Quran is God's trust accepted by Adam. According to Q 33:72, after the heavens, earth, and mountains refused, Adam agreed to make a covenant with God, which is understood to be God's giving humanity free will in return for humanity's worship of God alone.

The covenantal relationship is elevated to a new level with Moses, who serves as the mediator for establishing God's covenant with the entire nation of Israel (Exod 19, 24), an act that is symbolized by the writing of the tablets of the law and their deposition in the Ark of the Covenant. Yahweh's covenant with Israel is conditional upon their moral and cultic behavior, and is embodied metonymically in the two tablets of the Law (Exod 25:16). This same covenant, with associated blessings and curses, is expressed in the Quran as the blessings that God bestowed upon the Israelites in contrast to their continued disobedience (Q 2:47–61). Among the blessings given by God are "favoring the Israelites over all the worlds" (Q 2:47); dividing the sea and saving them from Egypt (Q 2:50); revelation of the Furqan and Torah (Q 2:53); the cloud, manna, and quails (Q 2:57); and the miraculous water from the rock (Q 2:60). Muslim exegetes add that God gave the Israelites kings, prophets, and books.

The theological application of a treaty explains the format of much of the Bible's legal materials, which scholars have shown largely follows the structure of Assyrian treaties. Thus, the legal materials contain a preamble (Exod 20:1; Deut 1:1–5), historical prologue (Exod 20:1; Deut 1:6–3:29), stipulations (Exod 20:2–14; Deut 4:1–26:19), list of curses and blessings (Lev 26:3–13; Deut 28:1–14), a description of the deposition of the law accompanied by a public reading (Exod 25:16; Deut 31:9–13), and list of witnesses (Deut 31:26). Several passages in the Quran extend the commercial understanding of contracts to the covenants between God and humans (Q 13:19–23, 23:1–11, 70:22–35). Q 5:1 enjoins Muslims to keep all covenants at the head of an outline of other ritual obligations such as the pilgrimage (5:1), the sacrifice (5:2), keeping of the food laws (5:3–5), marriage laws (5:5), purity laws (5:6), and almsgiving (5:12). This theme is repeated throughout the rest of the surah (Q 5) juxtaposing Muslims to the Israelites, Jews, and Christians who broke their covenants with God.

After Moses in the Bible, the covenant is renewed periodically in the history of Israel (e.g., Josh 24:25; Ezra 10:3). It is implicit in the covenant that Yahweh makes with David that establishes his dynasty in perpetuity (1 Kgs 2:4; Ps 132:12). In the ninth century BCE and thereafter, the covenant became a hallmark feature of the Classical Prophets, who often challenged traditional covenantal ideology by denying the permanence of Israel's cultic and religious life, and underscoring the conditional nature of Yahweh's covenant. Thus, Jeremiah prophesies the coming of a new and unbreakable covenant written on the hearts of the Israelites (Jer 31:27–37), a prophecy that becomes a centerpiece of later Christian theology. Muslim exegesis emphasizes that the Israelites were given multiple chances (prophets and revelations) but failed to fulfill their covenant with God, so the covenant was transferred to the Gentiles through the revelation of the Quran to the prophet Muhammad.

CULT. A system of worship and its accompanying rites. The Hebrew ['abodah] and Arabic ['ibadah] words most approximate to the English term *cult* have the meaning of "service" or the ritual obligations of God's worship.

In the Israelite context, the cult of Yahweh was accomplished by a number of priests (*see also* KOHEN; LEVITE; ZADOQITES) who tended to the Ark of the Covenant (Exod 27:19), tent of witness

(Exod 30:16), and other matters in the various sanctuaries and who performed sacrifices, each duty according to prescribed rules and various calendrical needs. In Mesopotamia and Egypt, a great deal of cultic effort was spent serving the daily needs of the cultic statue that occupied the center of the temple. The Israelites proscribed statues for their God (Exod 20:4; Deut 5:8), and thus, their cult centered on following and strengthening the covenantal precepts that Yahweh had established with Israel (Exod 20:3; Deut 5:7, 6:13). Also unlike many of the cults of Israel's neighbors, the Israelite cult apparently did not engage in cultic dramas with mythological bases outside of their historicized agricultural festivals.

With the construction of Yahweh's temple in the reign of Solomon (961–922 BCE) the cult was centralized in Jerusalem and other sanctuaries eventually outlawed (2 Kgs 18:4, 18:22, 23:1–37; Isa 36:7). When the kingdom divided after Solomon's death, King Jeroboam I (922–901 BCE) renewed the older cultic sanctuaries at Dan and Bethel to serve the needs of the northern kingdom (1 Kgs 12:27–30) and installed golden calves (i.e., young bulls) in the sanctuaries (cf., Exod 32). Though this act was viewed as apostasy by the cult in Jerusalem, the prophetic record appears rather ambivalent on the issue. The golden bulls, after all, did not represent the God himself, but rather served as his pedestal and as a symbolic embodiment of his strength. Numerous examples of cultic animal statues serving similar purposes can be found throughout the greater Near East. Thus, despite the fact that the prophets Elijah, Elisha, and Amos condemned the moral vicissitudes of the northern cults, they did not pronounce a single word against the golden bulls. On the other hand, the subtle distinction between the idol as a representation of God's power and its use as a representation of God could easily be lost. Thus, the prophet Hosea, who knew that the statues were not representations of God (Hos 8:5–6), condemned them for their apparent association with the worship of Baal (Hos 13:2; 1 Kgs 19:18). The prophet Ahijah also condemned the statues (1 Kgs 14:9).

The Quran makes a strong and distinct contrast between idolatry and "submission" [Ar. islam] to God. All of the prophets bring the message that there is only one God, and that all service is to be to this one God. Some prophets are credited with the institution of particular rites such as purification rituals (Adam, Abraham), prayer (Ishmael), almsgiving (Ishmael), fasting (Noah), and pilgrimage (Adam, Abraham), though the prophet Muhammad is said to have reinstituted all these and abrogated older rites during his mission.

CULTIC DRAMA. The ritual performance of religious traditions often at auspicious times (e.g., festival days) corresponding to seasonal changes. Cultic dramas are well known in the ancient Near East, both in Egypt and in Mesopotamia. The Babylonian creation myth, known as Enuma Elish, was read aloud and ritually reenacted on the fourth day of the Babylonian New Year's festival. Cultic dramas appear in the Bible as well, but only in reference to foreign cultic practice. In their contest with the prophet Elijah, the prophets of Baal partake in a ritual reenactment of the myth of Baal by gashing themselves, dancing, and prophesying ecstatically (1 Kgs 18:28). In his prophetic vision of the new temple, the prophet Ezekiel also refers to a cultic drama in which wailing women weep for the chthonic deity Tammuz (Ezek 8:14). Since the role of prophet and priest often overlapped, both in the greater Near East and in ancient Israel, some scholars see prophetic dramas as a related practice (*see also* PROPHETIC DRAMA).

CULTIC PROPHET. Term applied to prophets who also serve as functionaries in a particular cult. In Mesopotamia and Egypt, prophetic oracles often derived from cultic functionaries. In the biblical record there is evidence of the prophets of foreign gods apparently staffing their cults (1 Kgs 18:9, 18:20, 19:1, 22:6; 2 Kgs 3:13, 10:19; 2 Chr 18:5). Israel too had several cultic prophets. The patriarchs of Genesis, identified as prophets in Islam, had cultic functions in the establishment of sanctuaries and offering of sacrifices. Muslim sources make the prophets to be the originators of the Muslim cult. In the wilderness of wandering, Moses and Aaron had roles later associated with the priests, such as tending to the Tent of Meeting and its implements and presiding over sacrifices.

The prophet Samuel also served as a cultic functionary prior to the temple, offering sacrifices for the people in various cities (e.g., Bethel, Gilgal, Mizpah, Shiloh: 1 Sam 3:20–4:1, 7:15). After the construction of the temple, the Bible documents figures who are both prophets and priests, such as Jeremiah (Jer 1:1) and Ezekiel (Ezek

44:15–31). Isaiah too, apparently had access to the inner sanctum of the temple (Isaiah 6). Many scholars see the salvation oracles of Israel's cultic prophets as formal components of a sanctioned liturgy, and thus interpret their failure to materialize less as a prophecy, than as a formal expression of hope.

Zechariah, the father of John the Baptist, is associated closely with the temple in Q 19:11, and in Muslim sources he seems to be a temple officiant, though in Luke 1:8 he is said to serve his temple obligations in accordance with the familial duties prescribed in 1 Chr 24:10.

CYRUS II. The Persian king who ruled over Babylonia (559–530 BCE) and is hailed by Deutero-Isaiah as a messiah (Isa 45:1, 45:13). His lenient treatment of his subjects is evidenced in the biblical portrait of him allowing the Jewish exiles to return to Jerusalem (Isa 44:28) and to rebuild Yahweh's temple (Ezra 1:1–2, 1:8, 4:3; 2 Chr 36:22; Dan 1:21, 10:1).

– D –

DAHHAK. Name given in Arabic to the Persian king Biwarasb or Azdahaq with whom are associated many stories that make him out to be a villain comparable to or greater than the pharaoh of the Quran. He is said to have ruled over the entire earth and to have been a magician. The name is known from sources such as the *Bundahishn* and the Persian *Book of the Kings*. In Muslim exegesis and historiography, Dahhak is described as having seven heads, or two ganglia growing from his shoulders that he needed to anoint daily with human brains. Others say that the two ganglia moved when they were hungry and were like two snakes. He is said to have ruled 1,000 years, or to have ruled 1,000 and lived another 1,000. Other traditions identify Dahhak with Nimrod, whom Muslim and Jewish exegetical traditions identify as the tyrant who persecuted Abraham.

DAJJAL. Arabic term used as the title or name of the Antichrist in Muslim texts. The Arabic term is probably derived from a Syriac term [deggala] used as an adjective with the significance of "false" or "pseudo" when joined to other words like *Christ* [Syr. meshiha] or *Prophet* [Syr. nebiya]. The Dajjal, the time of his appearance, and his activities are described in detail in hadith reports transmitted from the prophet Muhammad as warnings to his followers. Some evince the possibility that the Dajjal was not necessarily an eschatological figure, but an historical personage in the lifetime of Muhammad's Companions. Other reports parallel descriptions found in non-Muslim apocalyptic traditions of the Antichrist as a herald of the end of time and the destruction of religion. As in other apocalyptic traditions, the revelation of the description and circumstances of the eschaton and the Antichrist serve to legitimize the prophetic character of Muhammad.

DAMASCUS. City located in the interior of Syria, at the foot of the Anti-Lebanon mountains and the edge of the desert extending east to the Euphrates and south to the Arabian Peninsula. The city dates at least to the fourth millennium BCE, and the first mention of it appears in a list of cities conquered by the Egyptian pharaoh Thutmoses III in the 15th century BCE. Damascus is mentioned in Gen 14:15, one of the oldest passages in the Bible, thus attesting to its existence at the beginning of the second millennium BCE. The city occurs again in the account of David's war with Zobah (2 Sam 8, 1 Chr 17), and in the eighth and ninth centuries BCE it became the capital of the Aramaean state that fought with the northern kingdom of Israel. The city was captured and incorporated into the Assyrian empire by Sargon II (721–705 BCE) and remained under Assyrian control until the seventh century BCE when it passed into Babylonian hands. After the campaigns of Alexander the Great (356–323 BCE), Damascus changed hands between the Seleucids and Ptolemies until the Nabataeans took control of the city in the first century BCE. Shortly afterward, Damascus fell under Roman rule. At the end of the fourth century CE, Damascus became part of the eastern Empire, and it was at this time that the defunct temple of Jupiter (previously devoted to the Aramaean stormgod Hadad) was rebuilt as the church of John the Baptist. When the city came under Muslim control in the seventh century CE a mosque was erected on the same spot by the Umayyads.

Damascus figures in a number of stories about the prophets. Abraham passed by Damascus on his way to Canaan and even employed an Aramaean servant named Eliezer (Gen 15:2), and the Israelites interacted with the city during the time of David and Solomon. Some Muslim exegetes report that the prophet Job, or his son Dhu al-Kifl, was sent to the people of Damascus. Damascus also is the city en route to which the apostle Paul encountered Jesus and became one of his followers (Acts 9:2–9).

DAMASCUS DOCUMENT. A Hebrew text extant in fragments from among the Dead Sea Scrolls and two manuscripts from the Cairo Geniza. The Geniza fragments were published under the titles *Zadoqite Work* and *Zadoqite Documents* on account of their references to the righteous "sons of Zadok" (Ezek 44:15) who were faithful when the other Israelites sinned. The titles "Damascus Rule" and "Damascus Document" derive from a reference to the new covenant mentioned in the document as being made in the land of Damascus. The text is divided into two parts. It begins with an opening exhortation to the faithful remnant of Israelites who were not destroyed by the Babylonian king Nebuchadnezzar II (r. 605–562 BCE). This section includes a sectarian and allegorical interpretation of biblical passages. Part two is a list of rules to be followed by the community, also derived from the interpretation of biblical passages and the examples of the prophets.

DANIEL. The latest book in the Hebrew Bible (c. 166 BCE) and the name of the main figure in that book. The text is cast in Babylon during the reign of Nebuchadnezzar II (605–562 BCE), but borrows on the themes of several other biblical traditions. Some connect the figure of Daniel with that of Dan-El, the hero of Ugaritic narrative poems mentioned also in the Bible (Ezek 14:4). Most scholars see the events cryptically described in the book as alluding to the reign of Antiochus IV (167–164 BCE), the Macedonian-Syrian conqueror who persecuted the Jews and forced their conversion to Hellenism. Antiochus also slaughtered a pig on the altar of the Jerusalem temple and erected a statue of Zeus in the Holy of Holies. Some of the features of the Daniel cycle of stories appear in earlier Near Eastern literature. The story of God punishing the Babylonian king with lycanthropy (Dan 4:15–32) finds a close parallel in the stories of the Babylonian king Nabonidus (555–539 BCE) and the Prayer of Nabonidus (4QPrNab) found at Qumran (75–50 BCE) (*see also* NABONIDUS; PRAYER OF NABONIDUS).

Daniel is not mentioned by name in the Quran, nor are any passages identified by Muslim exegetes as relating to him, but there are accounts of his prophethood in later Muslim literature. Muslim sources relate that Daniel was carried off to Babylon after Nebuchadnezzar destroyed Jerusalem. There he was thrown into a lion's den, but was rescued. In one such report, Daniel is aided by the prophet Jeremiah, who comes to Babylon from Jerusalem after receiving a revelation from God to help Daniel. A similar account appears in the Apocryphal Bel and the Dragon in reference to the prophet Habakkuk, who appears and transports food to Daniel in the pit. Tabari relates how Daniel, Hananiah, Azariah, and Mishael interpreted the dream of Nebuchadnezzar about the statue made of four metals destroyed by a rock from the heavens.

The tomb of Daniel is variously identified in Jewish and Muslim sources. Josephus (Antiquities 10.11.7) reports that Daniel built a tower at Ecbatana in Media, a tower that appears never to age, and in which the Median and Parthian kings are buried alongside Daniel. Later Jewish texts claim that Daniel is buried in Shushan (i.e., Susa), and that near Daniel's house was a stone under which he hid the vessels from the destroyed temple in Jerusalem. In other Jewish sources, Daniel is said to have been put in charge of returning the temple vessels to Jerusalem by Cyrus. There are a number of reports preserved in Muslim sources that the corpse of Daniel was discovered during the Muslim invasion of Iran. It is said that his body had been preserved since the time of his death, or that it was only a box containing his nerves and veins that was discovered. Other reports claim that the Muslims found a book that belonged to Daniel, a jar of fat, money, and a signet ring. The ring is reported to have had a stone engraved with two lions, between them a man being licked by the lions. Ibn Kathir relates that the corpse of Daniel was reburied, and the four who buried him were decapitated so that they could not tell anyone else the location of the tomb.

In the Bible, Daniel is nowhere called a prophet, though he is referred to as "the chief magician" (Dan 4:6). Nevertheless, he has several experiences that one might consider prophetic. Daniel is said to be better than all the king's soothsayers and magicians (Dan 1). He interprets dreams (Dan 2, 4), reads mysterious writing on the wall during the feast of Belshazzar (Dan 5), has a vision of four beasts

(Dan 7), has a vision of the Ram and Goat (Dan 8), delivers the prophecy of the Seventy Weeks (Dan 9), and has a vision of future events (Dan 10–12). In two of these instances (Dan 8, 9) the visions are explained to Daniel by the angel Gabriel. The nonattribution of the formal status of prophet to Daniel explains why, according to later Jewish tradition, prophecy ceased with Haggai, Zechariah, and Malachi (TB Sanhedrin 11a, Yoma 9b), though the rabbis also believed Daniel to have lived during the time of Nebuchadnezzar. The Talmud refers to Daniel as the Messiah who is mentioned in Jer 30:9 (TB Sanhedrin 98b) and related to Isaiah 56.

DAVID. King of united Israel (c. 1000–961 BCE), whose dynasty continued until the Babylonian destruction of Jerusalem in 586 BCE. Muslim exegesis sees David as a prophet who ruled for 40 years as God's caliph in Jerusalem. His rise to power is detailed in the biblical book of Samuel, which portrays him as an ambitious opportunist, brilliant military leader, and talented poet and musician. The youngest of eight children, he is credited with killing the Philistine giant Goliath (1 Samuel 17), though other biblical traditions bring this into question (2 Sam 21:19; 1 Chr 20:5). The Quran records nothing of David's family except that Solomon was his heir (Q 27:16). Muslim genealogists parallel David's descent to the genealogy given in 1 Chr 2:9–17 and Matt 1:1–17, but do not mention his brothers. The Quran refers to David's killing of Goliath (Q 2:251), but does not recount David's interaction with Saul.

According to the biblical book of Samuel, David's legendary friendship with Saul's son Jonathan, and his celebrated fame among the populace, made Saul envious of the young David, and drove him into fits of manic depression. David became king upon Saul's death and reigned from Hebron until he captured Jerusalem (then called Jebus), where he also housed the Ark of the Covenant. The Ark of the Covenant appears to confirm the kingship of Saul just before David's defeat of Goliath in the Quran as well (Q 2:248).

David also enlarged the borders of Israel from the Euphrates River in the east to Egypt in the south. The Quran credits David with extraordinary military ability. According to Q 21:80 God taught David the making of armor, and Q 34:10–11 states that God made iron soft for David so that he could make coats of mail with balanced perforations. Muslim exegetes explain that David was able to work with iron without need for fire or hammer, and that he was the first person to make armor from chain mail.

Some of David's exploits cast him in a very negative light, such as his adulterous affair with Bathsheba and his role in the deaths of her husband Uriah (2 Samuel 11), as well as his military general Joab (1 Kgs 2:6). Nevertheless, later generations viewed David as an ideal king whose family name bears with it the promise of the coming Messiah. Muslim exegetes do report that David had 100 wives, a fraction of the 1,000 wives attributed to his son Solomon, and that the mother of Solomon was the wife of Uriah. The Quran also refers to David's attributes, like strength (Q 38:17–20), which Muslim exegetes say refers to his obedience to God, his understanding of Islam, and his constant worship. Some Muslim exegetes assert that David used to sleep only half the night, then keep vigil in prayer, and that he fasted every other day.

David is renowned for his musical abilities. Several of the biblical Psalms are attributed to him, and later biblical tradition credits him a role in selecting and preparing a number of musical families for religious and prophetic service in the temple (2 Chr 35:3–15). Q 21:79 states that God made the mountains and the birds to sing praises along with David. Ibn Abbas reports that David's music and voice were so beautiful that the birds would stop in the air around him, and others report that wild animals used to stay by him until they died of thirst and hunger. The Quran states that God gave the Psalms to David (Q 4:163, 17:55), which is understood to mean that the Psalms were revealed to him by God during the month of Ramadan (*see also* ZABUR).

An Aramaic inscription discovered at Tel Dan in the north of Israel offers the only archaeological reference to the "House of David." Unfortunately it is rather fragmentary, and is not contemporaneous with David, who lived about a century and a half prior to the erection of the stele.

As with Moses, Baruch, and other pious men of ancient Israel, rabbinic writings record a tradition for David that describes his body as having avoided decomposition long after burial (TB Shabbath 152b, Baba Mezi'a 84b). The Roman emperor Hadrian (76–138 CE) is said to have opened David's tomb and was in awe at the preservation of his body. It is reported that after the emperor touched David's face, his blood again began to circulate.

DAY OF YAHWEH. Phrase found in prophetic texts in reference to a coming day of divine judgment and wrath in which evildoers will be destroyed and the righteous will be blessed. Amos 5:18–20 contains the earliest reference to the Day of Yahweh, and it is noteworthy that it is seen as a positive event. Ezekiel uses the expression in reference to what appears to be a specific battle against the Egyptian army (Ezek 30:3–5). Other prophets, like Isaiah (34:8), Jeremiah (46:10), Joel (1:15), Amos (5:18), Obadiah (15–21), Zephaniah (1:18), Zechariah (14:1), and Malachi (3:23) describe the Day of Yahweh as more of a vengeful eschatological event. For them it is a day of astral portents, celestial darkness, earthquakes, and divine battle. The belief in a Day of Yahweh appears to draw also on the tradition of Yahweh as warrior (Exod 14–15; Josh 10:8–14; Judg 5:20).

The Quran and Muslim exegesis also mention the Day of Judgment [Ar. yawm al-din] and the Day of Resurrection [Ar. yawm al-qiyamah], both of which closely relate to the biblical notion of the Day of Yahweh. The Arabic term [din] occurs numerous times in the Quran with the sense of "judgment" though the term also relates to "debt" [Aram. dayn] and "religion" or "revelation" [Pahl. den]. In Islam, the Day of Judgment refers both to the various times when God punishes the people on earth who have rejected his prophets and to the final day at the end of history when all people will be resurrected and judged for their deeds (*see also* ESCHATOLOGY).

DEAD SEA SCROLLS. Term applied to a number of texts discovered near the western shore of the Dead Sea since 1947, both in the vicinity of Qumran and including areas nearby. The texts were found in some 11 caves and include biblical texts, exegetical works (*see also* PESHER), law books, targums (*see* TARGUM), liturgies, apocalyptic and wisdom works, horoscopes, a treasure list, and a medical text. Most of the texts are in Hebrew or Aramaic, but some are in Greek, such as the Greek scroll of the Minor Prophets found at Nahal Hever.

Among the biblical texts found, all the books of the Hebrew canon with the exception of Esther are attested. These texts are significant because they provide evidence for a much earlier dating of the Hebrew text of the Bible. In most cases, the differences between the Hebrew biblical texts from Qumran and the Masoretic text are minimal, but in a few cases they help to explain divergences between the Bible's major textual witnesses (e.g., Septuagint, Targums, Vulgate). A fragment of a text attributed to Noah and Aramaic copies of passages from 1 Enoch and the related *Book of Giants* are among the texts, as are a number of scrolls related to the prophet and canonical book of Daniel (*see also* PRAYER OF NABONIDUS). The book of Jubilees also was discovered there, as were fragments related to the apocryphal Testaments of the Twelve Patriarchs.

There is much disagreement regarding the origins and dating of the texts found by the Dead Sea. Some scholars hold that the texts belonged to the library of a sectarian community at Qumran, and identify this community with the Essenes mentioned by a number of Hellenistic historians including Josephus. Some suggest that the community was an Essene splinter group. Other scholars have questioned elements of this view, suggesting that the texts may not have been a library per se, but rather a storehouse for texts removed from Jerusalem during the time of Roman upheaval. More recently, scholars have identified the Qumran community with the Sadducees (*see also* ZADOQITES) based on a letter found at Qumran that identifies and defines the cultic observances of the Qumran community. The dating of the texts depends to some degree on the identification of the group or groups responsible for placing the texts in the caves, but the date of the Qumran settlement is fixed archaeologically from the third century BCE to the first century CE, with most of the sites dating to the earlier part of this period. Some documents from outside of the immediate vicinity of Qumran date to the second century CE.

DEATH OF ADAM. Armenian text describing details from the last days of Adam's life and his death. The earliest manuscript of this text dates to the middle of the 14th century CE, but the contents relate closely to other apocryphal accounts of the death of Adam such as the Life of Adam and Eve and the Testament of Adam. According to the Death of Adam, when he was about to die Adam recounted to his son Seth what happened after the expulsion from the Garden of Eden. Adam explained how he fasted to atone for his sin, was brought tools for iron-working, and was instructed to use them by an angel. These elements parallel Jewish and Muslim accounts of Adam's first days outside of the Garden of Eden. The text also describes how Seth went to the Garden of Eden, took a branch from the Tree of Immortality, and planted it at Adam's tomb. It is said that from this branch grew a tree whose wood was used to construct the cross on which Jesus was crucified. The text describes Eve as having a vision of Adam's ascent into heaven and the divine temple there. It also states that Noah removed the bones of Adam from his grave and took them on the Ark during the time of the great flood.

DEBORAH. Prophet and judge of Israel whose story appears in the book of Judges (Judg 4:4–5:31). Referred to as the wife of Lappidoth, she prophesied from under a palm tree in the land of Ephraim, the same tree, according to Jewish tradition, as that under which Deborah, the nurse of Isaac's wife Rebekah, was buried (Gen 35:8, Jub 32:30). Deborah's leadership was instrumental in a victorious battle against Sisera, the military general of Jabin, the king of Hazor. The poem that encapsulates and epicizes the battle appears in Judges 5. The poem's first-person reference to Deborah as a "Mother in Israel" (Judg 5:7) is a title that may combine her attributes as leader with her prophetic connection to the palm tree (*see also* RHABDO-MANCY). The Talmud sees Deborah as the wife of Baraq (though the Bible does not state this) and recognizes her as one of seven female prophets mentioned in the Bible along with Sarah, Miriam, Hannah, Abigail, Huldah, and Esther (TB Pesahim 66b; Megillah 14a). Deborah also is mentioned among the prophets in the Armenian Prophet Lists. Since Deborah's song in Judges 5 was seen to be rather egocentric, rabbinic literature understood it as having been composed when the prophetic spirit briefly had departed from her (TB Pesahim 66b).

DEDANITE AND LIHYANITE. Two related North Arabic languages attested in inscriptions found primarily near al-'Ula (ancient Dedan) dating from the fifth and sixth centuries BCE. Dedan was an important trading site near an oasis in northern Arabia. Dedan is mentioned in the Bible as a descendant of Raamah son of Cush and Jokshan son of Abraham (Gen 10:7, 25:3). The Dedanite inscriptions are the earliest, coming shortly after some Akkadian inscriptions written in the North

Arabic script from the eighth and seventh centuries BCE. The Lihyan-ite inscriptions date from roughly the fifth century BCE to the first century CE. Most of the 500 or so inscriptions are cultic in nature, but also include references to ruling figures.

DEMON. A supernatural and liminal being that appears in many, often monstrous, forms, believed to afflict, torment, and possess humans. Belief in the existence of demons was widespread in the ancient world. Mesopotamians primarily saw demons as responsible for physical ailments, nightmares, and sexual dreams, as well as for ghostly appearances and strange sounds, though they also believed some demons to be benevolent. Both male and female, demons did not bear personal names, but instead belonged to a particular group, each responsible for a different realm of activity. Associated with cultic impurity, demons were believed to inhabit liminal zones like thresholds, allies, crevices, corners, ruins, and the underworld, and to be particularly active in the human world at night.

The earliest written records attest to a belief in demons. They are mentioned already at Ebla in various exorcist rites (*see also* EBLA). In Egypt, demons were driven out of patients as standard medical practice, and funerary spells invoked demons in an effort to prevent the deceased from being harmed when entering the next world. Ugaritic records attest to a belief in a demon named Haby, who is described as "a creeper with two horns and a tail." Apparently, this demon was known also to the prophet Isaiah (Isa 26:20).

Isaiah also refers to a different group of demons [Heb. se'erim] as frequenting desolate ruins along with Lilith (Isa 13:21, 34:14; *see also* LILITH). As the Hebrew term suggests, this type of demon was believed to resemble a he-goat (Zohar on Lev 17). Later biblical legislation uses the same term to refer to foreign gods (Lev 17:7). The Bible also refers to a figure named Azazel who is mentioned in connection with the Israelite "scapegoat" ritual performed on the Day of Atonement (Leviticus 16). In the ritual, a living goat is sent to Azazel in the desert after the sins of the nation have been transferred to it. The Peshitta, Targum, and Book of Enoch each treat Azazel as the prince of demons. Some scholars see a similar belief in demons as a backdrop for the ritual for leprosy in Lev 14, which requires the use of a red heifer and red water.

The New Testament sees demons [Gk. sing., diabolos] as belonging to the great Abyss (Luke 8:26–39), and capable of being exorcised by people, like Jesus, who possess authority over them (Mark 5:13). Jesus' exorcisms eventually led to the charge against him that he employed the power of the prince of demons (Matt 9:34). Exorcisms continued to be practiced among the early Christians (Acts 19:11–16). A belief in the existence of Satan (Heb. for "adversary") as the head of demons was already in place by the early Christian period (see also SATAN), and Luke 9:42 credits Satan with charge over legions of demons. The Greek world also believed in demons. Hellenistic philosophers describe them (i.e., daemons) as inferior deities, demiurgic beings, and deified heroes, who are capable of altering one's fate.

The Talmud discusses demons as well. As in Mesopotamia, they are seen as bringing lying dreams (TB Berakhoth 55b), but unlike in Mesopotamia, they often have personal names. The Talmud also records a performative spell for ridding a demon in order to cure an ulcer (TB Shabbath 67a). It gives the names of a number of demons responsible for health ailments (TB Shabbath 67a, 109a), including the famous Lilith, who is described as seizing those who sleep alone at night (TB Shabbath 151b), having long hair (TB Erubin 100b), and being the first wife of Adam (see also ALPHABET OF BEN SIRAH). She also is credited with giving birth to a demon named Hormin (elsewhere called Hormiz) (TB Baba Batra 73a). Adam too, and also Eve, are said to have begotten ghosts and demons (TB Erubin 18b, Genesis Rabbah 15:6). Demons are also associated with cemeteries (TB Sanhedrin 65b) and with tree stumps and various bushes for which protective amulets are made (TB Pesahim 111b). They are described as capable of changing color (TB Yoma 75a), haunting schoolhouses (TB Qiddushin 29a), and appearing as seven-headed dragons (TB Qiddushin 29b).

The Quran and Muslim exegesis also refer to demons and satans. The term *satans* [Ar. shayyatin], often translated as "demons," occurs 18 times in the Quran. The story of the creation describes how Iblis and the Jinn were like demons in their corruption of the earth before the creation of Adam. The banishment of the Jinn to the mountains and the islands of the sea may parallel accounts such as Genesis 6, and those found in the *Book of the Giants* in which "fallen angels" are associated with demons. Demons and Jinn also play important roles in the Quran's story of Solomon. Q 21:82 refers to the "demons and divers" assigned to Solomon, and Q 38:37–38 refers to "demons, builders, and divers" who are bound in fetters. This is paralleled in the Testament of Solomon. Muslim exegetes explain that the demons and Jinn were under Solomon's control because of a special ring he had. In one incident, related in the exegesis of Q 38:34, a demon is said to have stolen Solomon's ring and taken over his place on the throne for a period of time. Among other things, Solomon is said to have used the demons and Jinn to construct Jerusalem and various other cities. Such authority over demons also is attributed to Solomon on a number of late antique magic bowls discovered throughout the region of Mesopotamia.

DENKART. Canonical Zoroastrian texts redacted in Pahlavi in the ninth or 10th centuries CE which consist of nine numbered books, the first two of which are not extant. They represent an encyclopaedia of Zoroastrian knowledge. Book 3 is a treatise on Zoroastrian theology and a defense against Islam. Books 4 and 5 deal with controversies during the Sasanian and early Islamic periods, respectively. Book 6 is a compilation of moral precepts and wisdom traditions. Book 7 recounts the legend of Zoroaster. Book 8 lists and summarizes the Nasks of the Avesta, and book 9 summarizes the contents of the three Nasks, which comment on the Gathas, or hymns.

DEUTERO-ISAIAH. *See* ISAIAH.

DEUTERONOMY. The title of the fifth book of the Torah (Pentateuch) derives from the Septuagint, which recognizes that much of the legal material in the book repeats laws found in earlier books, hence "Deuteronomy" (Gk. for "second law"). The title of the Hebrew text [Heb. Debarim] derives from the "words" with which Moses addresses the Israelites in Deut 1:1. Many scholars identify the book, at least in part, with the scroll referenced in 2 Kgs 22:8–20, which is said to have been discovered by the high priest Hilkiah during the reign of Josiah (631–609 BCE). According to the account in 2 Kgs, the scroll's alleged discovery instigated massive reforms under the king. It is important to note, however, that the identification of this scroll with Deuteronomy (especially in its current state) is not without its difficulties. The book contains an admixture of narrative accounts that repeat the wilderness wanderings of the Israelites (Deut 1–4), a series of civil and religious laws (Deut 5–26), and the story of Moses' final words and death (Deut 17–34).

DHU AL-KIFL. Prophet mentioned in the Quran (Q 21:85, 38:48). Most Muslim exegetes identify Dhu al-Kifl as the son of the biblical figure Job, whom they see as a prophet as well. It is said that his name was Bishr, and that the title "Dhu al-Kifl" or "one who kept (commandments)" was given to him because of his character. Other exegetes identify him with the prophets Elijah and Zechariah. A number of different traditions associate Dhu al-Kifl with the prophet Elisha, some claiming that Dhu al-Kifl was Elisha, that he was Elisha's successor, or that he was an upright man whom Elisha imitated in fasting during the day and keeping vigil at night. Still other traditions report that he was not a prophet but an upright man who prayed 100 times a day. The Quran provides little information beyond listing him with Ishmael and Idris as being steadfast and upright (21:85), and with Ishmael and Elisha as being chosen (38:48).

Ahmad b. Hanbal relates a report from the prophet Muhammad that Dhu al-Kifl was an Israelite who became upright after a life-changing event. He had hired a prostitute who began to cry and explained that she had never done this sort of thing before. Dhu al-Kifl left her without having sex, renounced his sinful ways, and died the same day. In a report preserved in Tha'labi, it is said that Dhu al-Kifl was the son of Job, a prophet sent to the people of Rome. The people asked him for a sign and God granted them long life. When they began to multiply and not die, they filled the land and no longer had room to live unrestricted. So Dhu al-Kifl asked God to return them to their normal lifespans.

DHU AL-NUN AL-MISRI (796–861 CE). Muslim mystic from the town of Akhmim in Upper Egypt associated most closely with the notion of a secret knowledge of the attributes of divine unity. To Dhu al-Nun are attributed three alchemical treatises, and part of his fame may be due to the fact that his city of birth, Akhmim, was considered to be the place where Hermes Trismegistos received his revelations.

DHU AL-QARNAYN. Character mentioned in the Quran (Q 18:83–101). Many Muslim exegetes identify Dhu al-Qarnayn with Alexander the Great based on the similarities between the account in Q 18:83–101 and the episodes found in the Alexander Romance. Particular emphasis is placed on the account in Q 18:93–100 of Dhu al-Qarnayn's building of the gate against Gog and Magog, also found in many recensions of the Alexander Romance, going back to the Hellenistic period (*see also* GOG; MAGOG).

Other Muslim traditions claim that there were two figures named Dhu al-Qarnayn, one living in the time of Abraham, and the other living about 300 years before the time of Jesus. Tabari preserves an account that it was Dhu al-Qarnayn who judged in favor of Abraham's ownership of the well at Beersheba, and Ibn Kathir reports that Dhu al-Qarnayn was present when Abraham and Ishmael were building the Ka'bah in Mecca. It is this first Dhu al-Qarnayn who is associated with the prophet Khidr.

The name Dhu al-Qarnayn is interpreted in several ways by Muslim exegetes. They explain it by stating that it refers to two "horns" [Ar. qarnayn] on his head or by asserting that the sides of his head were brass or glowed as though he were horned. Other explanations attributed to the People of the Book, and possibly related to the vision of the horns in Dan 8, say that the two horns symbolize that Dhu al-Qarnayn was king over Rome and Persia. A third explanation is that Dhu al-Qarnayn traveled to the two ends of the earth where the "rim" [Ar. qarn] of the sun rises in the east and sets in the west.

Dhu al-Qarnayn is associated closely also with Moses, who in the Bible is said to bear horns when descending from the holy mountain (Exod 34:29; cf., Hab 3:4). In Muslim exegesis on Q 18:60–82, Moses is reported to have traveled to the ends of the earth searching for the water of life, where he instead found the prophet Khidr. In the Vulgate and in medieval European art Moses also is portrayed as being horned, as is Alexander the Great. In the long account of Wahb b. Munabbih, Dhu al-Qarnayn is said to have traveled to the cities at the ends of the earth, and to Jerusalem where he met a prophet named Khidr-Moses.

Other traditions preserved in Muslim exegesis and history identify Dhu al-Qarnayn with different pre-Islamic South Arabian kings. There also are traditions that Dhu al-Qarnayn was an angel or that he was a prophet.

DINAWARI. Abu Sa'id Nasr b. Yaqub al-Dinawari (d. 1009 CE) is the author of the earliest and most complete example of Muslim dream interpretation manuals. His work includes an elaborate introduction with chapters on the nature of sleep, conduct for the dreamer, different types of dreams, the angel of the dream, and the rules to be followed by the narrator of the dream and the interpreter. His work synthesizes the earlier works of Ibn Sirin and the Arabic translation by Hunayn b. Ishaq of the Greek work *Oneirocritica* by Artemidorus of Daldis (*see also* DREAMS AND DREAMS INTERPRETATION).

DIONYSIUS BAR SALIBI (d. 1171 CE). The West Syrian or Jacobite bishop of Mar'ash (from 1154 CE) and Mabbug (1155 CE). His writings include commentaries, only one of which is extant, on earlier theologians and philosophers, including Aristotle and Porphyry, and a work on the *Kephalia Gnostica* of Evagrius of Pontus. Dionysius bar Salibi produced a massive commentary on the Bible, the editing and publishing of which will be in preparation for some time. This commentary incorporates the exegesis of many earlier Syrian scholars and thus is an important source for the Jacobite interpretive tradition and its links to Jewish and Muslim exegesis.

DISCIPLE. One who intensely follows or attends upon a master scholar or teacher for the purpose of learning from him. A disciple can be understood also as an initiate into a body of knowledge. Several biblical prophets appear to have entered voluntarily into a disciple–master relationship. Elisha is said to have tended upon his master Elijah, and there are periodic references to the "sons" of prophets, a usage that cannot be taken literally in every case (*see also* SON OF THE PROPHETS). Prophetic discipleship societies were still in existence in the first century CE, as one can see by John the Baptist's disciples (Luke 7:18–30) and those of Jesus (Matt 10:1–5, Mark 3:16–19).

DISCIPLES OF JESUS. The followers of Jesus mentioned in the New Testament and referenced in the Quran (Q 5:112–115, 61:14). Muslim exegesis identifies the disciples as Peter, Andrew, Matthew, Thomas, Philip, John, James, Bartholomew, and Simon. The apostle Paul is mentioned as a follower, but not a disciple, as is Judas who took the place of Judas Iscariot after he betrayed Jesus. This definition seems to restrict the term *disciple* [Ar. sahabah] to those who followed Jesus while he was still on the earth, thus paralleling the general criterion for the Companions of the prophet Muhammad who followed him during his lifetime. The Quran seems to define the disciples as "helpers of God" (Q 61:14), and Muslim exegesis preserves the tradition that the disciples were sent to evangelize different lands: Peter and Paul to Rome, Andrew and Matthew to Ethiopia, Thomas to Babylon, Philip to Qayrawan and Carthage, John to Ephesus, James to Jerusalem, Bartholomew to Arabia (Hijaz), Simeon to the Berbers outside of North Africa, and Judas to Ariobus.

Q 5:112–15 describes how the disciples asked Jesus to send down a table to them from heaven, and in verse 114 Jesus requests the table from God so that they might have a "festival" or "feast" as a sign from God. Some Muslim exegetes claim that the table did not, in fact, come down from heaven because the disciples withdrew their request, but other exegetes explain that it provided an abundance of food. In some Muslim exegesis of the passage it is said that the feast was intended for the breaking of a fast the disciples were observing. Other traditions mention that the table contained seven fish and loaves, which fed thousands of people, and that those who were sick were healed when they ate the food. This seems to allude to the story of the fish and the loaves found in the New Testament (Mark 8:1–9; Matt 15:32–39), and it is possible that the Quran passage also alludes to the vision that Peter experienced of a sheet with animals on it that God sanctioned him to kill and eat (Acts 11:1–10).

Muslim exegesis also preserves an account of one of the disciples of Jesus attempting to walk on water, parallel to the account of Peter in the New Testament (Matt 14:22–33). Muslim exegesis on Q 36:13–29 reports that these verses refer to the sending of Simon, John, and Paul to the city of Antioch. This is rejected by other exegetes on the basis of Q 36:29 in which it is stated that the city was destroyed when it rejected the messengers, and thus many exegetes object because Antioch was not destroyed in the early Christian period but was the first city to believe in Jesus.

DIVINATION. The process of seeking divine will by way of mechanical praxis. Often accompanied by performative incantations, divination played a large role in ancient Mesopotamian religion, and to a lesser extent in ancient Egyptian religion. The biblical record makes it clear that divination was important in ancient Israelite religion as well. Sanctioned forms include the casting of lots, use of the ephod, Urim and Thummim, hydromancy, rhabdomancy, dreams, and oracles. Unsanctioned forms include necromancy, extispicy, astrology, augury, the consultation of teraphim, and divination by tossing arrows. Postbiblical forms of divination include the use of amulets, dreams, and bibliomancy.

Divination was a common practice in pre-Islamic Arabia, is associated with the Kahin, and is mentioned in the Quran. The main types of divination mentioned in Arabic and Muslim texts are varieties of physiognamancy [Ar. firasah], such as the reading of beauty spots and birthmarks, chiromancy, omoplatoscopy, observation of footprints, divination by morphoscopic and genealogical lines, observation of the ground, ornithomancy, geomancy, rhapsodomancy, oneiromancy, cleromancy, neromancy, capnomancy, anemoscopy, phyllomancy, and belomancy. In these sources, divination leads to knowledge of orientation in the wilderness, detection of minerals, detection of water, knowledge of rainfall, and the knowledge of past and future events.

DIVINE LIGHT. A concept central to Manichaean soteriology, but also found in other late antique and medieval traditions as a characteristic of savior and prophetic figures. In Western Manichaean texts the concept of the divine light is epitomized by its embodiment and suffering in Jesus, and all divine light that is trapped in material existence is called the "Jesus patibilis" or the "suffering Jesus" as cited by Augustine. In Eastern Manichaean tests, the divine light and its embodiment in matter is called "buddhagotra," which refers to the photonic or spiritual descendants of the Buddha.

Manichaean texts relate that the divine light was first trapped and made to suffer in Adam when he was bestowed with divine knowledge and wisdom. The divine light was then passed down through the prophets, including Jesus, until it was manifested in the prophet Mani, called the "Seal of the Prophets" in Middle Persian texts. Muslim sources also refer to the light of prophethood or the "Muhammadan Light" [Ar. nur Muhammadiyah], which passes from Adam through the prophets until the prophet Muhammad, and Muhammad also is called the "Seal of the Prophets." The Quran refers to a number of prophets as having received "knowledge and authority" from God, and this phrase usually is understood as referring to prophethood given by God. This notion of prophethood as a special knowledge or character is widespread in other traditions as well, such as those associated with the secret knowledge and divine character of Seth, Enoch, Solomon, Ezra, and Jesus.

DOCTRINE OF ADDAI. Composite Syriac text dating from the late fourth or early fifth century CE that narrates the mission of the apostle Addai to the city of Edessa. The text is preserved in Syriac, Armenian, Latin, Arabic, Persian, Old Church Slavonic, and Coptic. Eusebius mentions the first part of the story regarding the exchange of letters between Abgar and Jesus including a brief account of Addai's coming to Edessa and the conversion of the city in the year 340 CE (*see also* ABGAR LEGEND).

The Syriac Addai is identified with the Greek Thaddeus, mentioned as one of the 12 disciples of Jesus (Matt 10:3; Mark 3:18). In the Lukan list of apostles (Luke 6:14–16; Acts 1:13) Thaddeus does not appear, but his place is occupied by Judas son of James. Eusebius includes Thaddeus as one of the 70 apostles, claiming that he was sent to Edessa by Judas. The Acts of the Apostle Thaddeus, a text extant in Greek and Syriac, includes Thaddeus as one of the 70 apostles sent to Edessa. Another text extant in Arabic, Ethiopic, and Coptic fragments recount the acts of the apostle Judas Thaddeus, "brother of the Lord," who was sent to Syria and Mesopotamia. A Latin Passion of Simon and Judas Thaddeus contains an account of the martyrdom of Thaddeus by the priests of the Sun temple in Suanir.

There is also a well-known Manichaean apostle named Addai who is said to have been a missionary in the same area as the Christian Addai. According to Manichaean tradition, this Addai was one of the close followers of Mani and was endowed with the same healing powers as Mani. This connection has caused some scholars to speculate that the Christian "Addai" was adapted from Manichaean sources and grafted onto the stories of Thaddeus, and that the *Doctrine of Addai* was designed as anti-Manichaean polemic. According to Augustine, who himself was formerly a Manichaean, the Manichaeans claimed to have letters from Jesus, and Mani did write a letter to

Edessa claiming to be the Paraclete foretold by Jesus in John 16:7–8 (*see also* PARACLETE).

The *Doctrine of Addai* consists of three main parts. The first part is an account of the exchange of letters between King Abgar V of Edessa and Jesus, also known as the Legend of Abgar. Independently, this story was popularized through the reports of Eusebius. The *Doctrine of Addai* adds to the letter of Jesus a promise to protect the city, and reports that the letter was affixed to the gates of Edessa to protect the city. In the *Doctrine of Addai* it also is reported that Hanan, who bore the letters between Abgar and Jesus, painted a portrait of Jesus and returned it to Edessa. The second part of the text, also summarized in part by Eusebius, describes the sending of Addai to Edessa and the conversion of the city. It includes narratives of Addai's conversion of the pagan priests and Jews. The third part of the text is the legend of the discovery of the True Cross by Protonike, the supposed wife of Emperor Claudius, and includes anti-Jewish letters written between Abgar and Emperor Tiberius. The legend of the discovery of the True Cross is found also in Armenian, and is related to the accounts of the finding of the True Cross by Judas Kyriakos and Helena, the mother of Constantine.

DREAMS AND DREAM INTERPRETATION. Dreams and dream interpretation are widely attested in ancient Near Eastern records, the Bible and Quran, and Jewish and Muslim exegesis. In Mesopotamia, Egypt, Canaan, Israel, and ancient Greece, dreams were believed to be sent by the gods or by demons (nightmares, sexual dreams), and therefore provided a portal to the underworld. Scholars typically distinguish "message" dreams, in which a god or important figure appears in a dream and delivers an auditory missive to the dreamer (often to legitimate, support, or ease the political, national, or military concerns of the dreamer), from "symbolic" dreams, in which the dreamer witnesses enigmatic visual images that require an interpreter (oneiromantic). Some scholars also distinguish those dreams that involve prognostication as "mantic" or "prophetic." Each of these categories, while heuristically useful, nevertheless, remains typologically problematic, mostly because these categories overlap. Some symbolic dreams require no interpreter, and some message dreams do. There are prophetic message dreams and also prophetic symbolic dreams.

Unlike the Bible, which preserves only literary accounts of dreams and their interpretations, Mesopotamian dream accounts appear in a variety of textual genres including ritual, oracular, epistolary, historical, dedicatory, and literary texts. The abundant evidence cannot be used, however, to gauge the popularity of oneiromancy in Mesopotamia, for in the scholarly academies dream interpretation never achieved the status of other forms of divination such as extispicy (divining from animal viscera) and later astrology, which were viewed as more reliable and less subjective and therefore were used to authenticate a dream's interpretation. In Egypt, though dreams are mentioned quite early, the art of interpreting dreams did not come into vogue until later during the New Kingdom (1551–712 BCE), which may suggest some degree of earlier Mesopotamian influence (Mesopotamian influence also has been detected in Greek and Indian dream materials).

In the Bible, dreams also are regarded as legitimate means of divine communication. The Bible's "message dreams" closely resemble their Mesopotamian counterparts in terms of content and purpose and are experienced by a number of biblical figures (e.g., Abraham, Jacob, Joseph, Samuel, Solomon), whereas the "symbolic" dreams are reserved mostly for non-Israelites, though Israelites interpret their dreams. Inherent in this portrait is a polemic that casts foreign mantics as not having the divine wisdom, like Israelites, to decipher enigmatic dreams. Joseph must interpret the dreams of the pharaoh and his prisoners (Genesis 40–41) and Daniel must interpret the dreams of the Babylonian king (Dan 2 and 4). The only exception to this pattern is the dream of the Midianite soldier (Judg 7:13–15), which a fellow soldier interprets. Even here, however, the dream positions the import of its interpretation at an Israelite advantage. With the rise of Classical Prophecy in the eighth century BCE, attitudes toward dreams divide into two camps: those who view dreams as unreliable or unacceptable methods of divine revelation (as opposed to more direct auditory modes), and those who do not. Encapsulating the formative stage of this development is a statement in Num 12:6–8 that Moses is trusted since Yahweh speaks to him "plainly and not in riddles" (i.e., dreams). Coinciding with this development is a changing attitude toward prophecy as a cultural institution (*see also* PROPHECY).

Following the rise of Classical Prophecy, the auditory form of prophecy increasingly eclipsed dream interpretation as a legitimate mode of divine access (e.g., Isa 65:3–4), but it did not do so entirely. For as several biblical passages attest, dream interpretation continued to serve a productive social function in Israel, as it did in times past (e.g., 1 Sam 28:6), even if the interpreters were not to be trusted. The prophet Jeremiah thunders against dream professionals who falsify claims of divine inspiration (Jer 23:25–32, 27:9–10, 29:8–9), and the later prophet Zechariah harangues dreamers who speak lies and console with allusions (Zech 10:2). They do not speak against dreams as tools of divine revelation, but only against those who use dreams dishonestly.

A similar development occurs with regard to attitudes toward "visions," which a few prophets (e.g., Isaiah, Micah, and Ezekiel) view with suspicion when announced by figures whom they do not trust (e.g., Ezek 13:6–9, 13:23, 21:34, 22:28). When prophecy as a cultural institution went into gradual decline after the fifth century BCE, positive views toward dreams resurfaced. Hence, the positive and late apocalyptic views in the book of Daniel and Joel 3:1: "After that I will pour out my spirit on all flesh, your sons and daughters will prophesy; your old men shall dream dreams, and your young men shall see visions."

In the Quran, a dream that conveys symbolic significance is called a "vision" [Ar. ru'ya]. The term used in Islamic law to denote a "dream" in which nocturnal emission takes place [Ar. hulm] is sometimes used in reference to nocturnal visions that require interpretation (Q 12:44, 21:5). As in the Bible, dreams and visions are central to the Joseph story in the Quran (Q 12:4–5, 12:36, 12:43). Abraham also "sees in a dream" [Ar. manam] that he must sacrifice his son (Q 37:102, 105). The sights seen by the prophet Muhammad on his Night Journey and Ascent also are called a "vision" (Q 17:60).

Muslim scholars also connect dreams and prophecy in a more general way. The prophet Muhammad is reported to have said that at his death prophecy would cease but dreams continue, presumably as a means of communicating divine direction to people. Dream interpretation is traced back to the Companions of the prophet Muhammad, but some of the earliest extant works include an Arabic translation of the second-century CE *Oneirocritica* of Artemidorus by Hunayn b. Ishaq, a book concering visions attributed to Ibn Sirin, and the major oneiro-critical work of Dinawari. Dream interpretation also is discussed thoroughly in Muslim philosophical and mystical works such as those of Kindi, Farabi, Ibn Sina, and Ibn Rushd.

DRUGS. The use of drugs, especially alcohol (*see also* DRUNKEN-NESS), as a means of inducing or enhancing the prophetic experience is attested periodically throughout the ancient Near East, and is probably related to the mantic's role as an herbalist and medical practitioner (*see also* MEDICINE).

Evidence for opium use has been found throughout the ancient Near East, especially on Cyprus, though its connection to Cypriot cults has been questioned. The practice of inhaling intoxicating substances like cannabis and incense also appears in the written record. Herodotus (History 4.59–76) describes the use of hemp-seed as a tool in funerary rituals among the Scythians. Texts from Mari demonstrate that at least some prophets partook in excessive wine drinking as a means of accessing the divine. Ugaritic tablets also detail the events of the marzeah feast, a repast in which the city's dead kings were summoned to wine and dine with the living (*see also* NECRO-MANCY).

The practice of using drugs is condemned by the prophets in the Bible as excessive (Jer 16:5; Amos 6:7) and may lie behind the words of Isaiah, who rebukes those who seek oracles from the dead through inebriation (Isa 28:7–22). The commonly attested connection between mantic behavior and alcohol probably also explains the reference in the New Testament that some people thought Jesus to be a wine-bibber (Matt 11:19). The use of drugs was so closely tied to mantic practice that the Greek word for "drug" [Gk. pharmakea] eventually came to denote witchcraft (Gal 5:19–21).

DRUNKENNESS. There is much evidence throughout the ancient Near East, especially at Mari and Ugarit, for the use of alcohol, especially wine, as a means of achieving divine ecstasy or accessing the divine word. At Ugarit, the chief god El drinks to excess and flounders in his own vomit and feces, as a means of entering the underworld. At Mari too, prophets appear to have imbibed periodically in order to divine a god's will. Such mantic practices may lie behind the

words of the prophet Isaiah, who accuses the priest and prophet alike
of inebriated visions and judgment (Isa 28:7–8). They also probably
inform Deut 32:33, which associates wine drinking with foreign worship. The cults of certain gods in sixth-century BCE Greece, like that
of Dionysus, also were well known for their excessive drinking and
ecstatic behavior.

Despite such negative associations, wine drinking is never outlawed in the Bible, except for Nazirites and Rechabites (see Num 6:3;
Jer 35:2). It is said to "make the heart of man happy" (Ps 104:15), and
even appears as a drink-offering to Yahweh (Exod 29:40; Lev 23:13;
Num 15:5). The Quran contains a number of verses related to the prohibition of wine and intoxication (Q 2:219, 4:43, 5:90, 16:67), and
Muslim exegetes explicitly deny that, as a prophet, Noah could have
become drunk (cf., Gen 9:20–24). Sufi texts, on the other hand, often
use wine and drunkenness as metaphors for certain mystical states,
including the losing of one's self in the experience of God [Ar. fana'
al-nafs]. The biblical prophet Jeremiah uses drunkenness as a
metaphor for describing the impact of Yahweh's word on his people
(Jer 23:9), and Ps 78:65 similarly describes Yahweh awaking from
sleep like "a warrior shaking off wine." Because of its color, fer-
mented grape juice often was associated with blood, and became a
ritual symbol for it. As such it ultimately may be related to the practice of omophagia (though strictly forbidden by Israelites [Gen
9:4–5]). Thus, the cult of Dionysus viewed wine as the blood of the
god, an association that reverberates in a different cultural matrix in
the later Christian conception of the Eucharist.

– E –

EBLA. The ancient name of Tel Mardikh, a site in Syria excavated in
1975–85, which yielded several thousand cuneiform documents dating from 2400–2250 BCE. The documents are written in Eblaic, a language akin to Hebrew, though they antedate Hebrew by several centuries. In addition to providing a wealth of data on urban life in
ancient Syria during this period, and the oldest bilingual dictionary
on record, they attest to performative mantic practices including exorcism and prophecy. At least one Eblaic exorcist text records the

name of the demon Haby (as Habhaby), "he of two horns and a tail," mentioned also in Ugaritic texts and in Isa 26:20. The prophets mentioned in Eblaic texts appear to be rather peripatetic, plying their trade in various cities in and around Ebla. The term employed there for *prophet* [Ebl. nabiutum] is cognate to the Hebrew word used for the profession (*see also* NABI; PROPHET). The study of these texts is still in its infancy, and it is probable that they will shed a great deal more light on the early history of Syrian prophecy.

ECSTATIC. A prophet who exhibits entranced, possessed, frenetic, or enraptured behavior while prophesying. Ecstatic behavior can include unintelligible chanting and raving (*see also* GLOSSOLALIA), pronounced bodily movements and gestures, and frenzied dancing. Throughout the ancient Near East one finds ecstatic prophets. They are attested in Ugaritic and Hittite texts, Egyptian sources (*see also* TALE OF WEN-AMON), and in various texts throughout the Syro-Canaan area. In Mesopotamia and at Mari, there is record of the "ecstatic" [Akk. muhhu]. Mesopotamian records also attest the presence of two figures associated with dirt and self-inflicted wounds [Akk. zabbu], and with long hair [Akk. eshebu]. In many cases, these figures appear to have enjoyed the patronage of the royal court.

The biblical record also attests to ecstatic prophetic behavior. In some cases, the behavior appears to have been misunderstood as a sign of insanity or to have been used polemically [Heb. meshuga']. Thus, the king refers to the prophet Elisha as a mad ecstatic (2 Kgs 9:11). The prophet Jeremiah also underscores this misperception (Jer 29:26). The prophet Hosea, however, appears to classify this "insanity" as an outward sign of prophetic anxieties (Hos 9:7). Ecstatic speech (glossolalia) possibly appears in conjunction with King Saul and Samuel's band of prophets (1 Sam 10:5, 10:11), and the "raving" of the prophets of Baal (1 Kgs 18:29). The prophetic "ravings" of 70 elders chosen by Moses upon whom Yahweh descended in a cloud also perhaps constitute a form of glossolalia (Num 11:25–26). The prophet Isaiah possibly also alludes to the practice (Isa 28:10–13).

In some cases the ecstatic experience appears to have been rather traumatic. Daniel is drained of all strength and must remain in bed for several days (Dan 8:27, 10:17). Throughout the Near East, a conventional behavior of the ecstatic appears to have been standing on one's feet once the inspiration occurs (Num 11:17, 11:25, 11:26; Ezek 1:28, 2:2, 3:22–24; 2 Chr 24:20). The experience is variously described as an "onrush" of the spirit (Jug 14:6, 15:14) or being "clothed" with the spirit (2 Chr 24:20). The Bible also mentions self-inflicted wounds and long hair in connection with ecstatic prophets (1 Kgs 18:28, 20:35; 2 Kgs 1:18; Zech 13:4, 13:6). As a few of the latter examples demonstrate, ecstatic prophetic behavior may be related to the phenomenon of prophetic drama.

EDESSA. City located in Northwest Syria, identified as the modern city of Urfa in Southeast Turkey. To Edessa are attributed the origins of Syriac and Christianity in Syria. In the *Doctrine of Addai* and Eusebius there are reports of an exchange of letters between King Abgar V of Edessa and Jesus. Abgar invites Jesus to Edessa, and Jesus promises to send one of his apostles after his resurrection and ascension. The *Doctrine of Addai* narrates the coming of Christianity to Edessa. The city became an important center for Syriac Christianity, especially in the fourth through sixth centuries CE (*see also* ABRAHAM).

EFRIT. A type of Jinn, mentioned in the Quran as one of those who offer to bring the Queen of Sheba's throne to Solomon in Jerusalem (Q 27:39). Some Muslim scholars take this reference not as a special type of Jinn, but as an adjective meaning "rebellious" that describes one from among the Jinn. In later Islamic exegetical texts and folktales the Efrit is understood to represent a powerful class of Jinn closely related to the Marid (Q 37:7), also understood to be a type of Jinn.

EGIRRÛ. A form of minor prophecy known in Mesopotamia that is based on the omenistic "reading" of sounds. Sometimes associated with the divinatory practice of kledonomancy, it is probably related to the form of minor prophecy known as Bat Qol (lit. "daughter of a sound, echo") found in early Jewish literature. In Mesopotamia the egirrû is either favorable or unfavorable depending on when and where it is heard, and how it is interpreted. It can include many types of sounds including those of animals, birds, trees, and "accidental" noises.

EGYPT. Great Nile-centered civilization that was unified in the late fourth millennium BCE and continued to exercise a dominant role in the region until the fourth century BCE, after which it succumbed to massive cultural changes brought on by Hellenism and, a few centuries later, by Christianity. In several of the stories of the prophets, Egypt plays a significant role, including those of Abraham, Joseph, Moses, and Jesus. The Bible describes Abraham's visit to Egypt (Gen 12:10–20), and Sarah's handmaid Hagar also was Egyptian (Gen 16). Muslim exegesis also knows of Abraham's visit to Egypt, including his apparent lie about Sarah being his sister, but the story is not found in the Quran. The bulk of the Joseph story takes place in Egypt, and it is in Egypt that Joseph is raised to high rank, a position that enabled the Israelites to come to Egypt. Moses was born in Egypt and raised in the household of the pharaoh before being called as a prophet, and in the Quran Moses is sent to the pharaoh and the Egyptians. Egypt also figures prominently in the stories of Jesus. Muslim exegetes interpret the place to which Mary and Jesus flee in Q 23:50 as a reference to Egypt, and Matt 2:13–15 describes the flight of Mary, Joseph, and Jesus to Egypt as a fulfillment of Num 23:22. Local Egyptian traditions, both Muslim and Coptic, recognize a number of sites in Egypt where the Holy Family is said to have traveled and stayed during the childhood of Jesus.

ELCHASAI. A prophetic figure active in the second century CE, reported to have received a book from heaven and to have generated a following that is attested as late as the middle of the third century CE. Elchasai is known only from references in Christian sources, which considered him to be a heretic. There are various reports of his homeland including Iran and the general area east of the Jordan River. A cryptogram preserved in one of the extant fragments of the book attributed to Elchasai suggests that the language of the book and of Elchasai was Aramaic. The name Elchasai, also given as "Elxai," probably represents an Aramaic title [Aram. Heyl Kisai], which is translated as "Hidden Power," and may not be the proper name of the prophet. Followers of Elchasai seem to have been called "Sobiai" or the "Baptized" (from a Semitic root) and may be linked with the Sabians and/or the Mandaeans known from later sources including the Quran. Mani, the eponymous founder of the Manichaeans, reports that he lived in an Elchasaite community until he was 24 years old.

The book of Elchasai is not extant, but is summarized by hostile Christian sources. In some sources the book is said to have been revealed by a giant angel and a female figure, who are identified as the Son of God and the Holy Spirit. Other sources report that the book came out of the sky and hit Elchasai on the head. Forgiveness of sins is linked to a baptism invoking the seven witnesses: heaven, water, holy spirits, angels of prayer, oil, salt, and earth. Rather than facing east in prayer, the book seems to have commanded facing Jerusalem regardless of whether this required facing east or another direction. This prayer and the baptism seem to replace expiatory sacrifice and the cult associated with the former temple in Jerusalem. The book commands keeping the Sabbath and circumcision, and foretells an apocalyptic war between the godless angels of the north breaking out in the third year after the emperor Trajan (53–117 CE) subjected the Parthians. When read from the middle outward the extant cryptogram is an Aramaic phrase meaning "I am witness over you on the day of the great judgment," an expression that suggests prophetic intercession.

ELDAD AND MODAD. Names of two of the 70 elders who accompanied Moses on special tasks in the wilderness of wandering. The Bible states that Moses stationed the 70 elders around the Tent of Meeting and poured out upon them some of the spirit of prophecy that was on him, and they prophesied (Num 11:24–30). Eldad and Modad had stayed back at the camp, but the spirit descended upon them and they began to prophesy. In verse 25, the 70 at the tent only prophesied for a limited time, but in verses 28–30 Moses rebuffs Joshua's challenge that he stop Eldad and Modad from prophesying. Later exegetical traditions expand on the notion that Eldad and Modad continued to prophesy. Jewish sources report that there was a book that contained the prophesies of Eldad and Modad, among them information on the end of time, Gog and Magog, and the coming of the Messiah ben David. Jewish tradition also identifies these figures with Elidad and Samuel mentioned in Num 34:20–21 (Sifre Numbers 95, TB Sanhedrin 17a). The *Stichometry of Nicephorus* claims that the apocryphal book of Eldad and Modad contained 400 lines of prophesy, but all that is extant of this book is a four-word quotation found in the second-century CE text known as the Shepherd of Hermas (Vision 2.3.4) stating "The Lord is near to those who turn [to him]." The reference to Eldad and Modad in the Targum Yerushalmi on Num 11:26 is similar to this citation and so also appears to quote from this lost book.

ELIEZER. The name of Abraham's servant in the Bible, and a native of the Syrian city of Damascus (Gen 15:2). Talmudic tradition relates the rather homiletic account of a rabbi who, while visiting the tomb of Abraham, saw his servant Eliezer guarding the cave. After being told that Abraham was sleeping in the cave with Sarah, the rabbi was nonetheless allowed in since as Abraham told his servant "it is well known that there is no (sexual) passion in this world" (TB Baba Batra 58a). The Talmud also treats the famous line "Sit at my right hand, until I make your enemies your footstool" (Ps 110:1) as a quotation of Eliezer to Abraham (TB Sanhedrin 108b).

ELIJAH. Elijah the Tishbite was a prophet of Israel whose account is contained in 1 Kgs 17:1–2 and 2 Kgs 2:13. He prophesied during the reigns of Kings Ahab and Ahaziah (869–849 BCE). The biblical accounts about Elijah involve numerous miracles including withholding and sending rain, replenishing a widow's food, reviving her son from death, and summoning the fire of Yahweh down on a sacrifice in a competition against 400 prophets of Baal, a fire that licked up even the water that had been poured onto the sacrifice. 1 Kgs 19:15 also states that Elijah was responsible for anointing Hazael to be king over Aram. Q 37:123–132 also recounts the contest between Elijah and the people who worshipped Baal. Muslim exegetes report that Elijah was sent to the people of Baalbek, summoning them to reject the worship of their idol whom they called Baal. When the people of Baalbek tried to kill Elijah he is said to have hidden in a cave and been fed by ravens until he returned under a new king.

It has been observed that the biblical account of Elijah parallels the prophetic career of Moses. In each case the prophets begin a journey with a flight eastward to escape a persecuting king. Both prophets stay with families and return to challenge the king. Both Moses and Elijah go to Sinai or Horeb, and both experience mysterious deaths. The account of the Transfiguration in the New Testament also associates Elijah with Moses, though these figures may have been selected here to demonstrate that Jesus had the support of the law and prophets (Matt 17:1–8; Mark 9:2–8; Luke 9:28–36).

Instead of dying, Elijah is said to have been taken up in a miraculous whirlwind by a chariot and horses of fire, after which his disciple Elisha picked up the mantle of power he left behind and succeeded him as prophet (2 Kgs 2:13), though he had other disciples in Jericho and near the Jordan (2 Kgs 2:5, 2:7). His heavenly ascent was known to the historian Josephus (Antiquities 9.28) who remarked, "He disappeared from the sight of men, and no one knows where he is." Wahb b. Munabbih also reports that Elijah called upon God to remove him from the Israelites who rejected him, so God sent him a mount the color of fire, and on this steed Elijah was taken into heaven. There God clothed him in fire and gave him feathers, and ceased his need for food and drink, making him part human and part angel. The same motif also appears in the stories of Enoch.

Later Jewish traditions cast Elijah as a miracle worker even after his death, and the apocryphal Wisdom of Ben Sirah (48:1–14) similarly records that his corpse still prophesied and performed miraculous acts. The later biblical prophet Malachi prophesied that Elijah would return before the "great and terrible Day of Yahweh" (Mal 3:23), a theme that reverberates frequently in later Jewish tradition. The Mishnah associates Elijah with the resurrection of the dead (Sotah 9:15), and other texts assert that he will be one of the eight princes forming the cabinet of the Messiah. According to Seder Olam, Elijah will reappear at the coming of the Messiah and will be concealed once more until the time of Gog and Magog. The New Testament associates Elijah with Jesus (Matt 16:13–14; Mark 6:14–15, 8:27–28; Luke 9:7–8, 18–19) and John the Baptist (Matt 11:13–14, 17:10–13; Mark 9:11–13). Several of the texts known by the title Apocalypse of Elijah also describe Elijah's role in eschatological events.

Elijah has a good relationship with many rabbis of the talmudic period, often appearing to them as himself and instructing them in the mysteries of the world (TY Berakhoth 9:3). Later tradition also describes him as something of a shape-shifter. He appears in many forms, including an Arab merchant (TB Berakhoth 6b), horseman (TB Shabbath 109b), Roman official (TB Ta'anith 21a; TB Sanhedrin 109a; TB Avodah Zarah 17b), and even a harlot (TB Avodah Zarah 18b). Muslim exegetes report that the prophet Muhammad and a band of his followers once met Elijah on a journey outside of Mecca. Elijah served the prophet Muhammad with food from heaven and left on a cloud heading for the heavens. According to Jewish tradition, Elijah was responsible also for transmitting divine secrets (in the form of the Qabbalah) to the Nazarite rabbi Jacob; then to his disciple Abraham ben Isaac Ab Bet Din; and, finally, to the disciple of the latter, Abraham ben David. The Qabbalists in general possessed the power to conjure Elijah up by means of certain formulas. The Sufis also refer to Elijah and associate him closely with the prophet Khidr. It is reported by Ibn Kathir that every year during the month of Ramadan in Jerusalem the prophets Khidr and Elijah meet, and that they perform the pilgrimage to Mecca together each year.

ELIJAH, BOOKS OF. There are numerous references to texts, of both Christian and Jewish origin, attributed to the prophet Elijah. A reference to a book of Elijah appears in the list of apocryphal writings attached to the *Catalogue of Sixty Books* and also in the *Stichometry of Nicephorus*. Both Origen and Jerome state that the citation found in 1 Cor 2:9 can be found in a book attributed to Elijah.

The Hebrew Apocalypse of Elijah dates to the third century CE. It contains a revelation of the end times to Elijah by the archangel Michael; Elijah's journey through the world where he sees sinners punished; a discussion of the name of the last king; a description of the Antichrist; calendrical listing of events at the end of time; and five visions of Elijah including the resurrection, rewards and punishments of heaven and hell, three patriarchs, and the eschatological Jerusalem.

The Coptic Apocalypse of Elijah is extant in manuscripts dated to the fourth century CE but is assumed to be based on an earlier Greek text. It consists of five chapters including an introduction (ch. 1); an overview of the rulers of Egypt until the time of the Antichrist (ch. 2); a description of the Antichrist (ch. 3); the martyrdoms of Elijah, Enoch, and other righteous people (ch. 4); and a number of oracles describing events related to the salvation of the righteous and the defeat of the Antichrist (ch. 5).

Other references to an Apocalypse of Elijah include the description in the apocryphal Letter of Titus of a vision of Elijah in which the punishments of hell are detailed. Several references to Elijah's visions of hell are found in the Hebrew *Chronicles of Jerahmeel*, which appear related to Hebrew and Aramaic fragments from the Cairo Geniza.

There are also numerous fragments that report Elijah's visions of the Antichrist. Among these are Greek, Syriac, Latin, Ethiopic, Arabic, and Garshuni texts (i.e., Syriac written in Arabic characters). A Greek fragment exists, quoted by a Christian heresiographer, of a story involving Elijah and Lilith. A short Life of Elijah, perhaps derived from the Elijah portion of the Lives of the Prophets, exists in several Armenian recensions.

ELISHA. Son of Shaphat of Abelmeholah, the disciple and successor of the prophet Elijah. The accounts of his life appear primarily in 1 Kgs 19:19–2 Kgs 13:20, and contain stories that often parallel those of his master Elijah. His prophetic career took place during the reigns of Ahab, Ahaziah, and Jehoram (c. 850–800 BCE). Elisha is mentioned by name two times in the Quran (Q 6:86, 38:48), but no further information is provided. Unlike in the Bible where he is placed 150 years after King David, some Muslim exegesis sees Elisha as the prophet immediately preceding Samuel and the first kings of Israel. He is said to succeed Elijah, and to have been his nephew.

The Bible and Jewish tradition emphasize the similarities between Elijah and Elisha. Elisha too replenishes a woman's food (2 Kgs 4:2–7), restores her child to life (2 Kgs 4:34–35), parts the Jordan (2 Kgs 2:14), and appears powerful even after death. When a dead body being lowered into Elisha's sepulcher touched the latter's bones it revived immediately (2 Kgs 13:21). Elisha was closely tied to a group of ecstatics (2 Kgs 2:3–15), served a variety of sanctuaries (2 Kgs 2:1, 2:23), and apparently lived in Samaria (2 Kgs 6:32). Jewish exegesis states that Elisha had double the prophetic power that Elijah did, performing 16 signs or miracles whereas Elijah only performed eight. Though mentioned with some frequency in later Jewish texts, Elisha never became quite the figure that Elijah did in later tradition.

EMAR. Ancient city on the mid-Euphrates River known today as Tel Meskene. Situated about 85 kilometers West of Raqqa, Syria, the ancient city dates at least to the 24th century BCE and lasted as an important regional power until it was destroyed in 1187 BCE. Excavations conducted at Emar from 1972 to 1976 yielded hundreds of cuneiform documents, the great majority of which date to the period

1550–1200 BCE. The archival records attest to a number of religious institutions and festivals that share a great deal in common with those of the Israelites. The core of the archive was found in a temple, and the tablets' colophons identify them as belonging to the "diviner of the gods of Emar," a title closely associated with the word *prophet* [Emar. nabi], a term cognate with later biblical usage. The texts also describe a number of divinatory and performative practices including the use of lots, extispicy, and necromancy.

ENOCH. Son of Jared and father of Methuselah who lived 365 years and was "taken" by God (Gen 5:18–24). Though hardly mentioned in the Bible, a number of traditions concerning him circulated in antiquity. The New Testament states that Enoch was faithful and so did not die (Heb 11:5–6), and Jude 14–15 cites a prophesy of Enoch. His 365-year life span suggests a solar symbolism, and has been paralleled to the Sumerian king Enmeduranki, who was taught divination by the sun god and was listed seventh in line of antediluvian kings (Enoch is seventh in the line of Adam). The advisor of Enmeduranki, named Utuabzu, also is said to have ascended into heaven. Some associate the name Enoch with a word meaning "to found" and connect it with the founding of the first city, which is named after Cain's son Enoch (Gen 4:17). Others see in the name the meaning "initiate" on the basis of later traditions in which Enoch is initiated into heaven and the secret knowledge of God.

In Muslim exegesis, Enoch is identified with Idris, who is mentioned in the Quran two times (Q 19:56–57, 21:85–86). Like Enoch, Idris is associated closely with the origin of writing, divination, and other technical arts of civilization. The books of 1 Enoch, Jubilees, and the Testament of Abraham depict Enoch as a heavenly scribe, the first human to learn writing and the significance of astronomical phenomena. Eusebius cites a report that Enoch was the first to discover astrology, and identifies Enoch with Atlas, who is said by the Greeks to have discovered astrology (History 7.32.19). 2 En 68:1–2 states that Enoch wrote 365 books (thus, corresponding to the years of his life), which he handed down to his sons, that contained a complete knowledge of the heavens and the earth. There are three groups of texts, identified as 1, 2, and 3 Enoch, that describe Enoch's transfer into the heavens and the knowledge he acquired.

1 ENOCH. This title identifies a number of writings and traditions thought to have originated sometime between the fourth century BCE and the first century CE. The fullest text is an Ethiopic recension, the earliest manuscripts of which date to the 15th century CE, but earlier fragments of Greek and Aramaic texts also are extant. The book presents a series of revelations that Enoch transmitted to his son Methuselah for the righteous living at the end of time. Rich in apocalyptic, cosmological, and historical imagery, the Ethiopic Enoch contains materials closely related to a number of the stories of the prophets.

The composite 108 chapters of the Ethiopic text are divided into a series of "books" and other discrete units that are believed to have been collected and integrated into the Ethiopic recension. The major divisions of the text include the Book of the Watchers (1–36), Book of Parables (37–71), Book of the Heavenly Luminaries (72–82), Book of Dream Visions (83–90), Epistle of Enoch (92–107), and another Enoch Book (108). Also closely related to the Aramaic fragments of the Enoch texts is the *Book of the Giants*.

The Book of the Watchers, also called the Parable of Enoch, begins with an introduction describing Enoch as the seer of visions interpreted by angels and handed down for the righteous at the end of time. Chapters 6–11 expand upon Gen 6:1–4, which gives a report of demiurgic beings (lit. "sons of God") who descend and have sex with human women, thus producing giants. The Enoch tradition, however, characterizes them as fallen angels who also introduce magic and various arts of civilization to humanity. Chapters 12–16 describe Enoch's ascension and enthronement in heaven, his intercession for the fallen angels, and a series of visions. Chapters 17–36 narrate Enoch's journeys to the edges of the earth in the east and the west as a tour of the earth, hell, and the heavens.

The Book of Parables or Similitudes is an account of the visions seen by Enoch on his journeys and the interpretation of these visions by the angels. These visions include the judgment of the wicked and the abode of the righteous, worshipping angels, secrets concerning the courses of astronomical phenomena, the Son of Man, metal mountains, earthquakes, the monsters Leviathan and Behemoth, dimensions of the Garden of Eden, and the judgment of the great flood.

The Book of the Heavenly Luminaries includes an account of the movement and courses of the sun, the moon, the 12 winds and their gates, the four directions, the seven mountains and seven rivers, and the various names for the sun and the moon. The book ends with a restatement of Enoch's mission to transmit this information to the righteous at the end of time. Chapter 82 appends additional astronomical and calendrical visions that Enoch transmits to his son Methuselah.

The Book of Dream Visions recounts Enoch's visions of the great deluge, cows, fallen stars, heavenly beings, and an overview of Israelite history into the Hellenistic period and the coming messianic era. The Epistle of Enoch includes the Apocalypse of (Seven) Weeks and various admonitions to Enoch's descendants. The final book is an account of a vision of hell and various comments on the necessity of patience on the part of the righteous.

2 ENOCH. This title is given to a wide variety of Old Church Slavonic manuscripts with various titles and of varying lengths containing information about the life of Enoch and events up to the time of the great flood. Scholars hold different opinions regarding the origins and history of the traditions redacted in these manuscripts, but the main manuscripts of the longer and shorter recensions date to the 15th and 16th centuries CE.

The composite text used by scholars, both in the shorter and longer recensions, is lengthy and consists of 73 chapters. Various topics are addressed but fall into three main areas. First is Enoch's journey through the seven or 10 heavens (1–21). In these chapters, Enoch sees aspects of heaven and hell that closely parallel other ascension accounts: astronomical phenomena, angels in charge of natural phenomena, punishments of the wicked, gardens, chariot of the sun, the Phoenix, the phases of the moon, giants, angels worshipping God, and God himself. Second is Enoch's commission by God, his return to earth and instruction of his descendants, and his second ascension into the heavens (22–68). The third part (69–73) deals with the subsequent events surrounding the lives of Methuselah, Nir, Melchizedek, and the coming deluge. The longer recension ends with an account of Noah and the ark.

3 ENOCH. This text contains an account of Rabbi Ishmael's ascension into heaven and his visions, including an account of how Enoch was transformed into the angel Metatron. All the manuscripts of this work are in Hebrew and give various titles including "The Book of the Palaces" [Heb. Sefer ha-Hekhalot], the "Chapters of Rabbi Ishmael," and "The Elevation of Metatron." The work has been dated as early as the fifth and as late as the 15th century CE, and is thought to have originated in Babylon or Palestine. Among the extant manuscripts there are wide variations, and some more closely resemble anthologies or the private notebooks of scholars who collected Merkabah and Hekhalot traditions (see also MERKABAH [CHARIOT] MYSTICISM).

The composite text can be divided into four sections. Chapters 1–2 describe the ascension of Rabbi Ishmael, the angels' objecting to his entrance into the heavens, and the meeting of Metatron. Chapters 3–16 contain an account of the ascension of Enoch and his transformation into Metatron. In chapters 17–40 Metatron instructs Rabbi Ishmael in the hierarchies of angels and the order of the heavens. Chapters 41–48 continue this instruction, with Metatron discussing cosmogony, divine names, and the storehouses of the various souls including the souls of stars and angels. Manuscript A ends with Metatron's instruction on the end of time focused on the right hand of God, which was removed from earth when the temple in Jerusalem was destroyed. Numerous additions exist in other manuscripts, including a list of God's chariots, a list of 70 names of God, and the 70 names of Metatron.

EPHOD. Linen Israelite priestly vestment woven with gold threads or gold fittings referred to as an oracular device used by the priests (Exod 25:7, 29:5, 35:9). The ephod contained a bre1 Sam 23:10, 30:8). The ephod contained a breastplate, known as the "breastplate otained the Urim and Thummim. Other biblical texts suggest that the ephod served alone as an oracular device (1 Sam 23:10, 30:8), though such passages could simply be abbreviated references to the vestment along with the Urim and Thummim. The Israelites were not alone in attributing an oracular function to this garment, for the Midianites too possessed ephods (Judg 8:27). There is a comparable garment attested in Assyrian texts [Akk. epattu] and in Ugaritic texts [Ug. ipdk], worn by the goddess Anath. In some places the ephod's oracular function led to it becoming an object of worship (Judg 8:27, 17:5, 18:14, 18:20). After the reign of King David (c. 1000–961 BCE), the ephod does not appear to possess an oracular use, which has suggested to scholars the decreasing oracular role of the priesthood (*see also* ORACLE). The prophet Hosea, in fact, groups the ephod along with the other unsanctioned oracular devices in northern Israel including the massebah and teraphim (Hos 3:4; *see also* MASSEBAH; TERAPHIM).

EPHRAIM OF LUNTSHITS (1550–1619 CE). Ephraim Solomon ben Aaron of Luntshits (Lenczyca) was a Polish rabbi, preacher, and Bible exegete. His sermons on the Pentateuch and the Prophets were published under the titles *Precious Vessels* [Heb. Keli Yaqar] and *Vessels of Fine Gold* [Heb. Keli Paz] and are often reprinted in rabbinic Bibles. Ephraim's sermons often criticize the rich for not helping the poor as a sign of their spiritual pretensions.

EPHREM THE SYRIAN (c. 309–373 CE). One of the most famous scholars in Syriac Christianity. He was born in the city of Nisibis during the reign of the emperor Constantine (285–337 CE). He spent most of his time in monastic seclusion, first near Nisibis and later near Edessa. To Ephrem are attributed a vast number of works, which include biblical commentaries, sermons, and hymns. His sermons and commentaries on Genesis and Exodus are closely related to the interpretation and exegetical expansion of these same stories in Jewish and Islamic sources.

EPIC OF GILGAMESH. Ancient Mesopotamian poetic epic known in many recensions and translated into a number of ancient Near Eastern languages. The most ancient versions of the epic date to about 2100 BCE and appear as a cycle of separate stories involving the king of Uruk, Gilgamesh. These traditions were reworked into a unified series of tablets around 2000 BCE and achieved a more standardized form by around 1500 BCE, after which time the epic appears in various Mesopotamian recensions until the seventh century BCE.

The story describes the adventures of a semi-divine man named Gilgamesh, king of Uruk, and his quest for immortality. In the epic, Gilgamesh experiences dreams that his mother interprets as portending the coming of a man who will be Gilgamesh's equal. This man turns out to be Enkidu, a man who is said to walk on all fours and eat grass with the beasts of the field. Eventually, he is "civilized" into urban life by way of a harlot, and meets Gilgamesh, with whom he engages in a wrestling match that ends in a draw. Gilgamesh and Enkidu then become close friends. Much of the epic is concerned with his friendship and odyssey with Enkidu; together they battle the giant guardian of the Syrian forest Huwawa (Humbaba) and slay the Bull of Heaven. The latter is considered an act of hubris by the sun god Shamash, who retaliates by killing Enkidu. Upon seeing Enkidu die, Gilgamesh is confronted with thoughts of his own mortality and seeks immortality by journeying to the ends of the earth, where he meets a man named Utnapishtim. Utnapishtim tells Gilgamesh how he became immortal by building an ark, filling it with all living beings, and surviving a cataclysmic flood. Its closeness to the story of Noah and the flood in Genesis 6–9 attests to its influence in the region and to the mythological background of the Noah narrative. The epic's dream narratives also share a great deal in common with other ancient Near Eastern accounts of dream interpretation. That the epic's redaction in 1500 BCE was undertaken by an exorcist raises questions as to its import, and challenges some modern conceptions of ancient "literature." Gilgamesh's quest for the plant of immortality was also influential on later accounts associated with the various recensions of the Alexander Romance.

ESCHATOLOGY. Doctrine concerning the "last things" (i.e., the end of history), typically divided into two categories: mythical eschatologies (repeated and eternal battles between chaos and divine order in which the world is continually re-created) and historical eschatologies, which see the cataclysmic end of the cosmos as the final step in a divine process, one marked by important historical, and thus datable events.

While there is some limited evidence for mythical (and cosmically catastrophic) eschatological views in ancient Egyptian writings, a belief in an eschatology of the historical type appears to have been more widespread, especially in ancient Israel in the post-exilic period. This may be due to the influence of Iranian and Zoroastrian ideas of cosmic time and world history, as evidenced in later texts like the *Bundahishn*. Other scholars argue that apocalyptic and eschatological traditions developed when the Israelites, like other native peoples of the

Near East, lost their indigenous kingship and were ruled by foreign powers in the Hellenistic period.

The biblical doctrine of the eschaton (lit. "the end") has its origins in earlier beliefs concerning Israel's divine punishment for covenantal disobedience, but is tied also to expectations related to traditions concerning the Abrahamic promise, the rulership of David's house, and the Sinai covenant, with the return of Yahweh or his representative fulfilling God's promise to the Israelites or their ancestors. Such a doctrine is expressed in Isaiah, Amos, Hosea, and Micah, and especially Ezekiel, who interpret the exile as punishment for idolatry akin to the wandering of the Israelites in the wilderness. The eschatological views of these prophets envision a future temple and Jerusalem descending from heaven after a period of cleansing punishment. In the books of Maccabees, God's punishment is directed against the Hellenizing Jews and the foreign kings imposing their rule and religion upon the Jews, and the martyrdom of the non-Hellenizing Jews is tied to the expectation of future rewards. The link between punishment for covenantal disobedience and fulfillment of promise is a theme also found in apocalyptic works, early Christian literature, and the Quran (Q 2:48, 17:2–8).

According to the biblical record, the eschaton will be preceded by a messiah born of Davidic descent (Isa 11:1). The Messiah will then resurrect the dead (Dan 12:2) and commence with the Last Judgment, an event that will usher in a new period of peace during which God will reign supreme. Jewish and Islamic texts also have similar expectations about the eschaton, though the specifics vary from time and place, and tend to be rooted in the historical circumstances in which the expectations are expressed. In general the end is said to be preceded by a series of signs; a period of punishment and cleansing (often accompanied by the appearance of the Antichrist); the return of God through his messianic or prophetic representative(s); and the establishment of the promised kingdom of God on earth simultaneous with, or followed by, the Day of Resurrection and Judgment Day.

The imagery of the eschaton often derives from its use in prophetic contexts. The prophesies of Israelite prophets often are interpreted in later Jewish and Christian texts as referring not to the historical contexts of the prophets, but to future times on account of the apocalyptic language employed. Jesus uses eschatological imagery from the Israelite prophets to talk about his own fate, and Jesus is portrayed in the Gospels as an eschatological figure, especially in relation to his prophecies concerning the destruction of the temple and its link to his rejection and death. Throughout the Quran, the punishment of cities and peoples for rejecting their prophets is portrayed as eschatological destruction. Entire cities and peoples are destroyed by earthquake, screams, fire from the sky, rain of clay pellets, and are overturned or swallowed by the earth. Muslim exegetes contend that these stories were revealed to the prophet Muhammad as a warning to the people of Mecca, that they too would be destroyed if they did not accept the message and authority of the prophet Muhammad.

ESTHER. Name of a biblical book and the heroine whose story it contains. This book, known in Jewish tradition as the Megillah, takes place in Susa, the capital of the Persian empire, during the reign of King Xerxes (the text does not specify which Xerxes).

The ancient novella opens by describing how Xerxes, a cruel and egocentric king, decreed that all women should become slaves to their husbands after his wife Vashti refused to reveal her beauty to his drunken dinner guests. Vashti is removed, and the king launches a search for a new queen, which concludes when the king's servants find a beautiful Jewish woman named Esther. Talmudic tradition regards her, along with Sarah, Rahab, and Abigail, as one of the four most beautiful women in the world (TB Megillah 15a; Seder Olam 21). In the Bible, Esther, who is told not to reveal her Jewish identity to the king by her uncle Mordecai, becomes the next queen. Later Jewish tradition, seeing Mordecai as Esther's husband (LXX to Esth 2:7; TB Megillah 13a), attempted to soften the apparent adultery by claiming that God sent a female spirit to take the place of Esther, thus Esther never actually married Xerxes (Zohar III, 275b–276b). The biblical story unfolds when Mordecai overhears a plot to assassinate the king and informs Esther. She then tells the king and thus saves his life.

Unfortunately, though Mordecai's good deed is recorded, the credit for this act goes instead to a descendant of the Amalekites named Haman (*see also* HAMAN), who was rewarded with an important high-ranking office. When Mordecai refused to show him reverence, Haman provoked the king to issue an edict commanding the slaughter of all the Jews in Babylon (Esth 3:1, 3:6). For this he earned the title "enemy of the Jews" (Esth 9:24) and is treated as a prototypical anti-Semite in later talmudic tradition. Q 28:38 and Q 40:36 make Haman the vizier of the pharaoh to whom Moses spoke, and it is Haman whom the pharaoh orders to build the Tower of Babel. In the biblical account, the king is said to have eventually learned about Mordecai's deed, just about the time when Haman is preparing to hang Mordecai, and set the matter straight. Haman is killed, and Mordecai receives Haman's former office. Nevertheless, the edict could not be revoked, and so Mordecai encouraged the Jews to fight back; the Jews were victorious, and celebrated a feast, which is later celebrated annually as the Festival of Purim.

The book of Esther is noteworthy for its complete lack of reference to God, though the Septuagint lends the Festival of Purim a decidedly more religious character. The book's lack of reference to God led to the early debate regarding whether or not Esther was a divinely inspired book and should be accepted into the Jewish canon (TB Megillah 7a). Esther is also the only biblical book in the Hebrew canon that has not been found among the Dead Sea Scrolls. Since the names of the story's two main characters derive from Mesopotamian deities (Esther is the Hebrew reflection of Ishtar, the Babylonian Venus and goddess of fertility; Mordecai is cognate with the god Marduk), some scholars see in the story vestiges of an earlier Babylonian mythology, one whose ritual drama may lie behind the Festival of Purim. The story of Esther does not appear in the Quran or in Muslim exegesis besides the inclusion of Haman in the Moses story.

EUSEBIUS (260–339 CE). Christian author of several works, the most significant of which is his *History of the Church*, which includes important information on the early history of Christianity including Jesus, the disciples and apostles, important Christian writers, and some contemporaneous non-Christian figures and movements. Eusebius was born in Palestine, in the city of Caesarea, where he later studied with Pamphilus and was imprisoned for being a Christian in 309 CE. After a brief trip to Egypt, Eusebius was named bishop of Caesarea in 314 and had access to the library in Jerusalem founded by Bishop Alexander. Eusebius was in charge of the centrist group at the Council of Nicaea in 325 and was a leading figure in the Synod of

Jerusalem in 335. In 336 Eusebius delivered a panegyric for the emperor Constantine and was offered the bishopric of Antioch, which he declined. Eusebius used roughly 46 sources for his *History of the Church*, 15 of which are not extant, 10 of which are extant only in fragments, four of which are incomplete, one surviving in Syriac, one in Armenian and Latin, and fifteen are preserved intact. In addition to the *History of the Church*, Eusebius wrote exegetical works and studies of biblical geography along with letters on various subjects and polemical treatises.

EX EVENTU. The Latin term given by scholars to prophecies that have been composed "after the event" occurred, rather than before it. Some evidence exists for ex eventu prophecies, especially in extra-biblical materials such as the Marduk Prophecy, which purports to prophesy the return of the statue of the god Marduk from Elamite captivity, but which is known to have been composed during the reign of Nebuchadnezzar I (c. 1224-1103 BCE) after the statue was brought back to Babylon. The Egyptian Prophecy of Neferti also is an ex eventu prophecy.

EXECRATION TEXTS. Egyptian figurines or bowls of the Middle Kingdom (c. 2040-1750 BCE) inscribed with curses against Egypt's national enemies. The curses were put into effect when ritual experts smashed the bowls and figurines. The sympathetic process of destroying these texts has been compared to the prophetic drama of Jeremiah, who smashes a pot representing Jerusalem (Jer 19:10–11).

EXODUS. The second book of the Torah (Pentateuch), whose English title derives from the Greek title in the Septuagint meaning "going out" or "exiting" (i.e., from Egypt). The text's Hebrew title [Heb. Shemot, lit. "Names"] derives from the first line of chapter 1, which records the names of the sons of Israel. As with Genesis, earlier scholars attempted to delineate the various sources that were used while composing Exodus, though today this approach has proved less useful. The text of Exodus contains the birth and calling of Moses (Exodus 2–6), the contest against the pharaoh's magicians (Exodus 7), the ten plagues (Exodus 8–12), the departure from Egypt and parting of the Reed Sea (Exodus 13–15), the trek through the Sinai wilderness (Exod 15:22–18:27), and Moses' theophoric experiences on Mt. Sinai (Exodus 19–40) including the ten commandments (Exod 20:1–14) and the golden calf episode (Exod 32–34:9). The book also contains a number of civil laws (Exodus 21–24), laws detailing personal religious practice (Exod 34:10–35:3), and laws governing cultic practice and operation (Exod 25–31, 35:4–40).

EXTISPICY. Divination by means of reading the entrails of an animal, usually a sacrificial lamb or goat. The practice is widely attested in Mesopotamia and in Syro-Canaan. The interpretative process of "reading" the entrails was based on a variety of associative techniques, many of which treated the features of the exta as cuneiform signs. Hence, the practice of extispicy was considered the "writing of the gods." The prophet Ezekiel refers to it as a Babylonian practice (Ezek 21:26). Nevertheless, clay liver models for training in extispicy have been discovered at Ugarit and at Hazor in Israel. In the ancient Near East, the liver was considered the seat of the emotions, whereas the heart housed a person's intelligence and moral qualities. It is probable that the legal injunction commanding the sacrificial priests to burn the liver of the animal is a subtle response to this practice, since it makes extispicy impossible.

EZEKIEL. A prophet who lived through the destruction of Yahweh's temple and the Babylonian exile (539–586 BCE), and the name of the book of prophecies attributed to him. Arguably one of the strangest of all biblical prophets, Ezekiel appears to have been a Zadoqite priest (Ezek 44:15–31) who uniquely prophesied outside the land of Israel. He is said to have experienced a series of bewildering visions involving amalgamated beasts (Ezekiel 1–3), and engaged in a number of difficult prophetic dramas including laying on his side 390 days to symbolize exile of the northern kingdom (Ezek 4:5), eating a scroll (Ezek 3:1), not mourning the death of his wife as a symbol of Yahweh's attitude toward Jerusalem (Ezek 24:15–24), breaking food taboos (Ezek 4:9–17), and laying siege to a clay model of Jerusalem (Ezek 4:1–3). Muslim exegesis says that Ezekiel was called "Ibn al-Azuj" or "Son of the Old," because his mother asked God for a son though she was already old and barren.

Ezek 37:15–27 describes Ezekiel as experiencing a vision in which dry bones are resurrected, which is said to symbolize the reunification of the Davidic dynasty. Unlike his predecessors, Ezekiel also saw the wandering in the wilderness with Moses not as a golden age, but as a wicked age. Unlike Hosea and Jeremiah, who often blame Canaanite fertility cults for Jerusalem's faithlessness, Ezekiel places responsibility on each individual. Muslim exegesis usually associates Q 2:243, in which God kills and resurrects thousands of people, with the prophet Ezekiel. Muslim exegetes also record that the people in the verse are the Israelites who were afflicted with a disease, and that God showed their resurrection to Ezekiel; first the bones, then the flesh and skin, and then the spirits. In one account, this interpretation is presented to Umar b. al-Khattab by a group of Jews.

The book of Ezekiel also questions long-standing theological issues and positions, including the law of retribution in which the sins of the fathers are visited upon the sons (Ezek 18:1–4; cf., Exod 20:4–6). A vision of the restored temple concludes the book and offers a specific blueprint for the temple and for the future Israel, though sometimes in a way that contradicts the information found in the Torah (e.g., Ezek 44:9, 44:11, 44:31, 45:20). According to talmudic tradition, these contradictions caused some to "hide it" (i.e., suppress the book, TB Hagiga 13a–b) and others to debate whether it should enter the canon of sacred scripture (TB Shabbath 13b).

A Baraitha found in TB Hagiga 13b records a tradition that identifies the angel in Ezekiel's vision as Sandalphon (the angelic brother of Metatron). Ezekiel 1 eventually became a centerpiece of practice and belief in Merkabah mysticism for its recounting of Ezekiel's vision of God on his chariot (*see also* MERKABAH [CHARIOT] MYSTICISM). Later rabbinic traditions record a number of miraculous stories about Ezekiel. For example, Ezekiel's tomb is said to have provided pilgrims with miracles long after his death. The Zohar (II 166a) sees Ezekiel as an ancestor of Elihu, one of the friends of Job.

EZRA. The name of a priest and scribe who became the leader of Jewish exiles after returning from Babylon (Ezra 7–10, Neh 8–9), and the biblical book named after him. The biblical record suggests that Ezra's life overlapped with that of Nehemiah sometime during the reign of the Persian king Artaxerxes II (404–358 BCE), though a more precise statement in this regard is not possible. It seems likely that Nehemiah came to Jerusalem first, then returned to the Persian court, where he met Ezra, and returned to Jerusalem once again, this time with Ezra.

The books now identified separately as Ezra and Nehemiah were considered to be a single work but were separated into two books by Origen and Jerome. The division is not found in the Hebrew Bible, however, until after the 15th century CE. Distinguishing the many books associated with Ezra can be quite confusing. In the Septuagint, Ezra and Nehemiah are 2 Esdras. 1 Esdras is a paraphrase of 2 Chr 35–36, Ezra 1–10, Neh 7:38–8:12, and a tale about Zerubbabel and Darius (1 Esdr 3:1–5:6). In the Vulgate, Ezra is 1 Esdras, Nehemiah is 2 Esdras, and the Greek 1 Esdras is 3 Esdras. In the King James and Revised Standard versions Ezra and Nehemiah are separate books, and the Greek 1 Esdras is called 1 Esdras. The text known as 4 Ezra, not found in the Septuagint, is 4 Esdras in the Vulgate and 2 Esdras in English Bibles.

The Hebrew book of Ezra was composed sometime during the fourth century BCE, and some scholars identify its author (Ezra) as the author of Chronicles as well. The book describes the events leading to the construction of the second temple in Jerusalem and the restoration of worship. According to the Talmud (TB Sanhedrin 21b–22a), Ezra played an important role in translating the Hebrew texts into Aramaic for the populace (*see also* TARGUM). Ezra's importance in Jewish thought also led to his identification with the prophet Malachi (TB Megillah 15a; Targum to Mal 1:1), though he is never called a prophet in the Bible. Talmudic literature also debates whether Ezra brought the exiles from Babylon against their will (TB Qiddushin 69b), and sees Ezra as having been the pupil of Jeremiah's scribe Baruch (TB Megillah 16b).

According to the Muslim exegesis of Q 2:259, Ezra was not a prophet but a pious person who saw a city that was in ruins, was caused to die for 100 years, and was then resurrected. His food was in perfect condition after the lapse of time, but his donkey had decayed and deteriorated with age. Then God rejuvenated and resurrected the donkey as a sign to Ezra of his power to resurrect the dead. This same story appears in Muslim exegesis associated with the prophet Jeremiah.

The Quran asserts that the Jews say "Ezra is the son of God" (Q 9:30). Muslim exegetes explain that this does not refer to all Jews, but just a small group of Jews in Medina, or even a single Jew whom they identify by name. Others interpret the passage to be a reference to Enoch and Metatron traditions, which place a "second power" in heaven alongside God. Such traditions praising Ezra may relate to the high position given Ezra in postbiblical Judaism. According to the Talmud (TB Sanhedrin 21b–22a), had Moses not preceded him, Ezra would have been worthy of receiving the Torah for Israel. The Talmud (TB Megillah 16b) also claims that Ezra and the Torah surpassed the importance of the building of the temple.

Muslim exegesis on Q 9:30 explains that Ezra was one of the Israelite prophets coming between Solomon and John the Baptist. Ibn Kathir reports that one of the Companions of the prophet Muhammad related a story in which Ezra mourned over the fate of the Israelites, having been defeated and taken into exile, and having forgotten the Torah. Ezra was instructed to go to a river, purify himself, pray, and then receive three live coals in his mouth. After this episode Ezra was the most knowledgeable person in the Torah. He wrote out a copy of the Torah, which was compared to a copy hidden in the mountains, with which it was found to be identical. In 4 Ezra, Ezra drinks a fiery liquid from heaven and God sends five scribes who write day and night for 40 days while Ezra dictates the Torah. Ezra is said to have produced 94 books, 24 of which were public and 70 of which remained hidden.

EZRA, NON-CANONICAL BOOKS OF. Variety of non-canonical texts attributed to the prophet Ezra, outside of the texts known as 1–4 Esdras in the Vulgate and the Latin texts known as 5 and 6 Esdras. Most of these texts provide accounts of Ezra's intercessory activities and describe the secret knowledge acquired by Ezra during the course of his tours of heaven and hell. Some of them focus more on the fate of individual souls, and others primarily describe the geography of other realms or the cosmological and elemental details of such realms. The proliferation of Ezra books can, in part, be attributed to the tradition found in 4 Ezra of the 94 books ascribed to his redaction, 70 of which are considered to be hidden or apocryphal.

There are a number of separate texts known as the Apocalypse of Ezra, chief among them being the Greek, Syriac, and Ethiopic texts.

The Greek Apocalypse of Ezra consists of seven chapters and contains information on Ezra's intercession for sinners; visions of hell and heaven; signs of the Antichrist; and various information on medical, cosmological, and hagiographical matters. It is extant in two Greek manuscripts, the earliest dating to the 15th century CE, and the composition of the text is usually dated to sometime before the ninth century CE on the basis of a reference to a text with this title in the *Stichometry of Nicephorus*. The Syriac Apocalypse of Ezra includes a vision of four empires, a description of the Antichrist, and other materials. The material is related historically to the expansion of Islam and is addressed to Ezra's disciple, who is named Qarpos. There are fragments of this text also in Arabic. Closely related to the Apocalypses is the Vision of Ezra, attested in Latin manuscripts dating from the 11th to the 15th centuries CE. Like the Apocalypses of Ezra, the Vision of Ezra describes Ezra's journey through hell and heaven, and contains an account of Ezra's intercession for sinful souls. The Vision consists of only 66 verses but provides more elaborate information on the geography of hell and the punishments of particular categories of sinners than does the Greek Apocalypse of Ezra. The Ethiopic Apocalypse of Ezra includes a description of angelic functions, an account of the eschatological combat, calculations of the end time based on the generations since Adam, an account of the destruction of Jerusalem, and the coming of the Antichrist.

The Questions of Ezra is a non-canonical text detailing a series of questions Ezra poses to the angel of God about the fate of righteous and sinful souls after death. The text is preserved in two Armenian recensions (A, B) respectively dated to the 13th and 17th centuries CE. Recension A is 40 verses long, but there are also two lacunae in the manuscript following verse 10 and verse 40. Recension B is 14 verses in length and is missing the material of verses 11–30 found in recension A. The text describes how, after death, righteous souls rise through a series of seven steps up to God and the guardians of God's throne. The souls of the sinful are to be imprisoned by demons in the atmosphere until the Day of Judgment, but can be freed through intercessory prayer. Ezra also contends that souls that have experienced tortures on account of their faith, and those of the prophets and martyrs, will be forgiven their sins (A, 6-7). The effectiveness of the prayers of prophets such as Moses, Elijah, and Daniel is mentioned at the end of recension A. Recension B foretells the coming Day of Resurrection and Judgment. After judgment, righteous souls experience eternal light, whereas sinful souls are taken by an angel through frost, snow, darkness, hail, ice, storm, the hosts of Satan, streams, winds, rains, fiery rivers, and paths through narrow defiles and high mountains.

The Revelation of Ezra is a book of calendrical prognostications. It is extant primarily in Latin and Greek versions. Of the three Latin manuscripts, the earliest dates to the ninth century CE and gives the details of weather and the fertility of livestock and crops based on which day of the week on which the first day of January falls. This version is also found in Old French, Medieval Italian, German, and Czech recensions. The Greek versions define which days of the month are best for certain activities and accounts for days on which occurred the birth and death of certain biblical figures. Other such calendrical prognostications, known by the Greek word for this genre [Gk. kalandologia], are attributed to medieval scholars such as that attributed to Bede, the Church historian of the ninth century CE. The Revelation of Ezra also parallels earlier texts purporting to recount the contents of secret knowledge such as the Coptic Treatise of Shem.

4 EZRA. Also called 2 Esdras in English Bibles and 4 Esdras in the Vulgate. Properly, 4 Ezra is only chapters 3–14 of 2 Esdras. Chapters 1–2 are considered to be 5 Ezra and are sometimes called 2 Esdras in Latin manuscripts. Chapters 15–16 are considered to be 6 Ezra and are sometimes called 5 Esdras in Latin manuscripts. The text is attested in several Latin manuscripts, Syriac, Ethiopic, Armenian, Arabic, Coptic, Georgian, and Greek. Most scholars date the composition of 4 Ezra to the end of the first century CE and the addition of 5 and 6 Ezra to the end of the third century CE.

Chapters 3–14 recount seven visions of Ezra. The first vision (3:1–5:19) begins with a recounting of the stories of Noah, Abraham, Isaac, Jacob, and Esau, and references to Adam and David. The angel Uriel replies that God's justice is beyond human comprehension, and gives Ezra signs of the eschaton. In the second vision (5:21–6:34) Uriel explains the creation of successive generations, the divisions of the time, and more signs of the end. The third vision (6:35–9:25) is of the Day of Judgment and the fate of the righteous and the wicked. The fourth vision (9:26–10:59) is of the suffering and future transformation of Zion. In the fifth vision (11:1–12:39) Ezra sees the future rise of the Roman Empire and Uriel reveals that this empire will be punished by the Messiah. The sixth vision (13:1–58) is of a man rising from the sea with an army and destroying the enemy with fire from his mouth. In the seventh vision (14:1–48) Ezra is told to dictate 94 books over 40 days to five men. These are to become the 24 canonical books of the Bible and 70 hidden texts. The last vision also contains the account of Ezra drinking a liquid like fire that gives him the prophetic knowledge and wisdom to recite the sacred books. The Syriac, Ethiopic, Armenian, and one of the Arabic recensions add that, following his recitation, Ezra was taken up into heaven where he was called the "Scribe of God." Chapters 1–2 (5 Ezra) recount how Ezra was rejected by the Jews but is received by the Gentiles. Chapters 15–16 (6 Ezra) contain a number of denunciations and warnings of coming punishments.

– F –

FAKHR AL-DIN AL-RAZI (1150–1210 CE). One of the most famous Muslim intellectuals of his time, Fakhr al-Din al-Razi lived on the eve of the Mongol invasions. One of his best-known teachers was Majd al-Din al-Jili, the teacher of the famous Sufi philosopher Shihad al-Din Yahya al-Suhrawardi. He composed a Quran commentary that is not equally regarded as authoritative. It has been condemned by scholars such as Ibn Taymiyya and praised by others like Subki for its inclusion of philosophical and theological perspectives not normally found in other Quran commentaries. His commentary is organized according to different "questions" relating to the verses of the Quran much like other rational-theological works of the time. Some scholars believe Fakhr al-Din al-Razi died before the completion of his commentary, and that it was finished by his disciples.

FALSE PROPHETS. Label given in the biblical text for Israelite prophets who either deliberately utter false prophecies in the name of Yahweh or have deceived themselves into believing that their prophecies will come to pass (Isa 9:14; Jer 14:14, 23:5, 27:10, 29:9; Ezek

13–14; Hab 2:18; Zech 10:2). False prophecy must have been a widespread concern in the ancient Near East for there are several reports of attempts by the royal house to separate prophets and diviners into separate chambers in order to ascertain whether their prophecies are identical, i.e., said "with one voice" (e.g., Assyria, Mari, and 1 Kgs 21:13). Many biblical texts also refer to what appear to be false prophets, especially when referencing an official class of prophets, native or foreign, though the term "false, deceptive" [Heb. sheqed] does not appear (e.g., Isa 28:7; Jer 2:26, 4:9, 6:13; Zech 7:3; 2 Kgs 23:2; Neh 9:32; Lam 2:20; Ezek 7:26). Such prophets are described as obstructing knowledge (Isa 9:14; Hos 4:5, 9:7–8), leading the people astray (Mic 3:5), including other prophets (1 Kgs 13:20), interested only in wealth (Ezek 22:25), and are equated with diviners (Isa 3:2).

Several false prophets are known by name and figure prominently in prophetic narratives (*see also* HANANIAH; NOADIAH; ZEDEKIAH, SON OF CHENAANAH). The Bible's legal codes decide whether a prophet is a "true prophet" or not based on whether his or her prophecies come to pass (Deut 18:21–22), and the sentence for false prophecy is death. These legal materials also betray nationalist concerns and the influence of foreign modes of divine access, since they legislate against prophesying in the name of foreign gods (Deut 13:2, 13:4, 13:6). Such pronouncements, and the label "false prophet" reflect a growing tension between various competing prophetic groups, each positioning itself as an authoritative mediator of the divine word. Whether this development represents a reaction on behalf of the sanctioned authorities to direct or indirect Mesopotamian influence (as asserted in Isa 2:6), or whether such prophetic indictments represent polemical tools of self-identity (as found also in Assyria and Mari), is impossible to tell. According to the Talmud, a false prophet can be tried only before a 71-member Sanhedrin (TB Sanhedrin 2a), and if convicted, must die by strangulation (TB Sanhedrin 84b).

FORM CRITICISM. A critical approach to the biblical text originating in Germany in the 1900s [Ger. Formgeschichte] that aims to reconstruct the social institutions of ancient Israel by uncovering oral forms, conventional patterns, and genres [Ger. Gattungen] in the biblical text. Form criticism identifies these patterns by way of grammatical, formulaic, and other compositional and structural elements, and examines them to construct the specific social contexts [Ger. Sitz im Leben] for their use. Form criticism has been applied usefully to the study of prophetic oracles and has helped to distinguish various types of prophetic discourse and their purposes.

FORMER PROPHETS. The phrase employed in the Bible by the prophet Zechariah (Zech 1:4, 7:7, 7:12) to refer to the prophets who lived prior to the Babylonian exile (586 BCE), thus all biblical prophets with the exception of Haggai, Zechariah, and Malachi. The phrase represents a conscious conceptual distinction between pre-exilic and post-exilic prophecy. The Talmud sees the period between the former and latter prophets as a period in which the Urim and Thummim also ceased (TB Sotah 48a).

FURQAN. Arabic term attested seven times in the Quran that Muslim exegetes explain as related to the Arabic root [f-r-q] meaning to separate or distinguish one thing from another. Western scholars point out that the Aramaic term [Aram. purqan] to which the Arabic [Ar. furqan] is cognate occurs widely with the meaning "salvation" or "savior" in Syriac Christian writings. In the Quran the term *Furqan* seems to be employed as a name or descriptive epithet of the Quran (Q 25:1), and Muslim exegetes take it as such. The Furqan is said also to be sent down by God in Q 8:41 and Q 25:1 to "his servant," apparently referring to the prophet Muhammad's receipt of the Quran, or perhaps of something else. Q 21:48 states that God gave the Furqan to Moses and to Aaron, and Q 2:53 states that God revealed to Moses "the Book and the Furqan." Q 3:4 lists the revelation of the Furqan along with the revelation of the Torah and the Gospel. In Q 8:29 it is said that God will make a Furqan for those who fear God, redeeming them from their evil deeds and forgiving them. Muslim exegetes identify this Furqan as the Battle of Badr (624 CE), the first battle in which the Muslim community defeated the Meccans. In this context, the term also seems to have the semantic range of salvation and redemption.

– G –

GAD. Prophet mentioned only parenthetically in the biblical record. He appears to have plied his trade in the court of King David (1 Sam

22:5). Gad is called a "seer" in 2 Sam 24:11, 1 Chr 29:29, and 2 Chr 29:25. Some later rabbinic traditions group Gad among the Former Prophets. According to midrashic texts, Gad was slain by an "Angel of Mercy" along with David's elders and his four sons.

GELASIAN DECREE. A sixth-century CE text that includes a catalog of canonical texts, a list of synods and Christian writers, and a catalog of apocryphal and other nonauthoritative writings. The catalog of canonical texts includes the 27 books recognized as the canon of the New Testament today. Apocryphal works include a number of acts, gospels, epistles, the works of various writers, and amulets said to be compiled in the name of the angels. Unknown apocrypha include the Interdiction of Solomon, a book about the daughter of Adam, and a book about the giant Og and his fight with the dragon.

GEMATRIA. Greek term borrowed into Hebrew to denote the practice of reading letters of the alphabet as numbers, and thus treating numbers as equivalent to words, and reading words according to the sum value of their letters. This approach to the interpretation of words is used extensively in Jewish and Islamic exegesis of the Bible and Quran. The exegetical technique of gematria is attested first in Mesopotamia, where words were interpreted according to the numerical values of the signs or letters used to comprise them. In Mesopotamia, the cuneiform writing system also permitted many gods' names to be written as numbers (e.g., Ishtar as 14, Anu as 60, and Enlil as 50). In the later Seleucid period (312–64 BCE) gematria was employed in esoteric scribal colophons.

Gematria was adopted by the Jewish "scribes" [Heb. soferim], a term also understood to refer to the "counters" of letters. Jewish scribes equated the name of Abraham's servant Eliezer, whose letters total 318, with the 318 soldiers born into Abraham's household, whom Abraham rallied in his battle against the eastern coalition of kings (Gen 14:14). The device was known also to early Christians who read the name of the predicted beast as the number 666 (Rev 13:18), and to the Greek dream interpreter Artemidorus (second century CE) who employed it as a divinatory hermeneutic for deciphering dreams. Jewish exegesis of the Bible used gematria to determine the meaning of one word based on the sum of its letters being equal to the sum of the letters of another word, but also maintained that individual letters in words could be replaced and exchanged based on numerical equivalences.

Many of the surahs in the Quran begin with unconnected letters that are interpreted by some Muslim exegetes as numerical values with mystical or esoteric significance. The Arabic alphabet, containing 28 letters, is regarded by Muslims as the perfect alphabet for numerology. To assign numerical values to letters, 1–10 by ones, 10–100 by tens, 100–1000 by hundreds, requires 28 letters, and 28 is also considered to be the number of lunar mansions in Muslim cosmology. The Arabic science of letter numerology ['ilm al-huruf] and divination using it are based on three elements: the numerical value of individual letters, knowledge of the natural properties of the letters as derived from alchemy, and the astrological significance of the letters and their corresponding numbers. The 28 letters of the Arabic alphabet are grouped into four sets of seven letters corresponding to the four primary elements: fire, air, water, and earth. Various combinations of Arabic letters and numbers are used to signify different aspects of creation consisting of the combination of alchemical elements, and corresponding to the planetary spheres. In Jewish mysticism the Godhead is divided into 10 emanations connected with the 22 letters of the Hebrew alphabet. The emanation of the Godhead into the material world through letters of the Hebrew alphabet also appears in the *Sefer Yetzirah* that describes God's creation of the world using certain letters and numbers (*see also* SEFER YETZIRAH).

Among the types of hermeneutia related to gematria and used for the interpretation of the Quran and the Bible are the transposition of letters in one word to form another word, combination of letters in the divine name with those of words referring to other desired objects, substitution of one letter in a word by another letter according to certain tables of correspondences, and the formation of a word by combining the first letters of a word with the last letters of the preceding word in a phrase.

GENESIS. The first book of the Torah (Pentateuch), which describes the origin of the world and formative history of the Israelite nation including the lives of the patriarchs (Abraham, Isaac, Jacob, Joseph). The English name of the book means "Origins" and derives from the

Greek of the Septuagint translation of the first word of the Hebrew text [Heb. Bereshit], meaning "at the start" or "in the beginning." The oral traditions that comprise Genesis were passed down over countless generations and often share a great deal in common with the texts found at Ugarit, Mesopotamia, and Egypt. Though earlier scholarship has attempted to assign particular sections of the book to various sources, scholars today have seen greater literary unity in the book. While few would question that multiple sources lie behind the composition of Genesis, the criteria for delineating these sources has become methodologically questionable.

GENESIS APOCRYPHON (1QapGen). Aramaic paraphrase of Genesis found at Qumran as one of seven scrolls from Cave 1. The text consists of 23 columns of Aramaic, only three of which are preserved intact with another three partially intact. Only individual words or lines can be deciphered from the remaining columns. Paleography dates the text between 25 BCE and 50 CE, and the content of the text appears to relate to the book of Jubilees. Preserved is the story of Noah and the first part of the story of Abraham. Of note is the introduction of the motif of Sarah's beauty (20.2–8a) and Abraham's exploration of the boundaries of the promised land (21.15–22). The text also identifies Melchizedek as the king of Jerusalem in contrast to the juxtaposition of Shalem and Jerusalem in Gen 14:18 and Heb 7:1–2 but parallel with Ps 76:2 and Josephus (Antiquities 1.180).

GENESIS RABBAH. Large midrashic exposition on the biblical book of Genesis dated as early as the fifth century CE, though later redaction seems to have continued into the medieval period. The text significantly expands upon the biblical text by integrating a number of oral traditions, and by way of homiletic parables, sayings, and expositions. Its language is a form of Galilean Aramaic, as found also in the Talmud Yerushalmi. It is divided into 101 chapters and has been added to by later editors, as later editions show.

GERSHOM. Son of Moses and Zipporah (Exod 2:22). According to the Bible, Gershom's son Jonathan served as a priest before the idol in the sanctuary at Dan (Judg 18:30). Since the passage in Judges links a descendant of Moses to idol worship, the scribes responsible for the Masoretic Text suggested that a letter had dropped out of the manuscript through error, and that instead of reading here a reference to "the son Moses," it should be understood as "the son of Manasseh" (TB Baba Batra 109b). This reading is also evident in some early Muslim exegesis in which it is claimed that the Moses mentioned in Q 18:60 is not the famous Moses b. Imran, but rather Moses the son of Manasseh. The family of Gershom's son Shebuel eventually became the overseers of the treasures in Yahweh's temple (1 Chr 26:24). At least one rabbinic tradition sees Gershom as the son who was circumcised in the mysterious passage in Exod 4:24–26 (Mekhilta Yitro 1, 58a).

GLOSSOLALIA. An act of divine possession in which one speaks, chants, or sings unintelligibly or in a foreign language unknown to the speaker or listener. Though this sign of divine inspiration, also known as speaking in tongues, was practiced by early Christian communities (Acts 2, 19:61; Cor 12:10), it is attested more widely as an ancient Near Eastern mantic practice. When King Saul is taken up with a prophetic movement on his way to Gilgal, he also begins to "rave" (1 Sam 10:5, 10:11). Some scholars also see glossolalia in the "raving" behavior of the prophets of Baal (1 Kgs 18:29). Num 11:25–26 similarly describes the prophetic "ravings" of 70 elders chosen by Moses upon whom Yahweh descended in a cloud. The prophet Isaiah possibly also alludes to the practice (Isa 28:10–13). Glossolalia also appears to have been practiced by the muhhu-prophets of Babylon, Assyria, and Mari (*see also* ECSTATIC). Herodotus records the prophetic practice of speaking in a foreign tongue (in this case Carian) in an oracle delivered at the sacred precinct of Apollo Ptous (History 7).

GNOSIS AND GNOSTICISM. Terms used in reference to a variety of movements and texts that emphasize secret knowledge as a means of salvation from an imperfect material existence. The term *gnosis* often is used in a more generic sense to denote esoteric or special knowledge. The term *gnosticism* has been employed to lump together and reify a diversity of late antique views focusing primarily on the notion that the material world is a creation and under the management of the biblical "god," who is understood as a demiurge attempting to keep people from knowledge of the true, high God. The gnostic designation was applied to certain groups by Christian heresiographers and modern scholars, but these groups do not always use the term in reference to themselves. In some demiurgical myths, the prophet or savior figure is depicted as an emissary bringing knowledge of the true God and of the imperfection and illusion of the material world and its creator. Often this negative evaluation of the material world extends to human bodies, and some groups with demiurgical myths promote certain forms of sexual abstinence, diet, and behavior that are based on the notion of a "perfect" human. Other groups with demiurgical myths seem to promote asceticism and a freeing of the soul from its "material prison" in the body.

GOG. Ruler of Magog. *See also* MAGOG.

GOLDEN BOUGH. Name referring to a branch of gold mentioned in classical Greek sources and popularized by Sir James Frazer's *The Golden Bough*, first published in 1890. The golden bough is found in the sixth book of the Aeneid of Virgil (70–19 BCE) and appears to be connected with a particular tree in the commentary on Virgil by Servius in the fourth century CE. Servius gives different interpretations of the golden bough. Among them is the notion that the bough was used to gain entrance to the underworld, as exemplified in the Greek account of Persephone. Servius also refers to a tree whose branches were forbidden to be touched. In order to take one of its branches, one needed to fight and kill the warrior-priest who guarded the tree. A "golden bough" appears in Muslim exegesis as being in the possession of Abu Righal, one of the people of Thamud whom God destroyed for their rejection of the prophet Salih.

GOSPEL. Term used to translate an Arabic term that, according to 12 passages in the Quran, designates the book that was revealed to Jesus. The Arabic term [Ar. injil] appears to be a transliteration of either the Greek [Gk. engelion] or Ethiopic [Eth. wangel] words for "gospel," but is not necessarily understood as a particular gospel, text, or genre. The word often appears in conjunction with the Torah and the Quran, as being revealed to Jesus. Muslim exegetes are not entirely clear about the identification of the Gospel mentioned in the

Quran and extant books used by Christians. Some hold that the Gospel mentioned in the Quran refers to the words of Jesus, and thus, they relate it to the canonical gospels in the New Testament. Others hold that the Gospel mentioned in the Quran refers to a revelation no longer extant, and thus, they do not relate it to the New Testament.

GOSPEL OF THE EGYPTIANS. Extant in two versions among the tractates of the Nag Hammadi codices (III,2 and IV,2), this treatise is an account of the salvation history of the Sethian gnostics (*see also* GNOSIS AND GNOSTICISM). It also is entitled "The Holy Book of the Great Invisible Spirit." The text is attributed to the biblical figure of Seth and is divided into four main sections. Section one is a cosmogony that traces creation of the world down to the birth of Seth. Section two describes the coming of Seth to earth in the body of Jesus. Section three contains liturgical materials, and section four recounts the history of the writing of the text. According to this last section, Seth wrote the book in 130 years and placed it on a mountain, possibly the world-mountain, where it is supposed to remain until it is discovered at the end of time.

GREATNESS OF MOSES. Hebrew text [Heb. Gedulat Moshe] that describes Moses' ascent through the heavens and tour of hell. The text is preserved in a longer and a shorter recension. The shorter recension includes the names of key angels, omitted in the longer version, with whom Moses speaks during his ascent through the heavens. The longer version incorporates elements from the Bible, Talmud, and Zohar to expand on the basic account. According to the longer recension the ascension takes place when Moses first encounters God at the burning bush. In the first part of the text Moses ascends through the seven heavens, and in each of the heavens he meets angels. Throughout Moses is guided by Metatron, and his body is transformed into fire and into an angel-like state. Some of the angels Moses encounters are of gigantic size (with lengths the distance of a 500-year journey) and fantastic description (having 70,000 heads), and are associated with particular days of the weeks and natural elements (fire, hail, ice, snow). The longer recension identifies a few of the angels with passages from the Bible (Prov 8:4; Dan 4:10–14). After reaching the seventh heaven, Moses receives a Bat Qol from beneath the throne of

God and is given a tour of hell (*see also* BAT QOL). Then he is brought back to paradise and shown the Garden of Eden in which rest the Tree of Life and the thrones of Abraham, Isaac, and Jacob.

GREGORY OF NYSSA (c. 331–395 CE**).** One of the "Three Great Cappadocian Fathers" along with his older brother Basil and Gregory of Nazianzus. He was a student of Hellenistic culture and the sciences before he was ordained bishop of Nyssa (in Cappadocia) in 372. Gregory was in attendance at the Council of Constantinople in 381, where he was active in the debates against Arianism. He traveled to Roman Arabia (Bostra) and went on a pilgrimage to the holy sites in and around Jerusalem. Among his writings are works of Bible exegesis and an extended Life of Moses, which includes a christological interpretation of events from the life of Moses and the time of the Israelites.

– H –

HABAKKUK. Little is known about the biblical prophet Habakkuk. The apocryphal book of Bel and the Dragon asserts that Habakkuk was the son of Joshua, a man of Levitical descent, though scholars discount this as historically unreliable. The Seder Olam (20) also preserves a tradition that Habakkuk lived at the time of Manasseh (687–642 BCE). The biblical text he has left, however, appears to date between 605 and 598 BCE. The prophet's biggest concern is the rise of Babylonian power (Hab 1:6), but he also complains about the violence and lack of justice in the world (Hab 1:2–4). Yahweh's response in Hab 1:5 offers little solace, and instead promises a Babylonian onslaught. The prophet then continues by praising Yahweh's concerns for justice (Hab 1:12–2:1).

Some scholars see Habakkuk's prediction of doom against the evil men of Hab 2:6–19 as directed against King Jehoiachim, though the text remains vague in its harangue. The prayer in Habakkuk 3 is rich in mythological and historical allusions and has suggested to some that Habakkuk was a cultic prophet or that the chapter was a late addition. The lack of this chapter in the Commentary to Habakkuk found among the Dead Sea Scrolls suggests the latter, but may not be considered definitive evidence. The *Book of Josippon* (3.8b–8c) credits Habakkuk with having brought food to the prophet Daniel while the latter was in the lion's den. The Talmud also tells of Habakkuk stepping into a circle that he drew, and refusing to leave it until God told him his mysteries (TB Ta'anith 23a), a story later treated as an act of hubris (Psalms Midrash 90).

HADITH (pl. ahadith). Arabic term commonly used to refer to a report that can be traced back to the prophet Muhammad. According to Muslim scholars, hadith reports are of three types: those that preserve the sayings of Muhammad, those that preserve an account of his actions, and those in which he tacitly consented to what someone else said or did. Hadith reports were transmitted orally from the Companions of the prophet Muhammad to the earliest generations of their followers. In time, people began to record and collect hadith reports in writing. Some of these early collections, from the eighth and ninth centuries CE are still extant. In the 10th century CE the hadith reports considered authoritative were collected into six "books," the most authoritative of which are those collections attributed to Bukhari and Muslim.

Hadith reports play an important role in Quran interpretation. The earliest Quran interpretations were comments made by the prophet Muhammad or by his Companions and attributed to him. These comments were preserved and transmitted as hadith reports and became the basis for the bulk of later Quranic exegesis. Hadith reports also served to preserve the Quran in its different transmissions, and were formative in the construction of Islamic law.

HAGAR. Egyptian servant of Abraham's wife Sarah, who bore to Abraham a son named Ishmael (Gen 16:1–4). Although not mentioned by name in the Quran, Hagar is understood to be Ishmael's mother, alluded to in Q 14:37. According to the Bible, Hagar was an Egyptian slave-girl whom Sarah gave to Abraham as a wife (Gen 16:1–3). Jewish exegesis explains that Sarah had received Hagar from the pharaoh when Sarah and Abraham left Egypt (Genesis Rabbah 45:3), a tradition shared by Muslim exegetes. Other sources add that Hagar was the daughter of the pharaoh (Pirqe d'Rabbi Eliezer 25; Genesis Rabbah 45:1; Targum Yerushalmi on Gen 26:1).

The Bible and Muslim tradition (based on Q 14:37) agree that Hagar and Ishmael were sent out by Abraham because of Sarah's jealousy (*see also* ISHMAEL). Genesis preserves two accounts of Hagar's flight from Sarah (Genesis 16 and Genesis 21). The well discovered by Hagar appears to be identified with the well of Beersheba where Abraham makes the oath with Abimelech (Gen 21:22–34). Some Jewish exegetes maintain that the well was the "Well of Miriam," which would later reappear to the Israelites in the wilderness of wandering (Pirqe d'Rabbi Eliezer 30; Targum Yerushalmi on Gen 21:16).

Muslim exegesis explains that Ishmael was an infant when he and Hagar were driven into the wilderness (also suggested by Gen 21:14–15). Muslim sources narrate how when Hagar and Ishmael came to Mecca they were dying of thirst, and how Hagar ran between the hills of Safa and Marwah seven times before an angel appeared and revealed the well of Zamzam. The angel is said to have told Hagar not to fear because Mecca was the spot where Ishmael and Abraham would build the "House of God," a statement that is taken to refer to the Ka'bah. Yaqut identifies the biblical mention of Ishmael's home as "Paran" as being the word used in the Torah to refer to Mecca. Bukhari preserves a hadith report that adds that Hagar and Ishmael remained in Mecca until the Jurhum settled there, teaching Ishmael Arabic and providing him with his first wife.

Tabari and Tha'labi also attribute a number of "firsts" to Hagar, such as that she was the first woman to pierce her ears, the first to wear a girdle, and the first to be circumcised, perhaps relating to the Jewish exegesis in which Abraham tied a water barrel or veil around Hagar's waist to show that she was a bondswoman (Pirqe d'Rabbi Eliezer 30; Yalqut Shimoni, Gen 95, 1.424).

HAGGAI. The prophecy of Haggai records its own date: "the second year of Darius [I] the [Persian] king [582–486 BCE], in the sixth month, on the first day of the month" (Hag 1:1), that is, in 520 BCE. Its primary message is that Yahweh has ordained the rebuilding of his temple. Haggai was the official court prophet of Zerubbabel (Ezra 5:1, 6:4) whom Haggai regarded as offering the promise of continuing the Davidic line (Hag 2:23). He also prophesies the overthrow of the "throne of the kingdoms" (Hag 2:22), though Darius I remained on the throne, leaving this prophecy unfulfilled. The Talmud records a tradition in which Haggai, with the help of the angel Michael, showed the returnees in Jerusalem the exact location and plans for the altar (TB Zebahim 62a). He also is credited with having guided Jonathan ben Uziel when drafting his Targum of the Prophets (TB Yebamoth 16a; Qiddushin 43a; Nazir 53a; Hullin 137a).

HAMAN. Character who appears in the biblical story of Esther and the Quranic story of Moses. In the biblical book of Esther, Haman, the son of Hammedatha the Agagite, is a vizier of King Ahasuerus (Xerxes) who attempts to convince the king to eradicate all the Jews in the Persian empire. Haman's plan is foiled by Queen Esther, who gains the support of King Ahasuerus, and Haman is hanged from the gallows he had prepared for Mordecai the leader of the Jews. The Hebrew of the Masoretic text refers to Haman as the "Agagite," and the Babylonian Talmud (Megillah 13a) links Haman with Agag the king of the Amalekites who fought against Saul in 1 Samuel 15. The term *Agag* also is understood as a general appellative by which the kings of the Amalekites were known, and thus has general significance as a symbol for Israel's enemy, the Amalekites. Later traditions understood this as referring to Gog who is to lead the barbarians of the north against Israel at the end of time (Ezek 38–39); the name was thus understood by the Septuagint of Num 24:7. Other sources claim that Herod the Great (r. 37–34 BCE) was a descendant of Haman, and thus Agag, all persecutors of the Israelites or Jews. Rabbinic sources make Haman a descendant of Esau whereas Mordecai is a descendant of Jacob, and Rashi preserves a tradition in which Haman had sold himself as a slave to Mordecai for a loaf of bread during a war.

In the Quran, Haman is the vizier of the pharaoh with whom Moses has dealings. The name Haman appears six times, always with the pharaoh except for Q 28:38 and Q 40:36 where the pharaoh orders Haman to build a tower of clay brick so high that he might see the God of Moses. This appears to allude to the story of the Tower of Babel in Gen 11. Later Jewish exegetes identify Nimrod as the one who built the Tower of Babel. Muslim exegetes also claim that Nimrod is one of the two evil rulers (along with the pharaoh) of the whole earth. Muslim exegetes explain that the term *pharaoh* is the general title given to all the kings of the Amalekites, thus making reference to the pharaoh in the story of Abraham as well.

HANANI. Name of a seer who came to Asa, the king of Judah (r. 913–873 BCE), and predicted the escape of the Aramaean army before him (2 Chr 16:7). The prophecy so angered Asa that he threw Hanani into prison and oppressed some of the populace in retaliation (2 Chr 16:10), despite having married Hanani's daughter (2 Chr 16:7). Hanani's son, Jehu, also was a prophet and predicted the downfall of King Jehoshaphat (2 Chr 19:2), the son of Asa. Hanani's grandson was Eliezer, a prophet active during the reign of Jehoshaphat (2 Chr 20:37).

HANANIAH. Israelite prophet contemporary with Jeremiah who is said to be the son of Azur and a native of Gibeon (Jeremiah 28). Hananiah prophesied before Jerusalem's priests in the name of Yahweh, predicting that in two years Babylon would collapse; that its king Nebuchadnezzar II (r. 605–562 BCE) would return the ritual utensils he seized from Yahweh's temple; and that Jeconiah, the son of the Judaean king Jehoiachim would be restored to office. Jeremiah considered him a lying prophet (Jer 28:15) and prophesied that he would die in the same year (Jer 28:16–17). The clash between Hananiah and Jeremiah represents the tension and competition between various mantic groups in ancient Israel prior to the destruction of Yahweh's temple.

HANIF. Arabic term found ten times in the Quran (two times in the plural [Ar. hunafa']) apparently referring to a pre-Islamic monotheist. In most of the references, the word is associated with the prophet Abraham. Thus, following the religion of Abraham is to be considered being "hanif" (Q 2:135, 3:95, 4:125, 6:161, 16:123). It is neither Jewish nor Christian (Q 3:67) and is specifically opposed to idolatry (Q 10:105, 16:120, 22:31). Q 98:5 indicates that being hanif involves the worship of God alone, and Q 6:79 and Q 30:30 refer to being hanif as the original instinct of humanity. Modern scholars point out that the primary meaning of the term *hanif* in Jewish Aramaic is "heathen" or "pagan" and someone influenced by Hellenistic culture. It may also be related to pagan monotheists who worshipped in Jerusalem and at Mamre. In Arabic sources, the term appears in pre-Islamic Arabia, and Mecca in particular, to refer to monotheists who renounce idolatry and follow the example of Abraham.

HANNAH. Wife of Elkanah, who conceived and bore a son after praying to Yahweh at Shiloh. For providing her with a child, Hannah dedicated her son to the service of Yahweh, and this child grew up to become the prophet Samuel (1 Samuel 1–2). Though not called a prophet in the Bible, talmudic tradition lists her, along with Sarah, Miriam, Deborah, Huldah, Abigail, and Esther, as one of seven female Israelite prophets (TB Megillah 14a).

HARAM. Arabic term referring to a sanctuary, and related to terms meaning "sacred" or "forbidden." Having the significance of "sacred" or "inviolable," the term and its variations are found 31 times in the Quran, 15 of those being in the construct "Sacred Mosque" [Ar. al-masjid al-haram], an expression apparently referring to a place of prayer at Mecca. The Quran refers to the "Sacred House" (Q 5:2), and Q 5:97 mentions that God made the Ka'bah the sacred "house" or "temple" [Ar. bayt], the sacred months, the sacrificial animals, and their markings in order that people might learn that God knows all that is in the heavens and the earth. The noun [Ar. hurum] (Q 5:1, 5:95) is understood by Muslim exegetes to mean a person who is either in the sacred area [Ar. haram] of Mecca or in the sacralized state [Ar. ihram] of being a pilgrim.

In Islamic law, the sanctuary of Mecca is protected by certain restrictions both for pilgrims and for non-pilgrims in the area. The boundaries of the sacred area around Mecca extend far outside of the city itself and are specified in Islamic legal texts. Pilgrims are prohibited from wearing sewn clothing and perfume, cutting nails or hair, and sexual contact of any sort. Wild animals found in the sanctuary, and certain types of uncultivated plants, cannot be killed and eaten by either pilgrims or non-pilgrims. Most of these restrictions placed on ordinary behavior inside the sanctuary parallel conditions in the Garden of Eden. Muslim exegetes report that the sanctuary was first established by Adam, at God's command, as an earthly substitute for the Garden of Eden from which he was banished. After the first Ka'bah was taken into the heavens during the time of the great flood, Abraham and Ishmael rebuilt a new Ka'bah and established pilgrimage to the sanctuary for all people.

HARUT AND MARUT. Two angels mentioned in the Quran (Q 2:102) as the angels of Babylon who teach magic to people (*see also*

MAGIC). Muslim exegetes explain that Harut and Marut were challenged by God to be more righteous than human beings. When they came to earth they had sex with a woman and killed a man, and were subsequently sentenced to hang upside down in a well in Babylon. The theme of fallen angels copulating with women is often read into Gen 4:1–4, though the word "angels" does not appear there, and later apocryphal works associate the fallen angels with the origins of magic on earth. Some scholars identify the names Harut and Marut with Haurvatat and Ameratat, two angels found in Zoroastrian sources. Jewish tradition also preserves an account of two fallen angels, Azazel and Shemhazai, who criticize God because of human corruption. The two angels were sent to earth and slept with women. As penance, Shemhazai suspended himself between the heavens and the earth, but Azazel continued to sire gigantic offspring.

HASAN AL-BASRI (642–728 CE). Famous Muslim preacher born in Medina after his father was taken prisoner during the Muslim conquest of Sasanian Iraq. Hasan al-Basri was of the second generation of Muslims, and one of the followers of the Companions of the prophet Muhammad. He was best known for his preaching, which criticized the accumulation of worldly goods, and many of his sayings are repeated in later sources. He is credited with some unusual readings of the Quran and the transmission of hadith reports. Because of his fame, Hasan al-Basri is counted in the origins of many traditions including several orders of Muslim mysticism, alchemy, and the Mu'tazilah.

HAWTAH. Arabic term used to designate a sanctuary or sacred area, usually associated with a particular founding figure such as a holy man or prophet. The term is largely synonymous with the Arabic term *haram* but is limited almost exclusively to pre-Islamic sanctuaries. Some scholars speculate that the term might have South Arabian origins or that it signifies more of an agricultural cultic site than an urban one.

HEKHALOT LITERATURE. Term used to classify a number of Jewish esoteric texts composed roughly between the third and 10th centuries CE that record claims of access to divine mysteries by way of self-induced trances. The texts detail a number of supernatural and ritual acts. Practitioners are said to experience visions of the divine chariot known to the prophet Ezekiel (*see also* MERKABAH [CHARIOT] MYSTICISM), and thus to access and transcend divine "dwellings" or "palaces" [Heb. hekhalot]. Initiates are depicted as summoning angels to aid them in memorizing the Torah. The various texts collected under the label of Hekhalot literature show a number of influences from early apocalyptic literature, as well as from Egyptian and Mesopotamian performative ("magic") traditions. Perhaps the best known of these texts is 3 Enoch, also known by its Hebrew title [Heb. Sefer ha-Hekhalot].

HEMAN. Name of a royal seer whose descendants served as prophetic musicians in David's time (1 Chr 25:1), and performed for Yahweh's temple during the time of Josiah (640–649 BCE). They are notable for using music to inspire their prophecies. They appear alongside the families of Asaph and Jeduthun. The sons of Heman are Bukkiah, Mattaniah, Uzziel, Shebuel, Jerimoth, Hananiah, Hanani, Eliathah, Giddalti, Romamti-Ezer, Joshbekashah, Mallothi, Hothir, and Mahazioth. They are mentioned as prophetic musicians in 1 Chr 25:4. In all, Heman had 14 sons and three daughters (1 Chr 25:5), all of whom were trained in "cymbals, lyres, and harps, for the service of the house of God."

HERMES TRISMEGISTOS. Name of a deity-like prophetic figure associated with the Greek god Hermes and the Egyptian god Thoth, to whom many of the texts in the Corpus Hermeticum are ascribed. The name may derive from a Greek phrase [megistos kai megistos theos, megas Hermes] meaning "Greatest and Greatest God, Great Hermes" used of Thoth and Hermes in Hellenistic Egypt. Some sources claim that Hermes Trismegistos is the second Hermes who transcribed the teachings of Thoth, which were revealed to the first Hermes sometime before the great flood and subsequently stored in a temple in Upper Egypt. In the Corpus Hermeticum and associated texts, Hermes Trismegistos appears primarily as a god-like figure who reveals secret knowledge to select people, but in some texts he is the recipient of the revelation. Early Christian writers mention Hermes Trismegistos as an ancient sage, though most scholars date the redaction of the bulk of the Corpus Hermeticum to late antiquity.

Hermes Trismegistos is identified in Muslim sources with the prophet Idris or Enoch, though some exegetes dispute this identification. He is associated also with various other historical periods and figures in Arabic texts. In one account he is said to have hidden secret texts in a cave so that they would not be destroyed by the deluge (*see also* CAVE). Later these texts, identified in part with the Emerald Tablet and talismanic texts, were found by Apollonius and transferred to Aristotle and then to Alexander the Great. Other Muslim sources report that, according to the Sabians, Hermes Trismegistos was a prophetic figure. Hermes Trismegistos imparts secret knowledge to initiates in the Nag Hammadi texts known as the Asclepius fragment (VI,8) and the Discourse on the Eighth and Ninth (VI,6).

HERODOTUS (c. 490–425 BCE). Greek historian, called the "Father of History" because of the breadth of his well-known "Histories" [Gk. historiai], which cover the period of the Persian Wars (c. 519–487 BCE), but which also include a wealth of information on Egyptian and Persian history and religion. Book two, in particular, contains a rich description of Egypt and offers many comparisons with Greek and Persian culture.

HIDDEN TEMPLE VESSELS. A number of apocryphal sources make reference to the hiding or removal of the vessels from the temple in Jerusalem before the Babylonian destruction in 586 BCE. The motif of the hidden vessels usually appears in apocalyptic and eschatological contexts where the knowledge of their fate signifies the prophetic authority of the seer, and their future discovery is said to herald the beginning of a new eschatological age. 2 Macc 2:4–8 reports that Jeremiah hid the Tent, the Ark of the Covenant, and the Altar of Incense in a cave on a mountain outside of Jerusalem. 2 Macc 1:19 preserves a tradition related to the story of Hanukkah, that the oil from the Altar of Incense was removed from Jerusalem and hidden in a hole like a dry well. A similar account in the Lives of the Prophets credits Jeremiah with hiding the temple vessels. The Babylonian Talmud records that King Josiah (r. 640–609 BCE) hid the temple vessels under a rock in Jerusalem (TB Krithoth 5b; cf., Yoma 53b; Sanhedrin 26b). 2 Bar 6:7 claims that an angel removed the vessels from the temple during the destruction of Jerusalem.

2 Macc 2:8 also reports that the temple vessels will reappear at the end of time along with the glory of the Lord and the cloud that was seen in the time when Moses first supervised the creation of the vessels, and when Solomon built the temple. Book 2 of the Sibylline Oracles (188) and Jewish exegetical texts mention that Elijah is to restore the temple vessels at the end of time. Other sources, such as 2 Baruch, associate the reappearance of the vessels with the coming of the Messiah. Ibn Ishaq's biography of the prophet Muhammad includes a report that when Abd al-Muttalib (Muhammad's grandfather) recovered the well of Zamzam he also uncovered golden implements from an earlier temple including items from a mountain in Syria, suggesting that the prophethood of Muhammad be seen in terms of a sort of messianic eschatology.

HIJR. *See* MADA'IN SALIH; SALIH.

HIMA. Arabic term referring to a protected territory, usually reserved for the pasturage of particular animals and placed under the guardianship of the tribal deity. The usage is pre-Islamic and is found in Islamic literature referring to pre-Islamic practices, but the Quran's story of the prophet Salih does allude to the protected territory of the she-camel as the "land of God" (Q 7:73, 11:64). In pre-Islamic Arabian religions a domesticated animal, such as a camel, could be dedicated to a local deity as a "bloodless sacrifice" free to graze in the protected sanctuary of that deity.

HISTORY OF JOSEPH. An extremely fragmentary expansion of the story of Joseph related to the account in Genesis. The text is preserved in six Greek papyrus fragments that date to the sixth or seventh centuries CE. The story, as it appears in the text that is extant, follows the basic narrative structure of the Joseph story familiar from Genesis, but not much else can be discerned.

HISTORY OF THE RECHABITES. Text detailing the visit of Zosimus to a paradise-like island where he meets the Rechabites, a righteous people who were taken from among the sinful people of Jerusalem in the time of Jeremiah (cf., Jeremiah 35). The text is extant in many languages including Ethiopic, Greek, Syriac, Arabic,

Garshuni, Old Church Slavonic, and Armenian. Its composition has been dated as late as the sixth and as early as the first century CE, and the dated Syriac manuscripts appear to date from the 12th and 13th centuries CE.

The Syriac text contains 18 chapters, and the Greek includes an additional five chapters added at its end. Chapter 1 describes Zosimus, who lives in the wilderness by himself for 40 years not eating bread or drinking wine. He prays to God from a cave to see the "Blessed Ones" who were taken from the Israelites and the place where they now live. In chapter 2 Zosimus is taken by an angel and an animal until he reaches the great sea where he spots the cloud upon which the Blessed Ones dwell. Chapters 3–6 describe Zosimus's travel to the cloud as a trip to paradise where Zosimus meets Blessed Ones who wear no clothes and have faces like angels. Chapters 7–10 contain an account of how the Blessed Ones, who identify themselves as the Rechabites, were righteous among the sinful Israelites and were transported by God through the air on a cloud to their present dwelling (a detail that may reflect a combination of the etymology of the name Rechabite, lit. "chariot rider," with Yahweh's epithet, cf., Job 30:32).

Chapters 11–16 describe the edenic conditions of the Rechabites. They have none of the attributes or accoutrements of civilization: no agriculture, husbandry, wood, iron, houses, buildings, silver, or gold. Their food comes from wild trees and from manna, and their drink from tree roots. They have no clothing, but are covered with "glory" like that which covered the genitals of Adam and Eve. The people are never sick nor do they sin, experiencing only quietness and love toward God and one another. People who take wives do so only once and have sex only once, remaining abstinent for the rest of their lives. Pregnant women give birth to two children, one of whom can marry, the other of whom remains a virgin. The people rejoice at death while the angels carry their souls to heaven and prepare special sepulchers for their bodies. Because of its proximity to heaven, the people worship God in imitation of the praises of the angels and heavenly hosts, which they can hear.

Chapters 17–18 describe Zosimus's return to his cave on a cloud and the animal he rides. Chapters 19–23 in the Greek recension describe how Zosimus is tempted by Satan but then goes on to teach his testament to other ascetics in the desert. When Zosimus dies his body is buried, and his soul is said to shine brighter than the sun.

This text has much in common with other accounts of the righteous who are spirited away from among the sinful before their punishment and destruction, and the visits of later holy men and prophets to these people. Many of the accounts of the "People of Moses" and the "Lost Tribes" of Israel also recount similar miraculous journeys and edenic existences. The Ethiopic Christian text entitled the *Contending of the Apostles* also recounts the visit of Matthew to the lost tribes who neither eat meat nor drink wine, and lead perfect lives. Some of the accounts of the prophet Muhammad's Night Journey include his visits to two cities at the ends of the earth in which dwell the descendants of the followers of Hud and Salih or the People of Moses based on Q 7:129. Persian recensions of the Alexander Romance also recount Alexander's visit to the righteous living in two cities at the ends of the earth. Medieval Hebrew texts narrate Eldad ha-Dani's visit to the lost tribes in terms that also parallel these accounts.

HOREB. Apparently another name for Mt. Sinai, though some scholars see it as a different mountain in the same region. The Bible describes Horeb as the "Mountain of God" (Exod 3:1) from which Yahweh spoke to Moses (Deut 1:6, 4:15), and upon which Yahweh stands when Moses strikes the desert rock causing it to flow with water (Exod 17:6). It is from Horeb that Yahweh gave Israel the Torah (Deut 5:2; Mal 3:22) and where Israel transgressed the covenant by worshipping a golden calf (Ps 106:19). The tablets of the Law were placed in the Ark of the Covenant there (2 Chr 9:15). Horeb also is the site where the prophet Elijah witnessed a variety of theophoric events (1 Kgs 19:8). Rabbinic literature sees Mt. Sinai and Mt. Horeb as identical and explains the name Horeb by a clever play on words, noting that it was so called because "desolation [Heb. hurbah] to idolaters descended upon it" (TB Shabbath 89b). According to Josephus (Antiquities 2.12), Mt. Horeb was considered a holy mountain long before the Israelites, and for this reason, flocks were not allowed to pasture there. It is reported that some Christian monks at the St. Catherine Monastery took Horeb to be the northwestern end of Sinai, also known as "Ras Safsa'afah," whereas the traditional summit of the mountain is to be understood as Sinai.

HOSEA. Name of a biblical prophet who prophesied during the reigns of the Israelite kings Zechariah, Shallum, Menahem, and Pekahiah (746–736 BCE), contemporaneous with Jotham, king of Judah (r. 742–735 BCE), and the name of the book containing his prophecies. The book stands at the head of the minor prophets probably because of its size. The book is known for its nonnormative Hebrew (probably written in a northern dialect) and the difficulty of its interpretation. Yahweh's shocking command that the prophet marry a prostitute (Hos 1:2) has been understood in various ways. Some see it as a nonhistorical parable of God's love for Israel. Others have seen the reference as historical, but assert that Hosea married a woman who later became a prostitute. Still others have opined that the text is historical, but that he married a temple prostitute as an act of prophetic drama. This latter interpretation finds some support in Hos 4:9–14 in which Hosea attacks the practice of ritual prostitution.

In Hos 3:1, God commands the prophet to marry an adulterous woman, and scholars debate whether this woman is different from that in Hos 1:2. Most of Hosea's prophecies are attacks against his contemporaries. Hos 4:4–6 is directed against the priests and prophets for perpetuating the people's ignorance. Hosea also calls into question the sincerity of their ritual sacrifices (Hos 6:6). Hos 4:1–10 constitutes a lawsuit against Israel for breaking the covenant, and throughout the book, Hosea shares the Assyrian view that breaking a covenant leads to an entire nation's downfall (e.g., Annals of King Assurbanipal 5:130–6:10, 26–32, 44–47, 62–75, 78:68–74 [668–627 BCE]). His understanding of covenant also appears to be grounded in a knowledge of Israelite traditions as found in the Torah, especially the book of Genesis (Hos 6:7, 12:2–6, 12:12). The manner in which Hosea communicates with God appears to have involved a form of possession, for in Hos 1:2 Yahweh speaks "through" not "to" Hosea (*see also* POSSESSION). The prophet's reference to Yahweh's raising of Israel on the third day (Hos 6:2) later became a proof text for early Christians attesting to the resurrection of Christ.

HUD. The account of the Arab prophet Hud, sent to people of Ad, is found in Q 7:65–72, 11:50–60, 26:123–140, 41:15–16, and 46:21–25. His genealogy is given variously as Hud b. Shelah b. Arpachshad b. Shem b. Noah or Hud b. Abdallah b. Rabbah b. Ad b.

Uz b. Aram b. Shem b. Noah. The first genealogy seems to identify Hud with the biblical Eber (Gen 10:24), and the second makes the people of Ad descendants of Uz [Ar. 'Aws] b. Aram. Other traditions identify the Aram given here with the "Iram" of Q 89:7, which is said to be the name of the city in which the people of Ad lived, a city made of gold and silver that would move about the earth. The Quran places the people of Ad among the "winding sand-tracts" [Ar. al-Ahqaf], which usually is understood to be at the southern end of the Arabian Peninsula between Oman and the Hadramawt (Q 46:21). Ibn Kathir reports that Hud was the first to speak Arabic, and that the people of Ad were the "Original" Arabs, as opposed to the "Arabicized" Arabs who descended from Ishmael.

Other pre-Islamic references to the name Hud and the people of Ad also exist. The name is attested as a component of several biblical names as well. Ammi-Hud is the name of five individuals in the Bible (1 Chr 7:26; Num 34:20, 34:28; 2 Sam 13:37; 1 Chr 9:4). Abi-Hud is the name given for the grandson of Benjamin through Bela in 1 Chr 8:3. The name Hud also appears in pre-Islamic inscriptions in the Hadramawt. A Palmyrene inscription, dated to 267–272 CE, mentions a place or people called "Iyad," and Ptolemy refers to a people called the "Oaditai" or "Adites." Gen 10:19 lists the city of Admah as one of the cities of the plain associated with Sodom and Gomorrah. An Assyrian inscription of Sargon II, dated to 710 CE, mentions the Arab tribe of "Ibb-Ad" and Sargon's conquest of the fortress of Adu-mu in Arabia.

The Hud story epitomizes the prophetic cycle common to the early prophets mentioned in the Quran. Hud is sent to his people with the message to worship God only, acknowledging that God is the provider of their blessings. On the basis of Q 7:69, Muslim exegetes state that the people of Ad were gigantic in size, and that this was one of the blessings given to them by God. The people rejected Hud despite his warnings that they would be punished, and eventually they were destroyed.

The Quran describes the punishment as a violent wind that destroyed all of the people and left behind their buildings as a sign of their transgression (Q 51:41–42, 54:18–21, 69:6–8). Muslim exegesis includes an elaborate account of how when the people of Ad were afflicted with a drought, they sent a delegation to Mecca to pray for rain. God sent three clouds: white, red, and black. The leader of the delegation chose the black cloud thinking it contained the most rain, and it was this cloud that brought destruction to the people of Ad.

The tomb of Hud is said variously to be in the Hadramawt, at Mecca, or in the wall of the Umayyad Mosque in Damascus. In the Hadramawt there is a tomb that is the site of a yearly pilgrimage to visit the prophet Hud. At the tomb is a rock from which Hud is supposed to have made the call to prayer, and a well at the bottom of the valley. Some Muslim exegetes report that after the people of Ad were destroyed by God, Hud and his followers went to Mecca. Others state that the descendants of the followers of Hud are to be found in one of the two cities located at the ends of the earth.

HULDAH. Name of a female prophet of Jerusalem who prophesied during the reign of King Josiah (r. 631-609 BCE). According to 2 Kgs 22:14, she was the wife of Shallum, the son of Tikvah, the son of Harhas (2 Chr 34:22 reads "Shallum, son of Toqhat, the son of Hasrah). She is called also "the keeper of the wardrobe." Huldah is one of seven female prophets recognized by later Jewish tradition (TB Megillah 14a). The others include Sarah, Miriam, Deborah, Hannah, Abigail, and Esther. One talmudic tradition sees Huldah as a near relative of Jeremiah, another as a descendant of Joshua, and a third as a descendant of Rahab the prostitute (TB Megillah 14b).

– I –

IAMBLICUS (c. 245–330 CE). Neoplatonic philosopher who defended Hellenistic philosophy against Christianity and emphasized the soteriological value of theurgy [Gk. theurgia]. Iamblicus was born in Chalcis, Syria, and wrote an important work entitled *On the Mysteries of Egypt* in which he expanded Neoplatonic thought to include devotional and ritual elements. Among the elements he included was the notion that the *Chaldean Oracles* was a revealed text.

IBLIS. *See* SATAN.

IBN ABBAS (619–687 CE). Abdallah b. Abbas b. Abd al-Muttalib b. Hashim b. Abd Manaf b. Qusayy was a cousin and Companion of the prophet Muhammad. Ibn Abbas is one of the greatest of the early exegetical authorities on the Quran. He was 13 years old when Muhammad died, and when he died, at age 73, he was buried in Ta'if. His collection of sayings is one of the most important sources for hadith and Quran interpretation, and he often is credited as the founder of the science of Quran interpretation. Because of the extensive Israiliyat traditions attributed to him, Ibn Abbas is sometimes called the "Rabbi of the Arabs." His sayings are also responsible for establishing the significance of pre-Islamic Arabic poetry as a backdrop for understanding the Quran.

IBN AL-ARABI (1165–1240 CE). Muhyi al-Din Abu Abdallah Muhammad b. Ali b. Muhammad b. al-Arabi was a visionary, one of the most famous Sufis, and an author of many works related to Quran interpretation and prophethood. He was educated in Seville where he received his first vision, inspiring a pursuit for esoteric knowledge. His *Book of the Night Journey,* which recounts his ascent from the world of existence to God's presence, was written in Fez in 1198. In 1202 he went on pilgrimage to Mecca, passing first through Cairo and Jerusalem, where he began writing his magnum opus, the *Meccan Revelations*, outlining his views of knowledge and existence (the autographed text of the second recension dates to 1235–1239 and is 37 volumes in length). Ibn al-Arabi also traveled throughout Iraq, Syria, and Anatolia and eventually settled in Damascus around 1230. It was in Damascus that he wrote *Bezels of Wisdom*, a brief work extolling the virtues of 28 prophets from Adam to Muhammad. It is claimed that this text was revealed to Ibn al-Arabi by the prophet Muhammad in a dream.

IBN AL-ATHIR (1160–1233 CE). Izz al-Din Abu al-Hasan Ali b. Abi al-Karam was one of three well-known brothers who lived and wrote in northern Iraq in the 12th and 13th centuries CE. His brothers worked in the fields of hadith criticism (Majd al-Din Abu al-Sa'adat al-Mubarak, 1149–1210), and literary criticism (Diya al-Din Abu al-Fath Nasrallah, 1163–1239). Abu al-Hasan is best known for three works. The first is a reference work on the names of scholars. The second is a biographical dictionary devoted to the Companions of the prophet Muhammad. The third is a universal history from the creation to the year 1231. This last work includes much valuable information on Israelite history and the stories of the prophets from earlier sources such as the history of Tabari, and was influential on later works such as the history and stories of the prophets of Ibn Kathir.

IBN AL-NADIM (d. 995 CE). Famous author of the *Fihrist*, an "index" of Arabic books completed at the end of the 10th century CE. This index is an important source of information about early Islamic scholarship and attests to many texts that are no longer extant. The *Fihrist* is divided into 10 sections: scriptures (of Muslims, Jews, and Christians), language, history and genealogy, poetry, theology, law, philosophy and ancient sciences, folklore and magic, doctrines of other religions (Sabians, Manichaeans, Hindus, Buddhists, Chinese), and alchemy. Beyond simply listing the books in these fields, Ibn al-Nadim often provides information about the contents of the books, which is especially useful for understanding otherwise poorly attested areas. His information on the Sabians and Manichaeans, ancient sciences, and alchemy, for example, are particularly helpful.

IBN EZRA, ABRAHAM BEN MEIR (c. 1092–1167 CE). Spanish Jewish scholar, poet, astronomer, grammarian, traveler, and Neoplatonic philosopher renowned for his highly influential commentaries on biblical texts, including the books of Job, Daniel, and the Psalms, as well as the first five books of the Bible. His commentaries, often rather difficult if not cryptic in style, incorporate his philosophical, astrological, and numerological leanings, and reveal him to be a comparative philologist of the highest order. He also is responsible for translating a number of Arabic grammatical works into Hebrew.

IBN HAJAR (1372–1449 CE). Shihab al-Din Abu al-Fadl Ahmad b. Nur al-Din Ali is considered one of the greatest scholars of hadith reports. Ibn Hajar was born in Cairo, where his family had moved from Alexandria and originally from Ashkelon. His father was a rich merchant, but Ibn Hajar became a scholar. He was a lecturer, professor, head of a college, and judge, during which time he produced an immense amount of scholarly work, much of which focused on the study of hadith reports. Ibn Hajar wrote a number of influential and respected biographical dictionaries devoted to information on the lives of the Companions of the prophet Muhammad and later transmitters of hadith reports. He is perhaps best known for his lengthy commentary on the book of authoritative hadith reports compiled by Bukhari. This last work is said to have been collected from Ibn Hajar's lectures over a quarter of a century, and includes much information related to the interpretation of the Quran and the stories of the prophets.

IBN HAZM (994–1064 CE). Abu Muhammad Ali b. Ahmad b. Sa'id was a famous Spanish Muslim scholar of law, philosophy, history, and theology. He was educated in all the sciences of his time including grammar, rhetoric, lexicography, and the Muslim sciences of Quran and hadith criticism. Ibn Hazm was a prolific writer, and among his works is a compendium of "sects and heresies" [Ar. Milal wa Nihal] containing long discussions of Judaism and Christianity. He also wrote a separate treatise on the Bible critiquing what he considered to be alterations made by Jews to the original text. Running throughout his works is a view of prophecy that holds that true knowledge is gained only through revelation. The prophet Muhammad, being the "Seal of the Prophets," brought the final revelation that abrogates all others, though all prophets are to be venerated without distinction among them.

IBN ISHAQ (705–767 CE). Muhammad b. Ishaq b. Yasar al-Muttalabi al-Madani is well known as a historian, responsible for writing the earliest most widely known and cited biography of the prophet Muhammad in the middle of the eighth century CE. Ibn Ishaq was born in Medina to an Iraqi family, campaigned in Syria, and studied for some time in Egypt. After some scholarly disputes, he left Medina and went to Baghdad where he completed his biography of the prophet Muhammad. The first section of this biography, no longer extant, but cited extensively in later sources, is an account of the prophets and other figures from Adam leading up to Muhammad. It is cited extensively by later authors, especially Tabari and others' histories of the prophets and Quran commentaries. Ibn Ishaq is said to have transmitted hadith reports from his father and his paternal uncles Musa and Abd al-Rahman, on the authority of the prophet Muhammad. He also is reported to have traveled widely collecting information from prominent scholars on the history of Muhammad and earlier prophets.

IBN KATHIR (1300–1373 CE). Ismail b. Umar b. Kathir was born in Syria under the Mamluks. He studied in Damascus with the famous al-Mizzi and Ibn Taymiya, and later replaced Taqi al-Din al-Subki as director of the Dar al-Hadith al-Ashrafiyah in 1355, an important center for learning and a place of pilgrimage that enshrined one of the prophet Muhammad's sandals. At the age of 67 he was named professor of Quranic commentary at the Umayyad University in Damascus. He died shortly thereafter and was buried alongside Ibn Taymiya. Like other early Quran exegetes such as Tabari, Ibn Kathir also wrote both a world history and a Quran commentary. Ibn Kathir's commentary is regarded as one of the soundest in terms of its reliance upon authoritative hadith reports, though he also incorporates long quotations from the Bible and other Jewish and Christian sources. This Quran commentary is noteworthy for Ibn Kathir's careful comments on his evaluation of earlier opinions from scholars like Tabari.

IBN RUSHD (1126–1198 CE). Abu al-Walid Muhammad b. Ahmad b. Muhammad b. Rush al-Hafid, also known as "Averroës" in the Latin West where he was best known for his commentaries on the works of Aristotle. Ibn Rushd was born in Cordova to the grandson of a famous jurist, also known as Ibn Rushd (d. 1126). He studied Islamic law, theology, medicine, and other sciences related to Greek and Hellenistic thought. He spent the last part of his life (1153–1198) in Marrakesh under the Almohads. It is in Marrakesh that he worked on his commentaries and studied astronomy. Most of his works do not exist in Arabic but survive in Latin or Hebrew translations. They refine a philosophical definition of prophecy and knowledge acquisition based on the Quran but draw also upon Hellenistic notions of the soul and the intellect.

IBN SINA (980–1037 CE). Abu Ali al-Husayn b. Abdallah b. Sina, known in the Latin West as "Avicenna." Ibn Sina was born in Central Asia near Bukhara, and was regarded as a child protégé in the sciences, having famous physicians working under him when he was only 16. He is said to have mastered all the known sciences as the age of 18, and continued to develop his intellect in the investigation of Hellenistic and Eastern philosophies and their integration into Islamic thought. Some of his most important works are not extant, but his philosophical treatise *Kitab al-Shifa* is a synthesis of Aristotle, Plotinus, and Farabi. Ibn Sina outlines a world emanating from God in which the human soul attains the highest intellect and being through contact with the Active Intellect, which descends from the First Principle as the human soul ascends from earthly existence.

IBN SIRIN (654–728 CE). Abu Bakr Muhammad b. Sirin was considered to be the first well-known Muslim interpreter of dreams, and was highly regarded as a transmitter of hadith reports (*see* DREAMS AND DREAM INTERPRETATION). Later scholars cite his ideas, and beginning in the 10th century CE, a number of works were attributed to him in the field of dream interpretation. Some of these works are not extant, others remain unpublished, and still others can be attributed to later oneirocritics. A number of works extant in Turkish, Persian, Greek, and Latin are also listed as belonging to Ibn Sirin.

IDDO. Grandfather of the biblical prophet Zechariah, son of Berechiah (Zech 1:1). In Ezra 5:1 Zechariah is mentioned as the son, and not grandson, of Iddo, which may represent an abbreviated genealogy or variant tradition. In 2 Chr 12:15 Iddo is called a "seer" and is credited with having written a scroll of genealogies, which also recorded the "evil acts" of Rehoboam king of Judah. He apparently also wrote a scroll concerning Jeroboam son of Nebat (2 Chr 9:29), but none of these works have survived. Later talmudic tradition sees Iddo as the anonymous prophet mentioned in 1 Kings 13 (TB Sanhedrin 104a).

IDRIS. Mentioned in the Quran (Q 19:56–57, 21:85–86), Idris is identified by Muslim exegetes with the biblical Enoch (Gen 5:18). Along with Adam, Seth, and Noah, Idris is considered one of four Syrian prophets according to a report given on the authority of the prophet Muhammad. His genealogy is given as son of Jared b. Mehaliel b. Kenan b. Enosh b. Seth b. Adam, and he is said to have been the grandfather of Noah, though other exegetes assert that 1,000 years separated Idris and Noah. Suyuti reports that his name is derived from the Arabic word for studies [Ar. dirasah], and several exegetes mention that Idris was the first person to write with a pen. Many of the arts of civilization are said to have originated with Idris, such as making clothes and originating the use of slavery. He also is called the "Thrice-Great Hermes" [Ar. Hermes al-Haramisah] and the prophet of the philosophers. Of the 104 scriptures that are said to have been revealed to prophets, Idris is said to have received 30. Tabari reports that the "first scriptures" mentioned in Q 87:18 refers to the scriptures revealed to Seth and Idris. Some Muslim scholars identify Idris with Elijah and Khidr, perhaps in part because of the immortality of Idris. Based on the mention that God took Idris "up to a high place" in Q 19:57, Muslim exegetes hold that Idris was raised into heaven while still alive, and is one of four immortal prophets, two of which (Idris and Jesus) remain in the heavens.

IKHWAN AL-SAFA. Name given to an anonymous group of scholars who compiled 51 letters in Arabic accounting for all the sciences and knowledge of realities. The Arabic name "Ikhwan al-Safa" means "Brothers of Purity," and numerous identifications have been made concerning the identity of this group. Most claim that the collected letters were written by a Shi'i imam, and modern scholars attribute the letters to a group of Ismaili scholars who lived in the 10th century CE based on a comment in the Muslim philosopher Abu Hayyan al-Tawhidi. Though the text itself claims to consist of only 51 sections, the extant text of the letters contains 52 sections. The text is organized as a gradual progression from basic to abstract knowledge, which it groups into four sections: mathematics, logic, physics, and metaphysics or theology. Underlying the letters is the general notion that the material world is an emanation of the divine that only can be apprehended and understood for its true nature through the secret knowledge that supports, but is concealed in, the revelation and the law. Several prophets figure prominently in the unfolding of historical reality, including Adam, Noah, Abraham, Moses, Jesus, Muhammad, and a resurrected Muhammad, called the Qa'im. The story of Moses and al-Khidr, based on Q 18:60–82, is used to exemplify the distinction between the external knowledge of the law and secret knowledge of the living imams. The letters are a virtual encyclopedia of the ideas and traditions found in the early Islamic period and include the following: astrology (Babylonian, Indian, Greek), Bible and Judaism, New Testament and Christianity, Hermetic Corpus, alchemy, Haranian Sabianism, Aristotle, Plato, Porphyry, Plotinus and the *Enneads*, and Pythagoreanism supplementing Euclidean and Nichomachean geometry and number theory.

IMAM. Arabic term used in a wide variety of contexts with different meanings, but applied specifically by the Shi'ah to those holding the office of prophetic succession to Muhammad, beginning with Ali b. Abi Talib and his sons. Different groups within the Shi'ah claim the Imamate of different people, and hold different views regarding the Imamate.

The most general view is that the Imamate is a continuation of the religious office held by the prophets beginning with Adam and ending with Muhammad. Some Shi'i groups hold that the imam was divine or a partial manifestation of God, but others maintain that the imams only continued the religious office of the prophets, but did not receive new revelations or inspirations from God. The imams are said to have been created, along with the prophet Muhammad, before the creation of Adam, and are endowed with a special divine light. Imams are in possession of secret knowledge, not all of which derives from the prophet Muhammad. According to some Shi'i sources, the imam has in his possession certain books such as the *Divination* [Ar. Jafr], the *Scripture* [Ar. Sahifah], and the *Compilation* [Ar. Jami']. The *Scripture of Fatima* is a book said to have been revealed by Gabriel to Fatima, the daughter of the prophet Muhammad, and the imams are said to have in their possession the codex of the Quran made by Ali b. Abi Talib along with his own commentary on the revelation.

Throughout the history of the Shi'ah, treatises have been written about the Imamate, defining the office and promoting the necessity of following the imam. The imam is supposed to be designated by the previous imam and is said to be immune from sin and infallible. The imam is possessed of both secret knowledge and must be learned in the Quran and its traditional interpretation. According to the Imami or "Twelver" Shi'ah, the Twelfth Imam went into occultation and was hidden for a period of roughly a century during which time he was represented by select agents each called a "Gate" [Ar. bab] of the hidden imam. After this period of "Lesser Occultation" the Twelfth

Imam went into the "Greater Occultation" where he remains hidden until his return at the end of time as the Mahdi. Some sources claim that the hidden imam resides in one of the two cities, Jabalq and Jabars, located at the ends of the earth (*see also* JABAL QAF; JABAL SIN).

INFANCY GOSPELS. This expression refers to a number of different texts that narrate incidents from the infancy and childhood of Jesus. The best known of these infancy gospels is the Infancy Gospel of Thomas, which contains an account of the miracles performed by Jesus during his childhood. This gospel is extant in more than a dozen languages, including Syriac, Greek, Latin, Irish, Arabic, Armenian, Ethiopic, and Georgian. The earliest manuscripts appear to be a Latin palimpsest that dates to the fifth or sixth century CE, and a Syriac manuscript that dates to the second half of the sixth century CE. The Greek manuscripts date to the 15th and 16th centuries CE. The various miracles recorded in this gospel include Jesus bringing clay birds to life, raising the dead, healing the sick, reaping hundredfold from a single seed, and dumbfounding his teachers. The Quran states that Jesus claims to have brought a clay bird to life, healed the sick, and resurrected the dead (Q 3:49).

Another infancy gospel is that known as the Arabic Infancy Gospel, which was translated into Latin from a single manuscript that is now lost. Part of this also appears in the Syriac text entitled the "History of the Blessed Virgin Mary and the History of the Likeness of Christ" from a manuscript dated to the 13th or 14th century CE. In one of the incidents a woman salvages water used to wash Jesus and pours it over a girl, thus curing her of leprosy. In another the holy family meets two robbers whom Jesus identifies as the two to be crucified with him in Jerusalem. Jesus also causes a spring to gush from a tree and changes a group of children into goats, an episode also included in the Syriac text.

Another account of the childhood of Jesus is found in the Gospel of Pseudo-Matthew, so called because it was identified with the Latin translation of a Hebrew Gospel of Matthew mentioned by Jerome. The best manuscripts for this text date from the 14th and 15th centuries CE, but the composition of the text dates to as early as the eighth or ninth century CE. Among the incidents it includes is an account of a group of dragons worshipping the child Jesus. Other wild animals such as lions and leopards also worship Jesus, and all the oxen and asses come with the Holy Family on their journey to Egypt carrying their supplies. The Gospel of Pseudo-Matthew also contains a narrative of a palm tree bending down to provide Mary with fruit from its highest branches with a fountain of water gushing out from its roots. This same incident appears in the Quran (Q 19:24–26).

The Gospel of Pseudo-Matthew was later expurgated of certain elements, such as the earlier marriage of Joseph, and circulated under the title of the Gospel of the Birth of Mary. It was included in the *Golden Legend of Jaco of Voragine* at the end of the 13th century CE. Other extant sources for the childhood of Jesus include a Latin infancy gospel containing an account of Mary's midwife and the birth of Jesus in a cave. An Armenian infancy gospel expands on the narrative of the Wise Men, making them to be three kings ruling over Iran, India, and Arabia. Some of the Coptic literature about the birth of Mary appears in writings of Cyril of Jerusalem, Demetrius of Alexandria, and Cyril of Alexandria. Also dated from the sixth to ninth century CE is the Ethiopic Miracles of Jesus, which includes various episodes from the childhood of Jesus.

IRAM. City mentioned in the Quran (Q 89:7) and associated with the people of Ad to whom the prophet Hud was sent (*see also* AD; HUD). Q 89:7 gives the name as "Iram of the lofty pillars" [Ar. Iram dhat al-'Imad] though there is some difference of opinion about the exact interpretation of the phrase. Some exegetical sources hold that Iram is the name of a tribe and that Dhat al-Imad is the name of the city. Other traditions state that Iram was the name of a land, and not just a city. Still other sources identify the city as Alexandria or Damascus. It is said to be located in Yemen between the Hadramawt and Sana'a; to consist of castles made of gold, silver, and precious gems; and to have multiple rivers flowing beneath it. Other reports claim that the city moved around the earth from Syria to Yemen and to the Hijaz. The city is said to be square, and its size is given as 12 by 12 leagues. Its buildings are all said to be 300 cubits high, and stood for 500 years before they were destroyed by God. It is said that no one was allowed to enter the city, but its ruins were reported by one man in the time of the caliph Mu'awiyah. Later sources identify it with the city called Ubar, and there are reports of people visiting the city to obtain knowledge of secret and magical arts. It also is possible that the Quranic Iram is related to the biblical Aram, and thus refers to the Aramaean kingdoms located in southern Syria from the 11th to eighth centuries BCE.

IRENAEUS OF LYONS (f. 180 CE). Early Christian writer and bishop of Lyons. Irenaeus wrote an important work entitled *Against Heresies* [Lat. Adversus Haereses] in which he countered what he called gnosticism through his interpretation of the Bible (*see also* GNOSIS AND GNOSTICISM). He also appears to be the first person to refer to the canon of Christian texts as the "New Testament" (Against Heresies 4.9.1), and the first to interpret the Bible according to a thematic typology. Irenaeus also taught that the authority of biblical interpretation was based on apostolic succession starting from Jesus and continuing with his disciples who passed it on to the bishops of the Church.

ISAAC. Son promised by God to Abraham and his wife Sarah and born to them in old age. The story of the annunciation is found in the Bible (Genesis 17) and in the Quran (Q 11:69–74, 15:51–56, 51:24–30). Isaac is the son of Abraham and father of Jacob and Esau with Rebecca.

In the Bible, Isaac is the son through whom God establishes his covenant (Gen 17:15–21). It is Isaac whom Abraham nearly sacrifices on Mt. Moriah before being stopped by an angel (Genesis 22), an event and text known in later Judaism as the Binding [Heb. aqedah] of Isaac. The Quran does not identify the name of the son Abraham is to sacrifice (Q 37:99–111), but Q 37:112–13 refers to the annunciation of Isaac and states that God blessed Abraham and Isaac. Muslim exegetes are divided about the identification of the son. Many (including Tabari, Hasan al-Basri, Ali b. Abi Talib, and Ka'b al-Ahbar) state it was Isaac, but a number of exegetes also argue that it was Ishmael.

In the Bible, Isaac's connection to Yahweh's covenant earns him a place in the frequently occurring covenantal formula: such as "God of Abraham, Isaac, and Jacob" (e.g., Exod 6:8; 2 Kgs 13:23; Jer 33:26; Ps 105:9). This listing of three generations also occurs in the Quran (Q 38:45), sometimes with the addition of Ishmael (Q 4:163) and the "tribes" referring to the Israelites (Q 2:136, 2:140). The importance of the eponym is clear also by the prophet Amos's use of it in the expression "high places of Isaac," as a metaphor for Israel (Amos 7:9). Talmudic tradition credits Isaac with having dug a well that will eventually water Jerusalem in the days of the Messiah (Pirqe d'Rabbi Eliezer 35), and identifies Isaac with Elihu, the friend of Job (TY Sotah 5, 20d).

ISAIAH. The largest book of the major prophets, hence its placement in the Jewish canon at the head of the prophetic books. The book contains the prophecies of at least two different individuals, the first comprising chapters 1–39 and dating to 738–687 BCE, and the second (known as Deutero-Isaiah) comprising chapters 40–66 and dating to the sixth century BCE. Some scholars also propose the existence of a third individual (Trito-Isaiah) whose work appears in chapters 55–66 and dates to the sixth to fifth centuries BCE. The presence of a Deutero-Isaiah seems assured by the reference in Isa 45:1 to Cyrus the Persian king (559–530 BCE). Scholars who propose the existence of a Trito-Isaiah point to the critical attitude of the prophecies toward the restored community's failings.

The first Isaiah lived during the height of Assyrian power, especially under Tiglath-Pileser III, and witnessed the fall of Samaria and the northern kingdom of Israel, as well as the Assyrian invasions that took place during the reign of King Hezekiah (727–698 BCE). A member of the aristocracy and a statesman, this Isaiah was probably multilingual, may have held a priestly position (he has a vision in the temple), and appears to have been the head of a prophetic school. His wife also was a prophet (Isa 8:1). As a political thinker Isaiah advocates a policy of political isolationism and the avoidance of all foreign alliances, a position ultimately grounded in his conception of holiness (lit. "separateness").

Isaiah appears to have been preoccupied with knowing God and his name (Isa 12:4), and he placed great stock in the idea that Yahweh's temple was invulnerable to destruction. The failure of the Assyrian king Sennacherib to seize Jerusalem (Isaiah 36–37) only bolstered this belief. Isaiah also put great faith in Davidic kingship as a source of hope, though he was critical of the kings who sat on the throne. His emphasis on the Davidic line led ultimately to an early form of messianism (Isaiah 9, 11), and it is clear that he expected the appearance of a holy king in his own day. Isaiah's prophecies, especially his oracles against the nations (Isaiah 13–23), demonstrate an awareness of Assyrian oracular traditions. At times, Isaiah engages in shocking prophetic dramas including going naked and barefoot for three years (Isa 20:2–4).

Deutero-Isaiah probably derives from the same school as that of the first Isaiah. It is distinguished from first Isaiah, however, by its absolute monotheism (Isa 45:5–7), which also may reflect the dualism of Persian religion. Deutero-Isaiah places hope in the Persian ruler Cyrus, whom he calls a messiah (Isa 45:1). His message is primarily one of hope for the returning exiles.

Jewish tradition treats the prophecies of the two (or possibly three) authors as the work of a single individual, though the early rabbis were aware of the problems posed by this. At least one tradition sees the book of Isaiah as the work of Hezekiah and his colleagues, along with the books of Proverbs, the Song of Songs, and Qohelet (TB Baba Batra 15a). The first Isaiah's naked prophetic dramas were seen as unpalatable by the rabbis, who treated them as metaphors for prophesying in worn-out clothes and patched shoes (TB Shabbath 114a). Though the Bible is silent on Isaiah's death, talmudic tradition records his death at the hand of King Manasseh (TB Sanhedrin 103b). The Martyrdom and Ascension of Isaiah describes how he was sawn in half with a wooden saw, a martyrdom also attributed to Zechariah the father of John the Baptist by the Muslim exegete Wahb b. Munabbih.

ISHMAEL. Firstborn son of Abraham, born to him from his second wife, the Egyptian Hagar. Ishmael is regarded as the eponymous ancestor of several prominent Arab tribal groupings, and in Islam is considered the forefather of the prophet Muhammad.

In the Bible, Sarah, the first wife of Abraham, drives Ishmael and Hagar into the wilderness twice. In Genesis 16, Hagar is pregnant, and when she is driven away, receives a revelation in which God promises that Ishmael will father a great nation. In Genesis 21 Sarah incites Abraham to expel Hagar and Ishmael, and this time, God promises both Abraham and Hagar that Ishmael's descendants will be great. In both expulsion accounts, a miraculous well of life-saving water figures prominently. The Bible claims that Abraham dug this well (Gen 21:30), and places it in Beersheba (Gen 21:14). Gen 21:21–22 says that Ishmael made his home in the desert of Paran.

Muslim sources also narrate Abraham's expulsion of Hagar and Ishmael, and identify the biblical well (Gen 16:14, 21:19) with the well of Zamzam in Mecca. According to these sources, while searching for water for her son, Hagar ran back and forth between the hills of Safa and Marwah seven times. Then the well appears, thus making Zamzam the "Well of the Seven" [Ar. bi'r al-sab'a], the Arabic form of the name Beersheba. The reference to the sanctuary established by Abraham in Gen 21:33 is interpreted as Abraham's establishment of the sanctuary at Mecca. Abraham and Ishmael build the Ka'bah together (Q 2:125), and according to some Muslim exegetes, Ishmael is the son whom God commands Abraham to sacrifice at the completion of the sanctuary (Q 37:102–106).

Ishmael's name occurs six times in the Quran outside of the Abraham stories. Three of these references list Ishmael along with Abraham, Isaac, Jacob, and the Tribes (Q 2:136, 2:140, 4:163). Two other references list him together with Dhu al-Kifl (Q 21:85, 38:48). Q 19:54–55 states that Ishmael was a prophet who instructed his family in prayer and almsgiving. Muslim exegetes report that Ishmael was the first to speak proper Arabic, the first to tame horses, and the eponymous ancestor of the northern or "Arabicized" Arabs. It is said that Ishmael was sent as a prophet to the Jurhum, the Amalekites, and the people of Yemen.

Muslim exegesis also preserves the story of Abraham visiting Ishmael's wives. During the first visit Abraham is not treated well so he advises Ishmael to get another wife, which he does. The second visit Abraham is treated better and informs Ishmael to keep his wife. This story appears in Jewish sources too (Pirqe d'Rabbi Eliezer 30), but in Muslim sources it is specified that Ishmael's first wife was an Amalekite and his second was from the Jurhum. According to other Muslim sources, Ishmael passed on his prophethood to Isaac and married his daughter Nesmah to Esau, who together produced the Romans. It is said that Ishmael is buried in al-Hijr with his mother Hagar.

ISHMAELITES. A grouping of Arab peoples associated with the sons of Ishmael in the Bible and Muslim exegesis. The Bible often

identifies the Ishmaelites with the Midianites, though Midian elsewhere appears to descend from Abraham and his third wife Keturah
(Gen 25:4), rather than through Abraham's second wife Hagar.
Nevertheless, the Ishmaelites and Midianites sometimes appear
connected (Gen 37:27–28). 1 Chr 2:17 reports that one of David's
officials was an Ishmaelite, and 1 Chr 27:30 states that an Ishmaelite was in charge of David's camels.

Muslim exegesis attributes 12 sons to Ishmael from his Jurhumite
wife, and alleges that the People of the Book regard them as prophets
or apostles. Ibn Kathir states that the Arabs of the Hijaz are descendants of Nebaioth and Kedar, and it generally is held that the prophet
Muhammad descends from Kedar. The Bible gives the same list of 12
sons (Gen 25:12–17), though some of the names given differ from
those in the Arabic sources.

Some scholars hold that the biblical Ishmaelites are not the same
as the Ishmaelites attested in historical sources outside of the Bible.
Such scholarship reconstructs the nonbiblical Ishmaelites as a tribal
grouping (perhaps non-Arab) active in the desert of northern Arabia
during the heyday of the Assyrian empire. The eighth-century BCE annals of the Assyrian king Tiglath Pileser III record an Ishmaelite
group giving tribute to the king, and there seems to have been an Ishmaelite confederacy led by the tribe of Kedar in the vicinity of Duma
who fought with the Assyrians in the first part of the seventh century
BCE. It is likely that these Ishmaelites constituted at least some of the
tribal groupings that appear in the records of Nebuchadnezzar II and
later Achaemenid kings and were replaced by the Nabataeans in the
fourth century BCE.

Other scholars maintain that the sons of Ishmael mentioned in
the Bible are the eponymous ancestors of several important Arab
tribal groupings, and find their names mentioned in ancient nonbiblical sources. Nebaioth, Kedar, Abdeel, Mibsam and Mishma,
Tema, and Naphish are attested in Mesopotamian sources. Several
of these, as well as Massa and Haddad, appear in Thamudic and
other pre-Islamic North Arabic inscriptions too (*see also* DEDAN-
ITE and LIHYANITE; SAFAITIC;). Kedar and Tema appear
prominently also in the biblical books of Isaiah and Jeremiah. The
name Jetur, for example, is identified with the Ituraeans mentioned
in Greek and Latin sources.

The importance placed on the well of Lahai-Roi in Gen 16:13 has suggested to some that it may have served as a cultic site, though solid evidence is wanting. Archaeological and textual evidence testifies to an Ishmaelite cultic center at Duma. Tema seems to have been a major cultic and trade center until it was eclipsed by Dedan, the modern al-'Ula. These various centers and peoples often appear in Muslim exegetical works dealing with the pre-Islamic Arab prophets Salih, Shuayb, and Ishmael. Biblical passages also refer to "Ishmaelites" and the people of "Kedar" as generic terms for desert dwellers.

ISHOBAR NUN (c. 744–828 CE). Bible exegete and patriarch of the East Syrian or Nestorian Church (823–828 CE). He was born in Iraq and later stayed in a number of monasteries near Baghdad. His *Questions and Answers of the Scriptures* preserves the exegesis of earlier East Syrian scholars, and was translated into Arabic by Ibn al-Tayyib. He also wrote a cosmology drawing on a variety of source materials.

ISHO'DAD OF MERV. Bible exegete and East Syrian or Nestorian bishop of Hedatta in the ninth century CE. Isho'dad wrote a massive commentary on the Bible that was influential in the West Syrian or Jacobite Church. There it was used by Dionysius bar Salibi as a source for the biblical interpretations of East Syrian scholars.

ISRAFIL. Name of an angel who is responsible, in Muslim tradition, for announcing the Day of Judgment. Muslim exegetes see Israfil the first angel to prostrate himself before Adam (Q 7:11), and credit Israfil and Gabriel with appearing to Abraham and destroying Sodom and Gomorrah. Muslim sources also report that Israfil met with the prophet Muhammad for several years before the angel Gabriel came to give him the Quran. Some scholars suggest that the name Israfil and its variants (Sarafil, Sarafin) relate to a Hebrew word [Heb. serafim] meaning "burning," sometimes used in reference to heavenly amalgamated beings (Isa 6:2). Others connect the name with the angel Raphael mentioned in Tobit 12:15 who is one of seven angels standing ready to enter the presence of God, though the etymology for such a connection is uncertain.

ISRAILIYAT. Arabic term used by Muslim exegetes to designate Islamic traditions seen as deriving from the Hebrew Bible and later Jewish exegetical traditions, and stories about the Israelites derived from other sources such as the prophet Muhammad or his followers. These traditions most frequently appear in Quran commentaries and related works on the stories of the prophets. Some early Muslims were converts from Judaism and Christianity, and brought with them much lore from their own sources. These traditions were integrated into the earliest Quran commentaries and became a significant part of the Muslim exegetical tradition. One of the best-known transmitters of Israiliyat is Wahb b. Munabbih, who wrote a book, no longer extant, entitled *al-Israiliyat*, i.e., "Israelite Stories." Muslim scholars are not in total agreement about the authority of Israiliyat traditions, though they acknowledge that understanding many of the stories in the Quran often requires additional information supplied by the Israiliyat. Some later Muslim scholars, while preserving the traditions themselves in their commentaries on the Quran and stories of the prophets, are equivocal about the reliability of traditions transmitted on the authority of the Israelites or Jews. More recently, contemporary Muslim scholars have sought to downplay the significance of Israiliyat and to purge all Israiliyat from Quran commentaries.

– J –

JABAL QAF. The world-mountain, mentioned in the Quran (Q 50:1) and identified with the world mountains of other traditions such as the Iranian Mt. Burz and the Indian Mt. Sumeru (*see also* MOUNTAIN).

In the Persian recensions of the Alexander Romance, dated to the 11th through 13th centuries CE, Mt. Qaf is a mountain located at the ends of the earth, the location to which Alexander sets off in search of the water of life. There Alexander meets the angel Israfil standing on the mountain waiting to blow the trumpet on the Day of Judgment. In the Greek Alexander Romance, Alexander reaches the "Country of the Sun" and the "City of the Sun" after passing through the "Land of Darkness" when he comes upon a tall mountain on the top of which sits a Greek-speaking bird. Some Ethiopic recensions of the Alexander Romance include both the angel and the bird on the top of

Qaf. Muslim exegetes report that Alexander spoke with Mt. Qaf and discovered that it was the cause of all earthquakes that destroyed earlier peoples who rejected their prophets.

The Arab geographer Yaqut describes Qaf as a mountain that encompasses and encloses the earth. It is made out of blue or green crystal, and all mountains in the world are tributaries of Qaf. Mt. Qaf is associated with the city of "Jabalq," which can be read also as "Mt. Qaf" [Ar. Jabal-Qaf] in Arabic. This city is supposed to be located in the extreme east or west, at the edges of the earth. Qaf is also linked to the mountain on which Adam was supposed to have stood and peered into heaven after his expulsion from the Garden of Eden. In another Persian account, Alexander visits the tomb of Adam on Mt. Nod, which is understood to be a world-mountain like Qaf.

In some of the accounts of the Night Journey of the prophet Muhammad it is said that he visited the two cities at the ends of the earth: Jabalq and Jabars. The two cities have 10,000 gates and a change of 10,000 new guards each day. The inhabitants are said to be the remnants of those who believed in the prophets Hud and Salih, or the People of Moses as mentioned in Q 7:159 (*see also* HISTORY OF THE RECHABITES).

JABAL SIN. Name of a mountain located at the western edge of the earth, but also identified with Mt. Sinai in Muslim tradition. The name of the mountain appears related to the name of the two cities located at the edges of the earth: Jabalq and Jabars. Just as the name Jabalq can be read as the Arabic Jabal Qaf meaning "Mt. Qaf," so it is possible to read Jabars and its variants Jabals and Jabalsa as "Jabal Sin" and "Jabal Sina."

Arab geographers link this mountain to Mt. Sinai based on the pronunciation of the word and its variants. Muslim exegesis on Q 7:159 reports that the prophet Muhammad visited the remnants of the People of Moses during his Night Journey to the city of Jabars. In other accounts, the prophet Muhammad visits Sinai and the grave of Moses on the side of a mountain. Arab geographers also report that the inhabitants of Jabars are the People of Moses who were taken from the midst of the sinful Israelites during their wandering in the wilderness. The people of Moses were guided to this place by clouds and a pillar of fire just as reported of the Israelites in Exod 13:21–22.

The earth was "folded" [Ar. tuwiyat] for the People of Moses, a term seen to allude to the valley of Tuwa in Q 20:12 and Q 79:16 as the spot where Moses received the Torah.

Some accounts contain a variant spelling of Jabars with the Arabic letter *sad* instead of the letter *sin* at the end of the word. Some exegetes, such as Fakhr al-Din al-Razi, have compared the Arabic letter *qaf*, which appears by itself at the beginning of surah Qaf (Q 50:1), with the letter *sad*, which appears by itself at the beginning of surah Sad (Q 38:1). Other exegetes relate that the People of Moses were taken by God to a place beyond China, the Arabic term for "China" [Ar. Sin] being spelled with the letter *sad*, as in the variant spelling of the word *Jabars* (*see also* SINAI).

JABIR B. HAYYAN. The most famous of the early Muslim alchemists, who lived in the ninth century CE and produced a vast corpus of alchemical works. Whether the large list of works attributed to him is accurate, many of them are cited by later Arab alchemists. It is possible that some of these works were attributed to Jabir b. Hayyan only posthumously, perhaps by the end of the 10th century, and some Muslim historians even maintain that Jabir b. Hayyan was not a real person. The corpus attributed to him consists of six main areas: works on alchemical practice, systematic exposition of Jabir b. Hayyan's alchemical teaching, the theoretical foundations of alchemy, isolated treatises on specific subjects, alchemical commentaries on the works of Aristotle and Plato, and various treatises on related topics. In his writings, Jabir b. Hayyan claims that he was a disciple of the Imam Ja'far al-Sadiq and a South Arabian monk named Harbi.

JACOB. Also known by the name Israel, Jacob is the son of Isaac and Rebecca and the eponymous father of the Israelite tribes who descended from his 12 sons. The name Jacob [Heb. Ya'aqob, Ar. Ya'qub] derives from the word for "heel" [Heb. 'aqeb, Ar. 'aqb], because Jacob was born grasping the heel of his twin brother Esau (Gen 25:26).

The biblical cycle of Jacob stories appears in Gen 25:19–35:29, but Jacob plays a minor role also in the Joseph stories (Genesis 37–50). Jacob appears 16 times in the Quran, and most of these apart from the Joseph story are references to his prophethood and his descendency from Abraham and Abraham's son Isaac. Genesis 25 contains the account of the birth of Jacob and Esau, and Esau's selling of his birthright to Jacob for some stew, and in Genesis 27 Jacob cheats Esau out of their father's blessing. This also appears in Muslim exegesis, but not in the Quran. Genesis 28–31 contains the core of the Jacob cycle: his fleeing to Haran, where he marries Rachel and Leah while working for their father Laban, and his return to Canaan after causing Laban's sheep to bear speckled young. Jewish sources emphasize that, during his journeys and stay in Haran, Jacob was followed by miracles that included his dream at Bethel, his rolling back of the stone on the well, and his production of the speckled sheep. Muslim exegesis also knows the story of Jacob's flight to Laban and his labor in exchange for two wives. This whole account, including the episode of the speckled sheep, is attributed to Moses during his stay in Midian in Muslim exegesis on Q 28:21–28.

In the Bible, Jacob dreams of the stairway of a ziggurat (erroneously thought of as a ladder by later generations) upon which angels ascend and descend (Gen 28:10–22). The Bible identifies the place where Jacob slept as the "House of God" and the "Gate of Heaven," an appellation also signified by the Hebrew name Bethel (lit. "House of God") given by Jacob. Jewish exegesis identifies this location as the future site of the temple in Jerusalem on Mt. Moriah, the earth's foundation stone that reaches to the abyss (Pirqe d'Rabbi Eliezer 35, Rashi on Gen 28:18). The apocryphal text known as the Ladder of Jacob details the prophetic vision received by Jacob, and Jewish sources claim that Jacob received a vision of future events at this time.

According to Gen 32:23–33, Jacob wrestled with a being whom he identified as God. This apparently angelic being gave Jacob the name Israel because he had "striven with God," an ambiguous etymological derivation with both positive and negative import. The angel's injuring of Jacob's "thigh" (a euphemism for his testicles) provides an etiology for why Israelites do not eat the thigh sinew (Gen 32:33). Q 3:93 states that all food was allowed for the Israelites before the revelation of the Torah except that which Israel prohibited himself. Muslim exegesis explains that Jacob prohibited the eating of sinews or the eating of camel meat and milk in fulfillment of a vow he made to God since God cured him of the injury of his thigh. Jewish exegetes state that Jacob was attacked because he had promised, but had failed, to tithe his son to God if God kept him safe until he returned to his father (Pirqe d'Rabbi Eliezer 27; Targum Yerushalmi on Gen 32:25), a view found also in Muslim sources.

JACOB B. ASHER (c. 1270–1340 CE). A Spanish authority on Jewish law known usually by the title Ba'al ha-Turim because of his comprehensive legal work called *Four Rows* [Heb. Arba'ah Turim]. He also composed an influential commentary on the Pentateuch that drew upon materials from Sa'adia ha-Gaon, Rashi, Ibn Ezra, David Qimhi, and Ramban. Part of this commentary was an introductory treatise on Gematria and the Masorah, which he published separately. His Bible commentary often appears in the Miqra'ot Gedolot.

JACOB OF EDESSA (633–708 CE). West Syrian or Jacobite bishop of Edessa. Born in Andiba (near Antioch), Jacob studied at the Monastery of Qen-Neshrin in Syria before becoming bishop of Edessa, and then retiring to a number of different monasteries near Antioch where he taught Greek and biblical exegesis. His extant works include a Syriac grammar; a *Chronicle of Edessa*; and his *Enchiridion*, an encyclopedic philosophical dictionary. Jacob also contributed to later Syriac translations of the Bible from the Greek text.

JA'FAR AL-SADIQ (700–765 CE). Abu Abdallah b. Muhammad al-Bakir was the Sixth Imam, accepted by both the Imami and Ismaili Shi'ah. He was respected as a transmitter of hadith reports by many Sunni scholars, and is said to have been one of the teachers of Abu Hanifah; Malik b. Anas also studied with him. Because of Ja'far al-Sadiq's famed knowledge of Islamic law, the later Shi'i school of jurisprudence was called after his name (i.e., "Ja'fariyah"). He also is credited with a number of books, perhaps pseudepigraphically, on the subjects of alchemy and divination. One of these, entitled the *Divination* [Ar. Jafr], deals with foretelling the future primarily through the use of gematria and the numerical value of certain Arabic letters and words. This book is said to have originated as Ali b. Abi Talib's mystical interpretation of the Quran using gematria and was later passed on to Ja'far al-Sadiq (*see also* GEMATRIA). Unfortunately, the book is no longer extant, though portions of it are cited in later works.

JANNES AND JAMBRES. Two brothers identified in a variety of later traditions as the magicians who opposed Moses and Aaron before the pharaoh in Egypt. The names do not appear in the biblical account (Exodus 7). The Damascus Document mentions Jannes and his brother defying Moses, and 2 Tim 3:8 mentions both Jannes and Jambres. Pliny and other Hellenistic authors see Jannes and Jambres as magicians among the Jews along with Moses. The Targum Pseudo-Jonathan names Jannes and Jambres as having interpreted a dream of the pharaoh and predicting the birth of Moses (Exod 1:15), and identifies them as the two companions of the foreign prophet Balaam (Num 22:22). Other Jewish sources make Jannes and Jambres to be the sons of Balaam, but also give their names as Yachni and Mamreh (TB Menahot 85a). The Testament of Solomon (25:4) includes the remark from a demon of the Red Sea that he was the one called upon by Jannes and Jambres who fought Moses in Egypt. Bar Hebraeus mentions that Jannes and Jambres instructed Moses as a child in the pharaoh's house. Later Jewish texts claim that Jannes and Jambres died with the pharaoh in the Red Sea, though the Zohar claims that they were still alive and present with the Israelites in the wilderness of wandering, where they were responsible for making the golden calf (Zohar III, 194a–194b).

There also is an apocryphal work called the Book of Jannes and Jambres first mentioned by Origen in his commentary on Matt 27:9. It is listed also among apocryphal texts by Ambrose in the fourth century CE and in the Gelasian Decree in the sixth century CE. The Chronicle of John of Nikiu, a seventh-century CE work, also refers to a book by the magicians Jannes and Jambres. The text of the Book of Jannes and Jambres exists in Greek fragments of the third and fourth centuries CE. There also is a Latin text with an Anglo-Saxon translation dated to the 11th century CE.

JAPETH HA-LEVI (f. 950–980 CE). Ibn Ali Hasan al-Basri al-Lawi [Heb. ha-Levi] was a Karaite Bible exegete (*see also* KARAISM). Because of his fame he often is referred to as the "Teacher of the Exile" [Heb. Maskil ha-Golah]. His commentary on the Bible stresses grammar and lexicography in an attempt to demonstrate that exegetes are not bound by the oral tradition of rabbinic tradition. He also eschews allegorical interpretation, polemically distinguishes his

Karaite position from the rabbinic position, and criticizes various Muslim beliefs.

JEDUTHUN. According to the Bible (2 Chr 35:15), Jeduthun was a royal seer whose descendants served the court of David (r. 1000–961 BCE) and Josiah (r. 640–649 BCE). In 1 Chr 25:3 he is said to have prophesied by using a harp (*see also* MUSIC). His descendants appear along with the sons of Asaph and Heman as prophetic musicians established by David (1 Chr 25:1). Jeduthun's sons Gedaliah, Zeri, Jeshaiah, Hashabiah, and Mattithiah similarly prophesied by using music.

JEHU, SON OF HANANI. A biblical prophet who prophesied the destruction of King Jehoshaphat (2 Chr 19:2). Since he is said to have been the son of Hanani the seer, it appears that he was a member of a prophetic family, like Isaiah, though the word son can simply refer to disciples as well (Amos 7:14, *see also* SON OF THE PROPHETS).

JEREMIAH. Name of a prophetic book and the prophet credited with authoring the prophecies it contains. The prophet Jeremiah (640–587 BCE) prophesied during the reigns of several kings including Josiah, Jehoaz, Jehoiachim, Jehoiachin, and Zedekiah, and was a contemporary of the prophets Zephaniah, Nahum, and Habakkuk. His scribe, Baruch, is described as having penned the scroll that is now, at least in part, called the book of Jeremiah (Jeremiah 36), though the portions of the book so identified are not accepted as such by all scholars. The book's theology and periodic employment of Deuteronomistic words and phrases either reflect knowledge of the scroll discovered in the temple in the reign of Josiah or represent the hand of post-exilic editors.

The prophet Jeremiah was a priest and resident of the village of Anathoth with a large interest in international affairs. At first he advocated a policy of alliance with Egypt against Assyria (Jer 2:14–19, 2:36–37), but when Judah became a Babylonian province following the Babylon wars against Assyria and Egypt, Jeremiah advocated peaceful relations with the Babylonian king. When King Jehoiachin rebelled, Jeremiah warned him not to put his trust in the alleged invulnerability of Yahweh's temple, but to submit, a position that landed him in prison (Jer 26:8). The Babylonians then installed Jehoiachin's uncle, Zedekiah, in Jehoiachin's stead. When Zedekiah also rebelled, the Babylonians reacted with force. Jerusalem was razed and the temple was destroyed (Jeremiah 37–39), but Jeremiah was released from prison. After his release he advocated supporting Gedaliah, the Babylonian's new puppet-king, but Gedaliah was assassinated by his enemies who also kidnapped Jeremiah, and fled with him to Egypt, where he spent the rest of his life.

Jeremiah does not appear in the Quran by name, but some Muslim exegetes identify him with the person mentioned in Q 2:259 who passed by a ruined city and questioned whether God could bring it back to life. According to Muslim exegetes, Jeremiah was imprisoned when he warned the Israelites about Nebuchadnezzar II's upcoming destruction of Jerusalem. Nebuchadnezzar released Jeremiah from prison and then God sent Jeremiah to Jerusalem telling him that he was going to rebuild the city.

JEROME (c. 347–419 CE). Named Eusebius Sophronius Hieronymus, Jerome was one of the "Four Doctors of the Western Church," and is best known for his Latin translation of the Bible, which is contained in the Vulgate. Jerome was born in Stridon (Dalmatia) and studied in Rome for some time before moving to Antioch and becoming an ascetic in the Syrian desert (*see also* ASCETICISM). He served in Rome for a brief time under Pope Damasus before retiring to a monastery in Bethlehem. Pope Damasus commissioned Jerome to revise the Old Latin translation of the Bible. Jerome based his translation on the Hebrew rather than the Greek of the Septuagint, which he regarded as corrupt. Jerome referred to his method of translation as relying on the "Hebrew Truth" [Lat. Hebraica Veritas]. He also wrote commentaries on a number of biblical books and left behind an important work entitled *Hebrew Questions in Genesis*.

JERUSALEM. Capital of Israel founded under King David (c. 1000 BCE), and the site of central worship under his son King Solomon, who built Yahweh's temple there. The biblical text describes Jerusalem as inhabited by Jebusites before David conquered it (2 Sam 5:6), a people of unknown origin (but perhaps of Hittite or Hurrian affiliation).

Even before David had captured it, it was taken once by Judahites (Judg 1:8).

Earlier references to Jerusalem and its kings appear at Ebla, and in Egyptian execration (performative curse) texts dating to Senwosret I (1879–1842 BCE). There are mentioned the royal figures Yaqir-'Ammu and Saz'annu. The Amarna Tablets (c. 1360 BCE) also refer to one Abdi-Heba, a king whose name means "servant of [the Hurrian god] Hepa." The meaning of the city's name, though grammatically treated as a dual, is made clear by its appearance in the Amarna texts, which record it as Ur-Shalimu (City of [the god] Shalem).

In later Jewish literature the site of the temple is called "the navel of the earth," that is, the center of the universe, an umbilical tie to the birthing place of the cosmos (TB Sanhedrin 37a; Midrash Tanhuma, Way-yiqra' 13:23). This view may be anticipated in the prophet Ezekiel's reminder concerning Jerusalem: "Your birth and your origin is in the land of Canaan; your father was an Amorite, and your mother a Hittite. And as for your birth, in the day you were born your umbilical cord was never severed" (Ezek 16:3–4).

Muslim exegesis also refers to Jerusalem though the city is never identified by name in the Quran. Arabic and Muslim sources use different words for Jerusalem, including "al-Quds" (lit. "the holy"), which appears to be an abbreviation of the Arabic "Bayt al-Maqdis" (lit. "holy temple"). The latter apparently refers to Jerusalem as the site of Solomon's temple. In the earliest Muslim texts, Jerusalem is called "Aylah," an Arabic transcription of the Latin name of the city, "Aelia Capitolina," given when it was under Roman administration. Often the name Jerusalem appears in Muslim exegesis referring not only to the city, but to the larger area thought of as the Holy Land or the Land of Jerusalem, a usage which also may relate to Roman administrative divisions.

Q 17:1 refers to the "farthest mosque" [Ar. al-masjid al-aqsa] and "the area around which God blessed," and Muslim exegetes explain that this refers to Jerusalem visited by the prophet Muhammad during his Night Journey and from which he ascended into heaven. Muslim sources also regard Jerusalem as a city blessed with natural beauty and fertility, and with numerous prophets. Tabari cites reports that emphasize the remarkable fruit trees of Jerusalem, and others that refer to the many prophets buried there. Muslim exegetes stress that to no other city or people (i.e., the Israelites) were so many prophets sent, and that no other city or people rejected so many prophets.

The destruction of Jerusalem is said to have occurred two times according to the exegesis of Q 17:4–8. The first occurred under Nebuchadnezzar II (the stories of which are associated with the prophethood of Jeremiah, Daniel, and John the Baptist), and the second under the Romans. The second destruction of Jerusalem is regarded by many of the classical Muslim exegetes as the final destruction of the city, signaling the Israelites' loss of their chosen status, and coinciding with their rejection of Jesus the last of the Israelite prophets. A tie between the destruction of the city and the death of Jesus appears also in early Christian literature. Josephus links the destruction to the killing of John the Baptist (Antiquities 18.5.2), and Eusebius links it to the killing of James the Just, brother of Jesus and head of the Christian community in Jerusalem (History 2.9.2–3).

JESUS. Considered to be the "Seal of the Israelite prophets" in Muslim exegesis, and the last prophet sent by God to the Israelites before the coming of the prophet Muhammad. Jesus is mentioned by name 25 times in the Quran, and is called the "Christ" [Ar. masih] 11 times, a title not given to any other figure (*see also* MESSIAH). The Quran also calls Jesus a "prophet" (Q 19:30), an "apostle" (Q 4:157, 4:171, 5:75), the "voice of truth" (Q 19:34), and a variety of other titles associated with prophets. Some of the designations, including that of "prophet," are consistent with New Testament titles for Jesus, especially in the Gospel of Luke (Luke 7:39, 13:33).

The Quranic account of Jesus begins with the birth of Mary and her service in the Jerusalem temple under the guardianship of Zechariah, the father of John the Baptist (Q 3:33–37). In Q 3:42–47 and Q 19:16–26 Mary conceives Jesus while still a virgin through the intervention of the "spirit" of God, whom Muslim exegetes identify as the angel Gabriel (cf., Luke 1:26–38). Muslim exegetes explain that the angel Gabriel caused her to become pregnant by blowing into her womb through an opening in her clothing. According to Muslim exegetes, Joseph, who is not mentioned by name in the Quran, is said to have disavowed Mary because of the pregnancy until Mary convinced him that the pregnancy was from God. When Jesus was born, Mary was sitting beneath a palm tree from which dates fell and from under which a stream sprang forth. This episode parallels the account of the nativity in the Gospel of Pseudo-Matthew, demonstrating the wider influence of the more elaborate nativity traditions.

The Quran also states that God gave Mary and Jesus refuge on the "height" (Q 23:50), which Muslim exegetes interpret as a reference to the flight of the holy family to Egypt (Matt 2:13–15), a stay that they see as lasting 12 years. Many of the events of Jesus' childhood described in the Quran and Muslim exegesis also occur in the so-called Infancy Gospels. Thus, in the Quran Jesus speaks as a baby (Q 19:29–33). In Q 3:49 Jesus claims to bring a clay bird to life, heal the blind and leprous, resurrect the dead, and tell people what is hidden in their homes. Some of these events also appear in Q 5:110. Muslim exegetes describe how Jesus, while in Egypt, found a hidden treasure and caused 12 jars to fill with drink for the wedding party of a dignitary (cf., John 2:1–12).

The Quran also describes the prophethood of Jesus, but not in detail. Q 3:50 gives Jesus' proclamation that he comes as a fulfillment of the Torah, to allow some of that which was forbidden. Q 3:52–58 describes the calling of the disciples, and Q 5:111 makes a reference to God's revelation to the disciples to believe in Jesus. Muslim exegetes attribute a number of ascetic activities and sayings to Jesus including that he used to wear hair and eat the leaves of trees. He had no house or property and never saved food for meals. He used to sleep with a rock for a pillow. In one saying, Jesus proclaims that "seeing this world is like wanting a drink of sea water, for the more you drink, the more thirsty you become until you die." Another tradition preserves Jesus' prophecy concerning the destruction of the temple.

The crucifixion of Jesus and his ascension is narrated in Q 4:155–159. Q 4:157–158 states that Jesus was not killed, but only appeared to die, for God raised him up. Some Muslim exegetes understand this to mean that Jesus did not die on the cross and later ascended into heaven. Others say that Jesus did die but that God raised him from the dead. One report notes that a marker from the tomb of Jesus was found on a mountain near Medina with writing in a square Persian script. Some Muslims claim that Jesus emigrated to Kashmir after his apparent death at the crucifixion, and that he lived in Kashmir until the age of 120 (the same life span as Moses) and was buried in Srinagar. According to Muslim tradition, Jesus will return to earth at the end of time to kill the Dajjal (Antichrist) and reign on earth for seven years before his death. This statement is based on a variant reading of Q 43:61. According to Ibn Kathir, Jesus will return to earth on one of the minarets of the mosque in Damascus just as the dawn prayer takes place.

Most of the references to Jesus in the Quran concern refutations of what is taken as the Christian position that Jesus was God or the son of God. Most of these verses refute the notion that God would sire a son, or that God is a trinity. Q 5:75 states that both Jesus and Mary were human and ate food, and Muslim exegetes take the notion of the trinity to consist of God the father, Jesus the son, and Mary the consort of God (instead of the Father, Son, and Holy Spirit). According to the Quran (Q 61:6), Jesus claims he is the fulfillment of the Torah (also in John 15:25–26) and brings the good news of another prophet whose name is Ahmed. The Quran also refers to a gentile prophet mentioned in the Torah and in the Gospel (Q 7:157), and Muslim exegetes read this as a reference to the prophet Muhammad.

JETHRO. Moses' Midianite father-in-law and high priest of Yahweh (Exod 3:1), also called Reuel and Hobab (Exod 2:18; Judg 4:11), though Hobab is called Reuel's son in Num 10:29. Jewish tradition records several more names for him as well (e.g., Mekhilta Yitro 1, 57a). In the Bible it is Jethro who shows Moses where the mountain of God is (*see also* YAHWEH) and who instructs Moses on how to organize his administrative duties (Exodus 18). According to Jewish tradition, Jethro, along with Balaam and Job, was originally an advisor to the pharaoh before the exodus, but fled Egypt when the pharaoh decided to kill all the Israelite first-born males (Yashar Shemot, 138b; Targum Yerushalmi to Exod 2:23). Muslim tradition identifies Moses' father-in-law as Jethro, but also identifies him with the Arab prophet Shuayb who is sent to the people of Midian.

JINN. Arabic term referring to supernatural beings related to angels and demons. The word *jinn* occurs 22 times in the Quran. Q 55:15 states that the Jinn were created from a blazing tongue of fire, and Q 7:12 has Iblis state that he was created from fire (*see also* SATAN). In the exegesis of Q 2:30, it is said that before Adam was created, the Jinn lived on the earth causing corruption and bloodshed, and that Iblis was an angel. In Q 2:34 God addresses the "angels," and Iblis stands among them. Others report that Iblis was a Jinn and that his only connection with the angels was that they took him to heaven from the earth when he was young. Given the sound association with the Arabic term for the "garden" [Ar. jannah] of Eden, some exegetes explain that the name Jinn comes from Iblis who was put in charge of the Garden of Eden before his fall from heaven. Other lexicographers speculate that the name Jinn is to be understood in relation to the Arabic term meaning "hide" or "conceal" [Ar. ijtinan]. Modern scholars also suggest that the name derives from a Latin word [Lat. genius] and that the Jinn are connected with divinities in pre-Islamic Arabia.

Muslim attitudes toward the Jinn are mixed. Given the repeated mention of the Jinn in the Quran, many Muslim scholars accept the existence of the Jinn and attempt to define their natural and legal status. According to this perspective, the Jinn are different from humans in their substance, but are capable of either salvation or damnation. Muslim sources also mention different types of Jinn, such as those mentioned in the Quran, the Efrit (Q 27:39), and the Marid (Q 37:7). There are many accounts of sexual relations between humans and Jinn in classical Arabic literature, though some Muslim philosophers such as Ibn Sina and Ibn Khaldun appear to deny the physical existence of Jinn altogether. The Jinn play important roles in Arabic folklore and in the Muslim stories of the prophets. They play a prominent role in the stories of Solomon, where they aid demons in converting the Queen of Sheba and building the temple in Jerusalem.

JOB. Biblical book and the name of the man whose long suffering the book portrays. Job is mentioned by name in the Quran and is considered to be a prophet, though he is not necessarily sent to a particular people with a message (Q 21:83–84, 38:41–44). The Babylonian Talmud declares Job to be a prophet, but debates whether he was originally an Israelite (TB Baba Batra 14b–15a). Eusebius as well as some manuscripts of the Septuagint identify Job with Jobab, the son of Zerah, son of Reuel, son of Esau (Preparation, 9.25, 430d–431; LXX postscript to Job 42:17). Muslim genealogists claim that Job was son of Maws b. Rawh b. Esau b. Isaac b. Abraham, and debate whether he was Israelite or Roman.

The biblical book of Job is difficult to date, but most scholars place it sometime in the post-exilic period based on its language and theme of righteous suffering, which point to a period following the destruction of Yahweh's temple and Babylonian captivity. The exilic prophet Ezekiel also mentions Job (Ezek 14:14). The lack of clear reason given for why Job suffers in the book led later tradition to assume he had done something wicked. Thus, some rabbinic writings see Job as a counselor of the Egyptian pharaoh during the time of the Exodus, who stood silent when the pharaoh decided to kill all the Israelite first-born males (Yashar Shemot, 138b; Targum Yerushalmi to Exod 2:23). Other Jewish sources record a debate over the date of Job, with some placing him in the time of the patriarchs, others in the time of Moses, the Judges, Solomon, the Babylonian king Nebuchadnezzar II, and the Persian king Xerxes (TB Baba Batra 14b–15a).

The story of Job has the same basic outline in the Quran and Bible and involves a man who, though "blameless and upright" (Job 1:1), undergoes intense suffering after Satan inflicts upon him the loss of his family, home, and health. In rabbinic tradition, Satan's accusation coincides with New Year's Day and his affliction is abetted by the demoness Lilith (*see also* LILITH), also identified as the Queen of Sheba (Targum to Job 1:6, 1:15). In the Bible, when news of Job's suffering reaches his friends, they come to visit. Their several lengthy poetic dialogues with Job, which are framed by a prosaic prologue (Job 1:1–2:13) and epilogue (Job 42:7–16), are often argumentative, if not accusatory in character, and comprise most of the book. They accuse Job of having sinned, having little patience, and questioning God's ways. In the end, however, despite being scolded for his self-righteous attitude, Yahweh vindicates Job from a tempest and restores to him double what he once had (Job 42:10) and reprimands his friends for not speaking the truth (Job 42:7).

The Quran contains no discussion of Job's friends, but Muslim exegesis explains that Job had brothers who argued about the cause of his affliction, and a wife who did everything she could to stay by his side. The Quran makes brief mention of cold water that comes from the ground (Q 38:42), water that Job is to drink and use for washing. Ibn Kathir reports that God ordered Job to wash himself in this water as a means for healing his sickness. The Quran states that God returned to Job his family and "another like them" (Q 21:84, 38:43), which Muslim exegetes take to mean that God restored Job's health, family, and wealth twofold as a reward for being steadfast. Q 38:44 asserts that God found Job to be steadfast and an upright worshipper.

JOEL. Book of the minor prophets named after a prophet whose life and date are unknown. The book's mention of Greeks in Joel 3:6 is of little help in dating the book since the Greeks were known to have had access to the region already in Mycenaean times. The book's references to Judah's suffering and eschatological victory (Joel 3:19), and to the standing temple (Joel 1:14, 2:17), however, appear to place it in the post-exilic period, after the construction of the second temple. Joel's prophecy describes an invasion of locusts, which he interprets as a foreshadowment of the Day of Yahweh (Joel 2:2). He calls upon the people to repent and promises that in the future Yahweh will make agricultural yields abound, and that he will pour out his spirit on all humankind so that they again receive visions and divine dreams (Joel 2:28–29).

JOHN CHRYSOSTUM (c. 347–407 CE). Bishop of Constantinople (398–407) and author of a number of sermons that include much exegetical material on the book of Genesis and other biblical books, often avoiding allegorical interpretations. The Greek name Chrysostomos means the "Golden-mouthed," and was given to John because of the eloquence of his writing.

JOHN OF DAMASCUS (650–749 CE). Last of the "Cappadocian Fathers," John of Damascus was born in Damascus to an Arab family and was an official of the Umayyad Caliphate before retiring to the Mar Saba Monastery near Jerusalem. He is known for his work *Fount of Knowledge*, in which he catalogs heresies (including Islam) and has 100 chapters on theological questions pertaining to Christianity. His section on Islam makes reference to sections of the Quran that are not attested in any Muslim source.

JOHN THE BAPTIST. Prophet mentioned in the Quran only briefly in connection with his birth to Zechariah (Q 3:38–41, 19:1–15, 21:89–90). In the New Testament, John is responsible for the baptism of Jesus (Matt 3:11–17), and is sometimes identified with the prophet

Elijah (John 1:21). Muslim exegetes report, on the authority of Christian sources (e.g., Luke 1:36), that John was related by birth to Jesus, the father of John (Zechariah) and the father of Mary (Imran) marrying two sisters. Mary's mother is identified as Hannah, perhaps a reference to the biblical Hannah, mother of the prophet Samuel, and the name of John's mother is given as Elizabeth (see also Luke 1:13). John was born six months before Jesus, and later met Jesus and baptized him. It also is related that Jesus sent John out with 12 disciples, and among their teachings was the prohibition of marriage to a niece.

Muslim sources associate the martyrdom of John (Matt 14:1–12, Mark 6:16–29) with the destruction of Jerusalem by Nebuchadnezzar. Muslim exegesis of Q 17:4–8 narrates how the king of the Israelites killed John because the king desired to marry his own niece, a practice that John forbade (cf., Matt 14:3–4). Following John's death his blood is said to have boiled, and it was not possible to soak up the blood with sand, until it covered all of the city to the city walls. The blood only stopped boiling after Nebuchadnezzar destroyed the city. Josephus also reports that Herod killed John because of his growing popularity, and the Jews believed that the destruction of Herod's army was God's punishment for Herod killing John. The passage from Josephus appears also in Eusebius, and is followed by what is thought to be an apocryphal quotation from Josephus concerning the crucifixion and resurrection of Jesus.

JONAH. Name of a prophet and brief prophetic book that tells the story of Jonah and his prophetic mission. Jonah ben Amittai is known in historical texts as living in the eighth century BCE (2 Kgs 14:25), but the book of Jonah dates no earlier than the sixth century BCE. Suyuti identifies Jonah as the son of Mattai, but other Muslim exegetes claim that Jonah is the name of the people to whom the prophet was sent (Q 10:98, but Q 37:139). Jonah also is called "He of the Fish" [Ar. Dhu al-Nun] (Q 21:87) and "Person of the Fish" [Ar. Sahib al-Hut] (Q 68:48).

The biblical book of Jonah tells the story of the prophet Jonah, who upon being commanded by God to prophecy the destruction of Nineveh, the Assyrian capital, promptly boarded a ship and fled westward. While in the midst of the sea, the ship was caught in a tempest. The crew then singled out Jonah as the ultimate cause and tossed him overboard, at which time a great fish swallowed him. Jonah then prayed to Yahweh, who caused the fish to vomit him onto dry land. His mission in Nineveh was a success—not only did the Ninevites repent, but their animals did too. Yet, feeling that God should have destroyed Nineveh, Jonah became frustrated, and was rebuked by God for his lack of mercy by way of an allegory involving the miraculous growth of a tall gourd-like plant. This striking criticism of the prophet makes the book unique among the Bible's prophetic works.

The same basic story is found in the Quran and Muslim exegesis (Q 10:98, 21:87–88, 37:139–148, 68:48–50). Q 37:139–148 provides the fullest narrative, mentioning Jonah's flight to the ship, the casting of lots to ascertain who caused the storm, the fish's swallowing and vomiting of Jonah, and the growing of the plant that provided shade for Jonah. Muslim exegetes add to this that the fish that swallowed Jonah was swallowed by an even bigger fish, and the disagreement over the length of time Jonah spent in the fish's belly. The latter tradition may be reflected in Jewish midrashic expositions on Jonah, which describe him as entering the belly of one fish, only to be transferred to another (Pirqe d'Rabbi Eliezer 10). Ibn Kathir reports that the plant that provided shade for Jonah was a gourd, and that the flesh of the plant (including its seeds and shells) could be eaten uncooked. Other exegetes claim that what comforted Jonah was a special animal that came twice a day, giving Jonah its milk.

Bukhari and others record hadith reports from the prophet Muhammad to the effect that Jonah was the best worshipper of God. Other Muslim exegetes relate that the prophet Muhammad said Jonah had a special invocation that he used to call upon God from within the belly of the fish, an invocation that always receives a response from God.

JOSEPH. Son of Jacob and his wife Rachel (Gen 30:24) and eponymous ancestor of the tribes Ephraim and Manasseh (Num 1:32, 13:11). Initially these tribes of Joseph settled the central region of Canaan (Judg 1:22), with part of the tribe of Manasseh settling east of the Jordan River (Num 36:1, 36:5). In later works, however, the appellation "tribes of Joseph" is used of the northern region of Israel (Amos 5:15; Deut 27:12; Ezek 37:16; Ps 80:2).

Elements of the Joseph story have been found in a number of diverse cultures, and scholars have argued for various origins of the story. Of all the stories of the prophets, the story of Joseph is perhaps also the most widespread and frequently retold. The biblical account of Joseph is found in Genesis 37–47 and is considered to be a masterpiece of Hebrew literature. The Quran dedicates an entire surah (Q 12) to the Joseph story (though he is not mentioned by name elsewhere), and Joseph is the only figure, prophetic or otherwise, in the Quran whose story is the sole focus of a surah. Q 12:3 declares that the Joseph story is "the best of the stories" that God has revealed.

The basic outline of the Joseph story in the Bible and Quran agree, though the details differ and the focus of interpretation by Jews and Muslims tends to diverge. Jewish (and Christian) exegetes have seen in Jacob and Joseph the loss (symbolic death) and recovery (symbolic resurrection) of the beloved son, a motif also found in the stories of Abraham and his son Isaac. In his exegesis of Q 3:93, the Muslim exegete Qurtubi similarly reports that Jacob was attacked by God because he made a vow and then failed to sacrifice his son Joseph. The close relationship between Jacob and Joseph is reflected in Jewish exegesis, which says that of all of Jacob's sons, Joseph most closely resembled his father. Joseph is said to be the recipient of the secret prophetic knowledge that was passed from Shem and Eber, through Jacob (Genesis Rabbah 84:5, 87:8; Zohar 1, 180a, 182b, 222a). Q 12:6 states that God selected Joseph to receive special knowledge and perfected his blessing upon Joseph as he had perfected it on Abraham and Isaac.

The story of Joseph does not easily conform to the story of other prophets in the Quran. Joseph is not sent as a prophet to a particular people, nor does he proclaim a particular message. His story does not appear to relate directly to events occurring in the life of the prophet Muhammad. Nevertheless, Joseph does experience visions and is given the ability to interpret these, as well as the visions of others. Q 12:22 states that God gave Joseph "authority and knowledge," the marks of prophethood. The dramatic tension of the biblical story is absent in the Quranic account, as it is clear that Jacob knows from the beginning that Joseph is not dead (Q 12:13, 12:18, 12:87). Muslim exegetes stress that as a prophet, Jacob could not have been duped by his sons, nor would he have forgotten the initial dream that God gave Joseph, but which had not yet been fulfilled.

Some later Jewish and Muslim scholars regard the Joseph story as an allegory for the human soul. Joseph is the ideal soul to whom knowledge of its true divinity is revealed, but which must suffer patiently through the vicissitudes of earthly existence without denying God or allowing misfortune to cloud its focus on its origins and end with God. As in the Bible, the Quran makes it clear that Joseph was not at fault in the incident with his master's wife, but he is imprisoned nonetheless (Q 12:28–29, 12:35). Q 12:30–34 includes a scene of women cutting their hands because of Joseph's beauty, a scene found in later Jewish sources as well (Tanhuma Wa-yesheb 5). It is reported that the prophet Muhammad said Joseph was the most noble of people ever created, and Ibn al-Arabi interprets Joseph's beauty and nobility to mean that he was the perfect human being.

JOSEPH AND ASENATH. Story of Joseph's conversion and marriage to Asenath, the Egyptian daughter of Potiphar, which constitutes an expansion of the reference in Gen 41:45. The text is extant in numerous Greek manuscripts and various other recensions, and dates as early as the first century CE, though the earliest Greek manuscript dates to the 10th century. The earliest textual evidence for the text appears in the *Church History* of Pseudo-Zacharias, written at the end of the sixth century CE. Latin recensions of the story date to the 13th century, and the Ethiopian versions probably are based on a lost Arabic recension.

The text is divided into two parts. Part one (ch. 1–21) contains the story of Asenath's conversion on account of her desire for Joseph. In this section, Asenath renounces idolatry, is visited by a heavenly messenger who gives her the food of angels to eat, and is wed to Joseph. Part two (ch. 22–29) tells the story of the jealousy of the pharaoh's son who joins forces with some of Joseph's brothers to kidnap Asenath. During the foiled attempt, the pharaoh is fatally wounded, forcing Joseph to become the new king of Egypt.

Though Muslim sources do not record Joseph's marriage to Asenath, they explain that after Potiphar's death, Joseph was married to his wife, the woman who had originally tried to seduce Joseph. Muslim and Jewish sources provide the name Zuleikah for Potiphar's wife, and the romance of Joseph and Zuleikah is retold many times in a variety of exegetical and folkloric contexts.

JOSEPH FALAQUERA (1225–1290 CE). Shem Tov ben Joseph Falaquera (Palquera) was a Spanish Jewish thinker who combined Arabic,

Greek, and Jewish philosophical concepts in his work. Among his various writings are a treatise on dreams [Heb. Iggeret ha-Halom], Aristotelian ethics, the psychology of Ibn Sina, and a commentary on the philosophical work of Rambam. His works are known for their attempts to harmonize philosophy and religion, in particular demonstrating that the Bible and Talmud are consistent with rationalism.

JOSEPHUS, FLAVIUS (37–100 CE). Jewish historian and a military commander against the Roman army in the Galilee. While stationed there he was taken prisoner and brought to Rome where he eventually became an interpreter (and apparent Roman collaborator) under the Roman emperor Vespasian. After the destruction of Jerusalem and its temple in 70 CE he remained in Rome, where he wrote several works including *The Jewish War*, *The Jewish Antiquities*, *The Life*, and *Against Apion*, each of which are invaluable historical resources. His apparent collaboration with the Romans earned him ill repute in Jewish circles, and he is not even mentioned in the Talmud. His *Jewish Antiquities* is most relevant for the study of biblical prophecy. Completed in about 93 CE, this collection of "twenty books" sometimes mentions a prophet's intervention in connection with events on which the Bible is silent. With the exception of the prophets Hosea, Joel, Amos, Obadiah, Habakkuk, Zephaniah, and Malachi, Josephus discusses the biblical prophets with some frequency, placing the greatest emphasis on Jonah, Nahum, Isaiah, and especially Jeremiah. In many of his accounts Josephus diverges considerably from the biblical record, and he tends to pass over their symbolic actions and eschatological predictions. Many of the details found in Josephus also appear in other early Jewish and Christian exegesis.

JOSHUA. Name of Moses' successor, understood as a prophet by Muslim exegetes, and name of the sixth book of the Hebrew Bible, which narrates the calling and military exploits of Joshua. The highly epicized style and exaggerated claims of the biblical book of Joshua, and the difficulty of matching the narrative to archaeological remains, make it difficult to accept it as historically reliable, and it is probable that it underwent some editing in the post-exilic period. The literary portrait of Joshua is an evident attempt to parallel the life and mission of Moses. Like Moses, Joshua receives a theophoric experience in which he is asked to remove his sandals (Josh 5:15). Joshua too must send spies to reconnoiter the land (Josh 2:1), and like Moses, Joshua parts a body of water (Josh 3:15–17). Large parts of the book are concerned with the allotment of Canaanite land to the Israelite tribes.

Joshua is not mentioned by name in the Quran, but the exegetes know him as Joshua b. Nun b. Ephraim b. Joseph b. Jacob b. Isaac b. Abraham, and also see him as the prophetic successor to Moses. Tabarsi relates that Joshua was one of the 12 spies who had gone to reconnoiter the land who, along with Caleb, kept his promise not to tell the Israelites about the giants inhabiting the land (Q 5:20–26). Joshua and Caleb are said to be the only two people among the Israelites who began and did not die during the 40 years of wandering in the wilderness.

The Quran refers to the conquest of a city that is taken to be either Jerusalem or Jericho, that may reflect traditions concerning Joshua's conquest of Canaan (Q 2:58–59, 7:161–162). Reports given on the authority of the prophet Muhammad state that the sun stood still for Joshua so that he could conquer this city, a detail that is reminiscent of the story of Joshua's battle at Gibeon (Josh 10:12). Other accounts refer to Joshua's whittling down of his fighting force, a reference that recalls the scene in Q 2:249 and the biblical account of the judge Gideon (Judges 7).

JUBILEES. Apocryphal text, also known as the "Little Genesis," which purports to have been revealed to Moses and offers an account of the events described in Genesis and Exodus in units of "jubilees" (seven weeks of years = 49 years). Jub 6:22 refers to the "book of the first law," suggesting that Jubilees was regarded as the book of the "second law" transcribed from immutable heavenly tablets (Jub 6:23–31). These laws were transcribed by Enoch, passed to Methuselah, Lamech, Noah, Shem, Abraham, and Jacob, who passed them on to his son Levi and his descendants, the Levitical priesthood (*see also* LEVITE).

The entire text of Jubilees is extant in four Ethiopic manuscripts, the best preserved of which dates to the 16th century CE. Scholars speculate that the text was composed originally in Hebrew and then translated into Greek, but apart from some Hebrew fragments found among the Dead Sea Scrolls, no complete Hebrew or Greek text has survived. A Latin translation containing roughly one-fourth of the text appears in a palimpsest, and there is evidence of a Syriac translation in a number of citations found in an anonymous Syriac chronicle.

In addition to retelling many of the stories from creation to Moses, Jubilees reflects a greater concern for rituals and calendrical festivals than do the accounts in Genesis and Exodus. The text describes many of the patriarchs as offering sacrifices or giving instructions about rituals and purity laws. Jubilees also includes many expansions and interpretations that parallel other exegetical sources.

JUDGES. The biblical book of Judges contains the stories of 12 judges, charismatic military leaders who rose up in times of national emergency during the period 1150–1020 BCE. The 12 judges who are featured are Ehud, Deborah, Gideon, Abimelech, Jotham, Tola, Jair, Jephthah, Ibzan, Elon, Abdon, and Samson. Though they are 12 in number, they do not correspond to each of the 12 tribes of Israel. The book's portrait of these judges becomes increasingly less flattering as the stories proceed, thus bringing into relief a political tension between groups that advocate a continuation of the status quo, with its reliance on ad hoc military rule, and groups that desire monarchic rule. The book underscores this tension periodically and at its end (Judg 21:25) by the phrase, "In those days there was no king in Israel; everyone did what was right in their own eyes," an ambiguous line that can be interpreted positively or negatively. Though clearly filled with ancient traditions, the stories of the judges appear to have been edited to bring them into line with theological concerns of a later day, perhaps during the united monarchy or following the Babylonian destruction of the temple in 586 BCE.

Muslim sources such as Ibn Ishaq and Tabari refer to Samson as a prophetic figure who fought with the jawbone of a camel (Judg 15:15 refers to the animal as an ass) and had long hair, but they place his activities in the period following Jesus. Muslim exegetes also conflate the account of Gideon's attack on the Midianites and Amalekites in Judges 7 with Saul's battle against the Philistines in which David defeats Goliath (1 Samuel 17, Q 2:249).

JURHUM. Tribe closely associated with Mecca in the ancient period. The tribe is not mentioned in the Quran, but appears in Muslim exegetical remarks on the story of Ishmael and Hagar, especially Q 14:35–41. According to Muslim exegetes, when Ishmael and Hagar first arrived in Mecca the place was abandoned until after the well of Zamzam was uncovered and a group of the Jurhum settled there with Ishmael and Hagar. It is said that Ishmael learned Arabic from the Jurhum, and that he was the prophet sent to them, along with the Amalekites and the people of Yemen. Pre-Islamic poetry attributes the building of the Ka'bah to the Jurhum and the Quraysh, and the Roman geographer Pliny mentions an Arab tribe by the name of Charmai, which may be a reference to the Jurhum. Muslim genealogists identify the Jurhum as descendants of Qahtan, possibly identified with the biblical Joktan [Heb. Yoqtan] son of Eber (Gen 10:25–26). Some Muslim exegetes equate the name Joktan with Jokshan, the son of Abraham and Keturah, mentioned in Gen 25:2–3, thus linking the Jurhum to the Arab tribes who descended from the eponymous sons of Abraham and Keturah. Nevertheless, philological difficulties make this identification tenuous. Muslim exegetes also associate the Jurhum with the Amalekites located in Southern Arabia, the Hijaz and in Syria in Muslim sources, though biblical sources place the Amalekites in the territory of Edom (Gen 36:15–16).

JUST BALANCE. The Just Balance or "Merilo Pravednoe" is the title of a collection of East Slavonic writings that dates no later than the 13th century CE. This collection contains brief excerpts from Enoch materials that closely parallel chapters 42–65 of 2 Enoch.

– K –

KA'BAH. Cubical structure in the center of the mosque in Mecca, rebuilt many times, and said to have been first founded by Adam. Muslim sources refer to the Ka'bah as the "temple" or "house of God" [Ar. bayt Allah], which is the common designation for temples in Semitic languages (*see also* TEMPLE). The Ka'bah is the focus of Muslim worship, being the object that worshippers faced during prayer and around which circumambulations take place during the yearly pilgrimage. Using the temple as the direction of prayer and site of pilgrimage is widespread in other Near Eastern and Asian cultures as well. According to Muslim sources, the Ka'bah is the earthly counterpart to the throne of God in heaven around which angels circumambulate in praise of God.

In one corner of the Ka'bah is the "black stone," which worshippers address, touch, and kiss during the pilgrimage to Mecca. Muslim sources report that Adam brought this stone down with him from the Garden of Eden when he fell to the earth. At that time the stone was white. The blackness of the stone is attributed to the sins of humanity, and it is said that when the pilgrims touch the black stone their sins are forgiven. Other Muslim sources consider the black stone to be a meteorite.

The Ka'bah of Adam is said to have been a tent he pitched on the spot after he was expelled from paradise. This parallels the account found in other apocryphal texts such as the Life of Adam and Eve (1–4). The terminology used for the tent [Ar. 'arish, qubbah] is also used for the "Tent of Meeting" constructed by the Israelites for housing the Ark of the Covenant in the wilderness of wandering. Other Muslim sources state that the original Ka'bah was made of gems or crystal and was sent down to earth from paradise by God. This special Ka'bah was later raised up, during the deluge, to the middle heavens directly above the site of the earthly Ka'bah and directly below the location of God's throne. The raised Ka'bah is called the "inhabited" or "visited temple" [Ar. bayt al-ma'mur] since it is said to be visited by 70,000 angels every day praising God.

Muslim sources report that Abraham rebuilt the Ka'bah. The Quran relates that God instructed Abraham and Ishmael to reestablish the sanctuary at Mecca and the site as a place of pilgrimage (Q 2:125–129, 22:26–27). Muslim sources report that Abraham was guided by the Sakinah, or "presence of God," which appeared as a cloud hovering over the spot of the Ka'bah. It also is reported that Abraham built the Ka'bah out of the materials of five mountains, and that he was visited by Dhu al-Qarnayn during its building.

In the time of the prophet Muhammad the Ka'bah is said to have been filled with idols worshipped by the various tribes who lived in or visited Mecca. These idols were cleansed from the Ka'bah by Muhammad, and the sanctuary at Mecca was returned to the role it had been assigned in the time of Abraham.

Throughout Islamic history the Ka'bah has been destroyed, rebuilt, and renovated numerous times. Ibn Kathir preserves a tradition that the Ka'bah built by Abraham was much bigger than the structure that was rebuilt after the death of the prophet Muhammad by the Umayyad Caliph Abd al-Malik. It is also reported that early Muslim authorities were hesitant to encourage the renovation of the Ka'bah fearing that different rulers might embellish it for their own purposes. Many of the accounts of the destruction and rebuilding of the Ka'bah parallel the destruction and rebuilding of the temple in Jerusalem. The eschatological significance of the destruction of the temple and Ka'bah, and the return of a "new" one to the original site, is also similar in Jewish, Christian, and Islamic accounts (*see also* NEW JERUSALEM).

KA'B AL-AHBAR (d. 652 CE). Abu Ishaq b. Mati b. Haysu was a Yemenite Jew who converted to Islam shortly after the death of the prophet Muhammad. Some scholars speculate that "Ka'b" is derived from "'Aqiba" or "Ya'qub" and that the epithet "Ahbar" is a plural form of the word "Hibr" related to a Hebrew word [Heb. haber] used for "Rabbi." Muslim sources report that Ka'b al-Ahbar accompanied Umar b. al-Khattab to Jerusalem in 636 CE, and that he was asked by Mu'awiyah to serve in Damascus. He settled in Hims where he died. He is best known as the source of many Quran interpretations derived from the Bible and South Arabian sources, and for the introduction of traditions concerning the prophets and Israiliyat stories.

KAHIN. An Arabic pejorative term used in the Quran and Muslim exegesis for a soothsayer or false prophet. The term had a much richer significance in pre-Islamic Arabian religious contexts where it was used as a general designation for important cult officials and diviners. Etymologically, the Arabic term is related to the Hebrew term [kohen] that denotes an Israelite priest of Yahweh. Many of the functions of the pre-Islamic Arabian kahin also are associated with the prophethood of Muhammad.

In pre-Islamic Arabia, the kahin often was associated with belief in Jinn, the cult of ancestors, localized divinities, pilgrimage shrines, astral divinities, and both bloody and non-bloody sacrifices. Historically, the range of activities linked to the kahin are roughly those of other Near Eastern priest and prophet figures: cult official, diviner, and prophet.

The term *kahin*, when used of a diviner, refers to two types: ecstatic and non-ecstatic. Ecstatic divination and prophecy involved secret knowledge and sometimes possession by Jinn. Kahins are identified with a number of other names used for diviners based on the types of techniques employed. Non-ecstatic divination included providing oracles and bringing laws from the gods.

As guardian of the sanctuary, the kahin is described both as the founder of the sanctuary and as the caretaker. The founding of sanctuaries also relates to prophetic figures such as Adam, Abraham, and Muhammad, but also to local holy men in pre-Islamic Arabia. The kahin is called the "caretaker of the deity" [Ar. rabb dhi ilah] responsible for the upkeep of the sanctuary, a duty that involved keeping the keys to the sanctuary and carrying the portable shrine (*see also* LEVITE). Some scholars see the kahin's role as caretaker of the sanctuary as a distant echo of earlier ancient Near Eastern associations of the king as the "gardener," the one responsible for tending to the sacred garden with its tree and water of life. As cult officiant, the kahin both initiated and presided over ritual activities. This included the demarcation of sanctuaries and their regional rites, including various pilgrimages.

KARAISM. An eighth-century CE Jewish religious movement originating in Iran that held the Hebrew Bible as the only authoritative source of religious doctrine and practice. Consequently, Karaites stood in opposition to rabbinic Judaism, the Talmud, and the doctrine of Oral Torah. Originally, Karaites were known as Ananites, after Anan ben David, the sect's first major representative, but in the centuries that followed the term *Karaite* was adopted in order to highlight the importance that the movement placed on individual reading of Scripture [Heb. qara' for "read, recite"]. Though the movement was never very large (small groups of Karaites still exist today), Karaism eventually made its way west to Syria and especially Spain. Karaites also were known for their stringent asceticism, rejection of traditional Jewish ritual items, and marriage restrictions.

KASHANI (d. 1580 CE). Mulla Fath Allah Kashani was known as a jurisprudent, theologian, and Quran commentator though little is preserved about his life. He is known for his work on a collection of discourses from Ali b. Abi Talib, and three Quran commentaries (two in Persian and one in Arabic). The Arabic Quran commentary was completed in 1569 CE and contains Shi'i traditions along with references from earlier exegetes such as Zamakhshari and Tabarsi.

KEDAR. Second son of Ishmael and eponymous ancestor of a large tribal grouping that in the Bible often refers generically to nomadic peoples of the Arabian desert (Isa 21:17, Song 1:5). The tribe of Kedar was the most powerful of the Ishmaelite tribes whose activities were centered in northern Arabia from the eighth to fourth centuries BCE. The name is preserved in Assyrian and Neo-Babylonian texts, and appears as a personal name in Safaitic, Thamudic, Nabataean, and Arabic contexts.

There are a number of references to Kedar in the prophetic books of the Bible. Jeremiah uses the name in a merism in which the people of Kedar occupy the eastern edge of the world, and the people of Cyprus [Heb. kittim] the western edge (Jer 2:10). Jer 49:28–33 contains a prophecy addressed to Kedar and the kingdoms of Hazor, which some scholars see as a reference to Nebuchadnezzar II's campaign against the Arabs in 599 BCE. Several biblical passages seem to identify Kedar with the people of Edom (Ezek 27:21; Isa 21:16–17, 42:11), and the Septuagint on Isa 42:11 refers to the "rock people" as the inhabitants of Petra. Psalm 120 refers to the "tents of Kedar" in a way that suggests the lands east of Jerusalem. The Talmud records a tradition in which the people of Kedar worship water (TB Ta'anith 5b), and a discussion about whether sheep from Kedar were acceptable for sacrifice (TB Avodah Zarah 24a).

KETURAH. Third wife of Abraham and mother of the sons who were regarded as eponymous ancestors of significant Arabian and Aramaean peoples. The Bible lists the sons as Zimram, Jokshan, Medan, Midian, Ishbak, and Shuah (Gen 25:1–4). Jokshan is the father of Sheba and Dedan. The descendants of Dedan are the Asshurites, the Letushim, and the Leummim. The descendants of Midian are Ephah, Epher, Hanoch, Abida, and Eldaah. Because of the relation of these descendants to the Arabian incense trade in the eighth century BCE, some scholars derive the name Keturah [Heb. Qetura] from the word "incense" [Heb. qetoret]. Some Arab genealogists see Jokshan [Ar. Qahtan] as the ancestor of the southern Arabs.

Muslim exegetes state that all prophets after Abraham come from the descendants of Abraham. The prophet Muhammad descends from Ishmael, the Israelite prophets from Isaac, and the prophet Shuayb from Midian the son of Abraham and Keturah. Some Muslim genealogists claim Midian was the son of the daughter of Lot, and others link Shuayb to Abraham through both Sarah and Keturah by making Shuayb's genealogy to be Shuayb b. Issachar b. Midian b. Abraham (cf., Gen 30:17–18).

KHIDR. A prophet not mentioned by name in the Quran, but identified as the mysterious "servant of God" whom Moses finds and accompanies in Q 18:65–82. Muslim exegetes report differing opinions regarding the genealogy of Khidr and his status as a prophet. According to Ibn Hajar, Khidr was a prophet because he is described in the Quran as knowing more than the prophet Moses. Others claim that he was an angel who took human form or a saint, but not a prophet. It is reported also that he was one of the people who believed in Abraham and was with him in Babylon, and others say he was the son or the grandson of one of the pharaohs. Others say that he is the prophet Jeremiah. Those who claim Khidr is a prophet and is the one mentioned in Q 18:65–82 also maintain that, unlike the other prophets mentioned in the Quran, Khidr was not sent to a particular people but appeared only to interact with Moses.

Muslim exegetes explain that there are four prophets who have not yet died, two of whom live on the earth and two of whom live in heaven. The two who live on the earth are Khidr and Elijah, and the two in heaven are Idris and Jesus. Tabari explains that Khidr is Iranian and Elijah is Israelite, but that the two meet every year on their way to the pilgrimage in Mecca. The traditions of Khidr's immortality may also be related to the role of his character in the stories of Abraham and Dhu al-Qarnayn. According to some Muslim exegetes and historians, Dhu al-Qarnayn was the one who passed judgment in favor of Abraham at the well of Beersheba (Gen 21:22–34), and Khidr is said to have been over the vanguard of Dhu al-Qarnayn and was the one who drank from the water of life without knowing it. In another account, Khidr is described as being lowered into the sea to find its bottom, a story that is also told of Alexander the Great in some of the Greek recensions of the Alexander Romance. The same motif appears in the epic of Gilgamesh, where Gilgamesh descends to the bottom of the sea to obtain the plant of life. Most of the recensions of the Alexander Romance redacted after the time of the Quran, and the early Muslim commentaries, feature Khidr as one of the companions of Alexander the Great on his journeys to find immortality. The story of the lost fish in Q 18:60–64, which is interpreted to be the resurrection of the fish in the water of life, also is linked to stories in the Alexander Romance.

KINDI (801–862 CE). Abu Yusuf Yaqub b. Ishaq al-Kindi is known as the "Philosopher of the Arabs" and is credited with the introduction of Hellenistic thought into Arabic and Islamic philosophy. Not much is known of Kindi's life except that he was associated with the Abbasid Caliphs al-Ma'mun and al-Mu'tasim, and that he had a son to whom he dedicated some of his treatises. Among his works are several philosophical writings that deal with ideas and specific passages found in the Quran. He also wrote on medicine, mathematics, alchemy, and astronomy. Kindi takes a wide view of the acquisition of knowledge and perfection of the soul, attributing the source of all knowledge to God and explaining that this knowledge either is revealed through prophets or acquired by the human intellect.

KINGS. The title of this book in both the Septuagint and Hebrew Bible reflects its general subject matter, the roughly 400-year span of kings beginning with the death of King David (c. 960 BCE) and coronation of his son Solomon and concluding with the Babylonian exile under the reign of King Jehoiachim (598 BCE). In the Jewish canon, these books appear in the Prophets section, and in the Septuagint they comprise the third and fourth books of Kings (1 and 2 Samuel being the first and second books of Kings). The latter division and order is adopted by the Vulgate and later derivative translations.

In addition to providing a theologically charged historical outline of the later monarchies, the books of Kings describe the construction of Yahweh's temple under Solomon (1 Kings 6–7), the destruction and deportation of the northern tribes by the Assyrians (2 Kgs 17:14–21), and the eventual destruction of Jerusalem and the temple under the Babylonians (2 Kings 25). The book also contains stories about the prophets Elijah, Elisha, and (more briefly) Isaiah, though the historical events depicted in the book of Kings coincide with the lives of a number of other prophets as well (e.g., Amos, Hosea, Micah, Jeremiah, Zephaniah, Nahum, and Habakkuk). Much like in the books of Samuel, the portrait of Israel's kings is not flattering. Following the division of the kingdom into the northern (10 tribes) and southern (Judah and part of Benjamin) with its respective capitals in Samaria and Jerusalem, and respective temples in Dan and Bethel, and Jerusalem, all of the northern kings and most of the Judahite kings receive rebuff for their apostasy. Only the Jerusalemite kings Hezekiah (727–698 BCE) and Josiah (631–609 BCE) appear in a positive light, because of their attempts to centralize worship and follow the covenant established under Moses. The theological reflection on Israel's history, therefore, appears to be the result of a priestly editor of the post-exilic era.

KISA'I (f. 1100s CE). Muhammad b. Abdallah al-Kisa'i is the name attributed to the unknown author of the book known as the *Stories of the Prophets* [Ar. Qisas al-Anbiya'], which includes much information not found in earlier works, nor repeated in later exegesis. Kisa'i often expands on earlier exegesis by elaborating a fuller narrative story line and incorporating folkloric elements from otherwise nonextant oral traditions that often parallel stories from European and other traditions.

KOHEN. Hebrew term used in the Bible with the meaning of "priest." It appears in reference to early Canaanite kings who served also as high priests, such as Melchizedek (Gen 14:18), and occurs in conjunction with the priests of other religions. Examples include the Egyptian priest Potiphera (Gen 41:45), Jethro the father-in-law of Moses (Exod 3:1), Philistine priests (1 Sam 6:2), the priests of the god Baal (2 Kgs 10:19), Dagon (1 Sam 5:5), the Ammonite god Malcham (Jer 49:3), and the Moabite god Kemosh (Jer 48:7).

In Israelite society, the kohen occupied a hereditary position, and was responsible for bearing the Ark of the Covenant and the trumpets (Josh 3:13), and tending to the matters of the cult of Yahweh, especially the sacrifices and rituals of purification. Since the kohen was in charge of the Urim and Thummim (Exod 28:30), he also served in an oracular or divinatory capacity, and even had a role in coronating kings (1 Kgs

1:39). In post-exilic times the kohen also appears to have worked alongside the Levites (1 Chr 16:4–27), but had special status also as a teacher of the law (2 Chr 17:7–9). According to these passages, a kohen must descend from the tribe of Levi and the clan of Aaron (Lev 21:9). In the time of the judges, there is an Ephraimite named Micah bestowing the duties of a kohen upon his son (Judg 17:5) until he was able to locate a descendant of Moses (Judg 17:1). One of the last judges of Israel, Eli, also was called a kohen (1 Sam 1:9).

The Bible mentions a priestly center at Nob (1 Sam 21:2) where David sought refuge while fleeing from Saul. In retaliation, Saul nearly annihilated the entire priesthood (1 Sam 22:11–19). In David's time the Zadoqite family served as priests along with the Levites (2 Sam 15:27). Ezekiel's vision of the future priesthood is similarly reserved for the Zadoqites (Ezek 40:46; *see also* ZADOQITES). The term *high priest* [Heb. kohen gadol] is used first in reference to Aaron's oldest sons (Lev 21:10), but it does not appear to denote a special office until Jehoiada (2 Kgs 12:11), high priest in the reign of King Jehoash (802–786 BCE). Though the kohen was sometimes the object of prophetic rebuke (Hos 4:4), several prophets also served as priests including Isaiah (Isa 6:1), Jeremiah (Jer 1:1), and Ezekiel (Ezek 1:3). The status and influence of the kohen is evident in that the priests were deported along with other important persons to Assyria in 721 BCE (2 Kgs 17:27; *see also* KAHIN).

– L –

LACHISH LETTERS. Series of ostraca discovered at Lachish dating to c. 587 BCE which contain the correspondence of Lachish, a military outpost west of Jerusalem, and its military garrison(s). One of the Lachish letters provides the earliest extrabiblical reference to prophecy in Israel. Unfortunately, the letter is brief and the prophet is anonymous.

LADDER OF JACOB. Expansion on the biblical dream vision of Jacob found in Gen 28:11–22. This text is dated to the first century CE, but it is preserved in two Old Church Slavonic recensions dated to the 13th to 18th centuries, which are part of the *Explanatory Palaia*, a medieval Slavonic retelling of biblical stories. In the text Jacob has a vision of God on the chariot-throne and meets the archangel Sariel who is said to be in charge of interpreting dreams. The angel explains that the ladder symbolizes future events in Israelite history that culminate in the coming of the Messiah. Jewish exegesis on Gen 28:11–22 also records that Jacob's dream of the ladder was a revelation of future events.

LAMENTATIONS. Biblical book of poems written mostly in acrostic form and traditionally attributed to the prophet Jeremiah. Jewish tradition, in fact, sees Lamentations as the scroll mentioned in Jer 36:2 (TB Baba Batra 15a), and the Septuagint appends Lamentations to the end of the book of Jeremiah. Though Jeremiah elsewhere is referenced in the Bible as composing laments (Jer 7:29; 2 Chr 35:25), modern scholars disassociate the book from the prophet. The context for Lamentation appears to be the Babylonian destruction and deportation of Jerusalem in 586 BCE, which the poet accepts as God's punishment, though the poem provides no sure historical reference. The book's traditional association with Jeremiah and its moving call for justice in a time of overwhelming distress contributed to the later perception, in both Judaism and Christianity, that it was a prophetic text.

LATTER PROPHETS. Phrase employed by the rabbis in the Talmud in reference to the post-exilic prophets Haggai, Zechariah, and Malachi whose lives mark the end of prophecy (TB Sotah 48b). The expression is a logical correlate to the phrase "Former Prophets" employed by the biblical prophet Zechariah in reference to those prophets who lived before the destruction of Yahweh's temple in 586 BCE (Zech 1:4, 7:7, 7:12).

LEVI B. GERSHOM (1288–1344 CE). Also known as Ralbag and Gersonides, Rabbi Levi b. Gershom was a French polymath who wrote a series of commentaries on various books of the Bible. His best-known work is a philosophical commentary entitled the *Book of Wars of the Lord* [Heb. Sefer Milhamot Adonai], which includes discussion of the soul, dreams, divination, prophecy, gnosis, cosmogony, and the celestial spheres. In addition he wrote a treatise on mathematics and commentaries on Euclid, Ibn Rushd, Aristotle, and other rabbinic authors.

His commentary on the Bible covers the Pentateuch, Former Prophets, Job, Song of Songs, Ecclesiastes, Ruth, Esther, Proverbs, Daniel, Nehemiah, and Chronicles. His exegesis is rich in philosophical learning and from each of these books he extracted what he saw as the philosophical teachings represented in each.

LEVITE. Israelite priestly tribe descended from Levi, the third son of Jacob (Gen 29:34), whose male members were responsible for preparing the sacrifices, maintaining the tabernacle, and teaching the law (Deut 17:18, 33:10). For their service, the Levites received tithes. In order to perform their duties, they had to be free of physical defects (Lev 21:16–23). The Levites were not given a land allotment like the other tribes of Israel, but instead were given land estates in various cities throughout Israel (Judg 17:7–9, 19:1). Like resident aliens, their lack of tribal land led to the creation of special legal measures for protecting them (Deut 12:12, 14:29, 26:12), and they were not numbered when a census was taken (Num 1:47–49, 26:62).

Some scholars see the Levitical priesthood and its practices as heavily influenced by ancient Egypt. It is noteworthy that the stories in which the Levites emerge as a priestly tribe are set in Egypt during the time of the Exodus, and a great many of the names that appear in the Levitical genealogies are Egyptian. The Ark of the Covenant to which the Levites tended also shares a conceptual overlap with the divine barques transported by Egyptian priests. In this light it is tempting to see the Egyptian priesthood's ritual slaying of the serpent of chaos as a backdrop for the Bible's own dragon of chaos, the Leviathan, a serpent whose very name is etymologically related to that of the Levites.

Prior to the construction of Yahweh's temple, the Levites did not have a monopoly on the tribal priesthoods, for there are references to numerous non-Levites offering sacrifices without condemnation (Judg 17:5; 1 Sam 1:1, 7:1, 7:9; 2 Sam 8:18, 20:26). When the temple of Yahweh was built in Jerusalem, the Levites were joined to the Zadoqite priesthood who had served David in this capacity (2 Sam 15:24–25), and who probably had served as priests in Jerusalem before David conquered it (*see also* ZADOQITES). Later tradition casts the Zadoqites as original to the tribe of Levi (Ezek 40:46; cf., Samuel in 1 Chr 6:18–23).

Initially the Levites, like the Zadoqites (2 Sam 15:27), appear to have served an oracular role (Deut 33:8–10), but with the rise of Classical Prophecy in the eighth century BCE, the oracles increasingly fell into the domain of the prophets. The Levite does not appear to be distinguished from the "high priests" (*see also* KAHIN; KOHEN) in some texts (Deut 17:9; Josh 3:3; Jer 33:18), though elsewhere, especially in texts from the post-exilic period, it is clear that they serve very different functions (Ezra 8:15; Neh 12:23). Whereas the Levites prepare the sacrifice, the high priests offer them, and it is the high priest who has privileged access to the innermost sanctum of the temple. Eventually, the Levites appear as subordinate officials in the temple and as temple musicians (1 Chr 9:18, 15:16, 23:24, 23:28; 2 Chr 5:12).

The use of the term *Levite* not as a proper name, but as a common noun (e.g., Exod 6:19; Num 3:20; Deut 10:8) has led scholars to see the tribal name as a secondary development. The Hebrew root whence the name derives [Heb. lawa] means "join, attach to, twist," and may be attested in a fourth-century BCE Minaean inscription (ancient North Arabic) discovered in Dedan, modern al-'Ula. There the word appears in reference to an object given in pledge to a god. The connection of the Arabian usage to the Levites of Israel appears confirmed by circumstantial evidence. A Babylonian inscription discovered at Dedan states that the Babylonian king Nabonidus (r. 555–539 BCE) populated Dedan with soldiers from the western Levant, which probably included some Jews, and later Muslim writers mention that Dedan had a large Jewish community, and thus the Minaean inscription may reflect earlier Jewish usage.

LEVITICUS. Title of the third book of the Torah (Pentateuch), derived from the Latin of the Vulgate. The book's Hebrew title (Way-Yiqra'), meaning "He (Yahweh) said," is taken from the first word of the first verse. Leviticus details the laws enjoined upon the Levites, the priestly descendants of Levi, the third son of Jacob. Many scholars see the book's composition as the product of post-exilic priestly scribes (c. 500 BCE) concerned with sacrificial and purity laws (Leviticus 1–16, 27), though many of the laws it contains, such as the Holiness Code (Leviticus 17–26), may predate this considerably.

LIFE OF ADAM AND EVE. An account of episodes from the lives of Adam and Eve including an account of their fall, the fall of Satan, Cain and Abel, and the death of Adam. The text is considered to have originated in late antiquity though the earliest Latin manuscripts date to the ninth century CE. The closely related Apocalypse of Moses is attested in Greek manuscripts, the earliest of which dates to the 11th century CE. Elements of the text closely parallel accounts found in Jewish, Christian, and Muslim sources, demonstrating the widespread influence of these traditions and making it difficult to ascertain a more certain date and provenance for the text.

The text opens with Adam and Eve pitching a tent after being expelled from paradise and agreeing to perform penance for their sin of eating from the forbidden tree (1–4). For her penance, Eve must spend 40 days in the Tigris River with the water up to her neck, and Adam must spend the time in the Jordan River (6–8). Eve is seduced by Satan to leave the water earlier (9–10), and Satan gives an account of his being expelled from paradise (11–17). Chapters 18–24 give an account of Cain's birth and his murder of his brother Abel. In chapters 25–29 Adam explains to Seth how he was taken by the archangel Michael back into paradise where he repented to God. Chapters 30–44 describe Adam's final illness. Adam tells his son of his fall from paradise, and to relieve Adam's pain Seth and Eve set off to retrieve the oil that flows from the Tree of Life. Seth and Eve prostrate themselves at the gates of paradise but are not allowed to enter. The archangel Michael informs them that the oil will only be available at the end of time when the Messiah will anoint Adam and all the other believers who are raised from the dead. Four 15th-century manuscripts add here that Seth returned with a sapling or seeds from which grew the tree that supplied the wood for the cross of Jesus. Chapters 45–48 narrate Adam's death and his preparation for burial by the angels. In chapters 49–61 Eve instructs her children to inscribe the story and teachings of Adam and Eve on tablets that are to be preserved for later generations. An appendix, considered to be a later attachment, tells how Seth makes the tablets, which are unable to be read by anyone until the time of Solomon. Among the information Solomon finds on the tablets is the prophecy made by Enoch of the coming of the Messiah.

LILITH. Female demon and baby snatcher mentioned by the prophet Isaiah in conjunction with ruins (Isa 34:14) and known from Mesopotamian texts as a harpy-like figure with a woman's face and wings. The Talmud preserves ancient, and perhaps Babylonian, traditions of Lilith. It describes her as seizing those who sleep alone at night (TB Shabbath 151b), having long hair (TB Erubin 100b), being associated by name with performative medicine (Gittin 69b), and being credited with giving birth to a demon named Hormin (elsewhere called Hormiz) (TB Baba Batra 73a). The Medieval Jewish text known as Alphabet of Ben Sirah describes Lilith as the first wife of Adam.

LISHKAH. Hebrew term denoting a room or chamber of some ritual significance. The lishkah is described as a room in Yahweh's temple where the Rechabites were given wine (Jer 35:2), and a place where prophecies were recited (Jer 36:10). Jeremiah also refers to it as a scribe's room in the king's home (Jer 36:12). In Ezekiel's vision of the future temple it is described as a sacred room facing north (Ezek 46:19) used for eating the sacrificial meal with Yahweh (Ezek 42:13), and for storing the sacred garments (Ezek 44:19). By the time of the second temple it was used as a storeroom or treasury of sorts (Ezra 8:29; Neh 10:38). According to 1 Sam 9:22, the prophet Samuel invited about 30 guests to a sacrificial meal in a lishkah on a high place (1 Sam 9:25). The young Saul was bidden to eat last. The next morning Samuel secretly anointed him king. The word *lishkah* appears cognate with the Greek term for a sacred room associated with oracles (Gk. lesche), for example, the oracle of Apollo at Delphi.

LIVES OF THE PROPHETS. Text known from a number of Greek manuscripts and extant in Syriac, Ethiopic, Latin, and Armenian recensions, detailing the lives of 23 biblical prophets. Many scholars date the composition of the text to the first century CE, though the earliest Greek manuscript dates to the sixth century CE. It is unclear whether the text was originally composed in Hebrew or Aramaic, but no evidence exists from non-Christian sources, and some scholars have proposed that the original was Syriac. Some of the later Greek manuscripts include sections on Zechariah the father of John the Baptist, Simeon of Luke 2:25–35, and John the Baptist. The pre-Christian prophets mentioned include Isaiah, Jeremiah, Ezekiel, Daniel, Hosea, Micah, Amos, Joel, Obadiah, Jonah, Nahum, Habakkuk, Zephaniah, Haggai, Zechariah, Malachi, Nathan, Ahijah, Joad, Azariah, Elijah, Elisha, and Zechariah son of Jehoiada. The early Greek text contains few details not found in the biblical text but expands on the stories of Daniel, Ezekiel, Jeremiah, and Isaiah. Each section provides the prophet's place of origin and his place of death and burial. Many of the sections also include references to prophecies concering the coming of Jesus Christ. Jeremiah's remains are said to have been transferred by Alexander the Great and placed in a circle around Alexandria. The text also contains an account of Jeremiah causing the Ark of the Covenant to be swallowed up by a rock before the temple was destroyed. The episode of Nebuchadnezzar II's therianthropism also is expanded in the section on Daniel. Later Greek manuscripts and other recensions include additional materials.

LOST TRIBES. Expression used in reference to the 10 tribes of Israel that were attacked and deported in 721 BCE by the Assyrian king Sargon II (r. 721–705 BCE). Following their deportation, which is described in 2 Kings 18, they are lost in the historical record, thus becoming the "lost tribes." Later Jewish exegesis asserts that these tribes, or at least some of them, still exist at the edges of the earth, and are supposed to return to Israel at the end of time (*see also* HISTORY OF RECHABITES; PEOPLE OF MOSES).

LOT. Nephew of Abraham who is connected with the destruction of Sodom and Gomorrah and said to be the ancestor of the Moabites and Ammonites. Lot is a prophet in the Quran, sent to the people of Sodom. Gen 11:27–31 and Muslim exegesis make Lot to be the son of Abraham's brother Haran. Muslim genealogists disagree about the relation of Sarah to Lot. Some say that Sarah was the daughter of Haran and thus the sister of Lot. Others claim she was the daughter of Lot.

The Bible does not ascribe a prophetic role to Lot. He travels with Abraham to Canaan (Gen 12:4–5), takes the Jordan plain (Gen 13:1–13), is rescued by Abraham from kings of the East (Gen 14:1–16), and attempts to protect the angels sent to destroy Sodom (Gen 19:1–29). Gen 19:30–38 describes how the daughters of Lot get him drunk, have sex with him, and give birth to sons who become eponymous ancestors of the Moabites and Ammonites. Lot thus appears also in the book of Deuteronomy as having been promised the lands of Moab and Ammon (Deut 2:9, 2:19). Ps 83:3 depicts the Moabites and Ammonites as Israelite enemies, and Deut 23:3–6 prohibits these peoples from Israelite ritual, though Ruth was a Moabite and gave birth to Obed, the grandfather of David (Ruth 4:13–17) and ancestor of Jesus (Matt 1:5). The New Testament compares Lot to Noah as an upright man who was outraged by the sins of his people (2 Pet 2:5–10).

The stories of Lot occupy a relatively large space in the Quran (Q 7:80–84, 11:74–83, 15:61–77, 26:160–175, 27:54–58, 29:28–35, 37:133–138, 51:31–37, 54:33–40). Several of these passages put Lot in a line of successive prophets including Noah, Hud, Salih, and Shuayb. Q 21:71 refers to Lot and Abraham being delivered to the Holy Land, though some Muslim exegetes claim that the land to which they migrated was Mecca. Tabari reports that Lot settled in Jordan and God sent him as a prophet to the people of Sodom.

The people of Sodom are infamous in Muslim exegesis as the worst of sinners, their main sin being sodomy, but also highway robbery and rape. Q 29:32 alludes to Abraham's intercession on behalf of the people of Sodom, and Muslim exegesis explains that the city would only be spared if 10 upright people could be found in it, a tradition that reflects Abraham's words in Gen 18:16–33. The destruction of Sodom is mentioned several times and is described in various terms, as being overturned and as being rained upon with pellets of hardened clay. Q 53:53 refers to the "overturned cities" [Ar. mu'tafikah] destroyed by God, and Muslim exegetes explain that there were five cities destroyed: Sodom, Zeboiyim, Zoar, Gomorrah, and Admah, corresponding to the biblical "cities of the plain" (Gen 14:2–8).

The destruction of Sodom is repeated in later prophetic contexts as a paradigm for God's punishment of sinners. The Wisdom of Solomon (10:7–8) mentions the testimony of Sodom's destruction, as does Philo (de Abrahamo 141). Q 29:35 states that God left the city as a sign, and other passages make this point as well (Q 7:84, 15:77, 26:174). The biblical prophet Jeremiah compares the Jerusalem prophets to Sodom (Jer 23:14), and Isaiah compares the Israelites to Sodom and Gomorrah (Isa 1:10). In Jerome's commentary on Isaiah

1:10, it is said that one of the reasons Isaiah was killed by the Jews was because of this accusation. Some Muslim jurists refer to the raining of hardened clay upon the people of Sodom as justification for the stoning of adulterers.

LOTS. Sanctioned divinatory device, perhaps using stones, sticks, or potsherds, used widely in ancient Israel as a means of ascertaining God's will. Though the exact method by which they were used is uncertain, they appear to have been hidden in the fold of a garment or shaken in a vessel until one emerged. Alternatively, they could have been inscribed with names and selected by reaching into a vessel or by shaking the vessel until one remained. The belief in the accuracy of lots as a tool for ascertaining divine will can be seen by their use for a variety of important purposes.

Lots were used to divide the land of Israel according to tribe (Josh 18:6), select Saul as king (1 Sam 10:19–26), assign particular offices and positions (1 Chr 24:5, 25:8), select a sacrificial goat for the Day of Atonement (Lev 16:8), and allot slaves (Josh 4:3; Obad 11). Lots also were used to determine the guilt of an individual (Josh 7:16–19; 1 Sam 14:41; Jon 1:7; TB Sanhedrin 43b), and for selecting the wood for the sacrificial fire (Neh 10:35). The Israelites' use of Urim and Thummim may be a form of lots (*see also* URIM AND THUMMIM). The use of lots as a method for determining God's will was also used by the early Christians for selecting one of their apostles (Acts 1:26). Lots also continued to be used into the talmudic period (Shabbath 33a, 148b; Yoma 41a), and Jewish tradition states that each angel was assigned to each nation by casting lots (Pirqe d'Rabbi Eliezer 24; Targum Yerushalmi Gen 11:8 and Deut 32:8–9).

The Quran refers to, and prohibits, a special type of game [Ar. maysir] that may be related to divinatory practices involving lots (Q 2:219, 5:90). This game involved shooting colored and notched arrows by which a fixed number of players would claim the dismembered parts of a sacrificed animal. The prohibition of the game in the Quran may be related to the association of the arrows with other forms of belomantic divination (cf., Ezek 21:26).

LUQMAN. Mentioned in the Quran as a wise man (Q 31:12–19), Luqman is closely associated by Muslim exegetes with the story of Hud and the people of Ad. Some genealogists see him as the son of Ad, but other sources include him as one of the delegates sent to Mecca to pray for rain for the people of Ad in the time of the prophet Hud. Tabari reports that the length of Luqman's life was equal to the lifetimes of seven eagles. In the Quran, Luqman gives admonitions to his son, many of which parallel the admonitions found in other ancient Near Eastern literatures, especially those associated with the legendary figure Ahiqar. Muslim scholars also attribute a book of proverbs to Luqman, which is quoted in later sources and said to have been read by Wahb b. Munabbih. Ibn Ishaq records that Muhammad was shown the writings of Luqman, but that he declared that the Quran was better. Most Muslim exegetes claim that Luqman was not a prophet, but a pious and wise man. Other Muslim exegetes identify Luqman with the biblical Balaam. Later sources make Luqman to be the teller of fables, and many of those fables associated with Aesop in Europe were attributed to Luqman. The works of Rumi portray Luqman as a Sufi ascetic who voluntarily becomes a slave. In Turkish folklore Luqman appears as an Arab physician.

– M –

1 AND 2 MACCABEES. Apocryphal works found in the Septuagint and Vulgate but not in the Hebrew Bible. 1 Maccabees appears to have been composed near the end of the second or beginning of the first century BCE. Jerome and Origen claim that the book was originally composed in Hebrew. It consists of 16 chapters recounting the Maccabean revolt against the Hellenistic Seleucid kings of Syria. The focus is on Mattathias and his five sons. According to the account, Mattathias resisted and killed the Seleucid officer who came to impose the prohibition on study of the Torah, keeping the Sabbath, circumcision, and the temple service. Mattathias died around 166 BCE and his sons, headed by Judas, led an armed revolt against the Seleucid military forces and the Hellenizing Jews. Judas and his forces were eventually defeated in 160 BCE when fighting against a much larger force sent by King Demetrius. Judas the Maccabean is portrayed as a hero or savior figure infused with divine inspiration who establishes the rule of his house according to God's will.

2 Maccabees is a composite text consisting of a short introduction, two letters, and an excerpt from the history of Jason of Cyrene, and a conclusion. The letters are thought to have been composed originally in Aramaic or Hebrew and are dated to the last quarter of the second century CE, and the history of Jason of Cyrene was composed in Greek sometime after 160 CE. The first letter (1:1–9) is a brief and general document. The second letter (1:10–2:18) is longer and contains an account of the hiding of the sacred fire, Jeremiah's hiding of the temple vessels, and the contents of Nehemiah's library. The five books that made up the history of Jason of Cyrene are condensed into chapters 3–15 and provide a general overview of the events surrounding the Maccabean Revolt.

3 MACCABEES. Text describing events that occurred roughly 50 years before the Maccabean period and the events recounted in 1 and 2 Maccabees. The text is not included in the Catholic Bible or the Apocrypha since it was not included in the Vulgate, but it is found in other Greek Bibles and in the Syriac Peshitta. There are many Greek manuscripts, Syriac recensions, and an Armenian version.

3 Maccabees is divided into seven chapters. Chapter 1 recounts Ptolemy IV's visit to Jerusalem, his insistence that he enter the temple, and the protestation of the Jews. Chapter 2 describes the prayer of Simeon the high priest and God's punishment of Ptolemy with paralysis. Chapters 3–4 tell how Ptolemy persecuted the Jews of Alexandria, a plan that is frustrated in chapter 5. Chapter 6 contains the prayer of Eliezer, Ptolemy's change of mind, and the Jewish celebration for their deliverance. Chapter 7 contains a letter written by Ptolemy ordering that the Jews not be persecuted, and an account of the return of the Jews to their homes.

4 MACCABEES. An extended account and discourse upon the virtue of the martyrdoms of Eliezer, the mother, and her seven sons. The text is included in several manuscripts of the Greek Bible and the works of Josephus. It is not found in the Vulgate and so is not included in the Catholic Bible and the Apocrypha, but it does appear in the Peshitta.

4 Maccabees is divided into 18 chapters. Chapters 1–3 introduce the material with arguments concerning the virtues of reason and its

compatibility with the Law. Chapter 4 provides an account of the actions of Apollonius and Antiochus against the Jews and the temple in Jerusalem. Chapters 5–7 recount the martyrdom of Eliezer, chapters 8–13 the martyrdom of the seven sons, and chapters 14–16 the martyrdom of the mother. Chapters 17–18 contain additional exhortations on the example of martyrdom and perseverance of faith, citing examples from other stories of the prophets such as the murder of Abel, sacrifice of Isaac, imprisonment of Joseph, and Daniel's incarceration in the lions' den.

The motif of martyrdom is a significant part of prophethood and sainthood in other contexts. Persecution and martyrdom also play an important role in the stories of the Prophet of Ya-Sin (*see also* PEOPLE OF YA-SIN), Isaiah, John the Baptist and his father Zechariah, and Jesus.

MADA'IN SALIH. City identified as the place where the prophet Salih was sent to the people of Thamud. The Quran refers to the houses that the people of Thamud had hewn out of rock (Q 7:74, 26:149, 89:9), which Muslim exegetes associate with the Nabataean tombs and other monuments in the vicinity of the site. Muslim sources refer to the city as al-Hijr and understand this as related to the Arabic root meaning "forbidden" or "sacred" [h-j-r]. There are reports that the prophet Muhammad stopped at al-Hijr on his way to Tabuk and told his followers never to enter the city or drink from its water. It is understood that this prohibition is attached to God's punishment of the people of Thamud, and that the city is left as a reminder of their disobedience. The site of Mada'in Salih is rich in inscriptions in Arabic, Aramaic, Thamudic, Nabataean, Minaean, Lihyanite, Hebrew, Greek, and Latin attesting to its activity on the trade route.

MAGIC. Performative activity, often ritualistic in nature or context, involving the summoning or manipulation of supernatural forces or powers in order to influence people, events, and nature. These performative activities typically combine two components: a spoken (sometimes written) spell and a physical act of praxis (e.g., substitution, molding figurines, burning, burying, cutting, etc.). Often they require the practitioner to enter a state of ritual purity or other specific form of conditioning prior to performing the act.

The purposes of magic are numerous and varied and include obtaining love, power, and wealth; the procurement of fertility (both human and agricultural); the control of atmospheric phenomena; and the annihilation of one's enemies. Though it was formerly seen as a distinct conceptual category from that of religion, contemporary scholars have come to recognize the central and legitimate place of magic in ancient (and many modern) religious systems, and the role of societal mechanisms in determining views on magic. Many scholars see the label "magic" as determined entirely by social construct, and thus informed only by perspective. Often the word *magic* is employed in a pejorative sense to delegitimate another culture's religion; one culture's gods or demiurges often become another culture's demons, and thus, one culture's priests often become another's magicians (*see also* DEMON). The problematic aspects of the term *magic* have led some scholars to see it as devoid of any heuristic value, and to avoid it altogether.

An examination of the term as it is used in English translations of the Bible demonstrates well the problematic nature of the term. The Hebrew words often translated as magician [Heb. mekashef] (Deut 18:10) and [Heb. hartummim] (Exod 8:3) are foreign in origin (the first is Mesopotamian and the second Egyptian). They are treated with ridicule and contempt, though the same terms in Mesopotamia and Egypt denote legitimate religious practitioners, often supported by the central government and religious establishment. Similar remarks could be made with respect to other terms often associated with performative praxis. Witches, exorcists, necromancers, soothsayers, and wizards, as well as foreign prophets, each fall into this category. In biblical narratives, such figures often are pitted against Yahweh or his mantic practitioners, the Israelite prophets, and are discredited by them. Nevertheless, some would argue that there is little, other than the sanction of Yahweh and his worshippers, to differentiate some of the prophetic acts from those of their contemporary "magicians" and "diviners" (*see also* DIVINATION).

Among the stories of the prophets are numerous accounts of "magical" acts or comparisons of "magicians" and prophets. The Quran credits the angels Harut and Marut with bringing magical knowledge to the people of Babylon (Q 2:102). Seth, Shem, Abraham, and Daniel are all associated with astrology. Enoch and Idris are identified with Hermes Trismegistos and the origins of alchemy. Moses competes with Jannes and Jambres, the magicians of Egypt, and parts the Reed Sea (Exod 14:21) with a rod of power (*see also* ROD OF MOSES). There is an extant text entitled the *Sword of Moses*, a book of spells in Hebrew and Aramaic, and this is identified with the "sword of Moses" mentioned in Deut 33:29. The Testament of Solomon states that Solomon had a special ring that allowed him to bind all demons into his service for the building of Jerusalem. In the Bible, Elijah controls the weather (1 Kgs 17:1), Elisha makes an axhead float on water (2 Kgs 6:4–6), and both Elijah and Elisha resurrect dead children (1 Kgs 17:17–23; 2 Kgs 4:34–35). Daniel is compared to the magicians of Babylonia and is able to read secret writing on the wall. In fact, Dan 4:6 refers to him as "chief magician." Jesus, too, is closely associated with magic as evidenced by the accusations of this by some pagan polemicists in late antiquity.

The Quran mentions magic or sorcery [Ar. sihr, sihir] frequently as a common accusation made against prophets and their revelations. The accusation is made specifically against Abraham (Q 43:30), Moses and Aaron (Q 10:76, 27:13, 28:36), Jesus (Q 5:110, 61:6), and the prophet Muhammad (Q 74:24). The pharaoh accuses Moses of teaching magic to the Egyptians (Q 26:49), but the term also denotes the deception practiced by the Egyptian pharaoh in the story of Moses (Q 10:81). The label also is applied generally against prophets and their signs (Q 21:3, 34:43, 37:10, 46:7), their revealed books (Q 6:7), and God (Q 11:7, 52:15, 54:2). It seems to be a reality in other passages (Q 7:116), though placed in contrast to the "signs" of God. (*See also* ALCHEMY; ASTRONOMY AND ASTROLOGY; NECROMANCY; TERAPHIM).

MAGOG. Nation described by the prophet Ezekiel (Ezek 38:2, 38:14–22, 39:6), led by a king named Gog (also called the chief prince of Meshech and Tubal), that comes to attack Israel. It is not clear in the Ezekiel passage whether this battle refers to the eschaton, but since the name Gog [Akk. gagu] appears in Assyrian records as a king of a mountain tribe north of Assyria, an eschatological reading seems unlikely. In Gen 10:2, Magog also appears in the genealogy of Japheth, as the grandson of Noah (see also 1 Chr 1:5). Nevertheless, talmudic tradition reads Ezekiel's prophecy of the wars against Gog and Magog as a reference to the eschaton (TB Shabbath 118a), and understands Psalm 2 as a reference to the rebellion of Gog and Magog against God and the Messiah. The Talmud also tells the story of a man's discovery of a text written in Hebrew and Aramaic that places the war against Gog between God's battle against great sea monsters and the rule of the Messiah (TB Sanhedrin 97b). The New Testament also cites Gog and Magog in reference to the eschatological battle between God and the great dragon, Satan (Rev 20:8). The Quran describes Dhu al-Qarnayn's building of a wall to hold back Gog and Magog until they are set loose upon the earth at the end of time (Q 18:93–101).

MAHDI. Arabic term referring to the "guide" or "savior" who will come to earth at the end of time and usher in an era of peace and justice. There are numerous traditions, many conflicting, in both Sunni and Shi'i sources regarding the messianic figures who are to appear on earth at the end of time.

Muslim sources list and describe the signs of the coming of the Mahdi. They state that before the Mahdi comes the world will be filled with injustice and fighting, and that the Quran and knowledge of Islam will have all but disappeared. The Dajjal (Antichrist) will appear at the head of the armies of Gog and Magog who will break forth from the gate built against them by Dhu al-Qarnayn. The Mahdi is described as reviving the religion of the prophet Muhammad just as the prophet Muhammad revived the religion of Abraham. He will bring a new revelation and a new law, and will challenge those who interpret the Quran against him. Some sources report that the Mahdi will bring knowledge to supplement, but not necessarily abrogate, the knowledge revealed by the previous prophets.

Many Shi'i sources identify the Mahdi with one of the imams. The Imami or "Twelver" Shi'ah identify the Mahdi with the occluded Twelfth Imam, and the early Ismaili Shi'ah await the return of the Seventh Imam. Other figures are said to return with the Mahdi and are sometimes identified with him, including the Third Imam Husayn, who will return with the followers who were killed with him at Karbala; Jesus; earlier prophets and imams; and martyred followers of the prophet Muhammad.

MAIMONIDES. *See* RAMBAM.

MAJOR PROPHETS. Term referring to the prophetic books Isaiah, Jeremiah, and Ezekiel, so labeled because of their large size relative to those found in the Minor Prophets.

MALACHI. Last book of the minor prophets. The book tells little about its author. The title of the book literally means "my messenger," suggesting that it is not a personal name, but rather an appellation, perhaps derived from Mal 3:1. The date of the book is also uncertain, though most scholars place it in the mid-fifth century BCE after the restoration of the temple. Much of Malachi is taken up with cultic matters. Malachi indicts the priests for offering blemished sacrificial animals (Mal 1:13), allowing the worship of a foreign goddess as a wife of Yahweh (Mal 2:11), and neglecting tithes (Mal 3:10), and exhorts the people to obey Mosaic Law (Mal 4:4). The book ends by predicting the return of Elijah just before the Day of Yahweh arrives (Mal 3:23).

MANDAEANS. A group of people whose religious affiliation seems to have originated in late antiquity. The Mandaic term *mandayye* means "gnostics," and the group designates itself as "observants" [Mand. nasorayye]. It is possible that the Mandaeans are the "Sabians" referred to in the Quran as protected peoples along with Jews and Christians, based on the notion that the term refers to their practice of washing or baptism, which is central in Mandaean ritual.

Mandaean literature is found mostly in Mandaic, an eastern Aramaic dialect. There are six main bodies of texts considered authoritative by Mandaeans. The most significant is the *Ginza* or "Treasure," divided into the Right Ginza (18 treatises) and the Left Ginza (hymns of soul's ascent). Second is the *Book of John*, also called the *Book of Kings*, which consists of 37 mythological treatises centered around the epiphany of the heavenly man in Jerusalem. Third is the *Qolasta* or "Collection" of canonical hymns and prayers used for baptism, the mass of the soul, and ritual meals. Fourth are the Secret Scrolls, cultic texts accessible only to the priests describing the rite of marriage, ordination, the baptism of Abel, the Thousand and Twelve Questions, and commentaries on funeral rites. Fifth are the Diwans or "Collections" of texts, which include the Abatur and the Book of the Zodiac. Sixth are miscellaneous incantations and theurgic texts that are composed in

Mandaic and attributed to the Mandaeans such as incantation bowls and amulets.

MANI (216–277 CE). Eponymous founder of Manichaeism, Mani lived in third-century CE Iraq and Iran under the Sasanians. Manichaeans were persecuted in the Sasanian and Roman empires, though the religion spread and was successful in Central Asia, especially among the Uighir Turks. Later Christian and Muslim texts often accuse religious opponents of being Manichaeans and characterize their religion in terms not entirely consistent with the picture provided by the Manichaeans themselves.

Mani is said to have composed a series of treatises in Aramaic and in Middle Persian. These include the *Shahpuhr Book* addressed to the Sasanian Shahpuhr I (r. 240–272 CE), the *Living Gospel*, the *Treasure of Life*, the *Treatise*, the *Book of Secrets*, and the *Book of Giants*, the latter of which relates to the texts associated with the Enoch traditions (*see also* 1 ENOCH). Mani also produced a series of letters. Not all of these texts are extant, and many are attested only in Parthian, Middle Persian, Coptic, Soghdian, or Uighir, or are cited by non-Manichaean sources in Greek, Latin, Arabic, Persian, and Chinese.

Mani is portrayed as both a prophet and a savior figure. He is associated closely with both Jesus and the Buddha, and also with the transformed Enoch in some contexts. Mani is described as being the last in a line of prophets who, beginning with Adam, were the messengers of God or the Holy Spirit. Mentioned by name in this prophetic line are antediluvian figures such as Adam, Seth, Shem, Enosh, Enoch, and other major prophet figures such as Zarathustra, Jesus, and the Buddha. Mani is called the "Seal of the Prophets," a term also applied to the prophet Muhammad in the Quran, characterizing him as the culmination and last of the prophets.

MANICHAEAN HYMNS. Collections of hymns apparently recited in ritual contexts by different Manichaean groups. Many of the extant Parthian and Middle Persian Manichaean texts are hymns of this type. Among the Parthian texts are *Fortunate for Us* and *Rich Friend of the Beings of Light*. The first of these is extant in Uighur, and both describe the coming and saving acts of a savior figure with imagery associated with other soteriological traditions: intercession, purification, washing, healing, and heavenly ascension. The Middle Persian hymns include "The Speech of the Living Self" and "The Speech of the Light Self," both of which are attested in Soghdian fragments. These texts focus on the divine light trapped in the material prison of the body and the physical world.

MANICHAEAN MAGICAL TEXTS. Extant in Parthian and Middle Persian are incantations and amulets that are associated with Manichaean circles. These texts closely parallel information found in other esoteric textual traditions, including angelology, demonology, and the names of God, and refer to prophetic figures such as Adam and Jesus (*see also* MAGIC).

MANNA. Miraculous food with which God feeds the Israelites, along with quail, while they are wandering in the wilderness (Exod 16:14–30 and Q 2:57, 2:263, 7:160, 20:80). Scholars typically identify manna with the sticky sweet juice exuded by twigs and leaves of the turfa tree (a species of tamarisk) in the western Sinai between May and June. Muslim exegetes also report that manna is the gum of trees, something like a thick juice. The Hebrew word seems to indicate that the Israelites, bewildered by the substance, called it "manna," meaning "what (is it)?" (Exod 16:15). It appeared along with dew, looked like coriander seed, and had the yellowish color of bdellium (Exod 16:14; Num 11:7–9). After it was gathered, the people "ground it in mills, or beat it in a mortar, and baked it in pans, and made cakes of it; and the taste of it was like the taste of fresh oil" (Num 11:8). Muslim exegetes associate manna with the food given to Adam and Eve in the Garden of Eden, as they do the quail, which is said to be a special bird from the Garden of Eden. The last appearance of manna coincided with the Passover celebrated by Joshua, which marked the Israelite's entrance into Canaan (Josh 5:12).

Later legal tradition recalls the manna as evidence that humans "shall not live by bread alone" (Deut 8:3, 8:16). Its importance is signaled by its appearance in the liturgy, which refers to it as the "grain of heaven" (Ps 78:24), and by post-exilic recollections of Israel's early history (Neh 9:20). Talmudic tradition included manna as one of the 10 items created by God on the eve of the Sabbath at twilight (TB Pesahim 54a). Muslim exegetes refer to the manna as one of the blessings given by God to the Israelites with which they were not satisfied and for which they did not thank him. Both Jewish and Muslim tradition state that a jar of manna was among the contents of the Ark of the Covenant.

MARDUK PROPHECY. Mesopotamian text that claims to contain the words of the Babylonian god Marduk. In the prophecy Marduk describes the capture and journey of his cult statue from one city to another as intended by the god, despite the fact that the statue was captured by the Hittites in 1594 BCE, then taken from there to the city Assur by the Assyrians. It also tells of a brief stay in Elam to the east of Mesopotamia. In each place Marduk visited (except for Elam), the god's presence brought prosperity. Though the text also prophesies the rise of a Babylonian king who will take the statue back to Babylon and rebuild Marduk's temple, scholars have shown that it was written after the events it reports (*see also* EX EVENTU), during the reign of Nebuchadnezzar I (1224–1103 BCE), who succeeded in bringing it back from Elam. The prophecy is reminiscent of the biblical Ark of the Covenant, which was stolen by the Philistines and made a circuitous journey back to the Israelites, bestowing plagues upon the Philistines and blessing upon those who cared for it on its journey (1 Samuel 4:1–11, 5–6). It also raises questions with regard to the role of fictive elements and conventions in prophetic texts.

MARI. Mesopotamian site on the mid-Euphrates River that yielded more than 25,000 cuneiform documents during its many excavations from 1933 to 1955, only a small percentage of which have been published. The tablets date to the second millennium BCE (c. 1750–1697 BCE) and are the product of the Amorite civilization. Excavations at Mari uncovered a few dozen prophetic epistolary texts dating from the final decade of King Zimri-Lim (1730–1697 BCE) that closely resemble the prophetic materials found in the Bible, despite being separated in time by more than six centuries. In particular they offer the earliest attestation of intuitive prophecy; a "direct" type of revelation that apparently does not rely on mantic or divinatory devices (*see also* PROPHECY; PROPHET). It is unknown whether these prophecies were self-inspired or the result of divine initiative, but it is clear that the intuitive prophets of Mari, both male and female, existed alongside the more traditional mantics such as extispicers, dream interpreters, and readers of portents and omens (*see also* EGIRRÛ). In some cases, the same figure appears familiar with multiple methods of accessing the divine.

Scholars have distinguished the intuitive prophecies of Mari from the biblical prophecies by pointing to their tendency to be concerned with the well-being of the royal house, rather than with its excesses and the social and moral inequities they create. Nevertheless, the number of prophetic texts is still small, and the apparent lack of attestation could be an accident of discovery. Indeed, one Mari prophecy does command the king in the name of Adad, god of Aleppo, to judge the cases of his wronged subjects, a prophecy not unlike that found in Jeremiah (Jer 21:12, 22:3). Five kinds of prophets appear in the Mari texts: a "priest-prophet" [Akk. shangûm], "male cultic prostitute and transvestite" [Akk. assinum], "proclaimer" [Akk. qabbatum], "ecstatic" [Akk. muhhu], and "answerer" [Akk. apilum]. This last type apparently also prophesied in groups.

MARTYRDOM AND ASCENSION OF ISAIAH. Composite text describing the death of the prophet Isaiah and his visions as he ascends through the seven heavens. The complete text is extant only in Ethiopic, the earliest manuscripts dating to the 14th century CE, but the redaction of the composite text dates as early as the sixth century CE. Coptic fragments, composed in an archaic dialect (Proto-Subachimic) attest to the composite text in the fourth century CE. There also is a Greek legend of Isaiah in a 12th-century CE manuscript that incorporates the material from the composite text, but reverses the order of the two parts, putting the visions before the martyrdom.

The first five chapters describe the martyrdom of Isaiah and are thought to represent what was originally a separate work, composed in Hebrew and translated into Greek before being combined with chapters 6–11. A Greek fragment dating to the fifth or sixth century CE preserves portions of chapters 2–4, and the Old Church Slavonic recensions and the second Latin recension attest only to chapters 6–11. Some scholars also identify 3:13–4:22 as a later Christian addition entitled the Testament of Hezekiah, mentioned by an 11th-century Byzantine historian.

The text describes the conflict between Isaiah and the wicked Israelite kings (1:1–3:12), and contains a prophesy about the coming of the "Beloved" who is to be crucified, resurrected, and ascend to the seventh heaven (3:13–4:22). These verses also prophesy the future corruption of postapostolic Christianity, and the second coming of the Lord. Chapter 5 recounts the execution of Isaiah, sawn in half with a wooden saw. This martyrdom also appears in accounts of the killing of Zechariah, father of John the Baptist. Chapters 6–9 describe the ascent of Isaiah through the seven heavens, where he has various visions of angels and thrones. In the seventh heaven, Isaiah meets Abel and Enoch sitting on thrones like angels, and sees the record books of people's deeds. Chapters 10–11 narrate the commission of Jesus Christ, his descent and miraculous birth, his crucifixion and resurrection, and his ascent through the seven heavens. The text ends with Isaiah's instructions to Hezekiah concerning these visions.

MARY, MOTHER OF JESUS. Mary the mother of Jesus is found in the Quran (Q 3:33–47, 19:16–26) more often than in the New Testament. She is said to be the "daughter of Imran" (Q 3:35) and the "sister of Aaron" (Q 19:28), an apparent conflation of Mary the mother of Jesus with Miriam the sister of Moses and Aaron. The mother of Mary is not identified by name in the Quran, but Q 3:35 states that she made a vow to give Mary to God as a sacred trust. Muslim exegesis, like the account in the Protoevangelium of James, models the birth of Mary on the birth of Samuel and Samson, making Mary's mother to be Hannah. Hannah is said to have been barren until she asked God to give her a child whom she then vowed to consecrate to the service of God, as a servant of the temple in Jerusalem. The Quran also makes Zechariah, the uncle of Mary, to be the guardian of Mary during her service in the temple (Q 3:37). Muslim exegetes add that Mary stayed in her own cell in the temple, and that food miraculously appeared for her there: summer fruits in the winter and winter fruits in the summer. The annunciation and the nativity of Jesus also are described in the Quran and Muslim exegesis, and feature Mary. Muslim exegetes preserve a tradition that Mary is one of four women identified as the best women in the world along with Asiyah the wife of the pharaoh, Khadijah the first wife of the prophet Muhammad, and Fatima the daughter of the prophet Muhammad and wife of Ali b. Abi Talib. Abu Hurayrah reports that Mary was the only person born who was not attacked by Satan because she was protected by her mother, perhaps a reference to the immaculate conception.

MASORETIC TEXT. Present form of the biblical Hebrew text based ultimately on the textual tradition of Jewish scholars known as the Masoretes (eighth–ninth centuries CE). In order to preserve their recitation tradition, which was gradually falling into disuse under the spread of Arabic as a common tongue, the Masoretes invented a series of vowel points that they placed above and below the consonantal text. They also added a series of marginal notes (the Masorah) to assist a deeper study of the text. The system of vocalization and the critical apparatus allowed them to preserve their reading traditions while simultaneously leaving the sacred consonants intact. In the early period of masoretic transmission, the consonants were written by "writers, counters" [Heb. soferim], and the vowels by "pointers" [Heb. naqdim]. In late antiquity, there was a western Masoretic tradition, centered at Tiberius, and an eastern tradition, whose schools centered at Sura, Nehardea, and Pumbeditha in Mesopotamia. By the 11th century CE, however, only the western vocalization tradition remained in existence.

MASSEBAH. Hebrew term for standing stones of various heights used both as commemorative steles and cultic objects of worship. Some biblical texts refer to the erection of a massebah as a symbol of alliance (Gen 31:45; Exod 24:4; Isa 19:19–20), whereas others appear in sanctuaries (e.g., Shechem in Josh 24:26–27; Bethel in Gen 28:18, 31:31). Moses erected 12 standing stones near Yahweh's altar, which served to represent the 12 tribes of Israel (Exod 24:4).

Some scholars have suggested that the massebah has its origins in the cult of the dead, especially of one's ancestors and relatives, as a physical representation of the family line. Indeed, the patriarch Jacob sets up a massebah over Rachel's grave (Gen 35:20), and David's son Absalom erected one to mark his lack of progeny (2 Sam 18:18). The account of Jacob setting up a massebah at Bethel (lit. "House of God") in Gen 28:18 similarly appears in the context of the promise of progeny, though here it is taken also to be a memorial of the theophany. In other contexts, the standing stone was considered a god, for instance Baal (2 Kgs 3:2), and in other cases it is erected alongside an idol (Lev 26:1; Deut 7:5). Its association with male deities explains why biblical texts often mention it in connection with Asherah, both a goddess and sacred tree (Deut 12:3; *see also* ASHERAH). Asherah also was worshipped at Bethel (2 Kgs 23:15), the site where Jacob earlier had erected a massebah. Its association with unsanctioned forms of worship caused the erecting of a massebah to become illegal (Deut 12:3).

MECCA. City located in the middle of the Hijaz on the western coast of the Arabian Peninsula. Mecca is the cultic center of Islam. According to Muslim sources, Mecca was first established as a sanctuary by Adam, reestablished by Abraham, and finally returned to its rightful character by the prophet Muhammad. Mecca is the site of the Ka'bah, which is the focus of Muslim prayer and pilgrimage, and its sanctuary is considered the most sacred place on earth.

Adam is said to have established the sanctuary at Mecca after being expelled from the Garden of Eden. Muslim exegetes explain that Adam fell to Sri Lanka where he stood atop Mt. Nod and experienced the angels worshipping God in paradise. God ordered Adam to make a pilgrimage to Mecca and establish there a sanctuary as a temporary earthly substitute for the Garden of Eden. Several of the geographical features of Mecca are identified in etiological myths associated with Adam's meeting of Eve in Muzdalifah and Arafat. The well of Zamzam also first appears in Mecca to purify Eve from menstruation so that she could enter the sanctuary. God instructed Adam in the rites of the pilgrimage [Ar. hajj], which he performed to the amazement of the angels who perform similar rites around the throne of God in paradise. Adam's tent served as the first Ka'bah, and it is reported that God sent down a special gemstone or crystal Ka'bah from heaven that was later taken back up in the time of the deluge when Noah's ark circumambulated the site seven times.

Abraham is reported to have reestablished the sanctuary at Mecca, rebuilt the Ka'bah there, and reinstituted the practice of the pilgrimage to Mecca. Ishmael and Hagar first came to Mecca after they were expelled from Syria by Abraham and Sarah. Hagar ran between Safa and Marwah seven times looking for water for the infant Ishmael, thus establishing the rite of running between Safa and Marwah in the pilgrimage (*see also* HAGAR). Abraham visited Mecca when Ishmael was older, and the two of them were commanded by God to rebuild the Ka'bah and reestablish the pilgrimage (Q 2:125, 22:26–27).

Abraham is guided to the spot of the Ka'bah by the "presence of God" (Ar. sakinah) and is said to have built it out of materials taken from five mountains. The list is given variously including the following: Judi, Sinai, Zion, Olives, Tabor, Lebanon, and Hira. All of these mountains are associated with sanctuaries and revelations to other prophets, and suggest the notion of Mecca as the "navel" or center of the earth. Many of the traditions associated with cosmic mountains and with Jerusalem in particular are associated with Mecca also and the sanctuary there.

After reestablishing the sanctuary and the pilgrimage, Abraham is reported to have asked God to protect the people of Mecca (Q 2:126) and to raise a prophet from among them (Q 2:129). Ishmael was sent as a prophet to the Jurhum who resided in Mecca with Ishmael and Hagar, but Muslim exegetes interpret Q 2:129 as a reference to the coming of the prophet Muhammad who would descend from the line of Ishmael.

In the time of the prophet Muhammad, Mecca was in the hands of polytheists, except for a few people who seem to have followed the "religion of Abraham" and venerated the Ka'bah. After moving from Mecca to Medina, the prophet Muhammad changed the direction of prayer from Jerusalem to the Ka'bah in Mecca. The Quran refers to the "Place of Abraham" [Ar. maqam Ibrahim], which is regarded by early Muslim exegetes as encompassing all of the area of the sanctuary in Mecca (Q 2:125, 3:97). Other sources see the "Place of Abraham" as a particular spot or stone near the Ka'bah. The reference seems to relate to biblical and Jewish sources that regard Mt. Moriah and the temple in Jerusalem as the "place" or "house" of Abraham (Gen 22:4, Jub 22:24).

Also relating the sanctuary at Mecca to Jerusalem are the accounts of the rediscovery of the well of Zamzam by Abd al-Muttalib, the grandfather of the prophet Muhammad. Along with the well, Abd al-Muttalib also uncovered golden temple implements and other items from Syria, which may allude to other traditions in which the temple vessels from the temple in Jerusalem are said to have been hidden in the earth until the end of time (2 Macc 2:4–8; 2 Bar 6:7; 4 Bar 4; *see also* HIDDEN TEMPLE VESSELS).

Muslim eschatology states that at the end of time the Antichrist [Ar. Dajjal] will destroy the Ka'bah before the Day of Resurrection and Judgment. Some sources also refer to God's sending of an eschatological or "new" Ka'bah at the end of time (*see also* NEW JERUSALEM).

MEDICINE. In the ancient Near East, the medical arts were practiced by, or associated with, mantic professionals, because sickness and disease were perceived as acts of gods or demons (though not necessarily as divine punishments).

In ancient Egypt, medicine was intimately bound up in religious practices and frequently involved performative utterances (*see also* MAGIC), and physical treatments including the ingestion of potions (*see also* DRUGS). In Mesopotamia, the same figures who served as medical practitioners also performed exorcisms, spells, and prepared the remedies. Similar remarks could be made with regard to medical practices at Mari and Ugarit (*see also* SHAMAN).

The Hebrew Bible also testifies to the role of the mantic in medicine. The religious system of Israel permitted little room for agents of sickness other than Yahweh, however. It is Yahweh who wounds and heals (Exod 15:26; Job 5:18), and it is Yahweh who curses Israel with diseases should they break their covenantal agreement with him (Deut 28:15–22). Yahweh also inflicts diseases upon the Egyptians (Exodus 7–10), and Yahweh is considered the only true physician (Deut 32:39). Israelite conceptions of sickness and disease, therefore, are tied closely to those of divine transgression and ritual impurity (Exod 11:1; Deut 24:8; 1 Sam 6:8). Since prophets served as Yahweh's spokespersons, medicine and health care generally fell into their domain. Thus, the Bible tells how the prophet Elijah healed a widow's son of his terminal illness (1 Kgs 17:21–23; cf., 2 Kgs 4:34–35), and how an Aramaean king called upon the prophet Elisha to heal him of his leprosy (2 Kgs 5:3–14).

Medical services such as these often required that the prophet first seek an oracle (*see also* ORACLE) to ascertain whether the patient could be treated (2 Kings 1, 8, 20; 2 Chr 16:12). In exchange for his services the prophet was paid (1 Kgs 14:2–3). On some occasions music was employed as a therapeutic device (1 Sam 16:14), and on others, an implement or ritual object was used. Moses, for example, employed a bronze serpent to heal the people of their snake bites (Num 21:4–9). The implement apparently had later gained status as a relic of ritual use until King Hezekiah (715–687 BCE) had it removed from the temple and destroyed (2 Kgs 18:4; *see also* RELICS). Later Jewish tradition, especially the Talmud, preserves a great deal of medical knowledge as well, much of it attesting to Mesopotamian influence. For example, the Talmud contains a number of medical recipes and a collection of symptoms (TB Gittin 68b–70a), as well as a discussion of dreams used for therapeutic purposes (TB Berakhoth 57b).

The New Testament and Quran attribute healing powers to Jesus, and later exegetes explain that these miracles were evidence of his prophetic status. Often, Jesus' healing power is portrayed as the exorcism of demons, paralleling the role of prophets against affliction in the Hebrew Bible. In Matt 9:12 Jesus compares himself to a physician (cf., Luke 4:23), and Jesus is called the "Great Physician." Col 4:14 refers to Luke, the author of the Gospel of Luke and the Acts of the Apostles, as the "beloved physician." Later texts prescribe concoctions and elixirs designed to remedy specific diseases and ailments. Many of these texts are specifically attributed to prophets, are said to have been revealed by God for the prophets' use, and connect demon possession with disease.

MEDINA. City to which the prophet Muhammad emigrated in 622 CE and established the first Islamic society. The original name of the city, Yathrib, appears in Q 33:13 and is attested in Greek geographical works [Gk. Iathrippa] and in Minaean inscriptions. The name Medina derives from a common Arabic noun meaning "city" or "state." The noun occurs several times in the Quran in relation to the city, but may not have been taken as the proper name of the city until later.

Muslim sources report that the original inhabitants of the city were the Amalekites, and this may be related to traditions that conflate the Jurhum, who settled in Mecca at the time of Ishmael, with the Amalekites (*see also* AMALEKITES). From an early period there was a strong Jewish presence in the city, and at the time of the Hijrah (622 CE) there were three large Jewish groups in the city: the Qurayzah, Nadir, and Qaynuqa. These groups seem to have been in competition with two large Arab groups, the Aws and Khazraj, who traced their ancestry to Yemen. In the pre-Islamic period, the Aws and

Khazraj worshipped the god al-Manat at a shrine between Medina and Mecca. After the Hijrah the Islamic "community" [Ar. ummah] consisted of three clans from the Aws, two from the Khazraj, and the group of emigrants from Mecca. The Medinan Muslims were known as the "Helpers" [Ar. Ansar] and the Meccan emigrants were "Those who Made Hijrah" [Ar. Muhajirun]. In 624 CE the Qaynuqa Jews were expelled from Medina and in 625 the Nadir Jews were expelled. In 627 the Muslims massacred the Qurayzah Jews. These violent disputes with the Jews of Medina reflect social and economic concerns, but also indicate Jewish resistance to accepting the prophethood of Muhammad.

The prophet Muhammad died in Medina in 632 CE and was buried in his house. In time the Mosque of the Prophet in Medina and his tomb (known by the Ar. "hujra" meaning "room") became a place of pilgrimage. Also buried there are Aishah, the prophet's wife, and the first two caliphs, Abu Bakr and Uthman. Mecca and Medina together are called the "Two Sanctuaries" [Ar. Al-Haramayn], and Muslims going on pilgrimage to Mecca often append a visit to the Mosque and Tomb of the Prophet in Medina to their itinerary.

MEKHILTA. Nine-chapter midrashic text that deduces rules for living from the book of Exodus. The Mekhilta begins with Exodus 12 and continues to 23:19, though the legal statutes concerning the celebration of the Sabbath conclude the work (Exod 31:12–17, 35:1–3). Jewish tradition dates the Mekhilta to 90–130 CE, but it was edited and reworked in the centuries following.

MERISM. Common literary usage in the Bible in which two opposites are brought together to denote a totality. Thus, the tree of the knowledge of "good and evil" represents the tree of "all knowledge," the expression "from Dan to Beersheba" (1 Sam 3:20) means "all of Israel," and the famous periods of time listed by Qohelet, "A time to kill, and a time to heal; a time to break down, and a time to build up," represent times for all things (Qohelet 3).

MERKABAH [CHARIOT] MYSTICISM. Term derived from the Hebrew word [merkabah] meaning "chariot," described by the prophet Ezekiel (Ezekiel 1) as a throne of God. In later Jewish tradition, Ezekiel's vision became the prototype object of visionary contemplation. Merkabah mysticism began to take root in the first century CE, perhaps under the influence of groups whose mythology centered on a biblical demiurge. In the early and late Middle Ages, however, this movement was centered in Babylonia. At the heart of the merkabah mystic experience were ecstatic visions of God's throne and the celestial beings, and the ultimate goal was to see God's throne on the divine chariot. Later written tradition describes the ascent of the visionary as a dangerous journey through seven "heavenly dwellings," guarded by harmful angelic beings. In order to pass unharmed the initiate had to fast and recite performative formulae known as "seals." The Talmud tells of four men who attempted the journey: one died, one went insane, and one committed apostasy. Only the fourth, Rabbi Aqiba ben Joseph, had a successful visionary experience.

MESSENGER. The word *messenger* [Heb. mal'akh, Gk. angelos] appears in the Bible for humans (Gen 32:4; Judg 6:35) and divine figures, i.e., "angels" (Gen 19:1; 1 Kgs 13:18; Ps 103:20, 104:4; Job 33:23), whose primary role involves delivering a missive from one party to another. The Arabic term for messenger or apostle [Ar. rasul] occurs many times in the Quran, usually denoting a prophet, but also angels (*see also* APOSTLE). The use of the term *messenger* in reference to biblical prophets as "heralds of Yahweh" occurs only in post-exilic texts (Isa 42:19, 44:26; Hag 1:13; Mal 3:1; 2 Chr 36:15), thus suggesting a later development with regard to the conception of a prophet's mission. Some scholars see this change as representative of the impact of Mesopotamian heraldry on prophetic discourse.

MESSIAH. Title meaning "anointed one" that is applied in the Bible to priests, prophets, angels, and kings who have been anointed with oil by religious authorities (i.e., prophets and priests), thus marking them with special status and divine commission (*see also* ANOINT). The application of the title Messiah to the Persian king Cyrus (r. 559–530 BCE) in Isa 45:1 is a special case, since doubtless, the king was not physically anointed by Israelite religious authorities. The term also appears in the Quran 11 times as a title for Jesus.

A belief in a future messiah who will descend from King David and deliver Israel from a time of great distress is already in place by the eighth century BCE as is seen in the prophecies of Isaiah (Isa 9:5, 11:1–5), but these messianic expectations were not applied to the time of the eschaton until late in the post-exilic period (*see also* ESCHATOLOGY). Such messianism is reflected only in late psalms (e.g., Psalm 2, 72, 110) and biblical books such as the book of Daniel (Dan 9:25), and in the Dead Sea Scrolls in which one finds the expectation that two messiahs will come, one a priest, and the other a king (cf., Ps 110:4). Jewish messianic expectations, of course, also fueled the movement that later would become Christianity, though Jesus himself appears to have been rather reluctant to apply the title to himself (Mark 8:29–30).

Later Jewish tradition, like later Christian tradition, sometimes reinterprets biblical prophecies in a messianic light. To cite just one example with a counterpart in Christian exegesis, the Targum inserts the word *messiah* into its translation of the famous suffering servant poem of Deutero-Isaiah (Targum to Isa 53:10, 53:13). The Talmud too similarly treats certain biblical passages as esoteric references to the Messiah (TB Sanhedrin 98b). Messianic expectations and interpretations can be found also in a great number of Jewish midrashic, Hekhalot, and exegetical texts and continued to be relevant throughout the Islamic period.

METATRON. Figure in Jewish and Islamic texts closely associated with Enoch and the prophet Idris. The name Metatron also appears as "Maytatrun" or "Mitatron" and appears to be of Greek origin or perhaps represents an attempt to imitate a Greek name.

One of the earliest references to Metatron is in Muslim commentaries on Q 9:30–31 where Ezra, said to be seen by the Jews as the son of God, appears to represent a Jewish notion of a second power in heaven. The eighth-century CE Persian *Mother of the Book* [Pers. Umm al-Kitab] ascribes to Metatron the role of a demiurge in creating the earth. Several Muslim and Christian heresiographical texts refer to a Jewish group that worships a "Little God" or second minor power in heaven. The Alphabet of Rabbi Aqiba also refers to the "Lesser Yahweh," and this reference is repeated in Muslim texts as a designation of the angel who created the earth. Texts associated with Hekhalot mysticism assert that the "Angel of Yahweh" who appears to people on earth, and the image of God on the Divine Chariot, is not God himself, but Metatron, God's look-alike.

3 Enoch identifies Metatron with the transformed Enoch. Both 1 and 2 Enoch also describe the ascension of Enoch and his translation into heavenly status, but 3 Enoch specifically describes Enoch as being transformed into a visual replica of God. Enoch becomes Metatron when God increases his size, gives him a throne in heaven, clothes and crowns him in cosmic light, gives him wings, and transforms his body into fire. God also reveals to Metatron all the secrets of creation, and his crown is inscribed with the letters by which the cosmos was brought into being. Metatron is designated as the chief of the angels and the Prince of the Divine Presence [Heb. sar ha-shekhinah]. In Samaritan and later Hebrew incantation texts and amulets, Metatron appears as the "Prince of the Torah" [Heb. sar ha-Torah] because of his station next to God.

Metatron appears by name in a "Letter on the Invocation of Spirits" attributed to the Muslim philosopher Kindi (d. 866 CE), which Kindi says he borrowed from an earlier source. Here Metatron is one of the 12 "servants of the day" along with other spirits such as Immanuel and Elohim. Metatron also is conjured as a Jinn in the medieval Egyptian shadow play of Ibn Danyal. As an angel, Metatron occurs in the 13th-century CE magical collections of Ahmad al-Buni (d. 1225 CE). In these texts, though Metatron is pervasive, he is not always portrayed as the head of the angels. Buni refers to a "crown" and "lance" of Metatron, and the name of Metatron is said to be one of the names inscribed on the rod of Moses. The name also occurs on amulets and in incantations in Muslim contexts. In other places, Metatron is linked to the name of God and is said to be the chief angel who attends to the throne of God, which corresponds to the Jewish designation of Metatron as the Prince of the Torah. In the magic text of Ibn Hajj al-Tilimsani (16th century CE) Metatron is described similarly as having knowledge of the "Pen" of God, which writes on the "Preserved Tablet" (see Q 85:22).

MICAH. Book of the Minor Prophets that preserves the prophecies of Micah, a prophet from the village of Moresheth in Gath who prophesied during the reigns of Jotham (750–734 BCE), Ahaz (735–715 BCE), and Hezekiah (727–698 BCE) (Mic 1:1). The book of Jeremiah

(Jer 26:18) also mentions that Micah prophesied during the reign of Hezekiah. He thus was a contemporary of the prophet Isaiah, and some scholars even see him as Isaiah's disciple (compare Mic 4:1–4 and Isa 2:2–4). The book of Micah is concerned primarily with the excesses of the aristocracy, which the prophet holds responsible for the ensuing Assyrian threat. Some scholars see in the book signs of a later editor. Mic 7:8–10, for example, appears to refer to the Babylonian, not Assyrian destruction, and Mic 7:11–20 mentions the repairing of Jerusalem's walls and apparent return from exile. The prophecy in Mic 5:2–4 that Bethlehem will again be the site of another Davidic king is taken up in Christianity as a prophecy of the Christ.

MICAIAH. The prophet Micaiah, son of Imlah, appears in 1 Kings 22 as having worked in the court of King Ahab (r. 869–850 BCE), though 1 Kgs 22:8 states that Ahab disliked his prophecies because they always bade ill of him. Still, he was summoned by Jehoshaphat king of Judah while visiting Ahab's court, and asked for his prophecy concerning whether he should attempt to take Ramoth-Gilead back from the Aramaeans. Micaiah told him not to attempt it, and that if he did, the king would die. He was struck in the face by Zedekiah, son of Chenaanah, one of the other prophets working in the court, and thrown in prison. Despite Micaiah's warning, Ahab went to battle and was killed.

MICHAEL. Name of an archangel in Jewish and Islamic traditions. Michael is mentioned by name one time in the Quran (Q 2:98). Michael, the angel, is mentioned thrice in the Hebrew Bible (Dan 10:13, 10:21, 12:1), and twice in the New Testament (Jude 9; John 12:7–9). In the Muslim exegesis of Q 2:98 it is reported that the verse was revealed when the Jews of Medina challenged the prophet Muhammad to tell them the name of the angel bringing him revelations. When he responded that it was Gabriel, the Jews claimed that Gabriel was their enemy (Q 2:97), but Michael was the angel who revealed things to their prophets. Muslim exegetes also explain that whereas the name Gabriel means "worshipper of God" the name Michael means "lesser worshipper of God." In Jewish exegesis, Michael is said to be the greatest of the archangels who intercedes on behalf of the sinful. It is

Michael who makes revelations to the different nations, and who appeared to Moses in the burning bush. Michael is claimed to be one of the three messengers who appeared to Abraham before the destruction of Sodom and Gomorrah (Genesis 18), and his appearance is regarded as indicating the presence of God.

MIDIAN. Location named after the son of Abraham and Keturah corresponding to a large ethnic or political grouping somewhere in southern Jordan and northwest Arabia. The Midianites appear in several of the stories of the prophets. The Bible refers to the Midianites as merchants and seems to associate them with the Ishmaelites who take Joseph to Egypt (Gen 37:25–36). The Quran mentions Midian as the place to which the prophet Shuayb was sent. Muslim exegetes do not give a precise location for Midian but agree with the biblical genealogy that Midian was one of the sons of Abraham. Shuayb also is conflated with Jethro, the father-in-law of Moses from Midian, in the exegesis of Q 28:22–28. There are a number of links between Moses and Midian. In the Bible and Quran, Moses flees to Midian to escape the wrath of the pharaoh, and it is in Midian that God reveals himself to Moses in the burning bush (Genesis 2–4; Q 28:21–35). Mt. Horeb or Sinai, then, is to be located in Midian despite later Christian and Muslim identification of Sinai with Jabal Musa in the Sinai Peninsula (*see also* HOREB; SINAI). In The New Testament the apostle Paul refers to Sinai as a "mountain in Arabia," possibly with the meaning of Roman Arabia or the area controlled by the Nabataeans (Gal 4:25). Archaeological evidence from the northern Hijaz shows that Midian came into political prominence around the 13th century BCE, and that the Midianites were not merely a nomadic people. Evidence of walled cities, irrigation, mining operations, and refined pottery demonstrates the sophistication of the civilization in the area.

MIDRASH. Form of early Jewish commentary on biblical texts often homiletic or didactic in character and originating in an oral context. The hermeneutics employed in midrashic literature make the biblical texts appeal to a contemporary age. Prominent among midrashic hermeneutics is the use of word play as a means of connecting the original text to its new interpretation.

MIDRASH HA-GADOL. Name given to a midrashic commentary on the Torah compiled sometime in the early 13th century CE in Yemen. It contains a number of early midrashic traditions that are extant nowhere else.

MIDRASH TANHUMA. Name referring to various medieval compilations of Jewish exegesis of the Bible. Several related texts and fragments are extant, but there has been no successful attempt to trace these back to a single original text. There are two printed editions commonly referred to by the name Midrash Tanhuma, one edited by S. Buber (Jerusalem, 1964), and another reprinted many times as the "standard" edition.

MINOR PROPHETS. The 12 prophetic books of the Jewish canon, namely: Hosea, Joel, Amos, Obadiah, Jonah, Micah, Nahum, Habakkuk, Zephaniah, Haggai, Zechariah, and Malachi. They are called "minor" because of their size relative to the prophetic texts found in the Major Prophets.

MIQRA'OT GEDOLOT. Hebrew title (lit. "Great Readings") of a number of rabbinic Bible editions incorporating the Targum and various Jewish commentaries. Sometimes the Latin title Biblia Rabbinica is given to this type of Bible. The earliest edition was published in 1517 CE and includes the Hebrew text of the Bible, several of the Aramaic Targums, the commentaries of many rabbinic exegetes, and assorted other rabbinic treatises on Jewish law and interpretation. This was the first Jewish Bible to divide into two the books of Samuel, Kings, Chronicles, and Ezra and Nehemiah. Other early editions were published in 1525 (by Jacob ben Hayyim of Tunis) and 1546 (by Cornelius Adelkind). Also influential was the seventh edition (Amsterdam, 1724–28), which added a number of Jewish commentaries, especially from more recent European scholars. The latest edition is that published in Warsaw (1860–68), which includes 32 different commentaries in addition to the Hebrew text and Targums.

MIRIAM. Sister of Moses and Aaron (Exod 15:20; Num 26:59). In Exod 15:20 she is mentioned as a prophetic musician (*see also* MUSIC). Traditions concerning her prophetic influence appear to be negotiated during the journey through the wilderness, where she is summoned by Yahweh, along with her brother Aaron, to the Tent of Meeting, and told that Moses is preeminent among the prophets (Num 12:5). In an account of Miriam's competition with Moses for authority as a prophetic figure, Yahweh strikes her with ulcers of the skin (Num 12:10), from which she recovers only after Aaron and Moses pray for her (Num 12:11–14). For this act of hubris, she would become paradigmatic in the legal tradition (Deut 24:9). Nevertheless, later prophetic tradition recalls her positive attributes as a prophet (Mic 6:4).

Talmudic tradition recognizes Miriam as one of seven female prophets mentioned in the Bible, along with Sarah, Deborah, Hannah, Abigail, Huldah, and Esther (TB Megillah 14a). Rabbinic tradition also sees the well mentioned in Num 21:16–20 as the "well of Miriam." The well was one of the 10 items created on the eve of the Sabbath at twilight (TB Pesahim 54a), and followed the Israelites while wandering in the wilderness (TB Pesahim 54a). It dried up when she died (TB Ta'anith 9a), and her death is understood by Rashi (on Num 20:1) as atoning for the sins of the Israelites. Other traditions identify Miriam with the midwife Puah who helped to raise Moses (Exod 1:15; TB Sotah 11b) and with Azubah, the wife of Caleb (1 Chr 2:18; TB Sotah 12a).

The Quran does not refer to Miriam by name but mentions her as Moses' sister (Q 28:11–12). There are two references to a Mary who is the "daughter of Imran" (Q 3:35) and the "sister of Aaron" (Q 19:28), but these are taken by Muslim exegetes, largely based on the context, as references to Mary, the mother of Jesus.

MISHNAH. Earliest authoritative codification of Jewish oral traditions believed by rabbinic tradition to have accompanied the written law given to Moses by God on Mt. Sinai. The oral materials that comprise the Mishnah (Heb. for "Repeated [study]") were collected for centuries before being written down in the third century CE under the leadership of the Jewish scholar and religious leader Rabbi Judah ha-Nasi. The contents of the Mishnah represent an explanation and supplement for the legal materials found in the Torah, and are divided into six major sections, comprising a total of 63 tractates. In the centuries following the codification of the Mishnah, a tradition of exegesis developed around it that led to the creation of a commentary on the Mishnah known as the Gemara. Together, the Mishnah and Gemara make up the Talmud.

MONOLATRY. Term referring to the worship of one God while believing in the existence of many. Also referred to somewhat inaccurately as henotheism, which is, more aptly speaking, the belief in a hierarchy of deities who are embodied simultaneously in one Godhead. The monolatrous system characterized Israelite belief for most of its history. The national gods of other nations were recognized as existing (1 Sam 26:19), even though the Israelites chose to worship Yahweh alone (Deut 6:4). Monolatry gave way to ardent monotheism during and after the exilic period, perhaps under the influence of Iranian religion.

MONOTHEISM. Belief in and worship of a single God, to be distinguished from monolatry and polytheism. Though monolatry characterizes the religion of ancient Israel for most of its history, punctuated with brief periods of polytheism (1 Kgs 11:5), by the post-exilic period monotheism was the norm. Thus, Deutero-Isaiah asserts that Yahweh created both good and evil (Isa 45:7). Monotheism is the central and repeated message of prophets in the Quran, often expressed by variations of the phrase "There is no god but God."

MOSES. Hebrew leader and lawgiver, seen as the greatest prophet of Israelite tradition. The Quran focuses more attention on Moses than any other prophet, being mentioned by name 137 times (the next most frequently mentioned is Abraham, 69 times). Moses is the son of Amram [Heb. Amram, Ar. Imran] and Jochebed, and younger brother of Aaron (Exod 4:14, 6:20). He is a Levite both in the Bible and in Muslim genealogies.

The birth of Moses is described in terms similar to the nativity of Abraham and Jesus. Exod 1:15–22 narrates how the pharaoh ordered the killing of all male Israelite babies. Jewish and Muslim sources explain that the pharaoh did this because he had been told by his advisors that a savior would be born to the Israelites. The Targum Yerushalmi (Exod 1:15–16) and the Chronicles of Moses describe the pharaoh as having a dream about his demise, which is interpreted by

Jannes and Jambres, the two chief magicians of his court. The Quran indicates that Moses came to punish the pharaoh for exalting himself above God, and to show that the pharaoh could not escape what God had decreed for him (Q 28:6).

Moses was raised in the house of the pharaoh and received his education there. Exod 2:5 states that Moses was pulled from the water by a daughter of the pharaoh, but the Quran attributes the rescue and adoption to the wife of the pharaoh (Q 28:8–9). The New Testament states that Moses learned the "Wisdom of Egypt" (Acts 7:21–22), and Philo says that Moses learned all that could be known from the Egyptians, Greeks, Assyrians, and Chaldaeans (de Vita Mosis 1:23). Muslim exegetes explain that the pharaoh and his wife knew all along that Moses was an Israelite, and suggest further that they knew he was the one who would be the downfall of Egypt. The same point is made in accounts of Moses taking the pharaoh's crown and putting it on his own head as a child (Antiquities 2.232–23b; Exodus Rabbah 1.26).

Moses' killing of an Egyptian is recorded in Exod 2:11–15 and Q 28:14–21. Biblical texts explain that he killed the Egyptian man for treating an Israelite unjustly. Jewish exegetes explain that Moses knew that the man had raped an Israelite woman. Exodus Rabbah 1:29 asserts that Moses was clairvoyant, and that he killed the Egyptian taskmaster simply by speaking God's name. In the Quran Moses beats the man to death immediately following his receiving "authority and knowledge" from God (Q 28:14–15).

The flight and stay in Midian is greatly expanded in nonbiblical sources. A number of them, perhaps related to the reference to Moses' wife as an Ethiopian (Num 12:1), report that Moses spent time among the Ethiopians after leaving Egypt. Ibn Kathir reports that God sent an angel to guide Moses to Midian, and Kisa'i claims it was a magical lion that guided Moses. The *Book of Jasher* describes how Moses was imprisoned by Jethro and only succeeded in escaping with the help of his future wife Zipporah. Muslim exegetes conflate the entire Midian episode with the story of Jacob (Genesis 28–32). According to the Muslim exegesis of Q 28:21–28, Moses lifted a rock off the well in Midian and worked a number of years for Zipporah. Jethro's other daughter is said to have been named Leah, and Moses is only allowed to leave after causing Jethro's flocks to produce speckled sheep.

According to Exodus 3, Moses' revelation at the burning bush takes place during his stay in Midian. While standing on a mountain, Moses has a theophoric experience in which Yahweh appears to him in the form of a burning bush. The Quran places the revelation during his trip back to Egypt from Midian (Q 28:29). Moses received the name of Yahweh and was shown two miracles (the turning of his staff into a serpent and the striking of his hand with ulcerations of the skin), which convinced him of the veracity of the event and his calling to free the Israelites from bondage (Exodus 5, Q 20:9–24, 27:7–12, 28:29–35).

Moses is described as a man with a speech impediment (Exod 4:10), despite ironically being summoned as a spokesperson for God. The same motif occurs in Q 28:34, and Moses is called the "Speaker of God" [Ar. kalim allah] in Muslim exegesis. The Armenian biblical expansion on the history of Moses accounts for his impediment by explaining that he had burned his tongue when he was a child. In his homilies on Exodus, Origen ingeniously points out that Moses had been well educated and was eloquent before the revelation, so it must have been when he heard God speak that he felt his own speech was inadequate.

The interaction between Moses and the pharaoh is richly narrated in the Bible and Quran. Exodus 5–11 describes a series of 10 plagues that culminates in the death of all first-born sons and the first Passover. Interwoven throughout the narrative is the contest between Moses and Aaron and the Egyptian magicians, identified as Jannes and Jambres in extrabiblical accounts. Q 79:24 emphasizes that the contest between Moses and the pharaoh was really a contest between the pharaoh who claimed to be God and God working through Moses. Q 40:23–46 mentions only five plagues, and adds that the pharaoh commanded Haman to build a tower like the Tower of Babel, and that there was one Egyptian who believed in Moses. The parting of the sea, the miraculous escape of the Israelites, and the punishment of the pharaoh are interpreted by many exegetes to be ironic justice for the pharaoh's command to kill the Israelite babies by casting them into the sea. Exod 13:19 also notes that Moses took Joseph's bones with him out of Egypt because of the promise made in Gen 50:24.

During the Israelites' wandering in the wilderness Moses received the revelation of the tablets of the Law that embodied the legal and social covenant between God and the Israelites. According to Ezek 20:25–26 and some Christian and Muslim exegetes, the revelation of the Torah was a punishment for the sins of the Israelites, especially their worship of the golden calf. Other traditions refer to hidden revelations that were given to Moses, such as the Oral Torah and the book of the "second law" (Jub 6:22). Ibn Ishaq reports that when Moses came down from the mountain and saw that the Israelites were worshipping the golden calf, God took back part of the revelation that had been given to Moses.

Moses also plays an important role as leader of the Israelites. In addition to providing the Israelites with their laws and a means for administering them, Moses leads the Israelites in battle, reconnoiters the land, and repeatedly intercedes with God on behalf of the Israelites. Both Jewish and Muslim sources mention Moses' defeat of the giant Og (Deut 3:1–11). According to the Talmud, the height of Moses was 10 cubits, a stature that helped him to slay the giant Og by striking his ankle with an ax (TB Berakhoth 54b). Tabari and other Muslim exegetes explain that Og was one of the giants who inhabited the land that God told the Israelites to take.

In Judaism, Moses eventually obtains the authoritative title "Moses our Teacher" [Heb. and Aram. Moshe Rabbenu], and is said to have experienced two heavenly ascents. The first, at the burning bush, provided him with secret lore, redemptive knowledge, and spiritual illumination. The divine esoterica also included cosmological secrets, the dimensions and presence of God, and information concerning the coming of the Messiah. Upon his death, Moses' body was not subject to decay, and he achieved his second ascent, which gave him immortality (Rashi on Deut 34:7; TB Shabbath 152b; Baba Mezi'a 84b). Thus, Moses acts as courtier in God's palace, serving also as an intercessor (Esther Rabbah 7:13). Despite his importance, Moses never became the object of veneration in Judaism. There is no place in the liturgy for him, and while there are prayers to friendly ministering angels (e.g., Michael, Gabriel, Metatron) despite rabbinic disapproval (TY Berakhoth 9:1), and also prayers to the God of Abraham, Isaac, and Jacob, there are no prayers to Moses or the God of Moses.

In Islam, Moses often is compared to the prophet Muhammad. Exegetes explain the revelation of certain passages from the Quran as being directed at the Jews of Medina, reminding them of the Israelites' rebellion against Moses and God. Q 2:47–61 interprets all the events in the wilderness of wandering as a catalog of the Israelites' sins, blessings that the Israelites failed to acknowledge. Q 2:48, perhaps echoing Exod 32:33–35 and Rom 11:1–10, also states that the Israelites will be punished for these sins on the Day of Judgment with no one to intercede on their behalf. In contrast to Exod 32:30–35, Q 5:25 depicts Moses as refusing to intercede for the Israelites and asking God to separate Aaron and himself from them. This is interpreted by Muslim exegetes, such as Tabarsi, to mean that Moses asked God to send the Israelites to hell while he and Aaron enjoyed paradise.

MOUNTAIN. Mountains are closely associated with the divine throughout the ancient world. Due to their height they were considered closer to the divine realm, and therefore served as locations where the mortal and divine worlds could meet and interact.

Mountains are sometimes referred to as the abode of a particular god. Mesopotamian temples often are referred to as "Houses of the Mountain" [Sum. É.KUR], and the construction of ziggurats similarly appears to have been modeled on mountains. The pyramids of Egypt also may have been inspired by mountains. In Ugaritic mythology the god Baal dwells on Mt. Zaphon, and the Greek god Zeus lives on Mt. Olympus.

In the Bible, the God of Israel is conceived of as a mountain god (1 Kgs 20:23, 20:28), as is the Moabite god Kemosh (1 Kgs 11:12) and the local goddess Asherah (2 Kgs 23:15). Many scholars also see Yahweh's epithet "El Shaddai" as meaning "God of the Mountain" (based on the Akkadian cognate [Akk. shadu] meaning "mountain"). The theophanies of the patriarchs often occur on mountains (Gen 22:14, 28:17), and it is on Mt. Sinai (*see also* HOREB) that Yahweh established his covenant with the Israelites and where he forged the tablets of the Law (Exod 19:23, 31:18; Ps 68:16).

Prior to the construction of Yahweh's temple, mountain sanctuaries provided legitimate places for sacrifice. The prophet Samuel offered sacrifices on various high places (1 Sam 9:12). The Ark of the Covenant also was placed in mountain sanctuaries (1 Sam 7:1). Solomon too sacrificed on a mountain at Gibeon (1 Chr 16:39). When

Yahweh's temple eventually was built, it also was placed on Mt. Zion in Jerusalem (Ps 2:6, 78:68–69). Ecstatic prophetic behavior, both Israelite and non-Israelite, sometimes occurs on mountaintops (Num 23:3; 1 Sam 10:5; 1 Kgs 18:30). Ezekiel even prophesies to the mountains of Israel (Ezek 36:1–2). It is possible that the altar for sacrifice was conceived of as a miniature mountain similar to the "high places" (Heb. bamoth) on which non-Israelite sacrifices took place. Such a conception would explain why the altar was not to be constructed with hewn stone (Deut 27:5).

Muslim sources also associate specific mountains with the sanctuary at Mecca as a place of divine and historical significance. According to many creation accounts, God created the "mound" of the Ka'bah out of five mountains: Mt. Sinai, Mt. of Olives, Mt. Lebanon, Mt. Judi, and Mt. Hira. Sometimes the list includes Mt. Tabor. A similar tradition is connected to the account of Abraham's building of the Ka'bah in Mecca. Each of these mountains is associated with important prophetic figures: Mt. Sinai with Moses and Elijah, Mt. of Olives with Jesus, Mt. Lebanon with Solomon and the building of the temple, Mt. Judi as the spot where Noah's ark came to rest after the deluge (the Bible refers to it as the mountains of Ararat), and Mt. Hira as the place where the prophet Muhammad received his first revelation. Mt. Tabor is identified in early Christian tradition as the mountain on which the Transfiguration of Jesus took place (Matt 17:1–8; Mark 9:2–8; Luke 9:28–36; *see also* HOREB; JABAL QAF; JABAL SIN; SINAI).

MU'AWIYAH (r. 661–680 CE). Abu Abd al-Rahman Mu'awiyah b. Abi Sufyan, founder of the Umayyad dynasty and Companion of the prophet Muhammad.

MUHAMMAD (570–632 CE). The Quran defines the prophet Muhammad as the "Seal of the Prophets" (Q 33:40). He is regarded by Muslims as the last in a long line of prophets originating with Adam and including many biblical and nonbiblical figures.

The coming of Muhammad was foretold by earlier prophets and in earlier books. Q 2:129 reports that Abraham asked God to raise up a prophet from among the people of Mecca to teach them the "Book and Wisdom" and to purify them. Q 61:6 relates that Jesus claimed to be a prophet fulfilling the Torah and bringing the good news of a messenger who came after him (cf., John 15:25–26; Luke 4:16–22). Q 7:157 ambiguously refers to a Gentile [Ar. ummi] prophet whose coming is foretold in the Torah and the Gospel, perhaps an allusion to Isa 42:1–4. Muslim exegetes make reference to early reports that the Torah, before it was altered by Jews, contained numerous references to Muhammad. One of these, reported by Ka'b al-Ahbar, is supposed to have been God's word that he was sending the "New Torah" that Muhammad might open the eyes of the blind, the ears of the deaf, and the hearts of the uncircumcised (see Isa 42:1–4, 35:5).

Several of Muhammad's contemporaries are said to have seen or received signs foretelling the prophetic age. Ibn Ishaq reports that when Abd al-Muttalib visited Yemen the king told him about a secret book in which was found the description of a prophet named Muhammad who would lead the people to worship God, shun Satan, extinguish the fires of hell, and break idols. Also attributed to Abd al-Muttalib is the rediscovery of the well of Zamzam and the uncovering of the hidden temple vessels, both eschatological signs of the approaching new age. Ibn Ishaq reports that when Muhammad's mother was pregnant, she saw a light that came out of her and illuminated for her the castles of Syria. It also is reported that a Christian monk identified Muhammad as a prophet when he traveled to Syria as a merchant before his first revelation.

The life of the prophet Muhammad is normally divided into three parts. The first includes what happened to him before his first revelation and consists mostly of accounts of those who acknowledged his special character or future role as a prophet. The second part concerns his call to be a prophet and his early mission in the city of Mecca. The third part begins with his move to Medina and ends with his death. From references in Ibn Ishaq's biography of Muhammad, historians reconstruct the dates of significant events in these periods. Some scholars have questioned the validity of using later Muslim texts for this early history, and maintain that the biography of Muhammad, like the gospels, is less a "history" than an attempt to demonstrate the prophetic character of Muhammad.

It is said that the first revelation came to Muhammad when he was 40 years old, though the exact date is not known. If he was born in 570 CE, this would place his prophetic call in the year 610. Most exegetes agree that the first revelation was Q 96:1–3 and that Muhammad received these verses from the angel Gabriel while in seclusion in a cave on Mt. Hira. Other scholars record a tradition that for three years before the revelation of the Quran, the angel Israfil brought revelations to Muhammad in a language he could not understand (*see also* ISRAFIL; QURAN). Muhammad began his public preaching around 613 CE and around 615 CE a number of his early followers fled to Ethiopia to escape persecution in Mecca. In 619 CE Muhammad's uncle Abu Talib died, and without his protection, Muhammad sought refuge first in Ta'if and later in Aqabah, where he made an agreement with the people of Medina. The "Emigration" [Ar. hijrah] to Medina took place in 622 CE, the date on which the Islamic or "Hijri" calendar begins. There were several battles between the Medinan supporters of Muhammad and the Meccans, including the Battle of Badr (624 CE), Battle of Uhud (625 CE), and Battle of Khandaq (627 CE). The Meccans finally surrendered to Muhammad, probably because the Medinans were successful in cutting off food supplies to Mecca, and signed the Treaty of Hudaybiyah in 628 CE. In 629 CE Muhammad and his followers performed a pilgrimage to Mecca, and in 630 CE the Muslims occupied Mecca and began sending deputations to different parts of Arabia. After a final pilgrimage in 632 CE, Muhammad died and his body was buried in Medina.

Foremost among Muhammad's prophetic visions was his Night Journey [Ar. Isra] and Ascension [Ar. Mi'raj] referred to in Q 17:1. There are many different accounts of these two journeys, often linking the Night Journey and Ascension into a single event. In most of the accounts Muhammad is taken by means of a special animal named "Buraq" from Mecca to Jerusalem, and from Jerusalem Muhammad ascends through the seven heavens into the presence of God. In some accounts Muhammad meets various prophets in the different heavens through which he passes, and in other reports he meets all the prophets in Jerusalem and leads them in prayer. Some exegetes report that Muhammad traveled to various earthly sites associated with the prophets such as Mt. Sinai, the two cities at the edges of the earth, Bethlehem, and Jerusalem. During his trip through the heavens Muhammad is also shown the fate of sinners in hell and the rewards of the righteous in paradise. He sees the four rivers of paradise and the Lotus Tree, and is given the water of life (also identified as the river

Kawthar) to distribute to his followers. The accounts of Muhammad's Night Journey parallel the travels of Dhu al-Qarnayn, Alexander the Great, and Zosimos in the History of the Rechabites, and the accounts of his Ascension are similar to a number of the "tours of heaven and hell" found in texts such as the Apocalypse of Ezra.

MULLA SADRA (1571–1640 CE). Sadr al-Din Muhammad al-Shirazi, known as "Mulla Sadra," was one of the best known and original of Muslim philosophers. He lived during the early period of Safavid Iran and in his masterwork entitled "The Four Journeys" [Ar. al-Asfar al-Arba'a], he describes his own life as patterned after that of the prophet Muhammad. He studied Sufi thought, especially the works of Ibn Arabi and Suhrawardi, and relied most heavily on esoteric Shi'i traditions attributed to Ja'far al-Sadiq and Ali b. Abi Talib. Among his writings are Quran commentaries and philosophical works, the best known of which is his sophisticated mystical reflection on prophecy and theology entitled the "Wisdom of the Throne" [Ar. al-Hikma al-'Arshiyah].

MUSIC. Though attested only periodically in reference to prophecy, it is clear that music played an important role in Israelite prophetic circles, as it did elsewhere in the ancient Near East. Not only do prophecies appear in poetic forms that at times seem to have been sung (*see also* POETRY), but in some cases music served to induce the prophetic experience. According to the biblical record, Moses' sister Miriam, a prophet in her own right, is said to have sung her prophecies (Exod 15:20). The prophet Deborah also is known to have composed songs (Judg 4:4, Judges 5). The book of Samuel records that when King Saul was stricken with "an evil spirit of Yahweh" the young David would rid him of his distress by playing his lyre (1 Sam 16:23). King Saul too becomes enraptured in the prophetic spirit when he meets a band of prophets coming down from a high place prophesying to the music of "a lute, and a tambourine, and a pipe, and a lyre" (1 Sam 10:5).

– N –

NABI. Standard biblical Hebrew term for prophet with a long history in the ancient Near East (*see also* PROPHET). The term also appears in Arabic as the standard word for a prophet, and is used in the Quran roughly 50 times, though less frequently than the term often translated as "apostle" [Ar. rasul] (*see also* APOSTLE).

NABONIDUS. Last of the Babylonian kings (555–539 BCE) and a usurper who is referred to in Babylonian sources as having deserted Babylon and its god Marduk in favor of his hometown Haran and the worship of the moon god Sin. Afterward he fled to Tema in northern Arabia. For this act of hubris, the gods struck Nabonidus with lycanthropy; the text describes him as behaving like an animal. For this behavior he was remembered even beyond Babylon as an "insane" king. The descriptions of his act of hubris share much in common with the Prayer of Nabonidus (4QPrNab) found among the Dead Sea Scrolls (75–50 BCE), and his resulting divine lycanthropy closely resembles the description of the Babylonian king Nebuchadnezzar in the book of Daniel (Dan 4:15–32).

NAG HAMMADI. Site located near al-Qasr (ancient Chenoboskion), nine kilometers from the ruins of the Basilica of St. Pachomius, where 13 codices were discovered in 1945 dating back to the fourth century CE. Preserved in the codices are Coptic texts reflecting early Christian and other late antique religious ideas, including part of Plato's *Republic* and *Asclepius*. The texts appear to have been translated into Coptic from Greek by a number of different scribes thought by some scholars to be Pachomian Christian monks. The standard edition of the codices lists them according to the number of the codex and the number of the tractate in each codex (I,1-XIII,2). Some are extremely fragmentary, and others are attested by more than one copy. The types of texts found include apocalypses, commentaries on the Bible, gospels, letters, acts, doctrinal treatises, homilies, and prayers. Some are known from references in other sources, and most of them are clearly gnostic in character (*see also* GNOSIS AND GNOSTICISM). The discovery of these codices is comparable to the discovery of the Dead Sea Scrolls, having brought to light many otherwise unknown texts that help to fill out the rich spectrum of ideas found in late antiquity.

NAHUM. Book of prophecies of Nahum, a prophet whose hometown of Elkosh is unknown, and who apparently lived through the destruction of Nineveh in 612 BCE. Since the prophecy mentions the Assyrian sack of Thebes it cannot predate 663 BCE. The book is unique in that it contains no negative pronouncements of doom, but offers only a cry for joy over the fall of Nineveh.

NARSAI (c. 399–503 CE). East Syrian or Nestorian scholar, also known by "Narses," the Latinized form of his Persian name. Narsai was raised in a monastery and studied at the School of Edessa, over which he became director in 451 CE. He was a close follower of the theology of Theodore of Mopsuestia (c. 350–428 CE), who believed in the separate divine and human natures of Christ. Narsai wrote about 80 metrical homilies, which include much exegetical material.

NATHAN. Biblical prophet who prophesied during the reign of King David, and is credited with having composed a book in 1 Chr 29:29 and 2 Chr 9:29, though this work has not survived. Nathan was actively involved with royal affairs. He prophesied to David not to build a temple to Yahweh (2 Samuel 7), and was responsible for delivering David the parabolic news of Yahweh's punishment for his adulterous affair with Bathsheba (2 Samuel 12). Nathan also appears to have given David's son Solomon the supernomen Jedidiah (2 Sam 12:25), and had a hand, along with Zadoq the high priest, in anointing him as king (1 Kgs 1:45). His importance is signaled by the fact that he appears in the liturgy (Ps 51:2). Talmudic tradition credits Nathan, and Gad the seer, as being responsible for completing the book of Samuel (TB Baba Batra 15a).

NAZIR. Biblical Hebrew term for a man or woman specially dedicated or consecrated by a vow to serve Yahweh, the God of Israel. The term also is found in the Quran 44 times [Ar. nadhir] in reference to certain prophets, often paired with and contrasted to the "Herald" [Ar. basher], who brings good news.

The Bible characterizes Nazirs as ascetics. They are forbidden to drink intoxicants, come into contact with grapes or grape seeds, touch dead matter, or cut their hair (Numbers 6). Usually the vow was voluntary and temporary (Amos 2:11), and it could be imposed upon a child from birth (Judg 13:4–5). Only in rare cases was the vow taken for life (e.g., the judge Samson, Judg 13:5, 16:7). When the term of the vow was complete, the Nazir offered his or her hair on a burning altar as a sacrifice (Num 6:18), though the historian Josephus states that the Nazir would offer it to the priests (Antiquities 19.6.1).

Nazirite vows continued to be taken very late in post-exilic times, as is attested from a tomb inscription discovered on Mt. Scopus in Jerusalem that identifies the tomb as belonging to a family of Nazirites. Later Jewish tradition preserves a tension with regard to the Nazir, whose sometime rash vows often went unfulfilled. Thus, one midrashic text even refers to the Nazir as a sinner (Sifre Numbers 30). Other Jewish writings view the Nazir's holiness as comparable to the high priest (Mishnah Nazir 7:1; TB Ta'anith 11a–11b). Luke 1:15 describes John the Baptist as being a Nazirite from birth, and 2 Cor 6:17 seems to impose at least part of the Nazirite vow upon Christians.

Many of the prohibitions associated with the Nazirite vow are found in Muslim practice. The Quran and Islamic law forbid the drinking of wine, and this is specifically tied to being sober for the worship of God. In the state of sacralization during the pilgrimage [Ar. hajj], Muslim pilgrims do not cut their hair. The act of desacralization upon leaving the pilgrimage involves cutting the hair in a way that is similar to the offering made in the biblical Nazirite vow.

The use of the cognate term [Ar. nadhir] in the Quran usually is interpreted to mean a "warner" or a prophet who warns people of their punishment for not worshipping God. This scenario is generalized in Q 17:16 where it is implied that a warner is sent to all people, calling upon them to repent, before God destroys them (see also Q 43:23). Some verses use the term in reference to particular prophets such as Noah (Q 11:25, 71:2). Other passages refer to a "clear warner" [Ar. nadhir mubin] (Q 22:49, 29:50, 46:9, 51:51, 67:26). The Arabic word for "vow" [Ar. nadhr] is cognate to the Hebrew, and also appears as a reference to one consecrated to God through a vow outside of the Quran.

NECROMANCY. Practice of communicating with the dead in order to ascertain information, often oracles about the future. Necromancy is a widely attested divinatory art in the ancient Near East. Records from Mesopotamia refer to necromancy from very early times, but show a significant increase in the practice from the mid- to the end of the first millennium BCE. Necromancy was also practiced at sites peripheral to Mesopotamia such as Mari and Ugarit, though the archives of Ebla have yielded no evidence for it.

In Mesopotamia, and also among the Hittites, the practice appears to have involved the digging of pits. Texts describe the process as "raising the dead," thus demonstrating a possible conceptual relationship to later beliefs in resurrection. Ghosts of the dead also could be summoned by way of dreams, since dreaming served as a portal to the next world (*see also* DREAMS AND DREAM INTERPRETATION). In Mesopotamia and at Ugarit, the summoned dead are sometimes cited as "gods" [Akk. ilu, ilanu; Ug. ilu], which demonstrates the close tie that existed between necromancy and the cults of the dead. Texts from Ugarit, and later from Phoenicia, also detail the events of a special feast [Ug. Mrzh] at which Ugarit's dead kings are summoned to dine with the living. The feast and the praxis for summoning the dead involved excessive inebriation (*see also* DRUNKENNESS).

Necromancy was practiced in ancient Egypt too, though knowledge of the praxis involved is meager. It is known that especially during the New Kingdom period (1551–712 BCE) the Egyptians sometimes wrote letters to their dead in order to procure their help in earthly matters, and to receive from them messages by way of dreams.

Necromancy also appears in biblical texts. It is attested in monarchic times by the story of King Saul seeking the female necromancer [Heb. ba'alat 'ob, lit. "possessor of the ghost"] at Endor (1 Samuel 28). According to this text, Saul had outlawed the practice himself, but felt compelled to seek a necromancer to summon the dead prophet Samuel when other sanctioned divinatory means including the prophets, Urim (and Thummim), and dreams failed him (1 Sam 28:3, 28:6–7). The reference to dreams here may imply an incubatory rite by which one sought the dead through dreams (cf., Isa 65:4 in LXX). It is noteworthy that when he is summoned, the dead prophet Samuel is called an "elohim," the commonest Hebrew term for God in the Bible (1 Sam 28:13; see also Isa 8:19–23), though some scholars read the word as the plural "gods" and see it as referencing the necromancer's personal deities whom she summoned to help raise Samuel. The necromantic praxis is not detailed, but it is clear that while the necromancer sees the deceased, Saul does not (1 Sam

28:13), though he apparently hears him (1 Sam 28:15). Some scholars relate the Hebrew word "ghost" ['ob] to the Hebrew word for "father" ['ab], and see Israelite necromancy (as in Mesopotamia, Mari, and Ugarit) as closely tied to ancestral cults of the dead.

Some of the legal materials that proscribe necromancy do, in fact, draw a distinction between necromancy and the worship of Yahweh by underscoring Yahweh's "fatherly" relationship with the Israelites (Deut 14:1). Though banned by King Saul, necromancy continued to be practiced in Israel, especially during the reign of King Manasseh (687–642 BCE), which scholars attribute to Assyrian influence (2 Kgs 21:6). During the reign of Manasseh's successor Josiah (640–609 BCE), efforts were taken to eradicate the practice (2 Kgs 21:6, 23:24). Necromancy is banned also in the legislative code (Deut 4:1, 8:11).

The drinking feast known from Ugarit [Ug. mrzh] also appears in the Bible in the condemnations of the prophets (Jer 16:1–9, Amos 6:7). Its use of excessive drinking as a method for obtaining oracles is ridiculed by the prophet Isaiah (Isa 28:7–22), who elsewhere describes the praxis as involving ventriloquism and the eliciting of birdlike sounds (Isa 8:19–23, 28:10, 29:4). The mention of the "House of the Marzeah and Maioumas Festival" on a mosaic tile floor in Madeba (in modern Jordan) is the latest attestation of the feast and demonstrates its connection to the Greek drinking festival. Later Jewish tradition reads the incident at Baal-Peor (Num 25:2) as a reference to the marzeah as well (Targum Yerushalmi to Num 25:2; Sifre Numbers 131), but also knows of the "House of the Marzeah" simply as a house of mourning (TB Mo'ed Qatan 28b; Ketuboth 69b; Baba Batra 10a).

NEHEMIAH. Jewish governor of Judah in the post-exilic age and the name of the biblical book named after him. About the person Nehemiah very little is known. According to the Bible, he first served as the cupbearer for the Persian king Artaxerxes I (r. 465–424 BCE), and after being appointed governor in 445 BCE, he went to Jerusalem to oversee the construction of its walls amidst local strife and threatening regional opposition. After 12 years in Jerusalem, and before the project was completed, he went back to Persia (Neh 5:14), but returned to Jerusalem several years later (Neh 13:7). It is probably during this return trip that he brought the priest Ezra with him.

The book of Nehemiah details the historical events and difficulties of his governorship and describes a number of religious reforms undertaken by Ezra, including the reinstitution of the Feast of Booths [Heb. sukkoth] and the Sabbath, and the forbidding of mixed marriages (Neh 8:14, 9:1, 10:32). The Talmud (TB Sanhedrin 38a) regards Nehemiah as identical to the figure of Zerubbabel, who also is described as a Persia-appointed governor of Judah in charge of Jerusalem's building operations (Hag 1:1, 2:2; Zech 4:6–10; Ezra 4:1–3). Unlike Ezra, however, who is regarded as a second Moses, Nehemiah is treated less positively by later Jewish tradition. He sometimes is described as a rather self-interested man who looked down upon previous governors of Jerusalem, an attitude for which God punished him by taking one of the books he authored and attributing it to Ezra. Hence, the origin of the biblical book of Ezra (TB Sanhedrin 93b, Baba Batra 15a). 2 Macc 1:19–2:12 attributes to Nehemiah an important role in discovering the heavenly fire for lighting God's altar, which the prophet Jeremiah had hidden before the destruction by the Babylonians.

NEW JERUSALEM. The concept of a future Jerusalem as a new religious capital from which Yahweh will reign (Zech 14:16) and to which the nations will flock in pilgrimage (Zech 8:21). In the Bible, the concept appears only in prophetic texts of the post-exilic period, and probably is related to the vision of a new temple first articulated by the prophet Ezekiel (Ezekiel 40–42). Though the returning exiles did rebuild Yahweh's temple in Jerusalem (520–515 BCE) it was not as grandiose as the former temple constructed by Solomon, and in any event, was not the same temple as described by Ezekiel in his vision. Thus, later generations came to believe that the realization of Ezekiel's temple would occur in the future at the time of the eschaton (*see also* ESCHATOLOGY). Such a belief must have been widespread, for according to Josephus (Antiquities 13.68), the Jews of Heliopolis believed that the exiled high priest Onias would build a New Jerusalem there in accordance with the prophecy of Isa 19:18. Such a view is represented also by a number of fragments discovered among the Dead Sea Scrolls at Qumran, including the Temple Scroll (11QTemple), which details the dimensions of the future temple and describe its functionaries. These texts make it clear that the community that authored the scrolls expected the eschaton to occur in its lifetime. When the second temple was destroyed in 70 CE, the eschaton was put in the far more distant future, and along with it, the New Jerusalem.

Muslim exegesis of Q 17:4 refers to the "old Jerusalem" as having been destroyed twice, marking the end of the chosen status of the Israelites and of Jerusalem as the home of the prophets. There are many Muslim exegetical identifications of Mecca as the New Jerusalem in the sense that it is said to be the "desert Zion" (Isaiah 19–20, 35, 60; Psalm 153) or the "vine in the wilderness" (Ezek 19:10–14; Isa 54:1, Q 14:37). Other Muslim texts describe the cities at the edges of the earth (*see also* JABAL QAF; JABAL SIN) as having the dimensions and all the characteristics of the heavenly Jerusalem as described in Rev 21:1–22:5. Christian exegetes also apply biblical prophetic images of Jerusalem to Christians (2 Ezra 10:25–28; Rev 21:9) and to the person of Jesus (Mark 14:58).

NIMROD. Mythic hero and hunter whom the Bible mentions only very briefly as the son of Cush (Gen 10:8–9; 1 Chr 1:10), thus associating him with Ethiopia (Gen 10:6). The Quran does not mention Nimrod by name, but Muslim exegetes identify him as the tyrant king against whom Abraham contested in Babylon. The prophet Micah uses the expression "land of Nimrod" as a title for Assyria. Jewish tradition identifies Nimrod as Amraphel, one of the kings of the Mesopotamian coalition who warred against Abraham in Gen 14:1 (TB Erubin 53a). The Babylonian king Nebuchadnezzar II also is called the "descendant of Nimrod" (TB Pesahim 94a–94b), and thus, Nimrod is described as an idolater and self-proclaimed god.

By way of a word play on his name, the rabbis associated Nimrod with "rebellion" [Heb. marad], and thus with inciting the Babylonians to build the Tower of Babel in Genesis 11 (TB Pesahim 94b; Hagigah 13a; Avodah Zarah 53b; Hullin 89a). In the Quran it is the pharaoh and Haman who build the Tower of Babel (Q 28:38–42, 36–37). Nimrod also is credited with predicting the birth of Abraham by way of astrology, and with throwing him into a fiery furnace in the Talmud (TB Pesahim 118a) and Quran (Q 21:68, 29:24, 37:97). Elsewhere in midrashic texts Nimrod gives Abraham the giant named Og as a gift, who is identified also with his servant Eliezer. Nimrod was given the garments of skins that Adam and Eve wore by his father Cush, who had received them from his father Ham. The skins made Nimrod invincible (TB Pesahim 44b; Pirqe d'Rabbi Eliezer 24), and eventually were stripped from him when he died in battle against Esau. They eventually were passed on to Jacob and his son Joseph. Another tradition credits Esau with killing Nimrod's son (Pirqe d'Rabbi Eliezer 32; Targum Yerushalmi on Gen 25:25). Nimrod also is said to be the first person to eat meat. He is later identified with Zoroaster, and Muslim tradition asserts that he was one of four men to rule the entire earth.

NOADIAH. Name of a female prophet who lived in Jerusalem during the post-exilic period who uttered false prophesies to frighten Nehemiah into stopping the construction of Jerusalem's walls (Neh 6:14). She may be the one blamed by Nehemiah, along with other prophets and powerful individuals, for informing the Persian king that Nehemiah had hired his own prophets to proclaim the arrival of a king in Judah (Neh 6:7).

NOAH. Famous survivor of the great flood, considered a prophet in the Quran and Muslim exegesis. The story of a flood and a flood survivor is common in ancient mythologies. The Sumerian Deluge Story, preserved in six columns, recounts how Ziusudra son of Ubartutu of Shuruppak survives the flood and becomes immortal. The Epic of Gilgamesh (Tablet XI) refers to a flood that Utnapishtim (also called Atrahasis) survives because he was commanded by Enki to build a cubical ship. He is later made immortal. Zoroastrian texts relate the story of Yima, the first man and king who survives a flood with a number of animals on the instruction of Ahura Mazda. Indian and ancient Greek texts also describe cosmic floods.

Noah's story is contained in Gen 6:8–9:28, and is told in greater detail in Jub 4:28–10:17. Commanded to build an ark by God, Noah constructs what appears to be a large rectangular roofed barge into which he enters living species of all kinds in an effort to save them, and his family, from the impending deluge. Later Jewish tradition provides a far more complex picture of Noah and his story. Genesis Rabbah 36:4 explains that he became a castrate when a lion attacked him while leaving the ark. The Talmud relates that the biblical giant, and enemy of Moses, Og, survived the flood by sitting atop the ark (TB Niddah 61a). The Genesis Apocryphon adds details to the story of Noah, especially concerning his birth and the reaction of his father Lamech, a motif also found in 1 Enoch 106.

Noah also appears in other biblical contexts, especially associated with other prophetic figures. Exodus depicts Moses as a Noah figure. Both Noah and Moses are saved by an ark [Heb. teba] (Gen 6:14; Exod 2:3), and Moses leads the Israelites through the "flood" of the sea delivering them from the Egyptians (Exodus 15). In Isa 54:9–10 God compares the current situation of the Israelites to the days of Noah, especially the two covenants (Gen 9:16; Isa 54:10). Ezek 14:12–20 mentions Noah, Daniel, and Job as paradigms of righteousness. Matt 24:38–39 portrays Jesus as another Noah, 1 Pet 3:20 compares the flood to the baptism, and 2 Pet 2:5–6 sees both Noah and Lot as two righteous men. Heb 11:7 also lists Noah among other righteous men, a tradition that echoes Ezek 14:14.

The story of Noah appears also in the Quran, and plays a much more prominent role there than it does in Genesis (Q 7:59–64, 10:71–73, 11:25–49, 21:76–77, 23:23–30, 26:105–122, 29:14–15, 37:75–82, 54:9–17, 71:1–28). Noah is mentioned by name 43 times in the Quran as opposed to the brief reference to him in Genesis. In the Quran and in Muslim exegesis Noah is seen as the first of a series of prophets including Hud, Salih, Lot, and Shuayb who epitomize the regular prophetic pattern that includes a prophet being sent, rejected, and the destruction of those who rejected him.

Muslim exegesis on Q 29:14 states that Noah lived 950 years, was 480 years old when his prophethood started, was a prophet for 120 years, rode the ark when he was 600 years of age, and lived another 350 years after the flood. Tabari reports that the wood used to construct the ark was taken from a special tree that God ordered Noah to plant. The tree grew for 40 years while Noah prophesied to his people. Muslim exegetes describe the flood as coming from "pits" in the earth (Q 11:40), the gates of the sky (Q 54:11), and water boiling over the "oven" of Adam and Eve (Q 23:27). Q 11:42–44 refers to the fourth son of Noah, identified by Muslim exegesis as Yam (Heb. and Ar. for "sea"), who drowns in the flood. During the flood, the original Ka'bah is raised to heaven to become the "visited temple" [Ar.

bayt al-maʿmur], and the ark circumambulates its earthly location seven times before coming to rest on a mountain. According to Q 11:44, the resting place of the ark is on Mt. Judi, located in the land of Ararat in northern Mesopotamia (the biblical tradition has mountains [pl.] of Ararat, and the Mesopotamian tradition, Mt. Nisir or Nimush). Other Muslim exegetes state that Noah left the ark on the Day of Ashura of Muharram, and that this is the reason that one should fast on that day. Ibn Kathir reports that the grave of Noah is considered to be in Mecca or in a town known as Kurk Noah.

NUMBERS. The fourth book of the Torah (Pentateuch) takes its English title from the Greek of the Septuagint, which renders the "census" reported in Num 1:1–46. The Hebrew title [Heb. Be-Midbar] derives from its mention as the place (lit. "in the wilderness") where Yahweh spoke to Moses in Num 1:1. Many scholars see various sources present in Numbers, though the criteria used to delineate these sources are not without methodological problems. The book contains a mixture of historical narrative and legal statutes. It reports the Israelite registration of a census and military engagement (Numbers 1–3), the wandering of the tribes en route to Canaan, from Sinai to the Transjordan (Num 10:11–27, 32–34), and also contains a variety of priestly (Num 4:1–10:10), sacrificial (Numbers 28–29), and civil laws (Numbers 35–36).

NUSAYRIS. Muslim group, originating in ninth-century CE Iraq, which maintains the divinity of the Shiʿi imams and salvation through secret knowledge. The group traces its origins back to Muhammad b. Nusayr, who claimed to be the prophet of the divine Tenth Imam Ali al-Hadi (d. 868 CE). Nusayris hold that all souls are from a preexistent divinity and were cast to earth to be exiled in the material world. Knowledge of the true God comes to them through manifestations of his Essence [Ar. maʿna], his Name [Ar. ism], and the Gate [Ar. bab]. The earthly appearance of this "trinity" is identified with prophetic figures. The Essence was incarnated in Abel, Seth, Joseph, Joshua, Asaf, the apostle Peter, and Ali b. Abi Talib, who were followed by the first 11 Shiʿi imams. The Name was incarnated in Adam, Noah, Jacob, Moses, Solomon, Jesus, and Muhammad, each of whom was accompanied by an incarnation of the Gate. The Gate for the Essence of Ali b. Abi Talib and the Name of Muhammad was Salman al-Farisi. Muhammad b. Nusayr was the Gate of the Eleventh Imam Hasan al-Askari. Acknowledgment of the secret knowledge transmitted by this three-fold manifestation is said to result in an end to reincarnation in the material world and return of the soul to the astral plane where it resumes it original existence as a star.

– O –

OBADIAH. Book in the Minor Prophets and the prophet for which it is named. Nothing is known about the prophet Obadiah other than his very short prophecy, the shortest book in the Hebrew Bible, which appears to place him shortly after the destruction of Jerusalem (Obad 20 mentions the exiles). Obadiah's prophecy is aimed primarily at denouncing the nation of Edom for its role in the Babylonian invasion, but it ends on a positive note, the promise of Judah's return and destruction of its enemies. Though some have interpreted the final verse of the prophecy as an eschatological reference, its use of the term messiahs, in the plural, is usually taken as a reference to Judah's earthly anointed kings.

ODED. Biblical prophet mentioned in 2 Chr 15:8 along with his prophetic son (*see also* AZARIAH), and credited with him as responsible for encouraging the religious reforms of King Asa of Judah (913–873 BCE). After a bloody civil war during the reign of Pekah the king of Israel (736–732 BCE), Judah's army was routed and many of its soldiers taken captive as slaves. Oded prophesied to the Israelite soldiers in Samaria that Yahweh would execute his wrath on Israel if they retained the Judaean captives and the booty (2 Chr 28:9). The soldiers promptly responded by treating the captives kindly.

ODES OF SOLOMON. Collection of 42 hymns attributed to Solomon, extant in Coptic, Greek, and Syriac. The best attested of these are the Syriac, which has led many scholars to conclude that the hymns were originally composed in Syriac. The collection dates to the second or third century CE, though the earliest clear datable quotation is found in the work of a Christian scholar of the fourth century CE. A third-century Greek manuscript contains the 11th Ode, and the two Syriac manuscripts date to the 10th and 15th centuries, respectively. Throughout, the hymns display imagery that suggests connections with apocalyptic literature and the Gospel of John, as well as certain gnostic ideas.

OMEN. Any phenomenon or circumstance interpreted to portend good or evil, or to token a future event. In the ancient Near East, where gods were believed to influence all things in the natural world, there was, philosophically speaking, no room for coincidence. Therefore, any solicited or unsolicited occurrence within the realm of one's perception could be interpreted as an omen or divine missive (*see also* DIVINATION).

Though a belief in the veracity of omens as divine messages is attested among the earliest written records in Mesopotamia, the creation of extensive omen collections began first in the 21st century BCE and continued to expand until the connections became relatively standardized in the seventh century BCE. These often massive collections record the omenistic interpretations of dreams; assorted sounds; specific markings in animal viscera; sleeping and wakeful behavioral patterns; family relations; celestial and atmospheric phenomena; various types of sexual acts; the appearance of demons and ghosts; and the movements of a wide assortment of animals, reptiles, and birds. As such they represent the divinatory predictions of events, making them comparable to prophecy as a mode of divine communication.

A variety of figures are credited with the responsibility for interpreting such omens in Mesopotamia, the great majority of whom were highly erudite and trained with interdisciplinary mantic skills (*see also* MEDICINE; PROPHET). Omens are typically recorded as legal judgments with a protasis ("if such and such occurs. . . .") and an apodosis ("then it means the following. . . ."). The "if x, then y" formula represents a conditional circumstance with room for contingencies. To interpret an omen, a mantic would employ a variety of hermeneutical strategies, but foremost among them were the use of binary codes with attached values (e.g., right side = good, left side = bad) and punning (*see also* WORD PLAY).

Though there is less evidence for the interpretation of omens at Mari and Ugarit, it is clear that mantics in these locations were influenced by Mesopotamian conceptions. The Israelites too believed in omens as divine messages, but conceived of them through the lens of a very different religious system (*see also* MONOLATRY). The two Hebrew words most frequently translated as "omen" in the Hebrew Bible are often rendered "sign" [Heb. 'ot] and "wonder" [Heb. mophet]. In conception and function these terms overlap considerably with the Mesopotamian understanding of omens. In fact, the Akkadian term for "omen, sign" [Akk. ittu] is etymologically related to the Hebrew term "sign" ['ot] (*see also* SIGNS; WONDERS).

OMOPHAGIA. Practice of eating the raw flesh of an animal, usually after tearing it into pieces (*see also* SPARAGMOS). Omophagia is attested at Mari as the prophetic drama of an "ecstatic" [Akk. muhhu], along with sparagmos and prophetic nudity (cf., 1 Sam 19:20–24; Isaiah 20). In the Greek world it appears in Homeric accounts and was practiced periodically by followers of the god Dionysus. According to Saint Nilus, the practice survived into the fourth century CE among the Arabs of the Sinai Peninsula in practices surrounding the sacrifice known as "rending" [Ar. nikayah], a practice thought to be at the origins of certain views of sacrifice and the Christian Eucharist.

ORACLE. A medium, instrument, or agent through which deities speak or make known their intentions to humans, and the location where these divine intentions are revealed. As the etymology of the English word *oracle*, from the Latin term [Lat. orare] meaning "pray, entreat, speak," demonstrates, omens constitute a solicited form of divination in which a deity responds to human inquiry, usually in a time of personal or national crisis.

Methods for obtaining oracles in the ancient Near East were diverse and numerous (*see also* DIVINATION; DREAMS AND DREAM INTERPRETATION; OMEN; SIGNS). The Hebrew Bible refers to oracles simply as "the word of Yahweh," a designation used for unsolicited prophecies as well. The Hebrew word often translated in English Bibles as "oracle" [Heb. massa', lit. "burden, lifting up"] does not in itself clarify whether it was given in response to an inquiry (*see also* PROPHECY). Moreover, the Hebrew Bible provides numerous clear examples of oracles for which the term is not used. In some cases oracles appear to involve divinatory tools such as the Ark of the Covenant (Judg 20:27), lots (Jon 1:7), the ephod (1 Sam 23:10), and the Urim and Thummim (Deut 33:8), whereas other oracles require no tools or forms of praxis.

Typically priests or prophets serve as the mediums of oracles, and often oracles are sought in sanctuaries. The patriarchs obtain oracles at sanctuaries in Shechem (Gen 12:6–7) and Bethel (Genesis 28; 1 Kgs 12:31), and Moses consults Yahweh's word in the desert sanctuary known as the Tent of Meeting (Exod 18:15, 18:19, 33:7–11). Later during the time of the prophet Samuel and early monarchy, oracles are delivered at a sanctuary at Shiloh (1 Samuel 1–2). Large trees also served as places for receiving prophetic oracles (*see also* RHABDOMANCY).

In Israel's early history the priesthood (*see also* LEVITE) appears to have exercised a monopoly on divine oracles (Deut 33:8–10). The Levite Moses, for example, is given a privileged position as an oracular medium (Exod 33:7–11; Num 12:6–8). With the rise of Classical Prophecy in the eighth century BCE, however, the role of the priest as a medium of divine oracles diminished in favor of the prophet. Though lots continued to be used periodically, kings no longer sought oracles by way of the ephod and Urim and Thummim, both under the purview of the priesthood, but instead sought them from the prophets (Jer 37:3–10; Isa 37:5; 1 Kgs 22:5–12; cf., 1 Sam 23:2–6). In addition, some formerly sanctioned oracular devices now became illegitimate. The prophet Hosea condemns the use of the ephod, teraphim, and the massebah (Hos 3:4, *see also* MASSEBAH; SIBYLLINE ORACLES; TERAPHIM; URIM AND THUMMIM).

ORIGEN (c. 185–251 CE). Early Christian authority and important Bible exegete. Origen was born in Alexandria and was instructed in catechetical studies from his early twenties. He studied philosophy under Ammonius Saccas and other Neoplatonic theorists. He traveled to Rome, Caesarea, Anatolia, and Arabia, spending 18 years in Jerusalem and Caesarea. There are some 2,000 works attributed to him, including commentaries on almost every book of the Bible, though not all of them are fully extant. Of the 279 extant homilies on the Hebrew Bible, 21 are preserved in Greek. The rest are in Latin. Origen is famous for his allegorical or spiritualizing exegesis in which he applies typological and metaphorical models to the Bible.

– P –

PARACLETE. Term derived from the Greek word [Gk. parakletos] used five times in the New Testament in connection with Jesus (John 14:16, 14:26, 15:26, 16:7–8; 1 John 2:1). Muslim exegetes trace the term through Syriac, relating it to Q 61:6, and take it as Jesus' reference to the future coming of the prophet Muhammad.

In the New Testament Jesus is identified as the paraclete (1 John 2:1), commonly understood to mean an "advocate" or "one who intercedes" on behalf of his followers. Jesus also states that the Father will provide another paraclete (John 14:16), a "Spirit of Truth" whom the world can never accept. John 14:26 glosses paraclete with the term "Holy Spirit," and some Christian exegetes have understood this to be a reference to the sending of the Holy Spirit after Jesus as the third aspect of the Trinity. John 15:26 adds that the paraclete shall be Jesus' witness, and in John 16:5–15 Jesus delivers a farewell address, speaking about the paraclete. The paraclete is to be sent after Jesus, and will glorify Jesus and show the world how wrong they were about him.

Scholars have identified the paraclete with a number of figures, including the Mandaean Yawar, the prophet Elijah, or an anonymous prophetic figure who succeeds Jesus as Joshua did Moses and Elisha did Elijah. The Targum to Job 33:23 translates the "mediator" [Heb. melis] with "paraclete" [Aram. parakleta], which some understand to refer to the angel Michael. Texts from the Dead Sea Scrolls also conflate the angel Michael and a "Spirit of Truth," which echoes the references in the Gospel of John. According to Augustine, the Manichaeans claimed to have letters from Jesus, and it is known that Mani did write a letter to Edessa claiming to be the paraclete foretold by Jesus in John 16:7–8.

Q 61:6 appears to paraphrase John 15:25–26, but has Jesus state that the prophet who comes after him is called "Ahmad." Scholars have shown that the Arabic word *Ahmad*, meaning "someone worthy of praise," may show that the Greek term [Gk. parakletos] was understood to derive from the Greek term meaning "something praised" or "celebrated" [Gk. periklutos]. Others relate the Arabic term to a Syriac translation of the Greek term, which is attested in the Palestinian Syriac Lectionary [Syr. munahemana] with the meaning "comforter," but closely related to the Arabic word and name also meaning "someone worthy of praise" [Ar. muhammad]. Ibn Ishaq quotes John 15:25–26 and adds that the Syriac term is simply the Syriac for the name Muhammad, and although it is translated into Greek differently [Ar. baraqlitus], both terms are used as Jesus' references to the coming of Muhammad.

PARALLELISM. The commonest feature of biblical Hebrew poetry (found also in Ugaritic and Mesopotamian poetry), in which two or more poetic clauses or stichs parallel one another in thought (biblical Hebrew has no meter or rhyme). Much of the Quran also is composed in this way, and it is characteristic of pre-Islamic poetry as well.

The two clauses are separated by a brief pause and concluded by a longer final pause. To demonstrate, Ps 122:7 reads: (A) "Let there be peace within your ramparts; (B) tranquility within your fortress." Here the poetic stich marked (A) mirrors the (B) stich by paralleling "peace" with "tranquility," and "ramparts" with "fortress." The second stich is merely a reverberation of the preceding one with which it forms a single thought. The two main types of parallelism are antithetical parallelism (in which the parallels contrast one another), and synonymous parallelism (with parallel synonyms, as in the example from Psalm 127). Scholars have shown that in creating such poetic parallels poets culled from a stock repertoire of "word pairs" (i.e., synonyms, antonyms, and other words that tend to be grouped together). Since prophecies are written in verse, parallelism must be seen as a deliberate component of prophetic discourse, one that either was worked into a poem while performing it orally or which helped to structure the prophetic discourse in written form.

PARAPHRASE OF SHEM. Apocalyptic text describing a revelation to Shem, given by Derkeleas, a being identified as the likeness and son of the light. The Coptic text is the best preserved of all the Nag Hammadi codices (VII,1) and may relate to the "Paraphrase of Seth" mentioned by Christian heresiologists.

The text opens with Shem's mind separated from his body and ascending to the top of the world where there is no earthly material, only light. Shem is shown a cosmogony involving the mixing of Light, Darkness, and Spirit. From this interaction comes the creation of the material world, which the text describes in terms of demons, spirits, and beasts. Also portrayed are events from biblical history including the flood, destruction of Sodom, and the building of the Tower of Babel. Derkeleas descends to the lower realms in the form of body, but is not recognized as the savior. After completing his mission, Derkeleas ascends back into the upper realms, is clothed in glory, and communicates knowledge of his salvation to the elect race of Shem.

PASHUR. Son of Immer, a prophet (Jer 20:6), but also a priest and chief officer of Yahweh's temple (Jer 20:1, 20:6). When the prophet Jeremiah prophesied disaster for Jerusalem, Pashur had him flogged (Jer 20:2), for which Jeremiah retorted by predicting that he would go into exile along with other Babylonian captives.

PATRIARCHS. Though the term *patriarch* is sometimes applied to any male leader of a biblical tribe or clan, it is more commonly applied strictly to the founding fathers of the Israelite people and religion, Abraham, Isaac, and Jacob. Since the lives of the patriarchs, especially that of Jacob (who is surnamed Israel in Gen 32:29), represent the early history of Israel, the stories that relate them often are read allegorically (e.g., Gal 4:21–31).

PEOPLE OF MOSES. A group of Israelites who, in Jewish and Islamic traditions, are said to have abstained from the sins of the other Israelites, and to have been removed from regular human society and taken to the ends of the earth. Q 7:159 refers to the "People of Moses" who are guided by the truth and act justly according to it. Muslim exegesis explains that this refers to a group of Israelites, perhaps one of the tribes, who did not reject and kill the prophets sent to them by God. Because of this God removed this people from the midst of the Israelites and transported them to a city called Jabars or Jabalq, located at the eastern or western extremes of the earth (*see also* JABAL QAF; JABAL SIN). In some of these accounts God creates a subterranean passage through which the people pass to the ends of the earth. Some exegetes claim that the people were taken by God beyond China and were cut off from human society by a river of sand that only ceased flowing on the Sabbath. Others claim that the people were taken beyond Spain, and live in a place where all the pebbles are gems, mountains are of gold and silver, and all their food and clothing grows on special trees at their doorsteps. In some of the accounts of the prophet Muhammad's Night Journey it is reported that he visited the people at the ends of the earth. They are described as being "Muslims" before Islam, praying toward the Ka'bah in Mecca, believing in Muhammad, and renouncing the Sabbath.

The History of the Rechabites recounts the journey of Zosimus to visit the "Sons of Rechab" who were miraculously transported from Jerusalem to the edges of the earth in the time of the prophet Jeremiah. Like the prophet Muhammad, Zosimus is escorted by an angel and an unusual animal to this remnant of the Israelites who escaped Jerusalem before it was destroyed on account of the sins of the Israelites. The Sons of Rechab are clothed with the same garments worn by Adam and Eve before their fall, they eat manna, are never sick, and rejoice at the death of their members. A similar account referring to the "Lost Tribes" of the Israelites is found in the third-century CE Christian Latin poet Commodian and in the apocryphal Acts of St. Matthew.

Jewish writings state that the "Lost Tribes" and the "Sons of Moses" will return at the end of time. The Talmud mentions the three places of exile of the 10 lost tribes and their return to a rebuilt Jerusalem (TY Sanhedrin 10:5). It also explains, on the basis of Deuteronomy 9:14 and 1 Chronicles 23:15–17, that the "Sons of Moses" [Heb. Bnei Moshe] multiplied on account of God's promise to make a separate people out of his descendants (TB Berakoth 7a). Drawing upon Hosea 8:8, Zechariah 14:4, and Isaiah 49:21, a number of rabbinic sources describe how God will cause the lost tribes to tunnel underground and emerge from under the Mt. of Olives in Jerusalem at the end of time. The *Chronicles of Jerahmeel* also describes how a cloud brought the Sons of Moses to a place cut off by a river called "Sabbatianus" that is full of sand and stones (*see also* CHRONICLES OF JERAHMEEL). Among these people there are no unclean animals, and all the men are students of the law and are pious. Later medieval texts, such as the *Story of the Sons of Moses* [Aram. Agadata de-Bnei Moshe], also provide information about the People of Moses and their return to Jerusalem at the end of time.

PEOPLE OF THE BOOK. Term used in the Quran and in Muslim sources for Jews and Christians, but also extended to include Sabians, Zoroastrians, Hindus, and others. The Arabic term [Ahl al-Kitab] is found about 30 times in the Quran and refers strictly to Jews and Christians. The Sabians are grouped together with Christians and Jews in Q 5:69 and Q 2:62. Q 22:17 mentions the Christians, Jews, Sabians, and Zoroastrians, but these are not all considered People of the Book by Muslim exegetes. Muslim exegetes usually understand the term as a reference to the Jews and Christians, who are remnants of the Israelites who had received revealed books such as the Torah, the Psalms, and the Gospel. Q 5:47 specifically mentions the "People of the Gospel," apparently distinguishing Christians from Jews. Muslim exegetical interpretations often are given on the authority of the People of the Book, though more specific designations also appear, such as the "People of the First Book" or "People of the Torah," which refer to the Israelites or the Jews. References to interpretations given on the authority of the People of the Book do not normally appear to be taken from the Bible, but rather from Jewish and Christian interpretations or retellings of the Bible.

PEOPLE OF THE CAVE. Story of youths who slept in a cave for over 300 years, found in Q 18:9–26, and sharing affinity with a Christian story in which youths also sleep in a cave through periods of persecution. The Christian account, known as the "Seven Sleepers of Ephesus," was circulated in Greek and Syriac during late antiquity, and scholars generally date its composition to the sixth century CE. In this story, seven Christian youths flee into a cave near Ephesus where they sleep for centuries until they awake in the time of the Christian emperor Theodosius II (r. 408–450 CE). Their cave subsequently is made into a place of worship (*see also* CAVE). The Quran account states that the youths, whose number is given as three, five, or seven (Q 18:22), were fleeing to protect their worship of the one God (Q 18:16). The length of the sleep is given as 309 years (Q 18:25), though Q 18:26 states that God knows best the length of the sleep, and it appears variously in Muslim exegesis. The sleepers think they have slept only for a day, but discover it has been longer when they attempt to buy provisions in the city with their old money (Q 18:19). In Q 18:18, it is mentioned that the sleepers had with them a dog whose name is given as "Qitmir," a term used in Muslim contexts to protect against loss. Other exegetes claim the dog's name is "Raqim," mentioned in Q 18:9, but most exegetes understand "raqim" as a reference to an inscription placed over the site of the cave. The cave of Q 18:9–26 has been located variously in Ephesus, Jordan, Turkistan, and Spain. There also is an account of the Caliph Wathiq sending an expedition in the ninth century CE to locate the cave in the area of Cappadocia.

PEOPLE OF THE WELL. People to whom a prophet was sent, mentioned in Q 25:38 and 50:12. The Quran provides little information other than to list them along with the Ad, Thamud, people of Noah, the pharaoh, brothers of Lot, People of the Tanglewood, and the People of Tubba. All of these are people whom God destroyed when they rejected the prophets sent to them. Muslim exegetes locate the People of the Well in a district near the Thamud, in Yemen, and Azerbaijan. The prophet sent to the People of the Well is said to have been called Hinzalah b. Sifwan. The people rejected the prophet and threw him into a well, leaving him for dead. As a consequence of their actions they were afflicted with drought, their houses were destroyed, and they reverted to living among the Jinn and wild beasts of the area. It is reported also that one of the People of the Well believed in the prophet, a black slave who kept the prophet alive in the well by secretly providing him with food until the prophet reappeared to his people.

PEOPLE OF TUBBA. Mentioned in the Quran along with other people destroyed by God (Q 50:14, 44:37). Ibn Kathir reports that the People of Tubba are the people of Sheba, Arabs from Southern Arabia, and that Tubba was the title given to the kings of this people. It is also reported that one of the kings of Tubba wanted to destroy Mecca and Medina, but was stopped when two rabbis told him that a great prophet would live there at the end of time. According to this same account, the king circumambulated the Ka'bah and converted the people of Yemen to Judaism at a time before the coming of Jesus. It is said also that he sacrificed 6,000 animals at the Ka'bah. Some exegetes report that this happened when Mecca was in the hands of the Jurhum, and others report that it was about 700 years before the coming of the prophet Muhammad.

PEOPLE OF YA-SIN. Phrase used to refer to the "People of the City" mentioned in surah Ya-Sin (Q 36:13–29). According to the Quran, God sent three messengers to the city, but all the people rejected the messengers except for one, and God destroyed the city with a single scream. Muslim exegetes identify the city as Antioch, but disagree about the timing of the event. According to some, the three messengers were the followers of Jesus: Simeon, John, and Paul. A report given on the authority of the prophet Muhammad indicates that the three messengers sent to the People of Ya-Sin came after Jesus. Other exegetes claim that the three messengers were named Sadiq, Masduq, and Shalum, and that they were sent to ancient Antioch when it was ruled by a king named Antiochus b. Antiochus, at a time when the people worshipped idols. Muslim exegetes also identify the one faithful person as a man named Habib b. Mara. He is said to have been a carpenter, weaver, shoemaker, or fuller and to have been afflicted with leprosy. Q 36:26–27 gives the statement he makes upon entering paradise, and Muslim exegetes state that his people killed him and that God caused him to enter paradise immediately upon dying as a martyr.

PESHER. Type of early commentary on biblical texts found among the Dead Sea Scrolls. The word has its origins in the art of dream "interpretation" [Heb. pesher], and thus, in a similar way, seeks to reveal hidden meanings in the sacred text. The Pesher scrolls from Qumran are based largely on the prophetic corpus of scripture and interpret these texts in a way that justifies the needs and beliefs of the Qumran community.

PESHITTA. Name applied to the standard Bible of the Syriac Churches. The redaction of this translation is thought to have taken place by the third century CE though the earliest fragmentary manuscripts date to the end of the fifth century CE. By the seventh century CE a complete manuscript of the Bible is attested. In addition to the canonical texts and the Apocrypha, some Peshitta Bible manuscripts include 2 Baruch, 4 Ezra, 3 and 4 Maccabees, excerpts from Josephus, and Psalms 151–155. The Peshitta of the New Testament does not include 2 and 3 John, 2 Peter, Jude, and Revelation, and also lacks passages from some of the Gospels and the Acts of the Apostles.

The Bible in Syriac also is attested in the seventh-century CE Syro-Hexapla (a Syriac version of Origen's revision of the Septuagint) and the partially preserved translation of Jacob of Edessa in the eighth century CE. Earlier than the Peshitta of the Gospels was the Diatessaron, attributed to Tatian in the second century CE, and the Old Syriac version, attested in the Curetonianus and Sinaiticus manuscripts of the fifth century CE. Philoxenus, bishop of Mabbug, is credited with a revision of the Peshitta of the New Testament in the sixth century CE. The Harklean version of the New Testament is a Syriac translation attributed to Thomas of Harkel in the seventh century CE.

Some scholars point to a strong exegetical component in the Peshitta that suggests Jewish authorship. The Peshitta also often shows strong agreement with the Jewish Targums. It diverges from the Masoretic text, especially in the books of Chronicles, where several verses are missing. It also contains some verses in Chronicles not found in the Masoretic text. Interestingly, the book of Job follows the Torah (Pentateuch) in some Jacobite manuscript versions.

PESIQTA D'RAB KAHANA. Often called simply Pesiqta, the Pesiqta d'Rab Kahana is the oldest known midrash. It contains 32 midrashic homilies on the special Sabbaths for Jewish festivals. The work appears to have undergone some degree of reworking and editing, making it difficult to date, though most scholars place its author sometime around 800 CE, since the figure Mar Rab Kahana, to whom the text appears to be connected, lived at this time.

PESIQTA RABBATI. Compilation of Hebrew homiletic midrashim for the Sabbaths of Jewish festivals, beginning with the Sabbath for Hanukkah and ending with those for the Day of Atonement. It dates no earlier than the middle of the ninth century CE. It shares some of its homilies with Pesiqta d'Rab Kahana, but mostly contains independent material.

PHARAOH. Title used in reference to the kings of Egypt. Originally an Egyptian term meaning "big house," the word entered Hebrew by common usage. It appears 229 times in the Bible, but in only five cases is the pharaoh named (2 Kgs 23:29, 23:33, 23:34, 23:35; Jer 46:2). In each case the named pharaoh is Necho II (610–595 BCE).

This makes any historical reconstruction of the biblical texts that mention a pharaoh difficult at best. The Arabic term for the pharaoh [Ar. fir'awn] occurs 74 times in the Quran in relation to the stories of Moses and the Israelites. The term is understood by Muslim exegetes as a title and not a name, though some exegetes employ the title as if it were the name of the Egyptian king. In the Quran and Muslim exegesis, the pharaoh epitomizes the godless tyrant who denies God by claiming that he himself is God (Q 28:38). The pharaoh is paired with Haman in the Quran, both as archetypical enemies of the Israelites and Jews. The pharaoh exalts himself above the rest of the earth (Q 28:4), and is the one who orders the building of the Tower of Babel (Q 28:38, 40:36–37).

PHILO OF ALEXANDRIA (c. 20 BCE–50 CE). Hellenistic Jewish scholar who lived in Alexandria and who is regarded as one of the most important Jewish writers of the period. Philo came from a wealthy family. His brother was an important official in the Roman administration of Egypt, and Philo himself headed an Alexandrian Jewish delegation to Rome in 40 CE. The writings of Philo are divided generally into three categories: exposition or rewriting of the laws of Moses; exegesis of the Bible; and writings dealing with philosophical, historical, and apologetic topics. His works cover biblical topics from the creation to the life of Moses and his reception of the laws. Within this corpus are many expansions and interpretations found also in later biblical exegesis. Philo also wrote a series of works dealing with particular questions on the books of Genesis and Exodus that are largely extant in Armenian, but not in Greek. Philo's exegesis of Genesis is known for its allegorical interpretation, which he employs to counter more literal interpretations, to demonstrate that the text is consistent with Greek rationality, and to argue for a philosophical view of Judaism.

PHILO OF BYBLOS (c. 70–160 CE). Author of the *Phoenician History*, which is reported to be a Greek translation of the Phoenician work of Sanchuniathon of the eighth century BCE. The *Phoenician History* itself is not extant, but Eusebius quotes parts of it by including its account of the Phoenician cosmogony and the origins of civilized life (*see also* PHOENICIA). Parts of the cosmogony roughly parallel the biblical cosmogony of Genesis 1. The description of the originators of the arts of civilization is similar to descriptions in Genesis 4, and the discussion of the giants may relate to accounts of heavenly giants in the Septuagint of Genesis 6.

PHILOXENUS OF MABBUG (c. 440–523 CE). East Syrian or Nestorian scholar best known for his Syriac translation of the Bible from Greek. His name in Syriac is Akhsenaya. Philoxenus was born in Iran and educated at the famous School of Edessa. He became bishop of Mabbug in Syria in 485 CE but was exiled from 519 to 522 CE when the Roman emperor Justin I enforced the Creed of Chalcedon. In addition to his work on a new Syriac version of the New Testament, Philoxenus also wrote commentaries on several of the New Testament gospels.

PHOENICIA. Ancient maritime power consisting of city-states along the eastern Mediterranean Sea corresponding approximately with modern Syria and Lebanon. By 1250 BCE, the Phoenicians had established a number of colonies including Carthage [Phoen. Qar Hadash, lit. "New City"] in North Africa. They were responsible also for introducing the consonantal alphabet to the Greeks. In biblical times, Phoenicia's power was centered at Tyre and Sidon. Phoenician mercantilist abilities are portrayed in the Bible's descriptions of Israel's commercial and political ties, especially during the reigns of David and Solomon (2 Sam 15:11; 1 Kgs 9:26). Solomon also employed Phoenician artisans to design and construct Yahweh's temple in Jerusalem (1 Kgs 5:20, 5:32, 7:34–47). Phoenician influence can be seen also in the spread of the cults of Baal and Asherah during and after this period, an influence that frequently received prophetic rebuke (1 Kgs 18:19; Isa 65:11; Jer 32:35; Ezekiel 26–29).

PIRQE D'RABBI ELIEZER. Unfinished midrashic exposition written in Palestine sometime around the ninth century CE that aims to proclaim God's glory by tracing God's creative hand in the early history of Israel. It focuses on the history as found in the books of Genesis, Exodus, and Numbers, but also contains discussions of the story of Esther, Amalek's descendants, and the future age of God's redemption. Numerical compositional patterns are frequent in the book, especially based on tens, and it contains a number of Jewish traditions concerning biblical figures not found in the Bible. Much of the exegetical materials on the stories of Genesis closely parallel early Muslim exegesis of the same stories.

PLOTINUS (c. 205–270 CE). Founder of Neoplatonism. The story of his life can be found in the biography written by his student Porphyry. Plotinus combined elements from a number of Hellenistic traditions such as Platonism, Aristotelianism, and Stoicism into a particularly late antique approach to philosophy. The basic outline of Plotinus' thought was based on a tripartite division of existence into hypostases or "incarnations": God is transcendent, the Mind is the primary intellect that creates the material cosmos, and the Soul is the animated intellect representing an extension of the divine in the material cosmos. Neoplatonic thought formed a framework that allowed many Christians and Jews to interpret the Bible in a manner consistent with Greek thought.

POETRY. The most common form of prophetic discourse. Though distinguishing poetry from prose is often difficult in the Bible, the essential structural component of biblical poetry appears to be that of parallelism, a feature shared with Mesopotamian and Ugaritic texts (*see also* PARALLELISM). Hebrew prophets also employed other poetic features such as alliteration, assonance, word play, metaphor, simile, and chiasm, to name but a few. Hebrew poetry, however, possesses no meter or rhyme.

Though scholars have been accustomed to reading prophetic texts as poetry since the Humanist movement of the 18th century CE, it is unlikely that the biblical prophets would have considered themselves poets. When people charged the prophet Ezekiel of being a mere "singer of songs" (Ezek 21:5, 33:32), he took their statement as an accusation of false prophecy. This passage is an isolated example from the exilic period, but it probably represents a long-standing view. It also demonstrates the close relationship that existed in ancient Israel between poetry, prophecy, and music (*see also* MUSIC). Muslim sources record accusations against the prophet Muhammad to the effect that he was merely a poet possessed by Jinn. Such a tension between definitions of prophecy and poetry was present in ancient

Greece as well, where both the poet and prophet were inspired by muses, but where priests transcribed and reworked the unintelligible ciphers of prophets into poetic discourse.

Later Greek philosophical texts assert that all poets were liars, because they fabricated knowledge of the divine world. The rather sharp distinction between prophecy and poetry was maintained in early rabbinic culture as well. The distinction was again based on perspective. Since the very notion of poetry implies artistic skill and artifice, and since aesthetic skill cannot be attributed to God without some theological compromise, the category was deemed inappropriate for the study of God's word. On the other hand, a few of the medieval Jewish scholars, like Shem Tov Ibn Falaquera (1225–1295 CE) tried to distinguish three types of poems: those conveyed through prophecy (e.g., Deuteronomy 32, Exodus 15), those composed through the inspiration of the Holy Spirit (e.g., Psalms, Proverbs, and Song of Songs), and those of the skilled poets that are not found in the Bible. In his commentary to Exodus 15, Don Isaac Abravanel (1437–1508 CE) suggests that all poetry that one finds in prophetic speech has been arranged by the prophets themselves through the Holy Spirit, and is not the immediate recorded words of a prophecy. Many scholars today perceive the difference between poetry and prophecy as one of intent. Whereas ancient poetry aimed to entertain, persuade, and edify, prophetic discourse aimed to unleash the divine power of the word, and to activate God's plans and judgment by way of words.

POLYTHEISM. Worship and belief in multiple deities. Polytheism characterized the religious systems of Israel's neighbors, and periodically that of Israel as well (1 Kgs 11:5), despite oscillating efforts at state reform.

PORPHYRY (c. 232–305 CE). Neoplatonic philosopher famous for his biography of Plotinus and role in editing the *Enneads*. Porphyry was born in Tyre, and studied in Athens and then in Rome under Plotinus for six years. He wrote an introduction to Aristotelian logic and the influential *Life of Plotinus*. He was known for criticizing the Christian exegetes for relating the Bible to historical circumstances, but instead he favored a more allegorical or spiritual interpretation of texts.

POSSESSION. The state of being entered, dominated, and controlled by a god, demon, or other supernatural entity. In some contexts, the concept of possession also relates to a variety of terms translated into English as "inspiration," which refer to a god's breathing into or inflation [Lat. afflatus] of a human medium.

A belief that such entities periodically entered the human body was widespread throughout the ancient Near East, and played a large role in the diagnosis of sickness and disease (*see also* DEMONS; MEDICINE). Often the outward sign of possession was altered or frenetic behavior (*see also* ECSTATIC; GLOSSOLALIA). The Sibylline Oracles are described as having messy hair, wild eyes, and heaving breasts when they are possessed (*see also* ASCETICISM). Epilepsy and manic depression were widely believed to signal possession by a demon or harmful spirit (1 Sam 16:14). Gods too, could enter and control humans, and the result was often ecstatic prophecy (*see also* ECSTATIC; PROPHECY), which often appeared to others as temporary madness (2 Kgs 9:11). The experience is variously described as an "onrush" of the spirit (Judg 14:6, 15:14), or as being "clothed" with the spirit (2 Chr 24:20).

Sometimes, military success was credited to divine possession. Mesopotamian kings are said to enter the battlefield clothed by the radiant light of divinity. In the biblical story of the judge Samson (Judg 13:24–16:21), the onrush of Yahweh's spirit similarly moves Samson to fight. At times, divine possession appears to be a contagious phenomenon. King Saul begins prophesying when he comes into contact with a band of prophets enraptured in ecstasy (1 Sam 10:5, 10:11). Thus, possession also can be a group phenomenon, as is seen in the case of elders of Israel who are possessed simultaneously (Num 11:17, 11:25–26) and the foreign prophets of Baal (1 Kgs 18:29).

It is unclear in the Bible to what degree prophecy in general was viewed as divine possession. In some cases, especially those that result in outward behavioral changes, divine possession is clear (*see also* HOSEA), but elsewhere prophecy appears more as a form of communication with the divine. Such a distinction may be more apparent than real, however, as comparative evidence from Mesopotamia suggests. There the Assyrian goddess Ishtar speaks through her prophets, delivering divine missives that closely resemble biblical prophecies in form and content. Muslim sources attest to the fact that the prophet Muhammad's opponents often accused him of faking his revelations when he was really only possessed by a Jinn.

PRAYER OF JACOB. A fragmentary text that is preserved in a fourth-century CE Greek papyrus, though it is possible that the origins of the text are earlier. The prayer appears to be a type of invocation that is designed to transform the speaker into an angel on the earth after being recited seven times. Names and imagery in the prayer parallel other texts from Nag Hammadi and other magical texts. The speaker invokes God with several secret names to be empowered as an angel upon the earth and to be immortal.

PRAYER OF JOSEPH. Fragmentary text surviving only in the form of citations in the writings of several early Christian writers. There are three fragments. Fragment A is nine sentences long and is cited by Origen. In this fragment, Jacob gives details about his combat at Peniel (Genesis 32). He adds that the angel's name was Uriel, and that the angel was attempting to raise his status by attacking Jacob. Fragment B is one sentence in length and is found in Origen, as cited by the two Cappadocian fathers Basil and Gregory. Fragment B also is found in Eusebius and Procopius. In this fragment Jacob appears to speak to Joseph and also Ephraim and Manasseh, which may indicate that the fuller text was of the type found in the Testaments of the Patriarchs. Here, Jacob claims to have read "in the heavenly tablets" all the future events in the lives of Joseph and his sons. Fragment C is only one sentence in length and also is preserved in citations from Origen in Basil and Gregory. This fragment identifies Jacob as an angel named "Israel."

PRAYER OF NABONIDUS (4QPrNab). Fragmentary text discovered among the Dead Sea Scrolls that dates roughly to the period 75–50 BCE. The prayer shares a number of features with the Babylonian stories of King Nabonidus (r. 555–539 BCE), and with the biblical book of Daniel (chapter 4). The Prayer of Nabonidus mentions Nabonidus' perplexing dream (but is broken off at this point), and describes the king's seven-year inflammation that caused him to be "banished far from men" and was cured by an unnamed Jewish exorcist who forgave him his transgression. The shared elements in the

Prayer of Nabonidus suggest that the book of Daniel was employing well-known literary themes and traditions in its description of the king's madness in Daniel 4.

PRAYER OF THE APOSTLE PAUL. Brief text in Coptic from Nag Hammadi (I,1) invoking Jesus Christ to bestow authority, redemption, and secret knowledge. The prayer is said in the name of the "Evangelist" though the title at the end of the text is "Prayer of Paul, Apostle." The format of the prayer and its content are similar to other hermetical texts and rely upon the Psalms and epistles of Paul.

PROPHECY. An utterance or prediction believed to be a divinely given revelation of divine will, and the oral or written medium by which the utterance is conveyed (*see also* PROPHETIC DRAMA; SPEECH ACT THEORY). The contents and goals of prophecies can vary, but typically they serve as predictions of the future, and often they aim to alter the behavior of the people or nations at whom they are directed. They can be delivered in private or public settings.

Scholars usually distinguish between deductive and intuitive methods for obtaining prophecies. The former refers to prognostication based on deductive observations and their interpretations (*see also* DIVINATION; EGIRRÛ; EXTISPICY; MAGIC; NECROMANCY), whereas the latter involves inspiration induced either directly (the process is entirely unknown), or by way of various techniques (*see also* ASCETICISM; DRUGS; DRUNKENNESS; ECSTATIC; PROPHETIC NUDITY). Prophecies can be sought from the deity (*see also* ORACLE) or come unsolicited, and they can be received aurally or visually (*see also* VISION).

The earliest evidence for prophecy comes from texts found at Ebla (2400–2250 BCE), where a term for *prophet* [Ebl. nabi'utum] is attested, a word that is cognate with the later biblical Hebrew [Heb. nabi] and Arabic [Ar. nabi] terms for "prophet" (*see also* EBLA; EMAR). Whether these prophets received their prophecies by way of intuition or deductive techniques is unknown. Texts discovered on the mid-Euphrates at Mari (c. 1750–1697 BCE), however, reveal that early in the second millennium, intuitive and deductive forms of prophecy existed side by side as legitimate techniques of divine communication (*see also* MARI). In fact, often the same prophet appears skilled in both types, as prophets do also at Emar. In distinction to later types of intuitive prophecy found elsewhere, the primary focus of Mari prophecies appears to have been the material welfare, personal safety, and legitimation of the king.

In Mesopotamia proper, deductive techniques are attested quite early (*see also* DIVINATION), but intuitive prophecy does not appear to have been a major cultural phenomenon until the reign of the Assyrian king Esarhaddon (680–669 BCE). In this period are found prophets speaking in the name of Ishtar, the goddess of love and fertility. Sometimes these prophets are women, and at other times they appear to be transvestites. Male gods too appear in dreams and visions, though it is apparently only Ishtar who speaks directly through her prophets. Tools by which the prophets invoke intuitive prophecies in Assyria include excessive weeping, sighing, and praying. Devotees of the goddess Ishtar are called "criers of lamentations." The relationship between ritual weeping and prophecy is embodied in the Assyrian term meaning "speak, weep, lament" [Akk. nabû], again cognate with the terms found at Ebla and in the Hebrew Bible and Quran for prophesy. It is noteworthy that among later Jewish mystics, Christian ascetics, and Sufis, ritual weeping similarly served as a tool for ushering in divine revelation and obtaining God's mysteries.

Prophecy as a cultural institution also appears in ancient Egypt where it is closely tied to the priesthood. While predicting the future does appear to have been a significant function of the Egyptian prophet, his primary duties included offering the temple sacrifices, overseeing the procession of the sacred boats or arks (*see also* ARK OF THE COVENANT; LEVITES), ministering the food and drink offerings at the altar and at funerals, and the anointing of the king (*see also* ANOINT). Nevertheless, this figure also foretold agricultural yields and failures, atmospheric and celestial phenomena (*see also* ASTRONOMY AND ASTROLOGY), the appearance of diseases on humans and livestock (*see also* MEDICINE), and the coming of floods and earthquakes.

The most famous evidence for prophecy in the ancient Near East, however, comes from the Hebrew Bible, which characterizes the act of prophesying primarily as an intuitive process. As at Mari and in Mesopotamia proper, Israelite prophets display a wide variety of prophetic behaviors and experiences, and hail from a number of different social contexts. Some, like Gad and Nathan, are central to the royal house, while others, like Elijah and Elisha, are marginalized. A few have priestly status (e.g., Jeremiah, Ezekiel), whereas others, like Amos, have more humble beginnings. Though visual modes of divine communication appear with some frequency, the great majority of biblical references to prophecy underscore the central role that speaking plays in the prophetic experience, either as a medium of divine communication or in delivery of the prophecy. Hence, the English term *prophesy*, which derives from a Greek word meaning "speak before" [Gk. prophetes].

Terms employed in the Hebrew Bible in reference to both sanctioned and unsanctioned forms of prophecy are identical and include "a burden, a lifting up" [Heb. massa']; "envision" [Heb. hazah]; "see" [Heb. ra'ah]; "utter" [Heb. na'am]; and, most frequently, "speak" [Heb. naba']. While prophecy as a cultural phenomenon clearly played a role in the early history of Israel, as a cultural institution it appears to have taken root and burgeoned from the eighth to the fifth centuries BCE with the so-called Classical Prophets, a phrase used in reference to those prophets who have left literary works (*see also* CLASSICAL PROPHECY). This label, however, is somewhat misleading, for it masks a great deal of continuity that exists between earlier forms of prophecy as characterized by prophets like Abraham, Moses, Nathan, Elijah, Elisha, and the later classical forms. While the former figures appear only in narratives and not in prophetic works, the form and style of their prophecies, and the prophetic behavior these figures exhibit, is hardly different from later forms. In both periods one can find prophetic drama, pronouncements of weal and woe, performative mantic practices, and the delivery of prophecies in literary form (see, e.g., Nathan's deceptive parable in 2 Samuel 12:1–4; cf., 1 Kgs 20:35).

Where a more decisive change is discerned, however, is in the exilic and post-exilic periods, when prophecy became more apocalyptic, baroque, and eschatological in content (*see also* ESCHATOLOGY; EZEKIEL; LATTER PROPHETS). It is this period that also marks the end of Israelite prophecy as a cultural phenomenon and institution. Jewish tradition, as embodied in the Talmud, sees the destruction of the second temple in 70 CE as marking the end of Israelite prophecy. Nevertheless, it does recognize the survival and prophetic import of divine echoes and dreams (*see also* BAT QOL; DREAMS AND DREAM INTERPRETATION), though only as greatly reduced forms of prophecy. Some later Jewish mystical traditions do recognize intuitive prophecy as an active phenomenon. These traditions describe a process by which "God's glory" [Heb. shekhinah] speaks through the mouth of the practitioner during mystical union (*see also* HEKHALOT LITERATURE; MYSTICISM). Outside of early Judaism as well, prophecy continued to play a significant social role. Early Christianity, for example, viewed prophecy as an active phenomenon (Acts 11:28; 1 Cor 12:10), and prophesying similarly continued in gnostic circles (*see also* GNOSIS AND GNOSTICISM).

The Quran contains the stories of many prophets and their prophecies, not all of whom are identified by name. Most of the prophets in the Quran are to be identified with the same figures in the Bible and in Jewish exegesis, but significant others exist, such as Hud, Salih, Shuayb, and Dhu al-Kifl. Many of the references to prophets do not give specific accounts of what their prophecy was, but often prophets are said to reiterate that "there is no god but God" for the people to whom the prophet is sent. Prophets are described as condemning specific practices such as idolatry, cheating, and sodomy, but the overriding injunction is for people to acknowledge God and thank him for his provisions and gifts. The more detailed narratives, such as those related to the story of Moses, only elaborate on and emphasize this basic pattern.

Many prophets are responsible for bringing revealed "books" or "scriptures" to their people, and the Quran and Muslim exegesis often quote passages from earlier revealed books. Thus, Q 26:196 refers to the "scriptures of the first ones," and other passages refer to the "first scriptures" (Q 20:133, 87:18), which Muslim exegetes say refers to the books revealed to Adam, Seth, and Idris. The Quran also mentions "scriptures" [Ar. suhuf] revealed to Abraham (Q 53:36–37, 87:19), the Torah and the Furqan revealed to Moses (Q 2:53), the Psalms revealed to David (Q 4:163, 17:55), and the Gospel revealed to Jesus (Q 3:48). The Quran itself is the revelation to the prophet Muhammad, containing and superseding all earlier revelations to prophets.

PROPHECY OF NEFERTI. Egyptian prophetic text, also known as the prophecy of Neferohu, that dates to the Middle Kingdom (c.

2040–1750 BCE), but which claims to have taken place in the time of Fourth Dynasty pharaoh Snefru (r. 2613 BCE). As such, it represents the political propaganda of the pharaoh Amenemhet I (r. 1991–1962 BCE), the first king of the Twelfth Dynasty, who usurped the throne of Mentuhotep IV (r. 1992 BCE). It tells the story of how King Snefru summoned the magicians of his court for entertainment. One such expert, named Neferti, prophesied to Snefru that a series of catastrophes would devastate Egypt, but that a pharaoh king would arise, by the name Ameni (i.e., Amenemhet I), who would restore order. The text is a classical example of an ex eventu prophecy (*see also* EX EVENTU).

PROPHET. Man or woman recognized by a particular community as a spokesperson for a deity or other supernatural entity.

Throughout the ancient Near East, prophets exhibit a wide variety of prophetic behavior (*see also* ASCETICISM; ECSTATIC; PROPHECY), employ a number of techniques for obtaining the divine word (*see also* DIVINATION; PROPHECY), and serve a number of different social functions. In some cases, prophets serve as mediators between the divine and mortal realms, as priests do through ritual, and in some cases prophets even serve as priests. At other times, prophets function as social activists. At Mari, but especially in the Hebrew Bible and Quran, one finds prophets denouncing cases of injustice, social inequality, ethical violations, and religious impurity (2 Kgs 17–2; Kgs 2:18; Mic 6:8). Prophets thus serve to reinforce certain types of ethical, religious, and social behavior. In the Israelite context, this behavior is grounded in a conception of divine law (*see also* COVENANT), which commands that support be given to the less fortunate (Lev 19:9–10, 23:22). Israelite prophets often employ juridical formulae, frame their prophecies in a legal format, and pronounce judgment (Hab 1:12). The Quran makes numerous references to the covenant made between God and all people, a covenant about which prophets only serve as reminders (Q 7:172, 30:30, 33:7, 53:56).

The Hebrew Bible employs several terms to designate prophets, and throughout Israelite history both male and female prophets appear (Deborah, Huldah, Miriam, and Isa 8:3). The earliest term appears to have been *seer* [Heb. ro'eh] (1 Sam 9:9). As the term suggests, prophets served their communities primarily as prognosticators (Deut 18:22). The prophet Samuel is sought for his ability to locate lost asses, and is described as foretelling the future (1 Samuel 9). In exchange for their services, they received payments (1 Sam 9:7–8; Mic 3:11). A later term, roughly synonymous with *seer* is the "one who sees visions" [Heb. hozeh]. The most common term employed for prophet, however, is "prophet, spokesperson" [Heb. nabi], a title that is used for both sanctioned and unsanctioned prophets. This term is rendered in the Septuagint by a Greek term meaning "one who speaks before" [Gk. prophetes]. Hence, the English word *prophet*.

The etymology of the Hebrew term for prophet [Heb. nabi] denotes "speaking," and is related to a Mesopotamian word meaning "weeping" [Akk. nabu]. The latter meaning may be suggestive of an early technique for inducing prophecies. It is cognate with another form that appears first in Eblaic texts for "prophet" [Ebl. nabi'utum] (*see also* EBLA; NABI). The root [n-b-'] also appears meaning "prophet" at Emar (*see also* EMAR). The same etymology is present in the name of the Mesopotamian god Nabû, who is associated with scribes and writing, and therefore with the Tablets of Destiny (*see also* TABLETS). The cognate and its context perhaps inform the importance of writing among the biblical prophets (*see also* CLASSICAL PROPHETS), and relate (etymologically) to the biblical site Mt. Nebo, where the prophet and tablet-writer Moses is said to have died (Deut 34:1–6). Worship of Nabû spread beyond the confines of Mesopotamia to Egypt and Anatolia by way of Aramaic speakers in the fourth century BCE. The cult of Nabû survived in Syria through the Roman period into the second century CE, and later was identified by the Greeks with Apollo.

The Arabic term [Ar. nabi] used commonly in the Quran to designate a prophet is far less common than another Arabic term [Ar. rasul] also referring to a messenger or a prophet (*see also* APOSTLE). The Arabic term for "Messiah" or "Christ" [Ar. masih] is found 11 times in the Quran, though only with reference to Jesus. Muslim exegetes differentiate between the two terms: a generic prophet [Ar. nabi], and a prophet who brings a revealed book [Ar. rasul], but this distinction is not always consistent with the terminology used in the Quran for the different prophets. Muslim sources report that the total number of prophets sent by God is more than 200,000, though only a minute fraction of those are known by name.

With the exception of Egyptian prophets who were intimately connected to the priesthood, ancient Near Eastern prophets come from a variety of social backgrounds and are portrayed as having various roles. They often were distinguished as much by dress as by behavior. The Egyptian prophet, for example, is typically portrayed wearing a leopard-skin covering, and some of the Israelite prophets are similarly described as wearing mantles of hair (2 Kgs 1:8, 2:13–14; Zech 13:4). Prophets serving the cult of Ishtar, the Babylonian goddess of love and fertility, were transvestites. Some Israelite prophets appear to play a central role in the workings of the state and priesthood (e.g., Isaiah Jeremiah, Ezekiel), whereas others appear marginalized (Elijah). Both types often display subversive behavior and often have adversarial relationships with the monarchy and religious establishment, as well as with other prophetic groups (*see also* FALSE PROPHETS). Some appear to have lived in discipleship societies where they learned their trade from a master (Samuel, Elisha, Isaiah, Jeremiah), whereas others disclaim any connection to prophetic guilds (Amos 1:1, 7:14).

Muslim exegetes distinguish between two types of prophets with respect to social standing. The first type is the poor outcast represented by prophets like Hud, Salih, Abraham, Lot, Shuayb, Job, Jesus, and Muhammad. The second type is the prophet of high social standing such as Moses, David, and Solomon, who were all kings or leaders of the Israelites.

In the post-exilic period, Israelite prophets continued to issue their proclamations, but they do not appear to have been as numerous or productive as they were before the exile. With the death of the prophets Haggai, Zechariah, and Malachi, prophecy as an Israelite cultural institution came to an end (*see also* LATTER PROPHETS), and after the destruction of Yahweh's temple in 70 CE, only dreams and divine echoes were seen as possessing prophetic import (*see also* BAT QOL; DREAMS AND DREAM INTERPRETATION).

Throughout the Near East, the subjective nature of prophetic experience and interpretation precluded any possibility of prophetic infallibility. Numerous Mesopotamian epistolary texts attest to mistrust and competition between mantic groups, as do Israelite legislative texts (Deut 18:10–11), and the latter, in fact, define a "true prophet" as one whose prophecies comes true (Deut 18:22). Later Muslim scholars developed the notion of the infallibility of prophets, applying it first to the prophet Muhammad and then to all the prophets mentioned in the Quran, as well as others. This ideal is belied in part by the stories of the prophets found in the Quran and Muslim exegesis, but the veracity of the prophets' revelations is not questioned.

Unlike in Mesopotamia, Mari, or Egypt, the Israelite prophets often are characterized as performers of miraculous deeds (*see also* MAGIC). Thus, to cite a few examples, Moses parts the Reed Sea (Exodus 14–15), Joshua halts the sun and moon in the sky (Josh 10:12–13), Elisha makes an ax-head float on water (2 Kgs 6:4–6), and Isaiah makes the shadow on the sundial reverse direction (Isa 38:8). The prophetic employment of performative acts like these is modeled in part on that of Moses, who is described in the book of Numbers as a unique prophet, who alone had the privilege of speaking with Yahweh face to face (Num 12:6–8). The Quran and Muslim exegesis refer to the miracles of the prophets as "signs" given to them by God to demonstrate their prophetic status to the people (*see also* SIGN).

The Quran and Muslim creeds stipulate a belief in all the prophets and all the books revealed to them, without making any distinctions among them (Q 2:136, 3:84, 4:136, 42:13). For many Muslims this veneration includes pilgrimages to the tombs of prophets, such as the annual pilgrimage to the tomb of Hud in the Hadramawt and Shuayb in Yemen. There are 25 prophets mentioned by name in the Quran, though exegetes do not always agree on the identification of certain individuals. They are Adam, Idris, Noah, Hud, Salih, Abraham, Ishmael, Isaac, Jacob, Lot, Joseph, Shuayb, Job, Dhu al-Kifl, Moses, Aaron, David, Solomon, Elijah, Elisha, Jonah, Zechariah, John, Jesus, and Muhammad. Other passages refer to unnamed prophets, identified by exegetes, such as Khidr, Ezekiel, Samuel, Jeremiah, and Daniel.

PROPHETIC DRAMA. Many of the biblical prophets, as well as those from elsewhere in the ancient Near East, engaged in prophetic drama (also called symbolic action), a theatrical praxis that involves a sympathetic prediction or reenactment of words or events. Such dramas could be performed publicly or privately. Thus, Isaiah lived naked and barefoot for three years to symbolize the Assyrian deportation of Egyptians (Isa 20:1–4), and Jeremiah destroyed a pot before the populace to represent the fall of Jerusalem (Jer 18:10–11). In Ezek 3:1, the prophet Ezekiel devours a scroll before confronting the "House of Israel," and he later lays alone on his side 390 days to symbolize the exile of the northern kingdom (Ezek 4:5). Also of relevance here is Moses, who, when confronted with the transgressions of the Israelites after descending from Mt. Sinai, smashed the tablets of the Law (Exod 32:19). Prophetic drama may also be attested in the New Testament (Acts 21). Such prophetic actions, and there are many biblical and extrabiblical examples, are not only rhetorical acts, but are often understood to be performative means of achieving desired results through the effects of sympathetic actions.

PROPHETIC NUDITY. Stripping naked either as an ascetic ritual act associated with inducing the prophetic experience or as a form of prophetic drama (*see also* ASCETICISM; PROPHETIC DRAMA). The earliest attestation of prophetic nudity appears in the prophetic texts from Mari, where it is associated also with acts of omophagia and sparagmos. In the Bible, however, it is not connected with these acts. Instead, it is mentioned in reference to King Saul who lies naked an entire day and night prophesying before the prophet Samuel, a public behavior common enough to force the populace to question if Saul too "was among the prophets" (1 Sam 19:20–24). When reenacting a prophetic drama directed at Egypt and Cush (Ethiopia), the prophet Isaiah also goes naked for three years (Isa 20:2–3), an act that most scholars see as unlikely given the cold winter climate of Jerusalem.

PROTOEVANGELIUM OF JAMES. Account of the life story of Mary, the mother of Jesus. The text is extant in Greek, Syriac, Georgian, Arabic, Coptic, Ethiopic, Armenian, Old Church Slavonic, and Latin. The earliest Greek manuscript dates to the fourth century CE, the Syriac to the fifth century, Georgian to the seventh, and the Arabic and Coptic to the 10th century. By far, the most numerous manuscripts of the Protoevangelium are to be found in Old Church Slavonic, though the 169 attested manuscripts have not been adequately dated or studied. The text seems to have been known by the time of Origen and Clement of Alexandria in the early third century CE. The author claims to be James, presumably the brother of Jesus, but scholars have assigned a later date since the story relies on the canonical infancy stories, which were not well established until the middle of the second century CE.

Chapters 1–5 recount the birth of Mary to Joachim and Hannah, and are closely modeled on the story of Hannah and the birth of Samuel in 1 Samuel 1–2. Chapters 6–8 are of Mary's childhood. At the age of six months Mary is said to have set up a personal sanctuary in her bedroom, and when she was three years old she was given over to the service of the temple in Jerusalem. Chapter 9 describes Mary's betrothal to Joseph, and chapter 10 is an account of her sewing of the veil for the temple. The Annunciation takes place in chapter 11, Mary's visit to Elizabeth in chapter 12, and Joseph's vision of the angel in chapters 13–14. Chapters 15–16 recount the test of the "bitter water," probably a reference to the Israelite ritual known as the Sotah (Num 5:11–31), though there only the woman under suspicion for illicit sex is made to perform the ceremony. The birth of Jesus occurs in chapters 17–18, and the visit of the Magi is narrated in chapter 21. The last chapters (22–24) describe the martyrdom of Zechariah in the temple, repeating the conflation of Zechariah father of John the Baptist with the Zechariah mentioned in 2 Chr 24:20–22 and Luke 11:51.

The account of the birth and childhood of Mary is closely related to the information provided about her in the Quran and Muslim exegesis. Muslim exegesis of Q 3:33–37 states that Mary's mother, named Hannah, was barren, but made a vow that she would dedicate her child to temple service if God would allow her to give birth (Q 3:35). The bitter-water ordeal mentioned in the Protoevangelium (15–16) might also relate to Tabari's account of Mary and Joseph's collection of sweet water at a cave away from the temple. The Protoevangelium is also the most immediate source for the Gospel of Pseudo-Matthew and the Gospel of the Birth of Mary.

PROVERBS. Biblical book of proverbial aphorisms, practical wisdom, and moral advice traditionally attributed to King Solomon (Prov 1:1) and known for its poetic conciseness, allusive language, irony, word plays, and riddles (Prov 1:6). The book also is well known for its personification of Wisdom as a woman whose creation constituted the first act of God's creation (Prov 8:22–31). Despite the collection's ascription and the mention elsewhere in the Bible of Solomon's legendary talent for composing proverbs (1 Kgs 4:29–33), most scholars date the book to late in the post-exilic period. In fact, the book of Proverbs itself credits the authorship of its last two chapters to Agur ben Jakeh and Lemuel, king of Massa, figures not known elsewhere (Prov 30:1, 31:1). Some of its proverbs (Prov 22:17–24:22) also are strikingly similar to the collection of Egyptian proverbs known as the *Instruction of Amun-em-Opet* (c. seventh century BCE). Unlike other collections of proverbs from the ancient Near East, the biblical book contextualizes wisdom within the religious discourse of ancient Israel, crediting the ability to discover wisdom to the fear of Yahweh (Prov 1:7). Muslim tradition does not associate a book with Solomon, but does emphasize his wisdom (Q 21:79).

PSALMS. Biblical collection of 150 poems, not of all which are represented by the book's Hebrew title meaning "Praises" [Tehillim]. The book's Greek title [Psalmos] refers to the stringed instrument mentioned in the superscriptions of many of its poems, and encapsulates the fact that the poems were originally set to music.

According to early Jewish tradition, the book of Psalms was composed by King David, but modern scholars see it as an extremely diverse collection of poems composed and edited by a number of people and dating to various periods. Muslim tradition regards the Psalms (though not necessarily the text preserved in the Bible) to be a book revealed to David (*see also* ZABUR). Many of the poems also bear incipits that attribute their composition to others including Solomon, Moses, Asaph, and the sons of Korah, in addition to David. Psalm 137 refers to the Babylonian exile, which rules Davidic authorship out. Nevertheless, some psalms also mention kings, implying a date during the monarchic period (Ps 20:9, 21:1, 45:1). Other psalms show striking affinities with the Canaanite materials discovered at Ugarit, suggesting that they were composed early in Israel's history. Psalm 104 also has been shown to be a Yahwistic reworking of an Egyptian hymn to the god Aten.

Though the Bible testifies to the singing of hymns in the temple, the relationship of the psalms to the temple liturgy cannot be ascertained. In addition, some of the psalms clearly were written for other purposes including weddings (Psalm 45) and royal occasions like enthronement

(Psalms 2, 20, 21, 45, 61, 72, 110). Additional psalms were discovered among the Dead Sea scrolls found at Qumran. As poems, the psalms contained in the book of Psalms exhibit a number of poetic devices including parallelism, acrostics, and word play. Though the Bible does identify some of the temple musicians as prophets (1 Chr 25:1), there is no evidence that the Israelites ever considered their Psalms as prophecies. In the Middle Ages, however, a belief in the prophetic nature of the Psalms appears in Karaite commentaries to the book of Psalms that argue that the Psalms are prophetic prayers with eschatological import (*see also* KARAISM).

PSEUDO-CLEMENTINES. Works attributed to Clement of Rome (first century CE) describing his conversion to Christianity and travels with the apostle Peter. The text depicts early Christianity as having a strong Jewish character. Part of the text has survived in Greek manuscripts dating to the 11th and 14th centuries CE. There is a Latin recension that dates to the beginning of the fifth century CE and a Syriac version of the first part made about the same time.

PSEUDO-PHILO. Name applied to the author of an account of biblical history that had been attributed to Philo of Alexandria. Scholars typically date the text to the first century CE based on references to historical events, though the earliest manuscripts date to the 11th century CE. All of the extant manuscripts are in Latin and were transmitted along with Latin translations of Philo's works. The text contains 65 chapters, beginning with Adam and ending with the death of Saul. Portions of the text derive directly from the Bible, but most of the material expands upon and interprets the biblical materials.

PYTHAGORAS (c. 570–500 BCE). Greek philosopher to whom is attributed esoteric knowledge. Though little information is available about the life of the historical Pythagoras, his name was eponymous for different esoteric traditions in the Hellenistic and late antique periods. He was born on the Ionian island of Samos and later migrated to southern Italy where he died. His religious ideas centered on ritual purification and the strict secrecy of participants. His ideas were particularly influential on Neoplatonic thought, and Porphyry wrote a biography of Pythagoras. He sometimes is referred to as the "Hyperborean Apollo" and is said to have had the ability to predict the future and control animals. Most commonly associated with Pythagoras is the idea that the "occult self" or the "soul" [Gk. psyche] is the seat of truth and is separate from, and opposed to, the material body.

– Q –

QABBALAH. Name given to a form of esoteric Jewish mysticism in which initiates are allowed privileged and direct access to God's mysteries by way of meditation, visions, various ritual actions, and performative practices. The practices of Qabbalah (also spelled as Cabbalah and Kabbalah) ultimately derive from earlier Merkabah traditions (*see also* MERKABAH [CHARIOT] MYSTICISM), but the Hebrew term *Qabbalah* (lit. "received [tradition]") came to be used more commonly after the 12th century CE with the publication of one of the foundational texts of the Qabbalistic tradition, the *Sefer ha-Bahir* (lit. "Book of Lumination"). The Qabbalah has at its basis a belief that God's creation involved the use of 10 divine numbers [Heb. sefirot] and the 22 letters of the Hebrew alphabet. Each of the 10 numbers is equated with a particular aspect of God in his role as creator (*see also* SEFIROT). Together with the Hebrew alphabet, the numbers of the Sefirot were considered by practitioners of the Qabbalah as paths to divine knowledge.

QAZWINI (1203–1283 CE). Zakariyah b. Muhammad b. Mahmud al-Qazwini was a famous Muslim geographer and author of a well-known work, *The Wonders of Creation* [Ar. Aja'ib al-Makhluqat], which was the first systematic exposition of Islamic cosmography. Qazwini wrote the book in Arabic, but it also has been found in numerous Persian and Turkish translations. The manuscripts of this text often are illustrated with pictures of plants, animals, and other fantastic beings, which are described by Qazwini in the text. *The Wonders of Creation* is divided into two sections. The first deals with celestial phenomena (astral as well as heavenly) and matters of chronology, and the second describes terrestrial phenomena (four elements, winds, seven climes of earth, seas, earthquakes, mountains, wells) and includes a description of the different types of animals including humans and Jinn. Qazwini also wrote a geographical work that gives a more systematic description of the earth. Here, Qazwini also divides the inhabited earth into seven climes and describes each in alphabetical order. Both of these works include much information related to the stories of the prophets.

QISAS AL-ANBIYA. Arabic title given to a number of works and a genre devoted to the "Stories of the Prophets," closely related to Muslim exegesis of the Quran. Perhaps the earliest work devoted to the stories of the prophets is the first part of the biography of the prophet Muhammad by Ibn Ishaq in the eighth century CE. Muslim historians such as Yaqubi and Tabari in the ninth and 10th centuries also included extensive materials about the stories of the prophets in their historical accounts, which begin with creation and the story of Adam and Eve. Many of the best-known works on the stories of the prophets are attributed to scholars to whom Quran commentaries also are attributed, such as Tha'labi in the 12th century and Ibn Kathir in the 14th century.

Many of the earliest interpretations of the Quran, such as those attributed to the Companions of the prophet Muhammad and their followers may have originated as sermons or stories of the prophets rather than comments on particular verses of the Quran. A number of the works on the stories of the prophets, especially those produced in Iran and Central Asia, are illustrated with pictures depicting key scenes from the lives of the prophets. These illustrations seem to originate in the 12th and 13th centuries CE, but some of the best-preserved illustrated manuscripts were produced from the 15th to 17th centuries.

In addition to the prophets mentioned by name in the Quran, the stories of the prophets usually include accounts of other Quranic and non-Quranic figures. Other prophets not mentioned by name in the Quran include Khidr, Ezekiel, Samuel, Jeremiah, Daniel, the prophets sent to the People of the Well (Q 25:38, 50:12), and the People of the City mentioned in surah Ya-Sin (Q 36:13–29). Other non-prophetic figures mentioned in the Quran, such as Luqman, Dhu al-Qarnayn, the People of the Cave, and the Kings of Tubba, also are included in the stories of the prophets, as are figures such as Samson and St. George.

QOHELET. Biblical book of moral advice whose title means "Gatherer, Preacher" (also known by its Greek title "Ecclesiastes" with the same meaning). Arguably the most pessimistic book in the Bible, Qohelet argues that all human efforts are vain, and that all attempts to grasp the principles by which God governs the universe are futile at best. This skepticism is encapsulated in the book's repeated expression "vanity of vanities, all is vanity." For Qohelet, justice is not guaranteed (Qoh 9:11–12), and the most that one can do is live life as righteously as possible in fear of God (Qoh 8:10–13, 9:7, 12:1, 12:14). Though traditionally attributed to King Solomon (Qoh 1:12; TB Shabbath 20b) or King Hezekiah (715–687 BCE, see TB Sanhedrin 93b), the style of Hebrew in which Qohelet was written, and the philosophy expressed in the book (which appears rather Hellenistic), points to a date sometime in the third century BCE. The book's philosophy was deemed problematic by the later rabbis who debated whether to include it in the biblical canon (TB Shabbath 30b; Megilla 7a).

QUMRAN. Site lying on the western edge of the Dead Sea where most of the Dead Sea Scrolls were discovered in 1947 (*see also* DEAD SEA SCROLLS).

QURAN. Arabic text considered by Muslims to have been revealed by God through the intermediary of angels to the prophet Muhammad. According to Muslim scholars, the term *Quran* derives from one of two roots: [Ar. q-r-'] with the meaning of "read" and "recite" or [Ar. q-r-n] meaning "put together" and "assemble." Other scholars have pointed out that a Syriac term [Syr. qeryana] was used by East Syrian Christians with the meaning of "scripture reading" or "lesson," and may relate to the Arabic term used for the Muslim text.

In the text of the Quran, the term *Quran* is mentioned about 70 times. Q 56:77–80 states that the Quran is contained in a guarded book, something sent down from the Lord of the worlds, which only the ritually pure may touch. Q 20:2 and Q 76:23 refer to the Quran as a revelation, and other verses (Q 16:98, 17:45, 27:92) refer to it as a collection of revelations. Q 80:13 and Q 98:2 state that the Quran is contained in scriptures or scrolls [Ar. suhuf] written by the hands of scribes. Other passages in the Quran seem to use the term *Quran* in reference to only a part of the overall text (Q 72:1, 75:17). In Q 9:111

and elsewhere, the Quran is listed or compared with other scriptures such as the Torah and the Gospel. Some Muslim exegetes preserve traditions that the Quran is a "New Torah," and there are a number of verses that indicate that a "Quran" was revealed to Moses (Q 2:53) and to David (Q 4:163). According to Muslim scholars, there are 55 different names given to the Quran in the text of the Quran.

According to Muslim scholars the Quran was revealed in parts to the prophet Muhammad over a number of years until the time of his death. The Quran is considered to be the only text revealed to a prophet in parts, all the others having been revealed all at once to the prophets who received them. Some Muslim scholars also report that all scriptures were revealed in Arabic, but that earlier ones were subsequently translated into the languages of their people by their prophets. Q 85:21–22 states that the Quran is in the "Preserved Tablet," an inscribed tablet attached to the throne of God in the heavens. Q 3:7, 13:39, and 43:4 also mention the "Mother of the Book," which some scholars identify with the "Preserved Tablet," though the relationship of the two is not entirely clear. The words of the Quran were brought down from the heavens by Gabriel, though some traditions state that the angel Israfil also made revelations to the prophet Muhammad, and that other angels accompanied Gabriel and the revelation of specific parts of the Quran (*see also* ANGEL).

The Quran was revealed at different times and places, and in response to particular events that occurred in the life of the prophet Muhammad. Muslim scholars designate the 114 surahs of the Quran as being "Meccan" or "Medinan," these terms referring to where that portion of the Quran was revealed, when it was revealed, or to whom that portion of the Quran was addressed. The Quran was also revealed in locations outside of Mecca and Medina, including Jerusalem, the heavens, and underground. Certain verses were revealed more than once. According to Muslim scholars, most of the Quran was revealed five verses at a time, but some parts (such as Surah 6) were revealed all at once.

Muslim scholars record that the revelations to the prophet Muhammad were collected into the text of the Quran in three stages. The first stage was during his lifetime when it was memorized orally and written down by his followers. During the time of Abu Bakr and Umar b. al-Khattab, the first two caliphs who succeeded the prophet Muhammad, the entire text was recorded in writing, culled from written and oral testimony. This second stage is said to have been prompted by fear of losing the text with the death of a large number of those who had memorized its parts. The third stage was during the time of the Caliph Uthman, successor to Umar b. al-Khattab. Under Uthman the text was organized into a standard form, official copies were produced, and variant copies were supposed to be destroyed.

The text of the Quran consists of 114 surahs or "chapters" of varying lengths. The standardized text produced under Uthman arranged these surahs from longest to shortest, with the exception of the first surah, which is one of the shortest. Most Muslim scholars hold that the arrangement of the surahs is conventional, but the decision as to which verses belong in which surahs and in which order was considered to be according to divine revelation. Some surahs contain verses, the revelations of which are separated by many years.

There are numerous reports preserved in early Islamic sources, and repeated by later scholarship, that parts of the Quran were lost or excluded from the final text, and that other parts were abrogated and/or removed from the text. Some traditions report entire surahs that were abrogated and forgotten in the same night they were revealed. Muslim tradition also preserves a number of "readings" or recensions of the Quran text, which vary slightly. Also extant are several noncanonical codices attributed to the followers of the prophet Muhammad.

QURTUBI (d. 1272 CE). Muhammad b. Ahmad al-Qurtubi is the author of a respected and often-cited Quran commentary. Born in Spain, he traveled to Upper Egypt where he eventually died and was buried. Qurtubi's commentary is known for its inclusion of numerous hadith reports, many of which were not mentioned by earlier scholars like Tabari. Unlike Tabari, Qurtubi is more interested in the content of the hadith reports than the process of their transmission. Qurtubi's commentary focuses on the legal implications of the Quran, but has ample, often original, commentary on narrative passages including much from the Israiliyat.

– R –

RADAQ. Acronym for the name Rabbi David Qimhi (1160–1235 CE), a French Jewish scholar and Hebrew grammarian and lexicographer.

His grammatical treatise *Book of the Roots* [Heb. Sefer ha-Shoresh] was the most comprehensive work of its day, providing an examination of verbal conjugations, accents, and vocalization, as well as a lexicon in which he proposed many new Hebrew etymologies based on comparisons with Aramaic. It quickly became a popular standard. His commentaries on a number of biblical books were extremely influential, and are still printed, along with those of Rashi, in some rabbinic Bibles.

RAIN MAKING. Several prophets appear in connection with the production and cessation of rain. Throughout the ancient Near East, rain was associated with both punishment and fertility. In the Bible and Quran, God's might and wrath are portrayed in terms of storms, thunder, and lightning, and yet rain also appears as a metaphor for divine blessings. In the story of Noah, for example, rain serves as God's agent for both destroying and re-creating the world; it marks the beginning and end of chaos. Rain appears similarly in the Mesopotamian Epic of Gilgamesh.

Many prophetic stories involve making or withholding rain, and often such acts serve as a narrative device to prove the authority of God's prophet to his people. In the Bible, the prophet Elijah stops the rain at his bidding and resumes it again after defeating the prophets of Baal (1 Kgs 17:1, 18:42–45). Islamic sources similarly report the rain-making abilities of the prophet Hud before the people of Ad. God sent a drought against the people when they rejected their prophet, and when the people prayed for rain God sent them a dark cloud that instead brought about their destruction. The Talmud preserves a tradition about a righteous man named Honi, who, upon the pleading of the people, drew a circle and stood inside it in order to invoke rain through prayer. His method is said to have been so successful that eventually the people returned to him, asking him to make the rain cease (TB Ta'anith 19a, 23a).

The importance of water for survival in the desert climes of the Near East naturally led to its importance in prophetic stories and in ritual. Wells, rivers, cisterns, and pools all figure prominently in prophetic stories. In Islam, the purificatory aspects of water in ablution rituals, both as an expiation for sins and as a rite of initiation into paradise, are also tied to the authority of particular prophets, and praying for rain is a standard Muslim ritual. Such rituals also can be found in pre-Islamic South Arabian sacrificial rites [SAE. istisqa], which served to secure God's blessings (cf., Deut 28:12). These South Arabian rites, like those in other cultures and contexts, required specifically appointed and authorized cult officials to preside over the prayers for rain.

RAMBAM. Acronym commonly used for Spanish Jewish scholar, philosopher, physician, and jurist Moshe ben Maimon, also known as Maimonides and by the Arabic Musa b. Maymun (c. 1135–1204 CE). He is considered one of the most important Jewish intellectual figures of his day, and is responsible for a number of highly influential written works including a commentary on the Mishnah and the more famous *Guide for the Perplexed* [Ar. Dalalat al-Ha'irin]. When his native town of Córdoba was invaded in 1148 CE by the Islamic group known as the Almohads, he and his family were forced to practice Judaism furtively. A little over a decade later they moved to Fez. When a scholar with whom Rambam studied was executed, he again fled, this time to Palestine, where he stayed only briefly, before moving once again to Fustat, old Cairo in Egypt. Rambam is most remembered for his unique integration of Greek philosophy into Judaism. His works were translated into Latin and other European languages, and had a profound impact on later religious thought, Jewish and non-Jewish alike.

RAMBAN. Abbreviated name of the Spanish Jewish scholar and religious leader Rabbi Moses ben Nahman, also known as Nahmanides (c. 1194–1270 CE), who wrote commentaries on the Torah and Talmud. An interdisciplinarian, Ramban was a physician, philosopher, and accomplished poet. He also was an expert on the Qabbalah. Forced to flee Spain in 1263, Ramban went to Acre in Palestine, where he wrote his most famous scholarly works.

RASHBAM. Acronym commonly used of the Medieval Jewish exegete Rabbi Samuel ben Meir (d. 1174 CE), the grandson of Rashi. He finished the commentary to the talmudic tractate Baba Batra that Rashi had left unfinished when he died. He also contributed a commentary on the first five books of the Bible.

RASHI. Name in acronymic form for the Medieval Jewish exegete Rabbi Samuel ben Yitzhaq of Troyes, of northeastern France (1040–1105 CE). Rashi wrote a number of commentaries on biblical texts and on a number of talmudic tractates in which he combined literal with nonliteral methods of interpretation. He also authored a number of penitential hymns. These commentaries continue to be reprinted in published editions of the Talmud, appearing on the inner margins of the text, and in rabbinic Bibles (*see also* MIQRA'OT GEDOLOT). He received his training in Jewish learning in the great Jewish academies in Worms and Mainz, and later moved to Troyes, where he became the head of the Jewish community. Rashi's grandson Rashbam also was a famous exegete.

RELICS. Relics can be classified into two main types: corporeal relics, which are parts or remains of the body, and noncorporeal objects and places with which holy figures or their relics have come into contact. Corporeal relics include whole bodies, bones, and ashes, but also more disposable body parts such as fingernails, hair, and teeth. Noncorporeal relics include the personal property of holy figures, burial sites, coffins, shrines, reliquaries, and even footprints. Both corporeal and noncorporeal relics often become loci for pilgrimage and are used as the foundations for shrines, temples, and other places of ritual activity. Some traditions assign miraculous powers to relics, and with many relics are associated etiological narratives that link access to relics with a shared experience of events in the history of the community. Relics serve as a tangible link between the present and the past.

Relics appear in the ancient religious traditions of the Near East, the Hebrew Bible, Judaism, and Islam. A number of objects associated with the Egyptian pharaoh, a divinity in his own right, were venerated as sacred objects, including his ureaus and sacred boat. The burial sites of pharaohs were considered sacred territory. There is evidence at Saqqara to suggest that, due to the sacred character of the pharaoh's burial site, Egyptian priests desired to be buried near the body of the pharaoh. Reliquaries to the god Osiris also are known. In 2 Kgs 18:4 it is stated that King Hezekiah (727–698 BCE) ordered the destruction of Moses' bronze serpent because it had become an object of veneration. Moses had used the serpent in former times to heal people bitten by venomous snakes (Num 21:9). The Babylonian Talmud also preserves an argument over whether the bronze serpent was an idol (Abodah Zarah 44a), concluding that it was not an idol since technically it was the private property of Moses.

Many sources attest to the existence of the corporeal and noncorporeal relics of prophets. 2 Kgs 13:21 reports how a man's corpse was hastily put into the grave of the prophet Elijah, accidentally came into contact with the prophet's bones, and miraculously came to life. The bones of Ezra are located in a church in one of the monasteries of Wadi Natrun between Cairo and Alexandria. The head and body of John the Baptist are said to be held in the Umayyad mosque of Damascus or in a mosque on the site of the Herodian city of Sebastiyah near Nablus. There are several locations identified as the tomb of Jesus, and the tomb of Muhammad and the mosque in which it is placed in Medina are major pilgrimage sites. The relics of other figures closely related to prophets are also attested, such as the many relics of Christian and Muslim martyrs and saints, including the head of Husain b. Ali entombed in the Husain mosque in Cairo.

There is also evidence that the Ark of the Covenant was considered a type of relic or reliquary. According to the Bible, the Ark contained the tablets of the ten commandments, Aaron's rod, and a jar of manna, all of which might be considered relics in their own right. Q 2:248 states that the Ark contained the "remains" or "relics" of what was left by the family of Moses and Aaron. Muslim exegetes do not interpret this to mean corporeal relics but rather report that the ark contained the rods, clothes, and shoes of Moses and Aaron, the broken tablets of the Torah, and some manna.

Muslim sources also associate a number of relics with the prophet Muhammad. According to Bukhari when Muhammad performed his final pilgrimage at Mecca he clipped his hair and distributed it to his followers as relics. Other sources report that certain followers were buried with hairs and clothing from the prophet Muhammad, such as the first Umayyad Caliph who was buried with two shirts, hair, and fingernails from the prophet Muhammad. Many mosques and other buildings associated with Islamic ritual and learning incorporate relics from the prophet Muhammad such as hair, clothing, and other items said to have been owned by him during his life. Prominent noncorporeal relics include the prophet Muhammad's ring, his copy of the Quran, the pulpit from which he spoke, and a special awl for removing thorns which he received from the Negus of Ethiopia.

There are also a number of locations where footprints of prophets and related creatures can be found. There are many footprints of the prophet Muhammad, permanently marked in stone, such as the pair in the Qaitbey mausoleum in Cairo's City of the Dead, or the single print on the rock situated under the Dome of the Rock in Jerusalem. A footprint attributed to Jesus is located under the dome built by Salah al-Din on the top of the Mount of Olives near Jerusalem, and Muslim sources mention a footprint of Abraham in Syria. Other sources refer to a footprint left by the half-human, half-animal Buraq near the summit of Mount Sinai when Buraq carried the prophet Muhammad from Mecca to Jerusalem.

REMAQ (d. c. 1190 CE). Rabbi Moses Qimhi was a Jewish Bible exegete. His father was Joseph Qimhi (Riqam), and his brother was the famous David Qimhi (Radaq). Remaq's commentary focused on neglected books of the Bible including Proverbs, Ezra, and Nehemiah. He also wrote an ethical work on the book of Job.

RHABDOMANCY. Divination by means of wood. Some scholars see Ezekiel's reference to the Babylonian practice of divining by means of wooden arrows (Ezek 21:26) as a form of rhabdomancy, though more properly speaking it is a form of belomancy. A similar practice is known in Arab divination and may be related to the arrows used in a practice prohibited in the Quran (Q 2:219, 5:90). Several prophets similarly mention the divinatory use of wooden objects, though these could be metonymic references to idols made of wood (2 Kgs 19:18; Isa 37:19; Jer 2:27; Ezek 20:32; Hab 2:19).

Trees and plants have close associations with deities throughout the ancient Near East, especially "mother goddesses," and these associations may lie behind some biblical references. Yahweh appeared to Abraham near a terebinth tree (Gen 12:6, 13:18, 18:1), and Abraham also planted a grove in Beersheba for calling on El 'Olam (Gen 21:33). Muslim exegetes later associate this with Abraham's establishment of the sanctuary at Mecca. In the Bible, Jacob buries his household idols under an oak near Shechem (Gen 35:4), apparently the same location as "Yahweh's sanctuary" where Joshua later erected a "standing stone" [Heb. massebah] (Josh 24:26). The judge Deborah prophesied under a palm (Judg 4:5), and is called a "Mother in Israel" (Judg 5:7). Gideon also received the divine word near a terebinth (Judg 6:11), an anonymous prophet from Beth-El is reported to have performed his work beneath an oak (1 Kgs 13:14), and Yahweh appeared to Moses in the form of a burning bush (Exod 3:2). In Q 28:30, God calls to Moses from a tree.

Trees also were associated with idolatrous worship (Isa 1:29, 57:5; Ezek 6:13; Hos 4:13–14), often with the goddess Asherah (Deut 16:21, 2 Kgs 21:3; *see also* ASHERAH). It is of note that some scholars see the names of some biblical trees (e.g., Heb. 'allah for oak and 'elon for terebinth) as etymologically related to the word *el* meaning "god," though the connection is not without some philological difficulty.

RIQAM (c. 1105–1170 CE). Rabbi Joseph Qimhi was a Jewish exegete and father of another two well-known exegetes (*see also* RADAQ; REMAQ). He migrated from Spain to Narbonne and there wrote a Hebrew grammar, a commentary on the first five books of the Bible, and a commentary on the Prophets (not extant). His exegesis focuses on the plain meaning of the text, but also stresses grammar.

ROD OF MOSES. Moses' staff that he took with him in his dealings with the Egyptian pharaoh and while wandering in the wilderness. In the Bible and Quran, Moses' rod appears to have a role in affecting certain natural and supernatural events. The use of a staff as a tool by magicians is well known in the ancient world in divination (*see also* RHABDOMANCY) and in Egyptian ritual practices. Like his brother Aaron's rod (Exod 7:10), with which it often is confused, Moses' rod can transform into a serpent (Exod 4:2–4, 7:8–13; Q 20:17–23, 27:10, 28:31). In Exod 7:17 the rod is identified as Yahweh's rod. In the Quran it is the rod of Moses that swallows the rods of the other magicians (Q 20:65–69, 26:45). With the rod, Aaron and Moses strike the Nile, turning it into blood (Exod 7:19–20); transform sand into lice (Exod 8:13); summon fire and hail from the sky (Exod 9:23); call forth locusts with an east wind (Exod 10:13); and part the Reed Sea (Exod 14:6).

In the wilderness of wandering Moses uses the rod to lead the Israelites and to cause water to flow from rock (Exod 17:5–6; Num

20:8–11; Q 7:160). He also employs it to change the battle tide in a war against the Amalekites (Exod 17:11). Aaron's rod also miraculously buds, blossoms, and bears almonds (Num 17:23). Moses' rod is said to have been the weapon with which Moses defeated the giant Og and his army in the later exegesis of Num 21:21–25; Deut 3:1–11; and Q 5:20–26.

Later exegetes assert that Moses' rod was made from rock or metal, though the biblical tradition depicts the rod as made of almond wood (Num 17:23). Since the almond is the first plant to bud in the spring it was seen as especially auspicious. Hence, the words of Isaiah, which metaphorically depict the coming of a messianic figure as a rod stemming from the root of Jesse who will strike the earth with the rod of his mouth (Isa 11:1, 11:4; Mic 6:9). It is noteworthy that the prophet Jeremiah's prophetic call also involves a contemplation on the meaning of an almond tree (Jer 1:11–12).

Later Jewish and Muslim writings multiply the miraculous stories involving Moses' amazing rod. It is treated (like the tablets of the Law) as having been made from sapphire carved from the divine throne (Targum Yerushalmi on Exod 2:21, 4:20, 14:21; Deut 34:12). Muslim exegetes also explain that the rod was made of sapphire or emerald. A number of traditions see the rod as among God's first creations, and inscribed with his name (Targum Yerushalmi to Exod 14:21). The *Book of the Cave of Treasures* narrates how the rod was originally taken from the Garden of Eden by Adam, then passed down through the prophets until it ended in the hands of Moses. From Moses the rod passed down until its wood was used for the "True Cross." The Armenian Death of Adam similarly tells of a rod that Seth takes from the Tree of Life and plants at the tomb of Adam. This branch later becomes the tree from which wood is taken and used to construct the cross used for the crucifixion of Jesus.

Moses' acquisition of the rod also is expounded upon in Jewish and Muslim exegesis. According to one Jewish tradition, Moses' wife Zipporah told Moses how her father Jethro, while serving as the pharaoh's counselor, stole from the pharaoh's palace a divine rod inscribed with the name of God and the future 10 plagues of Egypt. According to Zipporah the rod was created by God during the twilight of the first Sabbath and given to Adam, who passed it on to Enoch, and on through his descendants until it was stolen from Joseph by the

Egyptians. The Pirqe d'Rabbi Eliezer (40) explains how Jethro struck the rod into the ground and it miraculously sprouted into a tree, which later devoured all unworthy suitors seeking to marry Jethro's daughters. A similar account in given in the *Book of Jasher* (*see also* BOOK OF JASHER).

Tabari explains that Zipporah gave Moses the rod, but that Jethro objected since it was a special rod, and the dispute was settled in Moses' favor by an angel who was passing by at the time. Other Muslim exegetes explain that the rod had been in the possession of the prophet Shuayb, identified as Jethro, and that it was the rod that Adam had taken from the Garden of Eden. In Zamakhshari's exegesis of Q 28:21–28, Moses uses the rod to slay a dragon that attacks him while he is sleeping.

Muslim exegesis also conflates the story of Moses and Jethro with that of Jacob and Laban. Thus, in the exegesis of Q 28:21–28 Shuayb/Jethro is described as blind, which forced him to feel the rod that Moses brought to him. Instead of using sticks with peeled bark from different trees like Jacob (cf., Gen 30:37), God commands Moses to strike his rod against all the sheep that come to the watering trough so that they produce speckled young.

RUMI (1207–1273 CE). Jalal al-Din Rumi b. Baha' al-Din Sultan al-'Ulama' Walad b. Husayn b. Ahmad Khatibi, also known as Mawlana, was a famous Persian poet and founder of the mystical Mawaliyah order of Sufis. Among his works is a verse rendition of the stories of the prophets, which provides an interpretation of the Quran that pays particular attention to the spiritual attributes of each prophet.

RUTH. Name of a biblical heroine from whom King David descends (Ruth 4:17), as well as the biblical book named after her. The story of Ruth takes place in the time of the Judges, though scholars date the book variously between the 10th and fourth centuries BCE. It tells the story of a woman named Naomi who, while living in Moab, experiences the loss of her husband Elimelech. When Naomi's sons also die, Naomi is faced with the possibility that her husband's name will be cut off, and so she and her daughter-in-law Ruth set out for Bethlehem. There, with the help of Naomi, Ruth finds love in the form of

Elimelech's kinsman Boaz, a wealthy man from the tribe of Judah. Since Ruth is a Moabite, and not an Israelite, but also a Yahwist who marries an Israelite, many scholars see the story as an apologia that seeks to justify King David's non-Israelite ancestry. Other scholars, however, who see the story as a later work, and interpret it as a polemic against the exclusive marriage policies of Ezra and Nehemiah. In Matt 1:5 Ruth appears in the genealogy of Jesus.

– S –

SA'ADIA HA-GAON (882–942 CE). Sa'adia ben Joseph was a famous Gaon (Aram. "leader") of the Jewish academy at Pumbeditha. He was born in Egypt and studied in Tiberius and Aleppo before moving to Iraq in the first part of the 10th century CE. He is well known for his polemics against the Karaites, and his treatises on philosophy, law, and Hebrew grammar. Sa'adia was the first to translate the Hebrew Bible into Arabic, and he wrote a commentary on the Bible that was rationalist in its outlook.

SABIANS. Name of a religious group, mentioned three times in the Quran (2:62, 5:69, 22:17), but identified variously in Muslim exegesis and by modern scholars. One interpretation is that the Arabic word *Sabian* [Ar. sabi'] refers to the ritual purification of "washing" or "baptism" [Ar. saba'] practiced by this group. Ibn al-Nadim mentions such a group living in the marshes of southern Iraq whose leader was named Elchasai, probably a reference to the Elchasaites with whom Mani claims to have grown up and lived in the early third century CE. This connection has caused some scholars to identify the Sabians of the Quran with the Manichaeans. Christian heresiographers mention that Elchasai passed on a revealed book to a figure named "Sobai," whom some scholars have taken as the derivation of the term *Sabians*, thus as followers of this figure. Other scholars have identified the Sabians and the Elchasaites with the Mandaeans based on frequent references in Arabic sources to the Mandaeans as "Washers" [Ar. subba] because of their regular ritualized washings.

Another interpretation of the term *Sabian* is that it refers to the Sabians of Haran in northern Mesopotamia. The Sabians of Haran were a pagan group whose ideas combined hermeticism, astrology, and alchemy. It is possible that this group claimed to be the Sabians mentioned in the Quran in order to claim the status of "People of the Book" or "Protected people" [Ar. ahl al-dhimmi] and protect their religious freedom. A number of treatises are attributed to, or associated closely with the Sabians of Haran. These include the *Secrets of Creation*, attributed to Apollonius of Tyana on the discovery of the Emerald Tablet; a manual of talismanic astrology translated into Latin as *Picatrix*; and a treatise recounting the secret knowledge revealed by the Sun, Moon, and Saturn to Adam and his son Seth.

SACRIFICE. A solemn consecration of a domesticated animal or other items (grains, liquids, hair) to God, often by killing the animal or burning it whole or in part. Sacrifice plays a significant role in a number of the stories of the prophets, as do related rites such as libations and communal feasts. Sacrifice is an ancient practice, at times associated with feeding the divine. It was practiced widely long before the first written records appear (c. 3400 BCE), and played a central role in the religious systems of the Levant, Mesopotamia, Egypt, Anatolia, and Greece. For most of this history, sacrifice constituted the only form of public ritual.

Sacrifice first appears in biblical narrative in the story of Cain and Abel. According to Genesis 4, Cain brought produce of the soil as an offering for Yahweh while Abel brought the first-born of his flock along with some of its fat. God looked with favor upon the offering of Abel, but not Cain, so Cain killed his brother Abel. Q 5:27 also states that the "two sons of Adam" presented sacrifice, and that one of the sacrifices was not accepted, but the verse does not identify the brothers by name, the nature of the sacrifices, nor which one was accepted. Muslim exegetes clarify that the sacrifice was ordered by Adam to decide between Cain and Abel, who both wanted to marry the same woman (Cain's twin sister). Jewish exegetes explain that Adam ordered the sacrifice because it was the appointed time, and the offering took place on the future site of the altar of the temple in Jerusalem. According to Muslim exegesis, Cain offered a fattened she-camel and Abel offered some of the undesirable part of his produce. A fire is said to have descended from heaven and consumed the sacrifice of Abel, but not that of Cain. Q 5:27 includes the statement of Abel that "God accepts only from the upright," suggesting that it was Cain's character, and not the content of his sacrifice, that was at issue. Jewish exegesis explains that Cain offered the best of his flock, while Abel ate a meal and offered only the leftovers to God.

Noah and his son Shem also are credited with one of the first sacrifices. Gen 8:20–22 recounts how Noah built an altar to God and offered a selection of the "pure" animals and birds from the ark. In return, God promised never again to destroy the earth on account of human wickedness. According to Jewish exegesis, Noah refused to exit the ark before God promised not to destroy the world again with a flood, and that the sacrifice was offered by Noah as an expiation for his building the ark to save himself, rather than for trying to convert the people of the earth from their evil ways. Jewish exegetes also explain that Noah's son Shem performed the priestly rite of the sacrifice because Noah had been maimed by a lion when disembarking from the ark. The Bible does not specify the animals sacrificed, but later Jewish exegetes record them as an ox, sheep, goat, two doves, and two pigeons, and the sacrifice is said to have taken place on the same spot as the sacrifices of Cain and Abel. Muslim exegesis does not mention a sacrifice, but recounts how Noah, his family, and all the animals of the earth fasted out of thankfulness to God on the day the ark rested on dry land.

The story of Salih, in the Quran and in Muslim exegesis, revolves around the bloodless sacrifice of the she-camel and its young. Drawing on a Quranic passage (Q 26:155–156), Muslim exegetes state that Salih produced a she-camel from the side of a mountain as a sign to the people of Thamud. The she-camel and the people had rights to the area's water on alternate days, but on the days they were restricted from the water the people could take milk from the she-camel. The protected status of the she-camel and its pasturing grounds is probably related to the pre-Islamic notion of a sacred enclosure [Ar. hima], and the nonviolent consecration of a special domesticated animal to God. The undoing of the people of Thamud comes when they hamstring the she-camel, not necessarily killing it, but restricting its free roam of the land.

Sacrifice also plays a central role in the biblical story of Abraham. In Genesis 15, Abraham offers a sacrifice that involves dismembering animals and birds and placing their halves on either side of a path, on which the fire of God proceeds. The ritual described in this pericope is reminiscent of Hittite and early Greek military treaty rituals, and it is noteworthy that the story follows closely upon that of Abraham's battles with the kings of the east (Genesis 14). According to Genesis 22, God commanded Abraham to offer his son Isaac as a burnt sacrifice on a particular mountain. Gen 22:11–14 recounts how the angel of God stopped Abraham from sacrificing his son, and provided instead a ram that Abraham sacrificed as a burnt offering. Both Jewish and Muslim exegetes refer to the sacrifice as one of the "trials" of Abraham, testing his faith or obedience to God. The Quran states that God redeemed Abraham's son with a "great sacrifice" (Q 37:107), which Muslim exegetes identify as a special ram that had been kept in paradise, it being the same one that Abel sacrificed to God. Jewish sources detail that the sinews of the ram were used to make the strings of David's harp, its skin became the girdle of Elijah, and its ashes were used to form the foundation of the altar of the temple in Jerusalem. Jewish sources take this sacrifice as expiatory, as an atonement for Israel. Muslim sources locate the sacrifice in Mecca and attach its significance to the establishment of the sanctuary at Mecca by Abraham and Ishmael.

The Bible also contains an account of the sacrifice made by Jethro, Moses' father-in-law, after the Israelites had crossed the sea and escaped from the Egyptians. According to Exod 18:12, Jethro made a burnt offering and offered other sacrifices to God while Aaron and the elders of Israel came and feasted with him in the presence of God. Jewish exegetes state that Jethro wished to convert to the religion of Moses, and made the offering because he was thankful to God for saving the Israelites. They explain the apparent absence of Moses from the feast with Jethro, Aaron, and the elders (Exod 18:12) by saying that he was serving them, and so was unmentioned.

1 Kings 18 recounts the sacrifice made by Elijah on Mt. Carmel in competition with the prophets of Baal. As in Jewish exegesis about the sacrifices of Cain and Abel, God sends down fire from heaven to consume the dismembered bull, despite that the whole altar and the area around it are drenched with water. Because of this display, the people believed in the prophethood of Elijah, who then slaughtered the 400 prophets of Baal. The Quran recounts the story of Elijah, but does not mention the competition of the sacrifices (Q 37:123–132).

Muslim exegetes also narrate the contest between Elijah and the people, and include his praying to God and the prophets' praying to their idols to bring rain. Jewish exegesis adds that the bull being offered to Baal spoke to Elijah and initially refused to be offered to another god. Elijah then convinced it to offer itself, and the victory of Elijah resulted in return of rain to the land.

The sincerity of those who offer sacrifices gradually comes under criticism in Israel beginning at the end of the 11th century BCE with the prophet Samuel (1 Sam 15:22–23). His views are echoed later by the prophets Amos (Amos 5:21–25), Hosea (Hos 6:6), Isaiah (Isa 1:11–14), Jeremiah (Jer 7:21–23), and Micah (Mic 6:6–9). Such prophetic rebuke probably also registers tensions between prophetic schools and the priesthood.

SAFA AND MARWAH. Two hills near Mecca. Muslim exegetes report that Hagar ran between Safa and Marwah seven times before the well of Zamzam appeared to save the infant Ishmael from dying of thirst. The seven-fold run may relate also to the conflation of Zamzam with Beersheba, the latter of which is understood in Arabic as meaning "Well of the Seven." Both of the words *Safa* and *Marwah* can be taken to mean "stone" in Arabic, and it is noteworthy that in the pre-Islamic period, pilgrims would run between these two hills and touch two stone idols (Isaf on Safa and Na'ilah on Marwah). In the exegesis of Q 2:153 it is said that Isaf and Na'ilah were people who profaned the Ka'bah, and as punishment were turned to stone.

SAFAITIC. Language attested in numerous pre-Islamic North Arabic inscriptions discovered near Safa in southern Syria, which date between the first century BCE and the fourth century CE. Safaitic is written in a script closely related to that used in South Arabian Epigraphic languages, and the inscriptions that preserve the script mostly list names and genealogical information. Some contain invocations of deities, and many feature pictures of camels or dancing girls. Other languages belonging to the group of early North Arabic languages are Thamudic, Taymanite, Dedanite, Lihyanite, and Hasaean.

SALIH. The story of the Arab prophet Salih, sent to the people of Thamud, is found in Q 7:73–79, 11:61–68, 15:80–84, 17:59, 26:141–159,

27:45–53, 41:17–18, 54:23–32, and 91:11–15. Salih's genealogy is sometimes given as Salih b. Ubayd b. Asif b. Masikh b. Ubayd b. Khadir b. Thamud b. Gether b. Aram b. Shem b. Noah with Thamud descending from Gether rather than Uz [Ar. Aws], as with the Ad. Tha'labi gives the genealogy as Salih b. Ubayd b. Asif b. Mashij b. Ubayd b. Hadhir b. Thamud b. Ad b. Uz b. Aram b. Shem b. Noah, making the Thamud to be descendants of Ad.

The city of Mada'in Salih, also called Magha'ir Salih and referred to as "al-Hijr" (Q 15:80), is located in the northern Hijaz at the site of some Nabataean ruins. Late antique Greek sources refer to the people of Thamud, though they place them considerably later in history than Muslim exegesis. The Assyrian king Sargon II also has left an inscription, which dates to 710 BCE and mentions Sargon's victory over an Arab tribe called Thamud. Muslim sources report that the prophet Muhammad passed by the former site of the people of Thamud and declared the area and its water off limits.

The story of Salih and the people of Thamud exemplifies the familiar cycle of a prophet rejected by his people who are then destroyed. Muslim exegetes claim that God had given the people of Thamud longevity, gardens and springs, and fertile crops, and had taught them to hew their houses out of mountains. The people are said to have asked Salih for a sign to demonstrate his prophethood, and he caused the she-camel to emerge from a mountain. Based on Q 26:155–156, Muslim exegetes explain that the she-camel and the people had rights to the area's water on alternate days, but that the people could take milk from the she-camel on the days they were restricted from the water. In addition, the people were not allowed to harm the she-camel. The punishment came when the people of Thamud hamstrung the camel. God destroyed the people by crushing and flattening them (Q 91:14), with an earthquake (Q 7:78) or a scream (Q 11:67, 15:83, 54:31).

In some Muslim sources there is a long account of the birth of Salih that closely parallels the account of the birth of Abraham found in Jewish and Muslim exegesis. Salih's father Kanuh is said to have served as a high priest for the idolatrous religion of Thamud. When Salih's birth was announced, all the idols fell down, and the king became afraid that Salih would destroy him. So Salih's father was put into a cave in the valley of al-Hira for 100 years. Salih's mother was guided to the cave by a bird from the Garden of Eden, and there conceived Salih.

It is reported that Salih and his followers moved to Mecca after the destruction of the people of Thamud. Other reports state that the descendants of the followers of Salih live in one of the two cities at the ends of the earth. Ibn Ishaq reports that the Golden Bough was found in the grave of Abu Righal, one of the people of Thamud who was destroyed outside of Mecca (*see also* GOLDEN BOUGH).

SALMON BEN JEROHAM [Ar. Sulaym b. Ruhaym]. Tenth-century CE Karaite scholar from Palestine who is known for his polemics against rabbinic views and for his Bible commentary, which attacks the rabbinic interpretations, especially those of Sa'adia ha-Gaon (*see also* KARAISM).

SALVATION ORACLES. Name given to biblical prophecies that predict for Israel a prosperous future in which the nation dwells securely under a Davidic king and Jerusalem becomes the centerpiece of world attention. Such prophecies of hope can be found in many of the prophetic books (e.g., Isa 2:2–4, 9:2–7, 11:1–9; Jer 31:31–34; Amos 9:11–15). Salvation oracles may have their origins in holy war oracles with which they share common features (e.g., Num 10:35; 2 Sam 22:15; 2 Chr 20:14–19). Unlike the numerous prophecies of imminent doom, which register critiques of contemporary society and which typically accurately prognosticated future events, biblical salvation oracles placed in the distant future apparently did not predict the future with any degree of accuracy.

SAMUEL. Name of a prophet and two biblical books associated with his prophecies and the first kings of the Israelites. Samuel is not mentioned by name in the Quran, but Muslim exegetes identify him as the prophet mentioned in Q 2:246.

In earlier Hebrew Bibles and Jewish tradition the books of 1 and 2 Samuel were combined with 1 and 2 Kings into one scroll, but were later divided into two sections (Samuel and Kings). The Septuagint separates these into four books (1, 2, 3, and 4 Kings), a division adopted by the Vulgate and later translations based upon it. The title for both the Hebrew and Greek text derives from the main character of the book, the judge and prophet Samuel, though the text continues long after his death has been narrated. The book describes the selection of Israel's first king Saul and Samuel's warnings against instituting a monarchy (1 Samuel 8) and details the monarchy's early formation, its political and military battles (mostly against the Philistines and Ammonites), and the tensions between the prophetic school of Samuel and the monarchic establishment.

In addition to providing a rough historical outline of the early monarchy and its political and personal intrigues, the book of Samuel mentions the existence of local sanctuary sites such as Mizpah (1 Sam 7:5, 10:17) and Shiloh (1 Sam 3:21), the latter of which served as an important quay for the Ark of the Covenant prior to the capture of Jerusalem and construction of the temple. It also provides a glimpse into the activities of the prophets Gad and Nathan, both of whom served the royal house during David's reign.

The book offers a dynamic and developing characterization of Israel's first two kings. As the earlier narratives continue, King Saul is increasingly cast in a negative light. He moves from being a charismatic military leader in his battles against the Philistines to a manic depressive fraught with an "evil spirit" from Yahweh (1 Sam 16:14, 19:9) and jealous of his son Jonathan's friend, the young upstart David. 1 Sam 15:10 narrates how his eventual rejection by Yahweh under Samuel led to the selection of David as king. According to 1 Samuel 28, upon Samuel's death, the rejected Saul, unable to receive divine word by way of dreams, Urim, or other prophets (1 Sam 28:6), sought the dead prophet's advice by way of necromancy, but even in death Samuel rejects Saul.

The portrait of David similarly undergoes a transformation in 1 and 2 Samuel. Initially an ambitious shepherd and talented musician, David becomes an effective military leader and king. The accounts of his battles are many and often epic in nature (e.g., his battle against the giant Goliath in 1 Samuel 17). His unsatiated appetite for power, however, encourages him to commit an adulterous affair with a married woman, Bathsheba, and the murder of her husband, Uriah the Hittite (2 Samuel 11–12). For these transgressions God brings upon him a series of punishments from which the royal house would not recover, including the death of his children, a number of ill-fated battles, and the attempted coup d'état of his son Absalom. The book closes with David's purchase of a threshing floor from a Hittite named Araunah (1 Chr 21:20 reads "Ornan") as a site for the Ark of the Covenant and future temple of Yahweh (*see also* THRESHING FLOOR). The date of the book's composition is debated, and much of the material appears to reflect contemporary concerns, though it appears that some editing also may have taken place sometime in the post-exilic period in order to bring it in line with later theological concerns.

The Quran provides little information on Samuel. Q 2:246–251 begins with the Israelites' request to their prophet (identified as Samuel by Muslim exegetes) for a king. Samuel gives them Saul [Ar. Talut, meaning "tall one"], whom they reject. Angels then return the Ark of the Covenant as a sign of Saul's legitimacy. Verse 249 describes Saul leading his forces into battle and a test at a river that thins his forces, closely paralleling the account of Gideon in Judg 7:1–8. Verses 250–51 describe David's victory over Goliath and end with an apparent justification for armed conflict.

Muslim exegetes assert that Samuel was one of the descendants of Aaron. They also describe how the last of the Israelite prophets, identified as Eli (cf., 1 Sam 4:18), died upon hearing about the capture of the Ark of the Covenant by the Amalekites (the Bible understands the enemies here as the Philistines). These Muslim sources also state that Samuel was born to the last living Levite woman (who already was pregnant before the attack of the Amalekites). Samuel was sent to the temple where he heard God calling him in the night to be a prophet to the Israelites.

SARAH. Wife of the patriarch Abraham, formerly called Sarai (Gen 17:15) and renowned for her physical beauty (Genesis 12 and 20; TB Megillah 15a; Seder Olam 21). The Quran does not mention Sarah's beauty, but Muslim exegetes tell the account of Sarah being taken by the tyrant (the pharaoh in some accounts) when Abraham said she was only his sister. Her inability to have children led her husband to seek an heir through his second wife Hagar, who bore to him a son named Ishmael (*see also* HAGAR; ISHMAEL). Though she already had reached menopause (Gen 18:11), Sarah eventually conceived and gave birth to a son, whom she named Isaac (Heb. meaning "he laughed" in Gen 21:6). The annunciation of Isaac also appears in the

Quran (Q 11:69–74, 15:51–56, 51:24–30). Isaac became the father of Jacob, and thus the eponymous grandfather of the tribes of Israel. Deutero-Isaiah recalls Sarah, along with Abraham, in its description of Israel's miraculous and historical past (Isa 51:2). Though the Bible never explicitly calls Sarah a prophet, it does state that Yahweh visited her (Gen 21:1). Thus, talmudic tradition recognizes Sarah, along with Miriam, Deborah, Hannah, Abigail, Huldah, and Esther, as one of seven female prophets in the Bible (TB Megillah 14a).

SATAN. Hebrew term meaning "adversary," used in the Hebrew Bible in reference to both human enemies (1 Kgs 5:18, 11:14, 11:23, 11:25) and angelic agents of Yahweh who instigate, provoke, and foster ill relations between humans and God. The term appears in the Quran, both in the singular [Ar. shaytan] and plural [Ar. shayatin], to refer respectively to the devil and demons.

In earlier biblical texts the term *satan*, when used for an angelic being (*see also* ANGEL), appears only as a common noun without specification (i.e., "a" satan, not "the" Satan). In the biblical story of Balaam, the enemy of Israel, Yahweh sends "a satan" to work on his behalf, and the angel is only "a satan" to Balaam (Num 22:22). In post-exilic texts, however, "satan" appears as a title (i.e., "the Satan"), denoting an angelic adversary par excellence. The book of Chronicles blames "the Satan" for provoking David to take a census (1 Chr 21:1). The prophet Zechariah's vision of Joshua the high priest (Zech 3:2) also entails the appearance of "the Satan" as an active member of the divine court. In the book of Job, "the Satan" similarly possesses heavenly status as one of the "sons of God" with access to Yahweh's court (Job 1:6), and though he is not described as a "fallen" angel, his home appears to be the earth, and not heaven, upon which he wanders to and fro (Job 1:7).

Most often the Septuagint renders the Hebrew term [Heb. ha-satan, i.e., "the Satan"] with "devil" [Gk. diabolos] (with the exception of one peculiar transliteration as simply "satan" in 1 Kgs 11:14), demonstrating that as late as the third and second centuries BCE, the Septuagint translators perceived the Hebrew term [Heb. satan] as a title and not as a personal name. The use of "Satan" as a proper name does appear in the New Testament (Matt 4:10; Mark 1:13; Luke 10:18) where it names a figure who has fallen from the heavens and who is capable of entering the human body (Luke 22:3; John 13:27). According to 2 Pet 2:4, other fallen angels were banned to Tartaros, a place the Greek world deemed lower than Hades. Satan also is said to have argued with the angel Michael in order to ascertain the whereabouts of Moses' grave (Jude 9).

Jewish folklore and theology of postbiblical times similarly treat Satan as a specific fallen angel bent on corrupting humankind. Apocryphal texts know of sinful angels and equate them with the "sons of God" mentioned in the book of Genesis (Gen 6:1–4) who corrupted humankind by having intercourse with mortals and introducing demons, witchcraft, and astrology to the world (Jub 4:14–15, 4:22, 5:1). In Genesis the angels are not described as fallen from paradise or leading a rebellion against God. 1 Enoch, however, portrays Satan as leading a rebellion of stars (angels) when creation began (1 En 18:15–16), a tradition picked up in later midrashic texts (Genesis Rabbah 27:7). Though later Jewish mystical traditions state that God chained the fallen angels to mountains and punished them by suspending them between earth and heaven (Zohar I, 96, 126a, III, 208a and 221a), there appears to have been a rather strong current in early rabbinic Judaism opposed to the notion that angels had fallen from heaven.

In the Muslim exegesis of the Quran verses on Adam and Eve, Satan is called Iblis. He was the first creature to be given authority over the earth and the sky. Iblis belonged to an angelic group of Jinn, or to a group of angels created from fire (Q 55:15). His name originally was al-Harith, and some report that it was Abu Kardus. Sources report that there was a war on earth among the Jinn, who were causing corruption and killing one another, so God sent angels from heaven. In some accounts Iblis was a young Jinn among other Jinn on the earth, and was taken back to heaven by angels where he grew up in their company. Other exegetes report that the Jinn were on the earth for 2,000 years before Adam, shedding blood, and that God sent against them an army of angels and cast them into the islands of the seas. It is said that it was the angels Harut and Marut who led God's forces when the angels came down upon the earth, but in other accounts Harut and Marut are fallen angels who taught magic to the people of Babylon (Q 2:102; *see also* MAGIC).

It is in heaven that Iblis, along with the other angels, is commanded by God to prostrate before Adam (Q 2:34). Iblis refused to follow God's command because he considered himself better than Adam. According to Ibn Abbas, Iblis used to be called 'Azazil, and was one of the most zealous and knowledgeable of the angels, but his position led him to be arrogant. He also was appointed as keeper of the Garden of Eden, and is said to have had four wings until his expulsion from paradise and transformation into the "stoned Satan" (Q 3:36, 16:98). Despite asking God for mercy, Iblis vowed to deceive Adam and his descendants, and turn them away from God. After his expulsion, Iblis sneaked back into the Garden of Eden in the mouth of a snake, or in some accounts with the help of a peacock. Once in the garden, Iblis convinced both Adam and Eve to eat from the Tree of Life, which they did, and they consequently were expelled to the earth. The snake, which previously had four legs, like those of a camel, was cursed to crawl on its belly, and was cast to earth in the vicinity of Isfahan (*see also* IBLIS).

SAUL. First king of Israel (c. 1020–1000 BCE) and descendant of the tribe of Benjamin, chosen for kingship on account of his height and charisma (1 Sam 9:2), and probably also because of his military prowess (1 Sam 9:1, 14:47–48). The Quran refers to Saul as the "Tall (one)" [Ar. talut], and Muslim exegetes narrate that Samuel was instructed to choose as king the person who was as tall as his rod. Q 2:247 records the objections of the Israelites to Saul's kingship on the grounds that he was not wealthy, and Muslim exegetes also report that the Israelites objected to Saul not being from the tribe of Judah. His lowly position is indicated in reports that he was a tanner or a water-carrier before becoming king. The Bible casts him as a sheepherder originally (1 Sam 11:5).

Saul's character is variable in the biblical account. He is described, for example, as a heroic leader in a decisive battle at Michmash where he defeated the Philistines (1 Sam 14:31) though his rash actions and disrespect for the protocols of ritual and holy war (1 Sam 13:8–14, 15:13–24) eventually led Yahweh and the prophet Samuel to reject him as king in favor of David (1 Sam 15:23). Q 2:249 describes a test Saul uses to thin out his fighting force, closely paralleling the account of Gideon in Judges 7. Though initially favored by Yahweh and even given to ecstatic prophecies (1 Sam 10:5, 10:11), Saul seems to have been unprepared for the pressures of kingship, and eventually succumbed to fits of manic depression (1 Sam 16:23) and jealousy, which he displaced onto the young David (1 Sam 16:8–9). Fatally injured in a battle on Mt. Gilboa, Saul finished his life by falling on his sword, and dying along with his son Jonathan. This tragic event caused David to compose a lament for them (2 Samuel 1). The Quran records nothing of Saul beyond the battle at which David defeats Goliath, and Muslim exegetes do not identify him as a prophet, leaving that role for Samuel.

SECOND TREATISE OF THE GREAT SETH. The only completely preserved tractate from Nag Hammadi (VII,2). It describes the coming to earth of a heavenly savior figure and his teachings (65:18 and 69:21–22). Though the title of the manuscript assumes the savior figure to be Seth, it appears to refer to Jesus Christ. The conflation of Seth and Jesus also appears in other texts such as the Gospel of the Egyptians. Scholars speculate that the text was translated into Sahidic Coptic from Greek, and that blocks of new material were inserted at that time. A number of prophetic figures including Adam, Abraham, Isaac, Jacob, Moses, David, Solomon, and John the Baptist are said to be false, because they did not know the true God whom this text describes as the Christ.

SEDER ELIAHU RABBAH. Rabbinic work of unknown origin and authorship mentioned in the Talmud as a text related to Rab Anan (c. 270 CE) directly by the prophet Elijah (TB Ketuboth 106a). It comprises one portion of a larger midrashic work known today as Tanna debe Eliahu, which in its present form dates to the 10th century CE. It contains comments on legal matters as well as a variety of narrative material such as parables, prayers, and first-person statements by the prophet Elijah.

SEDER OLAM (RABBAH). Name of a large narrative collection of ancient Jewish traditions and historical lore. Jewish tradition attributes authorship for Seder Olam to Rabbi Jose ben Halafta (c. 150 CE), but most scholars date it to the 12th century CE. The text begins with the story of Adam and concludes with Herod the Great (40–4 BCE).

SEER. *See* PROPHET.

SEFER HA-BAHIR. Hebrew title for a book meaning "Book of Lumination," also known as the "Midrash of Rabbi Nehunya ben ha-Qanah." Though the text is attributed to the first century CE, the earliest datable reference to this text appears in a text dated to the 13th century CE. *Sefer ha-Bahir* is an extended treatise explaining the mystical significance of the vowels and accents in the Hebrew Bible and containing an exegesis of the first chapters of the book of Genesis. The text is extant in 60 columns and takes the form of a dialogue between master and disciples. One of the main points of the treatise is that the world is preexistent like God, rather than created, and that it appeared as a manifestation of what was present already in the first sefirah ("emanation") of the Godhead (*see also* SEFIROT).

SEFER HA-RAZIM. Hebrew book whose title means "Book of Mysteries" and which contains the sacrifices and conjurations of various supernatural beings. It includes information on the seven heavens, incantations for gaining knowledge of the future, healing spells, and more than 700 names of angels. The text is written in mishnaic Hebrew, was found among the documents of the Cairo Geniza, and is extant in Latin and Arabic versions. Most scholars date the text no earlier than the eighth century CE.

SEFER YETZIRAH. Hebrew book whose title means "Book of Creation." The book is preserved in a composite form, and it is unclear when it first was composed, though scholars tend to date it to the middle of the 10th century CE based on references to a similar book by Sa'adia ha-Gaon and others. The first part of the text is also called the "Rules of Creation" [Heb. Hilkot Yetzirah], and is a thaumaturgical text that deals with how to create things using combinations of the letters of the Divine Name of God. The text may relate to a story in the Talmud (TB Sanhedrin 65b, 67b) that describes an incident in which Judah ha-Nasi (*see also* MISHNAH) and his pupils create a three-year-old calf using the letters of the Divine Name. A Greek text called *Cosmogony* [Gk. Kosmogonia] appears to have contained similar contents, and may have been in circulation as early as the Hellenistic period.

The second part of the *Sefer Yetzirah* is attributed to both Abraham and Rabbi Aqiba. It contains an extended treatise on the mystical and cosmogonic significance of the 22 letters of the Hebrew alphabet. According to the text, there are three "Mother Letters" (alef, shin, mem) from which all the others derive. The alef represents the air, the shin fire, and the mem water. This tripartite sequence also corresponds to the order in which the Godhead emanates. Following the three "Mother Letters" are the seven "Double Letters" (bet, gimmel, dalet, kaf, pe, resh, and teth), which correspond to the seven planets, days, and apertures in the human body. Following these are the 12 "Simple Letters" (all remaining letters), which correspond to the signs of the Zodiac and the organs of the human body.

SEFIROT. Term apparently coined by the author of the *Sefer Yetzirah* to denote the primordial "numbers" [Heb. safar, meaning "enumerate"] as the stages of God's emanation. Each sefirah (sing.) corresponds to one of God's manifested attributes emanating from the Godhead [Heb. Ein-Sof, lit. "without end"] to perceived reality. The relationship of the sefirot form a structure known as the "Sefirot Tree," which is supposed to display the units of all acts through which God reveals himself.

SELF-MUTILATION. *See* ASCETICISM.

SEPTUAGINT. Greek translation of the Hebrew Bible undertaken in Alexandria, Egypt, from the third to the second centuries BCE. The name Septuagint derives from the legendary tradition, as related especially in the Letter of Aristeas, that 70 (or 72) Jewish elders produced identical Greek translations though secluded from each other. Though the letter clearly intends to lend authority to the translation, the date of the translation is supported by the discovery of several second-century BCE Septuagint fragments found among the Dead Sea Scrolls. Scholars see the Hebrew text that was used in creating the Septuagint as differing a great deal from those that led to the Masoretic text, Targums, Vulgate, and Peshitta. The biblical books appear in a different order in the Septuagint than they do in the Hebrew canon, and some books (e.g., Jeremiah) even have different chapter arrangements. The Septuagint's order is based on genre, not on the Jewish liturgical calendar, and so the prophetic books appear after the legal, historical, and poetic works, an order that perhaps also reflects the historical stages by which these texts became canonized (though some Septuagint manuscripts place the prophetic works before the poetic texts). Though originally a product of Alexandrian Jews, the Septuagint was adopted by early Greek-speaking Christian communities, some of whose versions also contained the Apocrypha. This eventually led to its disuse among Jewish communities that sought to produce different Greek translations that reflected Jewish exegetical interests.

SETH. One of the sons of Adam and Eve, Muslim exegesis considers Seth a prophet, and he is closely associated with the origin and character of certain types of secret knowledge by other groups in late antiquity. According to Muslim exegetes, Seth is one of four Syrian prophets along with Adam, Noah, and Enoch.

According to the Bible, Seth was the third son of Adam and Eve, the father of Enosh, and lived to the age of 930 years (Gen 5:3–8). In Gen 4:25, Eve refers to Seth as a replacement for Abel, who was killed by Cain. Muslim exegetes also state that the name Seth was given to Eve by Gabriel, meaning "gift of God," as a replacement for Abel. Jewish exegesis claims that Seth was one of 13 men born circumcised, including Adam, who is said to have been created circumcised. Tabari reports that the People of the Book claim that though Adam and Eve always gave birth to twins (boy and girl), Seth was born without a twin.

Whereas Cain is the father of the wicked, Seth's descendants are the righteous and include Noah (Genesis 5) and Jesus (Luke 3:23–38). Muslim exegetes state that all humans now living descend from Seth through Noah. The Bible mentions the "Children of Seth" (Num 24:17), though some scholars read the name Seth here as a noun meaning "strife" or "devastation," as found in Jer 48:45 and Lam 4:47. Some gnostic groups in late antiquity took the name "Sethians," thus underscoring their roles as heirs to Seth and his secret knowledge. Later mystical Jewish exegesis records the tradition that the soul of Seth entered Moses and will enter the Messiah in the eschaton.

According to Muslim exegesis God sent 104 scriptures to prophets, and 50 of these were revealed to Seth. Ibn Ishaq reports that Adam commissioned Seth to succeed him as prophet, teaching him the hours of the night and day, and explaining what beings worshipped God in which of these hours. Adam also prophesied to Seth concerning the coming of the flood, and wrote a testament that he addressed to Seth.

In some apocryphal texts, such as the Testament of Adam and the Apocalypse of Adam, Adam explains to Seth astronomical phenomena and their relation to the beings that worship God, and Adam prophesies to Seth a series of future events including the flood. In other apocryphal texts, such as the Apocalypse of Moses and Life of Adam and Eve, Seth is associated with the quest for the oil of life, which flows from the Tree of Life in paradise. The testament that Adam addresses to Seth is said to have been placed in the Cave of Treasures with the body of Adam and the treasures that the Magi would present to Christ. The Gospel of the Egyptians and the Three Steles of Seth found at Nag Hammadi also purport to preserve the writings of Seth.

SFORNO, OBADIAH BEN JACOB (1475–1550 CE). Italian Jewish Bible exegete who also wrote on mathematics and Hebrew grammar, and authored a philosophical treatise using the Bible as a witness against Aristotelian theories. Sforno's biblical commentary focuses on the plain meaning of the text, and draws upon the works of Ibn Ezra, Rashbam, and Ramban, though also adding philological details not found in earlier works. In addition to the Pentateuch, Sforno comments on Psalms, Job, Jonah, Habakkuk, and Zechariah. He also wrote a preface to his commentary on the Pentateuch, which often is printed, along with his commentary, in the Miqra'ot Gedolot.

SHAMAN. Term used to describe practitioners of a wide variety of practices associated primarily with Central Asian and Siberian peoples, but also with Native Americans. The term comes into English through Russian from the Tunguz term *shaman*, which refers to a certain class of person responsible for spiritual matters in Siberian tribes. Many shamanistic practices and experiences parallel elements found in Near Eastern accounts of prophets and prophecy.

Among the main aspects of shamanism related to prophecy is a link established by the shaman between the material world and the spiritual or astral world. Shamans are selected by heredity or are called to their office. Initiates must undergo a symbolic death ordeal that involves lying inanimate for several days while the body is dismembered and stripped of its material existence by demons and spirits. The initiate is inflicted with every disease that inflicts humanity, and his soul is taken to the underworld, where it communes with the spirits of the dead. The primary technique of shamanism is an ecstatic trance and vision, though the shaman is also trained in the names and functions of the spirits, mythology and genealogical lore, and the secret languages of the spirits.

SHEM. One of Noah's three sons and survivor of the great flood. Shem is the eponymous ancestor of the Semites through his five sons Elam, Asshur, Arpachshad, Lud, and Aram (Gen 10:21–32; 1 Chr 1:17, 24). Among Shem's descendants are the Arabs and the Hebrews, and he is the forefather of all subsequent prophets mentioned in the Bible and Quran. Book 3 of the Sibylline Oracles identifies Shem with the Greek Titan Kronos.

Jewish traditions regarded Shem as the greatest, but youngest, son of Noah, who was born circumcised and served as a prophet for 400 years. Jewish exegesis on Gen 8:20 asserts that Shem performed the sacrifice after leaving the ark because Noah was maimed by a lion (Genesis Rabbah 36:4). Some sources also identify Shem with Melchizedek the enigmatic priest and king of Shalem (i.e., Jerusalem) mentioned in Gen 14:18–20. It is reported that Shem received the Hebrew script of the Torah along with 26 of the world's 72 languages and six of the world's 16 scripts. Shem is mentioned only one time in the New Testament, as an ancestor of Jesus (Luke 3:36). Muslim tradition agrees with the biblical references, that Shem was given the "middle of the earth" as his land (Q 37:77), and that he became the father of the Arabs, Persians, and Byzantines. Other Muslim sources report that the pit into which Joseph was cast was originally dug as a well by Shem. In some of the exegesis of Q 3:49, Shem is said to have been resurrected by Jesus to describe the construction of Noah's ark.

SHEMAIAH. Name of a prophet living at the time of King Rehoboam of Judah (r. 922–915 BCE) who prevented a civil war after Jeroboam I (922–901) had declared himself king of Israel by prophesying to

Rehoboam that the schism was God's doing (1 Kgs 12:22). In 917 BCE Shemaiah prophesied to Rehoboam that Yahweh would deliver him into the hands of the Egyptian pharaoh Sheshonq (r. 936–914 BCE), but when the king repented of the transgressions of which he was accused, Shemaiah returned to him with a new prophecy declaring that Rehoboam would not fall to Sheshonq, but that Sheshonq would reduce Jerusalem to vassalage (2 Chronicles 12). If Shemaiah is the same figure named in Jer 26:20 as Shemaiah of Kiriath-Jearim, then he also was the father of Uriahu, a prophet living at the time of Jeremiah (*see also* URIAHU). Shemaiah also is said to have composed a book of prophecies (2 Chr 12:15), which is not extant.

SHI'AH. Arabic term referring to the various groups in Islamic history that traced prophetic authority back to Ali b. Abi Talib and the subsequent imams among his descendants. Ali was one of the earliest followers of the prophet Muhammad, and he married the prophet's daughter Fatima. Shi'i scholars claim that the prophet Muhammad designated Ali as his successor, though he became caliph only after following three others, and his leadership was contested by the first Umayyad Caliph Mu'awiyah b. Abi Sufyan. Ali was assassinated in 661 CE by a group of his followers who objected to his arbitration with Umayyads, and was succeeded by his son (Muhammad's grandson) Hasan, who abdicated to the Umayyads and died in 669. His other son, Husayn, continued to oppose the Umayyads and was martyred in 680 CE.

From the earliest Imamate of Ali, different Shi'i groups have formed based on the grounds of doctrinal distinctions and questions of succession to the Imamate. Some of these groups proclaimed the divinity of Ali or a later imam, and had messianic and apocalyptic expectations. After the passing of the Fourth Imam, Zayn al-Abidin, the Zaydis claimed the Imamate of Zayd while others acknowledged the Imamate of Zayd's half-brother Muhammad al-Baqir. After the passing of the sixth Imam Ja'far al-Sadiq, the Ismailis claimed the Imamate of Ja'far al-Sadiq's eldest son Ismail, who had died while his father was still alive. Some of the Ismailis believed that Ismail did not die but went into occultation only to return at the end of time, while other Ismailis held that Ismail was succeeded by hidden imams, from whom came the imams who formed the Fatimid dynasty in Egypt

(909–1171 CE). The Imami or "Twelver" Shi'ah maintain that the Eleventh Imam Hasan al-Askari, who apparently died without a son in 874 CE, did have a son named Abu al-Qasim Muhammad, the twelfth and final imam, who went into occultation until his return at the end of time.

SHISHLAM. Appellation given by Mandaeans to the personification of perfected humanity, sometimes portrayed as a crowned and anointed king-priest, and other times as a divine man. The term appears in the coronation or ordination ritual of the Mandaean priest, which is described in mythical terms and is preserved in the Mandaic text entitled *The Coronation of the Great Shishlam*. The described ritual is one of initiation and parallels initiation rites found in the stories of the prophets such as washing and ritual purification, heavenly ascent, the acquisition of secret knowledge, and transformation into angelic or divine form. In this text, the initiate must be physically and ritually pure. He is stripped of his earthly body and "clothed" with a righteous soul symbolized by a white ritual dress. The initiate then enters a special structure accessible only to initiated priests. The building is described as a "temple," using the term used for the "Holy of Holies" in Nestorian worship [Syr. heykal]. There the initiate spends the night in vigil reciting words from books of secret knowledge. Upon emerging from the retreat, the initiate is crowned, and given other implements of kingship such as a ring and a staff. After initiation, the priest is a shishlam, a microcosmic representation of the truth.

SHUAYB. Prophet mentioned 11 times in the Quran, and associated with Jethro, the father-in-law of Moses. Shuayb was sent to the people of Midian (Q 7:85–93, 11:84–95) and to the People of the Tanglewood (Q 15:78–79, 26:176–191). Muslim exegetes disagree about whether these are the same people, and Suyuti reports that some exegetes claim that Shuayb was also sent to the People of the Well. Ibn Kathir maintains that the people of Midian and the People of the Tanglewood are identical. Kisa'i explains that these were originally two different peoples, but that the People of the Tanglewood moved to Midian and intermarried with the people of Midian. Kisa'i also claims that Shuayb was the son of the leader of the people of Midian, a man named Zion, son of Anaq, who married an Amalekite woman.

The narratives of Shuayb are grouped together with four other prophets: Noah, Hud, Salih, and Lot. Shuayb's prophethood comes at the end of this list just before the prophethood of Job, Dhu al-Kifl, and Jonah, but it is to Moses that Shuayb passes on the mantle of prophethood, symbolized by his rod that had been passed down to Shuayb from Adam through all the previous prophets. Muslim exegesis of Q 28:21–28 consistently identifies Shuayb with Jethro, Moses' father-in-law, though Ibn Kathir claims there would be a space of about 400 years between Shuayb and Moses assuming that Shuayb lived close to the time of Lot (Q 11:89). Most exegetes maintain that Shuayb was Moses' father-in-law, but some claim that Jethro was the nephew or cousin of Shuayb, or that Jethro was one of the people of Midian who believed in Shuayb.

The people of Midian are said to be the descendants of Midian the son of Abraham and Keturah, and the genealogy of Shuayb is given as son of Mikil b. Issachar b. Midian b. Abraham, associating Shuayb with both Sarah and Keturah. Wahb b. Munabbih says that Shuayb was one of the people in Babylon who believed in Abraham. The land of Midian is described as being on the edges of Syria, on the border of the Hijaz, close to the lake of the people of Lot (i.e., the Dead Sea).

Both the people of Midian and the People of the Tanglewood are accused of highway robbery and larceny. Qurtubi reports that the people of Midian blocked the way of those who believed in Shuayb. Ibn Abbas says that they were the first people to institute the collection of taxes, and that they took a 10 percent tax on all the people who moved through their territory.

The punishment meted out to the people of Midian is in the form of an earthquake (Q 7:91–92), which left the people lying face down in their homes as though they had never had the opportunity to live in and enjoy their homes. Thus the result of their punishment is that they prostrate themselves to God in death and can no longer enjoy the things obtained by their ill-gotten gains. Q 11:94–95 describes the punishment similarly except that it is not an earthquake, but a "scream" that brings about their demise. Q 26:189 refers to the "punishment of the day of shade," which is interpreted by Muslim exegetes to mean that God caused it to be very hot, then sent a cloud under which the people gathered, and caused fire to rain down upon them from this cloud. Ibn Kathir explains that when the heat hit the people they gathered under the cloud, at which point God then sent fire, an earthquake, and a scream, followed by a scorching wind.

SIBYLLINE ORACLES. Collection of prophetic sayings attributed to a female figure known as the Sibyl. In classical Greek and Latin sources the Sibyl was originally thought to be a single individual who was nearly immortal and moved from location to location. Later the term *Sibyl* is attributed to different individuals or collections of oracles identified by the location from which they originated (*see also* ORACLE). According to the anonymous preface to the standard collection of Sibylline Oracles, the Cumean Sibyl brought nine books to the ruler of Rome in the fifth century BCE. She demanded a price for them and when he would not pay she burnt three of them. She offered the remaining six for the same price, but he refused again, and so she burnt three more of them. He finally purchased them and entrusted them to special keepers, but the books were destroyed when the temple of Jupiter was burned in the first century BCE.

Roman tradition identified ten Sibyls: Persian, Libyan, Delphic, Cimmerian (Italy), Erythrean, Saian, Cumean, Hellepontic, Phrygian, and Tiburtine. Sometimes a Hebrew Sibyl is added to this list. The Sibylline Oracles are known in 14 books, but books 9 and 10 repeat material from books 4, 6, and 8, and are usually omitted. It is not possible to assign exact dates to the oracles, especially the form in which they are now extant. Much of the material, especially that in the earlier books, can be considered early, but book 14 reviews history down to the Arab conquest of Egypt in the seventh century CE.

Some of the Sibylline Oracles originated with Jews and Christians or were adapted by them. These include oracles from books 3–8, 11–14, and some fragments that are preserved in later works. Many of the oracles present overviews of history with eschatological overtones. Some of the oracles mix biblical history with Greek mythology; praise Jews; and warn against the destruction of empires, cities, and peoples. Several (e.g., book 8) mention Jesus Christ by name, detailing prophesies of his coming and his incarnation. Overall, the tone of the oracles is apocalyptic and eschatological, and they exhibit motifs and themes that are found in other Jewish and Islamic eschatologies.

SIFRE NUMBERS. Narrative midrashic exposition on the biblical book of Numbers that Jewish tradition dates to 90–130 CE. The text begins with Numbers 5 and continues to chapter 27, though some biblical stories are absent, including the account of the rebellion against Moses (Numbers 16–17) and the story of Moses' use of the bronze serpent (Num 20–24).

SIGNS. Events, acts, items, or persons that mark a divine occasion or are interpreted positively or negatively as possessing divine import. In the Hebrew Bible, the word *sign* [Heb. 'ot] often appears with the word *wonders* and represents the symbol, and therefore, pledge, attached to God's covenants. Thus, the rainbow is a sign (Gen 9:12), as is circumcision (Gen 17:11) and the Sabbath (Exod 31:17). The term also appears in reference to divine wonders (Exod 4:9, 8:19; Dan 3:33) and can mark sacred substances, like the blood on the doors over which the Angel of Death passes on the eve of the first Passover (Exod 12:13), or sacred objects, like the temple censers and Aaron's rod (Num 17:3, 17:25). Signs also refer to divine memorials (Josh 4:6), and can represent a mark or letter of the alphabet (Gen 4:15) as well as the standards or ensigns of Israel (Num 2:2; Ps 74:4). Often signs token a verification or vindication of past or future events (Exod 3:12; Ps 86:17), and thus serve to edify the person or persons for whom the sign is given. In this usage, signs cannot be distinguished from portents or omens. Prophecies and dreams also are called signs (Deut 13:2–6; 1 Sam 2:34, 10:9; 1 Kgs 13:3; 2 Kgs 19:29, 20:9; Isa 7:14, 20:3, 44:25; Ps 74:9), as are prophets themselves (Isa 8:18; Ezek 4:3, 12:11). Israelite kings, like Hezekiah (715–687 BCE), sought signs from God (Isa 38:22; 2 Chr 13:24), and the celestial bodies or patterns, especially when changed, are understood as signs (Gen 1:14; Jer 10:2; Ps 65:9).

Throughout the Quran prophets are given "signs" [Ar. sing. ayah, pl. ayat] to demonstrate their prophetic status. Often the sign is the prophet himself, or is a punishment for questioning the veracity of the prophet's words, or the remains of the people after having been punished by God. Rescuing Noah and his people in the ark while killing the rest with the flood is said to be a sign (Q 23:30, 26:121, 29:15, 54:15). The people of Hud were destroyed because they rejected God's signs (Q 7:72, 11:59, 41:15) and their punishment was a sign (Q 26:139). Salih brought the she-camel as a sign to the people of Thamud (Q 7:73, 15:81, 17:59, 26:154–155), which became the root of their own undoing (Q 27:52, 91:14–15). Abraham being saved from a fiery furnace is a sign for those who believe (Q 29:24). The destruction of Sodom is a sign (Q 7:84, 15:77, 26:174, 29:35, 51:37). Ibn Kathir says that Joseph's shirt that healed his father's blindness was one of the signs of the prophets. The People of the Tanglewood taunted Shuayb by asking him to cause a piece of the sky to fall upon them as a sign of his prophethood (Q 26:187). The plagues Moses brought to the Egyptians are signs (Q 17:101). Zechariah is cursed with the sign of not being able to speak because he doubted God's annunciation of John's birth (Q 3:41, 19:10–11). Jesus is said to have brought signs to the Israelites, but they called it magic (Q 61:6).

The Quran also refers to signs as evidence of God. Abraham saw the signs of the night and day (stars, moon, and sun) before discovering God (Q 41:37), and called upon God to raise up a prophet in Mecca who would recite the signs of God (Q 2:129). Shuayb seems to refer to himself as a sign to the people of Midian (Q 7:85). The miracles Moses performed before the pharaoh are signs of God's existence, disproving the pharaoh's claim to be God (Q 20:23–24, 43:46–56). The blessings of the Israelites in the wilderness of wandering are called signs, and the Israelites' rejection of the signs is tied to their punishment (Q 2:61). Samuel asserted that the return of the Ark of the Covenant was a sign of the kingship of Saul (Q 2:248). The prophet Muhammad was taken on the Night Journey and ascended into the heavens so that God might show him his signs (Q 17:1).

SINAI. Name of the desert peninsula that rests between the two finger-like channels of the Red Sea. In the Bible it is the region associated with Mt. Sinai, the mountain of God (*see also* HOREB) on which Moses experienced a number of theophanies and where Yahweh established his covenant with the Israelites (Exod 19:23; Ps 68:16). It is on Mt. Sinai that God provided Moses with the tablets of the Law, which he subsequently placed in the Ark of the Covenant (Exod 31:18).

The Quran refers to Sinai both as "Tur Sinin" (Q 95:2) and "Tur Sina" (Q 23:20), and the term *tur* [Ar. and Aram. "mountain"] is found another eight times in the Quran, seven of them in reference to

Sinai alone (2:63, 2:93, 4:154, 19:52, 20:80, 28:29, 28:46). Q 52:1 mentions "the mountain" [Ar. al-tur], which is associated with various mountains on which revelations were revealed, including Sinai. Muslim lexicographers claim that the term *sina* is Nabataean and that the term *sinin* is Ethiopic (*see also* JABAL SIN). The exact location of Mt. Sinai is unknown today, though a number of regional traditions have laid claim to its location.

SOLOMON. Son of David and king of Israel. Solomon is regarded as a prophet in the Quran and Muslim exegesis where he is the famous king who ruled the world from Jerusalem, having built the city with the aid of demons and Jinn.

According to the Bible, Solomon is responsible for instituting sweeping administrative changes, and for forging lucrative mercantilist relationships with the Phoenicians. Among his most famous achievements is the construction of Yahweh's temple, a monumental building effort that resulted in the unification of worship and the discredit of former sites of worship and pilgrimage. Though never explicitly called a prophet in the Hebrew Bible, Solomon does experience a theophoric dream (1 Kings 3) in which he receives his legendary wisdom, a dream in which Yahweh establishes his temple as an eternal sanctuary (1 Kgs 9:2), and an apparently more direct experience while building the temple (1 Kings 6).

The incipit for the biblical Song of Songs rather ambiguously relates the poem to Solomon, and the book of Proverbs also begins with an attribution to Solomon. Later Jewish tradition also attributes the book of Qohelet (Ecclesiastes) to him. Muslim exegetes do not attribute a book to Solomon, but the Quran refers to his famed wisdom in judgment (Q 21:78–79). Ibn Kathir repeats a report in which David makes a judgment and Solomon later offers a comment that would have made a more just settlement. The Bible contains the well-known passage in which Solomon decides between two mothers claiming the same child (1 Kgs 3:16–28). In later Christian and Jewish sources also, Solomon is known for his wisdom. The apocryphal book of Wisdom is attributed to Solomon, and to dream of Solomon is considered a sign of wisdom (TB Berakhoth 57b).

Solomon is said to have been given special gifts by God. The Bible describes Solomon's theophoric dream in which God grants him what he needs to govern his people (1 Kgs 3:4–15). The Quran states that Solomon was taught the speech of the birds and that "some of everything" had come to Solomon (Q 27:16). In Q 27:20–28 Solomon converses with the birds, the hoopoe bird in particular. Q 27:19 depicts Solomon as being able to understand the language of ants. He is given the wind to blow at his command (Q 21:81, 34:12, 38:36) and the command over demons and the Jinn (Q 21:82, 34:12, 38:37–38).

Though an immensely effective leader, prophetic tradition also sees Solomon in the light of his excesses (women, chariots, wealth, and foreign worship). Muslim sources say that Solomon had 1,000 women, 700 wives and 300 concubines, or 300 wives and 700 concubines. Bukhari preserves a report from the prophet Muhammad linking the number of Solomon's wives to his production of a fighting force for God. The link between Solomon's marriages and the extent of his dominion is found also in a Jewish midrashic text that relates the story of how an angel planted a reed in the sea upon which Rome was founded to mark Solomon's marriage to the pharaoh's daughter (Song of Songs Rabbah 1.6).

The Quran also contains an apparent indictment of Solomon (Q 38:30–33), which Muslim exegetes interpret as suggesting that Solomon forgot about the afternoon prayer because he was too busy admiring the beauty of some horses. For this Solomon flew into a rage and slashed all their throats and legs. Hasan al-Basri reports that it was a winged horse, but Tha'labi says it was 900 horses and that Solomon left 100, from which all Arabian horses descend.

Solomon's control of supernatural forces is found in both Jewish and Muslim sources. The Talmud, for example, states that Solomon reigned over all the higher beings including angels (TB Sanhedrin 20b). The Quran states that God gave Solomon control over demons and Jinn, and Q 34:13 indicates that this was for the purpose of building any monument Solomon wanted. Muslim exegetes say that Solomon used these beings to build Jerusalem, Istakhar, and Palmyra (*see also* TESTAMENT OF SOLOMON).

SON OF THE PROPHETS. Term used in the Bible to refer to an individual member of a class, order, or guild of prophets. There is much evidence to suggest that some of the biblical prophets, like those in Mesopotamia and Mari, received a formal training in prophetic schools, or like Elisha, entered into a discipleship relationship with a master prophet, with clear boundaries and expectations for succession. In some cases the relationship between disciple and master probably was hereditary (*see also* AZARIAH). The term *son of the prophets* most often represents a legitimate prophet sanctioned by the biblical authors (1 Kgs 20:35; 2 Kgs 2:3, 2:5, 4:1). Not all mantics, however, were so trained, as is evident from the prophet Amos, who disavows the title "son of the prophets" (Amos 7:14).

SONG OF SONGS. Biblical love poem of eight chapters traditionally ascribed to King Solomon (Song 1:1, hence the book's other name, the Song of Solomon), though most scholars date it to the post-exilic period. Comparativists looking to interpret the poem's meaning and the characters represented in its dialogues have looked to various Mesopotamian, Egyptian, Indian, and Arabic poetic genres, but no exact parallel has been found. It has been interpreted variously as an expression of erotic human love, an ancient fertility drama, a ribald satire, and an allegorical dialogue between God and Israel (or Christ and Christians). Others see the Song as a collection of smaller poems composed by different hands. According to the Mishnah (Yadayim 3:5), the Song of Songs would not have made it into the canon of sacred scripture had not some rabbis argued in favor of the poem's allegorical interpretation. Nevertheless, the eschatological interpretation of the Song cannot be traced back before 70 CE, and in Christian circles, the exegesis of the Song as historical allegory is rare before the time of Nicolas de Lyra (c. 1270–1349 CE), who himself was heavily influenced by Jewish sources, in particular the works of Rashi (*see also* RASHI).

SONG OF SONGS RABBAH. Allegorical exposition and interpretation of the biblical Song of Songs, also known as the Midrash Rabbah on Song of Songs. The midrashic text is marked by numerous repetitions and an uneven treatment of the Song's verses. Much of its material is borrowed from the Mishnah, Talmud Yerushalmi, and Genesis Rabbah, as well as the Pesiqta d'Rab Kahana, thus dating the work no earlier than the eighth century CE.

SOSHYANT. Avestan term originating in Zoroastrianism as the title of the future restorer of the earth who arrives just before the renovation of the cosmos. The *Denkart*, a ninth-century CE Zoroastrian encyclopedia, says that the Soshyant is the last bringer of religion for humanity from God. He is the last in a line of prophets that began with Gayomard, the first man. After the coming of the Soshyant there will be no need for religion or prophethood, for all people will walk in purity of their own accord. He will cause Zoroastrianism to spread over all the earth. The Soshyant is described as being at the head of an army that defeats the forces of evil on the earth in a way that is comparable to the messianic and prophetic figures of the eschaton in Judaism and Islam.

SOUTH ARABIAN EPIGRAPHIC. A family of ancient languages grouped as South Semitic along with Ethiopic, including Sabaean (attested sixth century BCE to the sixth century CE), Minaean (fourth to second centuries BCE), Qatabanian (fifth century BCE to third century CE), and Hadramitic (fourth century BCE to third century CE). These languages are attested only in inscriptions, found mostly in southern Arabia, but also in trading colonies elsewhere. Many of the inscriptions are dedicatory in nature, refer to royal edicts, or attest to religious rituals and various deities. Some of the ritual inscriptions provide information on cult officials, and several refer to ritual hunts.

SPARAGMOS. Practice of tearing a living animal into pieces, sometimes accompanied by omophagia, the eating of its raw flesh, and prophetic nudity. The practice is attested at Mari among ecstatics, who engaged in it as a means of inducing prophecy. The phenomenon and behavior may lie behind the account of Samson ripping up the lion after the spirit of Yahweh rushed upon him (Judg 14:6). The practice also is attested in the Greek cult of Dionysus, and according to Saint Nilus, survived into the fourth century CE among the Arabs of the Sinai Peninsula (*see also* OMOPHAGIA).

SPEAKING IN TONGUES. *See* GLOSSOLALIA.

SPEECH ACT THEORY. Theoretical approach to biblical texts, especially prophetic discourse, deriving from the disciplines of anthropology, sociology, and linguistics, which sees speech not merely as a means of reference, but as a device that combines word (logos) and action (praxis). Thus, by proclaiming a future event, a prophet is not merely suggesting that such an event will happen, but is making it happen. He is enscripting the future by deploying the inherent power of words, a belief that was widespread in the ancient Near East. This belief, and the Speech Act Theory that accounts for it, helps to explain a number of features in prophetic texts, including why prophets often speak about future events in the past tense. A belief in the performative dimension of words also lies behind prophetic word play (*see also* WORD PLAY).

SPIRIT. The word *spirit* [Heb. ruah, also meaning "wind, breath"] appears frequently in the Bible and in the Quran. It is used for the "breath of life" that God places into the nostrils of living things (Gen 6:17; Zech 12:1), and which departs upon death (Ps 78:39; Qoh 12:7). It also occurs in reference to the powerful command of God (Isa 34:16; Ps 33:6), the messianic king (Isa 11:4), and the wind of heaven (Gen 8:1). The prophetic tradition also associates the spirit of God with theophoric deep sleep [Heb. tardemah] (Isa 29:10, Mic 2:11), and the primary force involved with prophetic inspiration (Num 27:18; 2 Kgs 2:15), including frenetic or ecstatic prophetic behavior (Num 11:17; Hos 9:7; Ezek 2:2). Yahweh can send an "evil spirit," as he did to King Saul (1 Sam 16:15), a "lying spirit" to prophets (1 Kgs 22:22), and a "troublesome spirit," as he did to Job (Job 7:11). According to Exod 31:3 and 35:31, the divine spirit also endows some with technical and artistic skill, and Joel 3:1 describes the divine spirit as a future prophetic gift. Later prophetic tradition describes the divine spirit as an angelic being (Isa 63:9–10), who eventually is associated with the "divine presence" [Heb. shekhinah] (Ps 139:7).

The Quran makes specific reference to the "Spirit" [Ar. ruh] five times (Q 16:2, 17:85, 70:4, 87:38, 97:4) as an angelic being. It appears to be distinct from other angels, and Ibn Abbas claims that it is a special angel created higher than the others. Q 17:85 seems to identify the spirit with the "word" [Ar. amr] of God, and Q 97:4 connects it with the revelation of the Quran. There are also four references in the Quran to the "Holy Spirit" (Q 2:87, 2:253, 5:110, 16:102). All of these, with the exception of Q 16:102, refer to the Holy Spirit aiding

Jesus. Q 16:102 states that it was the Holy Spirit who revealed the Quran, and because of this reference, many Muslim exegetes identify the Holy Spirit with the angel Gabriel.

ST. GEORGE. An early Christian saint included in Muslim texts [Ar. Jiriyas or Girgus] as a prophetic figure. The story of St. George Megalomartyros is well known and widespread, especially in the Fertile Crescent and in Egypt. According to Christian accounts, George was a soldier, the son of a Palestinian Christian Arab who was martyred for refusing to sacrifice to the gods of Greece and Rome during the time of the Roman emperor Decius or Diocletian (third century CE). The major Christian versions of the story are extant in Syriac, Coptic, and Arabic accounts dating to the sixth and seventh centuries CE, and in Ethiopic sources from the 12th and 13th centuries CE.

In Islamic sources George is considered a prophetic figure who lived among a group of believers who had been in direct contact with the last of the disciples of Jesus. George is said to have been a rich merchant who opposed the erection of a statue of the god Apollo by the king of Mosul, named Dadan. After confronting the king, George was tortured many times to no effect, imprisoned, and aided by angels. Eventually George was able to expose that the idols were possessed by Satan, but was martyred when the city was destroyed by God in a rain of fire. The account closely parallels several other prophet stories, including the account of Abraham and the idols and Elijah's confrontation of the king.

Many of the accounts of St. George include the story of his defeat of a dragon, and many amulets and icons depict St. George on horseback lancing a dragon with his spear. Some identify the dragon with the emperor who tortured him, while others refer to it as the devil in reference to eschatological battles mentioned in apocalyptic texts. The dragon combat may also hearken back to ancient Near Eastern and Indo-European cosmogonies in which a beast of chaos is dismembered in the creation of the world.

According to several accounts, the emperor Diocletian personally attempted to destroy the shrine of St. George at Lydda in the late third and early fourth centuries CE, but was defeated and blinded. The shrine was later rebuilt as a church under the emperors Constantine in the fourth century CE and Justinian in the sixth century CE. This church apparently was destroyed and later rebuilt again during the Crusades of the 11th century CE to commemorate the help of St. George and the angels at the Crusaders' battle at Antioch. Other churches and shrines were built in honor of St. George throughout the Near East and in Europe, many of which housed relics associated with him.

According to Latin sources, Pope Zacharias discovered the head of St. George in the eighth century CE in a Vatican vault bearing an inscription identifying it. The head is said to have been kept there until it was moved to another church in the 17th century CE. The heart of St. George is reported to have been sent to King Henry V, who housed it in the Castle at Windsor. In the 13th century CE, the Syrian scholar Bar Sawma reported that he found a relic of St. George, which was placed in the church of St. George at Maraghah. Muslim geographers locate the tomb of St. George in Mosul.

STICHOMETRY OF NICEPHORUS. A catalog of canonical and apocryphal writings included in the *Chronography of Nicephorus*, patriarch of Constantinople (806–815 CE). Among the writings said not to be recognized as authoritative are 3 Maccabees, Wisdom of Solomon, Wisdom of Jesus Sirah, Psalms and Odes of Solomon, Esther, Judith, Susanna, and Tobith. Those of the New Testament include the Apocalypse of John, Apocalypse of Peter, Epistle of Barnabas, and the Gospel of the Hebrews. Apocryphal books of the Old Testament include the books of Enoch, Patriarchs, Prayer of Joseph, Testament of Moses, Assumption of Moses, Abraham, Eldad and Modad, Elijah, Zephaniah, Zechariah father of John, and Pseudepigrapha of Baruch, Habakkuk, Ezekiel, and Daniel. New Testament apocrypha includes the Acts of Paul, Peter, John, Thomas, the Gospel of Thomas, the Teaching of the Apostles, the books of Clement, and the writings of other early Christian authorities such as Ignatius and Hermes.

STRABO (64 BCE–c. 25 CE). Greek geographer and historian. Strabo traveled extensively from "Armenia to Etruria, from the Black Sea to the borders of Ethiopia" and wrote his *Geography* in about 7 BCE. His work *Historical Sketches* is not extant. Strabo's geographical work provides a wealth of information on the Mediterranean world, including Spain, Britain, Italy, Central Europe, Balkans, Greece, areas of the Black Sea and Caspian Sea, India, Persia, Mesopotamia, Palestine, Arabia, Egypt, Ethiopia, and North Africa. In addition to geographical descriptions, Strabo provides historical and economic information, and recounts other remarkable aspects of these different regions and peoples.

SUFISM. General term used for Muslim mysticism. The term derives from the Arabic term meaning "wool" [Ar. suf], though some see a connection with the Greek word for "wisdom" [Gk. sophia]. Sufis trace the origins of Sufism to the prophet Muhammad, and before him to the practices of the other prophets, back to Adam. Certain prophets are especially important to certain Sufi thinkers. Adam is the first man, created by the hand of God, and endowed with secret knowledge imparted directly from God. The heavenly ascent and physical transformation of Idris is a paradigm for later Sufi ascensional mysticism. Abraham's epithet "friend of God" often is taken as an indication of the closeness and representative of the love between God and humans. Khidr is particularly significant in Sufi texts as a "prophet of prophets," having been sent to Moses with secret knowledge. His immortality and association with fertility are utilized also in Sufi symbolism. Jesus is singled out as exemplifying the ascetic life that is central to many Sufi practices and theories of purification (*see also* ASCETICISM). All of these "virtues" are said to culminate in the prophet Muhammad, as described in the *Bezels of Wisdom* [Ar. Fusus al-Hikam], a book believed to have been communicated by the prophet Muhammad to the Sufi Ibn al-Arabi in the 13th century CE.

The mystical experiences of Sufis also parallel many of the experiences associated with the prophets. Sufis speak directly with God and act as the voice of God to other people. The experience of God is depicted by Sufis in terms of intoxication, ecstasy, dreams, and visions, as are many reports of prophetic experiences. Sufis often bring particular messages or books from God or previous prophets. The Sufi emphasis on spirituality often is compared to the message of the Israelite prophets, stressing the spirit rather than the outward trappings of ritual and the law.

SUHRAWARDI (1153–1191 CE). Maqtul Shihab al-Din Yahya al-Suhrawardi, also called the "Shaykh al-Ishraq," was a well-known

Sufi thinker, famous for his theory of illumination, the "wisdom of divine flashes" [Ar. hikmah al-ishraq]. This theory held that existence coincides with what is experienced as light. God is the essence of light and his revelations are illuminations, or flashes of divine insight that determine one's perceptual existence. Suhrawardi relied heavily on imagery derived from Iranian mythology, especially Zoroastrianism, and he considered himself the true representative of Hermes Trismegistos. He is said to have composed close to 50 Arabic and Persian books. Many of his ideas are expressed in allegorical tales drawn from the Quran and the stories of the prophets. Suhrawardi was executed in Aleppo for his religious and political views.

SUSA. Ancient city located in southwest Iran and identified with the modern city of Shush. The city of "Sus" is mentioned by Muslim exegetes as being the birthplace of Abraham. The reference, however, may be related to "Susa," since Susa was one of the oldest cities in the Near East, served as the capital of the Elamite empire in the fourth and third millennia BCE, and was an important city under the Achaemenids. Susa [Heb. Shushan] appears in Neh 1:1, Dan 8:2, and throughout the book of Esther. It is the city where the prophet Nehemiah served in the royal court of the Persian king Artaxerxes (r. 464–424 BCE). Susa also is the site of the tomb of the prophet Daniel, and continues to be a place of pilgrimage by Jews, Christians, Muslims, and others. Muslim geographers identify the tomb of Daniel as being in the city of Sus, but some reports place the city of Sus in Khuzistan.

SUYUTI (1445–1505 CE). Jalal al-Din Abd al-Rahman b. Abi Bakr b. Muhammad al-Suyuti is one of the most respected of Quran scholars. He is well known for his works in a number of fields related to the study of the Quran including his famous compendium of Quranic Studies and a voluminous Quran commentary. It is said that his written works number around 600.

SWORD OF MOSES. Hebrew and Aramaic text extant in several fragmentary manuscripts dating to the 13th and 14th centuries CE. A Greek papyrus dating to the third century CE closely relates to the contents of the *Sword of Moses*, but a specific connection has not been established. A book with the title "Sword of Moses" also is mentioned among the Gaonic Responsa of the 11th century CE. The name of the text probably derives from the reference in Deut 33:29 to the "excellent sword" of Moses, which is understood to represent a book of secret knowledge.

The text begins with a preface concerning proper handling of the book, requiring purification and a period of no sexual emissions. Most of the text is concerned with incantations that are affected by speaking the Divine Name of God and the names of various angels. Most of the spells are written rather than spoken and involve specific ritual actions. There are spells for sex, blinding, healing, snake bites, catching fish, sending dreams to people, speaking to the dead, and destroying houses. The text also includes instructions on the making of amulets.

SYMBOLIC ACTS. *See* PROPHETIC DRAMA.

– T –

TABARI (839–924 CE**).** Muhammad b. Jarir al-Tabari is the author of one of the earliest and best-known commentaries on the Quran and histories of early Islam (from the creation until his time). He is said to have memorized the Quran by age seven, and traveled widely for study in Rayy, Baghdad, Basrah, Kufah, Cairo, and parts of Syria. He founded his own school of law, called the Jaririyah, which did not survive past the fifth century CE. Tabari was a popular teacher in Baghdad, and was so prolific that his contemporaries joked about it. It was said that, divided over his entire lifetime, he wrote an average of 14 pages a day. His commentary on the Quran is particularly important as it preserves the first two and a half centuries of Muslim exegesis, and is known for its close dependence on hadith reports, which Tabari often gives in multiple versions and with differing interpretations of the same passages.

TABARSI (d. 1153 CE**).** Abu Ali al-Fadl b. al-Hasan al-Tabarsi was a noted theologian, jurist, and a master of Arabic learning. His commentary on the Quran is considered authoritative by Sunni and Shi'i

scholars alike. Although Tabarsi was a Shi'i and gives special prominence to Shi'i interpretations in his Quran commentary, he includes
the views of all the major exegetes in a comprehensive fashion, including some Mu'tazili exegetes. His commentary includes both lexical and grammatical questions, and a discussion of the different
views of earlier exegetes.

TABATABA'I (1903–1982 CE). Muhammad Husayn Tabataba'i was an
Iranian scholar who produced a monumental commentary on the
Quran. Tabataba'i came from a family claiming descent from the
prophet Muhammad, a family with a tradition of scholarship several
hundred years old. He was educated in Tabriz and later at Najaf. In
the realm of jurisprudence, he is said to have been one of the foremost Mujtahids. Alongside his Quran, hadith, and legal scholarship,
Tabataba'i also commented on the Sufi philosophical works of Ibn
Sina and Mulla Sadra. After World War II, he settled in Qum where
he taught Quran commentary and philosophical Sufism (influenced
by the comparative work of the French historian of religions Henri
Corbin). The Quran commentary of Tabataba'i, completed in 1972, is
very large (published in 20 volumes), and is aimed at young intellectuals of the Shi'i community. It treats verses in collective units rather
than individually, and treats Shi'i and Sunni hadith material after a
general overview of the passages.

TABLETS. Made of clay, and less often of stone, tablets comprised the
commonest medium for writing in ancient Mesopotamia. The concept of a "tablet" as a written record of something is used widely in
Jewish and Muslim sources as symbolic of heavenly records.

The importance and pervasiveness of tablets as a written medium,
coupled with a Mesopotamian belief in literate deities who keep
records on human affairs, were embodied in a widespread concept
known already in the early second millennium BCE as the "Tablets of
Fate." These tablets were the possession of the supreme deity and
played a central role in the continuation of his divine kingship. They
were conceived of as a divine link between heaven and earth, and
they imbued the god who possessed them with the power to control
the destinies of all peoples and events. They are described as clay
tablets containing cuneiform writing into which a divine seal impres-

sion was made, thus marking it as a binding legal treaty that could not be changed. Depending on which period one examines in ancient Mesopotamia, one can find a different deity in charge of them.

Tablets are often associated with the messages brought by prophets from God. Scholars have compared the Tablets of Fate to the stone tablets of the law that Yahweh inscribed for Moses (Exod 24:12, 31:18, 32:15–16), which Moses smashed in a dramaturgical act of anger while witnessing the transgression of his people (Exod 32:19), and which Yahweh forced him to rewrite (Exod 34:1; *see also* PROPHETIC DRAMA). Tablets also were used at times for prophetic composition, as the prophets Isaiah and Habakkuk evince, though as the passage from Habakkuk asserts, the medium probably was chosen to facilitate rapid reading (Isa 30:8; Hab 2:2). With the integration of the scroll as a written medium, the notion of Tablets of Fate was transferred to the scroll. Thus, the Psalms speak of a "scroll of life" (Ps 69:28), a concept echoed later in the New Testament (Phil 4:3; Rev 5:1, 20:12).

The Quran refers to a "Book of Record" or "Book of Fate," which is a record of all events and people. Q 35:11 says the life of all men is recorded in a book, and other passages refer to the time of death as being "written" (Q 3:145, 3:154). All things that happen are said to be "written" by God in a "book" (Q 9:51, 13:38, 57:22). Q 11:6 describes this as a "Clear Book," and Q 6:59 compares this book to the "keys to the hidden" about which only God knows. The contents of the heavens and the earth are also in the "Clear Book" (Q 27:75). There is also frequent mention of a "Book of Deeds" assigned to each person (Q 17:71, 18:49, 54:52, 78:29, 81:10–14). In addition, Muslim sources explain that all revelations to prophets come from the "Mother Book" [Ar. umm al-kitab], which is said to be attached to the throne of God in heaven (Q 3:7, 13:39, 43:4). This is sometimes identified with the "Preserved Tablet" [Ar. lawh mahfuz] mentioned in Q 85:21–22 (*see also* QURAN). Ibn Abbas states that Moses was given the Torah in the form of seven crystal tablets, and other exegetes describe the phenomenal height of these tablets when they were attached to the Lotus Tree in paradise.

TALE OF WEN-AMON. Egyptian tale dating to the 11th century BCE that reports the journey of an Egyptian named Wen-Amon to Byblos in Phoenicia. Wen-Amon was a high-ranking official of the god Amon who served the deity at Karnak in Thebes. In addition to providing a portrait of declining Egyptian power in this period, the text also makes reference to a young man, perhaps working in the court of the Phoenician king, who is seized one night in a state of frenzied prophetic ecstasy. Though a literary text, it nonetheless attests to the presence of prophetic activity in the Phoenician court in a period roughly contemporaneous with David and Solomon.

TALMUD. Term given to the two collections of ancient rabbinic writings that consist of the Mishnah (rabbinic oral and written laws organized into 63 tractates) and the Gemara (a commentary on the Mishnah), which comprise the basis for religious authority in rabbinic Judaism. The two collections, known as the Talmud Yerushalmi (also known as the Palestinian Talmud) and the Babylonian Talmud, were compiled between the years 200 and 500 CE. In addition to detailing discussions on a variety of laws on social, economic, and religious topics, the Talmuds contain a wealth of information on ancient Judaism and often cite ancient traditions concerning biblical figures and events not found in the Bible itself.

TARDEMAH. Biblical Hebrew word for a "deep sleep" often associated with theophoric experiences and prophecy. God caused a tardemah to fall upon Adam before extracting his rib and fashioning a woman from it (Gen 2:21). The book of Job associates the tardemah with divine dreams and visions (Job 4:13, 33:15), both of which constitute prophetic experiences. Jonah too experiences a deep sleep (Jon 1:5), as did Daniel, who was put into a deep sleep before experiencing visions (Dan 8:18, 10:9). The tardemah was perceived as conceptually close enough to death to become a metaphor for it (Ps 76:7). Its association with inactivity naturally led to its connection with laziness (Prov 19:15), and to its figurative use by the prophet Isaiah in his polemical description of the inabilities of other prophets (Isa 29:10).

TARGUM. Term used to designate the various Aramaic Jewish translations of the Bible. The Targums are not merely "literal" translations of the Hebrew Bible, but reflect the interpretive perspectives of those who produced them, and often include lengthy expansions or additions to what is found in the Hebrew and Greek texts of the Bible.

The process of translating biblical texts into the Aramaic language appears already in Ezra 4:7, a verse that reflects the impact of Aramaic on the Jewish communities returning from Babylon. The process thus achieved early status in ancient Judaism, as is attested also by several Targums found among the Dead Sea Scrolls. As the term *targum* (lit. "commentary, explanation, translation") attests, the Targums often represent exegetical paraphrasing more than word-for-word translations.

According to the Talmud (TB Megillah 3a), the Targum of the Pentateuch was composed by Onqelos the proselyte under the guidance of Rabbi Eliezer and Rabbi Joshua, and the Targum of the Prophets was composed by Jonathan ben Uzziel under the guidance of the prophets Haggai, Zechariah, and Malachi. This talmudic passage also relates that after the Targum to the prophets was completed, the land of Israel quaked and a Bat Qol exclaimed, "Who is this that has revealed my secrets to humankind?" (*See also* BAT QOL.) Jonathan ben Uzziel then stood up and said, "It is I who have revealed your secrets to humankind. It is fully known to you that I did not do this for my own honor or the honor of my father's house, but rather for your honor, so that dissension may not increase in Israel." This citation draws attention to this Targum's frequent treatment of prophetic verses as references to the messianic age.

The first five books of the Bible are attested in three major Targums. Targum Onqelos, probably redacted in its extant form in fourth- or fifth-century CE Babylon generally is regarded by Jews as the most authoritative Targum of the Pentateuch. It is not overly expansive of the Hebrew, leading some scholars to think that it was edited from a longer text. The name seems to be related to a Greek version of the Pentateuch produced by Aquila in the second century CE. The Targum Yerushalmi, also known as Targum Pseudo-Jonathan, because it was incorrectly linked to the Targum Jonathan on the prophetic books of the Bible, includes many interpretive expansions, being about two times the size of the original Hebrew text. Based on historical references, the Targum Yerushalmi is dated as early as the eighth century CE. The Codex Neofiti was found in a Vatican manuscript, and is dated to the 16th century CE, though its contents reflect earlier traditions. In addition to these three texts, there are also numerous fragmentary Targums, some of which are specific to the Cairo Geniza. There are also Targums on other specific books of the Bible outside of the Pentateuch and Prophets, including Job, Psalms, Proverbs, Lamentations, Song of Songs, Ruth, Ecclesiastes, Esther, and parts of Chronicles.

TEMPLE. A permanent sanctuary for a deity, often situated on or near mountains. The English word *temple* is derived from a Greek word denoting an "area marked off" [Gk. temenos], usually containing an altar [Gk. bomos]. It was also considered the house of the deity and thus also displayed the god's cult statue.

The Bible gives evidence for the existence of a number of sanctuaries in Israel prior to Solomon's construction of Yahweh's temple in Jerusalem (c. 950 BCE), but unlike their Egyptian, Mesopotamian, and Greek counterparts, Israelite sanctuaries did not house a cultic statue. There is mention of sanctuaries at Shechem (Josh 8:33), Bethel (Judg 20:27), Mizpah (1 Sam 7:5, 10:17), Shiloh (1 Sam 3:21), and Gibeon (2 Sam 21:6), which in Solomon's day was known as "the greatest high place" (1 Kgs 3:4–15). Such references evince that it was legitimate to sacrifice to Yahweh in a number of places in the region (*see also* SACRIFICE). Exod 20:24–26 permits the construction of altars to Yahweh in any place "where I shall remind men of my name." The Quran and Muslim sources refer to the Ka'bah as the "House of God" [Ar. bayt Allah] linking it with earlier temples in Semitic and Greek contexts (*see also* KA'BAH). The Arabic term for "temple" and "house" [Ar. bayt] is the common Semitic term for temple, found also in the Bible (e.g., "Beth-El" in Gen 28:10–22, 35:7, 35:15).

In some cases, it appears that sanctuary sites were places where the divine presence was somehow recognized through some sign or portent. Though many of the sites mentioned in the Bible were given special status, because they served at one time or another as resting places for the Ark of the Covenant, they probably already held cultic significance prior to the Ark's arrival. Thus it is said that David chose a Hittite threshing floor as a place for the Ark of the Covenant because an angel of Yahweh appeared there (2 Sam 24:16–25), though the site probably had long-standing cultic significance (*see also* THRESHING FLOOR). The location of the Ka'bah is said to have been designated by God to Adam first, and later to Abraham in a vision of God's Presence [Ar. sakinah], and many ancient Mesopotamian temples are said to mark the "navel" or spot where the heavens and the earth were once connected [Sum. duranki]. Throughout the ancient Near East, but especially in Mesopotamia, prophets and diviners were employed in order to establish whether or not a particular god approved the building of his or her temple, and to ascertain the proper time for doing so. According to the biblical text, though King David had desired to build a temple, the prophet Nathan instructed him to leave the construction for his son (2 Samuel 24), which he did (1 Kings 6–7). Nathan's prophecy to David not to build, and his instruction to Solomon to commence building, appears to fit well-established cultural and literary patterns in the ancient Near East.

Temple construction often is associated with cosmogonic and other natural models. Solomon's construction of Yahweh's temple is described as a seven-year process (1 Kgs 6:1, 6:37–38), a period, while though potentially accurate, is fortuitous given the widespread ancient Near Eastern emphasis on seven as a symbolic number associated with cosmogony, and other accounts of seven-day temple constructions at Ugarit and in Mesopotamia. The cedar walls of Solomon's temple were carved in the form of gourds and open flowers (1 Kgs 6:18). Gold-fitted cherubim, palm trees, and blossoms covered the temple doors (1 Kgs 6:35) and the doors to the great hall. The temple contained a room housing four rows of cedar columns that was called the "Lebanon Forest House" (1 Kgs 7:2).

The Islamic site of the Ka'bah and the mound upon which it is built are also said variously to have been constructed from the materials of seven mountains (Mt. Zion, Mt. Sinai, Mt. Judi, Mt. Lebanon, Mt. of Olives, Mt. Tabor, Mt. Hira). The cube of the Ka'bah corresponds to the four cardinal directions, the four alchemical elements, and the four universal elements of the emanated Godhead (Intelligence, Nature, Matter, Soul). To the six sides of the Ka'bah is added a "seventh," which is the throne of God, the heavenly archetype of the earthly temple.

The Bible provides fairly extensive descriptions of the architectural features and furnishings of the Jerusalem temple built by Solomon (1 Kings 6–7). It was a long rectangular building with one opening on its shorter side, built on a platform on a mountain (Ps 48:1–4). Inside the temple was divided into three sections, which were surrounded on three sides by a three-story building. At the front of the temple was the Ulam or front vestibule, before which stood two large pillars (1 Kgs 7:15–21) named Jachin (lit. "established") and Boaz (lit. "strength"), for which Phoenician analogs exist. Just behind the Ulam was the Hekhal (lit. "palace"), which might have been a place for worship. In the Hekhal stood the altar of incense (1 Kgs 6:20–21), the altar of gold (1 Kgs 7:48), the table of shewbread and 10 candlesticks (1 Kgs 7:48–49), and the bronze altar of sacrifice (1 Kgs 8:64, 9:25). At the heart of the temple, behind the Hekhal, and at an elevated level, was the Holy of Holies. The Hebrew term for the Holy of Holies [Heb. debir] etymologically relates either to being in the "back (room)" or to the act of "speaking." This innermost sanctuary was restricted architecturally, but also through a gradation of purity regulations, permitting only the high priest to enter, and only once a year, on the Day of Atonement.

The Bible also records alterations made to the Jerusalem temple under Kings Asa (1 Kgs 15:18), Joash (2 Kgs 12:1–16), Ahaz (2 Kgs 16:10–18), Hezekiah (2 Kgs 18:14–16), Manasseh (2 Kgs 21:3–5), and Josiah (2 Kgs 23:3–7; 2 Chr 34:8–13). The picture conveyed from the biblical text is not complete enough to provide a satisfying reconstruction of the Jerusalem temple, which has made it difficult to locate architectural analogs for Solomon's temple in the archaeological record of Israel's neighbors, though recently comparisons to the Hittite temple at 'Ain Dara have received notoriety. In 586 BCE, the Babylonian king Nebuchadnezzar II (605–562 BCE) destroyed the "House of God," and emptied it of its contents. Though both the biblical record and annals of Nebuchadnezzar II list the many items taken from the temple, they do not mention the Ark of the Covenant (*see also* HIDDEN TEMPLE VESSELS).

The destruction of the first temple inspired visions of future temples and the building of the second temple under Persian rule. During the exile (c. 571 BCE), the prophet Ezekiel experienced a vision in which he saw a new temple (Ezekiel 40–42). The image he describes is based on, though not identical with, Solomon's temple. Zech 1:7–6:15 also contain a series of "temple visions" with Jerusalem at the center of the cosmos. The Jerusalem temple was again rebuilt during the Persian period (Ezra 3), though it was smaller and very different from the one described by Ezekiel and Zechariah. This "second temple" is sometimes called the "Zerubbabel temple" since it was restored under Zerubbabel and the high priest Joshua (Hag 1:1). The second temple was enlarged and renovated by Herod the Great in 19 BCE and was completed in 64 CE, but was destroyed in 70 CE by the Romans. Visions of the future temple are found in the Dead Sea Scrolls, New Testament, and apocalyptic texts, and are associated with the revival of the sanctuary at Mecca in Muslim sources (*see also* NEW JERUSALEM).

TENT OF MEETING. Portable sacred tent in which Moses spoke face-to-face with Yahweh (Exod 33:7–11) during the journey through the wilderness. Even the priests were not privileged to enter the tent with him (Num 27:21). In some texts, the tent appears to house the Ark of the Covenant (Exodus 25–26, 36–40), which contained the tablets of the law, but elsewhere the Tent and the Ark of the Covenant appear as separate items (Exod 33:7–11; Num 10:33–36, 14:44; Deut 10:1–5, 31:14–15, 31:25–26). Some scholars compare the Tent of Meeting to the pre-Islamic "dome-tent" [Ar. qubbah] containing divine emblems. Ibn Kathir provides a detailed description of the Tent of Meeting, though he refers to it as the "Tent of Time" [Ar. qubbah al-zaman]. According to Ibn Kathir, this tent was the Ka'bah of the Israelites until they arrived in Jerusalem and built a more permanent site. The temple in Jerusalem continued to be the direction of prayer for all prophets, even the prophet Muhammad, until the direction of prayer was changed to the Ka'bah in Mecca after the Hijrah to Medina.

TERAPHIM. Household deities made of wood or stone variously described in the Bible as either miniature in size (Gen 31:34) or life-size (1 Sam 19:13). The Hebrew word [teraphim] probably derives from a Hittite word [tarpis] for the ancestral gods that tribes used as evidence of their status and ownership of estate. The stealing of them therefore represented the theft of a deed to property (cf., Genesis 31). They apparently also possessed a divinatory function (Hos 3:4), perhaps in connection with ancestor worship. The teraphim are mentioned as important items in a household shrine in Dan (Judg 17:5), and appear in conjunction with other divinatory techniques such as rhabdomancy, extispicy (Ezek 21:26), and dream interpretation (Zech 10:2). Their perceived connection with worship, whether real or apparent, led the prophet Samuel to refer to them as abominable idols (1 Sam 15:23), and they are listed in 2 Kgs 23:24 as among the items outlawed by the religious reforms of King Josiah (640–609 BCE).

TESTAMENT OF ABRAHAM. An account of Abraham's tour of the inhabited world in which he sees the sins of various peoples and a vision of judgment. This text is commonly grouped together as the Testaments of the Three Patriarchs along with the Testament of Isaac and the Testament of Jacob. The text is preserved in two recensions (A, B). The longer recension (A) is extant in partial Greek manuscripts and in Romanian, while the shorter (B) is attested in Greek, Slavonic, Romanian, Coptic, Ethiopic, and Arabic manuscripts. Though the earliest Greek manuscripts date to the 11th century CE, the text is thought to originate much earlier, and the other recensions are considered to derive from the Greek. Such tours of heaven and hell were popular in late antiquity and the medieval period in Judaism, Christianity, and Islam. The motif of a prophet being shown the world before dying is found also in the Testament of Moses and Jewish exegesis of Deut 34:1–4, which describe how Moses saw the land and future of Israel before his death. The Quran states that God showed Abraham the kingdom of the heavens and the earth so that he might be one who had certain belief (Q 6:75).

According to the Testament of Abraham, the archangel Michael was sent from heaven to tell Abraham of his death. Abraham refused to go until he was given a tour of the inhabited world and viewed all the creation of God. Michael took Abraham in a fiery chariot, along with a number of angels, to see various people on earth engaged in sinful activities. Then Abraham was led to the gates of heaven where he saw Adam and the two angels who record the sinful and righteous deeds of people. In recension B, it was Enoch whom Abraham saw recording the deeds of people. He is told that Abel is to judge first, then the 12 tribes of Israel, then God on the final Day of Judgment. Abraham is also described as interceding on behalf of a soul that was then spared. Michael returned Abraham to earth, but Abraham still refused to die, so God sent the Angel of Death to take him. Abraham then refused to go with the Angel of Death until the Angel of Death showed him his true hideous form, which the text then depicts with multiple heads and faces of dragons and flaming swords. In recension B the Angel of Death has only two faces, the face of a dragon and the face of a sword. The Angel of Death describes his various faces as the different ways of dying, and finally tricks Abraham into being taken.

TESTAMENT OF ADAM. An account of the knowledge passed from Adam to his son Seth concerning cosmology, angelology, and future events. The text is preserved in numerous recensions and versions, and its composition is sometimes dated as early as the fifth century CE. The Syriac manuscripts are thought to represent the earliest extant version of the text, and are dated to the ninth century CE. There are three sections to the text. First is the Horarium in which Adam speaks to Seth, lists the hours of day and night, and explains which parts of creation praise God at what times. Second is a prophecy in which Adam reveals the details of creation and the Fall, the coming flood, the life and death of Christ who is to be born of the virgin Mary, and the end of the world. The account of Christ is clearly influenced by the Christian account of Jesus, and mentions that Cain killed Abel because of his incestuous passion for his sister Lebuda (3:5). Seth seals the testament and places it in the Cave of Treasures with the body of Adam and the gold, myrrh, and frankincense that the Magi would take and present to Christ at the time of his birth (*see also* CAVE). The third section of the text is a hierarchy that is found in only one Syriac manuscript. It includes a list of the nine orders of heavenly beings, including angels and other beings, with an account of their function in the cosmos.

TESTAMENT OF ISAAC. This text narrates the testament given by Isaac to his son Jacob at the time of his death, including details of future history, Isaac's tour of hell, his visit to the heavens, and final ascent after his death. The text is preserved in Coptic, Arabic, and Ethiopic recensions, and relates closely to the Testament of Abraham and the Testament of Jacob. The Arabic manuscript dates to the 13th century CE, and the Coptic ones date to the ninth and 10th centuries. Because the text commemorates Isaac on a fixed day in the Coptic calendar, it is thought that it may have originated in Christian Egypt.

Chapters 1–2 provide the frame for the visions, narrating the interaction between Isaac and Jacob when the former learns of his impending death. Chapter 3 contains Isaac's telling of his vision to Jacob concerning the genealogy of Israel from Adam and Eve. This genealogy moves from Enoch to the 12 tribes to Jesus the Messiah born of the virgin Mary. Chapter 4 is an account of Isaac's asceticism and service to God, and includes Isaac's instructions to Jacob. Chapter 5 recounts Isaac's journey through hell and his seeing of the various punishments there. In chapter 6, Isaac is taken to heaven where he sees his father Abraham and speaks with God. Chapters 7–9 describe the death of Isaac, the ascent of his soul to heaven, and instructions to commemorate the day of his death.

TESTAMENT OF JACOB. An account of the death and final testimony of Jacob, appended to the Testament of Isaac. The text is extant along with the Testament of Isaac in the same manuscripts except for one of the Coptic (Sahidic) versions. In chapters 1–2 an angel is described as telling Jacob of his death and recounting to him the highlights of his life. Chapters 3–4 recount Jacob's instructions to his children, his specific instructions for Joseph to bury him with his forefathers, and his blessing of Joseph's sons Ephraim and Manasseh. In chapter 5 Jacob tells his sons of future events, and is taken on a tour of hell, seeing the punishments for different types of sinners. In the Coptic recension, chapter 5 also includes Jacob's ascent to heaven where he meets with Isaac and Abraham. It also includes an account of Joseph mummifying Jacob's body. Chapter 6 describes the burial of Jacob in the land of Canaan. Chapters 7–9 appear to be a later addition, exhorting readers to follow the patriarchs and to rely upon Jesus and Mary to intercede on their behalf on the Day of Judgment.

TESTAMENT OF MOSES. Text preserved only in a fragmentary Latin palimpsest, which describes the final testament of Moses to Joshua before he left the earth. The text is divided into two parts. The first part is an overview of Israelite history given by Moses as a prophesy to Joshua through the period of the destruction of the second temple and ending with eschatological events. The second is a dialogue in which Moses encourages Joshua in his leadership of the Israelites.

The date of the Testament of Moses is not certain though the single Latin palimpsest dates to the sixth century CE, and the original text is thought to date about a century earlier. This Latin text is apparently a translation from a Greek text, the composition of which some scholars date as early as the first century CE. The Acts of the Council of Nicaea (325 CE) lists a text called the "Assumption of Moses," which contains an account of Moses' ascent into heaven instead of dying. Such a notion may be alluded to in Jude 9, where the angel Gabriel and Satan fight over the body of Moses, but the Testament of Moses does indicate that Moses died. The relationship between the Assumption of Moses and the Testament of Moses is still unresolved, but both may relate to a medieval Hebrew text known as the Midrash on the Testament of Moses [Heb. Petirat Moshe], which describes the final words of Moses before his departure from the earth. Though there is no established date for this midrash, it is assumed to have originated sometime between the seventh and 14th centuries CE, and appears to relate to other rabbinic texts such as Deuteronomy Rabbah, Pesiqta Rabbati, and Pirqe d'Rabbi Eliezer. The midrash on the Testament of Moses includes information on the six days of creation, Adam, Noah, Abraham, Isaac, Jacob, Joseph, and the assumption of Moses' body into the heavens.

TESTAMENT OF SOLOMON. Composite text describing Solomon's binding of demons to help in the building of the temple in Jerusalem. The text is extant in Greek in a number of manuscripts dating to the 15th and 16th centuries CE. Some scholars date the text as early as the third century CE based on similar references in other texts, and the parallels between the specific details of the demonology in the Testament of Solomon and the Quran are particularly striking.

The text is divided into 26 chapters. Chapter 1 recounts how Solomon is given a magical ring by the archangel Michael from God, the "Lord Sabaoth," allowing him to imprison all demons to help in the building of Jerusalem. Some of the manuscripts include drawings of the seal said to be engraved on the ring; a thirty-one-letter word written in a series of concentric circles. The mention of Solomon with a magic ring also appears in Josephus (Antiquities 8.2.5). Chapters 2–7 describe Solomon's binding of five demons (Ornias, Beelzeboul, Onoskelis, Asmodeus, Lix Tetrax) with the help of the ring and different angels. Each of the demons are described, and under Solomon's interrogation, each of the demons explains its dwelling and its powers.

Chapters 8–17 narrate Solomon's interrogation and binding of another series of demons including the seven heavenly bodies of the world of darkness, a headless demon, a dog-like demon, a lion-shaped demon, a three-headed dragon spirit, Obyzouth a female demon with messy hair, a winged dragon, Enepsigos a two-headed female demon, Kunopegos a sea-horse demon, and the spirit of a slain giant. Various techniques are used to imprison the demons including the invocation and writing of names, magic bowls, and chains. Chapter 18 is a long catalog of the 36 heavenly bodies and Solomon's binding of them.

Chapters 19–26 contain various narratives, often apparently unrelated. Chapter 19 describes Sheba, Queen of the South, as a "witch" and refers to all the riches of Solomon. Chapter 20 returns to the demon Ornias and his connection to a boy (Chapter 1). In chapter 21 Sheba tours the temple and sees the angels and the wealth of Solomon. Chapters 22–23 describe Solomon's capture of the Arabian wind demon in a leather flask (See Q 21:81, 34:12, 38:36). In chapters 24–25 the demon Ephippas and the demon of the Red Sea (identified as Abezethibou in chapter 25) carry a pillar from Arabia, though this might refer to the transfer of Sheba's throne in Q 27:38–40. This last demon claims to be the one who aided Jannes and Jambres in their magic against Moses and Aaron. Chapter 26 contains a brief account of Solomon's lust for a Shummanite woman, which causes him to offer sacrifices to the gods Raphan and Molech, a motif found also in the Muslim exegesis of Q 38:34.

TESTAMENT OF THE THREE PATRIARCHS. This title refers to three separate texts that are sometimes collected together under this single rubric: the Testament of Abraham, the Testament of Isaac, and the Testament of Jacob.

TESTAMENT OF THE TWELVE PATRIARCHS. Text of the testaments given by the 12 sons of Jacob at the time of their death. The text exists in various languages though it is unclear whether it was originally composed in Hebrew, Aramaic, or Greek. The most complete manuscripts are in Greek and Armenian. The earliest Greek manuscript dates to the 10th century CE, and the extant Aramaic fragments were found in the Cairo Geniza.

TEXTUAL CRITICISM. Name given to the scholarly approach to biblical texts that aims to remove perceived textual errors that have crept into the text through many centuries of transmission, and seeks to restore "original" readings (i.e., the form of the text as transmitted in the fourth century BCE or later). The process involves a careful comparison of textual witnesses (e.g., Masoretic text, Septuagint, Targums, Vulgate, Peshitta) based on extant manuscripts.

THADDEUS. Mentioned as one of the 12 disciples of Jesus (Matt 10:3; Mark 3:18), but not in Luke, where the name Judas son of James is given (Luke 6:14–16; Acts 1:13). The Acts of Thaddeus, preserved in Greek and Syriac, describe how Thaddeus was responsible for bringing Christianity to the city of Edessa. Some scholars link the Greek Thaddeus to the Syriac "Addai" and identify Thaddeus with the main character who brings Christianity to Edessa in the *Doctrine of Addai*. This also may relate to the mention of Thaddeus as one of the 70 apostles (Eusebius, History 1.13).

THA'LABI (d. 1036 CE). Abu Ishaq Ahmad b. Muhammad b. Ibrahim al-Tha'labi al-Nisaburi is known for two works: a Quran commentary that draws heavily on earlier works such as Tabari, and a *Stories of the Prophets* [Ar. qisas al-anbiya'], which grew out of his Quran commentary. This latter work includes important materials not found in Tabari's works, but does not include some of the more fantastic elements found in the works of Kisa'i. The work of Tha'labi is an important source for Muslim materials on the stories of the prophets.

THAMUDIC. Language attested in pre-Islamic North Arabic inscriptions, largely in the area around Midian, in western and central northern Arabia, and in southern Palestine. The inscriptions date from the sixth century BCE to the fourth century CE, and usually are written in a square script related to South Arabian Epigraphic, though some Thamudic inscriptions are attested in Aramaic scripts (such as Nabataean). It is estimated that there are roughly 1,000 inscriptions in Thamudic, most of which are of a character similar to Safaitic inscriptions. Only one Thamudic inscription has been identified in Mada'in Salih, the site traditionally designated as the place mentioned in the Quran where the prophet Salih was sent to the people of Thamud.

THEODORE BAR KONI. Late eighth- to early ninth-century CE East Syrian or Nestorian Bible exegete who produced a massive Syriac encyclopedia, called the *Scholion*, which focuses on the Bible and preserves many exegetical comments from earlier authors.

THEODORE OF MOPSUESTIA (c. 350–428 CE). Identified as the first East Syrian or Nestorian scholar, Theodore of Mopsuestia proclaimed the two distinct natures of Christ. Though he seems to have written extensive Bible exegesis, some of this is extant only in the later works of scholars like Isho' bar Nun and Isho'dad of Merv.

THEODORET OF CYRRHUS (399–466 CE). West Syrian or Jacobite bishop of Cyrrhus and author of many works in Syriac. Among his works are a *History of the Monks of Syria*, a *History of the Church*, a heresiography, some 200 letters, and commentaries on a number of books from the Bible.

THEOPHANY. The appearance of God by way of dreams, visions, and visitations. Divine apparitions were enormously important for influencing decisions and establishing sacred territory for use as sanctuaries throughout the ancient Near East. It is presupposed in the divine command that sacrifices be performed wherever Yahweh allows his name to manifest (Exod 20:24). In Judg 6:4, the judge Gideon selects a spot for a sanctuary based on an angel's appearance (said to be a dream in Judg 6:25–26), and the site for Yahweh's temple in Jerusalem was selected in a similar way (2 Sam 24:16–25). The patriarchs all experience theophanies, and theophanies play instrumental roles in the calling of prophets. The Quran and Muslim exegetes specify that Abraham had a vision of God's Presence [Ar. sakinah] leading him to the spot at which to rebuild the Ka'bah. It also is said that the reading of certain surahs and verses in the Quran (e.g., Q 18) can cause the Sakinah to descend upon the reader.

THERIANTHROPISM. Term referring to deities and other creatures that combine human and animal traits. The word is derived from a Greek word meaning "wild beast" [Gk. ther] and another meaning "human" [Gk. anthropos]. Earlier scholars thought of therianthropism as characteristic of a certain stage in human development, corresponding to the stage of totemism coming after animism, but before religion. More recently, scholars have argued that it is not the animal nature that is emphasized in therianthropic beings, but rather the duality and ambiguity of the character who is so defined. The Bible gives the account of Nebuchadnezzar, who is transformed into a wild beast by a voice from heaven after he praised himself and his building of Babylon (Dan 4:25–31). Nebuchadnezzar is driven from human society, eats grass, drinks dew, and lets his hair grow like eagle feathers and his nails like a bird's talons. In the Prayer of Nabonidus, found in an Aramaic fragment among the Dead Sea Scrolls (4QPrNab), it is the Babylonian king Nabonidus (555–539 BCE) who is afflicted with therianthropism.

THEURGY. Term derived from a Greek word meaning "actuating the divine" [Gk. theourgia] or referring to actions that induce the presence of God or other divine beings. The *Chaldean Oracles*, attributed to Marcus Aurelius, but extant only in fragments assembled by Julian the Chaldean or his son Julian the Theurge, mention theurgy as a means for unification with the divine. The Greek conception of theurgy may relate to early Mesopotamian forms of prophesy and divination that involve ecstasy and spirit possession. Theurgy is used most widely in the Neoplatonic writings of Porphyry and Iamblichus (d. 325 CE). According to Iamblichus, in his treatise *On the Mysteries*, theurgy was practiced through offerings and led to divine possession. In later Christian mysticism, such as that of Pseudo-Dionysius the Areopagite, theurgy was an important means for describing the joining of the individual soul with the experience of God through Jesus.

THREE STELES OF SETH. Coptic text from Nag Hammadi (VII,5) that describes the revelation to Dositheos (perhaps the Samaritan teacher of Simon Magus) of three steles written by Seth, but previously lost. The three steles contain hymns to a Neoplatonic trinity of heavenly beings: the Self-Begotten [Gk. Autogenes], Barbelo, and the Unbegotten Father. Throughout, but especially in the first stele, the text reflects the social ascription of the Sethians and their place among other groups in late antiquity.

THRESHING FLOOR. In addition to being used for threshing grain, threshing floors throughout the ancient Near East were closely associated with sexual cultic practices and chthonic deities. In Mesopotamia the goddess Ishtar and her consort Dumuzi consummate their marriage on the threshing floor, a mythology that is embodied in the first millennium by the cultic practice of sacred marriage [Gk. hieros gamos]. At Ugarit, the threshing floor is the site of a necromancy ritual feast in which the ghosts [Ug. rp'm] of the dead kings share a meal with the living royal house. It also is a place for divine judgment, and the spot where the Ugaritic hero Aqhat experiences a vision of augury.

In the Bible, the Israelites held a "very great and solemn lamentation" at the threshing floor of Atad, a place where Joseph "observed a mourning period of seven days for his father" (Gen 50:10–11). The breach of Uzzah, who incurred the wrath of Yahweh for touching the Ark of the Covenant, took place when the Ark was on its way to "the threshing floor of Nachon" (2 Sam 6:6). Eventually, the Ark of the Covenant came to rest on the threshing floor of Araunah the Hittite (and possibly the Jebusite king, called "Ornan" in 1 Chr 21:18), which David purchased for the purpose (1 Kgs 8:65–66). It is the same place where Solomon eventually built Yahweh's temple. The connection between the threshing floor and the Jerusalem temple may be reflected also in the Quran's reference to the Israelites entering the "Hittah" gate (Q 2:58–59). According to Muslim exegetes, the word [Ar. hitta] means "wheat," but also constitutes a word play on the Hebrew word for sin [Heb. hata']. The two words are distinguished in Arabic [Ar. hittah for sin or atonement and Ar. hintah for grain]. Some scholars maintain that Q 2:58–59 is to be understood in relation to the saying of "shibboleth" in Judg 12:5–6, and could be related to another Arabic word for an ear of grain [Ar. sunbul, sunbalata].

In Judg 6:37, a threshing floor is the location of an oracle experienced by the judge Gideon. The threshing floor also appears in 1 Kgs 22:10 (= 2 Chr 18:9) as the place where Kings Ahab and Jehoshaphat sat to administer judgment, and where the prophet Micaiah and "lying prophet" Zedekiah son of Chenaanah delivered their prophecies (1 Kgs 22:22–23). The threshing floor's association with sexuality is perhaps reflected in Hos 9:1 and Ruth 3. The site retained its connection to judgment in later times as well, for according to the Talmud, the threshing floor was the place where the Sanhedrin met to adjudicate cases (TB Sanhedrin 36b).

TORAH. Term used in reference to the first five books of the Hebrew Bible (Genesis, Exodus, Leviticus, Numbers, and Deuteronomy). Also known by its Greek title as the Pentateuch. The Quran and Muslim exegetes often refer to the Torah denoting not only the Pentateuch, but all of the Hebrew Bible, and sometimes including Jewish exegesis or what might be considered oral Torah.

According to Jewish tradition the Pentateuch was authored by Moses, but already in the Middle Ages, Jewish scholars began to notice problems with this attribution (e.g., Moses dies in Deut 34:5–6 and the story continues). Most modern scholars see these texts not as the work of a single author, but as a composite of traditions compiled and edited by a number of people over a long period of time.

The term *Torah* derives from a Hebrew root that denotes shooting an arrow in a particular direction, a meaning that is inversely related to the word *sin* [Heb. hata'], which denotes missing one's target (Judg 20:16). The term already appears in the Bible hundreds of times meaning "direction, instruction, law." Its more general application appears in reference to a mother's instruction (Prov 1:8, 6:20), a father's teachings (Prov 7:2), and the wisdom of a poet (Ps 78:1). It is used of divine instruction as well (Job 22:22), often given by the prophets (Isa 30:9, Jer 8:8), and thus sometimes it appears in reference to a body of prophetic and priestly knowledge (Isa 42:21; Jer 9:12; Ezek 7:26; Hos 4:6). It also refers to specific laws like the Sabbath (Exod 16:4), religious festivals (Exod 13:9), and the legal obligations of the priests (Exod 12:49).

When the legal statutes were committed to writing they were referred to as the Torah. The term is used of God's covenant (Exod 24:12), also known as the "scroll of the Torah" (Josh 24:26). The book of Deuteronomy is called the Torah (Deut 1:5), and many scholars believe that the references to the Torah in the book of Psalms similarly refer to the book of Deuteronomy (e.g., Ps 1:2, 94:12, 119:18), as do some of the prophetic references (e.g., Mal 3:22; Dan 9:11). In the post-exilic period, however, the word *Torah* appears to represent the first five books known to the current canon (Ezra 7:6; Neh 8:2), though this is not certain.

Both pre-exilic and post-exilic prophets assert that Torah (i.e., "instruction") will take place in the messianic age (Isa 2:3, 51:4; Jer 31:33; Mic 4:4). Later Jewish tradition also maintains that when Moses received the written Torah from God on Mt. Sinai, he also was given an oral Torah (TB Shabbath 31a; Yoma 28b; Hullin 20b). The oral Torah continued to be passed down orally from generation to generation until it eventually was written down in the form of the Mishnah, the primary component of the Talmud (*see also* TALMUD). At the time of the Jewish revolt against Rome, known as the Bar Kokhba revolt (135 CE), the Roman authorities made it a capital offense to study the Torah (TB Yebamoth 108b).

In Q 3:48 the Torah is said to have been revealed to Moses, though some passages seem to associate the Torah with Jesus. In one case, God reveals to Moses the Torah and the "Furqan," a name used to designate the Quran according to Muslim exegetes (Q 2:53). Muslim exegetes explain that the Torah was contained on gigantic tablets stored in heaven, which described all things in the cosmos. These tablets were brought down to Moses on the mountain. Ibn Abbas says that when Moses saw the Israelites worshipping the golden calf, God recalled six of the seven tablets from Moses. Other verses in the Quran are taken by Muslim exegetes to refer to a loss of the Torah, especially associated with the loss of the Ark of the Covenant (Q 2:248).

Muslim exegetes generally interpret the Torah as having been revealed specifically for the Israelites. In the exegesis to Q 3:93 and other passages regarding food laws, Muslim exegetes claim that the Torah was revealed as a punishment for the Israelites. This is exemplified in the account of the red cow sacrifice (Q 2:67–73) where God continues to complicate his commands to the Israelites, because of their attempts to avoid following his original instruction. The Quran also refers to the Torah as containing references to the prophet Muhammad and Islam. In several places this theme is specifically associated with Jesus (Q 3:3–4, 3:50, 61:6), and may allude to Jesus' reading of Isa 61:1–2 (Luke 4:16–22).

TOSEFTA. Aramaic term meaning "supplement" that refers to the additional commentary on or oral traditions excluded from the redaction of the Mishnah. The author of the Tosefta is widely believed to have been Hiyya bar Abba II, an important rabbi of the third century

CE, though talmudic tradition also cites a tradition tracing it back to Nehemiah (TB Sanhedrin 86a).

TREATISE OF SHEM. An astrological treatise attributed to Shem, the son of Noah, divided into 12 chapters corresponding to the 12 signs of the Zodiac. The text is extant in a single 15th-century CE Syriac manuscript though it is likely that the materials go back to an earlier period. The chapters for each of the signs include general astrological information regarding the fate of people born under the sign in which the year begins, and include historical prognostications. The historical references are to events in Egypt, the Romans, Palestine (Galilee), and Syria (Damascus and Haran).

TREE OF LIFE. The concept of a sacred tree that gives life to those who eat its fruit or tend to its needs is widespread in the ancient Near East. In Mesopotamia, glyptic images of the sacred tree appear as early as the fourth millennium BCE, and in the millennia following one also can find such images in Syria, Egypt, Greece, and even India. By the middle of the second millennium BCE Mesopotamian iconographic reliefs depict the tree as a symbol often tended to by mythological hybrid griffin-genies, and closely associated with cosmic order, and thus also with the king who maintains the cosmic order. Elsewhere in the Near East the tree appears connected to fertility goddesses such as Asherah (*see also* ASHERAH; RHABDO-MANCY).

   In the Bible, the Tree of Life is described by God (or perhaps his angels) as located in the Garden of Eden and forbidden to humankind (Gen 3:22). When humankind is driven from Eden, God stations cherubims (i.e., griffins) and a continuously swirling sword of fire at Eden's entrance to guard it from violation. The expression "Tree of Life" appears elsewhere in the Bible only in the book of Proverbs as a reference to wisdom (Prov 3:18, 11:30, 15:4), and thus also to the teachings (i.e., Torah) of God (13:12–14). Later Jewish tradition describes the tree as hedged about by the Tree of Knowledge of Good and Evil, and bearing thousands of different fruits, each with a different exquisite taste. It grows in the center of Eden and provides shade to all of paradise (Zohar I, 140a), and from beneath it flows a spring that waters the entire earth (Genesis Rabbah 15:6). Since it is a life-giving source, it also is identified with the Torah (TB Berakhoth 32b). 1 En 8:3 identifies the tree as God's residence.

In the Muslim story of Adam and Eve the Tree of Life is the only special tree in the Garden of Eden, and it is from this tree that Adam and Eve must abstain (Q 2:35, 20:120). Muslim exegetes explain that because Adam and Eve were immortal already and did not need to eat from the Tree of Life, their sin of eating from the Tree of Life is to be understood as sheer disobedience to God. Some exegetes report that Eve made the tree bleed by eating from it, so God cursed her with menstruation. Other reports say the tree made those who ate from it defecate, so Adam and Eve had to leave, because feces were not allowed in the Garden of Eden. Wahb b. Munabbih describes the tree as having many branches from which the angels would eat, allowing them to live forever. The "Lote-tree" [Ar. sidrah] is mentioned three times in the Quran as being at the edges of the earth and near the "Garden of Shelter" [Ar. Jannah al-Ma'wa] (53:14–16), and it also is found at the center of paradise in the accounts of the prophet Muhammad's ascent into the heavens.

TRIBES. A term used in the Quran five times to refer to the Israelites (Q 2:136, 2:140, 3:84, 4:163, 7:160). In all but one of these references (Q 7:160), the term appears in a list with Abraham, Ishmael, Isaac, and Jacob. The Bible gives the sons of Israel as (by Leah) Reuben, Simeon, Levi, Judah, Issachar, and Zebulun; (by Rachel) Joseph and Benjamin; (by Bilhah) Dan and Naphtali; and (by Zilpah) Gad and Asher. Muslim exegesis preserves the list as (by Leah) Reuben, Judah, Simon, and Levi; (by Rachel) Joseph and Benjamin; (by Zilpah) Dan, Naftali, and Zebulun; (by Bilhah) Gad, Issachar, and Asher (Gen 35:22–26).

TRITO-ISAIAH. *See* ISAIAH.

TURFAN. City in the Uighir Sinkiang region of Chinese Turkistan. The city was an important station on the Silk Road between the Near East, India, and China, and as such, was home to a number of different religious traditions. Turfan was under Chinese influence until the locals converted to Buddhism from India in about the sixth century CE. About the same time Nestorian Christian missionaries established a presence in the city. Turfan next came under the control of the Uighir Kaghans from Mongolia, in the middle of the ninth century, who already had been converted to Manichaeism about a century earlier. Turfan did not come under Islamic influence until the 14th century. The city is best known for the discovery of a trove of texts in nearby caves (*see also* CAVE). The texts are mostly in Tokharian and Uighir, and represent a variety of traditions within Manicheism, Buddhism, and Christianity.

TUSI (995–1067 CE). Muhammad b. al-Hasan al-Tusi was a famous Shi'i Quran commentator. Born about 75 years after the death of Tabari, Tusi left Tus and moved to Baghdad where he studied with a number of Shi'i scholars, including Shaykh al-Mufid and Shaykh al-Murtada, and was appointed to the chair of theology. In 1056 CE Tusi moved to Najaf, to be near the tomb of Ali b. Abi Talib, and it was in Najaf that he died. Two of Tusi's books number among the four canonical books [Ar. al-kutub al-arba'ah] of the Imami Shi'ah. Tusi's commentary on the Quran is one of the earliest Shi'i commentaries and includes some unique exegetical features that helped to establish later conventions for Shi'i commentaries: variant readings, etymologies, word definitions, meanings of phrases, syntax, and the occasions of the revelations.

– U –

UBAYY B. KA'B (d. 653 CE). Abu al-Mundhir Ubayy b. Ka'b b. Qays was an early convert to Islam and a close Companion of the prophet Muhammad. Known as the secretary of the prophet Muhammad, Ubayy b. Ka'b is said to have helped in the collection of the Quran, and attributed to him is extensive knowledge of earlier revealed books and information on the Israiliyat.

UGARIT. Canaanite seaport known today as Ras Shamra, in Syria. Though the city is much older (dating to the Neolithic period), it became a Hittite satellite around 1350 BCE until it was destroyed shortly after 1200 BCE. Ugarit is especially known for the alphabetic cuneiform texts that were discovered there in 1929, whose contents share a great deal in common with biblical texts, especially the patriarchal narratives. Ugaritic priestly archives reveal an interest in mantic practices and divination and include texts that contain spells for curing snake bites, as well as dream, birth, and astronomical omina and necromantic materials. Liver and lung models used for training apprentices in the art of extispicy also have been found at Ugarit.

UMAR B. AL-KHATTAB (r. 634–644 CE). Abu Hafs Umar b. al-Khattab b. Nufayl b. Abd al-Uzzah, second caliph and one of the earliest Companions of the prophet Muhammad in Mecca. He also is known by his nickname "al-Faruq," which, according to some, was given to him by the People of the Book. Umar is highly respected as a transmitter of many hadith reports from the prophet Muhammad and is used as a source himself, based on his close relationship to Muhammad, for interpretations of the Quran, especially in matters of ritual and law. Many scholars, including Suyuti, report that some of the revelations contained in the Quran were revealed "on the tongue" of Umar, though there is some disagreement about what this means.

URIAHU. Prophet named as the son of Shemaiah of Kiriath-Je'arim (Jer 26:20), who also may have been a prophet (*see also* SHEMA-IAH). Uriahu prophesied during the reign of Jehoiachim, king of Judah (609–598 BCE) in accordance with the prophet Jeremiah against Jerusalem and Judah. When Uriahu heard that he was to become a victim of political assassination he fled to Egypt, but Jehoiachim's men went to Egypt and brought him back by force, where he was executed (Jer 26:20–24). Jewish tradition understands Uriahu as a relative of Jeremiah and also a priest of noble descent identical to the priest mentioned in Isa 8:2 (Targum to Isa 8:2). This is the atrocity that lies behind the Bible's reference to the king throwing his corpse into the graves of the commoners (Jer 26:23).

URIM AND THUMMIM. Divinatory objects of uncertain substance, origin, and etymology that were placed in a pouch attached to the breastplate of the priestly garment of Aaron and descendant high priests (Exod 28:30; Lev 8:8; Deut 33:8). Most scholars see the Urim and Thummim as precious stones, perhaps dark and light in color or brilliance, based on an analogy with the Assyrian practice of psephomancy, the divinatory use of precious stones with powerful properties. Some biblical texts refer to the Urim alone as a tool for obtaining divine will (Num 27:21), though this could be an abbreviated way of referencing both items. In 1 Sam 28:6, the Urim is mentioned along with dreams and prophets as a legitimate means of seeking Yahweh's will at the time of the early monarchy. Though they are mentioned in Ezra and Nehemiah (Ezra 2:63; Neh 7:65), the context leaves it unclear whether they were actually in existence. The Talmud sees the Urim and Thummim as having ceased with the death of the Former Prophets (TB Sotah 48a).

– V –

VISION. A visual experience of a prophetic or mystical nature, often symbolic in form and revelatory in character, that is witnessed through supernatural means (i.e., not by way of ordinary sight), either in a dream or in an altered state of consciousness (e.g., through trances, meditation, drug use, etc.).

Visions are usually, but not always, interpreted by a figure seen in the vision, or by the subject after the vision is complete. A number of ancient Near Eastern texts refer to visionary experiences. Ancient Egyptian records, especially of the New Kingdom period (1551–712 BCE) record a number of dream experiences that entail enigmatic visual images and their decipherment, but self-induced visions while awake do not appear. Visions experienced in dreams also are well-attested in the records of early Mesopotamia (*see also* DREAMS AND DREAM INTERPRETATION), but unlike in Egypt, ecstatic visions and trances also appear. They are attested only in the later periods, however, especially during the reign of Esarhaddon (680–669 BCE), when visions appear closely associated with the cult of the Babylonian Venus and goddess of love and fertility, Ishtar. Male deities too serve as sources of divine visions during this period, but less frequently. The prophetic fragments from Deir Alla in the Transjordan also label the prophet Balaam as the "man who sees the gods," but it is unclear whether or not Balaam experienced his visions in dream (*see also* BALAAM).

In ancient Israel, dreams certainly served as visionary media for patriarchs and prophets, but visions while awake also are well attested, and in fact, employ much the same vocabulary as that of dream experiences (Num 12:6; Job 33:15; Dan 2:19). In the Hebrew Bible, waking visions appear already in connection with Abraham who experiences a vision in which Yahweh promises him descendants and land (Gen 15:1). The foreign prophet Balaam is said to have experienced visions (Num 24:4, 24:16). While prophecy appears with some frequency in the period of the Judges, waking visions do not. In fact, according to the biblical text, prior to the time of the prophet Samuel, who is later called a "seer" (1 Sam 9:9; 1 Chr 9:22), visionary experiences are said to have been nonexistent (1 Sam 3:1, 3:15). It is of interest that such experiences coincide with the development of Israel's early monarchy. King David has two seers in his court, Gad and Nathan, who apparently experience waking visions (2 Sam 7:17, 24:11; 1 Chr 17:15), and following the political schism that divided the monarchy in 922 BCE, the phenomenon of waking visions appears to increase in frequency exponentially.

Many of the classical prophets refer to visions (Amos 7:1–3, 7:7–9, 8:1–3; Isaiah 6; Jer 1:11–14; Nah 1:1; Hab 1:1, 2:2; Lam 2:9), and the threat of not experiencing visions is regarded as a sign of Yahweh's wrath (Mic 3:6). As time progresses, however, the auditory form of prophecy increasingly eclipsed dream interpretation, and thus also visionary experiences, as legitimate modes of divine access (see, e.g., Isa 65:3–4), but they did not do so entirely. For as several biblical passages attest, visions continued to serve a productive social function in Israel, as they did in times past, even if those who claim to have experienced them were not to be trusted (Ezek 13:6–9, 13:23, 21:34, 22:28). During and after the period of the exile, visions take on their most complex, if not strangest, literary forms. The bewildering, and often apocalyptic and messianic, visions of the prophets Trito-Isaiah, Ezekiel, Haggai, and Zechariah are most representative (Isa 65:17, 66:22; Ezekiel 1; Hag 1:8; Zech 13:4). Despite these examples, experiences of waking visions appear to have come to an end late in the post-exilic period. It is only in such a context that the words of the prophet Joel are understood, as one who prophesies a future in which people will once again experience dreams and visions (Joel 3:1). Nevertheless, the late book of Daniel records a number of symbolic visions (Daniel 8, 10), and visions are mentioned with greater frequency again in postbiblical texts (2 Baruch, 4 Ezra).

The New Testament also makes reference to trance-like visions as a mode of divine communication (Matt 3:16; Acts 7:56–57, 10:10; 2 Cor 12:2; Revelation 7). The Dead Sea Scrolls also record a number of visions, some of which are not found in the Bible. According to the Temple Scroll (11QTemple) [Heb. Megillat ha-Miqdash] found at Qumran, Moses experiences a prophetic vision in which he sees the future temple of Jerusalem in a way that is very similar to the prophet Ezekiel (Ezekiel 40–42). Early rabbinic tradition, however, sees the prophets Haggai, Zechariah, and Malachi as marking the end of the prophetic period (Daniel is viewed as an earlier text), and thus, these prophets also signal the end of visions. References to visionary experiences in which an initiate sees "God's glory" [Heb. shekhinah] abound in later Jewish mystical texts (*see also* HEKHALOT LITERATURE).

The Quran and Muslim sources also discuss visions but they are not always distinct from dreams. The "signs" displayed by God may be understood as visions, especially those revealed specifically to prophets such as Abraham's vision of celestial phenomena and the prophet Muhammad's tour of the heavens (*see also* SIGNS). Apocalyptic texts also describe visions of heavenly objects and events that are said to represent future earthly objects and events.

VULGATE. Term used since the 16th century CE in reference to the Latin translation of the Bible made by Jerome (347–419 CE). Many scholars are careful to point out that Jerome did not translate the Apocrypha though these books are to be found in some manuscripts of the Vulgate. Jerome translated the Hebrew Bible (Old Testament) from the Hebrew using older Greek translations, and was responsible for revising the Old Latin versions of the Gospels. He referred to the Hebrew text as the "Hebrew Truth" [Lat. Hebraica veritas]. The rest of the New Testament generally is attributed to other scholars. The Vulgate seems to have been preserved in multiple codices until at least the seventh century CE when there is evidence of single complete codex of the Latin Bible. Chapter divisions were introduced in the 12th century, and the verse numbering used today goes back to the 16th century CE. It was at the Council of Trent in 1546 CE that the Vulgate was recognized by the Roman Catholic Church as the official version of the Bible.

– W –

WADD, SUWA, YAGHUTH, YA'UQ, NASR. The names of the false gods worshipped by the people of Noah, as mentioned in the Quran (Q 71:23). Muslim exegetes report that these names originally belonged to upright children of Adam. Later, upright people followed the example of these children of Adam, and in time people made images of them, and eventually turned to worshipping them.

WAHB B. MUNABBIH (655–732 CE). Abu Abdallah al-Abnawi Wahb b. Munabbih b. Kamil b. Sayij is widely cited as one of the followers of the prophet Muhammad's Companions. He is regarded as a sound transmitter of hadith reports and is attributed with many comments on the Quran, especially those related to biblical stories. He issued hadith reports on the authority of a number of respected Companions of the prophet Muhammad, but many of his interpretations originate from otherwise not extant oral traditions and accounts that are linked to Jewish and Christian exegetical traditions.

WELL. The motif of a well occurs in several of the stories of the prophets in the Bible and in the Quran. A number of Jewish sources record that "the well" was created at the beginning of time (Pirqe d'Rabbi Eliezer 30; TB Pesahim 54a; Sifre Deuteronomy 355; Mekhilta 51a). This is supposed to be the same well that Abraham dug at Beersheba (Genesis 21), at which Isaac met his wife Rebecca (Genesis 24), which Isaac claims at Beersheba (Genesis 26), at which Jacob meets his wife Rachel (Genesis 29), into which Joseph is thrown by his brothers (Genesis 37), at which Moses meets his wife Zipporah (Exodus 2), and from which the Israelites drank in the wilderness of wandering, also called the "well of Miriam."

Muslim exegesis recognizes some of these same connections, especially between Moses and Jacob. The exegesis of Q 28:21–28 conflates the story of Moses and Jethro with Jacob and Laban by way of the well motif. The well of Midian is associated with the "Meeting Place of the Two Waters" mentioned in Q 18:60–65 and identified by Muslim exegetes as the "water of life." In both instances Moses sets out on a wilderness journey led by a supernatural power. The well is identified as the "water of life," and in both cases Moses meets a prophet (Khidr, Shuayb) at the well who teaches him about prophethood.

In several instances the term *Beersheba* appears generically to refer to a number of different wells associated with the word *seven* [Heb. sheba', Ar. saba']. Thus, the number occurs in midrashic expositions in reference to the number of times Abraham and Isaac dug for wells (Pirqe d'Rabbi Eliezer 35) (*see also* BEERSHEBA). Muslim exegetes refer to the well of Zamzam as the "well of the seven," because Hagar ran between Safa and Marwah seven times looking for water.

Wells often are associated with purification and the forgiveness of sins. Rashi makes this explicit in a connection he draws between the death of Miriam in Num 20:1–2 (which atones for the sins of the Israelites, as the red heifer sacrifice is purificatory in Numbers 19) and the disappearance of the water in the wilderness before the Israelites enter the land of Canaan. Muslim scholars report the connection between ablutions and atonement, and preserve hadith reports from the prophet Muhammad in which he states that he will know his followers when he stands at his "Pool" [Ar. hawd] in paradise because their bodies will shine on those parts where they performed their ablutions.

The fate of wells also has eschatological significance. Ezekiel refers to the water welling up in Jerusalem with the arrival of the New Jerusalem and New Torah (Ezek 47:1–12). Zech 14:8 refers to the "living waters" that will flow from Jerusalem in the future (cf., Pirqe d'Rabbi Eliezer 35). In John 4:1–26, Jesus stands at the well of Jacob and promises the Samaritan woman the water of life, and she acknowledges him as the Messiah, a motif repeated again in John 7:37–38. The washing activities of John the Baptist are linked to his role as an Elijah figure and precursor of the Messiah. Muslim sources describe the recovery of the well of Zamzam by Abd al-Muttalib, the prophet Muhammad's grandfather, on the eve of Islam, signaling the beginning of a new prophetic age. A number of reports are preserved in Bukhari and other Muslim sources that at the end of time the well of Zamzam will overflow and be continuous with the heavenly pool of the prophet Muhammad, offering immortality to all Muslims.

WISDOM OF JESUS BEN SIRAH. Name of an apocryphal work (also known as Ecclesiasticus) originally composed in Hebrew sometime around 180–175 BCE, and translated into Greek after 132 BCE for Greek-speaking Jews. It is found in the Septuagint and is included in the Roman Catholic canon, but is not found in Jewish and Protestant Bibles. Much like the biblical books of Proverbs, Qohelet, and Job, the book offers moral advice for practical living. It also identifies the eternal Lady Wisdom [Gk. Sophia], whom it treats as an emanation of God, with the law of Moses. As such, it represents an early attempt to harmonize Hellenistic philosophy with Jewish customs. Hebrew and Greek fragments of the Wisdom of Jesus ben Sirah have been discovered among the Dead Sea Scrolls, and also among the cache of texts found in the Cairo Geniza.

WISDOM OF SOLOMON. Discourse on Wisdom attributed to Solomon, included among the deutero-canonical Apocrypha by the Council of Trent (1545–1563 CE), though excluded by Jerome from the Vulgate. The earliest Greek manuscripts date to the fourth century CE, but a Latin manuscript exists that dates to the second century CE. Many scholars date the composition of the text sometime at the end of the Hellenistic period, but no later than the first half of the first century CE. The text can be divided into two parts with two additional excursuses. Part 1 (1:1–6:21) deals with Wisdom and human destiny. Part 2 (6:22–10:21) is Solomon's quest for Wisdom. Part 3 (11–19) extols Wisdom's work in history with particular attention to the Exodus. The first excursus is an extension of part 3 (11:15–12:22), and the second is an indictment of idolatry (13–15).

WITCHCRAFT. The Hebrew word typically translated as "practice witchcraft" [Heb. kashaf] is used exclusively of unsanctioned manipulative practices, often derived from foreign nations. The Akkadian cognate [Akk. kashapu] also means to "cast spells." The Bible sees witchcraft as a capital offense (Exod 22:17), and Deut 18:10 lists the witch along with a number of other foreign, and therefore unsanctioned, practitioners. Despite the title "Witch of Endor" commonly attributed to her, the woman in 1 Samuel 28 who raises the prophet Samuel from the dead is more accurately speaking, a necromancer (*see also* NECROMANCY). Despite the legal injunctions, the historical texts make it clear that witchcraft at times was sanctioned by Israelite kings, such as Manasseh king of Judah (2 Chr 33:6). An analogous situation may obtain in the Middle-Assyrian legal codes that prohibit only certain types of witchcraft, especially those that disrupt commonly accepted social codes of behavior.

WONDERS. Miraculous events, acts, or people that are interpreted as displays or embodiments of divine power. In the Hebrew Bible, the word *wonder* [Heb. mofet] often appears in conjunction with the word *sign*. It is found in reference to the transformation of Aaron's rod into a serpent (Exod 7:9), the plagues of Egypt (Exod 11:10), and God's hand in shaping Israel's past (1 Chr 16:12; Ps 105:5). It also can token a future event like terrestrial and celestial events in the eschaton (Joel 3:3–4), and thus, at times is synonymous with prophecy (1 Kgs 13:3; 2 Chr 32:24) and prophetic dramas (Isa 20:3). Like the word *signs*, wonders can refer to the prophets themselves (Isa 8:18; Ezek 12:6, 24:24), or to people who bode well as omens (Zech 3:8). They also can be performed by false prophets (Deut 13:2; *see also* OMEN).

WORD PLAY. Ultimately grounded in divinatory hermeneutics, and in a belief in the inherent power of words, word play functions to enact and register divine judgment by means of literal correspondences based on linguistic correlations between the sign or vision and the interpretation it is given, or between the punishment and the name of the one being punished. Many types of word play are significant in prophetic discourse, such as those based on similarities in sound (paronomasia) and on the multiple meanings of words (polysemy). Other types of word play also exist including acrostics, atbash, and gematria.

– Y –

YAHWEH. Personal name of the God of Israel as found in the Hebrew Bible and on a number of ancient inscriptions (also periodically in abbreviated form as Yah or Yahu). The name means "He who exists" or "He who causes to exist." The four consonants that comprise the name (i.e., YHWH) are referred to as the tetragrammaton. In post-biblical times the name was regarded as too holy to pronounce, and a vocalization tradition was created to safeguard the name's pronunciation. Instead of reading the name "Yahweh," the reader was to substitute the noun *Adonai* (lit. "Lord"). This was accomplished by placing the vowels of the word *Adonai* over the consonants YHWH. Gradually, this reading tradition was forgotten and led to erroneous readings of the sacred name (e.g., Jehovah), and to the tradition of English translations that render Yahweh as "Lord" instead of transliterating the name (the Heb. term *Elohim* was rendered accurately as "God").

In the Bible, Yahweh's origins appear to be associated with the southern desert regions of Edom, Paran, Midian, and Seir (Deut 33:2; Judg 5:4). This association is supported by the influential role that the Midianite Jethro, Moses' father-in-law, plays on the development of Israelite religion. He is a high priest of Yahweh who shows Moses where the mountain of God is, and who instructs Moses on how to run civil affairs (Exod 18:14–27). Muslim exegetes identify Jethro with the Arab prophet Shuayb, who was sent to the people of Midian, and who passed on his prophethood to Moses. In addition, Egyptian documents dating to the reigns of Amenhotep III (r. 1417–1379 BCE) and Ramesses II (r. 1291–1224 BCE) describe the "nomads of Seir" as living in the "land of Yah." These facts have led scholars to see Yahweh as a deity originally at home in the Sinai. Indeed, the name Yahweh does not occur in the inscriptional materials at Ugarit, Mari, or Emar, though some have posited its existence in texts at Ebla. In any event, by the eighth century BCE, Yahweh appears to have been worshipped outside of Israel, especially among the Aramaeans. An Aramaic papyrus dating to c. 410 BCE reports the presence of a Jewish temple of Yaho at Elephantine, Egypt.

Yahweh appears originally to have been conceived of as a storm god (Psalm 29; Job 38) and the military head of a divine militia (2 Kgs 2:11; Hab 3:5; Psalm 18 and 50). Early in Israel's history he was apparently equated with El, the chief deity of the Canaanite pantheon (Exod 6:2–3). Consequently, other deities associated with El's pantheon, such as Baal and Asherah, also thrived in Israel, though the worship of Yahweh, as a national god, gradually displaced them (*see also* ASHERAH; BAAL). Though early in Israelite history Yahweh was thought of as not being located in a particular place, he nevertheless eventually was associated with Mt. Zion in Jerusalem (*see also* MOUNTAIN). It is this place that represented the site at which Yahweh would launch his cosmic battle against his enemies (Isa 31:4; Joel 3:16; Ps 48:2); a battle that is reminiscent of Yahweh's previous battle against the serpent of chaos Leviathan (Isa 27:1; Ps 74:13–14).

In the Bible, Yahweh is credited with inspiring the prophets to speak, and it is his covenant with the Israelites that forms the ideological basis for their prophecies. The biblical prophets' predictions of doom also often relate to the curses for disobedience found in the Israelites covenantal code (*see also* COVENANT). Although the Quran and Muslim tradition do not refer to God as "Yahweh" nor is Yahweh normally considered one of the 99 Names of God (*see also* ALLAH), some scholars have seen a reflex of the name in the many references in the Quran to God as "Huwa" (lit. "He" but also understood as one of the names of God).

YALQUT SHIMONI. Hebrew midrashic commentary on the entire Bible dating to the early 13th century CE. It was comprised of dozens of earlier works that it cites, and was named after a man named Shimon, about whom nothing is known. The commentary preserves a number of Jewish traditions concerning biblical figures in circulation during this time.

YAQUBI (d. 897 CE). Ahmad b. Abi Yaqub b. Ja'far b. Wahb was an Arab historian who lived in Armenia and wrote a history of the world from the creation to 872 CE. His history is divided into two parts. The first describes the different peoples of the world and their histories. Yaqubi begins with the Israelites and traces their history and their prophets to Jesus Christ and his disciples. He then treats the Assyrians, Babylonians, Indians, Greeks, Turks, Chinese, Egyptians, Ethiopians, and Arabs up to the time of the prophet Muhammad. Part 2 of the history covers Islamic history from the prophet Muhammad to 872 CE. Yaqubi also wrote a geographical work that includes important information on place names.

YAQUT (1179–1229 CE). Shihab al-Din Abu Abdallah Yaqub b. Abdallah al-Hamawi is the author of a well-known geographical dictionary. He was born in Roman territory to non-Arab parents, was later captured and sold as a slave to a merchant in Baghdad for whom he traveled. After he was manumitted (1199 CE), Yaqut traveled extensively and spent time researching geographical lore in libraries, especially in Aleppo where he died. His biographical dictionary includes information on real geography and on place names found in the Quran and Muslim exegesis.

– Z –

ZABUR. Arabic term (also Zubur) found nine times in the Quran referring to the book of the Psalms of David. Q 21:105 cites a verse from the Psalms (Ps 37:11, 37:29) about the upright inheriting the earth. Q 4:163 and Q 17:55 state that God gave David the Psalms, a reference that Muslim exegetes take to indicate that the Psalms were a revealed book. Some Muslim exegetes mention a report in which the Zabur is said to be one of the books revealed by God before the revelation of the Quran. A variant reading of Q 4:163, reported by Suyuti and other Muslim scholars, states that God gave David the "Quran" instead of "Zabur," leading some to speculate that the term *Zabur* is another name for the Quran. Q 3:184 and Q 35:25 list the Zubur along with "clear signs" and the "Book of Enlightenment" as revelations brought by previous prophets. Q 16:44 records the same, but without mention of the book. Q 26:196 also mentions the "Zubur of the first ones" apparently using "Zubur" to refer in a generic sense to scriptures revealed to earlier prophets. This generic sense of *scripture* also is apparent in the use of the term *Zubur* in Q 54:43 and Q 54:52.

ZADOQITES. Family name of the aristocracy and high priesthood of Jerusalem in the time of Abraham (Gen 14:18) and Joshua (Josh 10:1), who apparently also served King David as high priests after his capture of the city (2 Sam 20:25), along with the Levites. The later Chronicler attempted to resolve the apparent theological difficulty by making Zadoq, the priest in David's time, a descendant of Aaron, and therefore a Levite (1 Chr 6:1–8, 6:49–53). In Ezekiel's time the family of Zadoq continued to serve as priests (Ezek 40:46), but the family line was cut off when the Hasmonaeans seized the office in 171 BCE. Many scholars also identify the Zadoqites with the Sadducees and the community that produced and/or stored the Dead Sea Scrolls.

ZAKKUR INSCRIPTION. Historical inscription erected by the Aramaean Zakkur, king of Hamath and Lu'ath early in the eighth century BCE, and discovered in 1904 southeast of Aleppo. The stele was erected in honor of the dcity Ilu-wer, and the king's success over his enemies after having received a promise of victory from his ecstatic seers and diviners. As such it attests to the existence of the institution of prophecy in Aramaea, and to the employment of mantics in the Aramaean royal house.

ZAMAKHSHARI (1075–1144 CE). Mahmud b. Umar al-Zamakhshari was a well-known Quran commentator. Born in Central Asia, he studied in Khwarazmia and later traveled to Bukhara, Samarqand, and Baghdad. Later he moved to Mecca and stayed there long enough to acquire the name "Neighbor of God" [Ar. Jar Allah]. He is said to have been a rationalist and as such, his Quran commentary has been scrutinized by some Muslim cxcgetes, and an expurgated version was produced by later scholars. Zamakhshari's commentary is known for its reliance on reason rather than hadith reports, but also for its close study of philology and syntax. It is well regarded as a reference for apparent lexical and grammatical irregularities in the text of the Quran.

ZECHARIAH. Prophet and biblical book describing the visions of Zechariah. This difficult and obscure book contains the prophecies of Zechariah, the son of Berechiah and grandson of Iddo (Zech 1:1), though the book of Ezra (5:1) understands Zechariah as Iddo's son (the Hebrew term [ben] meaning "son" is ambiguous here). Much of the book is taken up with describing the difficult life of the Jews who returned from exile to Judah, but Zechariah, like the prophet Haggai, his contemporary, also calls for the rebuilding of Yahweh's temple. Comprising the core of the book of Zechariah are eight visions, each of which appear to share little in common other than an interest in consecrating the high priest

Joshua. The enigmatic material that appears in Zechariah 9–14 appears to be the work of a later hand, probably from the fifth to the fourth centuries BCE. Some scholars see this section as originally having been attached to the book of Malachi. It contains an attack on some prophets and prophecy (Zech 13:1–6), which signals the end of the prophetic era, and pronounces divine judgment on an unnamed Israelite leader. Zech 14:16 asserts that Gentiles also will be included in the salvation of Yahweh.

ZECHARIAH, FATHER OF JOHN. Prophetic figure mentioned in the Quran in conjunction with the birth of the prophet John the Baptist. The story of Zechariah is found in three places in the Quran (Q 19:1–15, 3:38–41, 21:89–90). The longest of these accounts narrates that Zechariah received a revelation from God about the future birth of his son John. Zechariah protested that he was old and that his wife was barren, so God gave him a sign—that he would not speak for three days and nights. According to Muslim exegetes this annunciation came to Zechariah when he was 92 years old, and he died after the death of his son John. Ibn Ishaq reports that the last three prophets sent to the Israelites, after their return from Babylon, but before the final destruction of Jerusalem, were Zechariah, John, and Jesus. Muslim genealogists give Zechariah's lineage as son of Berechiah b. Dan, or son of Iddo b. Meshullah b. Zadok b. Nachson b. Solomon b. David. The identification of Zechariah as the son of Berechiah also appears in Matt 23:34–36 and seems to conflate the father of John with the post-exilic prophet Zechariah (Zech 1:1), to whom the canonical book of Zechariah is attributed. Luke 1:5 refers to Zechariah as a member of the priestly division of Abijah (1 Chr 24:10), and in the Protoevangelium of James (23–24), Zechariah is killed by Herod in front of the temple, apparently a reference to the Zechariah, son of the high priest Jehoiada mentioned in Luke 11:51 and 2 Chr 24:20–22. Muslim sources also report that Zechariah was martyred by being sawn in half while hiding in a tree trunk, a martyrdom also attributed to the prophet Isaiah in other Christian and Jewish sources.

ZEDEKIAH, SON OF CHENAANAH. Prophet working in the court of King Ahab (c. 869–850 BCE) whom 1 Kings 22 labels as a "lying prophet." When the prophet Micaiah, son of Imlah, spoke out against Ahab and Jehoshaphat's intended battle against the Aramaeans, Zedekiah struck him in the face, after which Micaiah prophesied his eventual murder. Rabbinic tradition sees Zedekiah, the son of Chenaanah as the unnamed man in 1 Kgs 22:24, whose corpse came to life when it came into contact with the body of the prophet Elisha. According to this text, the dead Zedekiah came to life briefly in order that he might be buried elsewhere away from Elisha (TB Sanhedrin 47a; Hullin 7b; Tosefta-Targum 2 Kgs 13:21; Psalms Rabbah 26, 220).

ZEPHANIAH. Prophet and book of prophecies attributed to Zephaniah. Both date to the early part of King Josiah's reign (631–609 BCE). Zeph 1:1 provides the longest genealogy of any of the prophets, no doubt in order to inform the reader that he is related to David, since his great grandfather was King Hezekiah (727–698 BCE). His prophecy of the coming Day of Yahweh (Zeph 1:14–16) resounds Amos 5:18–20 and draws on the language and traditions of Genesis, especially those of Noah and the flood (Zeph 1:3), the Tower of Babel (Zeph 3:9), and Sodom and Gomorrah (Zeph 2:9). Yet for Zephaniah, the Day of Yahweh is to bring worldwide destruction, devastating especially Philistia, Moab, Ammon, Ethiopia, and Assyria (Zeph 2:4–15). Rabbinic literature credits Zephaniah as the teacher of the prophet Jeremiah and the great grandson of King Hezekiah (cf., Ibn Ezra and Radaq on Zeph 1:1). The Apocalypse of Zephaniah also is attributed to him.

ZERUBBABEL. Leader of the first group of returning exiles from Babylon responsible for overseeing the construction of Yahweh's temple (Hag 1:14; Ezra 2:2; Neh 7:7). According to 1 Chr 3:19 Zerubabbel is the grandson of King Jehoiachim (c. 598 BCE) and son of Pedaiah, but elsewhere, he is identified as the son of the Judean governor Shealtiel (Hag 1:1; Ezra 3:2). Since Zerubbabel was a Persian appointee, and apparently not anointed (*see also* ANOINT), scholars see his appearance in Haggai's prophecy and Zechariah's vision as prophetic efforts to legitimate him to the post-exilic community in Jerusalem (Zech 4:1–14). Rabbinic traditions identify Zerubbabel as Daniel (TB Sanhedrin 93b), and also as Nehemiah (TB Sanhedrin 38a), as well as an ancestor of the future Messiah (Targum to 2 Chr. 3:24). In various Hekhalot literatures, Zerubbabel is given access to divine mysteries such as the time of the Messiah's arrival and appears on friendly terms with the angel Metatron. When the Messiah returns Zerubbabel is supposed to authorize the angels Gabriel and Michael to release the prisoners in the underworld, and with Elijah, he will explain the meaning of all difficult biblical passages.

ZION. Name given to the Jebusite stronghold situated on the southern acropolis of the east hill of Jerusalem, and eventual site of David's royal palace (2 Sam 5:7; 1 Chr 11:5). Though sometimes Zion is distinguished from the area on which Yahweh's temple was built (1 Kgs 8:1; 2 Chr 5:2), it also is known as Yahweh's dwelling (Amos 1:2; Isa 31:9; Zech 8:3), and his "holy mountain" (Josh 2:1, 4:17; Ps 133:3), probably due to its proximity with the temple. Elsewhere it appears in reference to all of Jerusalem (Isa 14:32; Amos 6:7). Mt. Zion is envisioned in eschatological prophetic texts (*see also* ESCHATOLOGY) as the site to which people from all nations will come to worship (Isa 2:2–3; Mic 4:1–2) at Yahweh's future temple (Ezek 40:2).

ZIPPORAH. Wife of Moses and daughter of Jethro the Midianite high priest, mentioned only three times in the Bible (Exod 2:21, 4:25). The Quran does not mention Zipporah by name, but Muslim exegetes identify the wife of Moses as Zipporah [Ar. Safurah], and say that she had a sister named Leah. In a most enigmatic biblical passage she is described as circumcising her son to save Moses from an attack by Yahweh (Exod 4:25), and elsewhere Moses is said to have divorced her and sent her back to her father (Exod 18:2). Later talmudic tradition conflates her with the woman from Cush (Ethiopia) mentioned as Moses' wife in Num 12:1 and sees her as a paradigm of piety and beauty (TB Mo'ed Qatan 16b, Sifre Numbers 99). At least one Jewish tradition, however, identifies Moses' Cushite wife as an Ethiopian queen that Moses married when fleeing the Egyptian pharaoh (Targum Yerushalmi to Num 12:1).

ZOHAR. Aramaic and Hebrew text whose title [Heb. Sefer ha-Zohar] means the "Book of Splendor." The Zohar is attributed to Shimon bar Yohai who lived during the second century CE, though the text itself dates only to 13th-century CE Spain. It first appears in the writings of Moses de Leon (1240–1305 CE). The text is composite in nature, but consists in part of a "hidden midrash" of mystical exegesis in Hebrew and Aramaic of the Torah. There also are a number of "hidden books" within the Zohar including the Idra Rabbah and Idra Zutah, the Tiqqunei Zohar (70 interpretations of the first word of the Hebrew Bible), and the Raya Meheima (mystical interpretation of the revealed commandments).

ZOROASTRIANISM. Religion of ancient Iran, also called "Mazdaism" because of its veneration of Ahura Mazda (Av. For "Wise Lord") as God. The origins of Zoroastrianism go back to the prophet Zoroaster, who lived sometime between 1400 and 1200 BCE. Herodotus reports that he lived in the sixth century BCE and some modern scholars assign a date of 1000 BCE, when the Iranian tribes moved from Central Asia to the area now known as Iran. The only information available on the life of Zoroaster comes from the *Gathas* (hymns attributed to Zoroaster) and from a much later hagiographical biography.

Zoroastrianism first developed into a religion under the Achaemenids (c. 550–331 BCE) though the details of the religion are unclear. It appears that the "Magi" mentioned in various sources as accompanying Iranian rulers are Zoroastrian priests. Zoroastrian ideas appear in the Bible and in Judaism after the Babylonian exile, and become influential in the Mediterranean during the Hellenistic period. In the Parthian (141 BCE–224 CE) and Sasanian periods (224–651 CE), Zoroastrianism became more widely spread among the populace, especially after it became the official religion of the Sasanian empire. Most Zoroastrian texts were redacted during the ninth century CE, under the influence of Islam. At the end of the ninth century a group of Zoroastrians settled in Gujarat (western Indian subcontinent) and were subsequently called "Parsis" or "Persians," because of the origins of their religion. During the 17th century CE there was a renaissance of scholarship in Gujarati Zoroastrianism, which was responsible for the editing and publication of many earlier Zoroastrian texts.

Zoroastrian beliefs share some general features in common with later Jewish and Muslim exegetical traditions associated with prophets and prophecy. Thus, the *Bundahishn* describes the world as having a 12,000-year history, four 3,000-year periods, each one with its own prophetic figure. The first prophet was Zoroaster, and the subsequent three are called "sons" of Zoroaster. The *Denkart* describes the Soshyant who will appear at the end of time to restore the earth before renovating the cosmos. Most Zoroastrian writings can be traced back to the revelations of Zoroaster and commentaries on these revelations, though other visionary texts exist (*see also* BOOK OF ARDA VIRAF).

Appendix 1

List of Dictionary Entries

AVESTA
AZARIAH
AZRAEL

BAAL
BAALBEK
BALAAM
BAR HEBRAEUS
BARLAAM AND JOSEPHAT
BARUCH
2 BARUCH
3 BARUCH
4 BARUCH
BAT QOL
BEERI
BEERSHEBA
BEN SIRA
BENJAMIN
BIBLIOMANCY
BOOK OF ARDA VIRAF
BOOK OF JASHER
BOOK OF JOSIPPON
BOOK OF THE CAVE OF TREASURES
BOOK OF THE GIANTS
BUKHARI
BUKHTNASAR
BUNDAHISHN

CAIN AND ABEL
CAIRO GENIZA
CANON AND CANON LISTS
CANON MURATORI
CATALOGUE OF THE SIXTY BOOKS
CAVE
CHRONICLES
CHRONICLES OF JERAHMEEL
CHRONICLES OF MOSES
CLASSICAL PROPHECY

CLEMENT OF ALEXANDRIA
1 CLEMENT
2 CLEMENT
COLOPHON
CORPUS HERMETICUM
COSMOLOGY AND COSMOGONY
COVENANT
CULT
CULTIC DRAMA
CULTIC PROPHET
CYRUS II

DAHHAK
DAJJAL
DAMASCUS
DAMASCUS DOCUMENT
DANIEL
DAVID
DAY OF YAHWEH
DEAD SEA SCROLLS
DEATH OF ADAM
DEBORAH
DEDANITE AND LIHYANITE
DEMON
DENKART
DEUTERO-ISAIAH
DEUTERONOMY
DHU AL-KIFL
DHU AL-NUN AL-MISRI
DHU AL-QARNAYN
DINAWARI
DIONYSIUS BAR SALIBI
DISCIPLE
DISCIPLES OF JESUS
DIVINATION
DIVINE LIGHT
DOCTRINE OF ADDAI
DREAMS AND DREAM
    INTERPRETATION

HIMA
HISTORY OF JOSEPH
HISTORY OF THE RECHABITES
HOREB
HOSEA
HUD
HULDAH

IAMBLICUS
IBLIS
IBN ABBAS
IBN AL-ARABI
IBN AL-ATHIR
IBN AL-NADIM
IBN EZRA, ABRAHAM BEN MEIR
IBN HAJAR
IBN HAZM
IBN ISHAQ
IBN KATHIR
IBN RUSHD
IBN SINA
IBN SIRIN
IDDO
IDRIS
IKHWAN AL-SAFA
IMAM
INFANCY GOSPELS
IRAM
IRENAEUS OF LYONS
ISAAC
ISAIAH
ISHMAEL
ISHMAELITES
ISHO'BAR NUN
ISHO'DAD OF MERV
ISRAFIL
ISRAILIYAT

JABAL QAF
JABAL SIN

JABIR B. HAYYAN
JACOB
JACOB B. ASHER
JACOB OF EDESSA
JA'FAR AL-SADIQ
JANNES AND JAMBRES
JAPETH HA-LEVI
JEDUTHUN
JEHU, SON OF HANANI
JEREMIAH
JEROME
JERUSALEM
JESUS
JETHRO
JINN
JOB
JOEL
JOHN CHRYSOSTUM
JOHN OF DAMASCUS
JOHN THE BAPTIST
JONAH
JOSEPH
JOSEPH AND ASENATH
JOSEPH FALAQUERA
JOSEPHUS, FLAVIUS
JOSHUA
JUBILEES
JUDGES
JURHUM
JUST BALANCE

KA'BAH
KA'BAL-AHBAR
KAHIN
KARAISM
KASHANI
KEDAR
KETURAH
KHIDR
KINDI

KINGS

KISA'I

KOHEN

LACHISH LETTERS

LAMENTATIONS

LATTER PROPHETS

LEVI B. GERSHOM

LEVITE

LEVITICUS

LIFE OF ADAM AND EVE

LILITH

LISHKAH

LIVES OF THE PROPHETS

LOST TRIBES

LOT

LOTS

LUQMAN

1 AND 2 MACCABEES

3 MACCABEES

4 MACCABEES

MADA'IN SALIH

MAGIC

MAGOG

MAHDI

MAIMONIDES

MAJOR PROPHETS

MALACHI

MANDAEANS

MANI

MANICHAEAN HYMNS

MANICHAEAN MAGICAL TEXTS

MANNA

MARDUK PROPHECY

MARI

MARTYRDOM AND ASCENSION OF
    ISAIAH

MARY, MOTHER OF JESUS

MASORETIC TEXT

MASSEBAH

MECCA

MEDICINE

MEDINA

MEKHILTA

MERISM

MERKABAH (CHARIOT) MYSTICISM

MESSENGER

MESSIAH

METATRON

MICAH

MICAIAH

MICHAEL

MIDIAN

MIDRASH

MIDRASH HA-GADOL

MIDRASH TANHUMA

MINOR PROPHETS

MIQRA'OT GEDOLOT

MIRIAM

MISHNAH

MONOLATRY

MONOTHEISM

MOSES

MOUNTAIN

MU'AWIYYAH

MUHAMMAD

MULLA SADRA

MUSIC

NABI

NABONIDUS

NAG HAMMADI

NAHUM

NARSAI

NATHAN

NAZIR

NECROMANCY

NEHEMIAH

NEW JERUSALEM

NIMROD
NOADIAH
NOAH
NUMBERS
NUSAYRIS

OBADIAH
ODED
ODES OF SOLOMON
OMEN
OMOPHAGIA
ORACLE
ORIGEN

PARACLETE
PARALLELISM
PARAPHRASE OF SHEM
PASHUR
PATRIARCHS
PEOPLE OF MOSES
PEOPLE OF THE BOOK
PEOPLE OF THE CAVE
PEOPLE OF THE WELL
PEOPLE OF TUBBA
PEOPLE OF YA-SIN
PESHER
PESHITTA
PESIQTA D'RAB KAHANA
PESIQTA RABBATI
PHARAOH
PHILO OF ALEXANDRIA
PHILO OF BYBLOS
PHILOXENUS OF MABBUG
PHOENICIA
PIRQE D'RABBI ELIEZER
PLOTINUS
POETRY

POLYTHEISM
PORPHYRY
POSSESSION
PRAYER OF JACOB
PRAYER OF JOSEPH
PRAYER OF NABONIDUS
PRAYER OF THE APOSTLE PAUL
PROPHECY
PROPHECY OF NEFERTI
PROPHET
PROPHETIC DRAMA
PROPHETIC NUDITY
PROTOEVANGELIUM OF JAMES
PROVERBS
PSALMS
PSEUDO-CLEMENTINES
PSEUDO-PHILO
PYTHAGORAS

QABBALAH
QAZWINI
QISAS AL-ANBIYA
QOHELET
QUMRAN
QURAN
QURTUBI

RADAQ
RAIN MAKING
RAMBAM
RAMBAN
RASHBAM
RASHI
RELICS
REMAQ
RHABDOMANCY
RIQAM

ROD OF MOSES
RUMI
RUTH

SA'ADIA HA-GAON
SABIANS
SACRIFICE
SAFA AND MARWAH
SAFAITIC
SALIH
SALMON BEN JEROHAM
SALVATION ORACLES
SAMUEL
SARAH
SATAN
SAUL
SECOND TREATISE OF THE GREAT SETH
SEDER ELIAHU RABBAH
SEDER 'OLAM (RABBAH)
SEER
SEFER HA-BAHIR
SEFER HA-RAZIM
SEFER YETZIRAH
SEFIROT
SELF-MUTILATION
SEPTUAGINT
SETH
SFORNO, OBADIAH BEN JACOB
SHAMAN
SHEM
SHEMAIAH
SHI'AH
SHISHLAM
SHUAYB
SIBYLLINE ORACLES
SIFRE NUMBERS
SIGNS

SINAI
SOLOMON
SON OF THE PROPHETS
SONG OF SONGS
SONG OF SONGS RABBAH
SOSHYANT
SOUTH ARABIAN EPIGRAPHIC
SPARAGMOS
SPEAKING IN TONGUES
SPEECH ACT THEORY
SPIRIT
ST. GEORGE
STICHOMETRY OF NICEPHORUS
STRABO
SUFISM
SUHRAWARDI
SUSA
SUYUTI
SWORD OF MOSES
SYMBOLIC ACTS

TABARI
TABARSI
TABATABA'I
TABLETS
TALE OF WEN-AMON
TALMUD
TARDEMAH
TARGUM
TEMPLE
TENT OF MEETING
TERAPHIM
TESTAMENT OF ABRAHAM
TESTAMENT OF ADAM
TESTAMENT OF ISAAC
TESTAMENT OF JACOB
TESTAMENT OF MOSES

TESTAMENT OF SOLOMON
TESTAMENT OF THE THREE
   PATRIARCHS
TESTAMENT OF THE TWELVE
   PATRIARCHS
TEXTUAL CRITICISM
THADDEUS
THA'LABI
THAMUDIC
THEODORE BAR KONI
THEODORE OF MOPSUESTIA
THEODORET OF CYRRHUS
THEOPHANY
THERIANTHROPISM
THEURGY
THREE STELES OF SETH
THRESHING FLOOR
TORAH
TOSEFTA
TREATISE OF SHEM
TREE OF LIFE
TRIBES
TRITO-ISAIAH
TURFAN
TUSI

UBAYY B. KA'B
UGARIT
UMAR B. AL-KHATTAB
URIAHU
URIM AND THUMMIM

VISION
VULGATE

WADD, SUWA, YAGHUTH, YA'UQ, NASR
WAHB B. MUNABBIH
WELL
WISDOM OF JESUS BEN SIRAH
WISDOM OF SOLOMON
WITCHCRAFT
WONDERS
WORD PLAY

YAHWEH
YALQUT SHIMONI
YAQUBI
YAQUT

ZABUR
ZADOQITES
ZAKKUR INSCRIPTION
ZAMAKHSHARI
ZECHARIAH
ZECHARIAH, FATHER OF JOHN
ZEDEKIAH, SON OF CHENAANAH
ZEPHANIAH
ZERUBBABEL
ZION
ZIPPORAH
ZOHAR
ZOROASTRIANISM

Appendix 2
List of Prophets

This appendix provides the names of individuals recognized as prophets in the Quran and Islam, and in the Hebrew Bible and Judaism. As the entries in this dictionary testify, such lists can only be of heuristic value insofar as the many sources consulted present various definitions of prophethood and prophecy, use multiple terms for types of prophetic figures, and identify different people as prophets. The Hebrew Bible designates certain individuals as prophets who are not always regarded as such by Jewish exegetes, nor do Jewish sources always agree on the prophetic status of certain individuals. Some figures mentioned in the Quran are likewise regarded as prophets by only some Muslim exegetes, and in many cases Muslim exegetes disagree on which prophet is intended by the name given in the Quran. Nor are these lists complete. Muslim scholars state that many thousands of prophets were sent by God although only a select few are mentioned by name in the Quran, and other scholars recognize the existence of numerous prophetic figures outside the purview of the Bible. The following lists give only the names of those individuals for whom an entry can be found in this dictionary.

RECOGNIZED AS PROPHETS IN THE QURAN AND IN ISLAM

Aaron
Abraham
David
Dhu al-Kifl
Elijah
Elisha
Ezekiel
Ezra
Hud
Idris

Isaac
Isaiah
Ishmael
Jacob
Jeremiah
Jesus
Job
John the Baptist
Jonah
Joseph

Joshua
Khidr
Lot
Moses
Muhammad
Noah
Salih

Samuel
Seth
Shem
Shuayb
Solomon
Zechariah

RECOGNIZED AS PROPHETS IN
THE HEBREW BIBLE AND IN JUDAISM

Aaron
Abigail
Abraham
Amos
Balaam
David
Deborah
Elijah
Elisha
Esther
Ezekiel
Gad
Habakkub
Haggai
Hanani
Hananiah
Hannah
Hosea
Huldah
Iddo
Isaiah
Jacob
Jeduthun
Jehu, son of Hanani
Jeremiah
Jethro

Job
Joel
Jonah
Joseph
Joshua
Malachi
Micah
Micaiah
Miriam
Moses
Nathan
Noadiah
Obadiah
Oded
Samuel
Sarah
Saul
Shemaiah
Uriahu
Zechariah
Zedekiah, son of Chenaanah
Zephaniah

Bibliography

CONTENTS

INTRODUCTION

The following bibliography provides a broad overview of some of the many resources available for the further study of prophets and prophecy in Islam and Judaism. We have not attempted, nor are we able, to provide a comprehensive list of all relevant works. Instead, we have included works intended to facilitate, for non-specialists, in-depth research on the dictionary entries and related phenomena. The works listed in the General Reference Works section offer more detailed resources for future comparison of the sort we encourage here. We have also included a list of texts in translation, which includes texts and collections of texts in English translation directly relevant to the dictionary entries, though such a list is very limited and hardly reflects the breadth and depth of original textual resources available for the study of Islamic and Jewish views of prophets and prophecy.

Following these sections, the bibliography is divided into two main parts. The first part provides three bibliographies relative to prophecy in general: Ancient Near East and Israel; Hellenism, Judaism, Late Antiquity; and Islam. This division is roughly chronological, but readers may need to search more than one section when pursuing a specific topic. Historically speaking, the formative stages of Judaism, as a religious system distinct from Israelite religion, overlap with the end of prophecy as an Israelite cultural institution. Thus, in the bibliographic category on Prophecy in Hellenism, Judaism, and Late Antiquity we include works that discuss prophecy from later Jewish perspectives or that are relevant to the topic of Jewish mantic (and mystical) practices generally. Throughout, we have included relevant works dealing with exegesis as they relate to the stories of the prophets and prophecy.

The second part is divided into bibliographies corresponding to the prophets and prophetic figures mentioned in our dictionary entries, from Adam to Muhammad. We provide categories for individual prophets and figures associated with prophecy regardless of whether the figure is considered a prophet in both Islam and Judaism. Thus, the reader will find bibliographic categories for Adam and Eve, Noah, and Daniel, though these figures are considered prophets only in Islam. We have divided the bibliographic entries for the Israelite prophets into pre-exilic and post-exilic categories and have subdivided each of these groups by individual prophet. These are also arranged in a rough chronological order, and the bibliographies of some figures have been grouped together for convenience. Following these parts is a bibliography devoted to angels, demons, giants, and monsters, which includes references to many of the phenomena and issues mentioned in the dictionary in relation to prophets and prophecy.

ABBREVIATIONS USED IN THE BIBLIOGRAPHY

AA	*American Anthropologist*
AB	Anchor Bible
ACEBT	*Amsterdamse Cahiers voor Exegese en Bijbelse Theologie*
AE	*American Ethnologist*
AfO	*Archiv für Orientforschung*
AJA	*American Journal of Archaeology*
AJS	*American Journal of Sociology*
AJSL	*American Journal of Semitic Languages*
AJSR	*Association for Jewish Studies Review*
AnBib	Analecta Biblica
ANETS	Ancient Near Eastern Texts and Studies
ANRW	*Aufsteig und Niedergang der römischen Welt*
AO	*Acta Orientalia*
AOAT	Alter Orient und Altes Testament
AQ	*Anthropological Quarterly*
AR	*Archiv für Religionswissenschaft*
ARA	*Annual Review of Anthropology*
Arch	*Archaeology*
AS	*Assyriological Studies*
ASJ	*Acta Sumerologica*
ASR	*American Sociological Review*
ASTI	*Annual of the Swedish Theological Institute*
ATJ	*Ashland Theological Journal*
ATR	*Anglican Theological Review*
AulOr	*Aula Orientalis*
AUSS	*Andrews University Seminary Studies*
BA	*Biblical Archeologist*
BAR	*Biblical Archaeology Review*
BASOR	*Bulletin of the American Schools of Oriental Research*
BBR	*Bulletin for Biblical Research*
BibInt	*Biblical Interpretation*
BiOr	*Bibliotheca Orientalis*
BJRL	*Bulletin of the John Rylands University Library of Manchester*
BJS	Brown Judaic Studies

BK	*Bibel und Kirche*
BM	*Beth Miqra*
BN	*Biblische Notizen*
BR	*Biblical Research*
BRev	*Bible Review*
BRT	*Baptist Review of Theology/La Revue Baptiste de Théologie*
BS	*Bibliotheca Sacra*
BSOAS	*Bulletin of the School of Oriental and African Studies*
BTB	*Biblical Theology Bulletin*
BTFT	Bijdragen: Tijdschrift voor Filosofie en Theologie
BV	*Biblical Viewpoint*
BZ	*Biblische Zeitschrift*
BZAW	Beihefte zur ZAW
CA	*Current Anthropology*
CBQ	*Catholic Bible Quarterly*
CBQMS	*CBQ* Monograph Series
CHJ	*Cambridge History of Judaism*
CJ	*Concordia Journal*
ConB	Coniectanea biblica
CRAIBL	*Comptes rendus de l'Académie des inscriptions et belles-lettres*
CRBS	Currents in Research–Biblical Studies
CSR	*Christian Scholars Review*
CTR	*Concordia Theological Review*
CurTM	*Currents in Theology and Mission*
DBAT	*Dielheimer Blätter zum Alten Testament*
EB	*Estudios Biblicos*
ETL	*Ephemerides Theologicae Lovanienses*
ETR	*Études Theologiques et Religieuses*
EvQ	*Evangelical Quarterly*
FCLP	Feminist Companion to the Latter Prophets
FH	*Fides et Historia*
FRLANT	Forschungen zur Religion und Literatur des Alten und Neuen Testaments
GO	*Graecolatina et Orientalia*
GTJ	*Grace Theological Journal*
HAR	*Hebrew Annual Review*

HBT	*Horizons in Biblical Theology*
HDR	Harvard Dissertations in Religion
HO	*Handbuch der Orientalistik*
Hor	*Horizons*
HR	*History of Religions*
HS	*Hebrew Studies*
HSCP	Harvard Studies in Classical Philology
HSM	Harvard Semitic Monographs
HTR	*Harvard Theological Review*
HUCA	*Hebrew Union College Annual*
IBS	*Irish Biblical Studies*
IC	*Islamic Culture*
IEJ	*Israel Exploration Journal*
IJIAS	*International Journal of Islamic and Arabic Studies*
IJMES	*International Journal of Middle East Studies*
IOS	*Israel Oriental Studies*
IQ	*Islamic Quarterly*
IS	*Islamic Studies*
ISSB	*International Social Science Bulletin*
ITQ	*Irish Theological Quarterly*
JA	*Journal Asiatique*
JAAR	*Journal of the American Academy of Religion*
JANES	*Journal of the Ancient Near Eastern Society*
JAOS	*Journal of the American Oriental Society*
JBL	*Journal of Biblical Literature*
JBQ	*Jewish Bible Quarterly*
JCS	*Journal of Cuneiform Studies*
JEA	*Journal of Egyptian Archaeology*
JECS	*Journal of Early Christian Studies*
JESHO	*Journal of the Economic and Social History of the Orient*
JETS	*Journal of the Evangelical Theological Society*
JGES	*Journal of the Grace Evangelical Society*
JHS	*Journal of Hellenic Studies*
JJS	*Journal of Jewish Studies*
JJTP	*Journal of Jewish Thought and Philosophy*
JNES	*Journal of Near Eastern Studies*
JNSL	*Journal of Northwest Semitic Languages*

JQR	*Jewish Quarterly Review*
JR	*Journal of Religion*
JRAS	*Journal of the Royal Asiatic Society*
JRS	*Journal of Roman Studies*
JSAI	*Jerusalem Studies in Arabic and Islam*
JSJ	*Journal for the Study of Judaism*
JSNT	*Journal for the Study of the New Testament*
JSOT	*Journal for the Study of the Old Testament*
JSOTSS	JSOT Supplement Series
JSP	*Journal for the Study of the Pseudepigrapha*
JSQ	*Jewish Studies Quarterly*
JS	*Journal for Semitics*
JSS	*Journal of Semitic Studies*
JTS	*Journal of Theological Studies*
KI	*Kirche und Israel*
LTJ	*Lutheran Theological Journal*
LTQ	*Lexington Theological Quarterly*
LTS	*Lutheran Theological Studies*
MARI	*Mari-Annales de Recherches Interdisciplinaires*
MGWJ	*Monatsschrift für Geschichte und Wissenschaft des Judentums*
MQR	*Mennonite Quarterly Review*
MTSR	*Method and Theory in the Study of Religion*
MW	*Muslim World*
NABU	*Nouvelles Assyriologiques Bréves et Utilitaires*
NGTT	*Nederduits Gereformeerde Teologiese Tydskrif*
NHS	Nag Hammadi Studies
NRT	*Nouvelle Revue Théologique*
NT	*Novum Testamentum*
NTR	*New Theology Review*
NTS	*New Testament Studies*
OAC	Orientis Antiqui Collectio
OBO	Orbis biblicus et orientalis
OLZ	*Orientalistische Literaturzeitung*
Or	*Orientalia*
OS	Orientalia Suecana
OTE	*Old Testament Essays*
OTS	*Oudtestamentische Studien*

PEGLMBS	*Proceeding of the Eastern Great Lakes and Midwest Biblical Societies*
PEQ	*Palestine Exploration Quarterly*
PIBA	*Proceedings of the Irish Biblical Association*
PRS	*Perspectives in Religious Studies*
PSAS	*Proceedings of the Seminar for Arabian Studies*
PSB	*Princeton Seminary Bulletin*
QR	*Quarterly Review*
RA	*Revue d'Assyriologie et Archéologie orientale*
RB	*Revue Biblique*
RdQ	*Revue de Qumran*
REB	*Revue Études Byzantin*
REJ	*Revue des Études Juives*
RGRW	Religions in the Graeco-Roman World
RHPR	*Revue d'Histoire et de Philosophie Religieuses*
RHR	*Revue de l'Histoire des Réligions*
RO	*Revista Orientalia*
RQ	*Restoration Quarterly*
RSO	*Revista degli studi orientali*
RSR	*Religious Studies Review*
RTR	*The Reformed Theological Review*
SAAS	State Archives of Assyria Studies
SAOC	Studies in Ancient Oriental Civilization
SBLDS	Society of Biblical Literature Dissertation Series
SBLSS	Society of Biblical Literature Symposium Series
SBT	Studies in Biblical Theology
SBTS	Sources for Biblical and Theological Study
SC	*Sources chrétiennes*
Scrip	*Scriptura*
SCS	Septuagint and Cognate Studies
SEA	*Svensk Exegetisk Årsbok*
SEL	*Studi epigrafici e linguistici sul Vincino Oriento antico*
SH	*Scripta Hierosolymitana*
SI	*Studia Islamica*
SJOT	*Scandanavian Journal of the Old Testament*
SJT	*Scottish Journal of Theology*
SLAEI	Studies in Late Antiquity and Early Islam
SPat	*Studia Patristica*

SPAW	Sitzungsberichte der preusssischen Akademie der Wissenschaften
SR	*Studies in Religion*
StTh	*Studia Theologica*
SVTQ	*St. Vladimir's Theological Quarterly*
TA	*Tel Aviv*
TAPA	*Transactions of the American Philological Association*
TAPS	*Transactions of the American Philosophical Society*
TB	*Tyndale Bulletin*
TBT	*The Bible Today*
TCRPOGA	Travaux du Centre de Recherche sur le Proche-Orient et la Grèce Antiques
TD	*Theology Digest*
TE	*Theologica Evangelica*
TGUOS	*Transactions of the Glasgow University Oriental Society*
Them	*Themelios*
Theo	*Theology*
TJ	*Trinity Journal*
TJT	*Toronto Journal of Theology*
TS	*Theological Studies*
TT	*Theology Today*
TTZ	Trierer Theologische Studien
TUAT	Texte aus der Umwelt des Alten Testaments
TZ	*Theologische Zeitschrift*
UF	*Ugarit-Forschungen*
USQR	*Union Seminary Quarterly Review*
VE	*Vox Evangelica*
VT	*Vetus Testamentum*
VTS	*Vetus Testamentum* Supplements
WA	*World Archaeology*
WO	*Die Welt des Orients*
WTJ	*Westminster Theological Journal*
WUNT	Wissenschaftliche Untersuchungen zum Neuen Testament
ZA	*Zeitschrift für Assyriologie*
ZAW	*Zeitschrift für die Alttestamentliche Wissenschaft*
ZDMG	*Zeitschrift der Deutschen Morgenlandischen Gesellschaft*

ZDPV	*Zeitschrift des Deutschen Palästina-Vereins*
ZMR	*Zeitschrift für Missionwissenschaft und Religionswissenschaft*
ZNW	*Zeitschrift für die Neutestamentliche Wissenschaft und die Kunde des Urchristentums*
ZPE	*Zeitschrift für Papyrologie und Epigraphik*
ZRGG	*Zeitschrift für Religions- und Geistesgeschichte*
ZTK	*Zeitschrift für Theologie und Kirche*

GENERAL REFERENCE WORKS

Anchor Bible Dictionary. Ed. D. N. Freedman et al. 6 vols. New York: Doubleday, 1992.

Bahat, D. *The Illustrated Atlas of Jerusalem.* Trans. S. Ketko. New York: Simon and Schuster, 1990.

Baines, J., and J. Málek. *Atlas of Ancient Egypt.* New York: Facts On File Publications, 1980.

Black, J., and A. Green. *Gods, Demons and Symbols of Ancient Mesopotamia: An Illustrated Dictionary.* London: British Museum Press for the Trustees of the British Museum, 1992.

Browning, W. R. F. *The Oxford Dictionary of the Bible.* Oxford: Oxford University Press, 1996.

Cambridge History of Judaism. Ed. W. D. Davies and L. Finkelstein. Cambridge: Cambridge University Press, 1984.

Cambridge History of Later Greek and Early Medieval Philosophy. Ed. A. H. Armstrong. Cambridge: Cambridge University Press, 1967.

Cambridge History of the Bible. Ed. P. R. Ackroyd et al. 3 vols. Cambridge: Cambridge University Press, 1963–70.

Catalogue de l'ecole biblique et archéologique française de Jérusalem. Ecole biblique et archéologique française. Leiden, Netherlands: E. J. Brill, 2000.

Civilizations of the Ancient Near East. Ed. J. M. Sasson. 4 vols. New York: Scribner, 1995.

Cornell, T. *Atlas of the Roman World.* Oxford: Phaidon, 1982.

Critical Terms for Religious Studies. Ed. M. C. Taylor. Chicago: University of Chicago Press, 1998.

Day, J. *The Oxford Bible Atlas.* 3rd ed. Oxford: Oxford University Press, 1984.

Dictionary of Biblical Imagery. Ed. L. Ryken et al. Downers Grove, Ill.: InterVarsity Press, 1998.

A Dictionary of Biblical Interpretation. Ed. R. Coggins and J. Houlden. Philadelphia: Westminster, 1990.

Dictionary of Deities and Demons in the Bible. Ed. K. van der Toorn et al. Leiden, Netherlands: E. J. Brill, 1995.

Elenchus of Biblica. Roma: Pontificio Istituto Biblico, 1985–.

Encyclopaedia Judaica. Ed. J. Klutzkin and I. Elbogen. 10 vols. Berlin, 1928–34. Reprint, 16 vols. Jerusalem: Keter Publishing House, 1971.

Encyclopaedia of Islam. Ed. H. A. R. Gibb et al. 2nd ed. 11 vols. to date. Leiden, Netherlands: E. J. Brill, 1960–. 1st ed. Ed. M. T. Houtsma et al. 4 vols. Leiden, Netherlands: E. J. Brill, 1913–34.

Encyclopaedia of Religion and Ethics. Ed. J. Hastings. 13 vols. New York: Charles Scribner, 1951.

Encyclopedia of Archaeological Excavations in the Holy Land. Ed. M. Avi-Yonah. 4 vols. Englewood Cliffs, N.J.: Prentice Hall, 1975.

Encyclopedia of Biblical Interpretation. Ed. Menahem Kasher. 9 vols. New York: American Biblical Encyclopedia Society, 1953.

Encyclopedia of Judaism. 12 vols. New York, 1901–6. Reprint, New York: Continuum, 1964.

Encyclopedia of Mysticism and Mystery Religions. Ed. J. Ferguson. New York: Crossroads, 1982.

Encyclopedia of Religion. Ed. M. Eliade. 17 vols. New York: Macmillan, 1987.

Encyclopedia of the Dead Sea Scrolls. Ed. L. H. Schiffman and J. C. VanderKam. New York: Oxford University Press, 2000.

Encylopedia of the Quran. Ed. J. McAuliffe. 1 vol. to date. Leiden, Netherlands: E. J. Brill, 2001–.

Entsiklopedyah, 'Olum ha-Tanakh. Ed. M. Haran. Tel Aviv: Revivim, 1997.

Ginzburg, L. *Legends of the Jews*. Trans. H. Szold. 7 vols. Philadelphia, 1909. Reprint, Baltimore: Johns Hopkins University Press, 1998.

Groom, N. *A Dictionary of Arabic Topography and Placenames*. Beirut: Librairie du Liban, 1983.

Harding, G. L. *An Index and Concordance of Pre-Islamic Arabian Names and Inscriptions*. Toronto: University of Toronto Press, 1971.

Harper's Bible Dictionary. Ed. P. Achtemeier. San Francisco: HarperSanFrancisco, 1985.

The HarperCollins Atlas of the Bible. Ed. J. T. Pritchard. New York: HarperCollins, 1991.

The HarperCollins Dictionary of Religion. Ed. J. Z. Smith. San Francisco: HarperCollins, 1995.

Horovitz, J. *Jewish Proper Names and Derivatives in the Koran*. Hildesheim, Germany: G. Olms, 1964.

Jeffery, A. *The Foreign Vocabulary of the Qur'an*. Baroda, India: Oriental Institute, 1938.

———. *Materials for the History of the Text of the Qur'an: The Old Codices*. Leiden, Netherlands: E. J. Brill, 1937.

378 • BIBLIOGRAPHY

Kassis, H. E. *A Concordance of the Quran.* Berkeley: University of California Press, 1982.

Léon-Dufour, X. *Dictionary of the New Testament.* Trans. T. Prendergast. San Francisco: Harper and Row, 1980.

McKenzie, J. *Dictionary of the Bible.* Milwaukee: Bruce Publishing, 1965.

McKim, D. K. *Historical Handbook of Major Biblical Interpreters.* Downers Grove, Ill.: InterVarsity Press 1998.

Mir, M. *Dictionary of Quranic Terms and Concepts.* New York: Garland, 1987.

Neusner, J. *A History of the Jews in Babylonia.* 5 vols. Leiden, Netherlands: E. J. Brill, 1969–70.

The New Encyclopedia of Archaeological Excavations in the Holy Land. Ed. E. Stern. 4 vols. Jerusalem: Israel Exploration Society, 1993.

The New Jerome Biblical Commentary. Ed. R. Brown, J. Fitzmyer, and R. Murphy. New Jersey: Prentice Hall, 1990.

The Oxford Companion to the Bible. Ed. B. Metzger and M. Coogan. New York: Oxford University Press 1993.

The Oxford Dictionary of the Christian Church. Ed. F. L. Cross and E. A. Livingstone. 3rd ed. New York: Oxford University Press, 1997.

The Oxford Encyclopedia of Ancient Egypt. Ed. D. B. Redford. Oxford: Oxford University Press, 2000.

The Oxford Encyclopedia of Archaeology in the Ancient Near East. Ed. Eric M. Meyers. 5 vols. Oxford: Oxford University Press, 1995.

The Oxford History of Ancient Egypt. Ed. I. Shaw. Oxford: Oxford University Press, 2000.

The Oxford History of the Biblical World. Ed. M. D. Coogan. New York: Oxford University Press, 1998.

Penrice, J. *A Dictionary and Glossary of the Quran.* Delhi: Low Price Publications, 1873.

Reallexikon der ägyptischen Religionsgeschichte. Ed. H. Bonnet. Berlin: Walter de Gruyter, 1952–2000.

Reallexikon der Assyriologie und vorderasiatischen Archäologie. Ed. D. O. Edzard. Berlin: Walter de Gruyter, 1928–.

Reallexikon für Antike und Christentum. Ed. T. Klauser. 10 vols. Stuttgart, Germany: Hiersemann, 1950–78.

Roaf, M. *Cultural Atlas of Mesopotamia.* Oxford: Oxford University Press, 1990.

Rogerson, J. *Atlas of the Bible.* Oxford: Oxford University Press, 1986.

Schimmel, A. *The Mystery of Numbers.* Oxford: Oxford University Press, 1993.

Theological Dictionary of the New Testament. Ed. G. Kittel et al. 10 vols. Grand Rapid, Mich.: Eerdmans, 1964–76.

Theological Dictionary of the Old Testament. Ed. G. J. Botterweck et al. Trans. J. T. Willis et al. 11 vols. Grand Rapids, Mich.: Eerdmans, 1974–.

Tov, E. *Companion Volume to the Dead Sea Scrolls Microfiche Edition*. Leiden, Netherlands: E. J. Brill, 1995.

——. *Dead Sea Scrolls on Microfiche: A Comprehensive Facsimile Edition of the Texts from the Judean Desert*. Leiden, Netherlands: E. J. Brill, 1995.

——. *Textual Criticism of the Hebrew Bible*. Minneapolis, Minn.: Fortress, 1992.

Würthwein, E. *The Text of the Old Testament*. Grand Rapids, Mich.: Eerdmans, 1979.

TEXTS IN TRANSLATION

The Amarna Letters. Ed. W. Moran. Baltimore, The Johns Hopkins University Press, 1992.

The Ancient Near East in Pictures Relating to the Old Testament. Ed. J. B. Pritchard. Princeton, N.J.: Princeton University Press, 1969.

Ancient Near Eastern Texts Relating to the Old Testament. Ed. J. B. Pritchard. Princeton, N.J.: Princeton University Press, 1969.

The Apocrypha and Pseudepigrapha of the Old Testament in English. Ed. R. H. Charles. 2 vols. Oxford: Oxford University Press, 1913.

Aramaic Texts from Deir 'Alla. Ed. J. Hoftijzer. Leiden, Netherlands: E. J. Brill, 1976.

Armenian Apocrypha Relating to Adam and Eve. Ed. and Trans. M. Stone. Leiden, Netherlands: E. J. Brill, 1996.

Armenian Apocrypha Relating to the Patriarchs and Prophets. Ed. and Trans. M. Stone. Jerusalem: Israel Academy of Sciences and Humanities, 1982.

The Babylonian Talmud. 35 vols. London, 1935–48. Reprinted in 18 vols., London: Soncino Press, 1961.

The Book of Jasher. Trans. M. M. Noah. New York, 1840. Reprint, Escondido, Calif.: Book Tree, 2000.

Book of the Bee. Trans. E. A. W. Budge. Oxford: Clarendon, 1886.

Book of the Cave of Treasures. Trans. E. A. W. Budge. London: Religious Tract Society, 1927.

The Chronicles of Jerahmeel. Trans. M. Gaster. London, 1899. Reprinted in 2 vols. New York: KTAV Publishing, 1971.

The Chronography of Gregory Abu'l Faraj the Son of Aaron, the Hebrew Physician, Commonly Known as Bar Hebraeus. Trans. E. A. W. Budge. London: Oxford University Press, 1932.

The Context of Scripture. Ed. William W. Hallo and K. Lawson Younger. 3 vols. to date. Leiden, Netherlands: E. J. Brill, 1997–99.

Coogan, M. *Stories from Ancient Canaan*. Philadelphia: Westminster, 1978.

de Moor, J. *An Anthology of Religious Texts from Ugarit*. Leiden, Netherlands: E. J. Brill, 1987.

Documents from Old Testament Times. Ed. D. Thomas. New York, 1958.

The Early Church Fathers. Ed. P. Schaff and A. Roberts. 38 vols. Peabody, Mass.: Hendrickson, 1989.

Eusebius, *Ecclesiastical History.* Trans. C. F. Cruse. Peabody, Mass.: Hendrickson, 1991.

The Fathers according to Rabbi Nathan. (A) Trans. J. Goldin. New Haven, Conn.: Yale University Press, 1955. (B) Trans. A. Saldarini. Leiden, Netherlands: E. J. Brill, 1975.

Foster, B. R. *Before the Muses: An Anthology of Akkadian Literature.* 2 vols. Potomac: CDL Press, 1996.

García Martínez, F. *The Dead Sea Scrolls Translated: The Qumran Texts in English.* Leiden, Netherlands: E. J. Brill, 1996.

Gibson, J. C. L. *Textbook of Syrian Inscriptions.* 2 vols. Oxford: Oxford University Press, 1971–75.

Goodman, L. E. *The Book of Theodicy: Translation and Commentary on the Book of Job by Saadiah Ben Joseph al-Fayyumi.* New Haven, Conn.: Yale University Press, 1988.

Grossfeld, B. *The Targum Onqelos to Genesis.* Aramaic Bible, 6. Wilmington, Del.: Michael Glazier, 1988.

Hackett, J. *The Balaam Text from Deir Alla.* Chico, Calif.: Scholars, 1980.

Harari, Y. *Harba de-Moshe (The Sword of Moses): A New Edition and a Study.* Jerusalem: Akademon, 1997.

Hebrew-English Edition of the Babylonian Talmud. Ed. I. Epstein. 6 vols. London: Soncino, 1960.

Herdner, A. *Corpus des tablettes en cunéiformes alphabetiques découvertes à Ras Shamra-Ugarit de 1929 à 1939.* Paris: Impr. nationale, 1963.

The History of al-Tabari. Vol. 1: *From the Creation to the Flood.* Trans. F. Rosenthal. Albany: State University of New York Press, 1989. Vol. 2: *Prophets and Patriarchs.* Trans. W. M. Brinner, 1987. Vol. 3: *The Children of Israel.* Trans. W. M. Brinner, 1991. Vol. 4: *The Ancient Kingdoms.* Trans. M. Perlmann, 1987. Vol. 5: *The Sasanids, the Byzantines, the Lakhmids, and Yemen.* Trans. C. E. Bosworth, 1999. Vol. 6: *Muhammad at Mecca.* Trans. W. M. Watt and M. V. McDonald, 1988. Vol. 7: *The Foundation of the Community.* Trans. M. V. McDonald and W. M. Watt, 1987. Vol. 8: *The Victory of Islam.* Trans. M. Fishbein, 1997.

Ibn al-Arabi. *The Bezels of Wisdom.* Trans. R. W. J. Austin. New York: Paulist Press, 1980.

Ibn Kathir. *Stories of the Prophets.* Trans. S. Gad. Ed. H. R. Abo El-Nagah. Cairo, 2000.

Josephus. *The Works of Josephus.* Trans. W. Whiston. Peabody, Mass.: Hendrickson, 1987.

Kanaanäische und Aramäische Inschriften. Ed. H. Donner and W. Röllig. 3 vols. Wiesbaden, Germany: Otto Harrassowitz, 1966–69.

Klimkeit, H. J. *Gnosis on the Silk Road: Gnostic Texts from Central Asia*. San Francisco: HarperCollins, 1993.

Lauterbach, J. Z. *Mekilta de-Rabbi Ishmael*. 2 vols. Philadelphia: Jewish Publication Society, 1933.

Lichtheim, M. *Ancient Egyptian Literature: A Book of Readings*. 3 vols. Berkeley: University of California Press, 1973–80.

Life of Muhammad: A Translation of Ibn Ishaq's Sirat Rasul Allah. Trans. A. Guillaume. Oxford: Oxford University Press, 1955.

Manichaean Literature: Representative Texts Chiefly from Middle Persian and Parthian Writings. Ed. and Trans. J. P. Asmussen. Delmar, N.Y.: Scholars' Facsimiles and Reprints, 1975.

McGaha, M. *Coat of Many Cultures: The Story of Joseph in Spanish Literature, 1200–1492*. Philadelphia: Jewish Publication Society, 1997.

Midrash Rabbah. Trans. H. Freedman et al. 10 vols. London: Soncino, 1939.

Midrash Tanhuma. Trans. J. Townsend. Hoboken, N.J.: KTAV Publishing, 1989.

Midrash Tanhuma-Yelammedenu: An English Translation of Genesis and Exodus. Trans. S. A. Berman. Hoboken, N.J.: KTAV Publishing, 1996.

The Mishnah. Trans. H. Danby. Oxford: Clarendon Press, 1936.

Morgan, M. A. *Sepher Ha-Razim: The Book of Mysteries*. Chico, Calif.: Scholars, 1983.

The Nag Hammadi Library in English. Ed. J. Robinson. San Francisco: Harper and Row, 1990.

New Testament Apocrypha. 2nd ed. 2 vols. Ed. W. Schneemelcher. Trans. R. McL. Wilson. Louisville, Ky.: Westminster, 1991.

The Old Testament Pseudepigrapha. Ed. J. H. Charlesworth. 2 vols. Garden City, N.J.: Doubleday, 1983.

Parker, S. *Ugaritic Narrative Poetry*. Atlanta: Scholars, 1997.

Philo. *The Works of Philo*. Trans. C. D. Yonge. Peabody, Mass.: Hendrickson, 1993.

Pirke de Rabbi Eliezer. Trans. G. Friedlander. London, 1916. Reprint, New York: Sepher-Hermon Press, 1981.

Ramban (Nachmanides): Commentary on the Torah. Trans. C. Chavel. New York: Soncino, 1976.

Rashbam's Commentary on Exodus. Trans. M. Lockshin. Atlanta: Scholars, 1997.

Renard, J. *All the King's Falcons: Rumi on Prophets and Revelation*. Albany: State University of New York Press, 1994.

Stern, M. *Greek and Latin Authors on Jews and Judaism*. 3 vols. Jerusalem: Israel Academy of Sciences and Humanities, 1976.

The Tales of the Prophets of al-Kisa'i. Trans. W. Thackston. Boston: Twayne, 1978.

The Talmud of the Land of Israel. Trans. J. Neusner. 25 vols. Chicago: University of Chicago Press, 1982–.

The Talmud: The Steinsaltz Edition. Ed. A. Steinsaltz. 21 vols. New York: Random House, 1989–99.

Taylor, R. A. *The Peshitta of Daniel*. Monographs of the Peshitta Institute 7. Leiden, Netherlands: E. J. Brill, 1994.

The Torah: With Rashi's Commentary Translated, Annotated and Elucidated. Trans. Y. I. Herczeg et al. 5 vols. New York: Soncino, 1995.

Vermes, Geza. *The Complete Dead Sea Scrolls in English*. New York: Penguin, 1997.

Wheeler, B. *Prophets in the Quran: An Introduction to the Quran and Muslim Exegesis*. London: Continuum, 2002.

Wyatt, N. *Religious Texts from Ugarit: The Words of Ilimilku and His Colleagues*. Sheffield, England: JSOT Press, 1998.

The Zohar. Trans. H. Sperling and M. Simon. 5 vols. New York: Soncino, 1984.

PROPHECY: ANCIENT NEAR EAST AND ISRAEL

Ackerman, J. S. "Prophecy and Warfare in Early Israel: A Study of the Deborah–Barak Story." *BASOR* 220 (1975): 5–13.

Ackroyd, P. R. *Exile and Restoration*. Philadelphia: S.C.M. Press, 1968.

Akao, J. O. "Biblical Call Narratives: An Investigation into the Underlying Structures." *Ogbomoso Journal of Theology* 8 (1993): 1–11.

Albright, W. F. *The Biblical Period from Abraham to Ezra: An Historical Survey*. New York: Harper and Row, 1963.

Amsler, S. "Les prophètes et la communication par les actes." In *Werden und Wirken des Alten Testaments: Festschrift für Claus Westermann zum 70 Geburtstag*, 194–201. Neukirchen-Vluyn: Neukirchener Verlag, 1980.

Anbar, M. "Mari and the Origin of Prophecy." In *Kinattutu ša darâti: Raphael Kutscher Memorial Volume*. Ed. A. F. Rainey, 1–5. Tel Aviv: Institute of Archaeology, 1993.

Aro, J. "Remarks on the Practice of Extispicy in the Time of Esarhaddon and Assurbanipal." In *La Divination en Mésopotamie Ancienne et dans Les Régions Voisines*. (XIVe Rencontre Assyriologique International). Ed. D. F. Wendel, 109–77. Paris: Presses Universitaires de France, 1966.

Astour, M. C. "Sparagmos, Omophagia, and Ecstatic Prophecy at Mari." *UF* 24 (1992): 1–2.

———. "Une texte d'Ugarit récemment découvert et ses rapports avec l'origine des cultes bachiques grecs." *RHR* 164 (1963): 1–15.

Auld, A. G. "Prophecy and the Prophets." In *Creating the Old Testament: The Emergence of the Hebrew Bible*. Ed. St. Bigger, 203–26. Oxford: Basil Blackwood, 1989.

———. "Prophets through the Looking Glass: Between Writings and Moses." In *"The Place Is Too Small for Us": The Israelite Prophets in Recent Scholarship*. Ed. R. P. Gordon, 289–307. SBTS 5. Winona Lake, Ind.: Eisenbrauns, 1995.

———, ed. *Understanding Poets and Prophets*. JSOTSS 152. Sheffield, England: JSOT Press, 1993.

Avalos, H. *Illness and Health Care in the Ancient Near East: The Role of the Temple in Greece, Mesopotamia, and Israel*. HSM 54. Atlanta: Scholars, 1995.

Baltzer, K. "Considerations Regarding the Office and Calling of the Prophet." *HTR* 61 (1968): 567–81.

Barstad, H. M. "No Prophets? Recent Developments in Biblical Prophetic Research and Ancient Near Eastern Prophecy." *JSOT* 57 (1993): 39–60.

Barton, J. *Oracles of God: Perception of Ancient Prophecy in Israel after the Exile*. London: Darton, Longman, and Todd, 1986.

Becking, B., and M. Dijkstra, eds. *On Reading Prophetic Texts: Gender-Specific and Related Studies in Memory of Fokkelien van Dijk-Hemmes*. Leiden, Netherlands: E. J. Brill, 1996.

Beckwith, R. T., and M. J. Selman. *Sacrifice in the Bible*. Grand Rapids, Mich.: Eerdmans, 1995.

Begg, C. T. "The 'Classical Prophets' in Josephus' *Antiquities*." In *"The Place Is Too Small for Us": The Israelite Prophets in Recent Scholarship*. Ed. R. P. Gordon, 547–62. SBTS 5. Winona Lake, Ind.: Eisenbrauns, 1995.

———. "The Classical Prophets in the Chronistic History." *BZ* 32 (1988): 100–7.

Bellinger, W. H. *Psalmody and Prophecy*. JSOTSS 27. Sheffield, England: JSOT Press, 1984.

Benjamin, D. C. "An Anthropology of Prophecy." *BTB* 21 (1991): 135–44.

Ben Zvi, E. "History and Prophetic Texts." In *History and Interpretation: Essays in Honor of John H. Hayes*. Ed. M. P. Graham et al., 106–20. Sheffield, England: JSOT Press, 1993.

———. "Introduction: Writings, Speeches, and the Prophetic Books—Setting an Agenda." In *Writings and Speech in Israelite and Ancient Near Eastern Prophecy*. Ed. E. Ben Zvi and M. H. Floyd, 1–29. Symposium 10. Atlanta: Scholars, 2000.

———. "Prophets and Prophecy in the Compositional and Redactional Notes in I and II Kings." *ZAW* 105 (1993): 331–51.

———. "Studying Prophetic Texts against Their Original Backgrounds: Preordained Scripts and Alternative Horizons of Research." *In Prophets and Paradigms: Essays in Honor of Gene M. Tucker*. Ed. S. B. Reid, 125–35. JSOTSS 229. Sheffield, England: JSOT Press, 1996.

———. "Tracing Prophetic Literature in the Book of Kings: The Case of II Kings 15,37." *ZAW* 102 (1990): 100–5.

——. "Twelve Prophetic Books or 'The Twelve': A Few Preliminary Considerations." In *Forming Prophetic Literature: Essays on Isaiah and the Twelve in Honor of John D. W. Watts*. Ed. P. House and J. W. Watts, 125–56. JSOTSS Sup 235. Sheffield, England: JSOT Press, 1996.

Berger, P. "Charisma and Religious Innovation: The Social Location of Israelite Prophecy." *ASR* 28 (1963): 940–50.

Bickerman, E. J. *Four Strange Books in the Bible*. New York: Schocken, 1967.

Biga, M. G. "Omens and Divination at Ebla." *NABU* (1999): 103–4.

Biggs, R. "More Akkadian Prophecies." *Iraq* 29 (1967): 117–32.

Bin-Nun, S. R. "Some Remarks on Hittite Oracles, Dreams and Omina." *Or* 48 (1979): 118–27.

Blenkinsopp, J. *A History of Prophecy in Israel: From the Settlement of the Land to the Hellenistic Period*. Louisville, Ky.: John Knox, 1996.

——. *Prophecy and Canon: A Contribution to the Study of Jewish Origins*. Notre Dame, Ind.: University of Notre Dame, 1977.

——. *Sage, Priest, Prophet: Religious and Intellectual Leadership in Ancient Israel*. Louisville, Ky.: John Knox, 1995.

Bonechi, M., and J.-N. Durand. "Oneiromancie et magie à Mari à l'époque d'Ebla." *Quaderni di Semistica* 18 (1992): 151–59.

Bonner, C. "The Technique of Exorcism." *HTR* 36 (1943): 39–49.

Bos, J. W. H. "Who Speaks for God?" *Perspectives* 9 (1994): 8–9.

Bottéro, J. "Symptômes, signes, écritures en Mésopotamie ancienne." In *Divination et rationalité*. Ed. J. P. Vernat et al., 70–197. Paris: Éditions du Seuil, 1974.

Bourdillon, M. "Oracles and Politics in Ancient Israel." *Man* 12 (1977): 124–40.

Brenner, A. *A Feminist Companion to the Latter Prophets*. Sheffield, England: JSOT Press, 1995.

Brin, G. "Biblical Prophecy in the Dead Sea Scrolls." In *Sha'are Talmon: Studies in the Bible, Qumran, and the Ancient Near East Presented to Shemaryahu Talmon*. Ed. M. A. Fishbane, 101–12. Winona Lake, Ind.: Eisenbrauns, 1992.

Brown, J. P. "The Mediterranean Seer and Shamanism." *ZAW* 93 (1981): 374–400.

——. "Men of the Land and the God of Justice in Greece and Israel." *ZAW* 95/3 (1983): 376–402.

——. "The Templum and the Saeculum: Sacred Space and Time in Israel and Etruria." *ZAW* 98 (1986): 415–33.

Brown, R. M. "The Nathan Syndrome: Stories with a Moral Intention." *Religion and Literature* 16/1 (1984): 49–59.

Bruce, F. F. "Prophetic Inspiration in the Septuagint." In *"The Place Is Too Small for Us": The Israelite Prophets in Recent Scholarship*. Ed. R. P. Gordon, 539–46. SBTS 5. Winona Lake, Ind.: Eisenbrauns, 1995.

Brueggemann, W. "Israel's Social Criticism and Yahweh's Sexuality." In *A Social Reading of the Old Testament: Prophetic Approaches to Israel's Communal Life*. Ed. P. D. Miller. Minneapolis, Minn.: Fortress, 1994.

———. *Texts That Linger, Words That Explode: Listening to Prophetic Voices*. Minneapolis, Minn.: Fortress, 2000.

Brug, J. F. "Biblical Acrostics and Their Relationship to Other Ancient Near Eastern Acrostics." In *The Bible in the Light of Cuneiform Literature: Scripture in Context III*. Ed. W. W. Hallo et al., 283–304. ANTES 8. Lewiston, N.Y.: E. Mellen Press, 1990.

Buber, M. *Der Glaube der Propheten*. Zürich: Conzett and Huber, 1950.

———. *On the Bible*. New York: Schocken, 1982.

Burkert, W. "Itinerant Diviners and Magicians: A Neglected Element in Cultural Contacts." In *The Greek Renaissance of the Eighth Century B.C.: Tradition and Innovation*. Ed. R. Hägg, 115–19. Proceedings of the Second International Symposium at the Swedish Institute in Athens, 1–5 June. Stockholm: Svenska Institutet i Athen, 1983.

Burns, R. *Has the Lord Indeed Spoken Only through Moses?: A Study of the Biblical Portrait of Miriam*. Atlanta: Scholars, 1987.

Buss, M. J. "An Anthropological Perspective on Prophetic Call Narratives." *Semeia* 21 (1981): 9–30.

———. "The Social Psychology of Prophecy." In *Prophecy: Essays Presented to G. Fohrer*. Ed. J. A. Emerton, 1–11. BZAW 150. Berlin, 1980.

Butler, S. A. L. *Mesopotamian Conceptions of Dreams and Dream Rituals*. AOAT 258. Münster, 1998.

Carroll, R. P. "Ancient Israelite Prophecy and Dissonance Theory." In *"The Place Is Too Small for Us": The Israelite Prophets in Recent Scholarship*. Ed. R. P. Gordon, 377–91. SBTS 5. Winona Lake, Ind.: Eisenbrauns, 1995.

———. *From Chaos to Covenant*. New York: Crossroad, 1981.

———. "Inventing the Prophets." *IBS* 10 (1988): 24–36.

———. "Prophecy and Dissonance: A Theoretical Approach to the Prophetic Tradition." *ZAW* 92 (1980): 108–19.

———. "Prophecy and Society." In *The World of Ancient Israel: Sociological, Anthropological, and Political Perspectives*. Ed. R. E. Clements, 1–11. Cambridge, 1989.

———. *When Prophecy Failed: Reactions and Responses to Failure in the Old Testament Prophetic Traditions*. London: S.C.M. Press, 1979.

Cazelles, H. "The Canonical Approach to Torah and Prophets." *JSOT* 16 (1980): 28–31.

Childs, Brevard S. "The Canonical Shape of the Prophetic Literature." In *"The Place Is Too Small for Us": The Israelite Prophets in Recent Scholarship*. Ed. R. P. Gordon, 513–22. SBTS 5. Winona Lake, Ind.: Eisenbrauns, 1995.

Christensen, D. L. *Transformations of the War Oracles in Old Testament Prophecy*. HDR 3. Missoula, Mont.: Scholars, 1975.

Clark, D. J. "Sex-Related Imagery in the Prophets." *Bible Translator* 33 (1982): 409–13.

Clements, R. E. "The Form and Character of Prophetic Woe Oracles." *Semitics* 8 (1982): 17–29.

———. "Patterns in the Prophetic Canon." In *Canon and Authority: Essays in Old Testament Religion and Theology.*. Ed. G. W. Coats and B. O. Long, 42–55. Philadelphia: Westminster, 1977.

———. *Prophecy and Tradition*. Oxford: Blackwell, 1975.

———. "Prophets, Editors, and Tradition." In *"The Place Is Too Small for Us": The Israelite Prophets in Recent Scholarship*. Ed. R. P. Gordon, 443–52. SBTS 5. Winona Lake, Ind.: Eisenbrauns, 1995.

Clifford, R. J. "The Use of Holy in the Prophets." *CBQ* 28 (1966): 458–64.

Clines, D. J. A. "Language as Event." In *"The Place Is Too Small for Us": The Israelite Prophets in Recent Scholarship*. Ed. R. P. Gordon, 166–75. SBTS 5. Winona Lake, Ind.: Eisenbrauns,1995.

Cody, A. "The Phoenician Ecstatic in Wenamun." *JEA* 65 (1979): 99–106.

Coggins, R. "An Alternative Prophetic Tradition?" In *Israel's Prophetic Tradition*. Ed. R. Coggins et al., 77–94. Cambridge, 1982.

Cohen, N. G. "From *Nabi* to *Mal'ak* to 'Ancient Figure.'" *JSS* 36 (1985): 12–24.

Collins, T. *The Mantle of Elijah: Redaction Criticism of the Prophetical Books*. Biblical Seminar 20; Sheffield, England: JSOT Press, 1993.

Conrad, E. "The End of Prophecy and the Appearance of Angels/Messengers in the Book of the Twelve." *JSOT* 73 (1997): 65–79.

Cook, S. L. *Prophecy and Apocalypticism: The Post-exilic Social Setting*. Minneapolis, Minn.: Fortress, 1995.

Cooper, A. "Imagining Prophecy." In *Poetry and Prophecy: The Beginnings of a Literary Tradition*. Ed. J. L. Kugel, 26–44. Ithaca, N.Y.: Cornell University Press, 1990.

Cooper, J. "Assyrian Prophecies, the Assyrian Tree, and the Mesopotamian Origins of Jewish Monotheism, Greek Philosophy, Christian Theology, Gnosticism, and Much More." *JAOS* 120 (2000): 430–44.

Craghan, J. F. "The ARM X 'Prophetic' Texts: Their Media, Style, and Structure." *JANES* 6 (1974): 39–57.

Crenshaw, James L. *Prophetic Conflict: Its Effect upon Israelite Religion*. BZAW 124. Berlin: Walter de Gruyter, 1971.

Cryer, Frederick H. *Divination in Ancient Israel and Its Near Eastern Environment: A Socio-Historical Investigation*. JSOTSS 142. Sheffield, England: JSOT Press, 1994.

Culley, R. C., and T. W. Overholt, eds. *Anthropological Perspectives on Old Testament Prophecy*. Semeia 21. Chico: Scholars, 1981.

Davies, P. R. "The Audience of Prophetic Scrolls: Some Suggestions." In *Prophets and Paradigms: Essays in Honor of Gene M. Tucker*. Ed. S. B. Reid, 48–62. JSOTSS 229. Sheffield, England: JSOT Press, 1996.

Day, J. "Inner Biblical Interpretation in the Prophets." In *"The Place Is Too Small for Us": The Israelite Prophets in Recent Scholarship*. Ed. R. P. Gordon, 230–46. SBTS 5. Winona Lake, Ind.: Eisenbrauns, 1995.

Dearman, J. Andrew. *Property Rights in the Eighth-Century Prophets: The Conflict and Its Background*. SBLDS 106. Atlanta: Scholars, 1988.

Deist, Ferdinand E. "The Prophets: Are We Headed for a Paradigm Switch?" In *"The Place Is Too Small for Us": The Israelite Prophets in Recent Scholarship*. Ed. R. P. Gordon, 582–99. SBTS 5. Winona Lake, Ind.: Eisenbrauns, 1995.

DeVries, S. *Prophet against Prophet*. Grand Rapids, Mich.: Eerdmans, 1978.

Dietrich, M., et al. *Deutungen der Zukunft in Briefen, Orakeln und Omina*. TUAT 2. Gütersloh, Germany: G. Mohr, 1986.

Dietrich, M., and O. Loretz. *Mantik in Ugarit: keilalphabetische Texte der Opferschau, Omensammlungen, Nekromantie*. Abhandlungen zur Literatur Alt-Syrien-Palästinas, 3; Münster, 1990.

Dion, P. E. "The Horned Prophet (1 Kings xxii 11)." *VT* 49 (1999): 259–61.

Dossin, G. "Sur le prophétisme à Mari. " In *La divination en Mésopotamie ancienne et dans les régions voisines*. Ed. D. F. Wendel, 77–86. XIVe Rencontre Assyriologique Internationale. Paris, 1966.

———. "Une révélation du dieu Dagan à Terqa." *RA* 42 (1948): 125–34.

Duhm, B. *Die theologie der Propheten als Grundlage für die innere Entwicklungsgeschichte der israelitischen Religion*. Bonn, 1875.

Durand, J.-M. "La divination par les oiseaux." *MARI* 8 (1997): 273–82.

———. "In Vino Veritas." *RA* 76 (1982): 43–50.

———. "Les Prophéties des Textes de Mari." In *Oracles et prophéties dans l'antiquité: Actes du colloque de Strasbourg 15–17 juin 1995*. Ed. J. G. Heintz, 115–34. Travaux du Centre de Recherche sur le Proche-Orient et la Grèce Antiques, 15. Paris, 1997.

Eaton, J. H. "Festal Drama." In *"The Place Is Too Small for Us": The Israelite Prophets in Recent Scholarship*. Ed. R. P. Gordon, 247–51. SBTS 5. Winona Lake, Ind.: Eisenbrauns, 1995.

———. *Vision and Worship: The Relation of Prophecy and Liturgy in the Old Testament*. London, 1981.

Ellermeier, F. *Prophetie in Mari und Israel*. Herzberg: Verlag Erwin Jungler, 1968.

Ellis, M. de Jong. "The Goddess Kitium Speaks to King Ibalpiel: Oracle Texts from Ishchali." *MARI* 5 (1987): 235–61.

———. "Observation on Mesopotamian Oracles and Prophetic Texts: Literary and Historiographic Considerations." *JCS* 41–42 (1989): 127–86.

Everson, A. J. "The Days of Yahweh." *JBL* 93 (1974): 329–37.

Eynikel, E. "The Parable of Nathan (II Sam. 12, 1-4) and the Theory of Semiosis." In *Rethinking the Foundations*. Ed. T. Romer and S. McKenzie, 71-90. Berlin, 2000.

———. "Prophecy and Fulfillment in the Deuteronomistic History (1 Kgs 13; 2 Kgs 23,16–18)." In *Pentateuchal and Deuteronomistic Studies*. Ed. C. Brekelmans (1990): 227–37.

Fager, J.A. "Chaos and the Deborah Tradition." *QR* 13 (1993): 17–31.

———. "Miriam and Deborah." *TBT* 32 (1994): 359–63.

Fales, F. M., and G. B. Lanfranchi. "The Impact of Oracular Material on the Political Utterances and Political Action in the Royal Inscriptions of the Sargonid Dynasty." In *Oracles et prophéties dans l'antiquité: Actes du colloque de Strasbourg 15–17 juin 1995*. Ed. J. G. Heintz, 99–114. Travaux du Centre de Recherche sur le Proche-Orient et la Grèce Antiques 15. Paris, 1997.

Fenton, T. L. "Deuteronomic Advocacy of the *Nabi*: 1 Samuel IX 9 and Questions of Israelite Prophecy." *VT* 47 (1997): 23–42.

Fischer, J. A. "Notes on the Literary Form and Message of Malachi." *CBQ* 34 (1972): 315–20.

Fleming. D. E. "The Etymological Origins of the Hebrew *Nābî'*: The One Who Invokes God." *CBQ* 55 (1993): 217–24.

———. "*Nābû* and *Munabbiîtu*: Two New Syrian Religious Personnel." *JAOS* 113 (1993): 175–83.

Fohrer, G. "Die Gattung der Berichte über die symbolischen Handlungen der Propheten." *ZAW* 64 (1952): 110–20.

———. "Die Propheten des Alten Testaments im Blickefeld neuer Forschung." In *Studien zur alttestamentlichen Prophetie (1949–1965)*. BZAW 99. Berlin, 1967.

———. *Geschichte der israelitischen Religion*. Berlin: Walter de Gruyter, 1969.

———. *History of Israelite Religion*. Nashville, Tenn.: Abingdon, 1972.

———. *Symbolischen Handlungen der Propheten*. ATANT 25. Zurich, 1968.

Fontaine, C. "The Bearing of Wisdom on the Shape of 2 Sam 11–12 and 1 Kgs 3." *JSOT* 34 (1986): 61–77.

Gadd, C. J. "Some Babylonian Divinatory Methods, and Their Inter-relations." In *La divination en Mésopotamie ancienne et dans les régions voisines*. Ed. D. F. Wendel, 21–34. XIVe Rencontre Assyriologique Internationale; Paris: Presses Universitaires de France, 1966.

Gaster, T. H. *The Dead Sea Scriptures*. New York, 1976.

Geller, S. "Were the Prophets Poets?" In *"The Place Is Too Small for Us": The Israelite Prophets in Recent Scholarship*. Ed. R. P. Gordon, 154–65. SBTS 5. Winona Lake, Ind.: Eisenbrauns, 1995.

Gerstenberger, E. "The Woe-Oracles of the Prophets." *JBL* 81 (1962): 249–63.

Glahn, L., and L. Koehler. *Der Prophet der Heimkehr*. Giessen, 1934.

Glatt-Gilad, D. A. "The Role of Huldah's Prophecy in the Chronicler's Portrayal of Josiah's Reform." *Biblica* 77 (1996): 16–31.

Gordis, R. *Poets, Prophets, and Sages: Essays in Biblical Interpretation.* Bloomington, Ind., Books on Demand, 1971.

Gordon, C. H., and G. A. Rendsburg. *The Bible and the Ancient Near East.* New York: Books on Demand, 1997.

Gordon, R. P. "From Mari to Moses: Prophecy at Mari and in Ancient Israel." In *Of Prophets' Visions and the Wisdom of Sages.* Ed. H. A. McKay and D. J. A. Clines, 63–79. JSOTSS 162. Sheffield, England: JSOT Press, 1993.

———. "Present Trends and Future Directions." In *"The Place Is Too Small for Us": The Israelite Prophets in Recent Scholarship.* Ed. R. P. Gordon, 600–5. SBTS 5. Winona Lake, Ind.: Eisenbrauns, 1995.

———. "A Story about Two Paradigm Shifts." In *"The Place Is Too Small for Us": The Israelite Prophets in Recent Scholarship.* Ed. R. P. Gordon, 3–31. SBTS 5. Winona Lake, Ind.: Eisenbrauns, 1995.

———. "Where Have all the Prophets Gone? The 'Disappearing' Prophet against the Background of Ancient Near Eastern Prophecy." *Bulletin for Biblical Research* 5 (1995): 67–86.

———, ed. *"The Place Is Too Small for Us": The Israelite Prophets in Recent Scholarship.* SBTS 5. Winona Lake, Ind.: Eisenbrauns, 1995.

Gottwald, N. K. "The Biblical Prophetic Critique of Political Economy: Its Ground and Import." In *God and Capitalism: A Prophetic Critique of Market Economy.* Ed. J. M. Thomas and V. Visick, 11–29. Madison, 1991.

Grabbe, L. L. *Priests, Prophets, Diviners, Sages: A Socio-Historical Study of Religious Specialists in Ancient Israel.* Valley Forge, Penn.: Trinity Press, 1995.

Graffy, A. A. *Prophet Confronts His People: The Disputation Speech in the Prophets.* AnBib 104. Rome, 1984.

Grayson, K., and W. G. Lambert. "Akkadian Prophecies." *JCS* 18 (1964): 7–30.

Greenberg, M. "Biblical Attitudes toward Power: Ideal and Reality in Law and Prophets." In *Religion and Law.* Ed. E. Firmage, 101–25. Winona Lake, Ind.: Eisenbrauns, 1990.

Greenspahn, F. "Why Prophecy Ceased." *JBL* 108 (1989): 37–49.

Guillaume, A. *Prophecy and Divination among the Hebrews and Other Semites.* London: Hodder & Stoughton, 1938.

Gunkel, H. *Die Religion in Geschichte und Gegenwart.* Tübingen, Germany, 1930.

Gunneweg, A. H. L. *Mündliche und schriftliche Tradition ver vorexilischen Prophetenbücher als Problem der neuer Prophetenforschung.* FRLANT 73. Göttingen, Germany: Vanderhoeck und Ruprecht, 1959.

Habel, N. "The Form and Significance of the Call Narratives." *ZAW* 77 (1965): 297–323.

Hajjar, Y. "Divinités oraculaires et rites divinatoires en Syrie et en Phénicie à l'époque gréco-romaine." In *Aufsteig und Niedergang der Römischen Welt II: Principat 18.4: Religion.* Ed. W. Haase, 2236–320. Berlin, 1990.

Haldar, A. *Associations of Cult Prophets among the Ancient Semites*. Uppsala, Sweden, 1945.

Hanson, P. D. *The Dawn of the Apocalyptic*. Philadelphia, 1975.

———. *The People Called*. New York, 1986.

Haran, M. *Temples and Temple Service in Ancient Israel*. Winona Lake, Ind.: Eisenbrauns, 1995.

Hayes, J. H. "The Usage of Oracles against Foreign Nations in Ancient Israel." *JBL* 87 (1968): 81–92.

Heintz, J. G. "La 'fin' des prophètes bibliques? Nouvelles théories et documents sémitiques anciens." In *Oracles et prophéties dans l'antiquité: Actes du colloque de Strasbourg 15–17 juin 1995*. Ed. J. G. Heintz, 195–213. TCRPOGA 15. Paris, 1997.

———. "Prophetie in Mari und Israel." *Biblica* 52 (1971): 543–55.

Hendel, Ronald S. "Prophets, Priest, and the Efficacy of Ritual." In *Pomegranates and Golden Bells: Studies in Biblical, Jewish, and Near Eastern Ritual, Law and Literature in Honor of Jacob Milgrom*. Ed. D. P. Wright et al., 185–98. Winona Lake, Ind.: Eisenbrauns, 1995.

Heschel, A. *The Prophets*. New York: Harper and Row, 1962.

Hoffmann, Y. "The Day of the Lord as a Concept and a Term in the Prophetic Literature." *ZAW* 93.1 (1981): 37–50.

Hogenhaven, J. "Prophecy and Propaganda: Aspects of Political and Religious Reasoning in Israel and the Ancient Near East." *SJOT* 1 (1989): 125–41.

Holladay, J. S. "Assyrian Statecraft and the Prophets of Israel." *HTR* 63 (1970): 29–51.

Hölscher, G. *Die Profeten*. Leipzig: J. C. Hinrichs, 1914.

Hossfeld, F. L., and I. L. Meyer. *Prophet gegen Prophet*. Freibourg, 1973.

House, P. R. *The Unity of the Twelve*. JSOTSS 77. Sheffield, England: JSOT Press, 1990.

Houston, W. "What Did the Prophets Think They Were Doing?: Speech Acts and Prophetic Discourse in the Old Testament." In *"The Place Is Too Small for Us": The Israelite Prophets in Recent Scholarship*. Ed. R. P. Gordon, 133–53. SBTS 5. Winona Lake, Ind.: Eisenbrauns, 1995.

Huffmon, H. B. "The Expansion of Prophecy in the Mari Archives: New Texts, New Readings, New Information." In *Prophecy and Prophets: The Diversity of Contemporary Issues in Scholarship*. Ed. Y. Gitay, 7–22. Atlanta: Scholars, 1997.

———. "The Origins of Prophecy." In *Magnalia Dei—The Mighty Acts of God: Essays on the Bible and Archaeology in Memory of G. Ernest Wright*. Ed. F. M. Cross et al., 171–86. Garden City, 1976.

———. "Priestly Divination in Israel." In *The Word of the Lord Shall Go Forth: Essays in Honor of David Noel Freedman in Celebration of His Sixtieth Birthday*. Ed. C. L. Meyers and M. O'Connor, 355–59. Winona Lake, Ind.: Eisenbrauns, 1983.

Husser, J-M. *Dreams and Dream Narratives in the Biblical World*. Biblical Seminar 63. Sheffield, England: JSOT Press, 1999.

Hutter, M. "Der Legitime Platz der Magie in den Religionen des Alten Orients." *Granz Gebiete der Wissenschaft* 36 (1987): 315–28.

Janzen, W. *Mourning Cry and Woe Oracle*. BZAW 125. Berlin, 1972.

Jarick, J. "The Seven (?) Prophetesses of the Old Testament." *LTJ* 28 (1994): 116–21.

Jeffers, A. *Magic and Divination in Ancient Palestine and Syria*. Leiden, Netherlands: E. J. Brill, 1996.

Jeremias, J. *Kultprophetie und Gerichtsverkündigung in der späten Königszeit Israel*. Neukirchen, 1970.

Johnson, A. R. *The Cultic Prophet and Israel's Psalmody*. Cardiff: Univ. of Wales Press, 1979.

———. *The Cultic Prophet in Ancient Israel*. Cardiff: Univ. of Wales Press, 1944.

Johnston, A. "Prophetic Leadership in Israel." *TBT* 34 (1996): 83–88.

Keel, O., and C. Uehlinger. *Gods, Goddesses, and Images of God in Ancient Israel*. Minneapolis, Minn.: Fortress, 1998.

Kitchen, K. "The Patriarchal Age: Myth or History?" *BAR* 21 (March/April 1995): 48–57, 88–95.

Knight, H. *The Hebrew Prophetic Consciousness*. London: Lutterworth Press, 1947.

Koch, K. "Die Briefe 'Prophitischen' Inhalts aus Mari: Bermerkungen zu Gattung und Sitz im Leben." *UF* 4 (1972): 53–77.

———. *Die Profeten*. 2 Vols. Stuttgart: W. Kohlhammer, 1978.

Laato, A. *History and Ideology in the Old Testament Prophetic Literature: A Semiotic Approach to the Reconstruction of the Historical Prophets*. OTS 41. Stockholm, 1996.

Landsberger, B., and H. Tadmor. "Fragments of Clay Liver Models from Hazor." *IEJ* 4 (1964): 201–18.

Lang, B. *Monotheism and the Prophetic Minority: An Essay in Biblical History and Sociology*. Social World of Biblical Antiquity 1. Sheffield, England: JSOT Press, 1983.

———. "Prophetie, prophetische Zeichenhandlungen und Politik in Israel." *Tübinger Theologische Quartalschrift*. 161 (1981): 275–80.

Leavitt, J. "Poetics, Prophetics, Inspiration." In *Poetry and Prophecy: The Anthropology of Inspiration*. Ed. J. Leavitt, 1–60. Ann Arbor, Mich.: University of Michigan Press, 1997.

Lemaire, A. Les textes prophétiques de Mari dans leurs relations avec l'Ouest." In *Mari, Ebla et les Hourrites: Dix ans de travaux. Actes du Colloque International. (Paris, Mai 1993)*. Ed. J.-M. Durand, 427–38. Paris, 1996.

Lieven, Alexandra von. "Divination in Ägypten." *Altorientalische Forschungen* 26 (1999): 77–126.

Lindblom, J. "Die Religion der Propheten und die Mystik." *ZAW* 16 (1939): 65–74.

———. *Prophecy in Ancient Israel*. Oxford: Blackwell, 1962.

Lods, Adolphe. "Magie hébraïque et magie cananéenne." *RHPR* 7 (1927): 12–25.

Long, Burke O. "Divination as Model for Literary Form." In *Language in Religious Practice*. Ed. W. J. Samarin, 84–100. Rowley: Newbury House, 1976.

Long, B. O. "The Effect of Divination upon Israelite Literature." *JBL* 92 (1973): 489–97.

——. "Prophetic Authority as Social Reality." In *Canon and Authority: Essays in Old Testament Religion and Theology*. Ed. G. W. Coats et al., 3–20. Philadelphia: Fortress, 1977.

——. "Prophetic Call Traditions and Reports of Visions." *ZAW* 84 (1972): 494–500.

——. "Social Dimensions of Prophetic Conflict." In *"The Place Is Too Small for Us": The Israelite Prophets in Recent Scholarship*. Ed. R. P. Gordon, 308–31. SBTS 5. Winona Lake, Ind.: Eisenbrauns, 1995.

——. "The Social Setting for Prophetic Miracle Stories." *Semeia* 3 (1975): 46–63.

Loretz, O. "Nekromantie und Totenevokation in Mesopotamien, Ugarit und Israel." In *Religionsgeschichtliche Beziehungen zwischen Kleinasien, Nordsyrien, und dem Alten Testament: Internationales Symposion Hamburg 17.–21. März 1990*. Ed. B. Janowski et al., 285–318. OBO 129. Gottingen, Germany: Vanderhoeck und Ruprecht, 1993.

Lust, J. "On Wizards and Prophets." *VTS* 26 (1974): 133–42.

Malamat, A. "Episodes Involving Samuel and Saul and the Prophetic Texts from Mari." In *Hesed Ve-Emet: Studies in Honor of Ernest S. Frerichs*. Ed. J. Magness and Seymour Gitin, 225–29. BJS 320. Atlanta: Scholars, 1998.

——. *Mari and the Early Israelite Experience*. Oxford: Oxford University Press, 1989.

——. "A Mari Prophecy and Nathan's Dynastic Oracle." In *Prophecy: Essays Presented to G. Fohrer*. Ed. J. A. Emerton, 68–82. BZAW 150. Berlin, 1980.

——. "A New Prophetic Message from Aleppo and Its Biblical Counterparts." In *Understanding Poets and Prophets*. Ed. A. G. Auld, 236–41. JSOTSS 152. Sheffield, England: JSOT Press, 1993.

——. "Parallels between the New Prophecies from Mari and Biblical Prophecy." *NABU* 4 (1989): 61-64.

——. "Prophecy at Mari." In *"The Place Is Too Small for Us": The Israelite Prophets in Recent Scholarship*. Ed. R. P. Gordon, 50–73. SBTS 5. Winona Lake, Ind.: Eisenbrauns, 1995.

——. "The Secret Council and Prophetic Involvement in Mari and Israel." In *Prophetie und geschichtliche Wirklichkeit im alten Israel*. Ed. R. Liwak and S. Wagner, 231–236. Stuttgart: W. Kohlhammer, 1991.

——. "Two Parallels between New Mari Prophecies and Biblical Prophecy." In *Studies in the Archaeology and History of Ancient Israel in Honour of Moshe Dothan*. Ed. M. Heltzer et al. 107–10. Haifa, 1993 (in Hebrew).

Marcus, D. *From Balaam to Jonah: Anti-Prophetic Satire in the Hebrew Bible*. Atlanta: Scholars, 1995.

Marx, A. "Rahab, prostituée et prophetesse: Josue 2 et 6." *ETR* 55 (1980): 72–76.

Matthews, V. H. *Social World of the Hebrew Prophets*. Peabody, Mass.: Hendrickson, 2001.

Mayes, A. D. H. "Prophecy and Society in Israel." In *Of Prophets' Visions and the Wisdom of Sages*. Ed. H. A. McKay and D. J. A. Clines, 25–42. JSOTSS 162. Sheffield, England: JSOT Press, 1993.

Mays, J. L., ed. *Interpreting the Prophets*. Philadelphia, 1987.

McDermot, V. *The Cult of the Seer in the Ancient Middle East*. Berkeley, 1971.

McKane, W. "Prophet and Institution." *ZAW* 94 (1982): 251–66.

———. *Prophets and Wise Men*. Naperville: SCM Press, 1965.

Mead, J. K. "Kings and Prophets, Donkeys and Lions: Dramatic Shape and Deuteronomistic Rhetoric in 1 Kings xiii." *VT* 49 (1999): 191–205.

Melugin, R. F. "Prophetic Books and the Problem of Historical Reconstruction." In *Prophets and Paradigms: Essays in Honor of Gene M. Tucker*. Ed. S. B. Reid, 62–78. JSOTSS 229. Sheffield, England: JSOT Press, 1996.

Michaelsen, P. "Ecstasy and Possession in Ancient Israel: A Review of Some Recent Contributions." *SJOT* 2 (1989): 28–54.

Miller, J. E. "Dreams and Prophetic Visions." *Biblica* 71 (1990): 401–4.

Miller, P. D. "The Divine Council and the Prophetic Call to War." *VT* 18 (1968): 100–7.

———. "The Prophetic Critique of Kings." *Ex Auditu* 2 (1986): 82–95.

Moran, W. L. "New Evidence from Mari on the History of Prophecy." *Biblica* 50 (1969): 15–56.

Moriarty, F. L. "Word as Power in the Ancient Near East." In *A Light Unto My Path: Old Testament Studies in Honor of J. M. Myers*. Ed. H. N. Bream, et al., 345–62. Philadelphia, 1974.

Mowinkel, S. *Prophecy and Tradition: The Prophetic Books in the Light of the Study of the Growth and History of the Tradition*. Oslo, 1946.

———. "The 'Spirit' and the 'Word' in the Pre-exilic Reforming Prophets." *JBL* 53 (1934): 199–227.

Müller, D. H. *Die Propheten in ihre ursprünglichen Form*. Vienna, 1896.

Murray, D. F. "The Rhetoric of Disputation: Re-examination of a Prophetic Genre." *JSOT* 38 (1987): 95–121.

Nakata, I. "Two Remarks on the So-called Prophetic Texts from Mari." *ASJ* 4 (1982): 143–48.

Nicholson, Ernest W. "Prophecy and Covenant." In *"The Place Is Too Small for Us": The Israelite Prophets in Recent Scholarship*. Ed. R. P. Gordon, 345–53. SBTS 5. Winona Lake, Ind.: Eisenbrauns, 1995.

Niditch, S. *Ancient Israelite Religion*. Oxford: Oxford University Press, 1997.

———. *The Symbolic Vision in Biblical Tradition.* HSM 30. Chico, 1983.

Nissinen, M. *References to Prophecy in Neo-Assyrian Sources.* SAAS 7. Helsinki, 1998.

———. "The Socioreligious Role of the Neo-Assyrian Prophets." In *Prophecy in Its Ancient Near Eastern Context: Mesopotamian, Biblical, and Arabian Perspectives.* Ed. Martti Nissenen, 89–114. SBLSS 13. Atlanta: Scholars, 2000.

———. "Spoken, Written, Quoted, and Invented: Orality and Writtenness in Ancient Near Eastern Prophecy." In *Writings and Speech in Israelite and Ancient Near Eastern Prophecy.* Ed. E. Ben Zvi and M. H. Floyd, 235–71. SBLSS 10. Atlanta: Scholars, 2000.

Noegel, S. B. "Dreams and Dream Interpreters in Mesopotamia and in the Hebrew Bible (Old Testament)." In *Dreams and Dreaming: A Reader in Religion, Anthropology, History, and Psychology.* Ed. K. Bulkeley, 45–71. Hampshire, 2001.

———. *Puns and Pundits: Wordplay in the Hebrew Bible and Ancient Near Eastern Literature.* Bethesda, Md.: CDL Press, 2000.

Oppenheim, A. L. *The Interpretation of Dreams in the Ancient Near East: With a Translation of the Assyrian Dream Book.* TAPS 46.3. Philadelphia, 1956.

———. "Mantic Dreams in the Ancient Near East." In *The Dream and Human Societies.* Ed. G. E. von Grunebaum and Caillois, 341–59. Berkeley: University of California Press, 1966.

Osswald, E. *Falsche Prophetie im Alten Testament.* Tübingen, Germany: 1962.

Östborn, G. *Yahweh and Baal.* Lund: Guerup, 1956.

Overholt, T. W. *Channels of Prophecy: The Social Dynamics of Prophetic Activity.* Minneapolis, Minn.: Fortress, 1989.

———. "The End of Prophecy: No Players without a Program." In *"The Place Is Too Small for Us": The Israelite Prophets in Recent Scholarship.* Ed. R. P. Gordon, 527–38. SBTS 5. Winona Lake, Ind.: Eisenbrauns, 1995.

———. *Prophecy in Cross-Cultural Perspective.* SBLSS 17. Atlanta: Scholars, 1986.

———. "Prophecy in History: The Social Reality of Intermediation." In *"The Place Is Too Small for Us": The Israelite Prophets in Recent Scholarship.* Ed. R. P. Gordon, 354–76. SBTS 5. Winona Lake, Ind.: Eisenbrauns, 1995.

———. "Prophecy: The Problem of Cross-Cultural Comparison." *Semeia* 21 (1982): 55–78.

———. "Seeing Is Believing: The Social Setting of Prophetic Acts of Power." *JSOT* 23 (1982): 3–31.

Parker, S. B. "The Lachish Letters and Official Reactions to Prophecies." In *Uncovering Ancient Stones: Essays in Memory of H. Neil Richardson.* Ed. L. M. Hopfe, 65–78. Winona Lake, Ind.: Eisenbrauns, 1994.

———. "Official Attitudes toward Prophecy at Mari and in Israel." *VT* 43 (1993): 50–68.

——. "Possession Trance and Prophecy in Pre-exilic Israel." *VT* 28 (1978): 271–85.

——. *Stories in Scripture and Inscriptions: Comparative Studies on Narratives in Northwest Semitic Inscriptions and the Hebrew Bible*. New York, 1997.

Parpola, S. *Assyrian Prophecies*. SAAS 9. Helsinki, 1997.

——. "The Assyrian Tree of Life: Tracing the Origins of Jewish Monotheism and Greek Philosophy." *JNES* 52 (1993): 161–208.

——. "Mesopotamian Astrology and Astronomy as Domains of Mesopotamian 'Wisdom.'" In *Die Rolle der Astonomie in den Kulteren Mesopotamiens: Beiträge zum 3. Grazer Morganländischen Symposion [23.–27. September 1991]*. Ed. H. D. Galter, 47–59. Graz, 1993.

Patai, R. "The 'Control of Rain' in Ancient Palestine: A Study in Comparative Religion." *HUCA* 14 (1939): 251–86.

Paul, S. M. "Heavenly Tablets and the Book of Life." *JANES* 5 (1973): 345–53.

Person, R. F. "The Ancient Israelite Scribe as Performer." *JBL* 117 (1998): 601–9.

Petersen, D. L. "Ecstacy and Role Enactment." In *"The Place Is Too Small for Us": The Israelite Prophets in Recent Scholarship*. Ed. R. P. Gordon, 279–88. SBTS 5. Winona Lake, Ind.: Eisenbrauns, 1995.

——. "Israelite Prophecy: Change versus Continuity." In *Congress Volume Leuven 1989*. Ed. J. A. Emerton, 190–203. Leiden, Netherlands: E. J. Brill, 1991.

——. *Late Israelite Prophecy*. Missoula, Mont.: Scholars, 1977.

——. "Rethinking the Nature of Prophetic Literature." In *Prophecy and Prophets: The Diversity of Contemporary Issues in Scholarship*. Ed. Y. Gitay, 23–40. Atlanta: Scholars, 1997.

——. *The Role of Israel's Prophets*. JSOTSS 17. Sheffield, England: JSOT Press, 1981.

Philips, A. "The Ecstatics' Father." In *Word and Meanings*. Ed. P. R. Ackroyd and B. Lindars, 183–94. Cambridge: Cambridge University Press, 1968.

Plöger, O. *Theocracy and Eschatology*. Richmond: John Knox Press, 1968.

Porter, J. R. "Ancient Israel." In *Divination and Oracles*. Ed. M. Loewe and C. Blacker, 191–214. London, 1981.

Prophetie und geschichtliche Wirklichkeit im alten Israel. Ed. R. Liwak and S. Wagner. Stuttgart: W. Kohlhammer, 1991.

Rabin, C. "Notes on the Habakkuk Scroll and the Zadokite Documents." *VT* 5 (1955): 148–162.

Rabinowitz, I. *A Witness Forever: Ancient Israel's Perception of Literature and the Resultant Hebrew Bible*. Bethesda, Md.: Capitol Decisions Limited Press, 1993.

Rad, G. von. *The Message of the Prophets*. London, 1968.

——. "Origin of the Concept of the Day of Yahweh." *JSS* 4 (1959): 97–108.

——. *Theologie des Alten Testaments. Vol. 2: Die Theologie der prophetischen Überlieferungen Israels*. Munich, 1960.

Raitt, T. M. "The Prophetic Summons to Repentance." *ZAW* 83 (1971): 30–49.

Reiner, E. *Astral Magic in Babylonia*. TAPS 85.4. Philadelphia, 1995.

Renteria, T. H. "The Socio-Cultural Analysis of Prophets and People in Ninth Century BCE Israel." In *Elijah and Elisha in Socio-Cultural Perspective*. Ed. R. B. Coote, 75–126. Atlanta: Scholars, 1992.

Ricks, Stephen D. "The Magician as Outsider in the Hebrew Bible and the New Testament." In *Ancient Magic and Ritual Power*. Ed. M. Meyer and P. Mirecki, 131–43. RGRW 129. Leiden, Netherlands: E. J. Brill, 1995.

Ringgren, H. "Israelite Prophecy: Fact or Fiction?" In *Congress Volume: Jerusalem, 1986*. Ed. J. A. Emerton, 204–10. VTS 40. Leiden, Netherlands: E. J. Brill, 1988.

Ritner, R. K. "Dream Oracles." In *The Context of Scripture. Vol. I: Canonical Compositions from the Biblical World*. Ed. W. W. Hallo, 52–54. Leiden, Netherlands: E. J. Brill, 1997.

——. *The Mechanics of Ancient Egyptian Magical Practice*. SAOC 54. Chicago, 1993.

Ritter, E. K. "Magical Expert (= Ašipu) and Physician (= Asû): Notes on Two Complementary Professions in Babylonian Medicine." *AS* 16 (1965): 229–323.

Robinson, H. W. "Prophetic Symbolism." In *Old Testament Essays*. Ed. D. C. Simpson, 1–17. London, 1927.

Robinson, J. W. *Inspiration and Revelation in the Old Testament*. Oxford: Greenwood Publishing Group, 1946.

Robinson, T. H. *Prophecy and the Prophets in Ancient Israel*. London: Duckworth, 1923.

Rofé, A. "Classes in the Prophetical Stories: Didactic Legends and Parables." In *Studies on Prophecy,* 143–64. VTSup 26. Leiden, Netherlands: E. J. Brill, 1974.

——. "The Classification of the Prophetical Stories." *JBL* 89 (1970): 429–30.

——. *The Prophetical Stories*. Jerusalem: The Magnes Press, 1988.

Ross, J. "Prophecy in Hamath, Israel and Mari." *HTR* 63 (1970): 1–28.

Rowley, H. H. "The Nature of Prophecy in the Light of Recent Study." *HTR* 38 (1945): 1–38.

Saggs, H. W. F. *The Encounter with the Divine in Mesopotamia and Israel*. London: Athlone Press, 1978.

Sasson, J. M. "Water beneath Straw: Adventures of a Prophetic Phrase in the Mari Archives." In *Solving Riddles and Untying Knots: Biblical, Epigraphic, and Semitic Studies in Honor of Jonas C. Greenfield*. Ed. Ziony Zevit et al., 599–608. Winona Lake, Ind.: Eisenbrauns, 1995.

Sawyer, J. F. A. "Prophecy and Interpretation." In *"The Place Is Too Small for Us": The Israelite Prophets in Recent Scholarship*. Ed. R. P. Gordon, 563–75. SBTS 5. Winona Lake, Ind.: Eisenbrauns, 1995.

————. *Prophecy and the Biblical Prophets*. Oxford, 1993.

Schmidt, B. B. *Israel's Beneficent Dead: Ancestor Cult and Necromancy in Ancient Israelite Religion and Tradition*. Winona Lake, Ind.: Eisenbrauns, 1996.

————. "The 'Witch' of En-dor, 1 Samuel 28, and Ancient Near Eastern Necromancy." In *Ancient Magic and Ritual Power*. Ed. M. Meyer and P. Mirecki, 111–29. Leiden, Netherlands: E. J. Brill, 1995.

Schmidt, W. H. "Contemporary Issues." In *"The Place Is Too Small for Us": The Israelite Prophets in Recent Scholarship*. Ed. R. P. Gordon, 579–81. SBTS 5. Winona Lake, Ind.: Eisenbrauns, 1995.

Schmitt, A. *Prophetischer Gottesbescheid in Mari und Israel*. Stuggart, Germany: Kohlhammer, 1982.

Schniedewind, W. M. *The Word of God in Tradition: From Prophet to Exegete in the Second Temple Period*. JSOTSS 197. Sheffield, England: JSOT Press, 1995.

Scholem, G. *The Messianic Idea in Judaism*. New York: Schoken Books, 1971.

Scurlock, J. A. "Baby-Snatching Demons, Restless Souls and the Dangers of Childbirth: Medico-Magical Means of Dealing with Some of the Perils of Motherhood in Ancient Mesopotamia." *Icognita* 2 (1991): 137–85.

————. "Physician, Exorcist, Conjurer, Magician: A Tale of Two Healing Professionals." In *Mesopotamian Magic: Textual, Historical, and Interpretive Perspectives*. Ed. T. Abusch and K. van der Toorn, 69–79. Studies in Ancient Magic and Divination 1. Gröningen, Netherlands, 1998.

Seitz, C. "The Divine Council: Temporal Transition and New Prophecy." *JBL* 109 (1990): 229–47.

Seybold, K. *Satirische Prophetie: Studien zum Buch Zefanja*. Stuttgart, Germany: W. Kohlhammer, 1985.

Silberman, L. H. "Unriddling the Riddle: A Study in the Structure and Language of the Habakkuk Pesher." *RdQ* 11 (1961): 323–64.

Sister, M. "Die Typen der prophetischen Visionen in der Bibel." *MGWJ* 78 (1934): 399–430.

Soll, W. M. "Babylonian and Biblical Acrostics." *Biblica* 69 (1988): 305–22.

Sommer, B. D. "Did Prophecy Cease? Evaluating a Reevaluation." *JBL* 115 (1996): 31–47.

Sperling, D. "Akkadian *egerrû* and Hebrew *bt qwl*." *JANES* 4 (1972): 63–74.

Stacey, W. D. "The Function of Prophetic Drama." In *"The Place Is Too Small for Us": The Israelite Prophets in Recent Scholarship*. Ed. R. P. Gordon, 112–32. SBTS 5. Winona Lake, Ind.: Eisenbrauns, 1995.

Stone, M. *Scriptures, Sects, and Visions*. Philadelphia: Fortress & Blackwells, 1980.

Stuart, D. "Sovereign's Day of Conquest." *BASOR* 221 (1976): 159–64.

Tropper, J. *Nekromantie: Totenbefragung in alten Orient und im Alten Testament*. AOAT 223. Neukirchen-Vluyn: Neukirchener Verlag, 1989.

Tucker, G. M. "The Futile Quest for the Historical Prophet." In *A Biblical Itinerary: In Search of Method, Form and Content. Essays in Honor of George W. Coats*. Ed. E. E. Carpenter, 144–52. JSOTSS 240. Sheffield, England: JSOT Press, 1997.

———. "Prophetic Speech." In *Interpreting the Prophets*. Ed. J. L. Mays and P. J. Achtemeier, 27–40. Philadelphia, 1987.

———. "Prophetic Superscriptions and the Growth of a Canon." In *Canon and Authority*. Ed. G. W. Coats and B. O. Long, 56–70. Philadelphia: Fortress Press, 1977.

Uffenheimer, B. "Prophecy, Ecstacy, and Sympathy." In *Congress Volume: Jerusalem 1986*. Ed. J. A. Emerton, 257–69. VTS 40. Leiden, Netherlands: E. J. Brill, 1988.

Urbach, E. E. "When Did Prophecy Cease?" *Tarbiz* 17 (1946): 1–27.

Van Dam, C. *The Urim and Thummim: A Means of Revelation in Ancient Israel*. Winona Lake, Ind.: Eisenbrauns, 1997.

Van Winkle, D. W. "1 Kings 13: True and False Prophecy." *VT* 39 (1989): 31-43.

VanderKam, J. C. "The Prophetic-Sapiential Origins of Apocalyptic Thought." In *A Word in Season*. Ed. J. D. Martin and P. R. Davies, 63–76. JSOTSS 42. Sheffield, England: JSOT Press, 1986.

Vaux, R. de. *Ancient Israel*. 2 Vols. New York: McGraw-Hill, 1961.

Vawter, B. "Where the Prophets *nābî's?*" *Biblica* 66 (1985): 206-220.

Vermes, G. "Bible and Midrash: Early Old Testament Exegesis." In *Cambridge History of the Bible*. Vol. 1. Ed. P. R. Ackroyd et al., 199–231. Cambridge: Cambridge University Press, 1970.

Vidal, D. *L'ablatif absolu: théorie du prophétisme*. Paris, 1977.

Warner, S. M. "Primitive Saga Men." *VT* 29 (1979): 325–35.

Weinfeld, Moshe. "Ancient Near Eastern Patterns in Prophetic Literature." In *"The Place Is Too Small for Us": The Israelite Prophets in Recent Scholarship*. Ed. R. P. Gordon, 32–49. SBTS 5. Winona Lake, Ind.: Eisenbrauns, 1995.

Weippert, M. "Assyrische Prophetien der Zeit Asarhaddons und Assurbanipals." In *Assyrian Royal Inscriptions: New Horizons*. Ed. F. M. Fales, 71–115. OAC 17. Rome, 1981.

———. "The Balaam Text from Deir 'Alla and the Study of the Old Testament." In *The Balaam Text from Deir `Alla Reevaluated*. Ed. J. Hoftijzer and G. van der Kooij, 151–84. Leiden, Netherlands: E. J. Brill, 1991.

Weiss, M. "The Origin of the 'Day of the Lord'—Reconsidered." *HUCA* 37 (1966): 29–71.

Wellhausen, J. *Die kleinen Propheten*. Berlin, 1892. Reprinted, 1963.

Werblowsky, R. J. Z. "Mystical and Magical Contemplation." *HR* 1 (1961): 9–36.

Westermann, C. *The Basic Forms of Prophetic Speech*. Philadelphia: Westminster John Knox Press, 1967.

———. *Grundformen prophetischer Rede*. Munich: Raiser, 1960.

———. *Prophetic Oracles of Salvation in the Old Testament.* Louisville, Ky.: John Knox, 1991.

———. *Prophetische Heilsworte im Alten Testament.* FRLANT 145. Göttingen, Germany: Vanderhoeck und Ruprecht, 1987.

Widengren, G. *Literary and Psychological Aspects of the Hebrew Prophets.* Uppsala, Sweden, 1948.

Williams, J. "The Alas-Oracles of the Eighth Century Prophets." *HUCA* 38 (1967): 75–91.

Williams, J. "The Social Location of Israelite Prophecy." *JAAR* 37 (1969): 153–65.

Williams, J. G. "The Prophetic 'Father': A Brief Explanation of the Term 'Sons of the Prophets.'" *JBL* 85 (1966): 344–48.

Wilson, R. R. "Interpreting Israel's Religion: An Anthropological Perspective on the Problem of False Prophecy." In *"The Place Is Too Small for Us": The Israelite Prophets in Recent Scholarship.* Ed. R. P. Gordon, 332–44. SBTS 5. Winona Lake, Ind.: Eisenbrauns, 1995.

———. "Prophecy and Ecstacy: A Reexamination." *JBL* 98 (1979): 321–37.

———. *Prophecy and Society in Ancient Israel.* Philadelphia: Fortress, 1980.

———. "Prophecy in Crisis: The Call of Ezekiel." *Interpretation* 38 (1984): 117-130.

Wohl, H. "The Problem of the *Mahhû*." *JANES* 3 (1970): 112–18.

Wolff, H. W. "Prophecy from the Eighth through the Fifth Century." *Interpreting the Prophets.* Ed. J. L. Mays and P. J. Achtemeier, 14–26. Philadelphia, 1987.

Zevit, Z. *The Religions of Ancient Israel: A Synthesis of Parallactic Approaches.* London: Continuum, 2001.

Ziegler, J. *Duodecim prophetae.* Göttingen: Vanderhoeck und Ruprecht, 1943.

Zimmerli, W. "From Prophetic Word to Prophetic Book." In *"The Place Is Too Small for Us": The Israelite Prophets in Recent Scholarship.* Ed. R. P. Gordon, 419–42. SBTS 5. Winona Lake, Ind.: Eisenbrauns, 1995.

———. *The Law and the Prophets: A Study of the Meaning of the Old Testament.* Oxford, 1965.

———. "The Word of Divine Self-Manifestation (Proof-Saying): A Prophetic Genre." In *"I am Jahwe."* Ed. W. Brueggemann, 99–110. Atlanta: Scholars, 1982.

PROPHECY: HELLENISM, JUDAISM, AND LATE ANTIQUITY

Adorno, F., ed. *La cultura ellenistica.* 2 vols. Milan, 1977.

Ahrens, W. "Die magischen Quadrate al-Buni's." *Der Islam* 12 (1922): 167–77, 14 (1925): 104–10.

———. "Studien uber di magischen Quadrate der Araber." *Der Islam* 7 (1917): 186–250.

Alexander, P. "Bavli Berakhot 55a–57b: The Talmudic Dreambook in Context." *JJS* 46 (1995): 231–48.

Aune, D. E. *Prophecy in Early Christianity and the Ancient Mediterranean World.* Grand Rapids, Mich.: Eerdmans, 1983.

Bailey, H. W. *Zoroastrian Problems in Ninth-Century Books.* Oxford: Oxford University Press, 1943.

Bakan, D. *Maimonides on Prophecy: A Commentary on Selected Chapters of the Guide to the Perplexed.* London: Jason Aronson, 1991.

Bedhn, J. D. "Magical Bowls and Manichaeans." In *Ancient Magic and Ritual Power.* Ed. M. Meyer and P. Mirecki, 419–34. Religions in the Graeco-Roman World 129. Leiden, Netherlands: E. J. Brill, 1995.

Berlin, Adele. *Biblical Poetry through Medieval Eyes.* Bloomington: Indiana University Press, 1991.

Bernstein, M. S. "The Stories of the Prophets: Intertextuality in Judaism and Islam." *Journal of the Association of Graduate Studies in Near Eastern Studies* 1 (1990): 27–36.

Beyschlag, K. *Simon Magus und die christliche Gnosis.* WUNT 16. Tübingen, Germany: Mohr, 1975.

Bickerman, E. *Religion and Politics in the Hellenistic and Roman Periods.* Ed. E. Gabba and M. Smith. Como, 1985.

Bidez, J., and F. Cumont. *Les Mages Hellenisés.* 2 vols. Paris, 1938.

Boccaccini, G. *Middle Judaism: Jewish Thought 300 B.C.E. to 200 C.E.* Minneapolis, Minn.: Fortress, 1991.

Böhling, A. *Mysterion und Wahrheit: Gesammelte Beiträge zur spätantiken Religionsgeschichte.* Leiden, Netherlands: E. J. Brill, 1968.

Boyce, M. A. *History of Zoroastrianism.* 2 vols. Leiden, Netherlands: E. J. Brill, 1975, 1982.

———. "The Manichaean Literature in Middle Iranian." *Handbuch der Orientalistik* 4.2.1. Leiden, Netherlands: E. J. Brill, 1968, 67–76.

———. *Persian Stronghold of Zoroastrianism.* Oxford: Oxford University Press, 1977.

———. *Textual Sources for the Study of Zoroastrianism.* Manchester: Manchester University Press, 1984.

———. *Zoroastrians: Their Religious Beliefs and Practices.* 3rd ed. London: Routledge, 1987.

Brady, M., and J. C. VanderKam. *Prophetic Traditions at Qumran: A Study of 4Q383–391.* Ph.D. Dissertation, University of Notre Dame, 2000.

Brandt, W. *Die mandäische Religion.* Leipzig: J. C. Hinrichs, 1889. Reprint, Amsterdam: Philo, 1973.

Braun, H. *Spätjüdische-härestischer und frühchristlicher Radikalismus.* 2nd ed. 2 vols. BHT 24.1–2. Tübingen, Germany: Mohr, 1969.

Bréhier, E. *La Philosophie de Plotin*. Paris, 1928.

Brown, J. P. *Israel and Hellas*. Vol. 1. BZAW 231. Berlin: Walter de Gruyter, 1995.

———. *Israel and Hellas: Sacred Institutions with Roman Counterparts*. Vol 2. BZAW 276. Berlin: Walter de Gruyter, 2000.

———. "The Mediterranean Seer and Shamanism." *ZAW* 93 (1981): 374–400.

Brown, P. "The Rise and Function of the Holy Man in Late Antiquity." *JRS* 61 (1971): 80–101.

Bryder, P., ed. *Manichaean Studies: Proceedings of the First International Conference on Manichaeism*. Lovanii: International Association of Manichaean Studies, 1988.

Buber, M. *The Prophetic Faith*. New York: Harper, 1949.

Buck, C. "The Identity of the Sabi'un: An Historical Quest." *MW* 74 (1984): 172–86.

Burkert, W. *Greek Religion*. Trans. J. Raffan. Oxford: Basil Blackwell, 1985.

———. "Itinerant Diviners and Magicians: A Neglected Element in Cultural Contacts." In *The Greek Renaissance of the Eighth Century B.C. Tradition and Innovation*. Ed. R. Hägg, 115–19. Proceedings of the Second International Symposium at the Swedish Institute in Athens, 1–5 June 1981. Stockholm: Svenska Institutet i Athen, 1983.

———. *Lore and Science in Ancient Pythagoreanism*. Cambridge, Mass.: Harvard University Press, 1971.

Burkitt, F. C. *The Religion of the Manichees*. Cambridge: Cambridge University Press, 1925.

Casadio, Giovanni. "The Manichaean Metempsychosis: Typology and Historical Roots." In *Studia Manichaica II. Internationaler Kongress zum Manichäismus*. Ed. G. Wiessner and H -J. Klimkeit, 105–30. Wiesbaden, Germany: Otto Harrassowitz, 1992.

Christensen, A. *L'Iran sous les Sassanides*. Copenhagen: Levin and Munksgaard, 1936.

Chwolsohn, D. *Die Sabier und der Ssabismus*. 2 vols. St. Petersburg, 1856; reprint, Amsterdam: Oriental Press, 1965.

Collins, J. J. *Between Athens and Jerusalem*. New York: Crossroad, 1983.

———. *Seers, Sybils, and Sages in Hellenistic-Roman Judaism*. Leiden, Netherlands: E. J. Brill, 1997

———, et al., eds. *Death, Ecstasy, and Other Worldly Journeys*. Albany: State University of New York Press, 1995.

Colpe, C. "Anpassung des Manichäismus an den Islam." *ZDMG* 109 (1959): 82–91.

Coq, A. *Die buddhistische Spätantike II: Die manichäischen Miniaturen*. Berlin: D. Reimer, 1923.

———. "Ein christliches und ein manichäisches Manuskriptfragment in türkischer Sprache aus Turfan." *Sitzungsberichte der Königlichen Preusissischen Akademie der Wissenschaften* (1909): 1202–218.

Corbin, H. *Cyclical Time and Ismaili Gnosis*. London: Kegan Paul, 1983.

Culiano, I. P. *The Tree of Gnosis: Gnostic Mythology from Early Christianity to Modern Nihilism*. Trans. H. S. Wiesner. San Francisco: Harper and Row, 1992.

Cumont, F. "La propagation du manichéisme dans l'Empire romain." *Revue d'Histoire de Littérature Religeuse*, n.s. 1 (1910): 31–43.

——. *Oriental Religions in Roman Paganism*. Chicago: Open Court Publishing Company, 1911.

——, and M. Kugener. *Recherches sur le manichéisme*. 2 vols. Brussels, 1908–1919.

Decret, F. *Aspects du manichéisme dans l'Afrique romaine*. Paris: Etudes Augustiniennes, 1970.

——. *L'Afrique manichéene: Étude historique et doctrinale*. 2 vols. Paris: Etudes Augustiniennes, 1978.

——. *Mani et la tradition manichéene*. Paris: Etudes Augustiniennes, 1974.

Dietrich, A. Ed. *Synkretismus im syrisch-persischen Kulturgebiet*. Göttingen, Germany: Vanderhoeck und Ruprecht, 1975.

Droge, A. J. *Homer or Moses?* Tübingen, Germany: Mohr, 1989.

Drower, E. S. *The Mandaeans of Iraq and Iran*. 2nd ed. Leiden, Netherlands: E. J. Brill, 1962.

Duchesne-Guillemin, J. *La religion de l'Iran ancien*. Paris: Presses Universitaires de France, 1962.

——. *Zoroastre: Étude critique avec une traduction commentée des Gatha*. Paris: G. P. Maisonneuve, 1948.

Fahd, T. *La divination arabe*. Paris: Sindbad, 1987.

Feldman, L. "Prophets and Prophecy in Josephus." *JTS* 41 (1990): 402–11.

Figulla, H. "Manichäer in Indien und das Zeitalter des tamulischen Dichters Manikkavacagar." *Archiv Orientalni* 17 (1937): 112–22.

Flügel, G. *Mani: Seine Lehre und seine Schriften*. Leipzig: J. C. Hinrichs, 1862.

Frazer, J. G. *Adonis, Attis, Osiris*. 3rd ed. London: Macmillan, 1914.

Fück, J. W. "The Arabic Literature on Alchemy according to an-Nadim (AD 987): A Translation of the Tenth Discourse on the Book of the Catalogue (al-Fihrist) with Introduction and Commentary." *Ambix* 9 (1951): 81-144.

Gabain, A. von. *Das uigurische Königreich von Chotscho 850–1250*. 2 vols. Wiesbaden, Germany: Otto Harrassowitz, 1973.

Geiger, B. "The Middle Iranian Texts." In *The Excavations at Dura Europos. Final Report VIII: Pt. 1. The Synagogue*, 283–317. New Haven, Conn.: Yale University Press, 1956.

Gershevitch, I. "Old Iranian Literature." In *Iranistik*. Ed. B. Spuler, 1–30. HO 1.4.2.1. Leiden, Netherlands: E. J. Brill, 1968.

Gese, H., et al. *Die Religionen Altsyriens, Altarabiens und der Mandäer*. Die Religionen der Menschheit Bd 10, 403–64. Stuttgart, Germany: W. Kohlhammer, 1970.

Giversen, S. The Manichaean Coptic Papyri in the Chester Beatty Library. 4 vols. *Cahiers d'Orientalisme* 13, 15–17. Geneva, 1986–1988.

Gnoli, G. *Zoroaster's Time and Homeland.* Naples: Istituto Universitario Orientale, 1980.

Goldfeld, A. "Women as Sources of Torah in the Rabbinic Tradition." *Judaism* 24 (1975): 245–56.

Goldin, J. "The Magic of Magic and Superstition." In *Judah Goldin: Studies in Midrash and Related Literature.* Ed. B. Eichler and J. H. Tigay, 337–57. Philadelphia: Jewish Studies Program, University of Pennsylvania, 1988.

Green, P., ed. *Hellenistic History and Culture.* Berkeley: University of California Press, 1993.

Green, T. *The City of the Moon God: Religious Traditions of Harran.* Leiden, Netherlands: E. J. Brill, 1992.

Gruenwald, I. "Manichaeism and Judaism in Light of the Cologne Mani Codex." *ZPE* 50 (1983): 29–43.

Halperin, D. J. *The Faces of the Chariot: Early Jewish Responses to Ezekiel's Vision.* Texte und Studien zum antiken Judentum 16. Tübingen, Germany: Mohr, 1988

———. *The Merkabah in Rabbinic Literature.* New Haven, Conn.: Yale University Press, 1980.

Hamilton, J. R. *Les Ouighours à l'époque des cinq dynasties d'après les documents chinois.* Paris: Impr. Nationale, 1955.

Heinrichs, A. "The Cologne Mani Codex Reconsidered." *HSCP* 83 (1979): 339–67.

Henning, W. B. "The Book of the Giants." *BSOAS* 11 (1943): 52–74.

———. "Ein manichäisches Henochbuch." *SPAW* 5 (1934): 27–35.

———. "Mani's Last Journey." *BSOAS* 10 (1942): 941–53.

———. "Neue Materialien zur Geschichte des Manichäismus." *ZDMG* 90 (1936): 1–18.

———. "Two Manichaean Magical Texts with an Excursus on the Parthian Ending—*endeh.*" *BSOAS* 12 (1947): 39–66.

Henrichs, A. "Mani and the Babylonian Baptists: A Historical Confrontation." *Harvard Studies in Classical Philology* 77 (1973): 23–59.

———. "'Thou Shalt Not Kill a Tree': Greek, Manichaean and Indian Tales." *Bulletin of the American Society of Papyrologists* 16 (1979): 85–108.

Herrera, R. A. *Mystics of the Book: Themes, Topics, and Typologies.* New York: P. Lang, 1993.

Hinnells, J. R., ed. *Mithraic Studies.* 2 vols. Manchester: Manchester University Press, 1973.

Idel, M., and B. McGinn. *Mystical Union in Judaism, Christianity, and Islam: An Ecumenical Dialogue.* New York: Continuum, 1999.

Jackson, A. *Zoroaster, The Prophet of Ancient Iran.* New York: Macmillan, 1899. Reprint, 1965.

Jackson, A. V. W. *Researches into Manichaeism with Special Reference to Turfan Fragments.* New York: Columbia University Press, 1932.

Jonas, H. *The Gnostic Religion: The Message of the Alien God and the Beginnings of Christianity.* 2nd ed. Boston: Beacon, 1963.

Kaerst, J. *Geschichte des Hellenismus.* 3rd ed. 2 vols. Leipzig: J. C. Hinrichs, 1926–27.

Katz, S. T. *Mysticism and Sacred Scripture.* Oxford: Oxford University Press, 2000.

Kessler, K. *Mani: Forschungen über die manichäische Religion.* Berlin, 1889.

King, K., ed. *Images of the Feminine in Gnosticism.* Philadelphia: Fortress, 1988.

Klíma, O. *Mazdak: Geschichte einer sozialen Bewegung im sassanidischen Persien.* Prague, 1957.

———. "Mazdak und die Juden." *Archív Orientálni* 24 (1956): 420–31.

Klimkeit, H. J. "Der Buddha Henoch: Qumran und Turfan." *ZRGG* 32 (1980): 367–76.

———. *Gnosis on the Silk Road: Gnostic Texts from Central Asia.* San Francisco: HarperSanFrancisco, 1993.

———. *Manichaean Art and Calligraphy.* Iconography of Religions, 20. Leiden, Netherlands: E. J. Brill, 1982.

———. "Manichaean Kingship: Gnosis at Home in the World." *Numen* 29 (1982): 17–32.

———. "Manichäische und buddhistische Beichtformelen aus Turfan." *ZRGG* 29 (1977): 193–28.

Langermann, Y. Zvi. "Some Astrological Themes in the Thought of Abraham Ibn Ezra." In *Rabbi Ibn Ezra: Studies in the Writings of a Twelfth-Century Polymath.* Ed. Isodore Twersky, 28–85. Cambridge, Mass.: Harvard University Press, 1993.

Lesses, R. "The Adjuration of the Prince of the Presence: Performative Utterance in a Jewish Ritual." In *Ancient Magic and Ritual Power.* Ed. M. Meyer and P. Mirecki, 185–206. RGRW 129. Leiden, Netherlands: E. J. Brill, 1995.

Levine, L. I. *Judaism and Hellenism in Antiquity: Conflict or Confluence?* Seattle: University of Washington Press, 1998.

Lewy, H. *Chaldaean Oracles and Theurgy.* Ed. M. Tardieu. Paris: Etudes Augustiniennes, 1978.

Lieberman, S. *Hellenism in Jewish Palestine.* New York: Jewish Theological Seminary of America, 1950.

Liebes, Y. *Studies in the Zohar.* Albany: State University of New York Press, 1993.

Lieu, Samuel N. C. *Manichaeism in the Later Roman Empire and Medieval China: A Historical Survey.* Manchester: Manchester University Press, 1985.

——. *The Religion of Light: An Introduction to the History of Manichaeism in China.* Hong Kong: Centre of Asian Studies, University of Hong Kong, 1979.

MacKerras, C. *The Uighur Empire.* Columbia: University of South Carolina Press, 1972.

Macuch, R. "Anfänge der Mandäer." In *Die Araber in der alten Welt.* Ed. Altheim and Stiehl, 2:76–190. Berlin: Walter de Gruyter, 1965.

——, ed. *Zur Sprache und Literatur der Mandäer.* Studia Mandaica 1. Berlin: De Gruyter, 1976.

Malandra, W. *An Introduction to Ancient Iranian Religion.* Minneapolis: University of Minnesota Press, 1983.

Marcovich, M. *Studies in Graeco-Roman Religions and Gnosticism.* Leiden, Netherlands: E. J. Brill, 1989.

McAuliffe, J. D. "Exegetical Identification of the Sabi'un." *MW* 72 (1982): 95–106.

Ménard, J. *De la Gnose au Manichéisme.* Paris: Cariscript, 1986.

Menasce, J. de. "Zoroastrian Literature after the Muslim Conquest." In *The Cambridge History of Iran.* Ed. R. N. Frye, 4:543–65. Cambridge: Cambridge University Press, 1975.

Merkelbach, R. *Mani und sein Religionssystem.* Opladen, Germany: Westdeutscheer Verlag, 1986.

——. *Roman und Mysterium in der Antike.* Munich: Beck, 1967.

Milik, J. T. "The End of Prophecy and the End of the Bible in the View of Seder 'Olam, Rabbinic Literature, and Related Texts." *Sidra* 10 (1994): 83–94.

Miller, F. "Prophecy in Judaism and Islam." *IS* 17.1 (1978): 27–44.

Molé, M. *Culte, mythe et cosmogonie dans l'Iran ancien.* Annales du Musée Guimet. Paris: Presses Universitaires de France, 1963.

——. *La légende de Zoroastre selon les textes pehlevis.* Travaux de l'Institut d'Études Iraniennes de l'Université de Paris. Paris: Presses Universitaires de France, 1967.

Müller, W. "Mazdak and the Alphabet Mysticism of the East." *HR* 3 (1963–64): 72–82.

Müller-Kessler, C., and T. Kwasman. "A Unique Talmudic Aramaic Incantation Bowl." *JAOS* 120 (2000): 159–65.

Mylonis, G. E. *Eleusis and the Eleusian Mysteries.* Princeton, N.J.: Princeton University Press, 1961.

Nasr, S. H. *An Introduction to Islamic Cosmological Doctrines.* Cambridge: Belknap, 1964.

Newsome, James D. *Greeks, Romans, Jews: Currents of Culture and Belief in the New Testament World.* Philadelphia: Trinity Press International, 1992.

Nickelsburg, J. W. E. *Jewish Literature between the Bible and the Mishnah: A Historical and Literary Introduction.* Philadelphia: Fortress, 1981.

Nilsson, M. P. *Geschichte der griechischen Religion*. 3rd ed. 2 vols. Munich: München Beck'she, 1974.

Obolensky, D. *The Bogomils: A Study in Balkan Neo-Manichaeism*. Cambridge: Cambridge University Press, 1948.

Ort, L. J. R. *Mani: A Religio-Historical Description of His Personality*. Leiden, Netherlands: E. J. Brill, 1967.

Ostow, M., and J. A. Arlow. *Ultimate Intimacy: The Psychodynamics of Jewish Mysticism*. London: Karnac Books, 1995.

Pallis, S. A. *Essay on Mandaean Bibliography, 1560–1930*. London, 1933. Reprint, Amsterdam: Philo, 1974.

Parke, H. W., and B. C. McGing. *Sibyl and Sibylline Prophecy in Classical Antiquity*. London, 1988.

Patsch, H. "'Miszelle: Die Prophetie des Agabus." *TZ* 28 (1972): 228–32.

Pelliot. P. "Les influences iraniennes en Asie centrale et en extrême-orient." *Revue d'Histoire et de Litterature Religieuses*, n.s. 3 (1912): 97–119.

Peters, F. E. *The Harvest of Hellenism: A History of the Near East from Alexander the Great to the Triumph of Chrisitianity*. New York: Simon and Schuster, 1970.

Pétrement, S. *A Separate God: The Christian Origins of Gnosticism*. Trans. C. Harrison. San Francisco: HarperSanFrancisco, 1990.

———. *Le Dualisme chez Platon, les Gnostiques et le Manichéens*. Paris: PUF, 1947.

Potter. D. *Prophets and Emperors: Human and Divine Authority from Augustus to Theodosius*. Cambridge, Mass.: Harvard University Press, 1994.

Puech, H.-Ch. *Le Manichéisme: Son fondateur-sa doctrine*. Paris: Civilisations du Sud, 1949.

Quispel, G. "Jewish Gnosis and Mandaean Gnosticism." In *Les Textes de Nag Hammadi: Colloque sur la bibliotheque Copte de Nag Hammadi*. Ed. J. É. Menard, 82–122. Leiden, Netherlands: E. J. Brill, 1975.

———. "Mani the Apostle of Christ." In *Gnostic Studies*. Ed. Quispel, 230–37. Amsterdam: Philo, 1975.

Reeves, J. C. *Jewish Lore in Manichaean Cosmogony: Studies in the "Book of Giants" Traditions*. Cincinnati, Ohio: Hebrew Union College Press, 1992.

Reeves, M. "The Bible and Literary Authorship in the Middle Ages." In *Reading the Text: Biblical Criticism and Literary Theory*. Ed. S. Prickett, 12–63. Oxford: Oxford University Press, 1991.

Reitzenstein, R. *Das iranische Erlösungsmysterium*. Bonn: Marcus and Weber, 1921.

———. *Die Hellenistischen Mysterienreligionen*. Leipzig: J. C. Hinrichs, 1927.

———, and H. H. Schaeder. *Studien zum antiken Synkretismus aus Iran und Griechenland*. Studien der Bibliothek Warburg 7. Leipzig: B. G. Teubner, 1926. Reprint, Darmstadt: Wissenschaftliche Buchgesellschaft, 1965.

Ries, J. *Les études manichéens: Des controverses de la réforme aux découvertes du XXe siècle*. Louvain-la-Neuve, 1988.

Rose, E. *Die manichäische Christologie*. Studies in Oriental Religions 5. Wiesbaden, Germany: Otto Harrassowitz, 1979.

Rosenthal, F. "The Prophecies of Baba the Harranian." In *A Locusts Leg*. Eds. W. B. Henning and E. Yarshater, 220–32. London: Percy Lund, Humphries and Co., 1962.

Rudolph, K. *Gnosis*. Trans. R. Wilson. San Francisco: Harper and Row, 1983.

———. "Problems of a History of the Development of the Mandaean Religion." *HR* 8 (1969): 210–35.

———. *Theogonie, Kosmogonie und Anthropogonie in den mandäischen Schriften*. Göttingen: Vanderhoeck und Ruprecht, 1965.

Runciman, S. *The Medieval Manichee*. Cambridge: Cambridge University Press, 1947.

Ruska, J. "Alchemy in Islam." *IC* 11 (1937): 30–36.

———. *Tabula Smaragdina*. Leipzig: J. C. Hinrichs, 1926.

Schäfer, P. "Jewish Magic Literature in Late Antiquity and Early Middle Ages." *JJS* 41 (1990): 75–91.

Schenke, H. -M. *Der Gott "Mensch" in der Gnosis*. Göttingen, Germany: Vandenhoeck und Ruprecht, 1962.

Schiffman, L. H. *Reclaiming the Dead Sea Scrolls: The History of Judaism, the Background of Christianity, the Lost Library of Qumran*. New York: Jewish Publication Society, 1995.

Schneider, C. *Kulturgeschichte des Hellenismus*. 2 vols. Munich, 1967–69.

Scholem, G. *On the Kabbalah and Its Symbolism*. New York: Schocken, 1969.

Segelberg, E. *Masbuta. Studies in the Ritual of Mandaean Baptism*. Uppsala, Sweden, 1958.

Seidel, J. "Charming Criminals: Classification of Magic in the Babylonian Talmud." In *Ancient Magic and Ritual Power*. Ed. M. Meyer and P. Mirecki, 145–66. RGRW 129. Leiden, Netherlands: E. J. Brill, 1995.

Sharot, S. *Messianism, Mysticism and Magic*. Chapel Hill: University of North Carolina Press, 1982.

Smelik, K. "The Witch of Endor: 1 Samuel 28 in Rabbinic and Christian Exegesis till 800 A.D." *Vigiliae Christianae* 33 (1979): 160–79.

Solodukho, I. A. "The Mazdak Movement and the Rebellion of the Hebrew Population of Iraq in the First Half of the Sixth Century." In *Soviet Views of Talmudic Judaism*. Ed. J. Neusner, 67–86. Leiden, Netherlands: E. J. Brill, 1973.

Sperling, D. "Akkadian *egerrû* and Hebrew *bt qwl*." *JANES* 4 (1972): 63–74.

Spuler, B. "Die Uiguren, die Sogdier und der Manichäismus." *Handbuch der Orientalistik* 1.5.5 (1966): 148–62.

Steinmetz, D. "A Portrait of Miriam in Rabbinic Midrash." *Prooftexts* 8 (1988): 35–65.

Steinschneider, M. *Allgemeine Einleitung in die jüdische Literatur des Mittelalters: Vorlesungen*. Amsterdam: Philo, 1966.

Stemberger, B. "Der Traum in der rabbinischen Literatur." *Kairos* 18 (1976): 1–42.

Stroumsa, G. *Savoir et salut*. Paris: Editions du Cerf, 1992.

Sundermann, W. "Iranische Lebensbeschreibungen Manis." *AO* 26 (1974): 129–45.

———. "Namen von Göttern, Dämonen und Menschen in iranischen Versionene des manichäischen Mythos." *Altorientalische Forschungen* 6 (1979): 95–133.

Swartz, M. D. "Magical Piety in Ancient and Medieval Judaism." In *Ancient Magic and Ritual Power*. Ed. M. Meyer and P. Mirecki, 167–83. RGRW, 129. Leiden, Netherlands: E. J. Brill, 1995.

Tardieu, M. "Sabiens coraniques et 'sabiens' de Harran." *JA* 274 (1986); 1–44.

Tarn, W. W., and G. Griffith. *Hellenistic Civilization*. 3rd ed. London: E. Arnold, and Co., 1952.

Tavadia, J. C. *Die mittelpersische Sprache und Literatur der Zarathustrier*. Iranische Texte und Hilfsbücher 2. Leipzig: J. C. Hinrichs, 1956.

Tcherikover, V. *Hellenistic Civilization and the Jews*. Philadelphia: Jewish Publication Society of America, 1959–66.

Theiler, W. *Die vorbereitung des Neuplatonismus*. Berlin: Weidmann, 1934.

Vadja, G. "Les Zindiqs en pays d'Islam au début de la période abbaside." *Revista degli Studi Orientali* 17 (1937–38): 173–229.

Veltri, Giuseppe. *Magie und Halakhah: Ansätze zu einem empirischen Wissenschaftsbegriff im spätantiken und frümittelalterlichen Judentum*. Tübingen, Germany: Mohr, 1997.

Wallis, R. T., and J. Bregman, Eds. *Neoplatonism and Gnosticism*. Albany: State University of New York Press, 1992.

Wendland, P. "Symbolische Handlungen als Ersatz oder Begleitung der Rede." *Neue Jahrbücher für das klassiche Altertum* 19 (1916): 233–45.

Widengren, G. *Mani und der Manichäismus*. Stuttgart, Germany: W. Kohlhammer, 1961.

———. *Mesopotamian Elements in Manichaeism*. Uppsala Universitets Årsskrift 3. Uppsala, Sweden: Lundequistska Bokhandeln, 1946.

———, ed. *Der Mandäismus*. Wege der Forschung 167. Darmstadt, Germany: Wissenschaftliche Buchgesellschaft, 1982.

Wiessner, G., ed. *The Proceedings of the Second International Conference on Manichaeism*. Bonn, Germany: N.p., 1990.

Will, E., and C. Orrieux. *Ioudaïsmos-Hellènismos: Essai sur le Judaîsme judéen a l'époque hellénistique*. Nancy, France: Presses Universitaires de Nancy, 1986.

Williams, M. A. *Rethinking "Gnosticism" An Argument for Dismantling a Dubious Category*. Princeton, N.J.: Princeton University Press, 1996.

Wright, R. R., ed. and trans. *The Book of Instruction in the Elements of the Art of Astrology*. London: Luzac, 1934.

Yamauchi, E. *Pre-Christian Gnosticism: A Survey of the Proposed Evidences.* Grand Rapids, Mich.: Eerdmans, 1973.

Yoshida, Y. "Manichaean Aramaic in the Chinese Hymnscroll." *BSOAS* 46 (1983): 326–31.

Zaehner, R. C. *The Dawn and Twilight of Zoroastrianism.* London: Weidenfeld and Nicholson, 1961. Reprint, 1977.

———. *The Teachings of the Magi: A Compendium of Zoroastrian Beliefs.* London: Allen and Unwin, 1956. Reprint, 1975.

Zieme, P. "Ein uigurischeer Text über die Wirtschaft manichäischer Klöster im uigurischen Reich." *Researches in Altaic Languages.* Ed. L. Ligetti. Budapest: Akademiai Kiado, 1975.

PROPHECY: ISLAM

Abbott, N. *Studies in Arabic Literary Papyri. Vol. 2 Quranic Commentary and Tradition.* Chicago: University of Chicago Press, 1967.

Abdel-Razek, M. "La revelation dans l'Islam." *RHR* 100 (1929): 13–47.

Abdul, M. "The Historical Development of Tafsir." *IC* 15 (1971): 106–20.

Abdul-Hakim, K. "Religious Experiences or the Prophetic Consciousness." *IC* 16 (1942): 153–60.

Ahmad, I. *The Objective and Goal of Muhammad's Prophethood (SAW) in the Light of the Holy Qur'an.* Trans. A. Ahmad. Lahore, Pakistan: N.p., 1996.

Ahmad, R. "Quranic Exegesis and Classical Tafsir." *IQ* 12 (1968): 71–119.

Ahroni, R. "From Bustan al-'uqul to Qisat al-batul: Some Aspects of Jewish-Muslim Religious Polemics in Yemen." *HUCA* 52 (1981): 311–60.

Altizer, T. *Oriental Mysticism and Biblical Eschatology.* Philadelphia: Westminster, 1961.

Andrae, T. "Muhammad's Doctrine of Revelation." *MW* 23 (1933): 252–71.

Ansari, G. G. "The Concept of Prophethood." *Bulletin of Christian Institutes of Islamic Studies* 4 (1981): 146–54.

Arkoun, M. "The Notion of Revelation from Ahl al-Kitab to the Societies of the Book." *Die Welt des Islams* 28 (1988): 62–89.

Arnaldez, R. "Les elements bibliques du Coran comme sources de la theologie et de la mystique musulmanes." *Aspects de la foi de l'Islam.* Ed. J. Berque, 29–55. Brussels, 1985.

Asin Palacios, M. "La tesis de la necesidad de la revelacion, en el Islam y en la escolastica." *Al-Andalus* 3 (1935): 345–89.

Barth, J. "Midraschische Elemente in der muslimischen Tradition." In *Festschrift Abraham Berliner*, 33–40. Berlin: Druck von H. Itzkowski, 1903.

Bashear, S. "Quran 2:114 and Jerusalem." *BSOAS* 52 (1989): 215–38.

——. "Riding Beasts on Divine Missions: An Examination of the Ass and Camel Traditions." *JSS* 356 (1989): 37–75.

Bernstein, M. S. "The Stories of the Prophets: Intertextuality in Judaism and Islam." *Journal of the Association of Graduate Studies in Near Eastern Studies* 1 (1990): 27–36.

Bijlefeld, W. "A Prophet More Than a Prophet? Some Observations on the Quranic Use of the Terms 'Prophet' and 'Apostle.'" *MW* 59 (1969): 1–28.

Bouman, J. *Gott und Mensch im Koran*. Darmstadt, Germany: Wissenschaftliche Buchgesellschaft, 1977.

Bousquet, G. H. "Judaïsme, Christianisme, Islam, religions apparentées." *SI* 14 (1961): 5–35.

Bowker, J. "Intercession in the Quran and the Jewish Tradition." *JSS* 4 (1968): 183–202.

Bowman, J. "Banu Israil in the Quran." *IS* 2 (1963): 447–55.

——. "The Quran and Biblical History." *Ex orbe religionum: Studia Geo Widengren oblata* II (1972): 111–19.

Brion, F., trans. "Philosophie et révélation: Traduction annotée de six extraits du Kitab A'lam al-nubuwwa." *Bulletin de Philosophie Médiévale* 28 (1986): 134–62.

Brown, N. O. "The Prophetic Tradition." *Studies in Romanticism* 21 (1982): 367–86.

Bryan, J. "Mohammed's Controversy with Jews and Christians." *MW* 9 (1919): 385–415.

Buhl, F. "Eine arabische Parallele zu II. Chr. 35, 25." *ZAW* 29 (1909): 314.

Busse, H. "Die Kanzel des Propheten im Paradiesesgarten." *Die Welt des Islams* 28 (1988): 99–111.

Chapira. B. "Legendes bibliques attribuées à Ka'b el-Ahbar." *REJ* 69 (1919): 86–101.

Chodkiewicz, M. *Seal of the Saints: Prophethood and Sainthood in the Doctrine of Ibn Arabi*. Trans. L. Sherrad. Cambridge: Cambridge University Press, 1993.

Cohen, M. "Islam and the Jews: Myth, Counter-Myth, History." *Jerusalem Quarterly* 38 (1986): 125–37.

Colpe, C. "Das Siegel der Propheten." *Orientalia Suecana* 33–35 (1984–86): 71–83.

Cook, M. "Early Islamic Dietary Law." *JSAI* 7 (1986): 217–77.

Corbin, H. *The Man of Light in Iranian Sufism*. New York: Shambhala, 1978.

Denffer, A. von. *'Ulum al-Quran: An Introduction to the Sciences of the Quran*. Leicester, England: Islamic Foundation, 1983.

Elmore, G. T. *Islamic Sainthood in the Fullness of Time: Ibn al-Arabi's Book of the Fabulous Gryphon*. Leiden, Netherlands: E. J. Brill, 1999.

Ernst, C. *Words of Ecstasy in Sufism*. Albany: State University of New York Press, 1985.

Fahd, T. *La divination arabe: Études religieuse, sociologiques et folkloriques sur le milieu natif de l'Islam.* Leiden, Netherlands: E. J. Brill, 1966.

Friedländer, I. "A Muhammedan Book of Augury in Hebrew Characters." *JQR* 19 (1907): 84–103.

———. "Jewish Arabic Studies." *JQR*, n.s. 1 (1910–11): 183–215; 2 (1911–12): 481–516; 3 (1912–13): 235–300.

Friedmann, Y. "Finality of Prophethood in Sunni Islam." *JSAI* 7 (1986): 177–215.

Goitein, S. D. "Israiliyat." *Tarbiz* 6 (1936): 89–101.

Goldziher, I. "Hebräische Elemente in muhammedanischen Zaubersprüchen." *ZDMG* 48 (1894): 348 50.

———. "Isra'iliyyat." *REJ* 44 (1902): 63–66.

———. "Über Muhammedanische Polemik gegen Ahl al-Kitab." *ZDMG* 32 (1878): 341–87.

Hagemann, L. *Propheten–Zeugen des Glaubens: Koranische und biblische Deutungen.* Islam und Westliche Welt 7. Graz, Austria: Verlag Styria, 1985.

Halm, H. *Kosmologie und Heilslehre der frühen Ismailiya.* Wiesbaden, Germany: Otto Harrassowitz, 1978.

Halperin, D., and G. Newby. "Two Castrated Bulls: A Study in the Haggada of Ka'b al-Ahbar." *JAOS* 102 (1982): 631–38.

Hameen-Anttila, J. "Qur. 53:19, the Prophetic Experience and the "Satanic Verses"—A Reconsideration." *AO* 58 (1997): 24–234.

Heller, B. "Muhammedanisches und Antimuhammedanisches in den Pirke Rabbi Eliezer." *MGWJ* 69 (1925): 47–54.

———. "Récits et personnages bibliques dans la légende mahometane." *REJ* 85 (1928): 113–36.

Hilli, J. "A Study of Prophethood." Trans. I. K. A. Howard and S. M. W. Hasan. *al-Sirat* 2 (1976): 23–36.

Hinds, J. "God's Act of Saving Man: A Study of the Arabic Root 'njw' in the Quran." *Bulletin of Christian Institutes of Islamic Studies* 4 (1981): 5–20.

Hirschfeld, H. "Historical and Legendary Controversies between Mohammed and the Rabbis." *JQR* 10 (1898): 100–16.

———. *Jüdische und christliche Lehren im vor- und frühislamischen Arabien.* Krakow, Poland: Nakl. Polskiej Akademii Umiejetnosci, 1939.

Horst, H. "Israelitische Propheten im Koran." *Zeitschrift für Religions—und Geistesgeschichte* 16 (1964): 42–57.

Hourani, G. "The Qur'an's Doctrine of Prophecy." In *Logos Islamikos: Studia Islamica in honorem Georgii Michaelis Wickens.* Ed. R. M. Savory and D. A. Agius, 175–81. Papers in Medieval Studies 6. Toronto: University of Toronto Press, 1984.

Ibrahim, L. "The Place of Intercession in the Theology of al-Zamakhshari and al-Baydawi." *Hamdard Islamicus* 4.3 (1981): 3–9.

Jalal al-Haqq. "Epistemology of Prophethood in Islam." *al-Tawhid* 4.2 (1986–87): 53–71.

Jeffery, A. *The Quran as Scripture*. New York: R.F. Moore Co., 1952.

Jomier, J. "The Idea of the Prophet in Islam." *Bulletin Secretariatus pro non Christianis* 6 (1972): 149–63.

———. "Prophétisme biblique et prophétisme coranique: Ressemblances et différances." *Revue Thomiste* 77 (1977): 600–9.

Khoury, R. J., ed. *Les Légendes prophétiques dans l'Islam*. Wiesbaden, Germany: Otto Harrassowitz, 1978.

Kister, M. "'An Yadin (Quran IX/29): An Attempt at an Interpretation." *Arabica* 2 (1964): 272–78.

Knappert, J. "The Qisasu'l-anbiya'i as Moralistic Stories." *PSAS* 9 (1976): 103–16.

Kronholm, T. "Dependence and Prophetic Originality in the Koran." *Orientalia Suecana* 31–32 (1982–83): 47–70.

Kyrris, C. P. "The Admission of the Souls of the Immoral but Humane People into the Limbus Puerorum, according to the Cypriote Abbot Kaioumos (VIth Century A. D.) Compared to the Quran's al-Araf (Suras 7:44–46, 57:13f)." *Revue études sud-est Europe* 9 (1971): 461–77.

Lari, S. M. M. "The Necessity and Role of Prophethood." Trans. H. Algar. *al-Tawhid* 7 (1989): 135–56.

Lassner, J. "The Covenant of the Prophets: Muslim Texts, Jewish Subtext." *AJSR* 15 (1990): 207–38.

———. *Demonizing the Queen of Sheba: Boundaries of Gender and Culture in Postbiblical Judaism and Medieval Islam*. Chicago: University of Chicago Press, 1993.

———. "The 'One Who Had Knowledge of the Book' and the 'Mightiest Name' of God: Quranic Exegesis and Jewish Cultural Artifacts." *Studies in Muslim Jewish Relations* 1 (1991).

MacDonald, D. B. "The Doctrine of Revelation in Islam." *MW* 7 (1917): 112–17.

Macy, J. "Prophecy in al-Farabi and Maimonides: The Imaginative and Rational Faculties." In *Maimonides and Philosophy: Papers Presented at the Sixth Jerusalem Philosophical Encounter, May 1985*. Ed. S. Pines and Y. Yovel, 185–201. International Archives for the History of Ideas 114. Dordrecht: M. Nijhoff Publishers, 1986.

Madelung, W. "Apocalyptic Prophecies in Hims in the Umayyad Age." *JSS* 31 (1986): 141–85.

Marcotte, R. "Ibn Miskawayh: Imagination and Prophecy (nubuwwah)." *IC* 71 (1997): 1–13.

Marlow, L. "Kings, Prophets and the 'Ulama' in Medieval Islamic Advice Literature." *SI* 81 (1995): 101–20.

Massignon, L. "Salman Pak et le prémices spirituelles de l'Islam iranien." *Opera Minora* 1 (1969): 443–83.

Masson, D. *Monothéisme coranique et monothéisme biblique*. Paris: Desclée; DeBrouwer, 1976.

Michot, J. "Prophétie et divination selon Avicenne: Presentation, essai de traduction critique et index de l'Epitre de l'âme de la sphère." *Revue Philosophique de Louvain* 83 (1985): 507–35.

Miller, F. "Prophecy in Judaism and Islam." *IS* 17.1 (1978): 27–44.

Mingana. A. "Syriac Influence on the Style of the Kur'an." *Bulletin of the John Rylands Library* 11 (1927): 77–99.

Moubarac, Y. "Les noms titrés et attributs de dieu dans le Coran et les correspondents en épigraphie sud-sémitique." *Le Muséon* 68 (1955): 93–135, 325–68.

Nagel, T. *Die Qisas al-anbiya*. Bonn, Germany: N.p., 1967.

Nasr, S. H. "Ibn Sina's Prophetic Philosophy." *Cultures* 7 (1980): 165–80.

———. "The Prophet and Prophetic Tradition: The Last Prophet and Universal Man." *al-Sirat* 3 (1977): 3–10.

Newby, G. "Abraha and Sennacherib: A Talmudic Parallel to the Tafsir on Surat al-Fil." *JAOS* 94 (1974): 431–37.

Norris, H. T. "Qisas elements in the Quran." In *Arabic Literature to the End of the Umayyad Period*, 246–59. Cambridge: Cambridge University Press, 1983.

Noth, A. *Quellenkiritische Studien zu Themen, Formen, und Tendenzen frühislamischer Geschichtsüberlieferung*. Bonn, Germany: Selbstverlag des Orientalischen Seminars der Universität, 1973.

Obermann, J. "Koran and Agada: The Events at Mount Sinai." *AJSL* 58 (1941): 23–48.

Odumuyiwa, E. A. "Prophecy in the Bible and the Quran." *Orita* 15 (1983): 32–48.

O'Shaughnessy, T. "God's Throne and the Biblical Symbolism of the Quran." *Numen* 20 (1973): 20–21.

Pauliny, J. "Zur Rolle der Qussas bei der Entstehung und Überlieferung der populären Prophetenlegenden." *Asian and African Studies* (Bratislava) 10 (1974): 125–41.

Rahbar, D. *God of Justice: A Study in the Ethical Doctrine of the Quran*. Leiden, Netherlands: E. J. Brill, 1969.

Rahman, F. "The Qur'anic Concept of God, the Universe and Man." *IS* 6 (1967): 1–19.

Reissner, H. G. "The Ummi Prophet and the Banu Israil of the Quran." *MW* 39 (1949): 276–81.

Rippin, A. "The Commerce of Eschatology." In *The Qur'an as Text*. Ed. S. Wild, 125–35. Leiden, Netherlands: E. J. Brill, 1996.

Rodionov, M. "Prophetes et saints." *Saba* 3–4 (1997): 69–70.

Roest, C. A. A. *Thus They Were Hearing: The Word in the Experience of Revelation in Qur'an and Hindu Scriptures*. Rome: Università gregoriana, 1974.

Rosenblatt, S. "Rabbinic Legends in Hadith." *MW* 35 (1945): 237–52.

Rosenthal, F. "The Influence of the Biblical Tradition on Muslim Historiography." In *Historians of the Middle East*. Ed. B. Lewis and B. Holt, 35–45. London: Oxford University Press, 1962.

Roth, N. "Forgery and Abrogation of the Torah: A Theme in Muslim and Christian Polemic in Spain." *American Academy for Jewish Research: Proceedings* 54 (1987): 203–36.

Rubin, U. "Pre-Existence and Light: Aspects of the Concept of Nur Muhammad." *IOS* 5 (1975): 62–119.

———. "Prophets and Progenitors in the Early Shi'a Tradition." *JSAI* 1 (1979): 41–65.

Ruiz Gonzalez, G. "Aspectos diferenciales del concepto de profecia en el Islam, Judaismo y Cristianismo." In *Actas de la Jornadas de Cultura Arabe e Islamica* (Madrid, 1978): 359–64.

Ryan, P. J. "The Descending Scroll: A Study of the Notion of Revelation as Apocalypse in the Bible and in the Qur'an." *Ghana Bulletin of Theology* 4.8 (1975): 24–39.

Schapiro, I. *Die haggadischen Elemente im erzählenden Teil des Korans*. Berlin: H. Itzkowski, 1907.

Schuon, F. "Le mystère de la substance prophétique." *Etudes Traditionnelles* 83 (1982): 97–104.

Schwartzbaum, H. *Biblical and Extra-Biblical Legends in Islamic Folk Literature*. Walldorf-Hessen: Verlag für Orientkunde Dr. H. Vorndran, 1982.

Sidersky, D. *Les origines les légends musulmanes dans le Coran et dans les vies des prophetes*. Paris: N.p., 1933.

Stowasser, B. F. *Women in the Quran, Traditions, and Interpretation*. Oxford: Oxford University Press, 1994.

Takeshita, M. *Ibn Arabi's Theory of the Perfect Man and Its Place in the History of Islamic Thought*. Tokyo: Institute for the Study of Languages and Cultures of Asia and Africa, 1987.

Tardieu, M. "La chaîne des prophètes." *Cahiers d'Asie Centrale* 1–2 (1996): 357–66.

Tottoli, R. "Le storie dei profeti nella tradizione arabo-islamica." *Islam: Storia e Civiltà* 32.9 (1990): 171–77, 229–31.

———. "Un mito cosmogonico nelle Qisas al-anbiya di al-Talabi." *Annali di Ca Foscari* 28.3, *Serie Orientale* 20 (1989): 49–59.

Troll, C. W., trans. "The Fundamental Nature of Prophethood and Miracle: A Chapter from Shibli Nu'mani's Al-Kalam." *Islam in India* [1] (1982): 86–115.

Vajda, G. "Juifs et Musulmans selon le hadit." *JA* 229 (1939): 57–127.

———. "La contribution de quelques textes judéo-arabes à la connaissance du mouvement d'idées dans l'Islam du III–IXe siècle." *Élaboration de l'Islam* (1961): 87–97.

Von Grunebaum, G. E. "Islam: Experience of the Holy and Concept of Man." *Diogenes* 48 (1964): 81–104.

Wali Allah, S. *A Mystical Interpretation of Prophetic Tales by an Indian Muslim (Ta'wil al-ahadith)*. Trans. J. M. S. Baljon. Leiden, Netherlands: E. J. Brill, 1973.

Wasserstrom, W. M. *Between Muslim and Jew: The Problem of Symbiosis under Early Islam*. Princeton, N.J.: Princeton University Press, 1995.

Watt, W. M. "The Nature of Muhammad's Prophethood." *Scottish Journal of Religious Studies* 8 (1987): 77–84.

Weil, G. *Biblischen Legenden der Muselmänner*. Leipzig: J. C. Hinrichs, 1886.

Widengren, G. "Holy Book and Holy Tradition in Islam." In *Holy Book and Holy Tradition: International Colloquium Held in the Faculty of Theology, University of Manchester*. Ed. F. F. Bruce and E. G. Rupp, 210–36. Grand Rapids, Mich.: Eerdmans, 1968.

Wolfensohn, I. *Ka'b al-Ahbar und seine Stellung im Hadith und in der islamischen Legendenliteratur*. Frankfurt: Peter Lang, 1933.

Yahya, U. "Man and His Perfection in Muslim Theology." *MW* 49 (1950): 19–29.

Zwettler, M. "A Mantic Manifesto: The Sura of 'the Poets' and the Quranic Foundations of Prophetic Authority." In *Poetry and Prophecy: The Beginnings of a Literary Tradition*. Ed. J. L. Kugel. Ithaca, N.Y.: Cornell University Press, 1990.

ADAM AND EVE

Abdel-Haleem, M. "Adam and Eve in the Qur'an and the Bible." *IQ* 41 (1997): 255–69.

Alexander, P. "The Fall into Knowledge: The Garden of Eden/Paradise in Gnostic Literature." In *A Walk in the Garden*. Ed. P. Morris and D. Sawyer, 92–105. JSOTSS 136. Sheffield: JSOT Press, 1992.

Anderson, G. "Celibacy or Consummation in the Garden? Reflections on Early Jewish and Christian Interpretations of the Garden of Eden." *HTR* 82 (1989): 121–48.

———. "The Cosmic Mountain: Eden and Its Early Interpreters in Syriac Christianity." In *Genesis 1–3 in the History of Exegesis: Intrigue in the Garden*. Ed. G. A. Robbins, 187–224. Lewiston, N.Y.: Mellen, 1988.

———. "The Exaltation of Adam and the Fall of Satan." *JJTP* 6 (1997): 105–34.

———. "The Life of Adam and Eve." *HUCA* 63 (1992): 1–38.

———. "The Status of the Torah before Sinai." *DSD* 1 (1994): 1–29.

———, and M. E. Stone. *A Synopsis of the Books of Adam and Eve*. SBL. Atlanta: Scholars, 1994.

Bacher, W. "Lilith, Königen von Smargad." *MGWJ* 19 (1870): 187–89.

Barrett, C. K. *From First Adam to Last: A Study in Pauline Theology*. New York: Scribner's, 1962.

Baumgarten, J. M. "Purification and the Garden in 4Q265 and Jubilees." In *New Qumran Texts and Studies*. *STJD* 15. Ed. G. Brooke, 3–10. Leiden, Netherlands: E. J. Brill, 1994.

Beatty, A. "Adam and Eve and Vishnu: Syncretism in the Javanese Slametan." *Journal of the Royal Anthropological Institute* 2 (1996): 271–88.

Beck, E. "Iblis und Mensch, Satan und Adam. Der Werdegang einer koranische Erzählung." *Le Museon* 89 (1976): 195–244.

Bibby, G. *Looking for Dilmun*. New York: Knopf, 1969.

Brock, S. P. "Clothing Metaphors as a Means of Theological Expression in Syriac Tradition." In *Typus, Symbol, Allegorie bei den östlichen Vätern und ihren Parallelen im Mittelalter*. Ed. M. Schmidt, 11–40. Eichstatt, Germany: F. Pustet Regensburg, 1981.

Christensen, A. *Les Types du Premier Homme et du Premier Roi*. Archives d'Études Orientales 14. Leiden, Netherlands: E. J. Brill, 1943.

Cooper, J. "Assyrian Prophecies, the Assyrian Tree, and the Mesopotamian Origins of Jewish Monotheism, Greek Philosophy, Christian Theology, Gnosticism, and Much More." *JAOS* 120 (2000): 430–44.

Drower, E. S. *The Secret Adam*. Oxford: Clarendon, 1960.

Faris, N. A. "Khalifa or Khaliqa: A Variant Reading of Surah 2:28." *MW* 24 (1934): 183–86.

Greenfield, J. "A Touch of Eden." In *Orientalia J. Duchesne-Guillaume Emerito Oblata*, 219–24. Leiden, Netherlands: E. J. Brill, 1984.

Harl, M. "La prise de conscience de la 'nudité' de'Adam." *SPat* 92 (1966): 486–95.

Hassan, R. "Made from Adam's Rib: The Woman's Creation Question." Ed. J. Rooney. *al-Mushir* 27 (1985): 124–55.

Heller, J. "Der Name Eva." *AO* 26 (1958): 636–56.

Hermansen, M. K. "Pattern and Meaning in the Qur'anic Adam Narratives." *Studies in Religion* 17 (1988): 41–52.

Hirtenstein, S. "Lunar View, Air-Glow Blue: Ibn 'Arabi's Conversations with the Prophet Adam." *Journal of the Muhyiddin Ibn 'Arabi Society* 16 (1994): 51–68.

Jenkinson, E. J. "The Rivers of Paradise." *MW* 19 (1929): 151–55.

Khaja, K. "A Leaf from Sheyk-i-Akbar. The Bezel of Adam (Fas-i-Adamiyyah)." *IC* 1 (1927): 238–44.

Kikawada, I. M. "Two Notes on Eve." *JBL* 91 (1972): 33–37.

Kilpatrick, H. "Hawwa' bila Adam: An Egyptian Novel of the 1930's." *Journal of Arabic Literature* 4 (1973): 48–56.

Kister, M. J. "Adam: A Study of Some Legends in Tafsir and Hadith Literature." *IOS* 13 (1993): 113–74.

———. "Legends in Tafsir and Hadith Literature: The Creation of Adam and Related Stories. In *Approaches to the History of the Interpretation of the Qur'an*. Ed. A. Rippin, 82–114. Oxford: Oxford University Press, 1988.

Lachs, S. T. "The Pandora-Eve Motif in Rabbinic Literature." *HTR* 67 (1974): 341–45.

Lambden, S. "From Fig Leaves to Fingernails: Some Notes on the Garments of Adam and Eve." *In A Walk in the Garden*. Ed. P. Morris and D. Sawyer, 74–91. JSOTSS 136. Sheffield, England: JSOT Press, 1992.

Levison, J. R. "The Exoneration of Eve in the Apocalypse of Moses." *JSJ* 20 (1989): 135–50.

———. *Portraits of Adam in Early Judaism from Sirach to 2 Baruch*. JSP Supplement Series 1. Sheffield, England: JSOT Press, 1988.

Lewis, B. "An Ismaili Interpretation of the Fall of Adam." *BSOAS* 9 (1937–39): 691–704.

Marcus, R. "Tree of Life in Essene Tradition." *JBL* 74 (1955): 274.

———. "Tree of Life in Proverb." *JBL* 62 (1943): 117–20.

Matar, N. I. "Adam and the Serpent: Notes on the Theology of Mikhail Naimy." *Journal of Arabic Literature* 11 (1980): 56–61.

Meyers, C. *Discovering Eve*. Oxford: Oxford University Press, 1988.

Millard, A. "The Etymology of Eden." *VT* 34 (1984): 103–6.

Mir, M. "The Qur'anic Adam: The First Man and the First Prophet." In *Encyclopaedic Survey of Islamic Culture: Studies in Quran*. Ed. M. Taher, 76–85. Delhi, India: Anmol Publications,1997.

Nettler, R. L. "Ibn 'Arabi as a Qur'anic Thinker: Reflections on Adam in the Fusus al-Hikam." *Scottish Journal of Religious Studies* 13 (1992): 91–102.

Niditch, S. "The Cosmic Adam: Man as Mediator in Rabbinic Literature." *JJS* 34 (1983): 137–46.

Nolin, K. E. "The Story of Adam: Translation with Introduction and Notes of Dr. Muhammad Kamil Husayn's 'Qissat Adam' from His Collection of Essays Entitled: Mutanawwi'at, pub. 1961, 38–42." *MW* 54 (1964): 4–13.

Norris, P. *Eve: A Biography*. New York: New York University Press, 2001.

Orsatti, P. "La storia di Adamo in un commento corainico persiano." In *Yad-nama in Memoria de Alessandro Bausani*. Ed. B. S. Amoretti and L. Rostagno, 1:343–62. Università di Roma La Sapienza Studi Orientali 10. Rome, 1991.

Pagels, E. *Adam, Eve and the Serpent*. London: Random House, 1988.

Paret, R. "Der Koran und die Prädestination." *OLZ* 58 (1963): 117–21.

Parpola, S. "The Assyrian Tree of Life: Tracing the Origins of Jewish Monotheism and Greek Philosophy." *JNES* 52 (1993): 161–208.

Rasmussen, S. T. "Adam og Eva—associationer, etymologier og litteraer semantik: perspektivrids." In *Living Waters: Scandinavian Orientalistic Studies Presented to Professor Dr. Frede Lokkegaard on His Seventy-fifth Birthday, January 27th 1990*. Ed. E. Keck et al., 289–303. Copenhagen: N.p., 1990.

Reat, N. R. "The Tree Symbol in Islam." *Studies in Comparative Religion* 9 (1975): 164–82.

Rezvan, E. A. "Adam i banu adam v Korane (k istorii ponyatii 'pervochelovek' I 'chelovechestvo'). In *Islam: Religiya, obshchestvo, gosudarstvo*, 59–68. Moscow: N.p., 1984.

Rook, J. "The Names of the Wives from Adam to Abraham in the Book of Jubilees." *JSP* 7 (1990): 105–17.

Schöck, C. *Adam im Islam: Ein Beitrag zur Ideengeschichte der Sunna.* Islamkundliche Untersuchungen 168. Berlin: K. Schwarz, 1993.

Scholem, G. "Perakim hadashim me-inyane ashmeday ve-Lilit." *Tarbiz* 19 (1948): 165–75.

Scroggs, R. *The Last Adam: A Study in Pauline Anthropology.* Oxford: Blackwell, 1966.

Sharpe, J. L. "Second Adam in the Apocalypse of Moses." *CBQ* 35 (1973): 35–46.

Smith, J. I., and Y. Haddad. "Eve: Islamic Image of Woman." In *Women and Islam: Women's Studies International Forum.* Ed. Azizah al-Hibri, 135–44. Oxford: Oxford University Press, 1982.

Stillman, N. A. "The Story of Cain and Abel in the Quran and Muslim Commentaries." *JSS* 19 (1974): 231–39.

Stone, M. E. *A History of the Literature of Adam and Eve.* Atlanta: Scholars, 1992.

Wallace, H. N. *The Eden Narrative.* Atlanta: Scholars, 1985.

Watt, W. M. "Created in His Image: A Study in Islamic Theology." *TGUOS* 18 (1959–60).

Zandee, J. "Gnostic Ideas on the Fall and Salvation." *Numen* 11 (1964): 13–74.

Zayn, S. A. *Adam and the Creation [Adam wa al-Takwin].* Trans. A. L. Agha. Beirut, 1983.

Zwemer, S. M. "The Worship of Adam by Angels." *MW* 27 (1937): 115–27.

CAIN, ABEL, SETH

Aptowitzer, B. *Kain and Abel in der Agada.* Vienna: R. Loewit Verlag, 1922.

Bassler, J. "Cain and Abel in the Palestinian Targums." *JSJ* 17 (1986): 56–64.

Francis, F. T. "The Gnostics: The Undominated Race." *NT* 21 (1979): 271–88.

Goldber, J. "Kain: Sohn des Menschen oder Sohn der Schlange?" *Judaica* 25 (1969): 203–21.

Grattenpanche, J. "Caïn et Abel dans les légendes islamique." *Orientalia Lovaniensia Periodica* 24 (1993): 133–42.

Gutmann, J. "Cain's Burial of Abel: A Jewish Legendary Motif in Christian and Islamic Art." *Sacred Art Journal* 11 (1990): 152–57.

Huffmon, H. B. "Cain, the Arrogant Sufferer." In *Biblical and Related Studies Presented to Samuel Iwry*. Ed. A. Kort and S. Morschauser, 109–13. Winona Lake, Ind.: Eisenbrauns,1985.

Klijn, A. F. J. *Seth in Jewish, Christian and Gnostic Literature*. Leiden, Netherlands: E. J. Brill, 1979.

Kugel, J. L. "Cain and Abel in Fact and Fable." In *Hebrew Bible or Old Testament?* Ed. R. Brooks and J. Collins, 167–90. Notre Dame, Ind.: University of Notre Dame, 1989.

Layton, B., ed. *The Rediscovery of Gnosticism. II: Sethian Gnosticism.* Leiden, Netherlands: E. J. Brill, 1981.

Légasse, S. "L'oracle contre 'cette génération' (Mt 23,34–36 par Lc 1,49–51) et la polémique judéo-chrétienne dans la source des logia." In *Logia: Les Paroles de Jésus—The Sayings of Jesus*. Ed. J. Delobel, 237–56. Paris: Fischbacher, 1982.

Lewis, J. P. "The Offering of Abel (Gen. 4:4): A History of Interpretation." *JETS* 37 (1944): 481–96.

Mellinkoff, R. *The Sign of Cain*. Berkeley: University of California Press, 1981.

Pearson, B. "The Figure of Seth in Manichaean Literature." In *Manichaean Studies: Proceedings of the First International Conference on Manichaeism*. Ed. P. Bryder, 147–55. Lovanii: International Association of Manichaean Studies, 1988.

Sawyer, J. F. A. "Cain and Hephaestus: Possible Relics of Metalworking Traditions in Genesis 4." *Abr-Nahrain* 24 (1986): 155–66.

Schapera, I. "The Sin of Cain." In *Anthropological Approaches to the Old Testament*. Ed. B. Lang, 26–42. Issues in Religion and Theology 8. Philadelphia: Fortress, 1985.

Schenke, H.-M. "The Phenomenon and Significance of Gnostic Sethianism." In *The Rediscovery of Gnosticism: Proceedings of the International Conference on Gnosticism*. Ed. B. Layton, 2:588–616. Leiden, Netherlands: E. J. Brill, 1980–81.

Scott, A. B. "Churches or Books? Sethian Social Organization." *JECS* 3 (1995): 109–22.

Stillman, N. A. "The Story of Cain and Abel in the Qur'an and Muslim Commentaries." *JSS* 19 (1974): 231–39.

Stroumsa, G. *Another Seed: Studies in Gnostic Mythology*. NHS 24. Leiden, Netherlands: E. J. Brill, 1984.

Waltke, B. K. "Cain and His Offering." *WTJ* 48 (1986): 363–72.

Williams, M. A. *The Immovable Race: Gnostic Designation and the Theme of Stability in Late Antiquity*. Leiden, Netherlands: E. J. Brill, 1985.

———. "Stalking Those Elusive Sethians." In *The Rediscovery of Gnosticism: Proceedings of the International Conference on Gnosticism*. Ed. B. Layton, 2:563–78. Leiden, Netherlands: E. J. Brill, 1980–81.

ENOCH, IDRIS, HERMES TRISMEGISTOS, METATRON

Affifi, A. E. "The Influence of Hermetic Literature in Muslim Thought." *BSOAS* 13 (1950): 840–55.

Alexander, P. S. "The Historical Setting of the Hebrew Book of Enoch." *JJS* 28 (1977) 156–80.

Böttrich, C. "Recent Studies in the *Slavonic Book of Enoch*." *Journal for the Study of the Pseudepigrapha* 9 (1991): 35–42.

Casanova, P. "Idris et 'Ouzair." *JA* 205 (1924): 356–60.

Dimant, D. "The Biography of Enoch and the Books of Enoch." *VT* 33 (1983): 14–29.

Festugière, A. J. *Hermétisme et mystique païnne*. Paris: Aubier-Montaigne, 1967.

———. *La Révélation d'Hermès Trismégiste*. 4 vols. Paris: J. Gabalda, 1949–54.

Fowden, G. *The Egyptian Hermes: A Historical Approach to the Late Pagan Mind*. Cambridge, Mass.: Harvard University Press, 1986.

Gil, M. "Enoch in the Land of Eternal Life." *Tarbiz* 52 (1982): 1–15.

Grelot. P. "La géographie mythique d'Hénoch et ses sources orientales." *RB* 65 (1958): 33–69.

Heinrici, C. F. G. *Die Hermes-Mystik und das Neue Testament*. Ed. E. von Dobschütz. Leipzig: J. C. Hinrichs, 1918.

Himmelfarb, M. "A Report on Enoch in Rabbinic Literature." *SBL Seminar Papers* 13 (1978): 259–69.

Idel, M. "Enoch Is Metatron." *Immanuel* 24–25 (1990): 220–40.

Jansen, H. L. *Die Heochgestalt: Eine vergleichende religionsgeschtliche Untersuchung*. Oslo: N.p., 1939.

Jenkinson, E. J. "Did Mohammed Know Slavonic Enoch?" *MW* 21 (1931): 24–28.

Marquet, Y. "Sabéens et Ikhwan al-Safa." *SI* 24 (1966): 52–61.

Merkel, I., and A. B. Debus, eds. *Hermeticism and the Renaissance*. Washington, D.C.: Folger Shakespeare Library, 1988.

Milik, J. T. "Hénoch au pays des Aromates." *RB* 65 (1958): 70–79.

Moore, G. M. "Metatron." *HTR* 15 (1922): 62–85.

Moorsel, G. van. *The Mysteries of Hermes Trismegistos*. Utrecht, 1955.

Plessner, M. "Hermes Trismegistus and Arab Science." *SI* 2 (1954): 45–59.

Reitzenstein, R. *Die hellenistischen Mysterienreligionen*. 3rd ed. Leipzig: J. C. Hinrichs, 1927. Reprint, Darmstadt: Wissenschaftliche Buchgesellschaft, 1956.

———. *Poimandres*. Leipzig: J. C. Hinrichs, 1904.

Schäfer, P. *The Hidden and Manifest God: Some Major Themes in Early Jewish Mysticism*. Albany: State University of New York Press, 1992.

Scott, W. *Hermetica: The Ancient Greek and Latin Writings Which Contain Religious or Philosophical Teachings Ascribed to Hermes Trismegistos*. Oxford, 1924–36. Reprint, Bath, Avon, England: Solos Press; Lower Lake, Calif.: U.S. distributors, Atrium Pub. Co., 1993.

Segal, A. F. *Two Powers in Heaven: Early Rabbinic Reports about Christianity*. Leiden, Netherlands: E. J. Brill, 1977.

Siggel, A. "Das Sendschrieben das Licht uber das Verfahren des Hermes der Hermesse." *Der Islam* 24 (1937): 287–306.

Stone, M. E. "Enoch, Aramaic Levi, and Sectarian Origins." *JSJ* 19 (1988): 159–70.

Stroumsa, G. G. "Form(s) of God: Some Notes on Metatron and Christ." *HTR* 76 (1983): 269–88.

Suter, D. W. *Tradition and Composition in the Parables of Enoch*. Missoula, Mont.: Scholars, 1979.

Ubigli, L. R. "La Fortuna di Enoc nel giudaismo antico." *Annali di storia dell'esegesi* 1 (1984): 13–63.

Vadja, G. "Pour le Dossier de Metatron." In *Studies in Jewish Religious and Intellectual History*. Ed. S. Stein and R. Loewe, 345–54. Tuscaloosa: University of Alabama Press, 1977.

Vanderkam, J. C. *Enoch and the Growth of an Apocalyptic Tradition*. CBQ Monograph Series 16. Washington, D.C.: Catholic University of America, 1984.

Walker, J. "Who Is Idris?" *MW* 17 (1927): 259–60.

NOAH

Alexander, P. "The Targumim and Early Exegesis of the 'Sons of God' in Genesis 6." *JJS* 23 (1972): 60–71.

Bailey, L. R. *Noah: The Person and the Story in History and Tradition*. Columbia: University of South Carolina Press, 1989.

———. *Where Is Noah's Ark: Mystery on Mt. Ararat*. Nashville, Tenn.: Abingdon, 1978.

Baumgarten, A. I. "Myth and Midrash: Gen. 9:20–29." In *Christianity, Judaism and Other Greco-Roman Cults*. Ed. J. Neusner, 3:55–71. Leiden, Netherlands: E. J. Brill, 1975.

Bockmuehl, M. "The Noachide Commandments and New Testament Ethics." *RB* 102 (1995): 72–105.

Cohen, H. H. *The Drunkenness of Noah*. Tuscaloosa: University of Alabama Press, 1974.

Cryer, F. H. "The Interrelationship of Gen. 5:32, 11:10–11 and the Chronology of the Flood." *Biblica* 66 (1985): 241–61.

Dundes, A., ed. *The Flood Myth*. Berkeley: University of California Press, 1988.

Flusser, D., and S. Safrai. "Das Aposteldekret und die Noachitischen Gebote." In *Wer Torah vermehrt, mehrt Leben*. Ed. E. Brocke et al., 173–92. Neukirchen-Vluyn: Neukirchener Verlag, 1986.

Kikawada, I. M., and A. Quinn. *Before Abraham Was*. Nashville, Tenn.: Abingdon, 1985.

Lambert, W. G., and A. R. Millard. *Atra-hasis: The Babylonian Story of the Flood*. Oxford: Clarendon, 1969.

Lim, T. H. "The Chronology of the Flood Story in a Qumran Text." *JJS* 43 (1992): 288–98.

McClain, E. G. "The Kaba as Archetypal Ark." *Sophia Perennis* 4.1 (1978): 59–75.

Montgomery, J. W. *The Quest for Noah's Ark*. Minneapolis, Minn.: Fortress, 1972.

Novak, D. "Before Revelation: The Rabbis, Paul, and Karl Barth." *JR* 71 (1991): 50–66.

Suryakanta. *The Flood Legend in Sanskrit Literature*. Delhi, India: S. Chand, 1950.

VanderKam, J. C. "The Birth of Noah." In *Intertestamental Essays in Honour of Jozef Tadeusz Milik*. Ed. Z. J. Kapera, 213–37. Krakow, Poland: Enigma Press, 1992.

———. "The Granddaughters and Grandsons of Noah." *RdQ* 16 (1994): 457–61.

———. "Righteousness of Noah." In *Ideal Figures in Judaism*. Ed. J. Collins and G. W. Nickelsburg, 4–22. Missoula, Mont.: Scholars, 1980.

PRE-ISLAMIC ARAB PROPHETS

Abdalla, A. M., et al. *Studies in the History of Arabia. Vol. 1: Sources for the History of Arabia*. Riyadh, Saudi Arabia: King Saud University Press, 1979.

Ansari, A. R., ed. *Studies in the History of Arabia. Vol. 2: Pre-Islamic Arabia*. Riyadh, Saudi Arabia: King Saud University Press, 1984.

Beeston, A. F. L. The 'Men of the Tanglewood' in the Qur'an." *JSS* 13 (1968): 253–55.

———. "The Ritual Hunt: A Study in Old South Arabian Religious Practice." *Le Muséon* 61 (1948): 183–96.

Breton, J.-F. "Religious Architecture in Ancient Hadramawt." *PSAS* 10 (1980): 5–17.

———, and C. Darles. "Le tombeau de Hud." *Saba* 3–4 (1997): 79–81.

Canova, G. "Il serpente della Ka'ba: Una nota sulla Mecca preislamica." *Annali della Facoltà di Lingue e Letterature Straniere di Ca Foscari* 33, Serie Orientale 25 (1994): 421–25.

Caskel, W. *Das altarabische Königreich Lihyan*. Krefeld, Germany: Scherpe Verlag, 1950.

Chelhod, J., ed. *L'Arabie du sud, histoire et civilisations: Le peuple yéménite et ses racines*. Paris: G.-P. Maisonneuve et Larose, 1984–85.

Clemow, F. G. "A Visit to the Rock-Tombs of Medain-i-Salih, and the Southern Section of Hejaz Railway." *Geographical Journal* 42 (1913): 534–40.

Coussonnet, N., and F. Mermier. "Le pèlerinage au sanctuaire de Hud, le prophète de Dieu." *Saba* 3–4 (1997): 73–77.

Crowe, P. "A Trip to Madain Salih." *Royal Central Asian Journal* 51 (1964): 291–300.

Daum, W., ed. *Jemen*. Innsbruck, Austria: Pinguin-Verlag, 1987.

De Keroualin, F., and L. Schwarz. "Hud, un pelerinage en Hadramaout." *Quaderni di Studi Arabi* 13 (1995): 181–89

Dussaud, R. *La pénétration des arabes en Syrie avant l'Islam*. Paris: P. Geuthner, 1955.

Eph'al, I. *The Ancient Arabs: Nomads on the Borders of the Fertile Crescent, 9th–5th Centuries B.C.* Jerusalem: Magnes Press, 1984.

Gese, H., et al. *Die Religionen Altsyriens, Altarabiens und der Mandäer*. Die Religionen der Menschheit Bd 10. Stuttgart, Germany: W. Kohlammer, 403–64.

Ghul, M. A. "The Pilgrimage at Itwat." *PSAS* 14 (1984): 33–39.

Gibb, H. A. R. "Pre-Islamic Monotheism in Arabia." *HTR* 55 (1962): 269–80.

Gil, M. "The Origin of the Jews of Yathrib." *JSAI* 4 (1984): 203–23.

Grimme, H. *Texte und Untersuchungen zur safatensich-arabischen Religion*. Paderborn, Germany, 1929.

Halevy, J. "Le prophète Salih." *JA* 5 (1905): 146–50.

Hamblin, W. J. "Pre-Islamic Arabian Prophets." In *Mormons and Muslims: Spiritual Foundations and Modern Manifestations*. Ed. S. J. Palmer, 85–104. Provo, Utah: Religious Studies Center, Brigham Young University, 1983.

Höfner, M. "Die vorislamischen Religionen Arabiens." In *Religionen Altsyriens, Altarabiens und der Mandäer*. Ed. H. Gese et al., 233–402. Stuttgart, Germany: W. Kohlhammer, 1970.

Kawar, I. "The Last Days of Salih." *Arabica* 5 (1958): 145–58.

Knauf, E. A. *Ismael: Untersuchungen zur Geschichte Palästinas und Nordarabiens im 1. Jahrtausend v.Chr.* Wiesbaden, Germany: Otto Harrassowitz, 1985.

———. *Midian*. Wiesbaden, Germany: Otto Harrassowitz, 1988.

———. "Nomadischer Henotheismus? Bemerkungen zu altnordarabischen Stammesgöttern." In *XXII. Deutscher Orientalistentag vom 21. bis 25. März 1983 im Tübingen*. Ed. W. Rölling, 124–32. Stuttgart, Germany: W. Kohlhammer, 1985.

Kraemer, J. L. "The Andalusian Mystic Ibn Hud and the Conversion of the Jews." *IOS* 12 (1992): 59–73.

Krenkow, F. "The Annual Fairs of the Ancient Arabs." *IC* 21 (1947): 111–13.

Littman, E. *Thamud und Safa.* Leipzig: J. C. Hinrichs, 1940.

Milik, J. T. *Dédicaces faites par des dieux (Palmyre, Hatra, Tyr) et des thiases sémitiques à l'époque romaine.* Paris: Geuthner, 1972.

Moubarac, Y. "Les noms titres et attributs de dieu dans le Coran et les correspondents en épigraphie sud-sémitique." *Le Muséon* 68 (1955): 93–135, 325–68.

Nadvi, S. M. *A Geographical History of the Qur'an.* 2nd ed. Lahore, 1968.

Newby, G. *A History of the Jews of Arabia.* Columbia: University of South Carolina Press, 1988.

Oppenheim, A. L. "The Seafaring Merchants of Ur." *JAOS* 74 (1954): 6–17.

Potts, D. T. *Dilmun, New Studies in the Archaeology and Early History of Bahrain.* Berlin: D. Reimer Verlag, 1983.

Robin, C. "Judaisme et christianisme en Arabie du Sud d'après les sources épigraphiques et archéologiques." *PSAS* 10 (1980): 85–96.

———, and J.-F. Breton. "Le sanctuaire préislamique du Gabal al-Lawd (nord-Yémen)." *CRAIBL* (1982): 590–629.

Rothberg, B. *Timna.* Winona Lake, Ind.: Eisenbrauns, 1972.

Rothstein, G. *Die Dynastie der Lahmiden in al-Hira: Ein Versuch arabisch-persischen Geschichte zur Zeit der Sasaniden.* Berlin, 1899. Reprint, Hildesheim: G. Olms, 1968.

Ryckmans, G. "Les religions arabes préislamiques." In *Histoire Générale des Religions.* Ed. M. Gorce and R. Mortier, 200–28, 593–605. Paris, 1960.

Ryckmans, J. "Biblical and Old South Arabian Institutions: Some Parallels." In *Arabian and Islamic Studies: Articles Presented to R. B. Serjeant.* Ed. R. Bidwell and G. R. Smith, 14–25. London: Longman, 1983.

———. "De quelques divinités sud-arabes." *ETL* 39 (1963): 458–68.

———. "La chasse rituelle dans l'Arabie du Sud ancienne." In *al-Bahit: Festschrift Joseph Henninger*, 259–308. Bonn, Germany: Verlag des Anthropos-Instituts, 1976.

———. "Les confessions publiques sabéennes: Le code sud-arabe de pureté rituelle." *Annali dell'Istituto orientali di Napoli* 22 (1972): 1–15.

———. "Un rite d'*istisqa'* au temple sabéen de Marib." *Annuaire de l'Institut de Philologie orientales et slaves* 20 (1968–72): 379–88.

Sartre, M. *Bostra des origines à l'Islam.* Paris: Librairie orientaliste P. Geuthner, 1985.

Sawyer, J. F. A., and D. J. A. Clines. *Midian, Moab and Edom: The History of Archaeology of Late Bronze and Iron Age Jordan and Northwest Arabia.* Sheffield, England: JSOT Press, 1983.

Serjeant, R. B. "Hud and other Pre-Islamic Prophets of Hadramawt." *Le Muséon* 6 (1954): 121–79.

———. *South Arabian Hunt.* London: Luzac, 1976.

Sourdel, D. *Les cultes du Hauran à l'époque romaine*. Paris: Impr. Nationale, 1952.

Stetkevych, J. *Muhammad and the Golden Bough: Reconstructing Arabian Myth*. Bloomington: Indiana University Press, 1996.

Teixidor, J. *The Pagan God*. Princeton, N.J.: Princeton University Press, 1977.

———. *The Pantheon of Palmyra*. Leiden, Netherlands: E. J. Brill, 1979.

Van den Branden, A. *Histoire de Thamoud*. Beirut: Université Libanaise, 1960.

Wellhausen, J. *Reste arabischen Heidentums*. 3rd ed. Berlin: G. Reimer, 1961.

Wensinck, A. J. "Die Entstehung der muslimischen Reinheitsgestzgebung." *Der Islam* 5 (1914): 62–79.

Winnett, F. V. *The Arabian Genealogies in the Book of Genesis*. Nashville, Tenn.: Abingdon, 1970.

ABRAHAM, JACOB, ISAAC, ISHMAEL

Abdul, M. "The Role of Abraham in the Formation of Islam." *Orita* 8 (1974): 58–70.

Alder, W. "Abraham and the Burning of the Temple of Idols." *JQR* 77 (1986): 95–117.

Alexander, G. "The Story of the Ka'ba." *MW* 28 (1938): 43–53.

Alt, A. "The Gods of the Fathers." In *Essays on Old Testament History and Religion*. Trans. R. A. Wilson, 1077. Garden City, N.Y.: Doubleday 1966.

Aptowitzer, V. "Malkizedek: Zu den Sagen der Agada." *MGWJ* 70 (1926): 93–113.

Astour, M. C. "Political and Cosmic Symbolism in Genesis 14 and Its Babylonian Sources." In *Biblical Motifs: Origin and Transformation*. Ed. A. Altmann, 65–112. Cambridge, Mass.: Harvard University Press, 1966.

Barth, L. M. "Genesis 15 and the Problem of Abraham's Seventh Trial." *Ma'arav* 8 (1992): 245–63.

Bashear, S. "Abraham's Sacrifice of His Son and Related Issues." *Der Islam* 67 (1990): 243–77.

Baumbach, G. "Abraham unser Vater: Der Prozess der Vereinnahmung Abrahams durch das fruhe Christentum." *Theologische Versuche* 16 (1986): 37–56.

Beck, E. "Die Gestalt des Abraham am Wendepunket der Entwicklung Muhammeds. Analyse von Sure 2,118." *Le Museon* 65 (1952): 73–94.

Bell, R. "The Sacrifice of Ishmael." *TGUOS* 10: 29–31.

Bennett, C. "Is Isaac without Ishmael Complete? A Nineteenth-Century Debate Revisited." *Islam and Christian-Muslim Relations* 2 (1991): 42–55.

Bijlefeld, W. A. "Controversies around the Quranic Ibrahim Narrative and Its 'Orientalist' Interpretations." *MW* 72 (1982): 81–94.

Blenkinsopp, J. "Abraham and the Righteous of Sodom." *JJS* 33 (1982): 119–32.

——. "Biographical Patterns in Biblical Narrative." *JSOT* 20 (1981): 27–46.

Blum, E. *Die Komposition der Vatergeschichte.* WMANT 57. Neukirchen-Vluyn: Neukirchener Verlag, 1984.

Bohlig, A. "Jacob as an Angel in Gnosticism and Manicheism." *NHS* 14 (1978): 122–30.

Borrmans, M. "Abraham in the Qur'an." *Encounter* 222–23 (1995): 19–24.

Braun, F. M. "Le sacrifice d'Isaac dans le quatrième évangile d'apres le Targum." *NRT* 101 (1979): 481–97.

Brock, S. P. "Abraham and the Ravens." *JSJ* 9 (1978): 135–52.

Brodie, L. T. "Jacob's Travail (Jer 30:1–13) and Jacob's Struggle (Gen 32:22–32)." *JSOT* 19 (1981): 31–60.

Bruce, F. F. "'Abraham had two sons: A Study in Pauline Hermeneutics." *NTS* 22 (1975): 71–84.

Calder, N. "From Midrash to Scripture: The Sacrifice of Abraham in Early Islamic Tradition." *Le Museon* 101 (1988): 375–402.

——. "Tafsir from Tabari to Ibn Kathir: Problems in the Description of a Genre, Illustrated with Reference to the Story of Abraham." In *Approaches to the Qur'an.* Ed. G. R. Hawting and Abdul-Kader A. Shareef, 101–40. London: Routledge, 1993.

Clarke, E. G. "Jacob's Dream at Bethel." *SR* 4 (1974–75): 367–77.

Clements, R. *Abraham and David.* SBT 5. Nashville, Tenn.: T. Nelson, 1967.

Cohen, G. D. "Esau as a Symbol in Early Medieval Thought." In *Studies in the Variety of Rabbinic Cultures,* 243–69. Philadelphia: Jewish Publication Society, 1991.

Couffignal, R. *L'épreuve d'Abraham.* Publications de l'Université de Toulouse-Le Mirail A30. Toulouse, France: Association des Publications de l'Université de Toulouse-Le Mirail, 1976.

Cranford, M. "Abraham in Romans 4: The Father of All Who Believe." *NTS* 41 (1995): 71–88.

Cross, F. M. "Yahweh and the God of the Patriarchs." *HTR* 55 (1962): 236–41.

Daly, R. J. *Christian Sacrifice.* Washington, D.C.: Catholic University of America, 1978.

——. "The Soteriological Significance of the Sacrifice of Isaac." *CBQ* 39 (1977): 45–75.

Davies, P. R., and B. D. Chilton, "The Aqedah: A Revised Tradition-History." *CBQ* 40 (1978): 514–46.

Diebner, B. "'Isaak' und 'Abraham' in der alttestamentlichen Literatur ausserhalf Gen. 12–50." *DBAT* 7 (1974): 38–50.

Dreifuss, G., and J. Riemer. *Abraham, the Man and the Symbol: A Jungian Interpretation of the Biblical Story.* Wilmette, Ill.: Chiron Publications, 1995.

Du Mesnil Du Buisson, C. "Trois histoires arabes sur Abraham et Moise." *REJ* 99 (1934): 119–26.

Durand, X. "Le combat de Jacob: Gn 32,23–33." In *L'Ancien Testament: Approches et lectures*. Ed. A. Vanel, 99–115. Paris: Beauchesne, 1977.

Fekkar, Y. "Le mythe de Hajar." *Peuples Mediterranéens* 44–45 (1988): 235–45, 343.

Feldman, L. "Abraham the Greek Philosopher in Josephus." *TAPA* 99 (1968): 145–49.

———. "Josephus as a Biblical Interpreter of the Aqedah." *JQR* 75 (1985): 211–30.

Finkel, J. "An Arabic Story of Abraham." *HUCA* 12–13 (1938): 387–409.

Firestone, R. "Abraham's Son as the Intended Sacrifice (al-Dhabihi, Quran 37:99–113): Issues in Quranic Exegesis." *JSS* 34 (1989): 95–131.

———. "Difficulties in Keeping a Beautiful Wife." *JJS* 42 (1991): 196–214.

———. *Journeys in Holy Lands: The Evolution of the Abraham-Ishmael Legend in Islamic Exegesis*. Albany: State University of New York Press, 1990.

———. "Prophethood, Marriageable Consanguinity, and Text: The Problem of Abraham and Sarah's Kinship Relationship and the Response of Jewish and Islamic Exegesis." *JQR* 83 (1993): 331–47.

———. "Sarah's Identity in Islamic Exegetical Tradition." *MW* 80 (1990): 65–17.

Fishbane, M. "Composition and Structure in the Jacob Cycle." *JJS* 27 (1975): 15–38.

Fox, E. "Stalking the Younger Brother: Some Models for Understanding a Biblical Motif." *JSOT* 60 (1993).

Gispen, W. H. "A Blessed Son for Abraham." In *Von Kanaan bis Kerala: Festschrift für J.P.M. van der Ploeg*, 123–29. AOAT 211. Neukirchen-Vluyn: Neukirchener Verlag, 1982.

Greenspoon, L. J. "The Origin of the Idea of Resurrection." In *Traditions in Transformation*. Ed. B. Halpern and J. D. Levenson, 247–321. Winona Lake, Ind.: Eisenbrauns,1961.

Gunkel, H. *The Legends of Genesis*. Trans. W. H. Carruth. New York, 1901. Reprint, Schocken, 1964.

Guthrie, A. "The Significance of Abraham." *MW* 45 (1955): 113–20.

Gutmann, J. "Abraham in the Fire of the Chaldeans: A Jewish Legend in Jewish, Christian, and Islamic Art." *Fruhmittellterliche Studien* 7 (1973): 342–52.

Hackett, J. "Rehabilitating Hagar: Fragments of an Epic Pattern." In *Gender and Difference in Ancient Israel*. Ed. Peggy L. Day, 12–27. Minneapolis, Minn.: Fortress, 1989.

Hadas-Lebel, M. "Jacob et Esau ou Israël et Rome dans le Talmud et le Midrash." *RHR* 20 (1984): 369–92.

Hayward, C. T. R. "The Sacrifice of Isaac and Jewish Polemic against Christianity." *CBQ* 52 (1990): 292–306.

Hendel, R. S. *The Epic of the Patriarch.* HSM 42. Atlanta: Scholars, 1987.

Hillers, D. R. "Pahad Yishaq." *JBL* 91 (1972): 90–92.

Johns, A. H. "al-Razi's Treatment of the Qur'anic Episodes Telling of Abraham and His Guests: Qur'anic Exegesis with a Human Face." *Mélanges de l'Institut Dominicain d'Études Orientales du Caire* 17 (1986): 81–114.

Jomier, J. "La figure d'Abraham et le pélérinage musulman de la Mekke." *Mélanges Eugène Tisserant* I (1964): 229–44.

Kilian, Rudolf. *Isaaks Opferung.* Stuttgarter Bibelstudien 44. Stuttgart, Germany: W. Kohlhammer, 1970.

Kodell, J. "Jacob Wrestles with Esau." *BTB* 10 (1980): 65–70.

Kugel, J. L. "The Ladder of Jacob." *HTR* 88 (1995): 209–19

Kuschl, K.-J. "Eins in Abraham? Zur theologischen Grundlegung einer Friedenskultur zwischen Judentum, Christentum und Islam." *Zeitschrift für Kulturaustausch* 43 (1993): 85–97.

Lehmann, M. R. "Abraham's Purchase of Machpelah and Hittite Law." *BASOR* 129 (1953): 15–18.

Lemaire, A. "Les Bene Jacob: Essai d'interprétation historique d'une tradition patriarchale." *RB* 85 (1978): 321–27.

Mandel, P. "The Call of Abraham: A Midrash Revisited." *Prooftexts* 14 (1994): 267–84.

Martin-Achard, R. "La figure d'Isaac dans l'Ancien Testament et dans la tradition juive." *Bulletin des facultés catholiques de Lyon* 106 (1982): 5–10.

Mbon, F. M. *Abraham in the Qur'an.* Encyclopaedic Survey of Islamic Culture. Vol. 2: Studies in Quran. Ed. Mohammed Taher, 128–47. Delhi: Anmol Publications, 1997.

———. "A Hanif Resigned: Abraham in the Qur'an." *Islam and the Modern Age* 11 (1980): 121–48.

McEvenue, S. "A Comparison of Narrative Styles in the Hagar Stories." *Semeia* 3 (1975): 64–80.

McKenzie, S. "'You Have Prevailed': The Function of Jacob's Encounter at Peniel in the Jacob Cycle." *ResQ* 23 (1980): 225–32.

Mendenhall, G. "The Nature and Purpose of the Abraham Narratives." In *Ancient Israelite Religion: Essay in Honor of Frank Moore Cross.* Ed. P. D. Miller et al., 337–56. Philadelphia: Fortress, 1987.

Millard, A. R., and D. Wiseman, eds. *Essays on the Patriarchal Narratives.* 2nd ed. Winona Lake, Ind.: Eisenbrauns, 1983.

Moberly, R. W. L. "Abraham's Righteousness (Genesis XV 6)." In *Studies in the Pentateuch.* Ed. J. A. Emerton, 103–30. Leiden, Netherlands: E. J. Brill, 1990.

Morales Artega, T. "Dos profetas regatean por un pueblo: Abraham y Mahoma." *Actes du VI symposium international d'Études morisques sur: État des etudes de Moriscologie durant les trente dernieres annees. Études reunies et presentees par Abdeljelil Temimi. Waqa'i' al-Mu'tamar al-'Alami al-Sadis li-l-Dirasat al-Mawriskiya al-Andalusiya hawl: Wad'iyat al-dirasat al-Mawriskiya al-Andalusiya khilal al-thalathin sana al-madiya tahta ishraf 'Abd al-Jalil al-Tamimi*, 219–26. Centre d'études et de recherches ottomanes, morisques, de documentation et d'information. Zaghouan, Tunisia: 1995.

Morrison, M. A. "The Jacob and Laban Narrative in Light of Near Eastern Sources." *BA* 46 (1983): 155–64.

Moubarac, Y. *Abraham dans le Coran*. Paris: J. Vrin, 1958.

Musa, A. "The Role of Abraham in the Formation of Islam." *Orita* 8 (1974): 58–70.

Naimur Rehman, M. "The Qur'an on Nimrod's Fire." *Jha Commen Vol.* (1937): 297–308.

Naudé, J. A. "Isaac Typology in the Koran." In *De fructu oris sui: Essays in Honour of Adrianus van Selms*. Ed. I. H. Eybers et al., 121–29. Leiden, Netherlands: E. J. Brill, 1971.

Nestle, E. "Wie alt war Isaak bei der Opferung?" ZAW 26 (1906).

Nieswandt, R. *Abrahams umkäpftes Erbe*. Stuttgart, Germany: W. Kohlhammer, 1998.

Nöldeke, T. "Der Gott MRA BYTA und die Ka'ba." ZA 23 (1909): 184–86.

Oden, R. A. "Jacob as Father, Husband, and Nephew." *JBL* 102 (1983): 189–05.

Pellat, C. "Nemrod et Abraham dans le parler arabe des Juifs de Debdou." *Hesperis* 39 (1952): 121–45.

Pury, A. de. *Promesse divine et légende culturelle dans le cycle de Jacob, Genèse 28 et les traditions patriarcales*. 2 vols. Paris: J. Gabalda, 1975.

Reinink, G. J. "Ismael, der Wildesel in der Wüste": Zur Typologie der Apokalypse des Pseudo-Methodios." *Byzantinische Zeitschrift* 75 (1982): 336–44.

Renard, J. "Images of Abraham in the Writings of Jalal al-Din Rumi." *JOAS* 106 (1986): 633–40.

Rocalve, P. "Louis Massignon et Abraham." *Luqman* 13 (1997): 27–36.

Sandmel, S. "Abraham's Knowledge of the Existence of God." *HTR* 44 (1951): 137–49.

Schmid. H. "Ismael im Alten Testament und im Koran." *Judaica* 32 (1976): 76–81, 119–29.

Schützinger, H. *Ursprung und Entwicklung der arabischen Abraham-Nimrod-Legende*. Bonner Orientalistische Studien, n.s. 11. Bonn, Germany: N.p., 1961.

Segal, A. F. "'He who did not spare his only son. . . .' (Romans 8:32): Jesus, Paul, and the Sacrifice of Isaac." In *From Jesus to Paul*. Ed. P. Richardson and J. C. Hurd, 169–84. Waterloo, 1984. [="The Sacrifice of Isaac in Early

Judaism and Christianity." In *The Other Judaisms of Late Antiquity*, 109–30. BJS 127. Atlanta: Scholars, 1987].

Selman, M. J. "The Social Environment of the Patriarchs." *Tyn Bul* 27 (1976): 114–36.

Shafaat, Ahmed. "The Abrahamic Ummah." In *Islam in a World of Diverse Faiths*. Ed. D. Cohn-Sherbok, 188–200. Basingstoke, England: Macmillan, 1991.

Shinan, A., and Y. Zakovitch. *Abram and Sarai in Egypt*. Jerusalem: Hebrew University, 1983 [in Hebrew].

Siddiqui, N. "The Person Sacrificed Ismail or Ishaq? In the Light of Research into the Torah." *al-Serat* 1.2 (1975): 23–25.

Siker, J. "Abraham in Greco-Roman Paganism." *JSJ* 18 (1987): 188–208.

Snouck-Hurgronje, C. "La légende qorânique d'Abraham et la politique religieuse du prophète Mohammed. Traduit (avec la collaboration de G. W. Bousquet-Mirandolle) avec introduction et postface par G. H. Bousquet." *RA* 95 (1951): 273–88.

Spicehandler, E. "Shahin's Influence on Babai ben Loft: The Abraham-Nimrod Legend." In *Irano-Judaica II: Studies Relating to Jewish Contacts with Persian Culture throughout the Ages*. Ed. S. Shaked and A. Netzer, 158–65. Jerusalem: Ben-Zvi Institute for the Study of Jewish Communities in the East, 1990.

Spiegel, S. *The Last Trial: On the Legends and Lore of the Command to Abraham to Offer Isaac as a Sacrifice: The Akedah*. Trans. J. Goldin. New York: Jewish Lights Publications, 1967.

Steinmetz, D. *From Father to Son, Literary Currents in Biblical Interpretation*. Louisville, Ky.: John Knox, 1991.

Stetkevych, S. "Sara and the Hyena: Laughter, Menstruation, and the Genesis of a Double Entendre." *HR* 36 (1996): 13–41.

Swetnam, J. *Jesus and Isaac: A Study of the Epistle to the Hebrews in the Light of the Aqeda*. AB 94. Rome: Biblical Institute Press, 1981.

Talbi, M. "Foi d'Abraham et foi islamique." *Islamochristiana* 5 (1979): 1–5.

———. "La foi de Abraham: Le sens d'un non-sacrifice." *Islamochristiana* 8 (1982): 1-11.

Thompson, T. L. "Conflict Themes in the Jacob Narratives." *Semeia* 15 (1979): 5–26.

———. *The Historicity of the Patriarchal Narratives*. Berlin: Walter de Gruyter, 1974.

Troger, K.-W. "Mohammed und Abraham: Der Prozess der Ablosung des fruhen Islam vom Judentum und seine Vorgeschichte." *Kairos* 22 (1980): 188–200.

Van der Horst, P. W. "Nimrod after the Bible." In *Essays on the Jewish World of Early Christianity*, P. W. Van der Horst, 220–32. Göttingen, Germany: Vanderhoeck und Ruprecht, 1990.

Van Seeters, J. *Abraham in History and Tradition*. New Haven, Conn.: Yale University Press, 1975.

Von Rad, G. *Das Opfer des Abraham*. Munich: C. Kaiser, 1971.

Wacholder, B. Z. "Pseudo-Eupolymos' Two Greek Fragments on the Life of Abraham." *HUCA* 34 (1963): 83–113.

Wahl, H. M. "Die Jakobserzählungen der Genesis und der Jubiläern." *VT* 44 (1994): 524–46.

Ward, R. "Abraham Traditions in Early Christianity." *SCS* 2 (1972): 165–79.

Wheeler, B. "'The Land in Which You Have Lived': Inheritance of the Promised Land in Classical Islamic Exegesis." In *Flowing with Milk and Honey: Visions of Israel*. Ed. Leonard Greenspoon, 49–83. Omaha: University of Nebraska Press, 2002.

White, H. C. "The Initiation Legend of Isaac." *ZAW* 91 (1979): 1–30.

———. "The Initiation Rite of Ishmael." *ZAW* 87 (1975): 267–305.

Zakovitch, Y. "Juxtaposition in the Abrahamic Cycle." In *Pomegranates and Golden Bells: Studies in Biblical, Jewish, and Near Eastern Ritual, Law, and Literature in Honor of Jacob Milgrom*. Ed. D. P. Wright, 509–24. Winona Lake, Ind.: Eisenbrauns,1995.

JOSEPH

Apotwitzer, V. "Asenath, the Wife of Joseph: A Haggadic Literary-Historical Study." *HUCA* 1 (1924): 239–306.

Bechwith, R. T. "The Solar Calendar of Joseph and Aseneth." *JSJ* 15 (1984): 90–111.

Beeston, A. F. L. *Baidawi's Commentary on Surah 12 of the Quran: Text, Accompanied by an Interpretive Rendering and Notes*. Oxford: Clarendon, 1963.

Coats, G. W. *From Canaan to Egypt: Structural and Theological Context for the Joseph Story*. CBQMS 4. Washington, D.C.: Catholic Biblical Association of America, 1976.

Gutmann, J. "Joseph Legends in the Vienna Genesis." *Proceedings of the Fifth World Congress of Jewish Studies*. Jerusalem, 1973, 4:181–84.

Hameen-Antilla, J. "'We Will Tell You the Best of Stories': A Study on Surah XII." *Studia Orientalia* 67 (Helsinki ,1991): 7–32.

Hollander, H. W. *Joseph as an Ethical Model in the Testaments of the Twelve Patriarchs*. Leiden, Netherlands: E. J. Brill, 1981.

Horovitz, J. *Die Josephserzählung*. Frankfurt: Peter Lang, 1921.

Kraemer, R. S. *When Aseneth Met Joseph: A Late Antique Tale of the Biblical Patriarch and His Egyptian Wife, Reconsidered*. New York: Oxford University Press, 1998.

Kugel, J. L. *In Potiphar's House: The Interpretive Life of Biblical Texts*. 2nd ed. Cambridge, Mass.: Harvard University Press, 1994.

Levenson, J. D. *Death and Resurrection of the Beloved Son*. New Haven, Conn.: Yale University Press, 1993.

Lowenthal, E. I. *The Joseph Narrative in Genesis*. New York: KTAV Publishing, 1973.

MacDonald, J. "Joseph in the Quran and Muslim Commentary." *MW* 10 (1956): 113–31, 207–24.

Morris, J. "Dramatizing the Sura of Joseph: An Introduction to the Islamic Humanities." *Journal of Turkish Studies* 18 (1994): 201–24.

Rad, G. von. *Die Josephgeschichte*. Neukirchen-Vluyn: Neukirchener Verlag, 1956.

――――. "The Joseph Narrative and Ancient Wisdom." In *The Problem of the Hexateuch and Other Essays*. G. von Rad, trans. E. Dicken, 292–300. New York: McGraw-Hill, 1966.

Redford, D. B. *A Study of the Biblical Story of Joseph (Genesis 37-50)*. VTS 20. Leiden, Netherlands: E. J. Brill, 1970.

Schuller, E. "4Q372: A Text about Joseph." *RQ* 14 (1989–90): 349–76.

Seybold, D. A. "Paradox and Symmetry in the Joseph Narrative." In *Literary Interpretations of Biblical Narratives*. Ed. K. R. R. Gros-Louis et al., 59–73. Nashville, Tenn.: Abingdon, 1974.

Wilcox, M. "The Bones of Joseph: Hebrews 11:2." In *Scripture: Meaning and Method*. Ed. B. P. Thompson, 114–30. Hull, England: Hull University Press, 1987.

MOSES

Asmussen, J. P., and H. Dadkhan. "En jodisk-persisk beretning om profeten Moses og den jodiske religion." *Dansk Teologisk Tidsskrift* 58 (1995): 137–42.

Badawi, A. "Le problème de Haman." In *Studi in onore di Francesco Gabrieli nel suo ottantesimo compleanno*. Ed. R. Traini, 29–33. Rome: Università di Roma "La Sapienza," Dipartimento di studi orientali, 1984.

Beer, M. "The Riches of Moses in Rabbinic Aggada." *Tarbiz* 43 (1974): 70–87.

Belleville, L. *Reflections of Glory: Paul's Polemical Use of the Moses-Doxa Tradition in 2 Cor 3:1-18*. JSNT 42. Sheffield, England: JSOT Press, 1991.

Bienaimé, G. *Moïse et le don de l'eau dans la traditions juive ancienne*. Rome: Biblical Institute Press, 1984.

Bouguenaya Mermer, Y. "Islamisation of Knowledge: A Paradigm Shift—the Pharaoh's Sorcerers vs. the Staff of Moses." *Muslim Education Quarterly* 12 (1995): 4–29.

Buber, M. *Moses: The Revelation and the Covenant*. New York: Harper, 1958.

Buis, P. "Les conflits entre Moïse et Israël dans Exode et Nomres." *VT* 28 (1978): 267–70.

Cazelles, H., et al., ed. *Moïse: Homme de l'Alliance*. Paris: Desclee & Cie, 1955.

Chazon, E. "Moses' Struggle for His Soul: A Prototype for the Testament of Abraham, the Greek Apocalypse of Ezra, and the Apocalypse of Sedrach." *SC* 5 (1985–86): 151–64.

Chernus, I. *The Rebellion at the Reed Sea: Observations on the Nature of Midrash*. Chico, Calif.: Scholars, 1981.

Coats, G. W. *Moses: Heroic Man, Man of God*. JSOTSS 57. Sheffield, England: JSOT Press, 1985.

Daiches. D. *Moses: The Man and His Vision*. New York: Praeger, 1975.

Derrett, J. D. M. "The Bronze Serpent." *EB* 49 (1991): 31–39.

Derrett, J., and M. Duncan. "A Moses–Buddha Parallel and Its Meaning." *AO* 58 (1990): 310–17.

Dexinger, F. "Der Prophet 'Wie Mose' in Qumran und bei der Samaritanern." In *Mélanges bibliques et orientaux en honneur de M. Mathias Delcor*. Ed. A. Caquot et al., 97–111. Neukirchen-Vluyn: Neukirchener Verlag, 1985.

El'ad, A. "Some Aspects of the Islamic Traditions Regarding the Site of the Grave of Moses." *JSAI* 11 (1988): 1–15.

Elder, E. E. "Parallel Passages in the Koran—the Story of Moses." *MW* 15 (1925): 254–59.

Fitzmeyer, J. A. "Glory Reflected on the Face of Christ (2 Cor. 3:7–4:6) and a Palestinian Jewish Motif." *TS* 42 (1981): 630–44.

Fletcher-Louis, C. "4Q374: A Discourse on the Sinai Tradition: The Deification of Moses and Early Christology." *DSD* 3 (1996): 236–52.

Fodor, A. "The Rod of Moses in Arabic Magic." *AO* 32 (1978): 1–17.

Frankemölle, H. "Mose in Deutungen des Neuen Testaments." *KI* 9 (1944): 70–86.

Gager, J. G. *Moses in Greco-Roman Paganism*. Nashville, Tenn.: Abingdon, 1972.

Gressmann, H. *Mose und Seine Zeit: Ein Kommentar zu den Mose-Sagen*. Göttingen, Germany: Vanderhoeck und Ruprecht, 1913.

Gril, D. "Le personnage coranique de Pharaon d'après l'interprétation d'Ibn Arabi." *Annales Islamologie* 14 (1978): 37–57.

Gutman, J. "The Testing of Moses: A Comparative Study in Christian, Muslim and Jewish Art." *Bulletin of the Asia Institute*, n.s. 2 (1988): 107–17.

———, and V. B. Moreen. "The Combat between Moses and Og in Muslim Miniatures." *Bulletin of the Asia Institute* 1 (1987): 111–22.

Hafemann, S. J. "Moses in the Apocrypha and Pseudepigrapha: A Survey." *JSP* 7 (1990): 79–104.

Hamidullah, M. "The Name of the Pharaoh Who Died by Drowning." Trans. A. R. Momin. *Islam and the Modern Age* 12 (1981): 151–60.

Holladay, W. L. "Jeremiah and Moses." *JBL* 85 (1966): 17–27.

Horst, P. van der. 'Moses' Throne Vision in Ezekiel the Dramatist." *JJS* 34 (1983): 21–29.

Johns, A. H. "'Let my people go!' Sayyid Qutb and the Vocation of Moses." *Islam and Christian Muslim Relations* 1 (1990): 143–70.

Kister, M. "A Booth Like the Booth of Moses." *BSOAS* 25 (1962): 150–55.

Krauss, S. "A Moses Legend." *JQR*, n.s. 2 (1911–12): 339–64 with Note by I. Friedlaender 3 (1912–13): 235–36.

Künstlinger, D. "Tur und Gabal im Kuran." *RO* 5 (1927): 58–67.

Loewenstamm, S. "The Death of Moses." *Tarbiz* 27 (1958): 142–57. Trans. in *Studies in the Testament of Abraham*. Ed. G. W. E. Nickelsburg, Jr., 185–217. Missoula, Mont.: Scholars, 1976.

Maccoby, H. "Neusner and the Red Cow." *JSJ* 21 (1990): 69–75.

Meeks, W. A. "Moses as God and King." In *Religions in Antiquity: Essays in Memory of Erwin Ramsdell Goodenough*. Ed. J. Neusner. Leiden, Netherlands: E. J. Brill, 1968.

———. *The Prophet-King: Moses Traditions and the Johannine Christology*. Leiden, Netherlands: E. J. Brill, 1967.

Mellinkoff, R. *The Horned Moses in Medieval Art and Thought*. Berkeley: University of California Press, 1970.

Meyer, J. J. "Moses und Zarathustra, Jesus und Muhammed in einem Purana." *Wiener Zeitschrift fur die Kunde des Morgenlandes* 43 (1936): 1–18.

Meynet, R. "Le cantique de Moise et le cantique de l'Agneau (Ap. 15 et Exod. 15)." *Gregorianum* 73 (1992): 19–55.

Milgrom, J. "Magic, Monotheism and the Sin of Moses." In *The Quest for the Kingdom of God*. Ed. H. B. Hoffman et al., 251–65. Winona Lake, Ind.: Eisenbrauns,1983.

Milstein, R. "The Iconography of Moses in Islamic Art." *Jewish Art* 12–13 (1986–87): 199–212.

Moreen, V. B. "Moses in Muhammad's Light: Muslim Topoi and Anti-Muslim Polemics in Judaeo-Persian Panegyrics." *Journal of Turkish Studies* 18 (1994): 185–200.

Moubarac, Y. *Moise dans le Coran*. Paris, 1954.

Newsom, C. "4Q374: A Discourse on the Exodus/Conquest Tradition." In *The Dead Sea Scrolls: Forty Years of Research*. Ed. D. Dimant and U. Rappaport, 40–52. Leiden, Netherlands: E. J. Brill, 1992.

Noegel, S. B. "The Aegean Ogygos of Boeotia and the Biblical Og of Bashan: Reflections of the Same Myth." *ZAW* 110 (1998): 411–26.

———. "Moses and Magic: Notes on the Book of Exodus." *JANES* 24 (1997): 45–59.

Nordström, C. "The Water Miracles of Moses in Jewish Legend and Byzantine Art." *Analecta Suecana* 7 (1958): 78–109.

Pauliny, J. "'Ug ibn 'Anaq, ein sagenhafter Riese: Untersuchungen zu den islamischen Riesengeschichten." *Graecolatina et Orientalia* 5 (1973): 249–68.

Propp, W. H. "The Rod of Aaron and the Sin of Moses." *JBL* 107.1 (1988): 19–26.

Rajak, T. "Moses in Ethiopia, Legends and Literature." *JJS* 29 (1978): 111–22.

Rofé, A. "Moses' Mother and Her Servant according to an Exodus Scroll from Qumran." *BM* 40 (1995): 197–202.

Rudolph, U. "Christliche Bibelexegese und Mu'tazilitische Theologie: der Fall des Moses bar Kepha (gest. 903 n.Chr.)." *Oriens* 34 (1994): 299–313.

Schalit, A. *Untersuchungen zur Assumptio Mosis*. Leiden, Netherlands: E. J. Brill, 1989.

Schultz, J. P. "Angelic Opposition to the Ascension of Moses and the Revelation of the Law." *JQR* 61 (1970–71): 282–307.

Schwarzbaum, H. "A Jewish Moses Legend of Islamic Provenance." In *Fields of Offerings: Studies in Honor of Raphael Patai*. Ed. V. D. Sanua, 99–110. Rutherford, N.J.: Fairleigh Dickinson University Press, 1983.

———. "The Jewish and Moslem Versions of Some Theodicy Legends." *Fabula* 3 (1959): 119–69.

Seitz, C. R. "The Prophet Moses and the Canonical Shape of Jeremiah." *ZAW* 101 (1989): 3–27.

Shinan, A. "Moses and the Ethiopian Woman." *SH* 27 (1978): 66–78.

Silver, D. J. *Images of Moses*. New York: Basic Books, 1982.

Sirat, C. "Un midras juif en habit musulman: La vision de moïse sur le mont Sinaï." *RHR* 168 (1965): 15–28.

Smolar, L., and M. Aberbach. "The Golden Calf Episode in Postbiblical Literature." *HUCA* 39 (1968): 91–116.

Syed, S, M. "Haman in the Quran: A Historical Assessment." In *Encyclopaedic Survey of Islamic Culture: Studies in Quran*. Ed. M. Taher, 176–89. Delhi, India: 1997.

———. "Historicity of Haman as Mentioned in the Quran." *IQ* 24 (1980): 48–59.

Tonneau, R. M. "Moïse dans la tradition syrienne." In *Moïse: Homme de l'Alliance*. Ed. H. Cazelles et al., 247–65. Paris: Desclée, 1955.

Van Seters, J. *The Life of Moses: The Yahwist as Historian in Exodus-Numbers*. Louisville, Ky.: John Knox, 1994.

Weinfeld, M. "God versus Moses in the Temple Scroll." *RQ* 15 (1991): 175–80.

Wenham, G. J. "Aaron's Rod (Num 17:16–28)." *ZAW* 93 (1981).

Wheeler, B. "Moses or Alexander? Q 18:60–65 in Early Islamic Exegesis." *JNES* 57 (1998): 191–215.

———. *Moses in the Quran and Islamic Exegesis*. London: Curzon, 2002.

Williams, C. A. *Oriental Affinities of the Legend of the Hairy Anchorite.* 2 vols. Urbana: University of Illinois Press, 1925–26.

Winston, D. "Two Types of Mosaic Prophecy according to Philo." *JSP* 4 (1989): 49–67.

KHIDR, DHU AL-QARNAYN

Abel, A. "Dù'l Qarnayn: Prophète de l'universalité." *Annuaire de l'institut de philologie et d'histoire orientales (et slaves)* 11 (1951): 23–43.

Anderson, A. R. *Alexander's Gate, Gog and Magog and Enclosed Nations.* Medieval Academy of American Publications 12. Cambridge: Medieval Academy of America, 1932.

———. "Alexander's Horns." *American Philological Association Transactions and Proceedings* 58 (1927): 100–22.

Arkoun, M. "Lecture de la sourate 18." *Annales ESC* 35 (1980): 418–35.

Battye, N. "Khidr in the Opus of Jung: The Teaching of Surrender." In *Jung and the Monotheisms: Judaism, Christianity and Islam.* Ed. J. Ryce-Menuhin, 166–91. London: Routledge, 1994.

Bencheikh, J. E. "Sourate d'al-Kahf, neuf traductions du Coran." *Études arabes, Analyses théorie* 3 (1980): 1–51.

Clay, G. *The Medieval Alexander.* Ed. D. J. A. Ross. Cambridge: Cambridge University Press, 1956. Reprint, 1967.

De Ravignan, F. "Les sept dormants: Lieu de rencontre abrahamique." *Horizons Maghrebins* 20–21 (1993): 238–39.

Ethé, C. H. "Alexanders Zug zum Lebensquell im Land der Finsternis." *Sitzungsberichte der Bayerischen Akademie der Wissenschaften: Philosophisch-Historische Klasse* (München, 1871): 343–405.

Friedländer, I. "Alexandeers Zug nach dem lebensquell und die Chadirlegende." *AR* 13 (1910): 319–27.

———. *Die Chadirlegende und der Alexanderroman.* Leipzig, Germany: J. C. Hinrichs, 1913.

———. "Zur Geschichte der Chahdirlegende." *AR* 13 (1910): 92–110.

Heller, B. "Chadhir und der Prophet Elijahu als wundertätige Baumeister." *MGWJ* 81 (1937): 76–80.

Hopkins, E. W. "The Fountain of Youth." *JAOS* 26 (1905): 1–67.

Lidzbarski, M. "Wer ist Chadhir?" *ZA* 7 (1892): 104–6.

———. "Zu den arabischen Alexandergeschichten." *ZA* 8 (1893): 263–312.

Meissner, B. *Alexander und Gilgamos.* Leipzig, Germany: J. C. Hinrichs, 1894.

Paret, R. "Un parallèle byzantin à Coran XVIII, 59–81." *REB* 26 (1968): 137–59.

Virolleaud, C. "Khadir, Élie et Tervagant." *CRAIBL* (1950): 245–46.

——. "Khadir et Tervagant." *JA* 241 (1953): 161–66.

Vollers, K. "Chidher." *AR* 12 (1909): 234–84.

Wheeler, B. "The Jewish Origins of Q 18:65–82? Reexamination of A. J. Wensinck's Theory." *JAOS* 118.2 (1998): 153–71.

——. "The Prophet Muhammad Dhu al-Qarnayn: Early Islamic Exegesis of Q 17:1." *Byzantino-rossica* (2002, forthcoming).

Yamauchi, E. M. *Foes from the Northern Frontier*. Grand Rapids, Mich.: Baker Book House, 1982.

SAMUEL, DAVID, SOLOMON

Barthélemy, D., et al. *The Story of David and Goliath*. OBO 73. Göttingen, Germany: Vanderhoeck und Ruprecht, 1986.

Beuken, W. A. M. "I Samuel 28: The Prophet as 'Hammer of Witches.'" *JSOT* 6 (1978): 3–17.

Bowman, J. "David, Jesus Son of David and Son of Man." *Abr-Nahrain* 27 (1989): 1–22.

Brueggemann, W. *David's Truth in Israel's Imagination and Memory*. Philadelphia: Fortress, 1985.

Buber, M. *Kingship of God*. Trans. R. Scheiman. New York: Humanities Press International, 1967.

Campbell, A. F. *Of Prophets and Kings*. CBQMS 17. Washington, D.C.: Catholic Biblical Association of America, 1986.

Carlson, R. A. *David the Chosen King*. Stockholm: Almqvist and Wiksell, 1964.

Chastel, P. "La legende de la reine de Saba.'" *RHR* 119 (1916): 204–25, 120 (1917): 27–44, 160–74.

Clapp, N. *Sheba: Through the Desert in Search of the Legendary Queen*. New York: Houghton Mifflin, 2001.

Duling, D. C. "The Eleazar Miracle and Solomon's Magical Wisdom in Flavius Josephus' *Antiquitates Judaicae* 8:42–49." *HTR* 78 (1985): 1–25.

——. "The Legend of Solomon the Magician in Antiquity: Problems and Perspectives." *Proceedings of the Eastern Great Lakes Biblical Society* 4 (1984): 1–22.

——. "Solomon, Exorcism, and the Son of David." *HTR* 68 (1975): 235–52.

——. "The Testament of Solomon: Retrospect and Prospect." *JSP* 2 (1988): 87–112.

Flanagan, J. W. *David's Social Drama*. JSOTSS 73. Sheffield, England: JSOT Press, 1988.

Frontain, R. J., and J. Wojcik, eds. *The David Myth in Western Literature*. West Lafayette, Ind.: Purdue University Press, 1980.

Green, A. R. "Solomon and Siamun: A Synchronism between Early Dynastic Israel and the Twenty-first Dynasty of Egypt." *JBL* 97 (1978): 353–67.

Gunn, D. M. *The Fate of King Saul*. JSOTSS 14. Sheffield, England: JSOT Press, 1980.

———. *The Story of King David*. JSOTSS 6. Sheffield, England: JSOT Press, 1978.

Irwin, W. A. "Samuel and the Rise of the Monarchy." *AJSL* 58 (1941): 113–34.

Ishida, T. *The Royal Dynasties in Ancient Israel*. BZAW 142. Berlin: Walter de Gruyter, 1977.

———, ed. *Studies in the Period of David and Solomon and Other Essays*. Winona Lake, Ind.: Eisenbrauns, 1982.

Jackson, H. M. "Notes on the Testament of Solomon." *JSJ* 19 (1988): 19–60.

Jason, H. "The Story of David and Goliath: A Folk Epic?" *Biblica* 60 (1979): 36–70.

Jensen, P. "Das Leben Muhammeds und die David-Sage." *Der Islam* 12 (1922): 84–97.

Johns, A. H. "David and Bathsheba: A Case Study in the Exegesis of Qur'anic Story-telling." In *David and the Ambiguity of the Mizmar according to Arab Sources*. Ed. C. Poche. Basel: Barenreiter Kassel, 1983.

———. "Solomon and the Queen of Sheba: Fakhr al-Din al-Razi's Treatment of the Quranic Telling of the Story." *Abr-Naharain* 24 (1986): 58–82.

Kaiser, W. C. "The Blessing of David: The Charter of Humanity." In *The Law and the Prophets*. Ed. J. H. Skilton, 298–318. Nutley, N.J.: Presbyterian and Reformed Pub. Co., 1974.

Kugel, J. L. "David the Prophet." In *Poetry and Prophecy*. Ed. Kugel, 45–55. Ithaca, N.Y.: Cornell University Press, 1990.

Lassner, J. *Demonizing the Queen of Sheba: Boundaries of Gender and Culture in Postbiblical Judaism and Medieval Islam*. Chicago: University of Chicago Press, 1993.

Lindsay, J. E. "'Ali ibn 'Asakir as a Preserver of Qisas al-Anbiya': The Case of David b. Jesse." In *The Tower of David/Mihrab Dawud: Remarks on the History of a Sanctuary in Jerusalem in Christian and Islamic Times*. Ed. H. Busse. Jerusalem Museum of the History of Jerusalem, 1994.

Luke, K. "The Queen of Sheba (1 Kgs 10:1–13)." *Indian Theological Studies* 23 (1986): 248–72.

Malamat, A. "The Kingdom of David and Solomon and Its Contact with Egypt and Aram Naharaim." *BA* 21 (1958): 96–102.

McCarter, P. K. "The Historical David." *Interpretation* 40 (1986): 117–29.

Mendelsohn, I. "Samuel's Denunciation of Kingship in the Light of Akkadian Documents from Ugarit." *BASOR* 143 (1956): 17–22.

Mettinger, T. N. D. *King and Messiah*. Lund, Sweden: Guerup, 1976.

Pedersen, D. "Portraits of David: Canonical and Otherwise." *Iliff Review* 42 (1985): 2–21.

Press, R. "Der Prophet Samuel." *ZAW* 56 (1938): 177–225.

Preston, T. R. "The Heroism of Saul: Patterns of Meaning in the Narrative of the Early Kingship." *JSOT* 24 (1982): 27–46.

Pritchard, J. *Solomon and Sheba*. London: Phaidon, 1974.

Rösch, A. *Die Königin von Saba als Königin Bilqis*. Leipzig, Germany: J. C. Hinrichs, 1880.

Salzberger, G. *Die Sulomo-Sage in der semitischen Literatur*. Berlin: M. Harrwitz, 1907.

Schechter, S. "The Riddles of Solomon in Rabbinic Literature." *Folklore* 1 (1890): 349–58.

Schmidt, W. H. *Konigtum Gottes in Ugarit und Israel*. 2nd ed. BZAW 80. Berlin: Töpelmann, 1966.

Scott, R. B. Y. "Solomon and the Beginning of Wisdom." *VTS* 3 (1955): 262–79.

Soggin, J. A. "The Davinic-Solomonic Kingdom." In *Israelite and Judaean History*. Ed. J. Hayes and J. Miller, 332–80. London: S.C.M. Press, 1977.

Stehly, R. "David dans la tradition islamique à la lumière des manuscrits de Qumrân." *RHPR* 59 (1979): 357 67.

Weisfeld, I. H. *David the King*. New York: Bloch, 1983.

Whitelam, K. W. *The Just King*. JSOTSS 12. Sheffield, England: JSOT Press, 1979.

Willis, J. T. "Cultic Elements in the Story of Samuel's Birth and Dedication." *StTh* 26 (1972): 33–61.

PRE-EXILIC ISRAELITE PROPHETS

Amos

Andersen, F., and D. N. Freedman. *Amos*. AB 24A. New York: Doubleday, 1989.

Asen, B. A. "No, Yes and Perhaps in Amos and the Yahwist." *VT* 43 (1993): 433–41.

Barstad. H. M. *The Religious Polemics of Amos*. VTS 34. Leiden, Netherlands: E. J. Brill, 1984.

Barton, J. *Amos' Oracles against the Nations: A Study of Amos 1.3–2.5*. Cambridge: Cambridge University Press, 1980.

Bic, M. "Der Prophet Amos-Ein Haepatoskopos." *VT* 1 (1951): 293–96.

Carroll, M. D. "God and His People in the Nations' History: A Contextualized Reading of Amos 1 & 2." *TB* 47 (1995): 39–70.

Coote, R. *Amos among the Prophets: Composition and Theology*. Philadelphia: Fortress, 1981.

Escobar, D. S. "Social Justice in the Book of Amos." *Review and Expositor* 92 (1995): 169–74.

Eslinger, L. "The Education of Amos." *HAR* 11 (1987): 35–57.

Freedman, D. N. "Confrontations in the Book of Amos." *PSB* 11 (1990): 240–52.

Hasel, G. F. "The Alleged 'No' of Amos and Amos' Eschatology." *AUSS* 29 (1991): 3–18.

Heyns, D. "Space and Time in Amos 8: An Ecological Reading." *OTE* 10 (1997): 236–51.

Jeremias, J. *The Book of Amos*. Louisville, Ky.: Westminster John Knox Press, 1998.

King, P. J. *Amos, Hosea, Micah—An Archaeological Commentary*. Philadelphia: Westminster, 1988.

Landy, F. "Vision and Poetic Speech in Amos." *HAR* 11 (1987): 223–46.

Lang, B. "The Social Organization of Peasant Poverty in Biblical Israel." *JSOT* 24 (1982): 47–63.

Limburg, J. "Amos 7:4: A Judgment with Fire?" *CBQ* 35 (1973): 346–49.

Mays, J. L. *Amos*. Philadelphia: Westminster, 1969.

Murtonen, A. "The Prophet Amos—A Hepatoscoper?" *VT* 2 (1952): 170–71.

Paul, S. *A Commentary on the Book of Amos*. Minneapolis, Minn.: Fortress, 1991.

Pigott, S. M. "Amos: An Annotated Bibliography." *SWJT* 38 (1995): 29–35.

Schmitt, J. J. "The Virgin of Israel: Referent and Use of the Phrase in Amos and Jeremiah." *CBQ* 53 (1991): 365–87.

Smith, G. "Continuity and Discontinuity in Amos' Use of Tradition." *JETS* 31 (1991): 33–42.

Snyder, G. "The Law and Covenant in Amos." *RQ* 25 (1982): 158–66.

Wolff, H. W. *Amos the Prophet*. Philadelphia: Fortress, 1973.

Elijah and Elisha

Allen, R. B. "Elijah the Broken Prophet." *JETS* 22 (1979): 193–202.

Allison, D. C. "Elijah Must Come First." *JBL* 103 (1984): 256–58.

Battenfield, J. R. "YHWH's Refutation of the Baal Myth through the Actions of Elijah and Elisha." In *Israel's Apostasy and Restoration*. Ed. A. Gileadi, 19–37. Grand Rapids, Mich.: Eerdmans, 1988.

Begg, C. T. "The Chronicler's Non-Mention of Elisha." *BN* 7 (1988): 7–11.

Benjamin, D. C. "The Elijah Stories." In *The Land of Carmel: Essays in Honor of Joachim Smet, O. Carm*. Ed. P. Chandler and K. Egan, 27–41. Rome: Institutum Carmelitanum, 1991.

Bergen, W. "The Prophetic Alternative: Elisha and the Israelite Monarchy." In *Elijah and Elisha in Socioliterary Perspective*. Ed. R. B. Coote, 127–37. Atlanta: Scholars, 1992.

Bronner, Leah. *The Stories of Elijah and Elisha as Polemics against Baal Worship*. Pretoria Oriental Studies, 6. Leiden, Netherlands: E. J. Brill, 1990.

Cohn, R. "The Literary Logic of 1 Kgs 17–19." *JBL* 101 (1983): 333–50.

Coote, R. B., ed. *Elijah and Elisha in Socioliterary Perspective*. Atlanta: Scholars, 1992.

Dumbrell, W. J. "What Are You Doing Here: Elijah at Horeb." *Crux* 22 (1986): 12–19.

Fairstein, M. M. "Why Do the Scribes Say That Elijah Must Come First?" *JBL* 100 (1981): 75–86.

Fitzmyer, J. A. "More about Elijah Coming First." *JBL* 104 (1985): 295–96.

Frankfurter, D. *Elijah in Upper Egypt: The Apocalypse of Elijah and Early Egyptian Christianity*. Minneapolis, Minn.: Fortress 1993.

Hauser, A. J., and R. Gregory. *From Carmel to Horeb: Elijah in Crisis*. Sheffield, England: JSOT Press, 1990.

Hentschel, G. *Die Elijaerzählungen*. Leipzig, Germany: J. C. Hinrichs, 1977.

Montgomery, J. A. *A Critical and Exegetical Commentary on the Book of Kings*. International Critical Commentary. Edinburgh: T & T. Clark, 1960.

Nordheim, E. von. "Ein Prophet kündigt sein Amt auf (Elia am Horeb)." *Biblica* 59 (1978): 153–73.

Östborn, G. *Yahweh and Baal*. Lund, Sweden: C. W. K. Gleerup, 1956.

Overholt, T. W. "Elijah and Elisha in the Context of Israelite Religion." In *Prophets and Paradigms: Essays in Honor of Gene M. Tucker*. Ed. S. B. Reid. Sheffield, England: JSOT Press, 1996.

Parker, S. B. "KTU 1.16 III. The Myth of the Absent God and 1 Kings 18." *UF* 21 (1989): 283–96.

Rendsburg, G. A. "The Mock of Baal in 1 Kgs 18:27." *CBQ* 50 (1988): 414–17.

Renteria, T. H. "The Elijah/Elisha Stories: The Socio-Cultural Analysis of Prophets and People in Ninth Century BCE Israel." In *Elijah and Elisha in Socio-Cultural Perspective*. Ed. R. B. Coote, 75–126. Atlanta: Scholars, 1992.

Schmidt, H.-C. *Elisa: Traditionsgeschichtliche Untersuchungen zur vorklassischen nordisraelitischen Prophetie*. Gütersloh, Germany: Gütersloher Verlagshaus, 1972.

Schweizer, H. *Elischa in den Kreigen: Literaturwissenschaftliche Untersuchung von 2 Kön 3, 6,8-23, 6,24-7,20*. Munich: Kösel, 1974.

Steck, O. *Überlieferung und Zeitgeschichte in den Elia-Erzählungen*. Neukirchen-Vluyn: Neukirchener Verlag, 1968.

Stone, M. E., and J. Strugnell. *The Books of Elijah: Parts 1–2*. Missoula, Mont.: Scholars, 1979.

White, M. *The Elijah Legends and Jehu's Coup.* Atlanta: Scholars, 1997.

———. "Naboth's Vineyard and Jehu's Coup: The Legitimation of a Dynastic Extermination." *VT* 44 (1994): 66–76.

Hosea

Andersen, F. *Hosea.* AB 24. New York: Doubleday.

Bird, P. "'To Play the Harlot': An Inquiry into an Old Testament Metaphor." In *Gender and Difference in Ancient Israel.* Ed. P. L. Day, 75–94. Minneapolis, Minn.: Fortress, 1989.

Botha, P. J. "The Communicative Function of Comparison in Hosea." *OTE* 6 (1993): 57–71.

Brueggemann, W. *Tradition for Crisis: A Study in Hosea.* Richmond: John Knox, 1968.

Buck, R. *Die Liebe gottes beim Propheten Oseé.* Rome: Tipografia Pio X, 1973.

Burke, D. G. *The Poetry of Baruch: A Reconstruction and Analysis of the Original Hebrew Text of Baruch 3:9–5:9.* Chico, Calif.: Scholars, 1982.

Doorley, W. J. *Prophet of Love: Understanding the Book of Hosea.* New York: Paulist, 1991.

Dozeman, T. B. "Hosea and the Wilderness Wandering Tradition." In *Rethinking the Foundations: Historiography in the Ancient World and in the Bible.* Ed. T. Romer and S. McKenzie, 55–70. Berlin: Walter de Gruyter, 2000.

Emmerson, G. I. *Hosea: An Israelite Prophet in Judean Perspective.* JSOTSS 28. Sheffield, England: JSOT Press, 1984.

Fensham, F. C. "The Marriage Metaphor in Hosea for the Covenant Relationship between the Lord and His People." *JNSL* 12 (1984): 71–78.

Gordis, R. "Hosea's Marriage and Message." *HUCA* 25 (1954): 9–40.

Hall, G. "Origin of the Marriage Metaphor." *Hebrew Studies* 23 (1982): 169–71.

Hornsby, T. J. "'Israel Has Become a Worthless Thing': Re-reading Gomer in Hosea 1–3." *JSOT* 82 (1999): 115–28.

Irvine, S. A. "The Threat of Jezreel (Hosea 1:4–5)." *CBQ* 57 (1995): 494–503.

Kinet, D. *Ba'al und Jahweh: Ein Beitrag zur Theologie des Hoseabuches.* Frankfurt: Peter Lang, 1977.

King, P. J. *Amos, Hosea, Micah—An Archaeological Commentary.* Philadelphia: Westminster, 1988.

Kruger, P. A. "The Marriage Metaphor in Hosea 2:4–17 against Its Ancient Near Eastern Background." *OTE* 5 (1992): 7–25.

MacIntosh, A. A. *A Critical and Exegetical Commentary on Hosea.* Edinburgh: T & T. Clark, 1997.

May, H. G. "The Fertility Cult in Hosea." *AJSL* 48 (1931): 73–98.

McDonald, J. R. B. "The Marriage of Hosea." *Theology* 67 (1964): 149–56.

North, F. S. "Solution of Hosea's Marital Problems by Critical Analysis." *JNES* 16 (1957): 128–30.

Odell, M. S. "Who Were the Prophets in Hosea?" *Biblical Theology* 18 (1996): 78–95.

Peckham, B. "The Composition of Hosea." *HAR* 11 (1987): 331–53.

Rowley, H. H. "The Marriage of Hosea." *BJRL* 39 (1956): 200–33.

Schmidt, J. J. "Yahweh's Divorce in Hosea 2 — Who Is That Woman?" *SJOT* 9 (1995): 119–32.

Setel, T. D. "Prophets and Pornography: Female Sexual Imagery in Hosea." In *Feminist Interpretation of the Bible*. Ed. L. M. Russell, 86–95. Oxford: Blackwell, 1985.

Sherwood, Y. *The Prostitute and the Prophet: Hosea's Marriage in Literary-Theoretical Perspective*. Sheffield, England: JSOT Press, 1996.

West, G. "The Effects and Power of Discourse: A Case Study of a Metaphor in Hosea." *Scriptura* 57 (1996): 201–12.

Wolff, H. W. *A Commentary on the Book of the Prophet Hosea*. Philadelphia: Fortress, 1974.

Zobel, H. J. "Prophet in Israel und in Judah: Das prophetische Verständnis des Hosea und Amos." *ZTK* 82 (1985): 281–99.

Micah

Allen, L. *The Books of Joel, Obadiah, Jonah and Micah*. Grand Rapids, Mich.: Eerdmans, 1976.

Andersen, F. I. *Micah*. New York: Hi Marketing, 2000.

Ben Zvi, E. *Micah*. Grand Rapids, Mich.: Eerdmans, 2000.

———. "Micah 1.2–16: Observations and Possible Implications." *JSOT* 77 (1998): 103–20.

Dempsey, C. J. "Micah 2–3: Literary Artistry, Ethical Message, and Some Considerations about the Image of YHWH and Micah." *JSOT* 85 (1999): 117–28.

Elliger, K. "Die Heimat des Propheten Micha." *ZDPV* 57 (1934): 81–152.

Hillers, D. R. *Micah*. Philadelphia: Fortress Press, 1984.

Kaiser, W. *Micah, Nahum, Habakkuk, Zephaniah, Haggai, Zechariah, Malachi*. Nashville, Tenn.: Word Publishing, 1992.

King, P. J. *Amos, Hosea, Micah—An Archaeological Commentary*. Philadelphia: Westminster, 1988.

Mays, J. L. *Micah*. Philadelphia: S. C. M. Press, 1976.

McKane, W. *The Book of Micah: Introduction and Commentary*. Edinburgh: T. & T. Clark, 1998.

——. "Micah 2:1–5: Text and Commentary." *JSS* 42 (1997): 7–22.
Spaude, C. W. *Obadiah, Jonah, Micah*. Milwaukee, Wisc.: Northwestern Publishing, 2001.
Waltke, B. K., et al. *Obadia*. Downers Grove, Ill.: InterVarsity Press, 1988.
Wessels, W. J. "Conflicting Powers: Reflections from the Book of Micah." *OTE* 10 (1997): 528–44.
Wolff, H. W. *Micah: A Commentary*. Minneapolis, Minn.: Fortress, 1990.

Isaiah

Ackroyd, P. R. "The Biblical Interpretation of the Reigns of Ahaz and Hezekieh." In *In the Shelter of Elyon*. Ed. W. B. Barrick and J. R. Spencer, 247–59. Sheffield, England: JSOT Press, 1984.
Ahlstrom, G. W. "Some Remarks on Prophets and Cult." In *Transitions in Biblical Scholarship*. Ed. J. Rylaarsdam, 113–29. Chicago: University of Chicago Press, 1968.
Albertz, R. *Weltschopfung und Menschenschopfung untersucht bei Deuterojesaja, Hiob und in den Psalmen*. Stuttgart, Germany: Kohlhammer, 1974.
Anderson, G. W. "Isaiah XXIV–XXVII Reconsidered." *VTS* 9 (1963): 118–26.
Auld, A. G. "Poetry, Prophecy, Hermeneutic: Recent Studies in Isaiah." *SJT* 32 (1980): 567–81.
Auret, A. "The Theological Intent of the Use of the Names of God in the Eighth-Century Memoir of Isaiah." *OTE* 5 (1992): 272–91.
Barre, M. L. "Textual and Rhetorical-Critical Observations on the Last Servant Song (Isaiah 52:13–53:12)." *CBQ* 62 (2000): 1–27.
Barton, J. "The Law and the Prophets": Who Are the Prophets?" *OTS* 23 (1984): 1–18.
Berquist, J. L. "Reading Difference in Isaiah 56–66: The Interplay of Literary and Sociological Strategies." *MTSR* 7 (1995): 23–42.
Beuken, W. A. M. "Mishpat: The First Servant Song and Its Context." *VT* 22 (1972): 1–30.
Biddle, M. E. "The City of Chaos and the New Jerusalem: Isaiah 24–27 in Context." *PRS* 22 (1995): 5–12.
Boadt, L. "The Poetry of Prophetic Persuasion: Preserving the Prophet's Persona." *CBQ* 59 (1997): 1–21.
Bosman, H. J. "Syntactic Cohesion in Isaiah 24–27." In *Studies in Isaiah 24–27*. Ed. H. J. Bosman and H. van Gorl et al., 19–50. Leiden, Netherlands: E. J. Brill, 2000.
——, and H. van Grol. "Annotated Translation of Isaiah 24–27." In *Studies in Isaiah 24–27*. Ed. H. J. Bosman and H. van Gorl et al., 3–12. Leiden, Netherlands: E. J. Brill, 2000.

Brettler, M. Z. "Incompatible Metaphors for YHWH in Isaiah 40–66." *JSOT* 78 (1998): 97–120.

Brodie, L. "The Children and the Prince: The Structure, Nature and Date of Isaiah 6–12." *BTB* 9 (1979): 27–31.

Brueggemann, W. "Unity and Dynamics in the Isaiah Tradition." *JSOT* 29 (1984): 89–107.

———. "Weariness, Exile and Chaos." *CBQ* 34 (1972): 19–38.

Carlson, R. A. "The Anti-Assyrian Character of the Oracle in Is. IX 1–6." *VT* 24 (1974): 130–35.

Carr, D. "Reaching for Unity in Isaiah." *JSOT* 57 (1993): 61–80.

Carroll, R. P. "Ancient Israelite Prophecy and Dissonant Theory." *Numen* 24 (1977): 135–51.

———. "Prophecy and Dissonance: A Theoretical Approach to the Prophetic Tradition." *ZAW* 92 (1980): 108–19.

Ceresko, A. R. "The Rhetorical Strategy of the Fourth Servant Song." *CBQ* 56 (1994): 42–55.

Childs, B. S. "The Enemy from the North and the Chaos Tradition." *JBL* 78 (1959): 187–98.

———. *Isaiah and the Assyrian Crisis*. London: S.C.M. Press, 1967.

Clements, R. E. "Beyond Tradition History: Deutero-Isaianic Development of First Isaiah's Themes." *JSOT* 31 (1985): 95–113.

———. "The Immanuel Prophecy of Isa 7:10–17 and Its Messianic Interpretation." In *Die Hebraische Bibel und ihre zweifache Nachgeschichte*. Ed. R. Rendtorff, 225–40. Neukirchen-Vluyn: Neukirchener Verlag, 1990.

———. *Isaiah and the Deliverance of Jerusalem: A Study of the Interpretation of Prophecy in the Old Testament*. Sheffield, England: JSOT Press, 1980.

———. "Patterns in the Prophetic Canon: Healing the Blind and the Lame." In *Canon, Theology and Old Testament Interpretation*. Ed. G. Tucker et al., 189–200. Philadelphia: Fortress, 1988.

———. "The Prophecies of Isaiah and the Fall of Jerusalem in 587 B.C." *VT* 30 (1980): 421–36.

———. "The Unity of the Book of Isaiah." *Interpretation* 36 (1982): 117–29.

Clifford, R. J. *Fair Spoken and Persuading: An Interpretation of Second Isaiah*. New York: Paulist, 1984.

———. "The Function of Idol Passages in Second Isaiah." *CBQ* 42 (1980): 450–64.

———. "The Unity of the Book of Isaiah and Its Cosmogonic Language." *CBQ* 55 (1993): 1–17.

Coggins, R. J. "Do We Still Need Deutero-Isaiah?" *JSOT* 81 (1998): 77–92.

Cohen, C. "Neo-Assyrian Elements in the First Speech of the Biblical RAB-SAQE." *IOS* 9 (1979): 32–48.

Conrad, E. "The 'Fear Not' Oracles in Second Isaiah." *VT* 34 (1984): 129–52.

——. *Reading Isaiah*. Minneapolis, Minn.: Fortress, 1991.

——. "The Royal Narratives and the Structure of the Book of Isaiah." *JSOT* 41 (1988): 67–81.

——. *Reading Isaiah*. Minneapolis, Minn.: Fortress, 1991.

——. "Second Isaiah and the Priestly Oracle of Salvation." *ZAW* 93 (1981): 234–46.

——. "Two Unifying Females Images in the Book of Isaiah." In *Uncovering Ancient Stones*. Ed. L. Hopfe, 17–30. Winona Lake, Ind.: Eisenbrauns,1994.

Davidson, R. "Universalism in Second Isaiah." *SJT* 16 (1963): 166–85.

Day, J. "Echoes of Baal's Seven Thunders and Lightnings in Psalm 29 and Habbakuk 3:9 and the Identity of the Seraphim in Isaiah 6." *VT* 29 (1979): 143–51.

Driver, G. R. "Isaiah I–XXXIX: Textual and Linguistic Problems." *JSS* 13 (1968): 36–57.

Eaton, J. "The Origin of the Book of Isaiah." *VT* 9 (1959): 138–57.

Eder, A. "King Cyrus, Anointed (Messiah) of the Lord." *JBQ* 23 (1995): 188–92.

Evans, C.A. "On Isaiah's Use of Israel's Tradition." *BZ* 30 (1986): 92–98.

Exum, J. C. "Of Broken Pots, Fluttering Birds, and Visions in the Night." *CBQ* 43 (1981): 331–52.

Franke, C. "The Function of the Satiric Lament over Babylon in Second Isaiah (XLVII)." *VT* 41 (1991): 408–18.

Freedman, D. N. "Headings in the Books of the Eighth-Century Prophets." *AUSS* 25 (1987): 9–26.

Frohlich, I. "Daniel 2 and Deutero-Isaiah." In *The Book of Daniel in the Light of New Findings*. Ed. A. S. Van Der Woude, 266–70. Leuven, Belgium: Leuven University Press, 1993.

Gelston, A. "Universalism in Second Isaiah." *JTS* 43 (1992): 377–98.

Gerstenberger, E. "The Woe-Oracles of the Prophets." *JBL* 81 (1962): 249–63.

Ginsberg, H. L. "The Oldest Interpretation of the Suffering Servant." *VT* 3 (1953): 400–4.

——. "Reflexes of Sargon in Isaiah after 715 B.C.E." *JAOS* 88 (1968): 47–53.

Gitay, Y. "Deutero-Isaiah: Oral or Written?" *JBL* 99 (1980): 185–97.

——. *Isaiah and His Audience: The Structure and Meaning of Isaiah 1–12*. Assen, Netherlands: Van Gorcum, 1991.

——. "Isaiah—The Impractical Prophet." *Bible Review* 4 (1988): 10–15.

——. *Prophecy and Persuasion: A Study of Isaiah 40–48*. Bonn, Germany: Lingustica Biblica, 1981.

Gosse, B. "Isaie VI et la Tradition Isaienne." *VT* 42 (1992): 340–49.

Gottwald, N. K. "Immanuel as the Prophet's Son." *VT* 8 (1958): 36–47.

Graffy, A. "The Literary Genre of Isaiah 5, 1–17." *Biblica* 60 (1979): 400–9.

Gruber, M. "The Motherhood of God in Second Isaiah." *RB* 90 (1983): 351–59.

Haag, E. "Gott as Schopfer und Erloser in der Prophetie des Deuterojesaja." *TTZ* 85 (1976): 193–213.

Habel, N. "The Form and Significance of the Call Narratives." *ZAW* 77 (1965): 297–323.

———. "'He Who Stretches Out the Heavens.'" *CBQ* 34 (1972): 417–30.

Halpern, B. "'The Excremental Vision': The Doomed Priests of Doom in Isaiah 28." *HAR* 10 (1986): 109–21.

Hamborg, G. R. "Reasons for Judgement in the Oracles against the Nations of the Prophet Isaiah." *VT* 31 (1981): 145–59.

Hanson, P. *The Dawn of Apocalyptic*. Philadelphia: Fortress, 1979.

Hayward, R. "The Chant of the Seraphim and the Worship of the Second Temple." *PIBA* 20 (1997): 62–80.

Hogenhaven, J. "The Prophet Isaiah and Judaean Foreign Policy under Ahaz and Hezekiah." *JNES* 49 (1990): 351–54.

Hurowitz, V. "Isaiah's Impure Lips and Their Purification in the Light of Mouth Purification and Mouth Purity in Akkadian Sources." *HUCA* 60 (1989): 39–89.

Irsigler, H. "Speech Acts and Intentions in the 'Song of the Vineyard' Isaiah 5:1–6." *OTE* 10 (1997): 39–68.

Irvine, S. A. *Isaiah, Ahaz, and the Syro-Ephraimitic Crisis*. Atlanta: Scholars, 1990.

Jensen, J. *Isaiah 1–39*. Wilmington, Del.: M. Glazier, 1984.

———. "Weal and Woe in Isaiah." *CBQ* 43 (1981): 167–87.

Jeppesen, K. "From 'You, My Servant' to 'The Hand of the Lord Is with My Servants': A Discussion of Isaiah 40–66." *SJOT* 1 (1990): 113–29.

Johnson, D. G. *From Chaos to Restoration: An Integrative Reading of Isaiah 24–27*. Sheffield, England: JSOT Press, 1988.

Joines, K. R. "Winged Serpents in Isaiah's Inaugural Vision." *JBL* 86 (1967): 410–15.

Jones, G. H. "Abraham and Cyrus: Type and Anti-Type?" *VT* 22 (1972): 304–19.

Kapelrud, A. S. "The Main Concern of Second Isaiah." *VT* 32 (1982): 50–58.

Key, A. F. "The Magical Background of Is. 6:9–13." *JBL* 86 (1967): 198–204.

Knierim, R. "The Vocation of Isaiah." *VT* 18 (1968): 48–57.

Kuhrt, A. "The Cyrus Cylinder and Achaemenid Imperial Policy." *JSOT* 25 (1983): 83–97.

Laato, A. "Assyrian Propaganda and the Falsification of History in the Royal Inscriptions of Sennacherib." *VT* 45 (1995): 198–226.

———. *The Servant of YHWH and Cyrus*. Stockholm: Almqvist & Wiksell International, 1992.

———. *Who Is Immanuel? The Rise and the Foundering of Isaiah's Messianic Expectations*. Abo, Finland: Abo Academy Press, 1988.

Labahn, A. "The Delay of Salvation within Deutero-Isaiah." *JSOT* 85 (1999): 71–84.

Lacheman, E. "Seraphim of Isaiah 6." *JQR* 59 (1968): 71–72.

Lewis, T. J. "Death Cult Imagery in Isaiah 57." *HAR* 11 (1987): 267–84.

Machinist, P. "Assyria and Its Image in the First Isaiah." *JAOS* 103 (1983): 719–37.

MacKenzie, R. A. F. "The City and Israelite Religion." *CBQ* 25 (1963): 60–70.

Melugin, R. F. "The Conventional and the Creative in Isaiah's Judgment Oracles." *CBQ* 36 (1974): 301–11.

———. "The Formation of Isaiah 40–55." BZAW 141. Berlin: De Gruyter, 1976.

———. "The Servant, God's Call, and the Structure of Isaiah 40–48." *SBL Seminar Papers* (1991): 21–30.

Milgrom, J. "Did Isaiah Prophesy during the Reign of Uzziah?" *VT* 14 (1964): 164–82.

Millar, W. R. *Isaiah 24–27 and the Origin of Apocalyptic*. Missoula, Mont.: Scholars, 1976.

Millard, A. "Sennacherib's Attack on Hezekiah." *TB* 36 (1985): 61–77.

Miscall, P. D. "Isaiah: The Labyrinth of Images." *Semeia* 54 (1991): 103–21.

Na'aman, N. "Historical and Chronological Notes on the Kingdoms of Israel and Judah in the Eighth Century B.C." *VT* 36 (1986): 71–92.

Niccacci, A. "Isaiah xviii–xx from an Egyptological Perspective." *VT* 48 (1998): 214–38.

Nielsen, K. *There Is Hope for a Tree: The Tree as Metaphor in Isaiah*. Sheffield, England: JSOT Press, 1989.

Niessen, R. "The Virginity of the Almah in Isaiah 7:14." *Bibliotheca Sacra* 137 (1980): 133–50.

Noegel, S. B. "Dialect and Politics in Isaiah 24–27." *AulOr* 12 (1994): 1–42.

Oded, B. "The Historical Background of the Syro-Ephraimitic War Reconsidered." *CBQ* 34 (1972): 153–65.

Ogden, G. S. "Moses and Cyrus." *VT* 28 (1978): 195–203.

O'Kane, M. "Isaiah: A Prophet in the Footsteps of Moses." *JSOT* 69 (1996): 29–51.

Otzen, B. "Traditions and Structures of Isaiah XXIV–XXVII." *VT* 24 (1974): 196–206.

Overholt, T. W. "Seeing Is Believing: The Social Setting of Prophetic Acts of Power." *JSOT* 23 (1982): 3–31.

Pagán, S. "Apocalyptic Poetry: Isaiah 24–27." *Bible Translator* 43 (1992): 314–25.

Raabe, P. R. "The Effect of Repetition in the Suffering Servant Song." *JBL* 103 (1984): 77–81.

Ramsey, G. "Speech-Forms in Hebrew Law and Prophetic Oracles." *JBL* 96 (1977): 45–58.

Rendtorff, R. "The Book of Isaiah: A Complex Unity. Synchronic and Diachronic Reading." *SBL Seminar Papers* 30 (1991): 8–20.

Rice, G. "A Neglected Interpretation of the Immanuel Prophecy." *ZAW* 90 (1978): 220–27.

Roberts, J. J. M. "Does God Lie? Divine Deceit as a Theological Problem in Israelite Prophetic Literature." *SVT* 40 (1986).

———. "Double Entendre in First Isaiah." *CBQ* 54 (1992): 39–48.

———. "Isaiah and His Children." In *Biblical and Related Studies Presented to Samuel Iwry*. Ed. A. Kort and S. Morschauser, 193–203. Winona Lake, Ind.: Eisenbrauns, 1985.

Rófe, A. "Isaiah 66:1–4: Judean Sects in the Persian Period as Viewed by Trito-Isaiah." In *Biblical and Related Studies Presented to Samuel Iwry*. Ed. A. Kort and S. Morschauser, 205–18. Winona Lake, Ind.: Eisenbrauns, 1985.

Sawyer, J. F. A. "Daughter of Zion and Servant of the Lord in Isaiah: A Comparison." *JSOT* 44 (1989): 89–107.

Seitz, C. "The Divine Council: Temporal Transition and New Prophecy in the Book of Isaiah." *JBL* 109 (1990): 229–47.

———. "How Is the Prophet Isaiah Present in the Latter Half of the Book? The Logic of Chapters 40–66 within the Book of Isaiah." *JBL* 115 (1996): 219–40.

———. *Zion's Final Destiny: The Development of the Book of Isaiah: A Reassessment of Isaiah 36–39*. Minneapolis, Minn.: Fortress, 1991.

Sheppard, G. T. "The Anti-Assyrian Redaction and the Canonical Context of Isaiah 1–39." *JBL* 104 (1985): 193–216.

Skjoldal, N. O. "The Function of Isaiah 24–27." *JETS* 36 (1993): 163–72.

Steinberg, T. L. "Isaiah the Poet." In *Mappings of the Biblical Terrain*. Ed. V. Tollers, 299–310. Lewisburg, Pa.: Bucknell University Press, 1990.

Sweeney, M. *Isaiah 1–4 and the Post Exilic Understanding of the Isaianic Tradition*. BZAW 171. Berlin: Walter de Gruyter, 1988.

———. "Sargon's Threat against Jerusalem in Isaiah 10, 27–32." *Biblica* 75 (1995): 457–70.

———. "Structure and Redaction in Isaiah 2–4." *HAR* 11 (1987): 407–22.

———. "Textual Citations in Isaiah 24–27: Toward an Understanding of the Redactional Function of Chapters 24–27 in the Book of Isaiah." *JBL* 107 (1988): 39–52.

Terrien, S. "The Omphalos Myth and Hebrew Religion." *VT* 20 (1970): 315–38.

Thompson, M. W. W. "Isaiah's Ideal King." *JSOT* 24 (1982a): 79–88.

———. "Isaiah's Sign of Immanuel." *Expository Times* 95 (1983): 67–71.

Toorn, Karel van der. "Echoes of Judaean Necromancy in Isaiah 28,7–22." *ZAW* 100 (1988): 199–217.

Towner, W. S. "Tribulation and Peace: The Fate of Shalom in Jewish Apocalyptic." *Horizons in Biblical Theology* 6 (1984): 1–26.

Treves, M. "Isaiah 53." *VT* 24 (1974): 98–108.

Vermeylen, J. *Du prophète Isaïe à l'apocalpytique*. 2 vols. Paris: J. Gabalda, 1977–78.

Vriezen, T. C. "Essentials of the Theology of Isaiah." In *Israel's Prophetic Heritage: Essays in Honor of James Muilenburg*. Ed. B. W. Anderson and W. Harrelson, 128–46. New York: Harper, 1962.

Whedbee, J. W. *Isaiah and Wisdom*. Nashville, Tenn.: Abingdon, 1971.

Whitley, C. F. "The Call and Mission of Isaiah." *JNES* 18 (1959): 38–48.

Whybray, R. N. "Two Recent Studies on Second Isaiah." *JSOT* 34 (1986): 109–17.

Wilcox, P., and D. Paton-Williams. "The Servant Songs in Deutero-Isaiah." *JSOT* 42 (1988): 79–102.

Willis, J. "The First Pericope in the Book of Isaiah." *VT* 34 (1984): 63–77.

Wilshire, L. "The Servant-City: A New Interpretation of the 'Servant of the Lord' in the Servant Songs of Deutero-Isaiah." *JBL* 94 (1975): 356–67.

Zephaniah

Anderson, R. W. "Zephaniah ben Cushi and Cush of Benjamin: Traces of Cushite Presence in Syria-Palestine." In *The Pitcher Is Broken*. Ed. S. W. Holloway and L. K. Handy, 45–70. JSOTSS 190. Sheffield, England: JSOT Press, 1995.

Ball, I. J. *A Rhetorical Study of Zephaniah*. Berkeley: BIBAL Press 1988.

Berlin, A. *Zephaniah*. AB 25A. New York: Doubleday, 1994.

Christensen, D. L. "Zephaniah 2:4–15: A Theological Basis for Josiah's Program of Political Expansion." *CBQ* 46 (1984): 669–82.

House, P. R. *Zephaniah: A Prophetic Drama*. JSOTSS 69. Sheffield, England: JSOT Press, 1988.

Kapelrud, A. S. *The Message of the Prophet Zephaniah*. Oslo: Universitetsforlaget, 1975.

Lohlink, N. "Zephaniah and the Church of the Poor." *TD* 32 (1985): 113–18.

Nel, P. J. "Structural and Conceptual Strategy in Zephaniah, Chapter 1." *JNSL* 15 (1989): 155–67.

Roberts, J. J. M. *Nahum, Habakkuk, and Zephaniah*. Louisville, Ky.: Westminster/ John Knox, 1991.

Ryou, D. H. "A Form-Critical Reassessment of the Book of Zephaniah." *CBQ* 53 (1991): 388–408.

———. *Zephaniah's Oracles against the Nations: A Synchronic and Diachronic Study of Zephaniah 2:1–3:8*. Biblical Interpretation Series 13. Leiden, Netherlands: E. J. Brill, 1995.

Williams, D. L. "The Date of Zephaniah." *JBL* 82 (1963): 77–88.

Nahum

Arnold, W. R. "The Composition of Nahum 1:1–2:3." *ZAW* 19 (1901): 225–65.

Ball, E. "Interpreting the Septuagint: Nahum 2.2 as a Case-Study." *JSOT* 75 (1997): 59–75.

Cathcart, K. J. "The Divine Warrior and the War of Yahweh in Nahum." In *Biblical Studies in Contemporary Thought*. Ed. M. Ward, 68–76. Somerville: The Institute, 1975.

———. *Nahum in the Light of Northwest Semitic*. Rome: Biblical Institute Press, 1973.

Christensen, D. L. "The Acrostic of Nahum Once Again: A Prosodic Analysis of Nahum 1:1–10." *ZAW* 99 (1987): 409–14.

———. "The Acrostic of Nahum Reconsidered." *ZAW* 87 (1975b): 17–30.

———. *Transformation of the War Oracle in Old Testament Prophecy: Studies in the Oracles against the Nations*. Missoula, Mont.: Scholars, 1975.

Floyd, M. "The Chimerical Acrostic of Nahum 1:2–10." *JBL* 113 (1994): 421–37.

Haldar, A. *Studies in the Book of Nahum*. Uppsala, Sweden: Lundequistska Bokhandeln, 1947.

Nogalski, J. "The Redactional Shaping of Nahum 1 for the Book of the Twelve." In *Among the Prophets*. Ed. P. Davies and D. Clines, 193–202. JSOTSS 144. Sheffield, England: JSOT Press, 1993.

Roberts, J. J. *Nahum, Habakkuk, and Zephaniah*. Louisville, Ky.: Westminster/John Knox, 1991.

Vries, S. de. "The Acrostic of Nahum in the Jerusalem Liturgy." *VT* 16 (1966): 476–81.

Habakkuk

Barre, M. L. "Habakkuk 3:2: Translation in Context." *CBQ* 50 (1988): 184–97.

Brownlee, W. S. "The Placarded Revelation of Habakkuk." *JBL* 82 (1963): 319–25.

Carroll, R. P. "Eschatological Delay in Prophetic Tradition?" *ZAW* 94 (1982): 47–58.

Coleman, S. "The Dialogue of Habakkuk in Rabbinic Doctrine." *Abr-Nahrain* 5 (1964–65): 57–85.

Day, J. "Echoes of Baal's Seven Thunders and Lightnings in Psalm XXIX and Hab 3,9 and the Identity of Seraphim in Isaiah VI." *VT* 29 (1979): 143–51.

———. "New Light on the Mythological Background of the Allusion to Reshep in Habakkuk III 5." *VT* 29 (1979a): 353–55.

Eaton, J. H. "The Origin and Meaning of Habakkuk 3." *ZAW* 76 (1964): 144–71.

Emerton, J. A. "The Textual and Linguistic Problems of Habakkuk 2:4–5." *JTS* 28 (1977): 1–18.

Floyd, M. H. "Prophecy and Writing in Habakkuk 2,1–5." *ZAW* 105 (1993): 462–81.

———. "Prophetic Complaints about the Fulfillment of Oracles in Habakkuk 1:2–17 and Jeremiah 15:10–18." *JBL* 110 (1991): 397–406.

Gowan, D. E. "Habakkuk and Wisdom." *Perspective* 9 (1968): 157–66.

———. *The Triumph of Faith in Habakkuk*. Atlanta: Scholars, 1976.

Haak, R. D. "Poetry in Habakkuk 1:1–2:4?" *JAOS* 108 (1988): 437–44.

Hiebert, T. *God of My Victory: The Ancient Hymn in Habakkuk 3*. Atlanta: Scholars, 1986.

Irwin, W. A. "The Mythological Background of Habakkuk, Chapter 3." *JNES* 15 (1956): 47–50.

Janzen, J. G. "Eschatological Symbol and Existence in Habakkuk." *CBQ* 44 (1982): 394–414.

———. "Habakkuk 2:2–4 in the Light of Recent Philological Advances." *HTR* 73 (1980): 53–78.

Johnson, M. D. "The Paralysis of Torah in Habakkuk i 4." *VT* 35 (1985): 257–66.

Margulis, B. "The Psalm of Habakkuk: A Reconstruction and Interpretation." *ZAW* 82 (1970): 409–42.

Otto, E. "Die Theologie des Buches Habakuk." *VT* 35 (1985): 274–95.

Peckham, B. "The Vision of Habakkuk." *CBQ* 48 (1986): 617–36.

Roberts, J. J. M. *Nahum, Habakkuk, and Zephaniah*. Louisville, Ky.: Westminster/ John Knox, 1991.

Sanders, J. A. "Habakkuk in Qumran, Paul, and the OT." *JR* 39 (1959): 232–45.

Scott, J. M. "A New Approach to Habakkuk ii 4–5a." *VT* 35 (1985): 330–40.

Smith, R. L. *Micah–Malachi*. Waco, Texas: Word Books, 1984.

Southwall, P. J . M. "A Note on Habakkuk ii.4." *VT* 19 (1969): 614–17.

Sweeney, M. A. "Structure, Genre, and Intent in the Book of Habakkuk." *VT* 41 (1991): 63–83.

Torrey, C. C. "The Prophecy of Habakkuk." In *Jewish Studies in Memory of George A. Kohut*. Ed. S. Baron and A. Marx, 565–82. New York: Alexander Kohut Memorial Foundation, 1935.

Tsumura, D. T. "Hab 2,2 in the Light of Akkadian Legal Practice." *ZAW* 94 (1982): 294–95.

Obadiah

Allen, L. *The Books of Joel, Obadiah, Jonah and Micah*. Grand Rapids, Mich.: Eerdmans, 1976.

Barton, J. *Joel and Obadiah: A Commentary*. Louisville, Ky.: Westminster/John Knox, 2001.

Ben Zvi, E. *A Historical-Critical Study of the Book of Obadiah*. Berlin: Walter de Gruyter, 1996.

Brown, W. P. *Obadiah through Malachi*. Louisville, Ky.: Westminster/John Knox, 1996.

Davies, G. I. "A New Solution to a Crux in Obadiah 7." *VT* 27 (1977): 484–87.

Dick, M. B. "A Syntactic Study of the Book of Obadiah." *Semitics* 9 (1984): 1–29.

Lintzenich, R. *Hosea/Obadiah*. Nashville, Tenn.: Abingdon, 1999.

McCarter, P. K. "Obadiah 7 and the Fall of Edom." *BASOR* 221 (1976): 87–91.

Nogalski, J. D. "Obadiah 7: Textual Corruption or Politically Charged Metaphor?" *ZAW* 110 (1998): 67–71.

Raabe, P. *Obadiah*. AB 24D. New York: Doubleday, 1996.

Robinson, R. B. "Levels of Naturalization in Obadiah." *JSOT* 40 (1988): 83–97.

Snyman, S. D. "Cohesion in the Book of Obadiah." *ZAW* 101 (1989): 59–71.

Spaude, Cyril W. *Obadiah, Jonah, Micah*. Milwaukee, Wisc.: Northwestern Publishing, 2001.

Waltke, B. K., et al. *Obadiah, Jonah, Micah*. Downers Grove, Ill.: InterVarsity Press, 1988.

Watts, J. D. W. *Obadiah*. Grand Rapids, Mich.: Eerdmans, 1969.

Joel

Ahlström, G. W. *Joel and the Temple Cult of Jerusalem*. Leiden, Netherlands: E. J. Brill, 1971.

Allen, L. *The Books of Joel, Obadiah, Jonah and Micah*. Grand Rapids, Mich.: Eerdmans, 1976.

Andinach, P. R. "The Locusts in the Message of Joel." *VT* 42 (1992): 433–41.

Barton, J. *Joel and Obadiah: A Commentary*. Louisville, Ky.: Westminster/John Knox, 2001.

Bellinger, W. H. *Psalmody and Prophecy*. JSOTSS 27. Sheffield, England: JSOT Press, 1984.

Childs, B. S. "'The Enemy from the North' and the Chaos Tradition.'" *JBL* 78 (1959): 187–98.

Garrett, D. A. "The Structure of Joel." *JETS* 28 (1985): 289–97.

Kapelrud, A. S. *Joel Studies*. Uppsala, Sweden: Almqvist & Wiksells Boktryckeri, 1948.

Redditt, P. D. "The Book of Joel and Peripheral Prophecy." *CBQ* 48 (1986): 225–40.

Stephenson, F. R. "The Date of the Book of Joel." *VT* 19 (1969): 224–29.

Thompson, J. "Joel's Locusts in the Light of Near Eastern Parallels." *JNES* 14 (1955): 52–55.

Jeremiah

Ackroyd, P. R. "The Book of Jeremiah—Some Recent Studies." *JSOT* 28 (1984): 47–59.

Anderson, J. S. "The Metonymical Curse as Propaganda in the Book of Jeremiah." *BBR* 8 (1998): 1–13.

Applegate, J. "The Fate of Zedekiah: Redactional Debate in the Book of Jeremiah, Part I." *VT* 48 (1998): 137–60, 48 (1998): 301–8.

———. "'Peace, Peace, When There Is No Peace': Redactional Integration of Prophecy of Peace into the Judgement of Jeremiah." In *The Book of Jeremiah and Its Reception*. Ed. A. H. W. Curtis and T. Romer, 51–90. Leuven, Belgium: Leuven University Press, 1997.

Auld, A. G. "Prophets through the Looking Glass." *JSOT* 27 (1983): 3–23.

Berquist, J. L. "Prophetic Legitimation in Jeremiah." *VT* 39 (1989): 129–39.

Bright, J. "Jeremiah's Complaint—Liturgy or Expressions of Personal Distress?" *Proclamation and Presence: Old Testament Essays in Honour of Gwynne Henton Davies*. Ed. J. J. Burham and J. R. Porter, 189–213. Atlanta: Scholars, 1970.

———. "The Prophetic Reminiscence: Its Place and Function in the Book of Jeremiah." *Biblical Essays* (1966): 11–30.

Brueggemann, W. A. *A Commentary on Jeremiah: Exile and Homecoming*. Grand Rapids, Mich.: Eerdmans, 1998.

———. "Jeremiah's Use of Rhetorical Questions." *JBL* 92/3 (1973): 358–74.

Buss, M. J. "The Book of Jeremiah: Portrait of a Prophet." *Interpretation* 37 (1983): 130–45.

Carroll, R. *Jeremiah*. London: SCM Press, 1986.

———. "Poets Not Prophets: A Response to 'Prophets through the Looking Glass.'" *JSOT* 27 (1983): 25–31.

Castellino, G. R. "Observations on the Literary Structure of Some Passages in Jeremiah." *VT* 30 (1980): 398–408.

Crenshaw, J. L. "A Living Tradition: The Book of Jeremiah in Current Research." *Interpretation* 37 (1983): 117–29.

Dahlberg, B. T. "The Typological Use of Jeremiah 1:4–19 in Matthew 16:13–23." *JBL* 94 (1975): 73–80.

Davies, P. R. "Potter, Prophet and People: Jeremiah 18 as Parable." *HAR* 11 (1987): 23–33.

Fensham, F. C. "Nebukadrezzar in the Book of Jeremiah." *JNSL* 10 (1982): 53–65.

Fishbane, M. "Jeremiah 4:23–26 and Job 3:3–13, a Recovered Use of the Creation Pattern." *VT* 21 (1971): 151–67.

Frost, S. B. "The Memorial of a Childless Man, A Study in Hebrew Thought on Immortality." *Interpretation* 26 (1972): 437–50.

Gosse, B. "The Masoretic Redaction of Jeremiah: An Explanation." *JSOT* 77 (1998): 75–80.

Hobbs, T. R. "Some Proverbial Reflections in the Book of Jeremiah." *ZAW* 91 (1979): 62–72.

——. "Some Remarks on the Composition and Structure of the Book of Jeremiah." *CBQ* 34 (1972): 257–75.

Holladay, W. L. "The Background of Jeremiah's Self-Understanding." *JBL* 83 (1964): 153–64.

——. *A Commentary on the Book of the Prophet Jeremiah, Chapters 26–52.* Minneapolis, Minn.: Fortress, 1989.

——. "Enigmatic Bible Passages: God Writes a Rude Letter." *BA* 46 (1983): 145–46.

——. "The Identification of the Two Scrolls of Jeremiah." *VT* 30 (1980): 452–67.

——. "Jeremiah and Moses: Further Observations." *JBL* 85 (1966): 17–27.

——. "Prototype and Copies: A New Approach to the Poetry-Prose Problem in the Book of Jeremiah." *JBL* 79 (1960): 351–67.

——. "The Recovery of Poetic Passages of Jeremiah." *JBL* 85 (1966): 401–35.

——. "Style, Irony and Authenticity in Jeremiah." *JBL* 81 (1962): 44–54.

Holt, E. K. "Jeremiah's Temple Sermon & the Deuteronomists: An Investigation of the Redactional Relationship between Jeremiah 7 and 26." *JSOT* 36 (1986): 73–87.

Horwitz, W. J. "Audience Reaction to Jeremiah." *CBQ* 32 (1970): 555–64.

House, P. R. "Plot, Prophecy, and Jeremiah." *JETS* 36 (1993): 297–306.

Huffmon, J. "The Covenant Lawsuit in the Prophets." *JBL* 78 (1959): 287–88.

Isbell, C. D., and M. Jackson. "Rhetorical Criticism and Jeremiah vii 1–viii 3." *VT* 30 (1980): 20–26.

Jobling, D. "The Quest of the Historical Jeremiah: Hermeneutical Implications of Recent Literature." *USQR* 34 (1978): 3–12.

Lemke, W. E. "Nebuchadrezzar My Servant." *CBQ* 28 (1966): 45–50.

Lundbom, J. R. "Baruch, Seraiah, and Expanded Colophons in the Book of Jeremiah." *JSOT* 36 (1986): 89–114.

——. *Jeremiah 1–20.* AB 21A. New York: Doubleday, 1999.

——. "Jeremiah and the Break-Away from Authority Preaching." *SEA* 56 (1991): 7-28.

——. *Jeremiah: A Study in Ancient Rhetoric.* Missoula, Mont.: Scholars, 1975.

——. "The Lawbook of the Josianic Reform." *CBQ* 38 (1976): 293–302.

Magonet, J. "Jeremiah's Last Confession: Structure, Image and Ambiguity." *HAR* 11 (1987): 303–17.

Malamat, A. "The Historical Setting of Two Biblical Prophecies on the Nations." *IEJ* 1 (1950/1): 154–59.

Manahan, R. E. "A Theology of Pseudoprophets: A Study in Jeremiah." *GTJ* 1 (1980): 77–96.

McConville, J. G. "Jeremiah: Prophet and Book." *TB* 42 (1991): 80–95.

McKane, W. *A Critical and Exegetical Commentary on Jeremiah.* 2 vols. Edinburgh: T & T Clark, 1996.

Milgrom, J. "Concerning Jeremiah's Repudiation of Sacrifice." *ZAW* 89 (1977): 273–75.

Moore, M. S. "Jeremiah's Progressive Paradox." *RB* 93 (1986): 386–414.

Muilenberg, J. "The Terminology of Adversity in Jeremiah." In *Translating and Understanding the Old Testament: Essays in Honor of Herbert Gordon May.* Ed. H. T. Frank and W. L. Reed, 42–63. Nashville, Tenn.: Abingdon, 1970.

Mulzac, K. "The Remnant and the New Covenant in the Book of Jeremiah." *AUSS* 34 (1996): 239–48.

Noegel, S. B. "Atbash in Jeremiah and Its Literary Significance: Parts 1–2." *JBQ* 24 (1996): 82–89, 160–66, 247–50.

Overholt, T. W. "Jeremiah 27–29: The Question of False Prophecy." *JAAR* 35 (1967): 241–49.

———. "King Nebuchadrezzar in the Jeremiah Tradition." *CBQ* 30 (1968): 39–48.

———. "Remarks on the Continuity of the Jeremiah Tradition." *JBL* 91 (1972): 457–62.

Paterson, R. M. "Reinterpretation in the Book of Jeremiah." *JSOT* 37 (1987): 79–98.

Perdue, L. G., and B. W. Kovacs, eds. *A Prophet to the Nations: Essays in Jeremiah Studies.* Winona Lake, Ind.: Eisenbrauns,1983.

Reimer, D. *The Oracles against Babylon in Jeremiah 50–51: A Horror among the Nations.* San Francisco: Mellen Research University Press, 1993.

Roberts, J. J. M. "The Motif of the Weeping God in Jeremiah and Its Background in the Lament Tradition of the Ancient Near East." *OTE* 5 (1992): 361–74.

Rodd, C. S. "On Applying a Sociological Theory to Biblical Studies." *JSOT* 19 (1981): 95–106.

Roshwalb, E. H. "Build-Up and Climax in Jeremiah's Visions and Laments." In *Boundaries of the Ancient Near Eastern World: A Tribute to Cyrus H. Gordon.* Ed. M. Lubetski et al., 111–35. JSOTSS 273. Sheffield, England: JSOT Press, 1998.

Rowley, H. H. "The Early Prophecies of Jeremiah in Their Setting." *BJRL* 45 (1962/3): 198–234.

Rowton, M. B. "Jeremiah and the Death of Josiah." *JNES* 10 (1951): 128–30.

Schart, A. "Combining Prophetic Oracles in Mari Letters and Jeremiah 36." *JANES* 23 (1995): 75–93.

Seitz, C. R. "The Crisis of Interpretation over the Meaning and Purpose of the Exile." *VT* 35 (1985): 78–97.

———. "The Prophet Moses and the Canonical Shape of Jeremiah." *ZAW* 101 (1989b): 3–27.

———. *Theology in Conflict: Reaction to the Exile in the Book of Jeremiah*. Berlin: Walter de Gruyter, 1989.

Sharp, C. J. "The Call of Jeremiah and Diaspora Politics." *JBL* 119 (2000): 421–38.

Sisson, J. P. "Jeremiah and the Jerusalem Conception of Peace." *JBL* 105/3 (1986): 429–42.

Skinner, J. *Prophecy and Religion: Studies in the Life of Jeremiah*. Cambridge: Cambridge University Press, 1963.

Smith, D. L. "Jeremiah as Prophet of Nonviolent Resistance." *JSOT* 43 (1989): 95–107.

Sommer, B. D. "New Light on the Composition of Jeremiah." *CBQ* 61 (1999): 646–66.

Stipp, H. -J. "Zedekiah in the Book of Jeremiah: On the Formation of a Biblical Character." *CBQ* (1996): 627–48.

Stulman, L. "Insiders and Outsiders in the Book of Jeremiah: Shifts in Symbolic Arrangements." *JSOT* 66 (1995): 65–85.

Thompson, J. A. *The Book of Jeremiah*. Grand Rapids, Mich.: Eerdmans, 1980.

Tov, E. "The Book of Jeremiah: A Work in Progress." *BRev* 16/3 (2000): 32–38, 45.

Watts, J. W. "Text and Redaction in Jeremiah's Oracles against the Nations." *CBQ* 54 (1991): 432–47.

Weinfeld, M. "Jeremiah and the Spiritual Metamorphosis of Israel." *ZAW* 88 (1976): 17–56.

Weiss, H. "How Can Jeremiah Compare the Migration of Birds to Knowledge of God's Justice?" *BR* 2 (1986): 42–45.

Willis, J. T. "Dialogue between Prophets and Audience as a Rhetorical Device in the Book of Jeremiah." *JSOT* 33 (1985): 63–82.

Zimmerli, W. "Visionary Experience in Jeremiah." In *Israel's Prophetic Tradition: Essays in Honour of Peter R. Ackroyd*. Ed. R. Coggins et al., 95–118. Cambridge: Cambridge University Press, 1982.

Jonah

Ackerman, J. S. "Satire and Symbolism in the Song of Jonah." In *Traditions in Transformation: Turning Points in Biblical Faith*. Ed. B. Halpern, 213–46. Winona Lake, Ind.: Eisenbrauns, 1981.

Allen, L. *The Books of Joel, Obadiah, Jonah and Micah*. Grand Rapids, Mich.: Eerdmans, 1976.

Berger, B. L. "Picturing the Prophet: Focalization in the Book of Jonah." *Studies in Religion/Sciences Religieuses* 29 (2000): 55–68.

Bolin, T. M. "'Should I Not Also Pity Nineveh?' Divine Freedom in the Book of Jonah." *JSOT* 67 (1995): 109–20.

Cohn, G. H. *Das Buch Jona im Lichte der biblischen Erzählkunst.* Assen, Netherlands: Van Gorcum, 1969.

Craig, K. M. "Jonah and the Reading Process." *JSOT* 47 (1990): 103–14.

———. *A Poetics of Jonah: Art in the Service of Ideology.* Columbia: University of South Carolina Press, 1993.

Ferguson, P. "Who Was the 'King of Nineveh' in Jonah 3:6?" *TB* 47 (1995): 301–14.

Fretheim, T. E. "Jonah and Theodicy." *ZAW* 90 (1978): 227–37.

Frolov, S. "Returning the Ticket: God and His Prophet in the Book of Jonah." *JSOT* 86 (1999): 85–105.

Halpern, B., and R. E. Friedman. "Composition and Paronomasia in the Book of Jonah." *HAR* 4 (1980): 79–92.

Heerden, W. van. "Humour and the Interpretation of the Book of Jonah." *OTE* 5 (1992): 389–401.

Holbert, J. C. "'Deliverance Belongs to Yahweh!': Satire in the Book of Jonah." *JSOT* 21 (1981): 59–81.

Houk, C. B. "Linguistic Patterns in Jonah." *JSOT* 77 (1998): 81–102.

Limburg, J. *Jonah: A Commentary.* London: SCM Press, 1993.

Person, R. F. *In Conversation with Jonah: Conversation Analysis, Literary Criticism, and the Book of Jonah.* Sheffield, England: JSOT Press, 1996.

Ratner, R. J. "Jonah, the Runaway Servant." *Maarav* 5–6 (1990): 281–305.

Sasson, J. *Jonah.* New York: Anchor Bible, 1990.

Sherwood, Y. "Rocking the Boat: Jonah and the New Historicism." *BibInt* 5 (1997): 364–402.

Spangenberg, I. J. J. "Jonah and Qohelet: Satire versus Irony." *OTE* 9 (1996): 495–511.

Spaude, C. W. *Obadiah, Jonah, Micah.* Milwaukee, Wisc.: Northwestern Publishing, 2001.

Strickland, W. G. "Isaiah, Jonah, and Religious Pluralism." *Bibliotheca Sacra* 153 (1996): 24–33.

Waltke, B. K., et al. *Obadiah, Jonah, Micah.* Downers Grove, Ill.: InterVarsity Press, 1988.

EXILIC AND POST-EXILIC ISRAELITE PROPHETS

Ezekiel

Ackerman, S. "A *Marzeah* in Ezekiel 8:7–13?" *HTR* 82 (1989): 267–81.

Allen, L. C. *Ezekiel 20–48.* Dallas, Tex.: Word Books, 1990.

———. "Structure, Tradition and Redaction in Ezekiel's Death Valley Vision." In *Among the Prophets*. Ed. P. Davies and D. Clines, 127–42. Sheffield, England: JSOT Press, 1993.

Block, D. I. *The Book of Ezekiel, Chapters 1–24*. Grand Rapids, Mich.: Eerdmans, 1997.

———. "Gog in Prophetic Tradition: A New Look at Ezekiel 38:17." *VT* 42 (1992): 154–72.

Boadt, L. "The Function of the Salvation Oracles in Ezekiel 33 to 37." *HAR* 12 (1990): 1–21.

Bodi, D. *The Book of Ezekiel and the Poem of Erra*. Göttingen, Germany: Vandenhoeck & Ruprecht, 1991.

Borowski, E. "Cherubim: God's Throne?" *BAR* 21/4 (1995): 36–41.

Darr, K. P. "Ezekiel's Justifications of God." *JSOT* 55 (1992): 97–117.

Davis, E. F. *Swallowing the Scroll: Textuality and the Dynamics of Discourse in Ezekiel's Prophecy*. Sheffield, England: JSOT Press, 1989.

Fishbane, M. "Sin and Judgment in the Prophecies of Ezekiel." *Interpretation* 38 (1984): 131–50.

Frederisks, D.C. "Diglossia, Revelation, and Ezekiel's Inaugural Rite." *JETS* 41 (1998): 189–99.

Garfinkel, S. "Another Model for Ezekiel's Abnormalities." *JANES* 19 (1989): 39–50.

Greenberg, M. *Ezekiel 1–20*. AB 22. Garden City, N.Y.: Doubleday, 1983.

Halperin, J. *Seeking Ezekiel: Text and Psychology*. University Park: Pennsylvania State University Press, 1993.

Haran, M. "The Law Code of Ezekiel XL–XLVIII and Its Relation to the Priestly School." *HUCA* 50 (1979): 45–71.

Joyce, P. M. *Divine Initiative and Human Response in Ezekiel*. Sheffield, England: JSOT Press, 1989.

Lang, B. "Street Theater, Raising the Dead and the Zoroastrian Connection in Ezekiel's Prophecy." In *Ezekiel and His Book: Textual and Literary Criticism and Their Interrelation*. Ed. J. Lust, 297–316. Leuven, Belgium: Leuven University Press, 1986.

Lindars, B. "Ezekiel and Individual Responsibility." *VT* 15 (1965): 452–67.

Niditch, S. "Ezekiel 40–48 in a Visionary Context." *CBQ* 48 (1986): 208–24.

Odell, M. S. "You Are What You Eat: Ezekiel and the Scroll." *JBL* 117 (1998): 229–48.

Odendaal, M. "Exile in Ezekiel: Evaluating a Sociological Model." *NGTT* 40 (1999): 133–39.

Tanner, J .P. "Rethinking Ezekiel's Invasion by Gog." *JETS* 39 (1996): 29–46.

Tarlin, J. W. "Utopia and Pornography in Ezekiel: Violence, Hope and the Shattered Male Subject." In *Reading Bibles, Writing Bodies: Identity and The Book*. Ed. T. K. Beal and D. M. Gunn, 175–83. New York: Routledge, 1996.

Wahl, H.-M. "Noah, Daniel und Hiob in Ezechiel xiv 12–20." *VT* 42 (1992): 542–53.

Zimmerli, W. *Ezekiel 1*. Philadelphia: Fortress, 1979.

Haggai

Ackroyd, P. R. "Studies in the Book of Haggai." *JJS* 2 (1951): 163–76.

Bedford, P. R. "Discerning the Time: Haggai, Zechariah and the 'Delay' in the Rebuilding of the Jerusalem Temple." In *The Pitcher Is Broken*. Ed. S. W. Holloway and L. K. Handy, 71–94. Sheffield, England: JSOT Press, 1995.

Floyd, M. H. "The Nature of the Narrative and the Evidence of Redaction in Haggai." *VT* 45 (1995): 470–90.

Hildebrand, D. R. "Temple Ritual: A Paradigm for Moral Holiness in Haggai II 10–19." *VT* 39 (1989): 154–68.

Mason, R. "The Purpose of the 'Editorial Framework' of the Book of Haggai." *VT* 27 (1977): 413–21.

May, H. G. "'This People' and 'This Nation' in Haggai." *VT* 18 (1968): 190–97.

Meyers, C., and E. Meyers. *Haggai; Zechariah 1–8: A New Translation with Introduction and Commentary*. AB 25B. New York: Doubleday, 1987.

Petersen, D. L. *Haggai and Zechariah 1–8*. London: SCM Press, 1985.

Pierce, R. W. "A Thematic Development of the Haggai–Zechariah–Malachi Corpus." *JETS* 27 (1984): 401–11.

Redditt, P. L. *Haggai, Zechariah, Malachi*. Grand Rapids, Mich.: Eerdmans, 1995.

Smith, R. L. *Micah–Malachi*. Dallas, Tex.: Word Books, 1984.

Sykes, S. "Time and Space in Haggai—Zechariah 1–8: A Bakhtinian Analysis of a Problematic Chronicle." *JSOT* 76 (1997): 97–124.

Tollington, J. E. *Tradition and Innovation in Haggai and Zechariah 1–8*. JSOTSS 150. Sheffield, England: JSOT Press, 1993.

Wolff, H. W. *Haggai: A Commentary*. Minneapolis, Minn.: Fortress, 1988.

Zechariah

Bedford, P. R. "Discerning the Time: Haggai, Zechariah and the 'Delay' in the Rebuilding of the Jerusalem Temple." In *The Pitcher Is Broken*. Ed. S. W. Holloway and L. K. Handy, 71–94. Sheffield, England: JSOT Press, 1995.

Butterworth, M. *Structure and the Book of Zechariah*. JSOTSS 130. Sheffield, England: JSOT Press, 1992.

Cook, S. L. "The Metamorphosis of a Shepherd: The Tradition History of Zechariah 11:17–13:7–9." *CBQ* 55 (1993): 453–66.

Crotty, R. B. "The Suffering of Moses of Deutero-Zechariah." *Colloquium* 14 (1982): 43–50.

Finley, T. J. "The Sheep Merchants of Zechariah 11." *GTJ* 3 (1982): 51–65.

Fox, H. "The Forelife of Ideas and the Afterlife of Texts [Zech 14]." *RB* 105 (1998): 520–25.

Gordon, R. P. "Inscribed Pots and Zechariah xiv 20-1." *VT* 42 (1992): 120–23.

Hanson, P. D. "Zechariah 9 and the Recapitulation of an Ancient Ritual Pattern." *JBL* 92 (1973): 37–59.

Hoppe, L. J. "Zechariah 3: A Vision of Forgiveness." *TBT* 38 (2000): 10–16.

Kline, M. G. "The Structure of the Book of Zechariah." *JETS* 34 (1991): 179–93.

Larkin, K. *The Eschatology of Second Zechariah: A Study of the Formation of a Mantological Wisdom Anthology. Contributions to Biblical Exegesis and Theology* 6. Kampen, Netherlands: Kok Pharos, 1994.

LaRocca-Pitts, B. "Zechariah 6: A Vision of Peace." *TBT* 38 (2000): 23–28.

Mason, R. "The Relation of Zech. 9–14 to Proto-Zechariah." *ZAW* 88 (1976): 227–39.

———. "Some Examples of Inner Biblical Exegesis in Zechariah 9–14." *StEv* 7 (1982): 343–54.

Meyers, C., and Eric Meyers. *Haggai; Zechariah 1–8: A New Translation with Introduction and Commentary.* AB 25B. New York: Doubleday, 1987.

Nash, K. S. "Zechariah 4: A Vision of Small Beginnings." *TBT* 38 (2000): 17–22.

Person, R. E. *Second Zechariah and the Deuteronomic School.* JSOTSS 167. Sheffield, England: JSOT Press, 1993.

Petersen, D. L. *Haggai and Zechariah 1–8.* London: SCM Press, 1985.

———. *Zechariah 9–14 and Malachi.* Louisville, Ky.: Westminster/John Knox, 1995.

———. "Zechariah's Visions: A Theological Perspective." *VT* 34 (1984): 195–206.

Pierce, R. W. "A Thematic Development of the Haggai–Zechariah–Malachi Corpus." *JETS* 27 (1984): 401–11.

Portnoy, S. L., and D. L. Petersen. "Biblical Texts and Statistical Analysis: Zechariah and Beyond." *JBL* 103 (1984): 11–21.

Redditt, P. L. *Haggai, Zechariah, Malachi.* Grand Rapids, Mich.: Eerdmans, 1995.

———. "Israel's Shepherds: Hope and Pessimism in Zechariah 9–14." *CBQ* 51 (1989): 631–42.

———. "Nehemiah's First Mission and the Date of Zechariah 9–14." *CBQ* 56 (1994): 664–78.

———. "The Two Shepherds in Zechariah 11:4–17." *CBQ* 55 (1993): 676–86.

———. "Zerubbabel, Joshua, and the Night Visions of Zechariah." *CBQ* 54 (1992): 249–59.

Rudman, D. "Zechariah 5 and the Priestly Law." *SJOT* 14 (2000): 194–206.

Sykes, S. "Time and Space in Haggai–Zechariah 1–8: A Bakhtinian Analysis of a Problematic Chronicle." *JSOT* 76 (1997): 97–124.

Tollington, J. E. *Tradition and Innovation in Haggai and Zechariah 1–8.* JSOTSS 150. Sheffield, England: JSOT Press, 1993.

Van der Woude, A. S. "Zion as Primeval Stone in Zechariah 3 and 4." In *Text and Context.* Ed. E. Claassen, 237–48. Sheffield, England: JSOT Press, 1988.

Willi-Plein, I. *Prophetie am Ende: Untersuchungen zu Sacharja 9–14.* Cologne, Germany: P. Hanstein, 1974.

Malachi

Berquist, J. L. "The Social Setting of Malachi." *BTB* 19 (1989): 121–26.

Brown, William P. *Obadiah through Malachi.* Louisville, Ky.: Westminster/John Knox, 1996.

Coggins, R. J. *Haggai, Zechariah, Malachi.* Sheffield, England: JSOT Press, 1996.

Glazier-McDonald, B. "Mal'ak Habberit: The Messenger of the Covenant in Mal 3:1." *HAR* 11 (1987): 93–104.

Hartzell, Eric. S. *Haggai, Zechariah, Malachi.* Milwaukee, Wisc.: Northwestern Publishing, 1991.

Hill, Andrew. *Malachi.* AB 25D. New York: Doubleday, 1998.

Hinton, L. *Micah, Nahum, Habakkuk, Zephaniah, Haggai, Zechariah, and Malachi.* Nashville, Tenn.: Abingdon, 1994.

McKenzie, S. L., and Wallace, H. "Covenant Themes in Malachi." *CBQ* 45 (1983): 549–63.

Meyers, E. M. "Priestly Language in the Book of Malachi." *HAR* 10 (1987): 225–37.

O'Brien, J. M. "Judah as Wife and Husband: Deconstructing Gender in Malachi." *JBL* 115 (1996): 241–50.

———. *Priest and Levite in Malachi.* SBLDS 121. Atlanta: Scholars, 1990.

Petersen, D. *Zechariah 9–14 and Malachi.* Louisville, Ky.: Westminster/John Knox, 1995.

Pierce, R. W. "A Thematic Development of the Haggai–Zechariah–Malachi Corpus." *JETS* 27 (1984): 401–11.

Redditt, P. L. *Haggai, Zechariah, Malachi.* Grand Rapids, Mich.: Eerdmans, 1995.

Thompson, H. O. *Malachi: A Bibliography.* Delhi, India: 1995.

Ezra, Nehemiah, Daniel

Ackroyd, P. R. "The Jewish Community in Palestine in the Persian Period." *CHJ* 1 (1984): 130–61.

——. "The Temple Vessels—A Continuity Theme." *VTS* 23 (1972): 166–81.

Anderson, R. A. *Signs and Wonders: A Commentary on the Book of Daniel*. Grand Rapids, Mich.: Eerdmans, 1984.

Armerding, C. "Greek Culture and Jewish Piety: The Clash and the Fourth Beast of Daniel 7." *ETL* 65 (1989): 280–308.

——. "The Interpretation of the Ten Horns of Daniel 7." *ETL* 63 (1987): 106–13.

Ayoub, M. "'Uzayr in the Quran and Muslim Tradition." In *Studies in Islamic and Judaic Traditions: Papers Presented at the Institute for Islamic-Judaic Studies*. Ed. W. M. Brinner and S. D. Ricks, 3–18. Atlanta: Scholars, 1986.

Baumgartner, Walter. *Das Buch Daniel*. Giessen, Germany: A. Topelmann, 1926.

Blenkinsopp, J. *Ezra-Nehemiah*. London: SCM Press, 1989.

Boadt, L. *Ezekiel's Oracles against Egypt*. Rome: Biblical Institute Press, 1980.

Braverman, J. *Jerome's Commentary on Daniel: A Study of Comparative Jewish and Christian Interpretations of the Hebrew Bible*. Washington, D.C.: Catholic Biblical Association of America, 1978.

Buttenweiser, M. "The Date and Character of Ezekiel's Prophecies." *HUCA* 7 (1931): 1–18.

Carroll, R. P. "Coopting the Prophets: Nehemiah and Noadiah." In *Priests, Prophets and Scribes*. E. Ulrich et al., 87–99. JSOTSS 149. Sheffield, England: JSOT Press, 1992.

Cazelles, H. "La mission d'Esdras." *VT* 4 (1954): 122–30.

Cohen, S. *From the Maccabees to the Mishnah*. Louisville, Ky.: Westminster/John Knox, 1981.

Collins, J. J. "Apocalyptic Genre and Mythic Allusions in Daniel." *JSOT* 21 (1981): 83–100.

——. *The Apocalyptic Vision of the Book of Daniel*. Missoula, Mont.: Scholars, 1977.

——. "The Court-Tales in Daniel and the Development of Apocalyptic." *JBL* 94 (1975): 218–34.

——. *Daniel: A Commentary on the Book of Daniel*. Minneapolis, Minn.: Fortress, 1993.

——. *Daniel, First Maccabees, Second Maccabees*. Wilmington, Del.: Michael Glazier, 1981.

——. *Daniel with an Introduction to Apocalyptic Literature*. Grand Rapids, Mich.: Eerdmans, 1984.

——. *Seers, Sybils, and Sages in Hellenistic-Roman Judaism*. Leiden, Netherlands: E. J. Brill, 1997.

Cook, S. L. *Prophecy and Apocalypticism*. Minneapolis, Minn.: Fortress, 1995.

Coxon, P. "Nebuchadnezzar's Hermeneutical Dilemma." *JSOT* 66 (1995): 87–97.

Davies, P. R. "Reading Daniel Sociologically." In *The Book of Daniel in the Light of New Findings*. Ed. A. S. Van Der Woude, 345–61. Leuven, Belgium: University of Leuven Press, 1993.

Day, J. "Resurrection Imagery from Baal to the Book of Daniel." In *Congress Volume. Cambridge 1995*. Ed. J. Emerton, 125–33. Leiden, Netherlands: E. J. Brill, 1997.

Driver, S. R. *The Book of Daniel*. Cambridge: Cambridge University Press, 1912.

Dulin, R. "Leaders in the Restoration." *TBT* 24 (1986): 287–91.

Emerton, J. A. "The Origin of the Son of Man Imagery." *JTS* 9 (1958): 224–42.

Esler, P. F. "Political Oppression in Jewish Apocalyptic Literature: A Social-Scientific Approach." *List* 28 (1993): 181–99.

Ferch, A. J. "Daniel 7 and Ugarit: A Reconsideration." *JBL* 99 (1980): 75–86.

Ferguson, P. "Nebuchadnezzar, Gilgamesh, and the 'Babylonian Job.'" *JETS* 37 (1994): 321–31.

Flusser, C. "The Four Empires in the Fourth Sibyl and in the Book of Daniel." *IOS* 2 (1972): 148–75.

Galling, K. *Studien zur Geschichte Israels im persischen Zeitalter.* Tübingen, Germany: Mohr, 1964.

Garscha, J. *Studien zum Ezechielbuch*. Bern, Switzerland: Herbert Lang, 1974.

Ginsberg, H. L. *Studies in Daniel*. New York: Jewish Theological Seminary of America, 1948.

Gnuse, R. "The Jewish Dream Interpreter in a Foreign Court: The Recurring Use of a Theme in Jewish Literature." *JSP* 7 (1990): 29–53.

Goldingay, J. "The Stories in Daniel: A Narrative Politics." *JSOT* 37 (1987): 99–116.

Gosling, F. A. "Is It Wise to Believe Daniel?" *SJOT* 13 (1999): 142–53.

Grabbe, Lester, *Ezra–Nehemiah*. London: Routledge, 1998.

Hammer, Raymond. *The Book of Daniel*. Cambridge: Cambridge University Press, 1976.

Hanson, P. *The Dawn of Apocalyptic*. Philadelphia: Fortress, 1975.

Hartman, L. F., and A. DiLella. *The Book of Daniel*. AB 23. Garden City, N.Y.: Doubleday, 1978.

Heaton, E. W. *The Book of Daniel: Introduction and Commentary*. London: SCM Press, 1956.

Houtman, C. "Ezra and the Law." *OTS* 21 (1981): 91–115.

Koch, K. *Das Buch Daniel*. Erträge der Forschung 144. Darmstadt, Germany: Wissenschaftliche Buchgesellschaft, 1980.

———. "Is Daniel Also among the Prophets?" *Interpretation* 39 (1985): 117–30.

Kock, K. "Ezra and the Origins of Judaism." *JSS* 19 (1974): 173–97.

Laato, A. "The Seventy Year Weeks in the Book of Daniel." *ZAW* 102 (1990): 212–25.

LaCoque, A. *The Book of Daniel*. Atlanta: Scholars, 1979.

———. *Daniel in His Time*. Columbia: University of South Carolina Press, 1988.

Lawson, J. N. "'The God Who Reveals Secrets': The Mesopotamian Background to Daniel 2.47." *JSOT* 74 (1997): 61–76.

Lenchak, T. A. "Puzzling Passages: Daniel 7:7." *TBT* 36 (1998): 194.

Lucas, E. C. "Daniel: Resolving the Enigma." *VT* 50 (2000): 66–80.

———. "The Origin of Daniel's Four Empires Scheme Reexamined." *TB* 40 (1989): 185–202.

———. "The Source of Daniel's Animal Imagery." *TB* 41 (1990): 161–85.

Lust, J. "Cult and Sacrifice in Daniel: The Tamid and the Abomination of Desolation." In *Ritual and Sacrifice in the Ancient Near East*. Ed. J. Quaegebeur, 283–99. Orientalia Lovaniensia Analecta 55. Leuven, Belgium: University of Leuven Press, 1993.

Margalith, O. "The Political Role of Ezra as Persian Governor." *ZAW* 98 (1986): 110–12.

Mastin, B. A. "The Meaning of *hala'at* Daniel 4:27." *VT* 42 (1992): 234–47.

———. "Wisdom and Daniel." In *Wisdom in Ancient Israel: Essays in Honour of J. A. Emerton*. Ed. J. Day et al., 161–69. Cambridge: Cambridge University Press, 1995.

McComiskey, Thomas Edward. "The Seventy 'Weeks' of Daniel against the Background of Ancient Near Eastern Literature." *WTJ* 47 (1985): 18–45.

McNamara, M. "Nabonidus and the Book of Daniel." *ITQ* 37 (1970): 131–49.

Meadowcroft, T. "A Literary Critical Comparison of the Masoretic Text and Septuagint of Daniel 2–7." *TB* 45 (1994): 195–99.

Milik, J. T. "'Prière de Nobinide' et autre écrits d'un cycle de Daniel." *RB* 62 (1956): 407–15.

Montgomery, J. A. *A Critical and Exegetical Commentary on the Book of Daniel*. Edinburgh: T. & T. Clark, 1927.

Moore, M. S. "Resurrection and Immortality: Two Motifs Navigating Confluent Theological Streams in the Old Testament (Dan 12:1–4)." *Theologische Zeitschrift* 39 (1983): 17–34.

Morgenstern, J. "Jerusalem—485 B.C." *HUCA* 28 (1957): 17–47.

Mosca, P. G. "Ugarit and Daniel 7: A Missing Link." *Biblica* 67 (1986): 496–517.

Müller, Hans-Peter. "Magisch-mantische Weisheit und die Gestalt Daniels." *UF* 1 (1969): 79–94.

———. "Mantische Weisheit und Apokalyptik." *VTS* 22 (1972): 268–93.

Nickelsburg, G. *Jewish Literature between the Bible and the Mishnah*. Philadelphia: Fortress, 1981.

Patterson, R. D. "Holding on to Daniel's Court Tales." *JETS* 36 (1993): 445–54.

Pfandl, G. "Interpretations of the Kingdom of God in Daniel 2:44." *AUSS* 34 (1996): 249–68.

Plöger, O. *Historische und legendarische Erzählungen: Zusätze zu Daniel.* Gütersloh, Germany: Mohr, 1973.

Porter, P. A., *Metaphors and Monsters: A Literary-Critical Study of Daniel 7 and 8.* ConB 20. Lund, Sweden: Guerup, 1983.

Rowland, C. *The Open Heaven: A Study of Apocalyptic in Judaism and Christianity.* New York: SPCK Press, 1982.

Rowley, H. H. *Darius the Mede and the Four World Empires.* Cardiff: University of Wales Press Board, 1935.

———. "Nehemiah's Mission and Its Background." *BJRL* 37 (1955): 528–61.

Shea, W. H. "The Neo-Babylonian Historical Setting for Daniel 7." *AUSS* 24 (1986): 31–36.

Steinschneider, Moritz, "Da Traumbuch Daniels und die oneirokritische Literatur des Mittelalters." *Serapeum* 24 (1863): 193–216.

Stern, E. *Material Culture of the Land of the Bible in the Persian Period.* Jerusalem: Aris and Phillips, 1982.

Torrey, C. C. *Ezra Studies.* Chicago: University of Chicago Press, 1910.

Van der Toorn, K. "In the Lion's Den: The Babylonian Background of a Biblical Motif." *CBQ* 60 (1998): 626–40.

Welch, A. C. *Post-exilic Judaism.* Edinburgh: W. Blackwood & Sons, 1935.

Williamson, H. G. M. *Ezra–Nehemiah.* Sheffield, England: Sheffield Academic Press, 1987.

Wolters, A. "An Allusion to Libra in Daniel 5." In *Die Rolle der Astronomie in den Kulturen Mesopotamiens; Beiträge zum 3. Grazer Morgenländischen Symposium, 23.-27. September, 1991.* Ed. H. D. Galter, 291–306. Grazer Morgenländische Studien 3. Freiburg, Germany: Karl-Franzens Universität, 1993.

Woodard, B. L. "Literary Strategies and Authorship in the Book of Daniel." *JETS* 37 (1994): 39–53.

Yamauchi, E. M. "Mordecai, the Persepolis Tablets, and the Susa Excavations." *VT* 42 (1992): 272–75.

———. "Was Nehemiah the Cupbearer a Eunuch?" *ZAW* 92 (1980): 132–42.

Zechariah, John, Jesus

Abd El-Jalil, J. *Marie et l'Islam.* Paris: Beauchesne, 1950.

Addleton, J. S. "Images of Jesus in the Literatures of Pakistan." *MW* 80 (1990): 96–106.

Arnaldez, R. *Jésus fils de Marie prophète de l'Islam.* Paris: Desclée, 1980.

Badia, L. F. *The Qumran Baptism and John the Baptist's Baptism*. Lanham, Md.: Rowman & Littlefield, 1980.

Bainulabedeen, Md. "The Unnatural Birth of Jesus." *Bulletin of Christian Institutes of Islamic Studies* 8 (1985): 34–37.

Bammel, E. "John the Baptist in Early Christian Tradition." *NTS* 18 (1971–72): 95–128.

Basetti-Sani, G. "Christian Symbolism and Christological Typology in the Qur'an." *Bulletin of Christian Institutes of Islamic Studies* 4 (1981): 111–45.

Belli, A. "Stori meccana di Maria e di Gesù (Sura XIX, 1–35)." *Aevum* 24 (1950): 442–66.

Bishop, E. F. F. "The Son of Mary." *MW* 24 (1934): 7–26.

Blochet, E. *Le Messianisme dans l'hétérodoxie musulmane*. Paris: J. Maisonneuve, 1903.

Bousset, W. *Kyrios Christos: Geschichte des Christusglaube von den Anfängen des Christentums bis Irenaeus*. Göttingen, Germany: Vanderhoeck und Ruprecht, 1913.

Brown, R. E. *The Birth of the Messiah*. Garden City, New York: Doubleday, 1977.

———. "Gospel Infancy Narrative Research from 1976 to 1986." *CBQ* 48 (1986) 469–83, 661–80.

Bruce, F. F. *Jesus and Christian Origins outside the New Testament*. New ed. London: Hodder and Stoughton, 1984.

Bultmann, R. *Jesus Christ and Mythology*. New York: Scribners, 1958.

Busse, H. "Monotheismus und islamische Christologie in der Bauinschrift des Felsendoms in Jerusalem." *Theologische Quartalschrift* 161 (1981): 168–78.

Charfi, A. M. "Christianity in the Qur'an Commentary of Tabari." *Islamochristiana* 6 (1980): 105–48.

Chilton, B. *A Galilean Rabbi and His Bible*. Wilmington, Del.: M. Glazier, 1984.

Courtois, V. *Mary in Islam*. Calcutta: Oriental Institute, 1954.

Crossan, J. D. *The Historical Jesus: The Life of a Mediterranean Jewish Peasant*. San Francisco: HarperCollins, 1991.

Din, M. "The Crucifixion in the Quran." *MW* 14 (1924): 23–29.

D'Souza, A. "Jesus in Ibn 'Arabi's Fusus al-Hikam." *Bulletin of Christian Institutes of Islamic Studies* 6 (1983): 28–54.

Ferné, A. "La vie de Jésus dans Tabari." *Islamochristiana* 5 (1979): 7–29.

Field, C. H. A. "Christ in Mohammedan Tradition." *MW* 1 (1911): 68–73.

Fitzgerald, M. L. *Jesus in a Shi'ite Commentary*. Rome, 1996.

Geagea, N. *Mary of the Koran: A Meeting Point between Christianity and Islam*. Trans. L. T. Fares. New York: Philosophical Library, 1984.

Gibson, J. C. L. "John the Baptist in Muslim Writings." *MW* 45 (1955): 334–45.

Grant, R. M. *Christ after the Gospels: The Christ of the Second Century.* Louisville, Ky.: Westminster/John Knox, 1986.

Guthrie, A., and E. F. Bishop. "The Paraclete, Almunhamanna and Ahmad." *MW* 41 (1951): 251–56.

Hayek, M. *Le Christ de l'Islam.* Paris: Du Seuil, 1959.

———. "L'Origine des termes Isa, al-Masih (Jesus-Christ) dans le Coran." *L'Orient Chrétien* 7 (1962): 223–54, 365–82.

Hollenbach, P. "The Conversion of Jesus: From Jesus the Baptizer to Jesus the Healer." *ANRW* 2.25.1 (1982): 196–219.

Horsely, R. H. "Like One of the Prophets of Old: Two Types of Popular Prophets at the Time of Jesus." *CBQ* 47 (1985): 135–63.

Jomier, J. "Jesus tel que Ghazali le présente dans 'Al-Ihya.'" *Mélanges de l'institut dominicain d'études orientales du Caire* 18 (1988): 45–82.

Jones, L. B. "The Paraclete or Mohammed." *MW* 10 (1920): 112–25.

Khalidi, T. *The Muslim Jesus: Sayings and Stories in Islamic Literature.* Cambridge, Mass.: Harvard University Press, 2001.

Khan, Hayat. "Messiah, Jesus Son of Mary (His Ascension and Return) as Confirmed by the Quran." *Bulletin of Christian Institutes of Islamic Studies* 1.3 (1978): 2–13.

Khawam, R. R. "Témoignages de l'Islam sur Jesus." *Cahiers des Deux Mers* 1 (1995): 5–8.

Khoury, Th. "Die Christology des Korans." *ZMR* (1968): 49–63.

Knappert, J. "The Legend of the Virgin Mary in Islam." *Orientalia Lovaniensia Periodica* 18 (1987): 177–86.

———. "The Mawlid." *Orientalia Lovaniensia Periodica* 19 (1988): 209–15.

Kraeling, C. H. *John the Baptist.* New York, 1951.

Lawson, T. B. "The Crucifixion of Jesus in the Qur'an and Qur'anic Commentary: A Historical Survey." *Bulletin of Henry Martyn Institute of Islamic Studies* 10 (1991): 34–62.

Mack, B. L. *A Myth of Innocence: Mark and Christian Origins.* Philadelphia: Fortress, 1988.

Maier, J. *Jesus von Nazareth in der talmudischen Überlieferung.* Darmstadt, Germany: Wissenschaftliche Buchgesellschaft, 1978.

Marshall, D. "The Resurrection of Jesus and the Qur'an." In *Resurrection Reconsidered.* Ed. G. D'Costa, 168–83. Oxford: Oneworld Publications, 1996.

McAuliffe, J. D. "Chosen of All Women: Mary and Fatima in Quranic Exegesis." *Islamchristiana* (1981): 19–28.

———. *Qur'anic Christians: An Analysis of Classical and Modern Exegesis.* Cambridge: Cambridge University Press 1991.

McHugh, J. *The Mother of Jesus in the New Testament.* Garden City, N.Y.: Doubleday, 1975.

Michaud, H. *Jésus selon le Coran.* Cahiers Theologiques 46. Neuchatel, Switzerland: Éditions Delachaux et Niestlé, 1960.

Mourad, S. A. "A Twelfth-Century Muslim Biography of Jesus." *Islam and Christian-Muslim Relations* 7 (1996): 39–45.

Musk, B. "Encounter with Jesus in Popular Islam." *ERT* 10 (1986): 247–57.

Nazir Ali, M. "Christology in an Islamic Context." *al-Mushir* 24 (1982): 53–62.

Nistico, L. "I miracoli di Gesu nella tradizione islamica." *Islam: Storia e Civilta* 6 (1987): 77–83.

Nodet, E. "Jésus et Jean-Baptiste selon Josèphes." *RB* 92 (1985): 321–48, 497–524.

Parrinder, G. *Jesus in the Qur'an*. New York: Barnes and Noble, 1965.

Pauliny, J. "Buhtnassars Feldzug gegen die Araber." *Asian and African Studies* 8 (1972): 91–94.

———. "Islamische Legende über Bukht-Nassar (Nebukadnezar)." *GO* 4 (1972): 161–83.

Pawlikowski, J. T. "Mary in Judaism and Islam: International Symposium in Rome." *Journal of Ecumenical Studies* 23 (1986): 774–75.

Perrin, N. *Jesus and the Language of the Kingdom*. Philadelphia: Fortress, 1976.

Piemontese, A. M. "Storie di Maria, Gesu e Paolo nel commento coranico persiano di Surabadi." In *Orientalia Iosephi Tucci memoriae dicata*. Ed. G. Gnoli and L. Lanciotti, 1101–18. Rome: Istituto Italiano per il Medio ed Estremo Oriente, 1985–88.

Pinault, D. "Images of Christ in Arabic Literature." *Die Welt des Islams* 17 (1987): 103–25.

Pines, S. "'Israel, My Firstborn' and the Sonship of Jesus." In *Studies in Mysticism and Religion*. Ed. S. Pines, 177–90. Jerusalem: Magnes Press, 1967.

Räisänen, H. *Das Koranische Jesusbild: Ein Beitrag zur Theologie des Korans*. Helsinki: Missiologian ja Ekumeniikan, 1971.

Renard, J. "Jesus and Other Gospel Figures in the Writings of Jalal al-Din Rumi." *Hamdard Islamicus* 10 (1987): 47–64.

Riches, J. *Jesus and the Transformation of Judaism*. New York: Seabury Press, 1982.

Robinson, N. "Creating Birds from Clay: A Miracle of Jesus in the Qur'an and in Classical Muslim Exegesis." *MW* 79 (1989): 1–13.

Robson, J. "Muhammadan Teaching about Jesus." *MW* 21 (1939): 37–54.

———. "Stories of Jesus and Mary." *MW* 40 (1950): 236–43.

Rosch, G. "Die Jesusmythen des Islam." *Theologische Studien und Kritiken* (1876): 409–54.

Ross, J. M. "Which Zechariah?" *IBS* 9 (1987): 70–73.

Sanders, E. P. *Jesus and Judaism*. Philadelphia: Fortress, 1985.

Schall, A. "Die Sichtung des Christlichen im Koran." *Mitteilungen und Forschungsbeiträge der Cusanus-Gesellschaft* 9 (1971): 76–91.

Schedl, C. "Die 114 Suren des Koran und die 114 Logien Jesu im Thomas-Evangelium." *Der Islam* 64 (1987): 261–64.

Schimmel, A. *Jesus und Maria in der islamischen Mystik.* Munich: Kösel, 1996.

——. "Jesus and Mary as Poetical Images in Rumi's Verse." In *Christian-Muslim Encounters.* Ed. Y. Y. Haddad and W. Z. Haddad, 143–57. Gainesville: University Press of Florida, 1995.

——. "Jesus und Maria in der persischen Poesie." *Spektrum Iran* 6 (1993): 60–72.

Schumann, O. *Der Christus der Muslime: Christologische Aspekte in der arabischen-islamischen Literatur.* Cologne, Germany: Böhlau, 1988.

Scobie, C. H. H. *John the Baptist.* Philadelphia: Westminster, 1964.

Shaltout, Mahmoud. "The 'Ascension' of Jesus." *Majallat al-Azhar* 31 (1959–60): 189–93.

Smith, J. I. "The Virgin Mary in Islamic Tradition and Commentary." *MW* (1989) 79: 161–87.

Stern, S. M. "Abd al-Jabbar's Account of How Christ's Religion Was Falsified by the Adoption of Roman Customs." *JTS* 19 (1968): 129–76.

Swanson, M. N. "The Cross of Christ in the Earliest Arabic Melkite Apologies." In *Christian Arabic Apologetics during the Abbasid Period (750–1258).* Ed. S. K. Samir and J. S. Nielsen, 115–45. Leiden, Netherlands: E. J. Brill, 1994.

Theissen, G., and A. Merz. *The Historical Jesus: A Comprehensive Guide.* Philadelphia: Fortress, 2001.

——. *The Miracle Stories of the Early Christian Tradition.* Trans. F. Mc Donagh. Philadelphia: Fortress, 1983.

Thomas, D. "Abu Mansur al-Maturidi on the Divinity of Jesus Christ." *Islamochristiana* 23 (1997): 43–64.

——. "The Miracles of Jesus in Early Islamic Polemic." *JSS* 39 (1994): 221–43.

Trimmingham, J. S. *Christianity among the Arabs in Pre-Islamic Times.* London: Longman, 1979.

Troger, K.-W. "Jesus als Prophet im Verständnis der Muslime, Christen und Juden." *Kairos* 24 (1982): 100–9.

Vermes, G. *The Changing Faces of Jesus.* New York: Viking Compass, 2001.

——. *Jesus and the World of Judaism.* London: S.C.M. Press, 1983.

Wilken, R. L. *The Christians as the Romans Saw Them.* New Haven, Conn.: Yale University Press, 1984.

Winett, F. V. "References to Jesus in Pre-Islamic Arabic Inscriptions." *MW* 31 (1941): 341–53.

Wink, W. *John the Baptist in the Gospel Tradition.* Cambridge: Cambridge University Press, 1968.

Wismer, D. *The Islamic Jesus: An Annotated Bibliography of Sources in English and French.* New York: Garland, 1977.

Wright, G. R. H. "Tradition on the Birth of Christ in Christianity and Islam." *Saeculum* 35 (1984): 365–71.

Zahniser, A. H. M. "The Word of God and the Apostleship of 'Isa: A Narrative Analysis of Al 'Imran (3): 33–62." JSS 36 (1991): 77–112.

MUHAMMAD

Abdel-Malek, K. *Muhammad in the Modern Egyptian Popular Ballad*. Leiden, Netherlands: E. J. Brill, 1995.

Affifi, A. E. "The Story of the Prophet's Ascent (mi'raj) in Sufi Thought and Literature." *IQ* 2 (1955): 23–27.

Ahmad Khan, I. "Centres of Islam during Makkan Phase of Prophet Muhammad's Mission." *Journal of the Pakistan Historical Society* 44 (1996): 193–201.

Ahmed, B. *Muhammad and the Jews*. New Delhi, India: Vikas, 1979.

Altmann, A. "The Ladder of Ascension." In *Studies in Mysticism and Religion*. Ed. S. Pines, 1–32. Jerusalem: Magnes Press, 1967.

Alwaye, A. M. M. "al-Mi'raj: The Ascent of the Prophet." *Majallat al-Azhar* 45 (1972): 1–7.

——. "The 'Ascent' of the Prophet: Connecting the Islamic World with Jerusalem." *Majallat al-Azhar* (1968): 1–6.

——. "The Miraculous Journey of the Prophet from Mecca to Jerusalem." *Majallat al-Azhar* 47.5 (1975): 1–5.

——. "The Significance and the Importance of 'the Night Journey and the Ascent.'" *Majallat al-Azhar* (1969): 5–10.

Andrae, T. *Die Person Muhammeds in Lehre und Glauben seiner Gemeinde*. Uppsala, Sweden: P. A. Norstedt & Söner, 1917.

Asani, A. S., et al., *Celebrating Muhammad: Images of the Prophet in Popular Muslim Poetry*. Columbia: University of South Carolina Press, 1995.

Athamina, K. "Al-Nabiyy al-Umiyy: An Inquiry into the Meaning of a Quranic Verse." *Der Islam* 69 (1992): 61–80.

Azad, G. M. "Isra' and Miraj: Night Journey and Ascension of Allah's Apostle Muhammad (SAWS)." *IS* 22.2 (1983): 63–80.

Bashear, S. "The Mission of Dihya al-Kalbi and the Situation in Syria." *Der Islam* 74 (1997): 64–91.

——. "Riding Beasts on Divine Missions: An Examination of the Ass and Camel Traditions." *JSS* 356 (1991): 37–75.

Bell, R. "Muhammad and Previous Messengers." *MW* 24 (1934): 330–40.

——. "Mohammed's Call." *MW* 24 (1934): 13–19.

——. "Muhammad's Pilgrimage Proclamation." *JRAS* (1937): 233–44.

——. Muhammad's Visions." *MW* 24 (1934): 145–54.

Bennett, C. *In Search of Muhammad*. London: Cassell, 1998.

Benscheikh, J. E. *Le Voyage Nocturne de Mahomet*. Paris: Impr. Nationale, 1988.

Bevan, A. A. "Mohammed's Ascension to Heaven." In *Studien zur semitischen Philologie und Religionsgeschichte*. Ed K. Marti, 49–61. Giessen: A. Töpelmann, 1914.

Birkeland, H. *The Legend of the Opening of Muhammed's Breast*. Oslo: I Kommisjon hos J. Dybwad,1955.

——. *The Lord Guideth: Studies on Primitive Islam*. Oslo: I Kommisjon hos J. Dybwad, 1956.

Blachere, R. *Le problème de Mahomet, essai de biographie critique du fondateur de l'Islam*. Paris: Presses Universitaires de France, 1952.

Buaben, J. M. *Image of the Prophet Muhammad in the West: A Study of Muir, Margoliouth and Watt*. Leicester, England: Islamic Foundation, 1996.

Buhl, F. "The Character of Mohammed as a Prophet." *MW* 1 (1911): 356–64.

Buhl, F. "Ein paar Beiträge zur Kritik der Geschichte Muhammeds." *Orientalische Studien Th. Noeldeke gewidmet* 1 (1906): 7–72.

Busse, H. "The Destruction of the Temple and Its Reconstruction in Light of Muslim Exegesis of Sura 17:2–8." *JSAI* 20 (1996): 1–17.

——. "Jerusalem in the Story of Muhammad's Night Journey and Ascension." *JSAI* 14 (1991): 1–40.

Calder, N. "The Ummi in Early Islamic Juridic Literature." *Der Islam* 67 (1990): 111–23.

Conrad, L. I. "Abraha and Muhammad: Some Observations apropos of Chronology and Literary Topoi in the Early Arabic Historical Tradition." *BSOAS* 50 (1987): 225–40.

Cook, M. *Muhammad*. Oxford: Oxford University Press, 1983.

Crone, P. *Meccan Trade and the Rise of Islam*. Princeton, N.J.: Princeton University Press, 1987.

Eccel, A. C. "The Kinship-Based Cult of Muhammad among the Hamd of the Hawran." *Der Islam* 63 (1986): 323–33.

Faizer, R. S. "Muhammad and the Medinan Jews: A Comparison of the Texts of Ibn Ishaq's Kitab Sirat Rasul Allah with al-Waqidi's Kitab al-Maghazi." *IJMES* 28, 4 (1996): 463–89.

Fodor, A. "The Solar Bark in a Muhammadan Mi'raj Text." *Studia Aegyptiaca I, Recueil du textes dédiées à V. Wessetzky*, 83–87. Budapest: Eötuös Loránd Tudományegyetem, 1974.

Fück, J. W. *Muhammad ibn Ishaq: Literarhistorische Untersuchungen*. Frankfurt: Peter Lang, 1924.

——. "Muhammad-Persönlichkeit und Religionsstiftung." *Saeculum* 3 (1952): 70–93.

Fuda, A. R. "The 'Ascent' of the Prophet." *Majallat al-Azhar* (December 1964): 4–5.

Ganda, S. "Muslim Relics with the Sikh Rulers of Lahore." In *Essays in Indian Art, Religion and Society*. India History Congress Golden Jubilee Year Publication series 1. Ed. K. M. Shrimali, 282–88. Delhi, India: Munshiram Manoharlal Publishers, 1987.

Gil, M. "The Medinan Opposition to the Prophet." *JSAI* 10 (1987): 65–96.

———. "The Origin of the Jews of Yathrib." *JSAI* 4 (1984): 203–24.

Gilliot, C. "Muhammad, le Coran et les 'contraintes de l'histoire.'" In *The Qur'an as Text*. Ed. S. Wild, 3–26. Leiden, Netherlands: E. J. Brill, 1996.

Goldfeld, I. "The Illiterate Prophet (Nabi Ummi)." *Der Islam* 57 (1980): 58–67.

Goto, A. "Al-Madina: A Historical Analysis of the City at the Time of the Prophet Muhammad." In *Historic Cities of Asia: An Introduction to Asian Cities from Antiquity to Pre-modern Times*. Ed. M. Abdul Jabbar Beg, 203–21. Kuala Lumpur; Percetakan Ban Huatseng, 1986.

———. "Hadiths as Historical Sources for a Biography of the Prophet." *Orient* 30–31 (Tokyo, 1995): 82–97.

Griffith, S. H. "Muhammad and the Monk Bahira: Reflections on a Syriac and Arabic Text from Early Abbasid Times." *Oriens Christianus* 79 (1995): 146–74.

Guillaume, A. "The Biography of the Prophet in Recent Research." *IQ* 1 (1954): 5–11.

———. *New Light on the Life of Muhammad*. Manchester JSS Monograph 1. Manchester, England: Manchester University Press, n.d.

———. "Where Was al-Masyid al-Aqsà?" *al-Andalus* 18 (1953): 323–36.

Hartmann, R. "Die Himmelreise Muhammads und ihre Bedeutung in der Religion des Islam." In *Vorträge der bibliothek Warburg*. Ed. F. Saxl, 42–65. Leipzig, Germany: J. C. Hinrichs, 1930.

Hasan, P. "The Footprint of the Prophet." *Muqarnas* 10 (1993): 335–43.

Hawting, G. R. "The Disappearance and Rediscovery of Zamzam and the 'Well of the Ka'ba.'" *BSOAS* 43 (1980): 44–54.

———. "The Origins of the Muslim Sanctuary at Mecca." In *Studies on the First Century of Islamic Society*. Ed. G. H. A. Juynboll, 23–47. Carbondale, Ill., 1982.

Hoffman-Ladd, V. J. "Devotion to the Prophet and His Family in Egyptian Sufism." *IJMES* 24 (1992): 615–37.

Horovitz, J. "Biblische Nachwirkungen in der Sira." *Der Islam* 12 (1922): 184–89.

———. "The Earliest Biographies of the Prophet and Their Authors." *IC* 1 (1927): 535–59, 2 (1928): 22–50, 164–82, 495–526.

———. "Judaeo-Arabic Relations in Pre-Islamic Times." *IC* 3 (1929): 161–99.

———. "Muhammeds Himmelfahrt." *Der Islam* 9 (1919): 159–83.

———. "Zur Muhammadlegende." *Der Islam* 5 (1914): 41–53.

Idris, H. R. "Reflexions sur Ibn Ishaq." *SI* 17 (1962): 23–35.

Jeffery, A. "Was Muhammad a Prophet from His Infancy?" *MW* 20 (1930): 226–34.

Jomier, J. *Dieu et l'homme dans le Coran: L'aspect religieux de la nature humaine, joint à l'obeissance au Prophète de l'Islam*. Paris: Editions du Cerf, 1996.

Kakurawi, M., trans. *In Praise of the Prophet Muhammad: Qasida Poetry in Islamic Asia and Africa*. Ed. S. Sperl and C. Shackle. 2 vols. Studies in Arabic Literature 20. Leiden, Netherlands: E. J. Brill, 1996.

Kaptein, N. J. G. *Muhammad's Birthday Festival: Early History in the Central Muslim Lands and Development in the Muslim West until the 10th/16th Century*. Leiden, Netherlands: E. J. Brill, 1993.

Kister, M. J. "'Al-Tahannuth': An Inquiry into the Meaning of a Term." *BSOAS* 31 (1968): 223–36.

———. "Maqam Ibrahim. A Stone with an Inscription." *Le Muséon* 84 (1971): 477–91.

———. "The Market of the Prophet." *JESHO* 8 (1965): 272–76.

———. "Pare Your Nails: A Study of an Early Tradition." *Journal of the Ancient Near Eastern Society of Columbia University* 11 (1979): 63–70.

———. "The Sons of Khadija." *JSAI* 16 (1993): 59–95.

Knappert, J. "Utenzi wa Miiraji: The Ascension of the Prophet Mohammed, by Sh. Moh. Jambein." *Afrika und Übersee* 48 (1965): 241–74.

Landau-Tasseron, E. "Processes of Redaction: The Case of the Tamimite Delegation to the Prophet Muhammad." *BSOAS* 49 (1986): 253–70.

Lecker, M. "The Bewitching of the Prophet Muhammad by the Jews: Notes a propos 'Abd al-Malik b. Habib's Mukhtasar fi 'l-Tibb." *Al-Qantara: Revista de Estudios Arabes 13* (1992): 561–69.

———. *Jews and Arabs in Pre- and Early Islamic Arabia*. Brookfield, Vt.: Variorum, 1998.

———. *Muslims, Jews and Pagans: Studies on Early Islamic Medina*. Leiden, Netherlands: E. J. Brill, 1995.

———. "Yahud/'Uhud: A Variant Reading in the Story of the 'Aqaba Meeting." *Le Muséon* 109 (1996): 169–83.

Lings, M. *Muhammad: His Life Based on the Earliest Sources*. London: Islamic Texts Society, 1991.

Lüling, G. *Die Wiederentdeckung des Propheten Muhammad*. Erlangen, Germany: Lüling, 1981.

Madelung, W. *The Succession to Muhammad: A Study of the Early Caliphate*. Cambridge: Cambridge University Press, 1997.

Margoliouth, D. S. *Muhammad and the Rise of Islam*. London: Putnam, 1905.

Miskin, T. "The Miraj Controversy: Dante, Palacios and Islamic Eschatology." *IJIAS* 4.1 (1987): 45–53.

Morris, J. W. "The Spiritual Ascension: Ibn Arabi and the Miraj." *JAOS* 107 (1987): 629–52; 108 (1988): 63–77.

Newby, G. D. "Imitating Muhammad in Two Genres: Mimesis and Problems of Genre in Sirah and Sunnah." *Medieval Encounters* 3 (1997): 266–83.

———. *The Making of the Last Prophet.* Columbia: University of South Carolina Press, 1989.

———. "The Sirah as a Source for Arabian Jewish History: Problems and Perspectives." *JSAI* 7 (1986): 121–38.

Noeldeke, Th. "Die Tradition über das leben Mohammeds." *Der Islam* 5 (1914): 160–70.

Paret, R. "Das Geschichtsbild Mohammeds." *Welt als Geschichte* (1951): 214–24.

———. *Mohammed und der Koran.* Stuttgart, Germany: W. Kohlhammer, 1966.

Peters, F. E. *Muhammad and the Origins of Islam.* Albany: State University of New York Press, 1994.

———. "The Quest of the Historical Muhammad." *IJMES* 23 (1991): 291–315.

Phipps, W. E. *Muhammad and Jesus: A Comparison of the Prophets and Their Teaching.* London: Continuum, 1996.

Porter, J. R. "Muhammad's Journey to Heaven." *Numen* 21 (1974): 64–80.

Rahman, H. "The Conflicts between the Prophet and the Opposition in Madina." *Der Islam* 62 (1985): 260–97.

Raven, W. "Some Early Islamic Texts on the Negus of Abyssinia." *JSS* 33 (1988): 197–218.

Rodinson, M. "A Critical Survey of Modern Studies on Muhammad." In *Studies on Islam.* Trans. and Ed. M. L. Swartz, 23–86. New York: Oxford University Press, 1981.

———. *Muhammad.* Harmondsworth, England: Penguin, 1961.

Rubin, U. *The Eye of the Beholder: The Life of Muhammad as Viewed by the Early Muslims: A Textual Analysis.* SLAEI 5. Princeton, N.J.: Darwin, 1995.

———. "The Great Pilgrimage of Muhammad: Some Notes on Sura IX." *JSS* 27 (1982): 241–60.

———. "Hanifiyya and Ka'ba: An Inquiry into the Arabian Pre-Islamic Background of Din Ibrahim." *JSAI* 13 (1990): 85–112.

———. "Iqra' bi-smi rabbika." *IOS* 13 (1993): 213–30.

———. "Muhammad's Curse of Mudar and the Blockade of Mecca." *JESHO* 31 (1988): 249–64.

———. "The Shrouded Messenger: On the Interpretation of al-Muzzammil and al-Muddaththir." *JSAI* 16 (1993): 96–107.

Schimmel, A. *And Muhammad Is His Messenger: The Veneration of the Prophet in Islamic Piety.* Chapel Hill: University of North Carolina Press, 1985.

Schoeler, G. *Charakter und Authentie der muslimischen Uberlieferung über das Leben Mohammeds.* Studien zur Sprache, Geschichte und Kultur des Islamischen Orients 14. Berlin: Walter de Gruyter, 1996.

Sellheim, R. "Muhammeds erste Offenbarungserlebnis." *JSAI* 10 (1987): 1–16.
———. "Prophet, Chalif und Geschichte." *Oriens* 18–19 (1965–66): 33–91.
Shtober, S. "Muhammad and the Beginning of Islam in the Chronicle Sefer Divrey Yoseph." In *Studies in Islamic History and Civilization in Honour of Professor David Ayalon*. Ed. M. Sharon, 319–52. Jerusalem/Leiden: E. J. Brill, 1986.
Stroumsa, G. G. "'Seal of the Prophets': The Nature of a Manichaean Metaphor." *JSAI* 7 (1986): 61–74.
Tapper, N., and R. Tapper. "The Birth of the Prophet: Ritual and Gender in Turkish Islam." *Man* 22 (1987): 69–92.
Tottoli, R., trans. *La Ka'bah: Tempio al centro del mondo. Akhbar Makkah*. Trieste, Italy, 1992.
Tubach, J. "Eine christliche legende syrischer Herkunft in der Prophetenbiographie Ibn Hisams." *Orientalia Lovanensia Periodica* 26 (1995): 81–99.
Turkoglu, S. "The Sacred Relics." In *Economic Dialogue: Turkey*. Istanbul, [1986], 177–184.
Varisco, D. M. "Metaphors and Sacred History: The Genealogy of Muhammad and the Arab 'Tribe.'" *Anthropological Quarterly* 68 (1995): 139–56.
Wansbrough, J. *The Sectarian Milieu*. Oxford: Oxford University Press, 1978.
Watt, W. M. "His Name Is Ahmed." *MW* 43 (1953): 110–17.
———. "The Materials Used by Ibn Ishaq." In *Historians of the Middle East*. Ed. B. Lewis, 23–34. London: Oxford University Press, 1962.
———. *Muhammad at Mecca*. Oxford: Clarendon, 1953.
Waugh, E. H. "Following the Beloved: Muhammad as Model in the Sufi Tradition." In *The Biographical Process*. Ed. F. E. Reynolds and D. Capps. The Hague: Mouton, 1976.
———. "Religious Aspects of the Mi'raj Legends." *Actes XXIX CIO. 1975: Etudes arabes et islamiques 1. Histoire et civilisation* 4 (1975): 236–44.
Wensinck, A. J. *Muhammad and the Jews of Medina*. Trans. W. H. Behn. 2nd ed. Freiburg im Breisgau, Germany: K. Schwarz, 1975.
Wensinck, A. J. "Mohammed und das Judentum." *Der Islam* 2 (1911): 286–91.
———. "Muhammed und die Propheten." *AO* 2 (1924): 168–98.
Widengren, G. *Muhammad, the Apostle of God and His Ascension*. Uppsala, Sweden: Lundequistka Bokhandeln, 1955.
Yagmurlu, H. "Relics of the Prophet Muhammad." *Apollo* 92, no. 101 (1970): 50–53.

ANGELS, DEMONS, GIANTS, MONSTERS

Abusch, T. "The Demonic Image of a Witch in Standard Babylonian Literature: The Reworking of Popular Conceptions by Learned Exorcists." In *Religion, Science, and Magic: In Concert and in Conflict*. Ed. J. Neusner et al., 27–58. New York: Oxford University Press, 1989.

Albright, W. F. "What Were the Cherubim?" In *The Biblical Archaeologist Reader*. Ed. G. E. Wright and D. N. Freedman. New York: Anchor, 1961.

Alexander, P. S. "The Targumim and Early Exegesis of 'Sons of God' in Genesis 6." *JJS* 23 (1972): 60–71.

Awn, P. *Satan's Tragedy and Redemption: Iblis in Sufi Psychology*. Leiden, Netherlands: E. J. Brill, 1983.

Bartelmus, R. *Heroentum in Israel und seiner Umwelt*. Zürich: Theologischer Verlag, 1979.

Bauckham, R. J. "Early Jewish Visions of Hell." *JTS* 41 (1990): 355–85.

Benoit, P. "Pauline Angelology and Demonology: Reflections on the Designations of the Heavenly Powers and on the Origin of Angelic Evil according to Paul." *Religious Studies Bulletin* 3 (1983): 1–18.

Bietenhard. H. *Die himmlische Welt im Urchristentum und Spätjudentum*. WUNT 2. Tübingen, Germany: Mohr, 1951.

Bishop, E. F. F. "Angelology in Judaism, Islam, and Christianity." *ATR* 46 (1964): 142–54.

Black, J., and A. Green. *Gods, Demons and Symbols of Ancient Mesopotamia: An Illustrated Dictionary*. London: British Museum Press for the Trustees of the British Museum, 1992.

Bocher, O. *Christus Exorcista*. Stuttgart, Germany: W. Kohlhammer, 1972.

Caquot, A. *Génies, anges et démons*. sources orientales 8. Paris: Éditions du Seuil, 1971.

Cassuto, U. "The Episode of the Sons of God and the Daughters of Man." In *Bible and Oriental Studies*. Trans. I. Abrahams, 17–28. Jerusalem, 1973.

Clines, D. J. A. "The Significance of the 'Sons of God' Episode (Genesis 6:1–4) in the Context of the 'Primeval History' (Genesis 1–11)." *JSOT* 13 (1979): 33–46.

Dahl, N. A. "Die Erstegeborene Satans und der Vater des Teufels." In *Apophoreta: Festschrift Ernst Hänchen*. Ed. W. Eltester, 70–84. Berlin: Töpelmann, 1964.

Davies, T. W. *Magic, Divination, and Demonology among the Hebrews and Their Neighbors*. Reprint. Kila, Montana: Kessinger Publishing, 1993.

Day, J. *God's Conflict with the Dragon and the Sea*. Cambridge: Cambridge University Press, 1985.

Delcor, M. "Le mythe de la chute des anges et l'origine des géants comme explication du mal dans le monde dans l'apocalyptique juive: Histoire des traditions." *RSR* 190 (1976): 3–53.

De Menasce, P. J. "Une légende indo-iranienne dans l'angélologie judéo-musulmane: à propos de Harut et Marut." *Études Asiatiques* (1947): 10–18.

Deplace, C. *Le Griffon de l'archaïsme à l'époque impériale: Étude iconographique et essai d'interpretation symbolique*. Brussels: Institut historique belge de Rome, 1980.

Dickason, C. F. *Demon Possession and the Christian*. Wheaton, Ill.: Crossway Books, 1987.

Dimant, D. *The Fallen Angels in the Dead Sea Scolls, Apocrypha and Pseudepigrapha, and Related Writings*. Ph.D. Dissertation, Hebrew University, 1974.

Driver, G. R. *Mythical Monsters in the Old Testament*. Rome: Instituto per l'Orente, 1956.

Eitram, S. *Some Notes on the Demonology in the New Testament*. Oslo: Universitetsforlaget, 1966.

Elior, R. "Mysticism, Magic, and Angelology." *JSQ* 1 (1993).

Farkas, A. E., et al., eds. *Monsters and Demons in the Ancient and Medieval Worlds: Papers Presented in Honor of Edith Porada*. Mainz, Germany: P. von Zabern, 1987.

Fossum, J. E. *The Name of God and the Angel of the Lord*. WUNT 36. Tübingen, Germany: Mohr, 1985.

Gaylord, H. E. "How Satanael Lost His '-el.'" *JJS* 33 (1982): 303–9.

Goldziher, I. "La notion de la sakina chez les Mohametans." *RHR* 27 (1893): 296–308.

———. "Wasser als Dämonen abwehrendes Mittel." *AR* 13 (1910): 20–46.

Goodman, D. "Do Angels Eat?" *JJS* 37 (1986): 160–75.

Gunkel, H. *Schöpfung und Chaos*. Göttingen, Germany: Vanderhoeck und Ruprecht, 1895.

Hanson, P. "Rebellion in Heaven, Azazel, and Euhemeristic Heroes in 1 Enoch 6–11." *JBL* 96 (1997): 195–233.

Hendel, R. S. "Of Demigods and the Deluge: Toward an Interpretation of Genesis 6:1–4." *JBL* 106 (1987): 13–26.

———. "When the Sons of God Cavorted with the Daughters of Men." *BRev* 2 (1987): 813; 3 (1987): 837.

Hentschel, K. *Geister, Magier und Muslime: Damonenwelt und Geisteraustreibung im Islam*. Munich: E. Diederichs, 1997.

Himmelfarb, M. *Ascent to Heaven in Jewish and Christian Apocalypses*. Oxford: Oxford University Press, 1993.

———. *Tours of Hell: An Apocalyptic Form in Jewish and Christian Literature*. Philadelphia: Fortress, 1983.

Hull, J. M. *Hellenistic Magic and the Synoptic Tradition*. Naperville, Ill.: A. R. Allenson, 1974.

Hunter, E. C. D. "Who Are the Demons? The Iconography of Incantation Bowls." *SEL* 15 (1998): 95–115.

Johnston, S. I. "Defining the Dreadful: Remarks on the Greek Child-Killing Demon." In *Ancient Magic and Ritual Power*. Ed. M. Meyer and P. Mirecki, 361–87. Religions in the Graeco-Roman World 129. Leiden, Netherlands: E. J. Brill, 1995.

Kilmer, A. D. "The Mesopotamian Counterparts of the Biblical Nepilim." In *Perspectives on Languages and Text: Essays and Poems in Honor of Francis I. Andersen's Sixtieth Birthday.* Ed. E. W. Conrad and E. G. Newing, 39–43. Winona Lake, Ind.: Eisenbrauns,1987.

Koch, K. E. *Demonology Past and Present.* Grand Rapids, Mich.: Eerdmans, 1973.

Langton, E. *Essentials of Demonology: A Study of Jewish and Christian Doctrine, Its Origin and Development.* London: AMS Press, 1949.

————. *Good and Evil Spirits.* New York, 1942.

Lesses, R. M. *Ritual Practices to Gain Power: Angels, Incantations, and Revelation in Early Jewish Mysticism.* HTS 44. Harrisburg: Trinity Press International, 1998.

Lichty, E. "Demons and Population Control." *Expedition* 14 (1971): 22–26.

Littmann, E. "Harut und Marut." In *Festschrift Friedrich Carl Andreas zur Vollendung des siebzigsten Lebenjahres am 14.April 1916,* 70–87. Leipzig, Germany: J. C. Hinrichs, 1916.

Miller, P. D. *The Divine Warrior in Early Israel.* HSM 5. Cambridge, Mass.: Harvard University Press, 1973.

Montgomery, J. W., ed. *Demon Possession.* Minneapolis, Minn.: Fortress, 1976.

Mullen, E. T. *The Assembly of the Gods: The Divine Council in Canaanite and Early Hebrew Literature.* HSM 24. Chico, Calif.: Scholars, 1980.

Neugebauer, O. "Astronomy of the Book of Enoch." *Orientalia* 33 (1964): 48–61.

Newsom, C. *Songs of the Sabbath Sacrifice: A Critical Edition.* Atlanta: Scholars, 1985.

Nikiprowetzky, V. "Sur une lecture démonologique de Philon d'Alexandria, De gigantibus 6–11." In *Hommage à Georges Vajda: Etudes d'histoire et de pensée juives.* Ed. G. Nahon and C. Touati, 43–71. Leuven, Belgium: Peeters, 1980.

Oesterrich, T. K. *Possession: Demonological and Other.* London: University Books, 1930.

Pagels, E. *The Origin of Satan.* New York: Random House, 1997.

Petersen, D. L. "Yahweh and the Organization of the Cosmos." *JSOT* 13 (1970): 47–64.

Schäfer, P. *Rivalität zwischen Engeln und Menschen.* Studia Judaica 8. Berlin: Walter de Gruyter, 1975.

Scurlock, J. A. "Baby-Snatching Demons, Restless Souls and the Dangers of Childbirth: Medico-Magical Means of Dealing with Some of the Perils of Motherhood in Ancient Mesopotamia." *Icognita* 2 (1991): 137–85.

Segal, A. *Two Powers in Heaven.* SJLA 25. Leiden, Netherlands: E. J. Brill, 1977.

Segal, A. F. "Heavenly Ascent in Hellenistic Judaism, Early Christianity and Their Environment." *ANRW* 2.23.2 (1980): 1333–94.

Silva, A. da. "Dreams as Demonic Experience in Mesopotamia." *Studies in Religion/Sciences religieues* 22 (1993): 301–10.

Strugnell, J. "The Angelic Liturgy at Qumran." *VTS* 7 (1960): 318–45.

Trachtenberg, J. *The Devil and the Jews*. Philadelphia: Jewish Publication Society of America, 1943. Reprint, 1983.

Twelftree, G. *Christ Triumphant: Exorcism Then and Now*. London: Hodder and Stoughton, 1985.

Van der Osten-Sacken, P. *Gott und Belial*. Göttingen, Germany: Vanderhoeck und Ruprecht, 1969.

Van der Toorn, K., et al. *Dictionary of Deities and Demons in the Bible*. Leiden, Netherlands: E. J. Brill, 1995.

Van der Woude, A. S. "Melchisekek als himmlische Erlösergestalt in den neugefundenen eschatologischen Midraschim aus Qumran Höhle 11." *Oudtestamentlische Studien* 14 (1965): 354–73.

Vanhoye, A. "Médiateur des anges en Gal. 3:19–20." *Biblica* 59 (1978): 403–11.

Vermes, G. "The Archangel Sariel." In *Christianity, Judaism, and Other Greco-Roman Cults*. Ed. J. Neusner, 159–66. Leiden, Netherlands: E. J. Brill, 1975.

Whitney, K. W. *Two Strange Beasts: A Study of Traditions concerning Leviathan and Behemoth in Second Temple and Early Rabbinic Judaism*. Ph. D. Dissertation, Harvard University, 1992.

Wiggermann, F. A. M. "Exit *Talim*!: Studies in Babylonian Demonology, I." *Jaarbericht ex oriente Lux* 27 (1981-82): 90–105.

General Index

Index of References

About the Authors

Scott B. Noegel is associate professor of biblical and ancient Near Eastern studies at the University of Washington. Professor Noegel received his Ph.D. in 1995 from Cornell University in Semitic languages and literatures. He has published more than 50 articles on a variety of biblical and ancient Near Eastern topics, and is the author and editor of three books: *Janus Parallelism in the Book of Job* (Sheffield Academic Press, 1996), *Puns and Pundits: Wordplay in the Hebrew Bible and Ancient Near Eastern Literature* (CDL Press, 2000), and *Prayer, Magic, and the Stars in the Ancient and Late Antique World* (Pennsylvania State University Press). He coedits the latter work with Professors Brannon Wheeler and Joel Walker of the University of Washington. Professor Noegel intends to publish his latest monograph, *Nocturnal Ciphers: The Allusive Language of Dreams in the Ancient Near East*, later this year. Professor Noegel has given nearly 80 lectures on biblical and ancient Near Eastern topics at a number of colleges and universities. He is associate editor for the *Journal of Hebrew Scriptures* and the creator of *Okeanos*, an online resource devoted to the interdisciplinary study of the ancient Near East and Greece. His two films, *Descent of Ishtar* and the *Epic of Gilgamesh: Tablet XI*, have earned him international accolades. Currently, Professor Noegel is engaged in the creation of a *Teach Yourself Hieroglyphic Egyptian* CD-ROM. His name appears both in *Contemporary Authors* (Gale Group, 2001) and in the *International Directory of Distinguished Leadership* (American Biographical Institute, 2001).

Brannon M. Wheeler is associate professor of Islamic studies and chair of comparative religion at the University of Washington. Professor Wheeler earned his Ph.D. in Islamic studies from the University of Chicago and taught at Macalester College, Earlham College, Vanderbilt University, and Pennsylvania State University before coming to the

University of Washington. He has done postgraduate work and has been a visiting scholar at the Hebrew University in Jerusalem, the School of Islamic Law and Islamic Studies at Kuwait University, the American Research Center in Egypt, and the American Institute of Maghreb Studies in Tunisia. Professor Wheeler has published a number of books and articles on Islamic law, the Quran and its interpretation, and the study of religion including publications in Russia, Kuwait, Italy, Saudi Arabia, and Greece. He has also contributed entries to numerous encyclopedias including the *Encyclopedia of the Quran*, the *Oxford Dictionary of Islam*, the *Encyclopedia of Islam and Muslim Societies*, the *Encyclopedia of Women in Islamic Culture*, and the *Encyclopedia of American Studies*. Professor Wheeler has given invited lectures at a number of universities and colleges, including Yale, Syracuse, Claremont, University of Alabama, University of Chicago, Bard, Wooster, and the University of North Carolina at Chapel Hill. He has also lectured in Lebanon, Kuwait, Yemen, Saudi Arabia, Morocco, and Japan, and has appeared on television and radio programs in North America and the Middle East.